# MOON HANDBOOKS®

# NORTH CAROLINA

Pilot Mountain State Park

© ERIKA HOWSARE

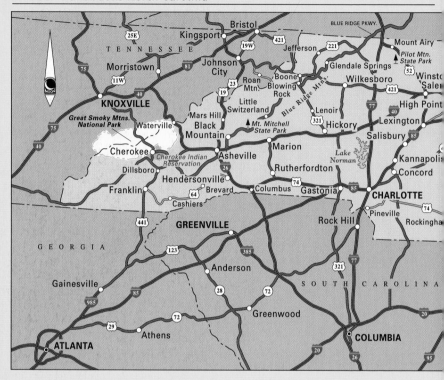

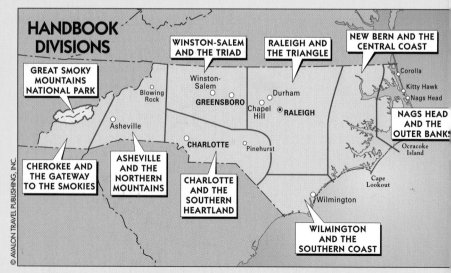

NORTH CAROLINA

© AVALON TRAVEL PUBLISHING, INC.

## MAP SYMBOLS

| | | | |
|---|---|---|---|
| ▬▬▬ Divided Highway | 🛡 ⬭ U.S. Interstate | ◉ State Capital |
| ▬▬▬ Primary Road | ⬭ U.S. Highway | ○ City/Town |
| ——— Secondary Road | ○ State Highway | ★ Point of Interest |
| - - - - - Unpaved Road | ✈ Airport | • Accommodation |
| —— - - State Boundary | ⚑ State Park | ▾ Restaurant/Bar |
| - - - - - Trail | ▲ Mountain | ▪ Other Location |
| ··········· Ferry | ⟆ Waterfall | ∆ Campground |
| | ⟆ Swamp | ⤙ Ski Area |

© AVALON TRAVEL PUBLISHING, INC.

© AVALON TRAVEL PUBLISHING, INC.

Mordecai Historic Park, Raleigh

© ERIKA HOWSARE

MOON HANDBOOKS®

# NORTH CAROLINA

**SECOND EDITION**

## MIKE SIGALAS

AVALON
TRAVEL

**Moon Handbooks North Carolina**
**Second Edition**

**Mike Sigalas**

Published by
Avalon Travel Publishing
1400 65th Street, Suite 250
Emeryville, CA 94608 USA

Please send all comments, corrections,
additions, amendments, and critiques to:

**Moon Handbooks North Carolina**
Avalon Travel Publishing
1400 65th Street, Suite 250
Emeryville, CA 94608 USA
email: atpfeedback@avalonpub.com
www.moon.com

Printing History
1st edition—1999
2nd edition—January 2003
5 4 3 2 1

ISBN: 1-56691-383-7
ISSN: 1540-3831

Editor: Kevin McLain
Series Manager: Erin Van Rheenen
Copy Editor: Emily McManus
Graphics Coordinators: Melissa Sherowski, Erika Howsare
Production Coordinators: Alvaro Villanueva, Darren Alessi, Jacob Goolkasian
Layout: Laura VanderPloeg
Cover Designer: Kari Gim
Interior Designers: Amber Pirker, Alvaro Villanueva, Kelly Pendragon
Map Editors: Naomi Adler Dancis, Olivia Sólis
Cartographers: Landis Bennett, Mike Morgenfeld, Naomi Adler Dancis
Indexer: Judy Hunt

Front cover photo: ©E. Poggenphol/FOLIO

Distributed by Publishers Group West

Printed in the United States by Malloy, Inc.

# ABOUT THE AUTHOR
## Mike Sigalas

Mike Sigalas's explorations of North Carolina began in boyhood, when he played in Smoky Mountain streams, reenacted Civil War battles with his siblings in nearby pastures, and visited the homes of his childhood heroes, Davy Crockett and Andrew Johnson. Later, as a college student visiting Great Smoky Mountains National Park on Spring Break, he awoke one morning in his freezing steel-walled utility van to find himself snowed in at the Smokemont Campground. On warmer days, Mike and his wife Kristin climbed mountain peaks, hiked to waterfalls, and rafted the Nantahala. Now a father, Mike achieves new feats, such as hiking to the top of Clingmans Dome while pushing a hefty two-year-old in a stroller.

Mike's professional writing career began providentially in 1987, while he was working as a steamboat pilot and Jungle Cruise guide at Disneyland. An off-duty Frontierland popcorn vendor slammed into Mike's 1970 Nova coupe in the employees' parking lot. Mike pounded out the dent himself and used the insurance money to buy his first word processor, a $350 Amstrad. On this, he tapped out his first published writing, supporting himself all the while in a variety of occupations, including blood bank distribution specialist, college-town rock singer, newspaper and magazine editor, and surf-band roadie.

*Moon Handbooks North Carolina* was written to the rhythm of clinking cups in various Lowcountry coffeehouses, to the creaking of a ceiling fan in a sticky upstairs room, and to the steady drumbeat of a toddler's fists on an office door. A stickler for authenticity, Mike consumed only hickory-smoked barbecue, sweet tea, and New Bern-born Pepsi-Cola as he worked. He is also the author of *Moon Handbooks Coastal Carolinas, Moon Handbooks South Carolina, Moon Handbooks Charleston & Savannah,* and the co-author of *Moon Handbooks Smoky Mountains.*

*For Kristin*

# Contents

**INTRODUCTION** ................................................... **1**

**THE LAND** ........................................................ **2**
The Carolina Coasts: Birthplace of the Deep South; Geography;
Regions; Rivers, Swamps, and Lakes; Climate

**FLORA AND FAUNA** ............................................... **10**
Vegetation Zones; Lowcountry Flora; Mammals; Aquatic Life;
Reptiles and Amphibians; Birds; Insects; Environmental Issues

**HISTORY** ........................................................ **15**
First Arrivals; British Proprietary Period; The Southern Colony Blossoms;
"Down with the Lords, Up with the King": End of the Proprietors' Era;
"Down with the King, Up with Liberty": The American Revolution in North
Carolina; Early Antebellum Old South; "The War for Southern Independence";
Reconstruction; The New South; Desegregation

**THE PEOPLE** ..................................................... **41**
Language; Terms of Address; Southern Subtleties: How to Read Southern Manners

### SPECIAL TOPICS

*Carolina's Bays* ........................ *5*    *The Scots-Irish* ........................ *24*
*Kudzu: The Vine that Ate the South* ........ *11*    *In Sherman's Words:*
*John Lawson and*                                        *Surrender at Bennett Place* ............. *34*
*   North Carolina's Animals* ............. *13*


**ON THE ROAD** ................................................... **44**

**RECREATION** .................................................... **45**
Water Sports; Fishing; Shrimping; Crabbing; Hiking; Bicycling; Hunting;
Skiing; Camping; Golf; Wine-tasting; Spectator Sports; Amusement Parks;
Music; Shopping

**ACCOMMODATIONS** ............................................... **56**
Hotels and Motels; Bed and Breakfasts; Cabins; Campgrounds and RV Parks

**FOOD** ........................................................... **58**
Seafood; Classic Carolina Eats; Alternatives; Beverages; Southern Restaurant
Chains; Buying Groceries

**TRAVEL BASICS** .................................................. **64**
By Car; By Air; By Train; By Bus; By Boat; Visas and Officialdom;
Special Interests; Health Maintenance; Natural Hazards; Crime; Other Issues

**COMMUNICATIONS, MEDIA, AND INFORMATION** .................... **76**
Postal Services; Telephones; Internet Access; Radio; Tourist Information; Money;
Odds and Ends

## SPECIAL TOPICS

Sight-Seeing Highlights ................. 45
North Carolina's Symbols and Emblems ..... 48
Small-Town Gems of North Carolina ....... 53
North Carolina Public Ferries ............ 66

# NAGS HEAD AND THE OUTER BANKS ......................... 81

## NAGS HEAD AND VICINITY ........................................ 83
Sights; Accommodations; Food; Entertainment; Sports and Recreation
## NORTH OF NAGS HEAD .............................................. 94
Duck; Corolla
## SOUTH OF NAGS HEAD ............................................. 98
Hatteras Island; Ocracoke Island; Portsmouth Island
## ROANOKE ISLAND ................................................... 105
Manteo; Accommodations; Food; Wanchese

## SPECIAL TOPICS

Outer Banks Highlights ................. 84
Lighthouses: The Outer Banks' Fab Four .... 85
Under the Floor ....................... 99

# NEW BERN AND THE CENTRAL COAST ........................ 110

## NEW BERN AND VICINITY ......................................... 112
History; Sights; Entertainment; Accommodations; Food; Getting There;
Getting Around; Information; North on Highway 17; Edenton; Hertford;
Elizabeth City; South on Highway 70
## BEAUFORT AND VICINITY ......................................... 130
Sights; Accommodations; Food; Recreation and Information; Atlantic Beach;
Points South

## SPECIAL TOPICS

Central Coast Highlights ............... 113
Down East .......................... 114
The Edenton Tea Party ................ 125

# WILMINGTON AND THE SOUTHERN COAST .................. 136

History
## WILMINGTON ...................................................... 140
Orientation; Sights; Accommodations; Food; Entertainment; Sports and
Recreation; Getting There; Getting Around; Information
## SOUTH OF WILMINGTON .......................................... 163
Southport; Bald Head Island; The South Brunswick Isles; Calabash

## SPECIAL TOPICS

Southern Coast Highlights . . . . . . . . . . . . . . 138
The Wilmington Ten . . . . . . . . . . . . . . . . . . 139
The Battle for North Carolina . . . . . . . . . . . 148
Simba, the Lion King of Tote-Em-In Zoo . . . 150

# RALEIGH AND THE TRIANGLE . . . . . . . . . . . . . . . . . . . . . . . . . . . . . . . . . . . . 167
History
## RALEIGH AND VICINITY . . . . . . . . . . . . . . . . . . . . . . . . . . . . . . . . . . . . . . . . . . 171
Sights; Tours; Accommodations; Food; Entertainment; Sports and Recreation;
Getting There: Getting Around
## DURHAM AND VICINITY . . . . . . . . . . . . . . . . . . . . . . . . . . . . . . . . . . . . . . . . . . 193
Sights; Accommodations; Food; Entertainment; Sports and Recreation;
Hillsborough
## CHAPEL HILL, CARRBORO, AND VICINITY . . . . . . . . . . . . . . . . . . . . . . . . . . 205
Sights; Accommodations; Food; Entertainment; Information
## SOUTHEAST OF RALEIGH . . . . . . . . . . . . . . . . . . . . . . . . . . . . . . . . . . . . . . . . . 212
Smithfield; Fayetteville; Pembroke

## SPECIAL TOPICS

Triangle Highlights . . . . . . . . . . . . . . . . . . . . 169
The War of Regulation . . . . . . . . . . . . . . . . . 170
WKIX—The Big Channel 85 . . . . . . . . . . . 185
Ava Gardner: Smithfield's Screen Siren . . . . 213
The Battle of Bentonville . . . . . . . . . . . . . . . 214

# CHARLOTTE AND THE SOUTHERN HEARTLAND . . . . . . . . . . . . . . . 216
## CHARLOTTE . . . . . . . . . . . . . . . . . . . . . . . . . . . . . . . . . . . . . . . . . . . . . . . . . . . . . 218
History; Sights; Accommodations; Food; Entertainment; Sports and Recreation;
Transportation
## NORTH OF CHARLOTTE . . . . . . . . . . . . . . . . . . . . . . . . . . . . . . . . . . . . . . . . . . 235
Lake Norman and Vicinity; Kannopolis; Salisbury
## SOUTH CAROLINA'S YORK COUNTY . . . . . . . . . . . . . . . . . . . . . . . . . . . . . . . 238
Rock Hill; Fort Mill; Paramount's Carowinds; South of I-85; York
## EAST OF CHARLOTTE . . . . . . . . . . . . . . . . . . . . . . . . . . . . . . . . . . . . . . . . . . . . 247
Reed Gold Mine State Historic Site; The North Carolina Sandhills; Pinehurst;
Southern Pines; Aberdeen

## SPECIAL TOPICS

Heartland Highlights . . . . . . . . . . . . . . . . . . 218
Pineville's James K. Polk . . . . . . . . . . . . . . . . 226

# WINSTON-SALEM AND THE TRIAD . . . . . . . . . . . . . . . . . . . . . . . . . . . . 253
## WINSTON-SALEM AND VICINITY . . . . . . . . . . . . . . . . . . . . . . . . . . . . . . . . . . 254
Sights; Accommodations; Food; Entertainment; Transportation; Mount Airy

## GREENSBORO AND VICINITY . . . . . . . . . . . . . . . . . . . . . . . . . . . . . . . . . . . . . . . 265
Sights; Accommodations; Food; Entertainment; Sports and Recreation;
North of Greensboro; South of Greensboro; High Point; Lexington

### SPECIAL TOPICS

*Triad Highlights* . . . . . . . . . . . . . . . . . . . . . *255*      *High Point's John Coltrane:*
*The Original Siamese Twins* . . . . . . . . . . . *264*          *Jazz Music's Patron Saint* . . . . . . . . . . . . *277*

## ASHEVILLE AND THE NORTHERN MOUNTAINS . . . . . . . . . . . . . . 281
History
## ASHEVILLE AND VICINITY . . . . . . . . . . . . . . . . . . . . . . . . . . . . . . . . . . . . . . . 285
Sights; Entertainment; Accommodations; Food; Shopping; Information;
Brevard; Hot Springs
## THE NORTHERN MOUNTAINS . . . . . . . . . . . . . . . . . . . . . . . . . . . . . . . . . . . . 296
Blowing Rock; Boone; North of Boone; South of Boone; East of Boone

### SPECIAL TOPICS

*Asheville Highlights* . . . . . . . . . . . . . . . . . . . *283*      *A Smoky Mountain Lingister* . . . . . . . . . . . *299*
*Race in 1885: A New Englander's View* . . . . *289*      *Boone and Valle Crucis in 1885* . . . . . . . . . *304*

## CHEROKEE AND THE GATEWAY TO THE SMOKIES . . . . . . . . . . 307
History; Orientation
## CHEROKEE . . . . . . . . . . . . . . . . . . . . . . . . . . . . . . . . . . . . . . . . . . . . . . . . . . . . 311
Sights; Entertainment; Accommodations; Campgrounds
## MAGGIE VALLEY . . . . . . . . . . . . . . . . . . . . . . . . . . . . . . . . . . . . . . . . . . . . . . . 315
Sights; Entertainment; Recreation; Accommodations; Food
## WAYNESVILLE . . . . . . . . . . . . . . . . . . . . . . . . . . . . . . . . . . . . . . . . . . . . . . . . . 322
Sights; Entertainment; Accommodations; Food
## DILLSBORO . . . . . . . . . . . . . . . . . . . . . . . . . . . . . . . . . . . . . . . . . . . . . . . . . . . 325
Sights; Shopping; Accommodations; Food; Getting There; Cullowhee
## BRYSON CITY . . . . . . . . . . . . . . . . . . . . . . . . . . . . . . . . . . . . . . . . . . . . . . . . . . 329
Recreation; Nantahala National Forest; Franklin; Highlands
## EAST OF BRYSON CITY . . . . . . . . . . . . . . . . . . . . . . . . . . . . . . . . . . . . . . . . . . 334
Fontana; Robbinsville; Murphy; Brasstown

### SPECIAL TOPICS

*Cherokee Area Highlights* . . . . . . . . . . . . . . *309*      *The Speech of Speckled Snake* . . . . . . . . . . . *313*
*Shades of Gray: Slaveholding and Rebellion*      *The Battle for Dupont State Forest* . . . . . . . *328*
    *in the Cherokee Nation* . . . . . . . . . . . . . . *310*      *Land of the Waterfalls* . . . . . . . . . . . . . . . . *330*

## GREAT SMOKY MOUNTAINS NATIONAL PARK .............. 337
History; Orientation
## SIGHTS ......................................................... 344
Elkmont; Cataloochee
## RECREATION .................................................. 347
Hiking; Biking; Fishing; Horseback Riding; Water Sports; Skiing
## ACCOMMODATIONS .......................................... 352
Campgrounds; Information

### SPECIAL TOPICS

Smoky Mountain Highlights ............ 339
Smoky Mountain Balds ................ 350
The Nation's Most Visited National Parks .. 340
Learning in the Smokies ............... 353
Smokies Hiking Reminders ............. 348


## RESOURCES .................................................. 357
Suggested Reading .................................................. 358
Internet Resources .................................................. 361
Index .................................................................. 362

# Maps

North Carolina . . . . . . . . . . . . . . ii-iii

## NAGS HEAD AND THE OUTER BANKS

Nags Head and the Outer Banks . . . . . 82
Kitty Hawk to Nags Head . . . . . . . . . 95
Nags Head to Bodie Island . . . . . . . . 98
Ocracoke . . . . . . . . . . . . . . . . . . . . . 102
Roanoke Island . . . . . . . . . . . . . . . . 106

## NEW BERN AND THE CENTRAL COAST

The Central Coast . . . . . . . . . . . . . . 111
New Bern . . . . . . . . . . . . . . . . . . . . . 112

## WILMINGTON AND THE SOUTHERN COAST

The Southern Coast . . . . . . . . . . . . . 137
Greater Wilmington . . . . . . . . . . . . . 141
Downtown Wilmington . . . . . . . . . . 142

## RALEIGH AND THE TRIANGLE

The Triangle . . . . . . . . . . . . . . . . . . . 168
Raleigh . . . . . . . . . . . . . . . . . . . . . . . 172
Downtown Raleigh . . . . . . . . . . . . . . 174
Downtown Durham . . . . . . . . . . . . . 194
Chapel Hill . . . . . . . . . . . . . . . . . . . . 207

## CHARLOTTE AND THE SOUTHERN HEARTLAND

The Southern Heartland . . . . . . . . . . 217

Charlotte . . . . . . . . . . . . . . . . . . . . . 219
Downtown Charlotte . . . . . . . . . . . . 222

## WINSTON-SALEM AND THE TRIAD

The Triad . . . . . . . . . . . . . . . . . . . . . 254
Winston-Salem . . . . . . . . . . . . . . . . . 256
Greensboro . . . . . . . . . . . . . . . . . . . . 265
Downtown Greensboro . . . . . . . . . . . 268

## ASHEVILLE AND THE NORTHERN MOUNTAINS

Asheville and the
   Northern Mountains . . . . . . . . . . . 282
Asheville and Vicinity . . . . . . . . . . . . 286
Asheville . . . . . . . . . . . . . . . . . . . . . . 288
The Northern Mountains . . . . . . . . . 296
Blowing Rock . . . . . . . . . . . . . . . . . . 298

## CHEROKEE AND THE GATEWAY TO THE SMOKIES

Cherokee and Vicinity . . . . . . . . . . . 308
The Quiet Side and Fontana Lake . . . 335

## GREAT SMOKY MOUNTAINS NATIONAL PARK

Great Smoky Mountains National Park
   and Vicinity . . . . . . . . . . . . . . . . . 338

# Abbreviations

**C.S.A.**—Confederate States of America
**I**—Interstate highway (e.g., I-95)
**N.C.**—North Carolina
**NPS**—National Park Service

**UNC**—University of North Carolina
**WPA**—Works Progress Administration

# Keeping Current

It's unavoidable: between the time this book goes to print and the moment you read this, a handful of the businesses noted in these pages will undoubtedly change prices, move, or close their doors forever. Other worthy attractions will open for the first time. If you see anything that needs updating, clarification, or correction, or if you have a favorite gem you'd like to see included in the next edition, I'd appreciate it if you'd drop me a line.

Address comments to:
*Moon Handbooks North Carolina*
Avalon Travel Publishing
1400 65th Street, Suite 250
Emeryville, CA 94608 USA
atpfeedback@avalonpub.com

*Carolina, I knew you before the highways got to you, and I loved you—and I still do.*

Wilmington native Charlie Daniels
in *"Carolina (I Remember You)"*

# Introduction

Taken as a whole, North Carolina is one of the most remarkable states in the union. Home to the Eastern United States' highest mountains, tallest waterfall, oldest river, largest wine industry, greatest gold strike, richest tobacco farms, busiest National Park, as well as a legendary shoreline and the early homes of four of the nation's most important presidents through WWI, it's hard to believe this could possibly be the state long dubbed the Rip Van Winkle State, and often celebrated as "a vale of humility between two mountains of conceit."

Blame the terrain: rugged mountains, unnavigable shores and rivers; impenetrable forests; uncountable creeks, sounds, and swamps, all of which separated would-be neighbors and encouraged the development of independent-minded sub-Carolinas from region to region, island to island, mountain to mountain, holler to holler. Even travelers had a rough time grasping the state as anything more than a collection of disconnected attractions; a New York couple might summer each year at Nags Head and spend every autumn in Highlands, but never in their lifetimes walk the streets of Raleigh.

Quirks of history roped together North Carolina's various regions as a political and economic unit; it was up to North Carolinians to bring an economically viable order from the cartographic chaos. Thus it is that from the beginning, "progress"-minded Carolinians have campaigned for better roads. Wood-plank roads built by African-American slaves linked one coastal river basin to another; others linked the promising farmlands of the Piedmont to the Cape Fear, the state's single major river, and thus to its greatest port, Wilmington, and points beyond. Later, railroads replaced the plank roads in the Piedmont and Coastal Plain and opened up the mountains to commerce and tourism; entrepreneurs tapped the idle rivers above their fall lines to provide electricity for industries that in turn provided the tax monies for more and better roads, as well as giving former subsistence farmers the factory wages with which they purchased their first Fords.

But though these sorts of changes were well in place by the advent of World War II, you'll still meet Tar Heels today who look at other parts of

Union Station, Aberdeen

the state as a foreign land; a native Charlottean, for instance, may have never visited Raleigh. Certainly, you'll find folks in Maggie Valley who know less about the Outer Banks than does the average New Yorker, and you'll find Bankers who have never seen snow.

Be that as it may, federal highways have pried open the oyster of North Carolina enough so that the riches inside are available for the plucking; and people have plucked. Northerners and other outlanders have poured in for years now and attacked the state with the enthusiasm of new converts, contributing—on the good side—to the preservation of many endangered historic districts and sections of land, but also inspiring the development of uninspired "golf course communities" and other exclusionary, prestige-minded developments that run counter to the Calvinist egalitarianism that has historically set North Carolina apart from its high-toned neighbors.

The best of North Carolina's new arrivals, however, seek to learn, and blend in with, the local culture, as do the state's more thoughtful visitors. The traveler to North Carolina today, in fact, arrives at an important epoch in the state's history. If North Carolina ever was the Rip Van Winkle State, Rip has woken up. But North Carolina is no doddering old mountaineer, confounded by the modern world and wondering where his best years have disappeared to; a better name might be the Cinderella State. After all, for years, North Carolina dutifully tended to its business while its sisters Virginia and South Carolina dominated much of Southern (and, until the Civil War, national) history. But North Carolina always knew she was great; always knew that her forests and peaks and rivers and sounds held untold treasures that only needed the right eyes to see them. At the dawn of the new millennium, North Carolina stands clad in beauties conjured by no human hand. Long-denied by an accident of birth, she has finally arrived at the ball.

## The Land

### THE CAROLINA COASTS: BIRTHPLACE OF THE DEEP SOUTH

To understand North Carolina history and culture, it helps to understand her relationship with her closest sister, South Carolina.

South Carolina, because of its deepwater ports in Beaufort, Georgetown, and, most important, Charles Town (later Charleston), quickly became one of the wealthiest British colonies in the New World. First lumber, then rice, indigo, and cotton all flowed out of the region, building a powerful aristocracy centered in Charleston, which, until the Civil War, dominated South Carolina politics and, in fact, the politics of the American South. General William T. Sherman, stationed at nearby Fort Moultrie before the war, recalled the Holy City in the 1840s as a "proud, aristocratic city," which had "assumed a leadership in the public opinion of the South far out of proportion to her population, wealth, or commerce."

Along coastal North Carolina, on the other hand, only the Cape Fear River flows to the ocean without first threading a gauntlet of coastal islands. At the mouth of the Cape Fear River grew the port town of Wilmington, but north of that the Outer Banks discouraged large cargo and passenger ships from reaching most of the state's 300 coastal miles. So even though the first English settlements in northeastern North Carolina began in the 17th century, that area developed very slowly. Even today towns like New Bern, Edenton, and Elizabeth City welcome legions of yachts, but none of the passenger liners and cargo ships you'll find docked at Wilmington.

A state's power tends to reside where its money is made, and in North Carolina, this ended up being inland, in the foothills. While development along most of the North Carolina coast stalled for lack of deepwater ports, the influx of flinty, small-scale farmers from Scotland and Pennsylvania during the 1700s to the state's Piedmont and Mountain regions quickly shifted the balance of power westward in the state. Wedged between haughty Tidewater Virginia and flamboyant coastal—or Lowcountry—South Carolina, North Carolina was shaped by nose-to-the-plow, Calvinist Presbyterians, not by the high-living, slave-owning, cotton- and rice-planting Anglicans of coastal Virginia and South Carolina.

North Carolina was first settled by small, diverse Native American tribes. Next came the Spanish, who poked around North Carolina's mountains looking for gold, attempted to colonize the Beaufort, S.C., area, and departed. And then came the British. Settlers started trickling down into the Albemarle region from Virginia's Jamestown settlement in the 1600s, living on scattered farms. North Carolina's first bona fide town, Bath, came along in 1705.

The towns along the coast generally date from the same period, and the romantic notions that spawned the antebellum excesses down in the regional capital of Charles Town influenced the wealthy in Wilmington as well, and, to a lesser degree, the wealthy of Albemarle towns like New Bern and Elizabeth City. All these port towns absorbed the goods and ideas spilling from visiting vessels, creating a cosmopolitan fabric in these larger waterfront communities.

## GEOGRAPHY
### Size and Area
North Carolina is the 28th-largest state, at 52,712 square miles in area. In some ways, it was America's proto-California. Before California was annexed into the United States, North Carolina boasted the nation's highest elevation, highest waterfall, and greatest wine production, and nearly all of its gold mining. Until gold was discovered in Georgia in 1829, North Carolina was the United States' *only* gold source. Today, North Carolina still boasts many of America's natural biggests and bests, but the claim is nearly always followed by the phrase "east of the Mississippi."

### Elevation
North Carolina slopes from northwest to southeast, and though the change is gradual, the overall effect is the largest elevation disparity in any

state east of the Mississippi. The highest spot is the top of Mount Mitchell, at 6,684 feet. The lowest elevation in the state, as you might expect, is sea level at the ocean's edge—or at the bottom of whatever pit the most energetic Carolinian child has dug in the sand on a given day.

## REGIONS

It's easiest to understand North Carolina by dividing it into four strips. From east to west they are: the **Tidelands,** which encompass the outer coastal areas, including the Outer Banks, but also the coastal inner banks; the sandy-soiled **Coastal Plain,** of which the capital would be Fayetteville or perhaps Greenville; the **Piedmont,** home of most of North Carolina's biggest cities and industry; and the **Mountains,** which shares duties with the Tidelands as the state's top area for tourism. For this book I've subdivided these areas into likely travel destinations.

### The Albemarle Region
The first sector of the Carolinas successfully settled by the English was the Tidelands region called the Albemarle. In the broadest use of the term, "the Albemarle" describes all of the northeastern corner of North Carolina. Technically the term describes the mainland inland of the Outer Banks, along the Albemarle Sound. The sound itself, the end of seven different rivers, slices 55 miles into the continent. Those seven rivers intersecting the region create a very watery area, mostly consisting of marsh, maritime forest, wetlands, and bait shops.

Today numerous state- and federally designated areas, such as the Alligator River National Wildlife Refuge, preserve the area's unique and graceful natural resources.

### The Outer Banks
Technically all the coastal islands off the North Carolina shore—all the way down to the Brunswick Isles south of Wilmington—qualify as outer banks, but in common parlance, the "Outer Banks" refers to the islands from the Virginia border south to Ocracoke Island, in the Tidelands area. Much of this land, fortu-

nately, has been preserved as national and state preserves and parks, including **Mackay Island National Wildlife Refuge,** near the Virginia border; **Currituck National Wildlife Refuge,** near Corolla; **Jockey's Ridge State Park,** near Nags Head; and especially the large **Cape Hatteras National Seashore.** South of Ocracoke, all of Portsmouth, Lookout Island, and the Shackleford Banks have been preserved as the **Lookout Island National Seashore.** This last is perhaps the most pristine of all the preserves. These islands give visitors the chance to visit virtually untouched Atlantic coastline—and they're unreachable except by boat.

### The Central Coast

This Tidelands region has taken to calling itself the Crystal Coast, maybe to attract more New Age travelers. The Core Banks and the Bogue Banks make up most of the central coastline. The Bogue Banks have been developed as a sort of minor-league Nags Head, but the Core Banks remain relatively untouched.

### The Cape Fear Coast

The Cape Fear Coast, for the purposes of this book, includes all of the Tidelands area from the Wilmington beaches—Topsail Island southward—to Kure Beach.

### Brunswick Isles

The Tidelands-area islands south of Wilmington have become increasingly popular in recent years, as Myrtle Beach expands upward and Wilmington expands southward. Inland from the Brunswick Isles, developed but still largely a regional—not national—destination, lies little Calabash, the tiny fishing town near the South Carolina border that has given its name to a style of seafood.

### The Sandhills

In the Coastal Plain region between the Pee Dee and the Cape Fear Rivers, the Sandhills of North Carolina were created, most scientists say, during their days millions of years back when they did service as Carolina's coastline. There wasn't much anybody could do with the land around here; George Washington passed through in 1791 and—gentleman farmer that he was—proclaimed the land worthless. Later military men would disagree; Fort Bragg, near Fayetteville, is

© MIKE SIGALAS

## CAROLINA'S BAYS

No, these oval or elliptically shaped depressions didn't get their name because they look like little self-contained bays, but because of the bay trees that usually grow around them. Look hard enough and you'll find nearly half a million Carolina bays in the coastal plain from Maryland to Florida, but you'll find them most commonly in South and North Carolina. If you drive by one (and you will), you might assume it's just an isolated swamp, but from the air, or on a topographic map, their distinctive shapes make them easy to identify.

So where did they come from? That's what scientists would like to know. Here are the facts: All of North Carolina's bays face in a northwest-southeast direction. Sometimes a sandy ridge will encircle the bay, but almost always only on the southeastern rim.

Is it possible that these bays are the result of a single catastrophic event? Some scientists believe the bays are scars from a meteorite that exploded into thousands of pieces just before hitting the earth. If a meteor hit the earth headed in a northwesterly direction, this would explain the identical direction of the bays and would explain the oblong shape—as meteorite pieces burrowed to a stop in the ground.

It's a fine theory. Unfortunately, no one has found any remnants of a meteor anywhere around the bays, nor have they detected the magnetism normally found around remnant areas.

A second theory, less exciting, argues that the bays' unique shape comes from the area's constant exposure to prevailing southwesterly winds. The ridge of sand around the southeast rim of many of the bays might be the result of occasional strong northwesterly winds from rare winter storms.

Nobody knows for sure. But wherever they come from, the bays are worth visiting. The smallest bays are around four or five acres in area, some serving as private ponds.

the largest U.S. military installation on the East Coast. And golfers would disagree too—the courses of Pinehurst, Southern Pines, and Aberdeen have harvested bushels of tourism receipts annually for nearly 100 years.

### Piedmont
The Piedmont area is home to North Carolina's two famed trios of cities: the Triad (Greensboro, Winston-Salem, High Point), and the Triangle (Raleigh, Durham, Chapel Hill), as well as its largest city, Charlotte. This is the heartland of the state.

### Northern Mountains
The famed resort towns of Asheville and Blowing Rock are here, as is the best skiing. The Blue Ridge Parkway weaves through the region.

### Southern Mountains
Home to the state's best whitewater rafting and some of its most pristine hiking, this region doubles as the quiet underside of outrageously popular Smoky Mountains National Park.

### Great Smoky Mountains
Both nature and the National Park Service have rendered this region a world unto itself. It's the most popular national park in the nation; gateway towns like Cherokee and Maggie Valley have built up attractions—both worthwhile and not-so—to snag dollars from the pockets of tourists passing through into the park. The massive Harrah's complex in Cherokee is home to the state's only true casino.

## RIVERS, SWAMPS, AND LAKES

North Carolina's coast stretches for 300 miles if you fly above it, northeast to southwest, in a straight line. But the true coast has no relation to hypothetical flight paths. Serving as the ocean end of the Roanoke-Dan, Cape Fear, Neuse, Tar, and Chowan river basins, the jagged land fingers of the coast touch more than 1,500 miles of waterfront and contain more than 3,000 square miles of water surface. And that's when the region's not flooded.

The rest of North Carolina is not exactly

parched. While no North Carolina rivers are particularly long (none over 200 miles in length) or wide, there are certainly a lot of them. As one old North Carolina schoolbook explained to children:

*Instead of having a few huge rivers and lakes, North Carolina is lucky to have lots of small ones. It is like having many small meals each day instead of having only one huge meal only once a week. Which would you rather have? . . . A person cannot ever be very far from fresh water **anywhere in North Carolina!***

The story of North Carolina's rivers, to a large degree, is the story of the state. The Chowan, Pamlico, Neuse, and Cape Fear Rivers attracted the first settlers to the coast and defined its settlement patterns—farms and plantations usually spread up the river from the coast—and its trade patterns. Inland, the fact that the Great Pee Dee River flowed across the line into South Carolina helped exacerbate the cultural differences between the settlers of central and western North Carolina and the settlers along the coast. The Winston-Fayetteville plank road was built in 1854 to connect the western part of the state with the inlandmost navigable point of the Cape Fear River, which led to the state's chief port at Wilmington. Daniel Boone and a generation of frontiersfolk who would push over the mountains into Tennessee and Kentucky and parts further west grew up along the Yadkin River in the north part of the state; the clear waters of the French Broad and Nantahala Rivers in the western part of the state, formerly the lifeblood of the region's Native Americans, are now the lifeblood of the frontier folk's descendants, and of Western Carolina's large tourism industry.

## Lakes

The only lakes of any size along the North Carolina coast are **Lake Mattamuskeet, Phelps Lake, Alligator Lake,** and **Pungo Lake,** all south of the Albemarle Sound. In a water-rich area like this, it's easy to see how even the largest natural lake in all of North Carolina—Mattamuskeet—could be taken for granted. It was the center of an

Lake Norman

© ERIKA HOWSARE

Indian reservation in 1715, but over the years local residents have twice drained it and used the lakebed for farming. Fortunately, in 1934 Mattamuskeet became a United States Wildlife Refuge.

Apparently because of their greater age, the Appalachian chain isn't home to the sort of natural, glacial-residue lakes found in the Rockies and Sierras. Most of North Carolina's biggest lakes—including Lakes Wylie and Norman, near Charlotte, and Lakes Jordan and Harris near Raleigh—are man-made.

## Other Waterways

Saddled at the south with Cape Fear and at the north with the Great Dismal Swamp Canal—and that's not even to mention Bodie (pronounced "body") Island on the Outer Banks—it's a wonder North Carolina's grimly named coast ever caught on with vacationers. And yet, despite its self-deprecating name, the Great Dismal Swamp Canal is a favorite of the yachtsy set, who often turn up in Elizabeth City (where, whenever five or more yachts are gathered in the marina, the Rose Buddies will show up, bringing rosebuds, wine, and cheese to the floating visitors). The **Intracoastal Waterway** also slides down the inside of the states, landward of barrier islands, down rivers, and through man-made canals. Running from Norfolk, Virginia, to Miami, the waterway allows boaters to travel up and down the southern East Coast without worrying about storm waters or the Gulf Stream's prevailing northerly current.

## CLIMATE
### When to Visit

Most Carolinians will tell you that the best times to see North Carolina are in the autumn and in the spring. And there's some sense to this.

In autumn, the temperature, humidity, and bug count are down. And the crops are in: roadside stands brim with peaches, apples, and vegetables, hot boiled peanuts, and hot apple cider. In fact, in North Carolina (as in much of the South) most state fairs and county fairs are held in the fall rather than midsummer, to capitalize on the more merciful weather. Around Brevard and Blowing Rock, the leaves explode like a Gerard Manley Hopkins poem transposed into brilliant oranges, yellows, and reds.

On the coast, fall is hurricane season. But hurricanes generally come along a handful of times each century, while *every* fall features some beautiful cool weather.

In the spring, the dogwood and azalea blossoms are out and the weather is a blessed mix: not too cold, not too hot, but just right. In the mountains, the creeks and rivers are full of rain, pleasing waterfall hikers and whitewater paddlers alike.

In truth, though, for people without limitations on their breathing, summer in North

> *Most Carolinians will tell you that the best times to see North Carolina are in the autumn and in the spring. Around Brevard and Blowing Rock, the leaves explode like a Gerard Manley Hopkins poem transposed into brilliant oranges, yellows, and reds.*

Carolina is not all that bad, and it has its own likable nuances. The ocean waters are warm and swimmable, and even the mountain creeks are relatively warm. The kids are out of school and fill the parks. It's also true that a midsummer lightning storm over the Pamlico Sound is an experience not to be missed. And you will certainly being able to say you've experienced the South's legendary humidity at its high-water mark.

So if you're planning a lot of sight-seeing—as opposed to just lolling by the pool, on the lake, or at the ocean—then think twice before visiting between June and September. And this is doubly true if you're planning on camping and hiking, both of which at this time of year become a life struggle against the insect kingdom. If you're already familiar with the South or come from a place that enjoys a similar climate, then you won't have a problem. But if you're flying in from London or San Francisco and stepping off the plane into a Charlotte August, you're going to need at least a few days, and possibly some grief counselling, to adjust.

Winter in North Carolina is a much milder experience than it is in northern states, but the higher mountains get goodly amounts of snow, augmented on the slopes by snowmaking machines, and all the little towns—Dillsboro, Highlands, Blowing Rock—that look cute all year turn into something from an old-fashioned Christmas card. Even foothills towns like Charlotte and Raleigh take a dusting or two, closing things down until all the cars that have slid into ditches can be towed away.

Though temperatures stay relatively warm—almost always above freezing—on the coast, a trip at this time of year is a different sort of vacation than it is in the summer, having less to do with coconut oil and more to do with steaming bowls of clam chowder. The Atlantic is too cold to swim, though surfers brave it with wet suits. Fortunately the large number of evergreen pines throughout the coastal region keeps the area looking lush even in the winter.

## Precipitation

First-time visitors to the American South always comment on "how green everything is." The South in general, and the Carolina coast in particular, is a very damp place. Even the hottest day of the year might have a rain shower. In fact, some parts of Carolina receive as much as 81 inches of rain annually (most of Hawaii gets only 45 inches). The statewide average in North Carolina is around 49 inches of rain annually. Cape Hatteras gets 56 inches; Wilmington 54; and even Charlotte gets 43 inches of rain. But the mountains get by far the most—in fact, they get more rain than anywhere else in the continental United States: Mount Mitchell, the state's high point, receives 74 inches of rain a year, in addition to 58 inches of snow.

One thing that many non-Southerners don't realize is that summer is the rainy season in the South. Convectional rain comes on humid days in the summer. As the sun heats the earth, the earth in turn warms the air layers just above it. Pretty soon you've got convection currents—movements of warmed air pushing its way upward through cooler air. Eventually this rising moisture reaches an elevation where it begins to cool and condense, creating cumulus clouds. As the clouds thicken and continue to cool, they create the dark thunderclouds that send picnickers and beachgoers scurrying for cover.

In a land this humid, every sunny day holds a chance for scattered showers. Bring an umbrella; if you're camping, consider tarping your tent and gear before leaving for any long hike—you don't want to return to a soggy sleeping bag and waterlogged supplies. If you get hit by a particularly heavy storm while driving, do what the locals do: pull off under an overpass and wait it out. These types of heavy torrents don't usually last more than a few minutes.

As opposed to convectional precipitation—a warm-weather phenomenon—frontal precipitation nearly always takes place during the winter. Frontal precipitation also differs in its general lack of drama—instead of a rapidly forming and short-lived torrent, it normally takes the form of a steady rain or drizzle, with little or no lightning and thunder. It almost always means chilly and sometimes polar air masses, but most cold fronts coming down from the north are diverted by the Blue Ridge Mountains. Warm air from the Caribbean often can keep the thermostat at a bearably warm level in the winter.

Frontal precipitation brings what little snow comes to North Carolina. Coastal towns sometimes get a little snow; Raleigh averages about 8 inches, and Asheville gets 14 inches. But the higher mountains get more than four times that much. If you're renting a cabin for in the winter, come prepared with a couple extra days' worth of food and water in case you're snowed in.

## Hurricanes

It seems as if every generation of Coastal Carolinians has its own Day 1, its own hurricane from which to date the events of their lives. As in, "Our Honda's only a couple years old. But we've had that old truck since before Floyd."

North Carolina ranks third, after Florida and Texas, in the number of hurricane strikes since 1899.

Hurricane Hazel of 1954, Hugo of 1989—which caused extensive damage in Charlotte and other inland areas—and Bertha, Fran, Dennis, and Floyd in the late 1990s are the hurricanes that stick out in the minds of many living North Carolinians. Hazel killed 95 people from South Carolina to New York, including 19 in North Carolina, not to mention perhaps as many as 1,000 in Haiti and 78 in Canada. It sent 90-mph winds as far west as Raleigh.

The storm tide at Calabash was boosted by the fact that Hazel came a-calling on the night of the October full moon, the highest lunar tide of the year. On this night, the dotted lines in the centers of island streets normally soak in seawater anyway; with this high tide beneath it, Hazel's storm surges, pushed by 150-mph winds, reached 18 feet at Calabash.

Holden Beach, Little River Inlet, Oak Island, and Wrightsville Beach also took the worst of it. And all the grief wasn't on the barrier islands:

Wilmington cowered under near-100 mph winds. Hazel destroyed more than 15,000 homes and structures, and damaged more than twice that many, creating $136 million in estimated property losses—in 1954 dollars.

The following year, 1955, Hurricanes Connie, Diane, and Ione all hit North Carolina, causing extensive damage. And then things were relatively quiet—for a while. Most every year came watches, with occasional small strikes. But this lull in Mother Nature's war with Carolinians allowed for large-scale development along most of the North Carolina coast.

The rush to build, of course, just set up more pins for Hurricane Hugo to knock over. Hugo blew into the region in 1989, featuring 135-mph winds and a 20-foot storm surge down in Bull's Bay, north of Charleston, S.C.—the highest storm surge in United States history. But Hugo's effect on North Carolina was inland; in the Piedmont area, Hugo destroyed more than six billion board feet of timber.

Several lesser hurricanes hit the coast between 1989 and 1996, including Emily, which did considerable damage along the Outer Banks in 1994. In July 1996, Bertha hit hard and unexpectedly, turning from a dispersed and dispersing storm into a Category 2 hurricane that blew across Cape Fear. Fran blasted her way through much the same areas in September that same year, tearing down thousands of half-rebuilt structures and razing the morale of the region, before turning west and battering Raleigh to the tune of $1 billion. Bonnie followed in 1998, throttling Carolina Beach and surrounding areas.

But none of this prepared North Carolinians for 1999, when Hurricane Dennis skimmed up the Carolina Coasts and then dropped anchor a few hundred miles from Cape Hatteras, giving Bankers a chance to see what it would feel like to live inside a car wash for five days. After finally downgrading to a tropical storm, Dennis headed inland to pour out some eight inches of rain in one day, causing widespread flooding.

This would have been all right, as far as natural disasters go, but two weeks later, before the local news shows could even finish up with the post-Dennis human interest stories, Dennis's bigger brother Floyd came barreling in, dropping 20 inches in some areas—and raising flooding to unprecedented heights. The Tar River had posted a record crest of 23.9 feet during the rainy March of 1998, but after Floyd, it reached 34 to 35 feet.

Nearly every year brings two or three hurricane watches, but this doesn't keep people from building expensive multimillion-dollar homes right on the oceanfront. And why should it? The Housing and Urban Development Act of 1968 (amended in 1969 and 1972) made federal flood insurance available to homeowners and developers, subsidized by taxpayer money. Thus it is that after each hurricane, homeowners and developers replace the old rambling beach houses of yesteryear with beachfront mansions on stilts.

# Flora and Fauna

## VEGETATION ZONES

For the following information I owe much to Audubon International; to the fine *Landscape Restoration Handbook* by Donald F. Harker, Gary Libby, Kay Harker, Sherri Evans, and Marc Evans; and to George Sigalas III, horticulturist at Reynolds Plantation resort in Greensboro, Georgia.

## LOWCOUNTRY FLORA

### Coastal Vegetation

Among the native vegetation you'll see along the coast are the South Carolina state tree, the cabbage palmetto *(Sabal palmetto)*, along with dwarf palmetto *(Sabal minor)* and the groundsel bush *(Baccharis halimifolia)*, covered with what look like tiny white paintbrushes in late summer and fall. You'll also see grand live oak *(Quercus virginica)* and laurel oak *(Quercus laurifolia)* shading the coastal cities.

Many of these trees hang thick with Spanish moss *(Tillandsia usneoides)*, which is not, as many people believe, parasitic. Instead, it's an epiphyte, similar to bromeliads and orchids. These plants attain their nutrients from the air, not from their host plants. Many oaks are also adorned with resurrection fern *(Polypodium polypodioides)*, which looks shriveled up and often blends in with the bark of the tree it is climbing. When it rains, however, the fern unfolds, and its dark green fronds glisten like green strands of jewels.

Sea oats *(Uniola paniculata)* grow among the sand dunes on the coast. Waving in the ocean breezes, they look like something out of a scenic calendar. Because of their important role in reducing beach erosion, sea oats are protected by state law.

### Freshwater Marsh

The North Carolina coast has many freshwater marshes, characteristically thick with rushes, sedges, grasses, and cattails. Many of the marshes and associated swamps were diked, impounded, and converted to rice fields during the 18th and 19th centuries; today many of these impoundments provide habitat for waterfowl. Characteristic plant species include swamp sawgrass *(Cladium mariscus)*, spike-rush, bulrush, duck-potato, cordgrass, cattail, wild rice *(Zizania aquatica)*, southern wax myrtle *(Myrica cerifera)*, and bald cypress *(Taxodium distichum)*.

### Southern Floodplain Forest

Southern floodplain forest occurs throughout the coastal plain along large and medium-size rivers. A large part of the floodplain lies saturated during the winter and spring—about 20 to 30 percent of the year. In these areas you'll find abundant amounts of laurel oak and probably willow oak *(Quercus phellos)*, sweet gum *(Liquidambar sturaciflua)*, green ash *(Fraxinus pennsylvanica)*, and tulip tree *(Liriodendron tulipifera)* as well.

In higher areas on the coastal plain, swamp chestnut oak *(Quercus michauxii)* and cherrybark oak *(Quercus pagoda)* dominate; in lower areas, you're more likely to find bald cypress, water tupelo *(Nyssa aquatica)*, and swamp tupelo *(Nyssa biflora)*, along with southern magnolia *(Magnolia grandiflora)*, American beautyberry *(Callicarpa americana)*, common papaw *(Asimina triloba)*, southern wax myrtle, dwarf palmetto, trumpet creeper *(Campsis radicans)*, groundsel bush, Virginia sweetspire *(Itea virginica)*, cinnamon fern *(Osmunda cinnamomea)*, sensitive fern *(Onoclea sensibilis)*, and the carnivorous pitcher plant.

If the last item on that list piques your interest, consider this: the famous **Venus flytrap** is indigenous to only one place in the world: the area surrounding Wilmington, N.C.

## MAMMALS

Scientists have claimed that in ancient days, camels and even elephants roamed Carolina. Early settlers referred to bison, elk, wolves, and panthers. But you won't find any in the wild today-except for elk that have been reintroduced

# KUDZU: THE VINE THAT ATE THE SOUTH

Although Asians have harvested kudzu for more than 2,000 years—using it for medicinal teas, cloth, paper, and as a baking starch and thickening agent—the fast-growing vine wasn't introduced to the United States until it appeared at the Philadelphia Centennial Exposition of 1876. Southern farmers really first became acquainted with it when they visited the Japanese pavilion at the New Orleans Exposition of 1884–86. For some 50 years afterward, although a few visionaries proclaimed the vine as the long-awaited economic savior of the South, most Southerners thought of it largely as a garden ornamental. They called it "porch vine" because many trained it up trellises to provide shade for swings.

After the boll weevil infestation of the 1920s wiped out Carolina cotton crops, and as years of single-crop farming began to take their toll on the soils of the South, the U.S. Department of Agriculture under Franklin D. Roosevelt imported vast amounts of kudzu from Japan, and the Civilian Conservation Corps planted some 50,000 acres of the vine for erosion control and soil restoration. Down-and-out farmers could make as much as $8 an acre planting kudzu, and in the midst of the Depression, few could refuse the offer.

And that was the last time many of those acres saw sunlight. The problem, it seems, is that kudzu's insect nemeses had no interest in immigrating to America along with the vine, so kudzu actually grew better in the United States than in Asia—often a foot or more a day. Soon, kudzu had covered fences, old cars, and small houses. It swallowed whole trees, depriving their leaves of sunlight and killing them. And this happened at about the time that many farmers realized that loblolly pine timber, not kudzu, could bring them back to prosperity.

Today, a wiser Department of Agriculture categorizes kudzu as a weed. Millions of dollars are spent each year trying to eradicate the stubborn

vine, whose roots survive the South's mild frosts and most available herbicides. Some say it covers more than two million acres across the South.

Read any Southern newspaper long enough and you'll run across a dozen varieties of the same story: "Kudzu May Contain Cure for $X$." Nobody can believe that the plant could be as annoying as it is without also providing some major benefit to humanity. One thing we do know for sure: as a member of the bean family (*Fabaceae*), kudzu's roots contain bacteria that fix atmospheric nitrogen and thus help increase soil fertility.

And Southerners know how to make the best of things. Down in Walhalla, South Carolina, Nancy Basket creates kudzu paper and then uses it in multicolored collages celebrating rural life and Native American themes. Others weave thick baskets from the mighty vine. Some farmers have experimented with grazing goats and other livestock on kudzu, which not only provides free food for the animals but also seems to be one of the few dependable ways to constrain the plant.

Although there may be less kudzu in North Carolina than there was a few years ago, don't worry—you'll still find kudzu all across the Sea Island coast, climbing and covering trees, inching toward the edge of the road. It's everywhere. Are you parked on a Lowcountry roadside as you're reading this? Reach over, open your glove box, and you'll probably find some kudzu.

If you'd like to find out more about the vine that ate the South, go to the website www.cptr.ua.edu/kudzu.html, which will in turn lead you to several other sites dealing with the vine. A documentary, *The Amazing Story of Kudzu*, has been distributed to public TV stations nationwide, so watch your local listings to see when it might be broadcast in your town. Or you can purchase a copy of the video by calling 800/463-8825 (Mon.–Fri. 8 A.M.–5 P.M. Central time). Tapes run about $21.

within Great Smoky Mountains National Park. A similar reintroduction of wolves failed in the 1990s. In the mountains and a few other spots, including the Alligator River National Wildlife Refuge near the Outer Banks, it's possible, but unlikely, that you'll encounter a black bear.

However, you may well see raccoons, badgers, beavers, possums, and a variety of squirrels, though you'll need a flashlight to catch the nocturnal flying squirrel. River otters, beavers, rabbits, deer, and the seldom-seen bobcat also dwell in the forests. Along the coastal marshes and river bottoms, you'll find the rice rat, which, like the marsh rabbit, can take to the water if circumstances require it. Brevard is famous as home to a rare breed of white squirrels; along the swamp ridges and coastal islands you might spot a southern fox squirrel, one of the better looking squirrels nature has produced.

Ocean mammals include the playful bottle-nosed dolphin and the rare, gentle manatee, which attempts to dwell peacefully in the coastal inlets but often ends up playing speed bump to the many leisure craft swarming the waters.

## AQUATIC LIFE

Featuring everything from clear mountain streams to saltwater marshes and the Atlantic itself, North Carolina's diverse waters provide a correspondingly wide variety of fish and other sea life.

### Coastal and Ocean

The tidal rivers and inlets teem with flounder, sea bass, croaker, drum, and spot. Deep-sea fishing—particularly as you head out toward the Gulf Stream—includes bluefish, striper, flounder, drum, Spanish and king mackerel, cobia, amberjack, shad, and marlin, to name only a few. Above Hatteras, the Gulf Stream veers northeast away from the Atlantic coast, marking a sort of Mason-Dixon line for anglers: north of here, ocean fishing reaps such cold-water fish as cod, haddock, and common mackerel; south of Hatteras, the warm waters produce snapper, barracuda, and other warm-water fish.

Off the coast, sharks, sailfish, and small barracuda abound.

Other sealife includes numerous types of jellyfish, starfish, conch (pronounced "conk" hereabouts), sand dollars, sea turtles, numerous species of shark (many of them edible), rays, shrimp, and Atlantic blue crabs. You'll also find oyster beds along the coast, though, due to pollutants, most of the oysters here are no longer safe for consumption.

### Sounds

Currituck and Albemarle Sounds are mostly freshwater, and so you'll find large-mouthed bass and perches and other freshwater fish there. To the south, the sounds are saltwater and home to croaker, bluefish, and small sharks.

### Rivers

Brook and speckled trout are native to the mountains' streams and rivers; the rainbow trout has invaded, after being introduced by fishermen. The rainbow's exploding populations have made the brook trout rare, and they—the exotic rainbow, not the brook trout—are fair game.

## REPTILES AND AMPHIBIANS

The Tar Heel State hosts a small population of one of the most feared reptiles—the **alligator.** Generally inhabiting the low-lying areas of the coastal plain, alligators prefer fresh water; only very rarely will you find them in the ocean—a fact for which the coastal tourism industry is eminently grateful. Although Carolina alligators are not nearly as large as their counterparts in Florida, they can reach up to six feet or so, plenty big enough to do damage to a human being. While alligator attacks on people are very rare, exercise caution if you see one—these loglike creatures can move mighty quick when food is involved.

**Water brown snakes** often grow as long as four feet. You'll find them all along the coastal plain. The water brown is also a tree-climbing snake; sometimes you'll see them enjoying the sun on tree limbs overhanging rivers, streams, and swamps. They feed mainly on catfish. In blackwater swamps you'll find **black swamp snakes,** usually just over a foot long.

But these aren't the kinds of snakes most

visitors have on their minds when they're hiking in the South. North Carolina, after all, features six different slithering creatures that can bring on trouble with a bite: copperhead, canebrake rattlesnake, eastern diamondback rattlesnake, pigmy rattlesnake, cottonmouth (water moccasin), and the eastern coral snake. Fortunately none of these animals are aggressive toward humans; you'll probably never even see one. If you do, just stay away from them.

Most snakebites occur when someone is picking up or otherwise intentionally disturbing a snake.

## BIRDS

Along the North Carolina coast, bird-watchers have spotted more than 400 different species—accounting for more than 45 percent of the bird species found on the continent.

## JOHN LAWSON AND NORTH CAROLINA'S ANIMALS

The British Surveyor-General of North Carolina and an enthusiastic explorer and chronicler of the land, John Lawson came to the Carolinas in 1700 and traveled approximately 1,000 miles through their dense marshlands and forests. Lawson described the flora and fauna of Carolina for fascinated European readers in *A New Voyage to Carolina* (1709), later reissued as *The History of Carolina*. One of the ablest of the early settlers, Lawson helped found Bath, North Carolina's first town, and later helped found New Bern.

After a laundry list of the native wildlife, which included buffalo ("I have known some kill'd on the Hilly Part of Cape-Fair-River,"), bears, panthers, mountain lions, wildcats, wolves, polcats (skunks, "they smell like a Fox, but ten times stronger,") and "Tygers," though he said that while of course he'd seen one once, fleetingly, they mostly lived westward, near the Mississippi. Below, Lawson describes the Carolina panther, once the most feared animal in the backcountry, and today absent from the state except as the mascot of Charlotte's Carolina Panthers, though the animal Lawson describes is closer to what is commonly called a mountain lion:

*The Panther is of the Cat's kind; about the height of a very large Greyhound . . . he climbs Trees with the greatest Agility imaginable, is very strong-limb'd, catching a piece of Meat from any Creature he strikes at. His Tail is exceeding long; his Eyes look very fierce and lively, are large, and of a grayish Colour; his Prey is, Swines-flesh,*

*Deer, or any thing he can take; no Creature is so nice and clean, as this, in his Food. When he has got his Prey, he fills his Belly with the Slaughter, and carefully lays up the Remainder, covering it very neatly with Leaves, which if any thing touches, he never eats any more of it. He purrs as Cats do; if taken when Young, is never to be reclaim'd from his wild Nature. He hollows like a Man in the Woods, when kill'd, which is by making him take a Tree, as the least Cur will presently do; then the Huntsmen shoot him; if they do not kill him outright, he is a dangerous Enemy, when wounded, especially to the Dogs that approach him. This Beast is the greatest Enemy to the Planter, of any Vermine in Carolina. His Flesh looks as well as any Shambles-Meat whatsoever; a great many People eat him, as choice Food; but I never tasted of a Panther, so cannot commend the Meat, by my own Experience. His Skin is a warm Covering for the Indians in Winter, though not esteem'd amongst the choice Furs. This Skin dress'd, makes fine Womens Shooes, or Mens Gloves.*

Though Lawson was one of the first to protest white mistreatment of the Indians, two years after the publication of *Voyage*, he was captured by Native Americans and tortured to death, beginning the Tuscarora War.

Along the coasts, look for various wading birds, shorebirds, the wood stork, swallow-tailed kite, brown pelican, marsh hen, painted bunting, seaside sparrow, migrant ducks and waterfowl, black-necked stilt, white ibis, the marsh wren, the rare reddish egret and Eurasian collared doves, and the yellow-crowned night heron. Popular birding sites include **Pea Island National Wildlife Refuge** and **Cape Hatteras National Seashore, Cape Lookout National Seashore,** the west side of **Sunset Beach,** and Fort Caswell on the eastern tip of **Oak Island** near Southport.

## INSECTS

The members of North Carolina's vast insect population include **fireflies, mosquitoes,** and **no-see-ums.** The first of these are an exotic sight for those who haven't seen them before; people traveling with kids might want to ask around to find out where they can hope to spot some fireflies come sundown.

Don't worry about where to find mosquitoes and no-see-ums—they'll find you. If you're visiting between spring and late fall and plan to spend any time outdoors, bring insect repellent.

## ENVIRONMENTAL ISSUES

As opposed to, say, most parts of California, where landscapers must intentionally plant grass and trees—along with artificial watering systems—North Carolina is so fertile that at times it seems that if you don't hack nature back, it might swallow you up. Farmers complain about "wet" summers here. Grass grows to the very edge of the highways. Pine trees grow everywhere they haven't been cut down, and kudzu grows over everything not in motion.

Consequently, while there have always been a number of farsighted environmentalists in the region, many Carolinians have been slow to see a need for conserving natural resources and preserving places of wild scenic beauty. A common Carolina practice when building a home, for instance, is to a) clear-cut the entire property of native scrub pine; b) build the home; c) plant a lawn, along with a few nursery-bought oaks or willows for shade.

But this view of nature-as-adversary is slowly changing. With the arrival of so many emigrants and tourists from denuded areas, the Carolinas have of late come to see the beauty that some residents had taken for granted. Of course, some native Carolinians—not uncommonly those who bear long-held deeds to now-developable land—complain that activists so recently arrived from bombed-out northern climes have no business preaching the gospel of conservation in their new home. Fortunately many native Carolinians have noticed the declining quality of life and are just as eager, if not more eager, than the transplants to keep chaos out of the order of nature. Rapidly developing trails systems and the acquisition of endangered properties by both the state, and such private organizations as the Nature Conservancy bode well for the future of North Carolina's remaining wilderness.

Perhaps the darkest cloud North Carolina lives under is its need to contain suburban sprawl. The state's cities have grown big over the past 20 years, and they have not, by and large, grown well. The tendency of new arrivals to purchase large lots in cul-de-sac-gnarled "plantations" is one problem to overcome. These huge, upscale developments promise to create an exclusive community for their residents, and not only do these plantations hoard community interest and activities from residents of the surrounding neighborhoods, but they most commonly are built just outside of town, thus requiring the destruction of free space. They also increase local traffic levels, since people who work in town have to drive to and from their new homes on the outskirts. Fortunately, the growing popularity of Traditional Neighborhood Developments (TNDs), with smaller lot sizes, sidewalks, and mixed-use grid layouts that allow people to walk to work or to the market show some promise of creating the sort of environments that will encourage and sustain the friendly, people-oriented demeanor of Tar Heel society for generations to come.

# History

Because North Carolina first developed along the coast, much of the early history of the state centers there, in cities such as Bath, Edenton, New Bern, and Wilmington. But because the state's power shifted so early to the heartland, you'll find important historical sites across the state. The first European colony in North America nestled, if briefly, near Wilmington, N.C. (or Georgetown, S.C.). The first attempted English colony—the famed Lost Colony—was set on North Carolina's Roanoke Island. Such were the beginnings, if by false start, of Europe's conquest of North America. More than 300 years later, humans first propelled themselves into flight from a sand dune in Kill Devil Hills on the Outer Banks, the beginnings of the human conquest of air and space. In the years between, North Carolina saw the vanquishing of ancient empires, the birth of revolts and revolutions, the enslavement and emancipation of a race. She saw the youth of four future U.S. presidents, as well as the rise and fall of coastal pirates, the Confederacy, and King Cotton.

## FIRST ARRIVALS

Ethnologists estimate that about 30,000 to 75,000 indigenous Americans lived in North Carolina at the time of European contact. By 1715 this number had been halved by European diseases and war, and by the time of the American Revolution, the population was a small fraction of its former size. Two hundred years later, most of the Native Americans in North Carolina (less than one percent of the total population) were descendants of the Cherokee who, when told to hit the Trail of Tears, instead disappeared into the mountains.

The numbers of people claiming indigenous

*The first attempted English colony—the famed Lost Colony—was set on North Carolina's Roanoke Island. More than 300 years later, humans first propelled themselves into flight from a sand dune in Kill Devil Hills on the Outer Banks, the beginnings of the human conquest of air and space.*

blood is on the rise, however. Though still only a tiny minority numerically, Native American Carolinians are being lured out of the genetic shadows by the increased celebration of Native American heritage in US popular culture.

## Prehistoric Peoples

If these people had only known they'd end up lumped for all eternity in a dimly lit category called "prehistory," they no doubt would have kept better notes. What many scientists theorize, based on the little existing evidence, is that migrating peoples reached the Carolinas some 15,000 years ago. This was still at the end of the ice age, but they found megafauna such as mammoth, mastodon, and great bison. All we know about these early people is that they made primitive tools and hunted.

Toward the end of the Pleistocene epoch, the Paleo-Indian appeared—that is to say, descendants of the same early people, but with better tools. The culture—primarily defined by its use of Clovis points on spears—spread, apparently, from the Great Plains toward the Atlantic. The Paleo-Indians were North Carolina's first great big-game hunters. They went after mammoth and mastodon; one of their tricks was to burn out a marsh or woods, driving the animals that hid within to slaughter. They may have also added some gathering to their prodigious hunting efforts.

When the ice age finally ended, North Carolina's physical environment, including flora and fauna, went through some predictably large changes. The early Americans adapted to these changes, creating a society fed on fish, shellfish, small mammals, and fowl. With the greater abundance of game, and the resulting leisure time,

reconstructed Native American village in Hillsborough

you might think that a "high" culture would have developed at this point, but the living was so easy, and apparently the existing philosophies were so comfortable, that little change is noticeable in the artifacts of these cultures, though they're separated by thousands of years.

During this, the Archaic period, Carolinians apparently spent spring and summer near a major body of water—a river, marsh, or the Atlantic; shell middens and shell rings identify these sites. The people would move to higher regions to hunt white-tailed deer in the fall, returning to their waterside digs for the winter. Trade may have also begun during this period: tools made of Piedmont materials have been found along the coast; coastal plain materials have been found at Archaic sites in the mountains.

Pottery some experts date to between 2500 B.C. and 1000 B.C. first appeared along the Savannah River around the time Moses and the Israelites were waiting for a ferry on the shore of the Red Sea. Archaeologists have found these simple ceramics around the shell middens along the coast.

During the late Archaic period, domestication of such plants as beans, squash, sunflower, and sumpweed began, though apparently corn was not a big crop in the Southeast until much later.

During the Woodland period—1000 B.C.–1000 A.D.—Native Americans began to rely increasingly upon agriculture. Farming both permitted and required a less mobile lifestyle, which in turn gave rise to further development of ceramics (now that nobody had to lug the pots from mountains to sea anymore) and permanent structures. Being tied to one area also meant that hunters needed to be able to kill more of an area's available wildlife instead of moving on to easier pickings elsewhere; to that end, the bow and arrow—developed around this time—came in handy.

The Mississippian period (named because this type of culture seems to have first appeared in the middle Mississippi Valley region) was a time of great advances. Cultural nuances such as ritual burial practices, platform mounds, and a hierarchical structure organized under village chiefs suggest a sophisticated religio-socio-political system. Along North Carolina's fall line, in the decades after 1150 A.D. or so, as the French were constructing Chartres Cathedral, Mississippians were battling their way eastward into the pristine world of the well-established Woodland Indians.

Because the Mississippians were an unwelcome, invading force, their early sites in the state feature encircling palisades—defensive structures for protecting themselves against the hostile Woodland peoples. Eventually, the Mississippians, and the Mississippian way of life, won out.

Mississippians tended to plant their crops in the rich bottomlands beside rivers, building their villages up on the bluffs overlooking them. One of the best—and only—descriptions of one of these towns comes from Hernando de Soto. When de Soto explored western South Carolina and North Carolina in 1540 (on his way to discovering the Mississippi River), he encountered Cofitachequi, an important Mississippian town on the banks of the Wateree River in today's Kershaw County. Ruled by a female chief, Cofitachequi consisted of temple mounds and a number of rectangular, wattle-and-daub, thatched-roof houses, with storehouses of clothing, thread, deerskins, and pearls.

The pearls suggest that the good folks of Cofitachequi traded with coastal Indians—an interpretation further bolstered by the fact that they were well versed in the existence of the Spanish, whose only other presence in the region had been established 14 years earlier, on the coast, at the failed colony of San Miguel de Guadalupe.

All the Native Americans who dwelt in North Carolina at the time of the European invasion derived from Iroquoian, Siouan, Algonquian, and Muskogean language groups. Northeast of the Catawba-Santee waterway lived the numerous Siouan tribes, the southern portion of the Sioux Nation extending to the Potomac River near what would later become Washington, D.C. At the coast, where the living was easy, tribes tended to be small but plentiful: the Croatan, Tuscarora, Combahee, Edisto, Kiawah, Etiwan, Wando, and Waccamaw. The fewer tribes of the Upcountry—the Cherokee, Lumbee, and Creek, for instance—were larger and stronger.

For instance, the most powerful tribe, the Cherokee, ruled a 40,000-square-mile region—the northwestern third of modern-day South Carolina and North Carolina—though they were constantly at battle with the more warlike Creeks and the Chickasaws of northern Mississippi and western Tennessee, and the Choctaw in the southern Mississippi region. Only with the Cherokees' help during the Yamasee Wars did the Carolinian colony survive.

Out on the Outer Banks, archaeologists think that 5,000 Native Americans known as the **Croatan** may have populated Hatteras Island from as early as 1000, primarily in the Buxton Woods Maritime Forest on the south end of the island. After European contact, however, the story of the Croatan falls into a familiar pattern: exposure to European diseases and other hardships eliminated all traces of the original Bankers by the 1770s. In the 16th and 17th centuries, two tribes from other regions settled into North Carolina. The English in 1584 estimated that some 7,000 Algonquians lived in modern-day North Carolina, but the most powerful group, the **Tuscarora,** were relative newcomers to the Southeast, having recently moved down from New York in a series of migrations. Down in what would become known as South Carolina, the Yamasee Indians, who had had clashes with the Spanish further south in modern-day Georgia, moved up into the Sea Islands around Beaufort after receiving the go-ahead from British colonials in Charles Town. The proactivity that caused the tribes to seek out better living places would later cause them to strike out against encroaching settlers, leading to the Tuscarora and Yamasee Wars.

North Carolinian Indians contributed many things to the Carolinian way of life, most notably place-names. Whether you're surfing off Cape Hatteras, fishing the Roanoke River, or biking the worldclass trails in the upstate's Tsali Wilderness, take time to reflect on the Native Americans who gave the name to your location.

## BRITISH PROPRIETARY PERIOD

Though the 16th century brought a handful of reconnaissance missions and attempts at colonization by Spain and France, the Spanish had nearly all disappeared by the turn of the following century. Except for a handful of Spanish Jesuit priests in modern-day South Carolina, the Carolinas were left again to the indigenous Americans—for 83 years.

But this didn't mean that Europeans had forgotten about Carolina. By the second quarter of the 17th century, Spain's power had declined to the point where British monarch Charles I began to assert England's historic claims to the coast, founded on the discoveries of the Cabots. The king was prompted by his need to do something with the French Huguenots who had taken refuge in England. In 1629 he granted his attorney general, Sir Robert Heath, a charter to everything between latitudes 36 and 31 (more or less from the present-day Georgia-Florida line to the North Carolina-Virginia line) and all the way west to the Pacific. In the charter, Charles lists the name of the region as "Carolana," a transmogrification of "Charles." Despite one failed attempt (the *Mayflower* miscalculated and landed its French Huguenot passengers in Virginia), no one ever settled in South Carolina under the Heath Charter.

### Establishment of the Lords Proprietors

While the Heath Charter was gathering dust, Cromwell and the Puritans beheaded Charles I and took control of England. Upon Cromwell's death, Charles II was restored to the throne, largely due to the efforts of the English nobility. The king was short of funds but wanted to show his gratitude to his allies, so in 1663 he regranted most of the Heath Charter lands to a group of eight noblemen: his cousin Edward, the Earl of Clarendon; his cousin and counselor George Monck, Duke of Albemarle; William, the Earl of Craven; Lord John Berkeley; Anthony Ashley-Cooper; Sir George Carteret; Sir John Colleton; and Sir William Berkeley. This grant was ex-

panded in 1665 into an even larger swath encompassing everything from 65 miles north of St. Augustine to the bottom of Virginia.

Of course, the successors of Robert Heath had a legal right to Carolina (Charles II had changed the "a" to an "i"). To mollify them, the king promised future lands, which eventually turned out to be 100,000 acres in interior New York. The original grants were made null and void, and Carolina thereby gained eight lords proprietors.

The term "lords proprietors" does a good job of explaining both the nobles' roles and their motives in the early settlement of Carolina. As lords, they had penultimate say over what life would be like for settlers in this new land. As proprietors, they had an almost purely financial interest in the venture. Certainly none of them came to Carolina to live. The weaknesses inherent in this government-by-the-barely-interested were to become apparent before long.

### Settlement of the Albemarle Region

Perhaps the first problem the lords proprietors faced was the defiant attitudes of the settlers who since at least 1657 had been trickling down from the thriving colony at Jamestown, Virginia, and purchasing land from the Native Americans around the Albemarle Sound at the mouth of the Chowan River. Unlike later settlers, these first Albemarle settlers had lived—and due to the fuzzy boundaries between Virginia and North Carolina, emigrated believing they would continue to live—under crown authority. For all its faults, royal colonial rule meant that the colony received the attention of the king and his underlings, full-time governing professionals with extensive financial resources. These ex-Virginians tired quickly of the all-too-often amateurish, vacillating, talk-to-me-next-month governing style of the lords proprietors.

The king himself had his suspicions about the lords proprietors' abilities, and so they set out to prove themselves able governors. First, they divided Carolina into three counties: Albemarle; Clarendon, which stretched south from the Chowan River to the Cape Fear Valley; and Craven, which covered the area south of Cape Romaine, south of present-day Georgetown and including present-day Charleston. The Carolina lands outside these counties—which, on paper, extended westward to the Pacific Ocean—could be settled later, as circumstances permitted.

## The Barbadians

After assigning the Albemarle a governor in October 1664, the proprietors went to work on the two counties to the south. Happily, a number of settlers from the successful British colony of Barbados showed interest in exchanging the West Indies' hurricanes, tropical illnesses, unbearable humidity, and already crowded conditions for the chance to settle Carolina. The lords sent the self-named "Barbados Adventurers" an enthusiastic letter promising to assist them "by all way and means" and asking them to spread the word about Carolina among their planter neighbors.

The influence these Barbadians and other planters from the West Indies would have on the structure and flavor of Carolina culture is hard to overstate. With them, they brought a tropical strain of European feudalism that took root in Clarendon and Craven Counties. Their experience raising rice largely determined the economy of South Carolina's Lowcountry through the Civil War, and their preference for West African slave labor would shape Carolina society into the present day.

In 1663 the eager Barbadians had sent William Hilton sailing along the Carolina coast, looking for a good site for settlement, but other than his discovery and naming of Hilton Head Island, nothing much had come of the expedition. In the fall of 1665, Barbadians established Charles Town in the short-lived County of Clarendon at the mouth of the Cape Faire (now Cape Fear) River. Before long, things in the first Charles Town began to resemble a particularly hard-edged episode of *Survivor*. Shipwreck, dissent, Indian trouble, and other problems distressed the settlement, though its population rose to 800 before residents finally abandoned shore and headed for the ships again. Before they did, they sent an exploratory mission captained by Robert Sandford southward to explore the Port Royal area. There Sandford visited with the friendly Edisto Indians. When the ship left to return to Cape Faire,

Dr. Henry Woodward stayed behind to explore the interior and study the native languages.

When Sandford returned to the failing settlement in Clarendon County, he added to the general discontent with glowing reports of the Port Royal region down in Craven County—as yet unsettled.

## The Treacherous First Passage

Port Royal became the new focal point for the proprietors and for their Barbadian clients. Advertisements and pamphlets in England proclaimed the glories of Carolina, and recruitment rolls began to fill with adventurous and sometimes desperate men and women of all circumstances.

After many, many delays, in August 1669 the first three ships (the *Mayflowers* of South Carolina, more or less), named *Carolina, Port Royal,* and *Albemarle,* sailed from England to Barbados, arriving in late fall. Actually the *Albemarle* turned out to be the *Santa Maria* of the journey—it sank off Barbados. After gathering up proprietor-prescribed farming supplies, *Carolina* and *Port Royal* set sail again, with the sloop *Three Brothers* replacing *Albemarle*. Not long afterward, the ships were separated by a storm. *Port Royal* drifted and was lost for six weeks (running out of drinking water in the process) before finally wrecking in the Bahamas. Though 44 persons made it safely to shore, many of them died before the captain was able to build a new vessel to get them to the nearest settlement. On the new craft, they reached New Providence, in the Bahamas, where the captain hired another boat that took most of the surviving passengers to Bermuda. There they caught up with the *Carolina*.

In Bermuda, an 80-year-old Puritan Bermudan colonist, Colonel William Sayle, was named governor of the settlement in the south part of Carolina. Under Sayle, the colonists finally reached Port Royal, on March 15, 1670. As settler Nicholas Carteret reported, the Edisto Indians who greeted the settlers on shore made fires and approached them, "whooping in their own tongue and manner, making signs also where we should best land, and when we came ashore they stroked us on the shoulders with their hands, saying 'Bony Conraro, Angles,' knowing us to be English by our color." These Indians spoke broken Spanish, a grim reminder that Spain still considered Carolina its land. The main Spanish base, in St. Augustine, was not all that far away.

Running across overgrown remnants of Spanish forts on Santa Elena Island—and remembering the not-so-long-ago Spanish massacre of a French colony there—no doubt made the English reconsider the wisdom of settling at the hard-to-defend Port Royal. Neither did the Edistoes seem thrilled to have the English as neighbors. Fortunately for the Brits, the cassique (chief) of the Kiawah Indians, who lived farther north along the coast, arrived to invite them to settle among his people, in exchange for help in beating back the ever-threatening Spanish and their Westo Indian allies.

The settlers agreed to the terms and sailed for the region now called West Ashley, just south of Charleston Peninsula. There, in early April at Albemarle Point on the shores of the Ashley River (the site of present-day Charles Towne Landing), they founded Charles Town. The name honored their king.

On May 23 the *Three Brothers* struggled into Charles Town Bay, minus 11 or 12 of its passengers, who had gone ashore for water and provisions at St. Catherine's Island, Georgia, and run into Indians allied with the Spanish. In fact, of all the several hundred who had begun the journey from England or Barbados, only 148 survivors stepped ashore at Albemarle Point. Three were African slaves.

### Carving Out a Home

The settlers immediately set about protecting themselves against the Spanish and their Indian allies, and not a moment too soon. In August the Spanish at St. Augustine sent forth Indians to destroy Charles Town. Fortunately Dr. Henry Woodward, who had been left behind by Sandford four years earlier, was now able to help. When the Spanish and Indian aggressors arrived, Woodward had just returned from a diplomatic journey throughout the region, in which he had convinced the Lowcountry's many small tribes to

unite with the English into a single, powerful defense league against the hated Spanish.

Facing the united tribes and a well-warned British militia, the arriving Spanish and Westoes decided they didn't really want to attack after all. The Spaniards went back to St. Augustine and decided to get serious about making that a permanent, well-fortified city.

## THE SOUTHERN COLONY BLOSSOMS

By the following February, 86 Barbadians had joined the Charles Town settlement. Shortly after that, steady old Governor Sayle died, replaced by the temporary Governor Joseph West, one of the state's most capable Colonial-era leaders. On September 1, 1671, Barbados governor Sir John Yeamans showed up with nearly 50 more Barbadians. Yeamans eventually replaced West as governor.

In its earliest days, the economies of both the Albemarle and Charles Town depended largely on trade with the Indians. To coax the continent's furs from the indigenous peoples, traders went deep into the territory—some as far as the Mississippi River—bearing metal tools, weapons, and other things for which the Native Americans were willing to trade pelts.

This same sort of trade was taking place up in the Albemarle, but the lack of a deepwater port kept large ships from being able to haul the riches back to England. So while the Albemarle remained small, unprofitable, and unruly, "Carolina"—as the proprietors now referred to the Charles Town region—grew quickly in population and in prosperity. By 1700 it was inarguably the crown jewel of England's North American colonies. However, with so much land and a crop system that required a great amount of labor, the bulk of South Carolina's first immigrants came as indentured servants or slaves to work for those Barbadians already building plantations among the coastal Sea Islands and up the rivers. Since they could legally be kept as slaves for life, and because many of them had experience growing rice back in their native country, West Africans were the preferred import.

Yet while the traders were penetrating the interior, and the plantations spread over vast fields, in *South Carolina: A Geography,* Charles Kovacik and John Winberry estimate that even as late as 1715, 90 percent of South Carolina's European and African population lived within 30 miles of Charles Town. The danger from the Spanish and Westoes was simply too great for most would-be pioneers to venture farther.

Those whites who did live out on the plantations lived largely among their own slaves, with African-American bond servants outnumbering free persons often as much as 10 to 1 in some districts. The voices of whites who warned that planters were setting themselves up for an insurrection were lost amid the clinking of gold in the planters' coffers. The Barbadians had turned a wild land into a boom economy before, and they were certain that slavery was the way to do it.

The lords proprietors, who were all for government by the elite, weren't too concerned about the explosion of slavery in Carolina. Neither were the royals, since slavery was still legal in the British Empire. What concerned them was Carolina's exports: Carolinian rice (and, after 1740, indigo) was extremely valuable to the empire; in the 1730s, England even made a point of settling Georgia to act as a buffer zone between the prized plantations of Carolina and the Spanish at St. Augustine.

By 1680 Charles Town settlers had decided that Albemarle Point was too unhealthy and hard to defend; some settlers began moving north to Oyster Point, site of the present-day Charleston Battery. It really *was* a better spot. Because it was low on the peninsula, coastal planters both north and south of the town could easily transport their goods to Charleston's port using tidal creeks.

## Rebellion in Albemarle

Meanwhile, TK miles northeast in the neglected Albemarle region, the crusty old Virginia settlers had had enough. In 1677 they staged the Culpeper Rebellion, jailing the governor of Albemarle and electing an assembly to carry on the lords proprietors' business honestly for a change. Historians consider this one of the very first political uprisings in Euro-American history.

For once, the lords proprietors paid attention to the grievances of the Albemarle settlers and promised to provide a man of justice and integrity to replace the former governor. To find

© ERIKA HOWSARE

**The High Point Museum features historic 18th-century buildings.**

such a man, of course, the proprietors felt they must choose a man of their own social rank, and so they chose Seth Sothel, who had recently bought one of the original proprietors' shares.

A strange thing happened to Sothel on his way to the governor's seat. A boatload of Turkish pirates captured his ship and took him to North Africa, where he was tortured and forced into hauling bricks as a slave.

Sothel escaped the next year and dutifully headed on to Carolina to assume the position. Settlers who may have hoped that his spell at the bottom of the social ladder would help Sothel empathize with their woes quickly realized that rather than easing their pains, the post-prison Sothel seemed more interested in spreading his own. He ignored the instructions of the other proprietors, jailed Carolinians who opposed him without benefit of trial, and when asked to help settle some private estates, seized them for himself. By 1689 the Albemarle assembly brought him up on charges and found him guilty. They banished him from the colony for a year and from public office for a lifetime.

Fortunately for the colony, accepted standards for political stability were low in the 17th century, and new colonists continued to arrive, rebellions or no. Boats full of French Huguenot Protestants began arriving in 1680; France's 1685 repeal of religious freedoms for non-Catholics accelerated this process.

By now the Spanish had agreed to stop harassing the English settlement at Charles Town, but they forbade any further encroachment to the south. In 1684 a group of Scottish religious dissenters had tried to start up a community at Port Royal, but the Spanish raided it and slaughtered most of the residents. In 1686, 100 Spanish, free blacks, and Indians landed at Edisto Island and broke into Governor Joseph Morton's house, stealing his valuables and kidnapping and then murdering his brother-in-law. They also kidnapped/liberated/stole 13 of Morton's slaves. Normally the Spanish offered liberty to escaped English slaves. In this case, though, whatever they offered these 13 didn't appeal to two of them; they escaped and returned to Morton.

Back in the Albemarle region, the conflicts were still largely internal. The red-faced proprietors had apologized formally for the actions of Governor Sothel and then appointed Phillip Ludwell as governor—and in doing so, made an important distinction. Ludwell's commission described his domain as containing not just Albemarle County, but also the former Clarendon County as well. The concept of the Carolinas as two distinct entities, north and south, and not one or three, had begun to take root.

But after Sothel and some of the scoundrels who had come before him, many Albemarle residents had lost trust in the proprietors' human resources department. Before Ludwell could even get used to the humidity, John Gibbs, who claimed that Sothel had appointed him upon leaving, took two magistrates prisoner and, with a body of 80 rebels, declared himself the true governor of the Albemarle.

Of course the problem with heading a successful rebellion is that you find yourself trying to govern rebels. Gibbs' government proved to have the staying power of a paper submarine, but the rebels had certainly caught the proprietors' attention. After humoring the yokels, the proprietors now felt certain that the northern part of Carolina was far too undisciplined to exist as a separate political unit. Consequently, beginning in 1691, and continuing through 1705, the northern colony labored under the watchful eye of the governor of South Carolina, who per proprietors' instructions, appointed a deputy governor for Albemarle.

Not that the residents of the southern settlement didn't have their own business to attend to. By 1695 Charles Town's citizens (or rather, their slaves) had built thick stone walls and six bastions, making the city into an armed fortress. By 1702 England was embroiled in Queen Anne's War with France and Spain. Since the French were now in the Mississippi Valley to the west, and the Spanish in Florida to the south, the penned-in Carolinians decided to take the initiative and attack the Spanish stronghold of St. Augustine. Unfortunately, though Moore's men were able to clean out smaller Spanish settlements between the rival capitals, the War of Augustino ended in failure—the Spanish would stay in control of Florida until the United States purchased it from them in 1819.

## Towns Come to the North

It says something about the different character of the North and South Carolina coasts—and the proprietors' beliefs about their relative potential for profitability—that though North Carolina received its first English settlers 17 years earlier, the state wouldn't have its first permanent town until 35 years after the founding of Charles Town. Nonetheless, in 1705 disgruntled French Huguenots leaving Virginia began bridging the gap between the two colonies by founding the town of Bath south of the Albemarle region on the Pamlico River. In 1710 a Swiss company settled Swiss, English, and German colonists even further south, along the Neuse River. They called the new settlement New Bern, named after the city in Switzerland. Though settlement continued to accelerate, the first part of the 18th century brought numerous problems to the Carolina coasts—pirates and the Tuscarora and Yamasee Wars principal among them. In each case, when the colonists pleaded with England for help, the proprietors took a deep breath, rolled up their puffy sleeves, and . . . did nothing.

The Carolinians ended up using their own abilities to solve the crises. Consequently, though they certainly didn't mean to do it, it was the proprietors who convinced the Carolinian settlers that they didn't need lords proprietors at all.

## "DOWN WITH THE LORDS, UP WITH THE KING": END OF THE PROPRIETORS' ERA

Though North Carolina would continue on under proprietor rule until King George II bought rights to the colony in 1729, by 1719, south of the Cape Fear, it was time for a revolution, South Carolina style.

It was a very polite and orderly revolution. Everyone said "please," "thank you," and "yes, ma'am." No one was killed.

In a sense, the South Carolina Revolution of 1719 was the opposite of the Revolution of 1776. Colonists in 1776 tended to feel some fidelity

to the distant King George, even while hating the governors and soldiers he had installed over them. But the revolutionists of 1719—which, again unlike 1776, included just about everyone—very much respected proprietary governor Robert Johnson, who had, after all, just saved Charles Town from pirates. But Johnson wasn't popular enough to atone for the sins of the lords proprietors back home. In November 1719, Carolina elected James Moore as governor and sent an emissary to England to ask the king to make Carolina a royal province with a royal governor and direct recourse to the English government.

The royal government—which had interest in Carolina's exports and realized that the lords proprietors were not up to the task of protecting the colony—agreed. While this was all worked out, South Carolina was a self-ruling nation for two years. At the end of this time, Carolinians elected Robert Johnson, the old proprietary governor, as the first royal governor.

Now that the boundaries of South Carolina were more or less defined (though disputes with Georgia over the exact border extended into the 1980s), Johnson set about trying to encourage settlement in the western frontier—both to make Charles Town's shipping more profitable and to provide a buffer against whomever might next want to cause the Carolinians grief. The western frontier at this point meant just about everything beyond the coastal inlets and river mouths.

Settlement continued between the established Carolina colonies too: the first construction in modern-day Edenton began around 1715; the town of Beaufort, N.C., was laid out in 1722, and the town of Brunswick was settled along the Cape Fear in 1725. In 1733 New Town, later Wilmington, was founded further up the river.

## The Plaid Menace: The Highland Scots Arrive

After the king bought out the lords proprietors in North Carolina—with the exception of Lord Granville, who would later sell Moravians the site for Salem—North Carolina began a period of prosperity that would carry it through to the American Revolution. Inland settlement began in

## THE SCOTS-IRISH

Though the original British-American colony in North Carolina was founded by the English, with the exception of African-Americans no single ethnic group has affected the development of North Carolina culture as powerfully as the Scots-Irish. North Carolina claims three native-born U.S. presidents, and all three—Jackson, Polk, and Andrew Johnson—came from Scots-Irish stock. For that matter, so did sometime Tar Heel Woodrow Wilson.

With few exceptions, the Scots-Irish weren't actually Irish at all. They were plain old Scots who came to North Carolina by way of Pennsylvania, by way of Ireland.

At the same time as the founding of Jamestown, Virginia (1607), emigrants from the Scotch Lowlands began to trickle, and then pour, into the north of Ireland—at the rate of 3,000 to 4,000 a year. Hungry for land and Presbyterian by faith, they settled among themselves, mostly in the Ulster region. And there they prospered. And prospered some more. They prospered altogether too much, in the British view. Soon, English parliament prohibited the export from Ireland to England and Scotland of cattle, beef, pork, and dairy products. Due to the Scots-Irish dominance of the wool trade, Ireland was forbidden to ship its manufactured wool *anywhere*.

The Scots were understandably irate, but Parliament made things worse. Presbyterians were already forced to contribute to the Church of England, but in 1704, England began forbidding non-Anglicans from holding governmental or military office. Its pastors were even fined for marrying Presbyterian couples.

Something needed to change, and the Scots-Irish decided it was the scenery. With the dawn of the new century began a flood of Scottish immigrants to the North American colonies. Most Ulsterites arrived in Delaware, Philadelphia, or Boston. By 1749, according to Benjamin Franklin, they made up a full one-quarter of the population of Pennsylvania, and by 1774, the future Quaker State's 350,000 Scots-Irish made up a third of its population.

Pennsylvania's land prices shot up exponentially, and the Scots-Irish farmers began looking elsewhere for cheaper acreage; that's when they heard that North Carolina's Lord Granville was asking three shillings for 640 acres, and was even giving away land free to large groups. The land rush along the Yadkin and Catawba River valleys began as early as 1740. From 1732 to 1754, the population of North Carolina more than doubled, and most of the new arrivals were Scots-Irish.

The independent spirit of the Scots-Irish benefited from the Presbyterian emphasis on education. It is not coincidence this most Presbyterian colony in the nation was the first to erect a state university, and it's no coincidence that the long-oppressed Scots-Irish farmers of North Carolina, alone of all the colonies, refused to ratify the U.S. Constitution without first seeing a Bill of Rights. A century later, their grandchildren would drag their feet about joining the Confederacy.

---

earnest, largely by Scottish Highlanders, who came as early as 1732 and en masse after their defeat at Culloden in 1746. North Carolina, in fact, received more Scots than did any other North American province. Though the exodus of Scots spiked following their loss at the Battle of Culloden, many historians argue that the causes of migration were more economic than political. A population explosion in the Highlands after about 1730 had made it even harder to make a living there.

Though there had been several settlements of Lowland Scots in North Carolina before 1700, the first settlement of Highlanders on the Cape Fear was probably in 1732, and by 1776 the number of Highlanders living on the Cape Fear, primarily around the village of Cross Creek (now Fayetteville), numbered somewhere around 12,000. In fact, so notable was the flight of Scots to America that not long before hostilities began in the American Revolution—in which most Highlanders would side with England—Samuel Johnson, visiting in North Britain, spoke of "an epidemick of wandering which spreads its contagion from valley to valley."

*Inhabitants flock in here daily, mostly
from Pensilvania and other parts of
America, who are over-stocked with people and Mike directly from Europe, they
commonly seat themselves towards the
West, and have got near the mountains.*

> Gabriel Johnston, Governor
> of North Carolina, to the Secretary of
> the Board of Trade, February 15, 1751.

Meanwhile, Scots-Irish and Germans also poured down from Pennsylvania looking for fertile land with fewer Indian tensions. Though light in numbers until after 1739, by 1760 Scots nearly equaled the number of English, though they didn't have much of a presence on the coast; the vast majority of them settled inland, up to the foot of the Blue Ridge Mountains. Future presidents Andrew Jackson and Andrew Johnson would come from the marriage beds of Scots-Irish pioneers.

People of the same ethnic mix were also continuing on through into South Carolina's Midlands and Upcountry, with its rivers leading to South Carolina ports at Charles Town and Georgetown. But with no north-south waterways to travel, North Carolinians—even among the Chowan, Albemarle, and Pamlico sounds—were isolated from one another. North Carolinians quickly realized that they needed to capitalize on their one genuine port—Wilmington, on the Cape Fear River. As early as 1715, the colonial assembly had allotted funds for a 100-plus-mile road connecting New Bern to the Cape Fear. More than 100 years later, a fine plank road would connect Salem and the rest of the heartland to the same river. So it was that the eastern North Carolinians discovered how to turn the toil of their western neighbors into money for themselves. While farmers in the Piedmont toiled, the traders and merchants in the coastal region grew richer and richer.

But no other English colony enjoyed the amount of wealth concentrated in the South Carolina Lowcountry. Plantations generated more than one million British pounds annually, allowing planters to hire private tutors for their children and to send their sons to England for further education. It was these well-educated

planters' sons—familiar with but not unduly impressed by the subtleties of English law—who would eventually lead the charge for the colonies' independence from the mother country.

But while the wealthy were essentially being raised to lead, the Carolinas' constant battles with Indians, the French, and the Spanish were enhancing the average colonist's feelings of military competence and independence.

## "DOWN WITH THE KING, UP WITH LIBERTY": THE AMERICAN REVOLUTION IN NORTH CAROLINA

The popular consciousness has so intertwined the American South with the Civil War that it's often forgotten that the Revolution was also fought here. It's said that history is written by the victor, and in an odd way, the North's triumph in the Civil War long gave Northern academia—centered in Boston, the self-proclaimed "Athens of America"—the job of telling the American story. And in the Northern version, the Revolutionary battles fought in New England and thereabouts are given much of the emphasis. As a result, many people are surprised to find that North and South Carolina were the site of any Revolutionary action at all. (They're even more surprised when (and if) they learn that 137 significant Revolutionary battles were fought within South Carolina's borders—more than in any other state.)

North Carolina agitated less than its southern neighbor before the war, and when the war came, little of it took place within North Carolina's borders. Nonetheless, North Carolinians took part in many of the war's most important battles, and the incidents that took place within its borders were important ones.

Though Loyalist support was stronger along North Carolina's coast than in its mountains, when an impoverished crown began taxing the American colonies, state residents felt put upon. The 1765 Stamp Act drew demonstrations and even armed uprisings in Brunswick and Wilmington; no revenue stamps were ever sold in the state. In 1767 North Carolinians banded together again to boycott a new set of taxes, the Townsend Acts, that levied duty on glass, wine, oil, paper, tea, and other goods.

In 1774, royal governor William Tryon sent British troops inland to the area around Hillsboro to trounce the Regulators, a Loyalist militia composed of inlanders who had tired of being abused and ignored by the eastern-run colonial government. After his victory at the Battle of Alamance, west of Hillsborough, the capable Tryon left Carolina (he'd never much liked it) to become governor of New York. At this point the British might have looked for an able governor who could help quell the general resistance to Parliament control, but instead, as they'd done so often before in North Carolina, the British sent a petty tyrant to do a statesman's work. Josiah Martin, the 34-year-old new governor, paid precious little respect to the elected legislature, fueling the Carolinians' worst fears about the crown's dismissive attitude toward their attempts at self-government.

*The popular consciousness has so intertwined the American South with the Civil War that it's often forgotten that the Revolution was also fought here. Many people are surprised to find that North and South Carolina were the site of any Revolutionary action at all.*

Disgruntled North Carolinians flocked to New Bern—then the colony's capital—to attend a convention and elect delegates to attend the first Continental Congress, in Philadelphia. When the Revolution broke out in April 1775, Governor Martin headed north and a temporary colonial government established itself and prepared for war with the British.

Of course, as in every other colony, not all North Carolinians wanted to go to war. This was particularly true in the western part of the state, where many of the Scottish Highlanders, devout Presbyterians, had signed an oath before emigrating to never again take up arms against the British government. True to their word, most of these men refused to fight on the American side, and many served as Loyalist (Tory) troops.

Nonetheless the Loyalists were badly outnumbered, particularly close to the coast. Governor Martin began mulling over the idea of arming the coast's huge slave population, but the audacity of this pushed the Patriots to the limit. In May 1775, as Minutemen marched on the governor's palace in New Bern, Governor Martin fled to Fort Johnston at the mouth of the Cape Fear River. This didn't stop the Minutemen—500 of them marched to see the governor at the fort, but he slipped away onto a British war sloop anchored off shore.

With no governor left to disobey, the revolutionists, or "Whigs," got serious about governing themselves. At the August 1775 congress in Hillsborough, leaders from around the colony formed a provisional government and began organizing an army to defend colonial interests from the British. That December, more than 700 North Carolinians marched off to western South Carolina to put down the Loyalists there. Others headed north to establish Continental rule in Norfolk, Virginia.

## The Battle for North Carolina

But Governor Martin was not through yet. He recruited Loyalists throughout the colony, including the Highland Scots of the west, and the Black Pioneers, a group of free African-Americans and slaves promised their freedom for service to the Crown.

With war erupting in and around Boston, the British had decided that their best strategy was to take advantage of the strong Loyalist support in the Southern colonies. They planned a military drive from Wilmington or Charles Town that might sweep through the South Carolina Upcountry, then on through North Carolina and Virginia, gathering men along the way with whom to attack Washington in the north.

Martin's plan was for the Highland Scots to march eastward in February and rendezvous with British general Charles Cornwallis, who would be coming south by ship to begin his conquest of the South. Unfortunately for Mar-

INTRODUCTION

© ERIKA HOWSARE

**The House in the Horseshoe, near Carthage, still has bullet holes from the Revolutionary War.**

tin's plan, the Scots got there too early, and the Brits got there too late. When General Donald MacDonald's 1,600 Highlanders marched toward Wilmington in February 1776, the Minutemen were waiting for them at Moore's Creek Bridge. At night, the Patriots removed the planks from the bottom of the bridge, and waxed and soaped the bridge's runners.

The following morning, an hour before sunrise, Patriot sharpshooters lay in wait as the first Highlanders approached the bridge in the fog. The Scots tried to walk across the slippery runners, but sure enough, most fell. As the creek filled with drowning and floundering Scotsmen, the sharpshooters opened fire, slaughtering 30 of them and drowning even more. They took 850 prisoners, guns, wagons, and medical supplies.

Cornwallis finally showed up with his 2,000 troops in June. He sent scouts ashore, and they learned that Wilmington had been lost completely to British rule. He likely found this easy to believe, as Governor Josiah Martin asked (and received) asylum aboard Cornwallis's vessel. Wisely, Sir Henry Clinton of the BritishNavy moved on, but not so wisely, in late June 1776 he tried to land the same troops in Charles Town, at

Sullivan's Island. When the South Carolinians under William Moultrie brought Clinton a stunning defeat there, they gave the American army its first major victory. The news reached the colonial delegates up in Philadelphia a few days later, and it emboldened them to write up and sign a Declaration of Independence from England.

The Sullivan's Island debacle also caused the British to rethink their strategy—and they abandoned the South for nearly three years.

Next for North Carolina came the Fourth Provincial Congress, on April 12, 1776, at Halifax. Here Patriot leaders authorized their delegates to the Continental Congress to "concur with the delegates of other Colonies in declaring Independency." According to many historians, though many Americans had been talking about outright independence from Britain in conversation, this was the first time it had been formally and explicitly called for by any colony. Later in the year, the Fifth Provincial Congress approved the first state constitution, which included a bill of rights, three branches of government, voting rights for free blacks, and provision for public education.

In 1777 the new State Legislature began to

systematically confiscate Tory property. This had the desired effect, causing half-hearted Tories to consider their other ventricles, and sending diehards out of the colony altogether.

## The Tide Turns in the Upcountry

By 1780 the British had seen enough success up north to attempt the 1776 south-to-north strategy a second time. With George Washington's troops now mired down in the North, the idea was to sandwich them by pushing troops up from the South while Washington tried to defend himself to the North.

At Kings Mountain on October 7, 1780, British major Patrick Ferguson—who had issued threats to the mountain men of North Carolina and Tennessee that they would be hung if they tried to oppose his Loyalist troops—was attacked on a hilltop by a body of North and South Carolinians under South Carolinian Andrew Pickens. The "Over-mountain Men" charged up the mild hillside without breaking a sweat and proceded to massacre the British—some 900 in all, including Ferguson. It was a major victory and a horrible slaughter; the British death count was nearly four times the losses suffered by Custer and his men a hundred years later.

The startling news of this major victory for the Patriots—particularly since it was won by militiamen and not trained Continentals—provided a great swing of momentum for the fence-sitting Upcountry citizens who had grown tired of British brutality. Because of this, King's Mountain is considered by some to be the turning point of the Revolution—especially since it forced General Cornwallis to split his troops, sending Lieutenant Colonel Banastre "No Quarter" Tarleton into the South Carolina Upcountry to win the area back for the British. This division of his forces made it impossible for Cornwallis to move on his plan for a major push through North Carolina and on to Washington's army, since that plan required a Loyalist body of troops to stay behind and keep the peace in the Carolinas.

Finally that December, Washington's right-hand man, General Nathanael Greene, arrived with an army of Continental troops. He promptly sent many of them under General Daniel Morgan toward the British-held star fort at Ninety-Six, South Carolina. Tarleton caught wind of the maneuver and—as Greene had hoped—split his own troops to pursue Morgan. They caught up with him upon the shores of the Broad River, at Hiram Saunder's cow pens, on January 17, 1781.

Pickens and his guerrillas joined up with Morgan just before the battle. Morgan felt they were still too weak to take on Tarleton's trained troops and, in order to secure a chance of retreat, wanted to cross a river that would have separated them from the British. Pickens convinced him to stay on the British side of the river, so that they'd have to fight it out. And fight they did, in what some military historians consider the best-planned battle of the entire war. Knowing that many of his undisciplined militiamen would turn and run when the superior force of elite British regulars approached, Morgan put his militiamen in front, and instructed them to fire three rounds, then retreat behind the body of Continental troops. Tarleton's spies told him of Morgan's position and he couldn't believe the Americans' ignorance. He rolled forward his small cannons to disperse the militiamen, but to his surprise, they held their ground. Tarleton's troops were already moving forward at this point, and it was too late to call them back, even after the marksmanship of the mountaineers began dropping the British like so many squirrels. The redcoats faltered and hesitated, until they saw what they'd expected to see—the militiamen were turning tail and running scared.

Or so it seemed. In truth, Morgan had played upon British expectations brilliantly. The regrouped redcoats, augmented by the fresh, hard-fighting troops of the 71st Highlanders, chased after the retreating Patriot militia. And as they did, they found themselves facing the furious fire of Continental regulars. Patriot calvary swooped around the British right rear, and then the mountain militia hit their left rear, having circled around after their strategic retreat. More than 1,000 British and Highlanders were killed or captured. It was another stunning loss for the British—even more so than Kings Mountain, in that the Patriots had defeated the supposedly unstoppable British Regulars.

After Moore's Creek, North Carolina itself didn't see much Revolutionary action until 1781, when North Carolinians helped thin out Cornwallis' men—fresh from King's Mountain—at Guilford Courthouse. North Carolinian men, however, served all throughout the war. Many of the men who spent the bitter winter of 1777 with Washington at Valley Forge were North Carolinians. The war did come to North Carolina in 1780 and 1781, when Cornwallis, having gained control of South Carolina at last, headed to Charlotte. While there he received word that his left flank had been destroyed by North Carolinians at Kings Mountain, South Carolina. Now with South Carolina back in the throes of rebellion, and his men encountering bitter resistance in Charlotte ("The hornets' nest" of Revolution, Cornwallis called the Queen City), the British general set after Greene and his troops. The British chased them clear across the state and up into Virginia, which was precisely Greene's plan—he hoped to separate Cornwallis' men from their supply lines. While Greene gathered new recruits ready to take on the invading British, Cornwallis' troops were disappearing one by one into the villages along the way, tired of fighting and ready to make a life in the colonies. Consequently, by the time Cornwallis finally encountered Greene directly at Guilford County courthouse on March 15, 1781, he had only 2,253 men, while Greene had 4,400. What Cornwallis' men had on their side was experience, and they managed to take a brutal toll on the Continentals; but they also took devastating losses. When Greene finally pulled his men from the field, Cornwallis stood among the dead and dying of his army and realized that this "victory" had likely caused him to lose the war.

Cornwallis marched across the state to Wilmington, which was in British hands. From there he decided to give up trying to take the Carolinas and headed north. Before he left, however, he proclaimed all of North Carolina back under Royal authority and handed over the reins to the dogged Josiah Martin. But if Cornwallis was deluded enough to believe his own proclamation, Martin clearly wasn't. Not long after Cornwallis marched away, he boarded a ship to England and said good-bye to Southern hospitality forever. Cornwallis, meanwhile, with the Carolinas to thank for his army's anemic condition, marched up to Yorktown, where Washington sunk his ivory teeth into the redcoat army's withered remains and effectively ended the American Revolution.

## Forming a Nation

North Carolinians contributed much at the Constitutional Convention. Convention delegate Hugh Williamson suggested, for instance, that the president should be removable by impeachment. He proposed that a two-thirds vote—and not a three-fourths vote—should be sufficient for successful impeachment. North Carolina–born Andrew Johnson would be the first president impeached under this provision.

The fight to ratify the Federal Constitution was heated in North Carolina. The small backcountry farmers, who valued freedom and autonomy above just about everything, largely opposed the document, while Easterners, who saw profits in the stability a strong central government could bring, favored it. When the vote came in August of 1788, the anti-Federalists won out, by a vote of 184 to 84. The convention recommended a bill of rights, and proposed 25 amendments. Together with Rhode Island, North Carolina stayed outside the new Union of States. Pro-Federalists sent out pamphlets to help people understand the document better, but it was only when it became clear a bill of rights would soon be added that North Carolina agreed to ratify the Constitution on November 16, 1789—too late for Carolinians to cast a vote for George Washington for President.

## EARLY ANTEBELLUM OLD SOUTH

Faced with growing tension between the traditional eastern power elites and the inland farmers who made up an increasing majority of North Carolina's population, the state government came up with a compromise. In 1788, the state purchased 1,000 acres near the Wake County courthouse in the center of the state, and plotted the town of Raleigh, named after the English investor who had first attempted to colonize the region. In 1793, the state laid the cornerstone of the first building of what would become the University of North Carolina, Chapel Hill. It was the first state-run university in the new nation.

It was after the 1793 invention of the cotton gin, however, that a different series of events caused the Upcountry and Lowcountry to see eye to eye. The Lowcountry had grown rich on long staple cotton, while the short staple cotton supportable by Upcountry soils took too much time to separate by hand. Eli Whitney's invention of the gin near Savannah, Georgia, changed all that. Now the heartland's short staple cotton couldn't be grown quickly enough.

In North Carolina, the increase in cotton's profitability led to an increase of slaveholding throughout the state. Slaves also made tobacco harvesting more profitable. Predictably, though, this race for wealth caused planters to be reckless with their lands. During the winters, they used slaves to tear out woods and prepare new lands for planting more, more, more . . . rather than fertilizing and thus preserving the quality of the land they'd already planted. Soon, the inevitable happened; soil was destroyed and planters found they needed to move westward to new lands in Alabama, Arkansas, Texas, and Louisiana. Combined with the general depression following the panic of 1819, soil depletion caused a third of North Carolina's population to flee the state between 1815 and 1850. At the same time the coastal counties of North Carolina clung to their rule of state politics, though by 1840 over half the state's population lived west of Raleigh.

## Resentment of the North

In 1811 British ships plundered American ships, inspiring the Carolinas' outraged "War Hawk" representatives to push Congress into declaring the War of 1812. During the war, tariffs on exported goods were raised to support America's military efforts, but afterward Northern lawmakers continued to vote for higher and higher levies on exports and imports. These surcharges mainly punished the South for selling its goods in Europe instead of in the North. Not surprising-

ly, other laws also forced the South to buy its manufactured goods from the North.

Concluding that they were at the hot end of the poker, many Carolinians—particularly South Carolinians—began to talk of seceding from the union to operate as an independent state with trade laws tailored to its own best interests. Even South Carolina–born vice president John C. Calhoun, who had begun as a Federalist favoring a strong centralized government, began to doubt the wisdom of this vision as he saw the rights of Southern states trampled for the "good" of the more powerful North. However, he also saw the political dangers in dissolving the federal union.

## The Nullification Crisis

In 1828 Calhoun decided upon the doctrine he would espouse for the rest of his life—the primacy of "states' rights." He believed that constitutionally, the government of each state had more power within that state than the federal government. Consequently, if a state deemed it necessary, it had the right to "nullify" any federal law within its state boundaries.

Many North Carolina Unionists believed that while a state had the full right to secede from the Union if it chose, it had no right, as long as it remained a part of the Union, to nullify a federal law. (This same theory has been modified and codified by millions of parents of teenagers as the "As Long as You're Sleeping Under My Roof" Law.)

Not surprisingly, the federal government saw the whole idea of nullification as an attack upon its powers, and when in 1832 South Carolina's houses quickly "nullified" the hated federally mandated tariffs, President Andrew Jackson (ironically, South Carolina's only native-born president, who had spent a reckless youth in and about Salisbury, N.C.,) declared this an act of rebellion and ordered U.S. warships to South Carolina to enforce the law.

In December 1832 Calhoun resigned as Jackson's vice president (making him the only vice president to resign until Spiro Agnew, some 150 years later) so that he could become a senator and stop South Carolina's destructive run toward secession, while solving the problems that had so inflamed his fellow Carolinians.

Before Federal forces arrived at Charleston, Calhoun and Henry Clay agreed on a compromise tariff that would lower rates over 10 years. The passage of this tariff pacified everyone just enough to prevent immediate armed conflict. But the debate between the relative importance of states' rights versus federal power became a dividing line between the North—whose majority position gave it power over federal decisions—and the South—which, because it had a different economy and social structure from the North, knew that it would rarely be in the majority opinion on a federal vote.

## The Abolitionist Movement and Southern Response

By this time the fact that most of the slaves in the Northern states had been freed made it much easier for Northerners to be intolerant toward the sins of their Southern neighbors. Most abolitionists were Christians who saw the protection of African-Americans, along with any other unfortunates, as a God-given responsibility. Southern slaveholders—most of them at least nominally Christian, and many quite devout—generally saw their opponents as dangerous, self-righteous meddlers who would be better off tending to their own sins than passing judgment on the choices of others.

The journal of Mary Boykin Chesnut, native of Camden, S.C., and the daughter, granddaughter, and great-granddaughter of plantation slave owners, shows how one Southern woman perceived the similarities and differences between abolitionists and slave owners. Except for a small group of Southern extremists, both sides agreed that the slave trade was immoral and should remain illegal. The question then was how best to treat the African-Americans already in the country. On one side of the issue, she writes, lay the abolitionists, in "[n]ice New England homes . . . shut up in libraries," writing books or editing newspapers for profit—abolitionist books and tracts sold extremely well in the 1850s and early 1860s. "What self-denial do they practice?" she asks her journal. "It is the cheapest philanthropy trade in the world—easy. Easy as setting John Brown to come down here and cut our throats in Christ's name."

As for Southerners, she argues, "We [are] not as much of heathens down here as our enlightened enemies think. Their philanthropy is cheap. There are as noble, pure lives here as there—and a great deal more of self-sacrifice." Plantation masters and mistresses, she points out, had been "educated at Northern schools mostly—read the same books as their Northern contemners, the same daily newspapers, the same Bible—have the same ideas of right and wrong—are highbred, lovely, good, pious—doing their duty as they conceive it."

Many pro-slavery apologists argued that Northerners had no place in the debate over the morality of slavery, because they could not own slaves and would therefore not suffer the societal impacts that manumission would mean to the South.

The crux of the question lay in the debate over the extent of the humanity of slaves. Slaveholders contented themselves that Africans, while admittedly sharing many traits of human beings, were somehow less than fully human, making the slaves' own views about their enslavement unworthy of consideration—any more than a child would be allowed to choose her own curfew. Many believed that blacks were on their *way* to becoming "elevated" as a race but needed close interaction with whites (even at gunpoint) to help them along.

The effect of bloody slave rebellions, such as the Stono revolt in South Carolina and John Brown's massacre at Harper's Ferry in 1859, embarrassed more moderate abolitionists into silence—particularly in the South. Meanwhile, pro-slavery Southerners perceived these isolated incidents as indicative of the "true" ends and means of all abolitionists, inflaming and galvanizing Southerners-even many North Carolinians who had never owned a slave—into a reactionary anti-abolitionist stance that effectively ended reasoned debate on the issue. To most abolitionists the question was one of man's duty to respect other human beings as children of God; to many Southerners, it was a question of to use modern terminology, "choice": slave owner or not, they didn't want anybody taking away their legal right to own slaves. They feared that "somebody" would be the U.S. government, ruled by a majority of non-slaveholding states. As the 19th century pressed on, Southerners gradually realized that as a perennial minority faction, their only hope for self-determination on the slavery issue was to ensure continued state autonomy. Hence the "states' rights" argument: defending a state's right to determine what was best for its own people.

## The Cult of Slavery: Slavery as Intrinsically Good

Carolinians had earlier tolerated slavery more or less as a necessary evil. But largely in reaction to the continual sparring with abolitionists, in the last decades before the Civil War many people in North Carolina reached a new height of sophistry, proclaiming slavery a positive good: a benefit to the enslaved, and a proper response to the "natural" differences between whites and blacks. Apologists such as Thomas Harper argued that the wage-employee system of the North was irresponsible—and more exploitive than slavery itself. The Southern slaveholder, after all, paid room and board for a slave even when the slave was too young, too sick, or too old to work. Meanwhile the Northern capitalist paid his wage earners only for the hours they worked. When they were sick, or when they got too old, or when a new technology came along that they were not trained for, the wage payer could fire the employees, and his responsibility for their welfare was considered finished. (Some historians argue that the average slave was actually paid 90 percent of his or her life's earnings by the time of death.) Virginian George Fitzhugh, in such 1850s titles as *Sociology for the South* and *Cannibals All!*, argued that slavery, being the most humane and efficient system, was destined to regain its popularity throughout the world.

Though Fitzhugh's prediction was off by a mile, certainly slavery was "popular" in North Carolina before the war, and not only among wealthy whites. Abolitionist *London Times* reporter William Howard Russell, observing the impoverished villages of the Dismal Swamp in the first days of the Civil War, suggested a psychological motivation: "the poor whites here are rabid to have a class below them," he explained, "ergo they are all for slaves." In South Carolina, a

movement was even launched to require every white man in the state to own at least one slave, the idea being that, as with home ownership (long an accepted requirement for voting), *slave* ownership would help instil in the lowliest Sandhills farmer the maturity and responsibility desirable in a gentleman citizen.

In 1838, when most Cherokee left North Carolina on their forced walk to Oklahoma, 10 percent of them left with the black slaves they owned. Historian Richard Rollins estimates that by 1860, a full 25 percent of all free Southern blacks legally owned slaves. Some were family members purchased by free blacks, but most were purchased to act as the owners' servants or workers.

## The Mexican War

The 1846 war with Mexico affected the Carolinas considerably. For North Carolinians, what was at stake was the acquisition of additional lands open to slavery—and hence more representation in the U.S. Congress for slaveholding states. Though North Carolina contributed only one regiment, which saw no significant action, it was Pineville-born President James K. Polk—who had moved on to Tennessee in earlier years—who sent them into action. In fact, many former North Carolinians fought in the war, including James Pinckney Henderson, born near Lincolnton. He returned from Mexico to serve as the first governor of Texas, and later, as U.S. Senator.

Even with its much smaller population, the South as a whole, in fact, sent and suffered the loss of more soldiers, furnishing 43,232 men in the Mexican War while the North, whose pundits had disapproved of the effort, sent along only 22,136 troops. Hence the Wilmot Proviso, a proposal by a Pennsylvanian legislator to ban slavery within all territory acquired as a result of the Mexican War, struck Carolinians as extremely unjust: Southerners who had risked their lives to win over the new Southwest were now being told they could not expect to bring their "property" with them if they settled there. John C. Calhoun successfully rallied the rest of the slaveholding states to oppose Wilmot's plan as yet another effort to tighten the noose around slavery's neck. The Southern-led Senate blocked the bill.

But the question of slavery's status in the expanding nation's new and future territories now lay out in the open. The issues raised by the acquisition of the American West in the Mexican War made plain to Northerners and Southerners their different visions of America's destiny and accelerated the nation's tailspin toward civil war. In the North, many of those willing to tolerate the cancer of slavery in states that already practiced it could not with good conscience watch it spread to new lands beneath the shadow of the Stars and Stripes. The South, which had held a hope that territorial expansion and the spread of slavery might allow the region to ascend again to equality or even dominance in national politics, finally had to confront the fact that the North would never allow this to happen. As long as the South remained in the Union, it would always be the oppressed agricultural region, its interests continually overlooked for those of the industrialized North.

Of course, Calhoun had been telling the rest of the South this since the Nullification Crisis twenty years before.

### Eruption of Secessionism and the Descent into War

Though the Coffin brothers and other Quaker Abolitionists in the Piedmont courageously spirited escaped slaves northward along the Underground Railroad, few North Carolina whites saw general emancipation as a viable option. Even Abraham Lincoln believed the races couldn't live together peaceably as equals; he supported the notion of sending slaves—American-born or not—to Africa. Many slaves and free blacks shared this viewpoint, believing that white prejudice was so ingrained that the establishment of a separate black republic was the only solution. Not only would it destroy the economy, affecting the slaveholding minority and non-slaveholder majority alike, but whites feared the "Africanization" of their cherished society and culture, as they had seen happen after slave revolutions in some areas of the West Indies.

Carolinian leaders had long divided up between devoted Unionists, who opposed any sort

of secession, and those who believed that secession was the sacred right of any state that had chosen to join the union in the first place. Calhoun proposed that Congress could not exclude slavery from the territories and that a territory, when it became a state, should be allowed to choose which type of economy it wanted—free labor or slave. But after Calhoun's death in 1850, the South was left without a leader great enough, both in character and in national standing, to stave off the more militant Carolinian factions' desire to secede immediately.

## "THE WAR FOR SOUTHERN INDEPENDENCE"

When Lincoln was elected, a number of conventions around the Deep South organized to discuss their options. South Carolina's assembly met first, at Columbia on December 17, 1860. States with strong pro-secession movements like Alabama and Mississippi sent delegates to the convention, where they advised the Carolinians to "take the lead and secede at once."

Thus it was that on December 20, 1860, South Carolinian delegates in Charleston voted to secede from the Union.

Six days later, on the day after Christmas, Major Robert Anderson, commander of the U.S. garrisons in Charleston, withdrew his men against orders into the island fortress of Fort Sumter in the midst of Charleston Harbor. South Carolina militia swarmed over the abandoned mainland batteries and trained their guns on the island. Sumter was the key position to preventing a sea invasion of Charleston, so Carolina could not afford to allow the Federals to remain there indefinitely. Rumors spread that Yankee forces were on their way down to seize the port city, making the locals even itchier to get their own troops behind Sumter's guns.

Meanwhile the secessions continued. Mississippi seceded only a few weeks after South Carolina, and the rest of the lower South followed. On February 4, a congress of southern states met in Montgomery, Alabama, and approved a new constitution—which, among other things, prohibited the African slave trade.

# IN SHERMAN'S WORDS:
## SURRENDER AT BENNETT PLACE

At Bennett Place in Durham, N.C., Virginia-born Confederate general Joseph E. Johnston surrendered to Union General William T. Sherman in April 1865, effectively ending the American Civil War. The generals' first meeting came 17 days after Lee's surrender in Appomattox and on the very morning that Sherman had received a telegram telling of President Lincoln's assassination. Years later, in his autobiography, Sherman remembered the meeting:

*We rode up the Hillsboro' road for about five miles, when our flag bearer discovered another coming to meet him: They met, and word was passed back to us that General Johnston was near at hand, when we rode forward and met General Johnston on horseback, riding side by side with General Wade Hampton. We shook hands, and introduced our respective attendants. I asked if there was a place convenient where we could be private, and General Johnston said he had passed a small farmhouse a short distance back, when we rode back to it together side by side, our staff-officers and escorts following. We had never met before, though we had been in the regular army together for thirteen years; but it so happened that we had never before come together. He was some twelve or more years my senior; but we knew enough of each other to be well acquainted at once. We soon reached the house of a Mr. Bennett, dismounted, and left our horses with orderlies in the road. Our officers, on foot, passed into the yard, and General Johnston and I entered the small frame-house. We asked the farmer if we could have the use of his house for a few minutes, and he and his wife withdrew into a smaller log-house, which stood close by.*

*As soon as we were alone together I showed him the dispatch announcing Mr. Lincoln's assassination, and watched him closely. The perspiration came out in large drops on his forehead, and he did not attempt to conceal his distress. He denounced the act as a disgrace to the age, and hoped I did not charge it to the Confederate Government. I told him I could not believe that he or General Lee, or the officers of the Confederate army, could possibly be privy to acts of assassination; but I would not say as much for Jeff. Davis, George Sanders, and men of that stripe. We talked about the effect of this act on the country at large and on the armies, and he realized that it made my situation extremely delicate. I explained to him that I had not yet revealed the news to my own personal staff or to the army, and that I dreaded the effect when made known in Raleigh. Mr. Lincoln was peculiarly endeared to the soldiers, and I feared that some foolish woman or man in Raleigh might say something or do something that would madden our men, and that a fate worse than that of Columbia [SC, which Sherman's men had burned to the ground] would befall the place.*

As it turned out, Secretary of War Edwin Stanton was concerned that Sherman's terms were too generous, and he suspended Sherman's orders and sent General Grant hustling down to evaluate the situation. In the end, Johnston's troops were given the same terms as Lee's at Appomattox. Both Union and Confederate troops waited in the area for several days, during which they raided a local tobacco warehouse and quickly became addicted to Bull Durham tobacco, thereby ensuring the region's economic survival in the grim years to come.

Sherman and Johnston went on to become good friends. After Sherman's death, one of the men serving as his pallbearer was Joseph E. Johnston.

© ERIKA HOWSARE

**Bennett Place**

Lincoln, and other Unionists, argued that the United States was "one nation, *indivisible*," and denied the Southern states' right to secede. Raleigh-born congressman Andrew Johnson of Tennessee, alone among Southern legislators, refused to abandon the Congressional chamber with his fellow Southerners, but instead publicly dedicated his very "blood" to saving the Union.

While Johnson's former neighbors in North Carolina didn't all share the vehemency of his belief, neither had they thrown in their hats with the Confederacy. Unionism was extremely popular among Tar Heels, who in their independent-minded thinking had no desire to place themselves under the thumb of Charleston or Richmond any more than they wanted to be under Washington's. It looked as if a war were imminent. Virginia, which had not yet seceded, called for a peace conference, and North Carolina, similarly uncommitted, sent delegates. But it didn't matter; Washington ignored the conference's suggestions. Even the best efforts of reasonable minds couldn't pierce the accumulated bitterness on both sides of the Mason-Dixon line.

When, on January 9, 1861, the U.S. ship *Star of the West* approached with provisions for the soldiers in Fort Sumter, two Citadel cadets fired what was arguably the first shot of the War between the States in Charleston Harbor—a cannon shot meant to warn the vessel off. One of the ship's officers quipped, "The people of Charleston pride themselves on their hospitality. They gave us several balls before we landed."

Then, for the rest of the month and through February and March, nothing happened. Finally Virginian orator Roger Pryor barreled into Charleston, proclaiming that the only way to get Old Dominion to join the Confederacy—and thus bring along North Carolina and the border states—was for South Carolina to instigate war with the United States. The obvious place to start was right in the midst of Charleston Harbor.

On April 10 the *Mercury* reprinted stories from New York papers that told of a naval expedition sent southward toward Charleston. The Carolinians could wait no longer if they hoped to take the fort without having to take on the U.S. Navy at the same time. Some 6,000 men were now stationed around the rim of the harbor, ready to take on the 60 men in Fort Sumter. At 4:30 A.M. on April 12, after days of intense negotiations, and with Union ships just outside the harbor, the firing began. Thirty-four hours later, Anderson's men raised the white flag and were allowed to leave the fort with colors flying and drums beating, saluting the U.S. flag with a 50-gun salute before taking it down. During this salute one of the guns exploded, killing a young soldier—the only casualty of the bombardment and the first casualty of the war.

Again South Carolina's instigation persuaded others to join the Confederacy. British journalist William Howard Russell, travelling in the South at the time of the firing on Fort Sumter, described the scene at Goldsboro:

> *At Goldsborough & elsewhere [there is] much excitement & a good deal of drink. State volunteers [are] going out to seize the U.S. fortresses Macon & Caswell & of course [they are] ungarrisoned. Ladies [stand] waving kerchiefs from the public house to drunken [marching] men, [whose] arms [are] bad. [They are] splendid long-legged chaps tho', very often handsome faces. . . . Lincoln's proclamation calling 75,000 out is all laughed at & derided.*

The next night, on April 15, Russell's train arrived in Wilmington:

> *[I] walked across [the] platform to [a] room where [a] rude supper was spread & slaves waited— . . . [The]Vigilance Comm[itt]ee would not permit my telegraph to go. They were all drunk. I refused to see them . . . [they told] coarse jokes about old Abe, [though] some said Anderson could not help defending Sumter.*

In summarizing his findings in a hastily scribbled letter to British Minister Lord Lyons a few days later, Russell wrote:

> *North Carolina was in revolt—that is, there was no particular form of authority to rebel against, but the shadowy abstractions in lieu of it were treated with deserved contempt by the "Citizens" who with flint muskets & quaint uniforms were ready at the various stations to seize on anything—particularly whiskey— which it occurred to them to fancy. At Wilmington I sent a message to the electric telegraph office for transmission to New York, but the "Citizens" of the Vigilance Committee refused to permit the message to be transmitted, & were preparing to wait upon me with a view of asking me what were my general views on the state of the world, when I informed them peremptorily that I must decline to hold any intercourse with them—which I the more resolved to do in that they were "highly elated & excited" by the news from Sumter.*

Even if they weren't all elated, the entire South was excited. When Lincoln demanded troops from Southern states, Virginia, Arkansas, North Carolina, and Tennessee, now certain that the President meant to use force to keep their fellow Southern states under federal rule, seceded one by one.

Of these Johnny-Reb-Come-Latelies, North Carolina came nearly last of all. In fact, though it would lose more men than any other Southern state to Yankee bullets, North Carolina was always divided in its feelings, even after the war began, resenting the high-handedness of Jefferson Davis and the Confederate government nearly as much as it did the encroachments of the Federals. In Greensboro, Quaker farmer Vestal Coffin and his cousin Levi sheltered hundreds of escaping slaves; Levi later moved up to Ohio, where he oversaw the Underground Railroad and became known in Abolitionist circles as its president. In addition, the very inflammatory and influential 1857 book, *The Impending Crisis of the South: How to Meet It,* circulated by Republicans in 1860 as an antislavery tract during the election, had been penned by Davie County native Rowan Helper. And whereas South Carolina's coastal residents, ruled by its large plantation owners, led the charge into the fray, the independent folks of the Outer Banks, at least, saw no benefit in protecting the rights of wealthy slave-owning mainlanders.

All told, North Carolina in 1860 had just

34,658 slave owners out of a white and free-black population of more than 660,000. Those 34,658 owned over 330,000 slaves, and each slave counted for three-fifths of a vote—to be cast by their owners—but even this didn't give slaveholders a majority in the Tar Heel State. Nonetheless, most North Carolinians subscribed to the states' rights doctrine, and on general principle resented the intrusion of the federal government into state affairs. Though Governor John Ellis waited to see whether or not Lincoln would send troops to try to hold the more radical Deep Southern states in the Union, North Carolinians would not stand to see Federals march through their state to fight their Southern brethren.

On January 8, 1861, a day before the firing on Fort Sumter, overeager North Carolina troops disobeyed their governor and seized Fort Caswell and Fort Johnston at the mouth of the Cape Fear River. Ellis, not wanting to provoke the Union to violence, ordered the rebels to return the forts to federal hands.

On March 15, North Carolina Senator Thomas L. Clingman—for whom the Smokies' highest peak is named—and Senator Stephen A. Douglas proposed evacuating nearly all the forts in the seceded states, including Forts Johnston and Caswell, and Fort Sumter in Charleston. They thought (rightly) that this would defuse the most obvious flashpoints for confrontation between Federals and local secessionists, allowing time for peaceable discussion of the issues. It was rumored that Lincoln planned to carry out this idea, despite the fact that his old Illinois enemy Douglas had proposed it. Then, unexpectedly, Lincoln sent Federal ships to Charleston to reprovision the soldiers in Fort Sumter, which led Charlestonians to fire the first shot of the war.

In truth the outgunned, outmanned, and virtually navy-less South had no chance against the North. Federal ships sailed along the southern coastline, sealing off one important port after another.

After the weakly defended Fort Hatteras fell to Federal troops in August 1861, the pro-Union locals held a convention proclaiming secession null and void, and declaring the village of Hatteras itself the capital of "the true and faithful State of North Carolina." In November the Outer Bankers elected Marble Nash Taylor as their governor. Like the western Virginians, they sent delegates to Washington, D.C., with hopes of being seated in the U.S. Congress. Unlike the Virginian Appalachians, whose region became the state of West Virginia, the Banker delegation never convinced the right people to take them seriously, and they were never seated or recognized.

After capturing Fort Hatteras, the Federals took Roanoke Island in February 1862, New Bern and Washington in March. One of the Union soldiers in this operation was George Washington Whitman, younger brother of poet Walt Whitman, who described a part of the Roanoke rout to his mother:

*We . . . started after the rebels, quite a number of whom had broke for the shore about a mile off. The way was pretty well strewn with blankets and coats thrown off by the rebels as they ran. A few of them escaped in boats, but we got 40 or 50 there. . . . After travelling about an hour we found two dead rebels lying in the woods and farther on lay another just dying, the top of his head being shot off. . . . We met . . . a party with a flag. They said they came from a large force and wanted to make terms for a surrender . . . they had had enough for one day and stacked their arms and wilted without a struggle.*

The same systematic closing of ports and taking of port towns took place in South Carolina. What the Federals *couldn't* do was take Wilmington or Charleston, and this fact allowed blockade runners to bring in needed supplies to the Southern armies, protracting America's bloodiest war by several years.

North Carolina lost more men in sheer numbers than any other state: 19,673 killed in battle, a full one-fourth of all Confederate battle deaths. It also lost more men to desertion (23,000) than any other state—as well it should have, given the way the North Carolinians felt the Confederate government mistreated them.

For instance, complained former Unionist and North Carolina Governor Zebulon B. Vance, by drafting Tar Heels into the army and then marching them off to fight in other states, the Confederate Government had carelessly left North Carolina's mammoth coastline vulnerable to attack. Vance also protested that, due to Jefferson Davis' resentment and distrust of North Carolinians for their slowness at seceding, a glass ceiling kept worthy Confederate North Carolina officers from receiving the general's commissions they deserved, thus depriving Tar Heel soldiers of serving under Tar Heel generals, who, presumably, would treat them with paternal concern. Given the high death rate of North Carolinians on the battlefields of Virginia and Pennsylvania, it's easy to understand Vance's concern.

Sherman's 1865 march through Georgia and the Carolinas resulted in the burning of Atlanta and Columbia, but confident that the South's spirit had been crushed, and acknowledging North Carolina's reluctance to secede in 1861,North Carolina escaped relatively unscathed—despite the fact that most of Sherman's incendiary legions were stationed in Raleigh when news came of Lincoln's assassination. At the Bennett farmhouse near Durham, Confederate General Joseph Johnston—leader of the last major Confederate army in the field—surrendered to Union General William T. Sherman. The generals' first meeting came 17 days after Lee's surrender at Appomattox and on the very morning that Sherman had received a telegram telling of President Lincoln's assassination. Illinois Sergeant George F. Cram, one of Sherman's troops, described the effect of this news on Raleigh's citizens and occupying soldiers:

> *Yesterday our camps were filled with intense sorrow over the death of Mr. Lincoln. A shadow was thrown suddenly over our rejoicing and the feeling in the entire army is deep mourning. The citizens of this place held a meeting yesterday and made some resolutions expressing their sorrow at the occurrence and even the old rebels seem to feel a kind of horror at such a dastardly deed.*

That night, drunken and distraught Federals attempted to burn Raleigh to the ground; that they didn't is due to the courage of Union Major General John "Black Jack" Logan. The general, whom Sherman had demoted out of concern for his pre-war role as a Democratic "Copperhead" congressman and for his suspected continued pro-Southern sympathies, rode into the midst of the marching crowd and announced that if they were going to burn Raleigh, they'd have to shoot him first. The crowd backed down, and Raleigh was spared. (Logan would return to Washington as a Republican senator after the war, and ironically would be one of the mob of Radical Republicans who would try to bring down the presidency of Raleigh-born President Andrew Johnson.)

# RECONSTRUCTION

Though they had long made up a sizeable portion of North Carolina's population, African-Americans played a prominent role in governing North Carolina for the first time when Federal troops occupied the state after the war.

Just as Jefferson Davis would have predicted, to a degree, North Carolina went along with the occupying Federals. Many believed that white Carolinians would do well to accept President Andrew Johnson's terms for re-entry to full participation in the Union. However when the powerful "radical" anti-Southern Congress seized control of the Reconstruction process, things got harder for white Carolinians. The idea of these Republicans was to establish a solidly Republican South by convincing blacks to vote Republican and then keeping former Confederates from voting for as long as possible. Northern industrialists, increasingly powerful in the postwar years, had every reason to support the party that promised to keep Southern agricultural interests selling at depressed prices for years to come.

North Carolina's federally mandated new constitution of 1868 brought democratic reforms, but by now most whites viewed the Republican government as representative of black interests only and were largely unsupportive. Laws forbidding former Confederates—which included much of the white male population of North Carolina—from bearing arms only exacerbated the tensions, as rifle-bearing black militia units began drilling in the streets.

Added to the brewing interracial animosity was many whites' sense that their former slaves had betrayed them. Before the war most slave-holders had convinced themselves that they were treating their slaves well and had thus earned their slaves' loyalty. Understandably most slaves had been willing to give their masters the impression that they were indeed devoted to the household. Hence, when the Union Army rolled in and slaves deserted by the thousands (though many did not), slaveholders took it as a personal affront—a sort of treason.

And thus went Reconstruction in North Carolina: the black population scrambled to enjoy and preserve its new rights while the white population attempted to claw its way back to the top of the social ladder by denying blacks those same rights.

Perhaps predictably, Ku Klux Klan raids began shortly thereafter, terrorizing blacks and black sympathizers in an attempt to re-establish white supremacy. The blatant corruption of the "carpet-bagger" Republican Governor William Holden and of the legislature, combined with the Klan's success at stifling black voting, led to the election of a Democrat majority in the state legislature in 1870. A year later, the Democrats had impeached Governor Holden; four years later, Democrats amended their state constitution in 1875 and returned wartime governor Zebulon Vance to office in 1876. After the white majority's essential aims were met, the Klan largely disbanded.

But racial antagonisms were far from over. Another "vigilance" group, the Red Shirts of South Carolina, showed up just before the 1898 elections in Wilmington, a town long dominated by Republicans. They stirred up whites and frightened blacks, though at first there was no violence. Their aims, however, were clear: just before the election, the chairman of the state Democratic party issued an appeal to white Tar Heels to turn out for the vote, asserting that "North Carolina is a WHITE MAN'S STATE, and WHITE MEN will rule it." Begrudging the

continued Republican rule in the black-majority region, and inflamed by alleged aspersions cast upon white women by the editorials of a local black newspaper, some 600 to 2,000 armed whites burned the newspaper offices. Though reports varied, rioters by most accounts killed some 14 blacks, jailed 10 others, and ran the "negro political leaders," including the white Republican mayor, out of town. This coup d'état ended with the establishment of a Democratic former Confederate officer as mayor. The following year, the triumphant leaders of the Wilmington Riot led the movement for the establishment of the Grandfather Clause, which effectively disenfranchised the black population of North Carolina, ensuring Democratic rule for the next sixty years.

## THE NEW SOUTH

In 1886 Atlanta newspaper publisher Henry W. Grady, speaking before a New York audience, proclaimed his vision of a "New South"—a South, that is, based on the Northern economic model. By now the idea had already struck some enterprising North Carolinians that all that cotton, tobacco, and hardwood lumber they were sending north at cut rates could be processed just as well in-state, while allowing Carolinians to prosper not only from its harvesting, but from its processing. Factories arose along the powerful rivers of the Piedmont, making cigarettes, textiles, and furniture. In 1880, the state began its "Cotton Mill Campaign," a propaganda program to educate people about the benefits of industrializing the state to process the raw materials grown there in the state. It worked.

By the end of the 19th century, the textile industry was exploding across Piedmont, with its powerful turbine-turning rivers—at last bringing relief from the depressed sharecropper economy. The growing popularity of the Piedmont's bright leaf tobacco helped many farmers recover, though not all Carolina farmers were able—because of soil conditions—to grow it.

James Duke's development of mass-production cigarettes brought a true upper caste to historically egalitarian North Carolina. Massive grants from wealthy benefactors would enlarge the state's universities and prepare the way for North Carolina's rise in the late 20th century.

On another front, after 1886, in Winston, former Confederate soldier and farmer Leonidas LaFayette Polk began to publish *The Progressive Farmer*, to teach farmers the latest in farming techniques, and to attack what he saw as unfair tariffs passed by the Northern-led congress on Southern exports. Polk would go on to run for president on the Populist ticket.

North Carolina, at the forefront of this Progressive cause, passed a law instituting the statewide prohibition of alcohol long before the rest of the country, in 1907—presumably to give Tar Heel moonshiners a jump-start on mastering the craft.

Just as in the Mexican-American War (James K. Polk) and the tail end of the Civil War (Andrew Johnson), World War I found a onetime North Carolina resident in office—Thomas Woodrow Wilson, of Davidson College and Wilmington. Wilson appointed his Tar Heel supporters to important positions: he named Washington, N.C.–born Josephus Daniels, a Raleigh newspaperman, as Secretary of the Navy, and Aberdeen's Walter Hines Page as ambassador to England.

The invasion of the boll weevil, beginning in 1919, destroyed the cotton crop, which, though it hadn't paid well since before the Civil War, was nonetheless still the "other" big crop, along with tobacco. Thus, just as they were coming out of their post–Civil War slump, North Carolina and other cotton states toppled into their own Depression 10 years before the rest of the nation. Blacks and low-income whites left in droves for better jobs up north. Tobacco became more important to the state economy than ever. By the mid-1930s, the state's tobacco crops were bringing in a combined $141 million; the cotton crop was worth only $41 million, while corn brought in $32 million.

The establishment and expansion of military bases during World War II, as well as domestic and foreign investment in manufacturing in more recent decades, have revitalized the state.

## DESEGREGATION

Compared to hot spots such as Mississippi and Alabama, desegregation went relatively smoothly during the 1950s and 1960s in North Carolina. The first sit-in of the Civil Rights era took place in Greensboro, N.C., in February 1960.

Another front of the Civil Rights battle revolved around voting rights, which had been largely denied blacks in North Carolina since the 1870s. In North Carolina in 1958, for instance, while whites only made up 80 percent of the population, a full 90 percent of all voters were white. Throughout the 1960s, restrictions were lifted and blacks began to vote in larger numbers. However, the flight of African-Americans to the north during the Jim Crow era left few counties with black majorities. Nonetheless, here and there, African-American legislators, mayors, and judges began to win elections.

Blacks, who tended to be poorer than whites,

the Bank of America tower in Charlotte

© ERIKA HOWSARE

favored the Democratic Party, with its greater funding of government-run social programs. Whereas the Southern Democratic party had long been the "white man's" party, during the Kennedy/Johnson years, conservative Southern Democrats found themselves unwelcome in their own party. In 1964 Barry Goldwater's platform galvanized South Carolina's "Dixiecrats" and led to major defections into the Grand Old Party. Further uproars were caused by the forced implementation of busing in Charlotte and other towns as a means of addressing the de facto segregation by neighborhoods. By 1972, Tar Heels surprised even themselves by voting in Republican James E. Holshouser as governor—the first GOP governor since Reconstruction. A year later, 1973, North Carolina was even ready to elect its first Republican senator in several decades—Jesse Helms. For the next 27 years, Helms of course was fixed in the Washington firmament, no matter what artillery Democrats might use to try to bring him down. He finally left office, of his own accord, in 2002.

Since the early 1970s, more and more Northerners have discovered North Carolina, many of them attracted to the high-paying jobs generated by the creation of Research Triangle Park in the nexus between Raleigh, Durham, and Chapel Hill. Many others have visited the coast for years and have, in their later years, chosen to move down permanently, especially as the nation's collective memories of Southern race riots and lynchings continue to dim. Many descendants of black Carolinians who moved out of the South during the Jim Crow years have moved back.

And with all these new arrivals has come much material and cultural wealth, and not a little bit of modern society's bad side, too. Crime rates in Charlotte, the Triangle, and the Triad surged outrageously in the 1980s and 1990s. In 2002, Charlotte and the Triangle were both named as among the American cities with most polluted air. And every midsized and larger city has had to rework its transportation system to deal with the increased demands on area roadways.

Some of these things should resolve themselves in time in these North Carolina towns, long humble in spirit but lofty in their ambitions.

## The People

North Carolinians are proud of their humilty—you could call them famously humble. Rarely has a state fielded so many likeable characters, from Andy Griffith to Rick Dees, from presidential candidate Elizabeth Dole to Charles Kuralt of *On the Road*. Despite all its physical beauty, despite its music, its food, the pounding of its mountain whitewater and the salty aroma of its coastal marshes, the very best thing about North Carolina is its people.

Unless they leave home, Carolinians cannot escape their past: a white Middleton may well share a classroom with a black Middleton, one the likely descendant of the other's great-great-great-grandfather's slaves—and the two of them quite possibly distant cousins.

Perhaps because so much of their history has been spent withstanding the tugs and blows of other regions that commanded them to change,

Tar Heels are none too quick to equate change with progress.

Their understanding of people as intrinsically flawed creatures also makes Carolinians value traditions and manners more than many—for in a culture where human nature is seen as inherently flawed, "self-expression" and "doing what you feel" are not necessarily good things. To Tar Heels some parts of the self are . . . well . . . just selfish. Hence Carolinians use ritualized courtesies copiously to smooth the rough edges of humanity. Tar Heels are taught to say "yes, ma'am," "no, sir," "please," and "thank you," whether or not their inner children feel like it.

One of the most charming things about North Carolinians is how they're nearly always genuinely surprised to hear that non-Southerners have bothered to come all this way just to see their little state. Most Tar Heels are proud of where they live and usually quite happy to show you around.

## LANGUAGE

*If you meet a man without stopping, the salutation here always is, "How d'ye do, sir?" never "Good morning," and on parting it is, "I wish you well, sir," more frequently than "Good-bye." You are always commanded to appear at the table . . . in a rough, peremptory tone, as if your host feared you would try to excuse yourself.*

*"Come in to supper." "Take a seat." "Some of the fry?" "Help yourself to anything you see that you can eat."*

*They ask your name but do not often call you by it, but hail you "Stranger," or "Friend."*

**Northern-born Frederick Law Olmstead, describing North Carolina etiquette in The Cotton Kingdom, 1861**

One of the things outsiders often notice about Southerners is the Southern way with figurative language. To some degree this is derived from the strong Biblical tradition of the region; for centuries Southern evangelical Christians have striven to illustrate the intangibles of life with easy-to-visualize parables, following the example of Jesus, who used illustrations drawn from situations familiar to his unschooled 1st-century audiences (a shepherd's concern for his sheep, wheat planted among briars, a disobedient son returning home) to explain complex theological doctrines.

Hence if you're butting into a conflict between two Tar Heels, you may be reminded that "y'all don't have a dog in this fight." If you think a person is smart just because he went to school, you're forgetting that "livin' in a garage don't make you a Ford." My personal favorite, though I only heard it once, describes a thoughtful person who apparently was "sweeter than sugar cubes in syrup." Makes you want to brush your teeth just hearing it.

Carolinians don't think or figure, they "reckon." They don't get ready, they "fix," as in, "I'm fixing to head down to Charleston." They don't push buttons, they "mash" them. They "cut" lights on and off, "carry" people around in their cars, accomplish urgent tasks in a "skinny minute," and push shopping "buggies" around the Winn-Dixie. If a Carolinian is a stranger to a subject, she "doesn't know 'boo'" about it. If she's never met you before, she doesn't know you from "Adam's house cat." If she *does* know you and sees you, she won't just hug you, she'll "hug your neck." And if a Carolinian says he really needs to "take a powder," it probably just means he has a headache and is taking a dose of Goody's powder (a regional remedy—essentially crushed aspirin). If he tells you he's "like to pass out," it means he's very tired, not drunk.

Tar Heels never pop in to say "hello" or "hi"—they stop by to say "hey." In fact you'll rarely hear "hi" in public—it's usually "hey."

Fairly well known is the preference for "y'all," or the more formal "you-all." (Some Carolinians argue that "y'all" is actually more politically correct than the Yankee "you guys," since it's not gender-exclusive.) It's usually the first linguistic nuance you'll pick up when you're in the state, and it's one of the hardest for displaced Tar Heels to mask when they're outside of Dixie. It just sounds friendlier. If you meet more than one person walking together on the street, it's proper and friendly to say, "Hey, you-all."

Pronunciation counts too. Though there's not the space to go into all the regional variations, just remember that cautious Carolinians buy "IN-surance" on their house, which will pay for the family to stay in a "HO-tel" if the house burns down.

In the Upcountry particularly, the "s" on the ends of plurals is often dropped, as in, "That Co-Cola is sixty-five cent."

## TERMS OF ADDRESS

One of the most admirable qualities of Southern culture is its resistance to the Cult of Youth. Although perhaps less so along the coastline, North Carolina is in general a place where it's not against the law to get old. Here age is generally still respected, and one way of showing and reinforcing this respect is the customary respectful way of referring to elders as "ma'am" and "sir." For example:

"Excuse me, ma'am, but could you tell me where to find the trailhead?"

"Didn't y'all see the sign back away? Where the two magnolia used to be?"

"No, ma'am."

Note that visitors don't *have* to say "ma'am" and "sir"—Southerners expect non-Southerners to be ill-mannered—but doing so might help you blend in a little better.

Children address adults normally with "Mr.," "Miss," or "Mrs." attached to the adult's first name or last name. Family friends or other adult friends are often addressed by the first name, preceded by Mr. or Miss—whether or not the woman in question is married. Hence, to our friends' children my wife and I are Miss Kristin and Mr. Mike. It's a typically Carolinian compromise, reinforcing societal roles and responsibilities by keeping the generations separate, yet also encouraging intimacy with first names.

Note too that if a large age difference exists between you and another (older) person, it's proper to address an elder as Mr., Ms., Mrs., or Miss.

What with the arrival of so many people from other parts of the country and the world, many of North Carolina's bigger cities have found their manners slipping. In May 2000, North Carolina State Senator Beverly Perdue introduced a bill authorizing local school boards to require students to use "Yes, ma'am," "Yes, sir," "No, sir," and "No, ma'am" in the classroom and at school-sponsored functions, and to provide state funding to support local programs on respectful address outside of the school day for students who repeatedly violated the rule.

## SOUTHERN SUBTLETIES: HOW TO READ SOUTHERN MANNERS

You and your travel companion meet a nice Carolinian couple, who invite you to their home for dinner. You eat, you adjourn to the porch for beverages, and then you sit around talking. It gets a little late, but your hosts seem so eager to continue the conversation that you linger. It gets later. You really *should* go, but as you rise, your hosts offer another round of drinks. Finally you decide you must go. You leave, while your hosts openly grieve your departure. You're begged to return again when "y'all can stay a little longer."

What the average unsuspecting non-Southerners don't realize is that they have just committed a major faux pas. Though you of course had no way of knowing, your hosts were ready for you to leave right after dessert, but offered drinks on the porch only because you showed no signs of leaving, and they wanted to be polite.

So what's the rule of thumb when visiting with Southerners you don't know very well? Leave about when you first suspect you should, only an hour earlier.

# On the Road

*I want to say just a few words about North Carolina, my home state, possibly the finest state in this entire union. We got industry of all kinds, pretty country; raise corn, cotton, tobacco, peaches, peanuts, all like that; got colleges all over the state, fine quality, pretty girls; and run off the finest white lightning made anywhere.*

*Mount Airy native Andy Griffith, 1950s*

From primeval granite peaks to quaint colonial fishing villages; from surf competitions to steam trains to the Appalachian Trail, from homegrown bluegrass parlors and barbecue shacks to Raleigh's bistros and Charlotte's skyscrapers, Wilmington's film debuts, Chapel Hill's Bohemian coffeehouses, and Harrah's 80,000-square-foot, full-bore casino in Cherokee, North Carolina offers travelers a wealth of diverse vacations within one state. It also offers some fairly sizeable distances if you're trying to cover the entire state in one trip.

Most people focus on exploring one region of North Carolina at a time; I've divided the chapters of this book along some of the more common destination groupings. Anyone with a healthy appetite for local culture and profound interactions with native residents can spend a week's time exploring within the boundaries described by each chapter. Another option is to explore a larger section of the state less deeply; it's common for travelers to take in the entire coastal region, for instance, in one trip, or to spend a week exploring the upper and lower mountains.

If you're planning a statewide speed-read of the regions, you'll want to read this book carefully, plan on some long drives, and choose your destinations thoughtfully—perhaps using the Highlights chart in this chapter. Though this sort of trip will give you only a quick taste of each region, it will help you immensely in planning for your next trip to the Tar Heel State.

City Market, Raleigh

© ERIKA HOWSARE

## SIGHT-SEEING HIGHLIGHTS

**Nags Head and the Outer Banks**
Cape Hatteras National Seashore
Jockey's Ridge State Park
Manteo waterfront
Ocracoke Village
Wright Brothers National Landmark

**New Bern and the Central Coast**
Beaufort waterfront
Edenton's historic district
Ferry ride (take your pick)
New Bern's historic district

**Wilmington and the Southern Coast**
Wilmington's historic district
Southport

**Raleigh and the Triangle**
Brightleaf Square, Durham
Historic Hillsborough
Mordecai Historic Park and President Andrew
Johnson's Birthplace, Raleigh

**Charlotte and the Southern Heartland**
Historic Salisbury
Mint Museum of Art
Town Creek Indian Mound State Historic Site

Reed Gold Mine State Historic Site

**Winston-Salem and the Triad**
International Civil Rights Museum
Lexington
Mount Airy
North Carolina Zoological Park
Old Salem
Seagrove Pottery Studios

**Asheville and the Northern Mountains**
The Biltmore Estate and Winery
Biltmore Village
Pack Place: Education, Arts and Science Center

**Cherokee and the Gateway to the Smokies**
Great Smoky Mountains Railroad, Dillsboro
Highlands
Maggie Valley Opry House
Oconaluftee Indian Village
Rafting the Nantahala Gorge

**Great Smoky Mountains National Park**
Cades Cove
Cataloochee Valley
LeConte Lodge
The Appalachian Trail

ON THE ROAD

# Recreation

## WATER SPORTS

### Surfing

Yes, Carolinians surf. What's even more startling to some first-time visitors is that the North Carolina hosts a full-blown surf subculture as well, with surf shops, board makers, and not a little attitude. The enthusiasm for the sport runs high along the coasts—much higher than the waves, in fact. The Outer Banks have a long and distinguished history of surfing, dating back to the 1960s. Stellar local surf shops include **Corolla Surf Shop,** in the Corolla Light Village Shops, 252/453-9283, website: www.corollasurfshop.com, which includes a

surfing museum inside the store. Down on Hatteras you'll find **Ocean Roots,** across from the Avon Pier, 252/995-3369.

The southern North Carolina coast enjoys pretty decent surf for this side of the country, and a very active surf scene. The Wilmington area alone boasts well over a dozen surf shops. East Coast surfers congregate hereabout for surf contests each summer. The best spot in the region is arguably the Crystal Pier, but it's also often the most crowded. Good spots include the north end of Wrightsville Beach in front of Shell Island Resort; I've also seen some great surf off Fort Fisher, and Maryland Avenue, Carolina Beach, and Kure Beach can all be good under the right conditions. So can Bald Head Island, though it's a pain to get there. As anywhere, stop by a surf shop, strike up a conversation with some locals, and find out where they're breaking the day you're there. Check out www.snc-surf.com before you come out; it's a great website for planning your Wilmington area surfing.

**Sailing, parasailing,** and **windsurfing** are all popular along the Carolina coast. On the Outer Banks, they're legendary.

### Diving

North Carolina's long history of shipwrecks makes the waters offshore a virtual wonderland for divers. However, winter's rough, cold waters can make offshore diving pretty inhospitable between October and May.

Hearty people dive in North Carolina's historic rivers and sounds year-round; expect water temperatures in the 50s.

### Canoeing and Kayaking

North Carolina is a paddler's paradise: the challenging Appalachian whitewater bookends the coast's peaceful blackwater rivers, swamps, sounds, and inlets teaming with wildlife, and challenging Atlantic beach paddles. On the Outer Banks, outfitters run a variety of creative, quality paddling excursions and sea island overnights through such pristine areas as Pea Island National Wildlife Refuge, Alligator River National Wildlife Refuge, Cape Hatteras National Seashore, and the Kitty Hawk Maritime. On the Central Coast, people paddle the Rachel Carson Reserve, Cape Lookout, and the Shackleford Banks.

### Whitewater Rafting

North Carolina's mountains are rich with good whitewater. Pick up a copy of the pamphlet titled **"Paddle North Carolina"** at any state tourism office, or see it online at www.paddlenorth-carolina.org. **Nantahala Outdoor Center** is one of the state's largest and most experienced outfitters; it's at 13077 U.S. 19 W., 800/232-7238 or 828/488-6900, website: www.noc.com; or try **Nantahala Rafts,** Gorgarama Park, 14260 U.S. 19 West, 828/488-2325.

## FISHING

The person who invents the all-in-one driving iron and fishing pole will make a quick fortune in the North Carolina—beyond golfing, Carolinians like most to fish.

Off the coast, boaters enjoy Gulf Stream fishing for amberjack, marlin, sailfish, tuna, dolphin, and wahoo. Closer in, you can still hope to land mackerel, blackfin tuna, cobia, and shark. Surf, pier, and jetty fishing includes channel bass, Spanish mackerel, shark, flounder, croakers, and whiting. For sans-boat angling, public and private piers jut from Carolina deep into the waters of the Atlantic. Approximately 730 miles of trout streams thread through Great Smoky Mountains National Park alone, and bass-filled Fontana Lake lies on the southern border. You'll also find fishing throughout the Nantahala and Pisgah National Forests, and in the DuPont State Forest near Brevard. The Smokies are one of the last refuges of the brook trout, the only species native to these parts; if anglers catch one, they must release it. Efforts to restore brook trout populations have led to the closing of some streams, and rangers at visitors centers in the park can advise which ones to avoid. The rainbow trout, however, are fair game.

Trout season never ends in the Smokies; visitors can fish all year. A Tennessee or North Carolina fishing license enables you to fish all over the park. Trout stamps are not required, but you can use one-hook artificial lures only—no bait allowed. You can pick up a fishing license at a bait store, or online from the Tennessee Wildlife Resources Agency at www.state.tn.us/twra. Contact the North Carolina Wildlife Resources Commission at 1709 Mail Service Center, Raleigh, NC 27699-1709, 919/662-4370. Or see the commission's site online at www.state.nc.us/Wildlife. Licenses cost around $15 for the year, or $5 for three days. The two states have a very limited reciprocal agreement, which means that only in very limited areas of Tennessee can you use a North Carolina license, and vice versa. But within the park, either state's license will do.

Even within the National Park, while your

© MIKE SIGALAS

fisherfolk at Oregon Inlet

ON THE ROAD

choice of bait is limited, your choice of location is not. You can fish right beside the road or backpack into the most remote streams in the park. Or you can hire guides who will take you to the best places. Many of them are based over the border in Gatlinburg, and include **Old Smoky Outfitters,** 511 Parkway in the Riverbend Mall, 865/430-1936, website: www.oldsmoky.com; **Smoky Mountain Angler,** at 376 E. Parkway, 865/436-8746; and **Smoky Mountain Guide Service,** 800/782-1061 or 865/436-2108. A good book for independent anglers is Don Kirk's *Smoky Mountains Trout Fishing Guide.*

## SHRIMPING

For shrimping, you'll need a cast net and an ice chest or some saltwater. A cast net is round, with weights all along the rim; you throw a cast net somewhat the way you'd throw a Frisbee, though in truth it flies closer to the way an uncooked pizza would. Which is one way of saying this might take a little practice. But what's a half hour or hour's practice when it teaches you how to catch shrimp?

After you've thrown a perfect loop—so that the

net hits the water as a circle, its weights bringing the net down in a perfect dome over the unsuspecting shrimp—wait for the weights to hit the bottom. This is something you just have to sense, since you can't see or feel it. Now jerk on the center line that draws the weights together, closing the bottom of the dome into a sphere, and trapping the shrimp.

You can rent a small johnboat or outboard, or you can throw from some inlet bridges; it's up to you, but most people seem to feel that ebb tide is the time to throw, since this is when the shrimp, who spend high tide spread out and frolicking in the marsh grasses, are the most concentrated in the creekbeds. Cast your net toward the side of a waterway, just on the edge of the grasses, and you may well snag a number of these mobile crustaceans.

## CRABBING

Crabbing has to be one of the easiest ways to catch some of the best food found in the ocean. Oh, you can charter your boats far out to sea, slaphappy on Dramamine, but you'll find *me* in the shallows with a bucket, a string, a sinker, a net, and some ripe chicken backs. That's pretty much all you need to land a good supper's worth of **blue crab** in North Carolina. Here's how:

1. Tie the string to a piece of chicken and the sinker.
2. Wade out in the water about waist-high.
3. Hold onto one end of the string, and drop the chicken and sinker into the water.
4. Wait for the crabs to come scuttling over for supper.
5. When you feel a tug on the chicken, pull up on the string and swoop beneath the crab with your net.
6. Call me; invite me over for dinner.

A few rules here:
• If the crabs have yellow eggs (roe) on the underside, the law requires you to toss them back.
• If the crab is less than five inches wide across its back, you'll need to toss it back, too.
• Drop the "lucky" ones who pass these two tests into an ice chest and keep them cold until you cook them.

## HIKING

North Carolina features a number of excellent hiking trails. Though I've covered a number of my favorite hikes in this book, serious hikers will want to pick up a copy of Randy Johnson's *Hiking North Carolina*, or a similar guide, for details on all the best trails in the state.

If you're hiking in heavily wooded North Carolina, keep this in mind: though it won't help your wildlife-viewing any, during hunting season, wear some fluorescent orange. Better yet, you'll find plenty of great trails in hunting-free state parks and nature preserves to keep you busy until the smoke clears at the end of hunting season. Just to be safe, however, it won't hurt to wear some orange here also—to keep safe against poachers.

If you're hiking with a dog, make sure Fido's wearing some orange, too.

### Some Notable Trails

Northernmost of the great trails is the **Tracks in**

### NORTH CAROLINA'S SYMBOLS AND EMBLEMS

Beverage: milk
Bird: cardinal
Boat: shad boat
Colors: red and blue
Dog: Plott hound
Fish: channel bass
Flower: dogwood
Insect: honey bee
Mammal: gray squirrel
Motto: *Esse quam videri,*
    "To be, rather than to seem"
Nickname: the Old North State, or
    the Tar Heel State
Reptile: eastern box turtle
Rock: granite
Shell: Scotch bonnet
Song: "The Old North State"
Stone: emerald
Tree: pine
Vegetable: sweet potato

**the Sand Trail** at Jockey's Ridge State Park, a self-guided, 1.5 mile trek past more than a dozen interpretive stations that point out the local ecosystems. The **Cape Hatteras Beach Trail** is the most oceanward trail you'll encounter—and the easiest to follow. From Whalebone Junction south of Nags Head, turn right, stick to the shoreline, and head south 75 miles (one-way), through the length of Hatteras and Ocracoke Islands. You'll need to cross some bridges and take a ferry, but this is the best possible way to get a thorough Banks experience. For something much less ambitious, south of New Bern in Croatan National Forest, the 1.4 mile **Cedar Point Tideland Trail** makes a loop through hardwood and pine-laced estuary and tidal marsh areas. You can hide behind wildlife viewing blinds along the way and take some great nature shots. Even shorter, but memorable, the **Flytrap Trail** at Carolina Beach State Park near Wilmington carries you through a rare growth of Venus flytraps.

Even just within the National Park boundaries, you'll find more than 800 miles of trail awaiting you in the Smokies. But there's no reason to only hike within the park—good trails with beautiful views, usually involving a waterfall, wind all throughout the mountain region.

Incidentally, if you want to camp along any trail in the park, you'll need to pick up a permit from a ranger station.

## Appalachian Trail

The most famous trail in America plunges southwesterly from Virginia into Tennessee and then lopes back and forth across the Tennessee/North Carolina border, in between the Cherokee and Pisgah National Forests. Then it enters the National Park and pushes along the mountain ridge for 68 miles (a solid week's worth of hiking in itself) before exiting due south to spend some quality time with North Carolina alone, passing through the Nantahala National Forest and toward the trail's southern terminus in Georgia.

Along most of the Appalachian Trail in this area, you'll find whatever solitude you might hope for on a trail as famous as this one. But in the National Park, Maine-to-Georgia hikers tramp alongside weekend hikers, who mingle with day-trippers who want to experience the famous trail. As a result, the in-park trail sections, especially near Newfound Gap, can be very crowded.

## Other National Park Hikes

A couple of great hikes leave from the park's midway point at the Newfound Gap parking lot. From the lot, you can hike east for four miles to **Charlies Bunion,** a sheer drop of 1,000 feet. A spectacular view awaits. From Newfound Gap you can also hike to **Clingmans Dome,** along a 7.5-mile section of the Appalachian Trail, the highest in the park. Or you can get dropped off in the parking lot at Clingmans Dome and hike downhill, assisted by gravity.

Leaving from Cades Cove, the five-mile roundtrip **Abrams Falls** hike is a good one for people with kids; they love to play in the water at Abrams Creek, which drains Cades Cove. The

**Rich Mountain** trail begins on a one-way road out of Cades Cove and offers a good view of the mountains and the cove itself.

**Mount LeConte** features not only magnificent views but a rustic lodge at the top, and for this reason, no less than five trails lead to its summit: the **Boulevard Trail** and the **Alum Cave Trail** are two of the best. For optimal sightseeing, take the former on the way up, and the latter on the way down.

If you're staying in Gatlinburg and feeling guilty about that heavy breakfast buffet, you might consider taking the **Bullhead Trail,** a 7.25-mile one-way hike that gains 4,017 feet. It begins in the Cherokee Orchard parking lot near Gatlinburg. Right outside Gatlinburg on the Newfound Gap Road is one of the more popular trails in the park. **Chimney Tops** is only two miles one-way, with an elevation gain of 1,335 feet. By the steep end, most people are using hands and feet—but the view is worth it.

© MIKE SIGALAS

**Great Smoky Mountains hiking trail**

The 1.5-mile one-way **Grotto Falls** hike is cool on the hottest days. Hikers gain only 500 feet in elevation and can look for members of the park's 23 species of salamanders on the way. The trail ends at a waterfall.

So does the mild, four-mile **Hen Wallow Falls** hike, which gains just 600 feet through a forest of magnificent poplars and hemlocks. The namesake falls are two feet wide at the top and 20 feet wide at the bottom.

The Ramsay Cascades trail leads to its 100-foot high namesake. While they're not a straight, Niagara-like drop, the cascades are the park's highest waterfall.

### Other Hikes

The waterfalls of the Nantahala National Forest offer an excellent end point for hikers who need motivation. Even falls with parking lots and overlooks can entice would-be couch potatoes with the promise of a better view from a different angle.

An excellent guidebook for hiking is *Hiking Trails of the Smokies,* which covers 149 trails with a detailed narrative, full-color map, and trail profile charts for 165 trails. Printed on lightweight paper, it's easy to carry, costs $16.95, and is available at visitors centers' gift shops.

## BICYCLING

North Carolina has taken the lead in providing nine different State Bicycling Highways. The **Virginia to Florida Bicycle Route** is perhaps the most ambitious. It enters the eastern part of the state on N.C. 32 near Corapeake, travels mostly flat two-lane roads along the Coastal Plain, and threads through New Bern and Edenton before ending in Wilmington. You can find more information on the route from the folks at Bikecentennial, P.O. Box 8308, Missoula, MT 59807. Another route, the **Ocracoke Option,** covers 175 miles from Wilson in the center of the state to Cape Hatteras National Seashore. A third traces the Cape Fear River, ending in Southport. For information on these or any of the other North Carolina State Bicycling Highways, contact the Bicycle Program at the N.C. Depart-ment of Transportation in Raleigh, 919/733-2804, website: www.ncdot.org.

See individual chapters for specifics. A very dependable ride anywhere on the coast is to simply take your bike along the hard-packed sand on the beach.

Riding a bike in **Great Smoky Mountains National Park,** the most crowded park in the country, is not easy. First of all, there's no biking on any of the park's trails. Second, with all the vehicular traffic, if you're going to bike the park's roads, you'd best get out there early.

The park's best biking area is Cades Cove. A concessionaire at the campground store rents bikes, or BYOB. The best *time* to ride there is on Saturday and Wednesday mornings (before 10 A.M.) in the spring and summer, when Cades Cove Loop Road is closed to motor traffic. It also closes at sunset each evening, so if you've got a bike light or really good vision, you might try a moonlight ride.

A few unimproved roads make for good in-park mountain-bike riding. Try the Cataloochee Valley on the eastern end of the park, or the Parson Branch Road out of Cades Cove, but keep in mind that it is one-way out of the cove.

In North Carolina's Nantahala National Forest, the famed **Tsali** area offers more than 40 miles of single-track trails, as well as a campground at the trailhead. For more information contact the USFS at 865/479-6431 or Nantahala Outdoor Center at 865/488-6737. Some say it's getting a bit crowded, but most agree that the Tsali trails, located as they are on a peninsula in Fontana Lake with the Smokies as a backdrop, provide the best all-around mountain biking on the North Carolina side. Then again, it's hard to beat all the scenery and choices at **DuPont State Park** between Hendersonville and Brevard—though at present, much of it involves riding on roads, not single-track.

Down in Asheville, if you're visiting the Biltmore Estate, you're welcome to bike the trails criss-crossing the extensive grounds, but only after you've paid your admission fee. For more information on trails in the region, see the Mountain Bike Western North Carolina site at www.mtbikewnc.com.

# HUNTING

For many Carolinians, a crisp fall day just isn't complete without heading out into the woods to go hunting. Few instincts seem to be as ingrained in humans as the instinct to hunt prey, and the activity ("sport" seems somewhat misleading—as if the animals had to kick in a league fee to join the fun) has a long history in the South, and in the cultures from which modern-day Southerners descend.

You'll find white-tailed deer, wild turkey, ruffed grouse, quail, squirrels, and other small mammals just a-beggin' to be gunned down in national and state forests, national wildlife refuges, and wildlife management areas.

Get the specifics for North Carolina hunting by contacting the Wildlife Resources Commission at 512 Salisbury St., Raleigh, 919/733-7291.

*Few instincts seem to be as ingrained in humans as the instinct to hunt prey, and the activity ("sport" seems somewhat misleading—as if the animals had to kick in a league fee to join the fun) has a long history in the South.*

# SKIING

If you've come to the Smokies in pursuit of the world's best ski slopes, you'd best recheck your sources. However, Tar Heel skiing is decent, and it's here all season long—the snowmakers see to that. **Ski Beech,** 1007 Beech Mountain Parkway, 800/438-2093 or 704/387-2011, website: www.skibeech.com, offers 15 slopes, seven chairlifts, and the highest skiing in eastern North America—5,505 feet into the Appalachian sky. Other popular resorts include three-slope, two-chairlift **Appalachian Ski Mountain,** 3 miles off U.S. 321, north of Blowing Rock, on the road to Boone (follow the signs), 704/295-7828, website: www.appskimtn.com, and the state's biggest facility, 18-slope, 5-lift **Sugar Mountain,** in Banner Elk, 704/898-4521, website: www.skisugar.com. **Cataloochee Ski Area** above Maggie Valley has nine slopes (seven with snowmaking equipment), three ski lifts and a rope tow. Night skiing is available too.

# CAMPING

North Carolina has thousands and thousands of camping spaces across the state. I've listed some campgrounds in individual chapters, but for a more complete list, pick up a *Woodall's,* or similar camping guide.

## Backcountry Camping

For even more privacy than you'll find in Cataloochee, Great Smoky Mountains National Park also offers close to 100 backcountry sites for backpackers. Reservations are required for some sites, but there is no charge. Write to Backcountry Permits, Great Smoky Mountains National Park, Gatlinburg, TN 37738 or call 865/436-1231.

Park rangers are very strict about camping in unauthorized places. This means campers cannot spend the night in a parking area or picnic area or on the side of the road, even if all the campgrounds are full and it is 10 P.M. on Saturday night. The same holds true for the backcountry. Allow enough time to get to your destination before nightfall.

# GOLF

North Carolina is a golfer's dream; the state is home to around 600 golf courses, including some of the top links in the nation. The Pinehurst area in the state's sandhills region is known in some quarters as world's golf capital: Pinehurst, Southern Pines, and Aberdeen together offer duffers 25 courses. For a comprehensive guide to North Carolina's courses, call 800/8474862, or see www.visitnc.com, and request a copy of the yearly *North Carolina: The Official Golf Guide.*

# WINE-TASTING

Believe it or not, the Smokies region contains the most-visited winery in America. The 96,500-

square-foot **Biltmore Winery** is on the grounds of the Biltmore Estate in Asheville. You'll need to pay to get onto the grounds, but if you're visiting them anyway, you may want to stop by to sample the extensive list of wines, including nonalcoholic sparkling drinks. Over in Pigeon Forge, **Mountain Valley Vineyards,** 2174 Parkway, 865/453-6334, produces 16 different kinds of wine—mostly sweet and medium sweet. Muscadine wine is the best-selling one, although berry wines run a close second. Visitors can watch wine being made in August and September. Mountain Valley is open for tastings all year seven days a week.

## SPECTATOR SPORTS

### Football

Though the NFL's Carolina Panthers, based in Charlotte, have drawn a following over the past years, it's *college* football that still dominates North Carolina. Even people who never got around to completing eighth grade take intercollegiate ball very seriously. Most Carolinians choose the Duke Blue Devils, UNC Chapel Hill Tar Heels, or NCSU Wolf Pack early on and go with it for life, even while passing through a variety of romantic relationships, political views, and theologies.

Consequently, getting tickets to a big game can be a challenge, but check the sports page in whatever town you're in and if it's pigskin season you'll find a college playing somewhere nearby.

### Auto Racing

They say that auto racing has made such a big hit in North Carolina because the people here have historically valued their freedom more than most. As rural Tar Heels gradually rose from poverty in the early part of the 20th century, they seized upon car ownership as a chance to break free from the traditional limitations of their time and place, and it was only natural that the fastest drivers would soon become heroes to the general population, especially when they were people like Junior Johnson, who learned his driving skills dodging federal agents while defiantly running moonshine from North Carolina's mountains.

It's a theory. What's certain is that racing is

Historic Durham Athletic Park

# SMALL-TOWN GEMS OF NORTH CAROLINA

**Beaufort**
Beaufort's lively waterfront and closeness to the beach make this a fine vacation destination.

**Blowing Rock**
Dazzling (and full) in the autumn and cute all year round; Jan Karon's fictional Mitford is a real-world delight.

**Brevard**
Classical music, mountain views, and white squirrels. What else could you want?

**Edenton**
Still looking back across the tranquil waters of Albemarle Sound to Mother England, colonial Edenton is a outstanding place to spend a quiet couple of days.

**Highlands**
A near-perfect little mountain town.

**Hillsborough**
Colonial flashpoint; today its well-preserved downtown features plenty of historic homes.

**Manteo**
Contains a couple of very nice B&Bs and provides lots of dining/shopping opportunities as well as

Roanoke Island Festival Park, just across the river.

**Mount Airy**
Andy Griffith's hometown; the model for Mayberry, archetypical American small town.

**Oriental**
A favorite stopover from New Bern; great seafood restaurants and a low-key attitude.

**Ocracoke Village**
Sure, it's metacute—a cute village that continues to exist by being a cute village—but for feeling away from it all without formally leaving North America, it's hard to beat Ocracoke.

**Southport**
In a coastline of tourist-driven burgs, Southport stands out as the real thing: a salty fishing town. Nice maritime museum, shops, historic buildings.

**Runners-Up:** Aberdeen, Bath, Dillsboro, Elizabeth City, Salisbury, Seagrove, Waynesville

**Possibly in a Few Years:** Hertford, Washington

**Other Downtowns Worth Exploring:** Chapel Hill, New Bern, Old Salem, Old Greensborough, Wilmington

ON THE ROAD

*big* here. Home to racing legends like Richard Petty and Junior Johnson, North Carolina is today home of more than 46 Winston Cup and 36 NASCAR teams, two major NASCAR events (the Coca-Cola 600 and UAW-GM Quality 500), as well as numerous races throughout the state annually

## Minor League Baseball

Major League baseball is tough to take seriously these days; it's hard to see much drama in a game when you're looking out at a diamond full of players who, win or lose, are cumulatively worth more than the GM board of directors. But Minor League baseball is, as they

say, a whole 'nother ballgame. Watching 18- and 19-year-olds, who are making less than a middle manager at Hardee's, battle for The Bigs may remind you why you fell in love with the game in the first place.

North Carolina is blessed with no less than *14* minor league baseball teams across the state, including the world's most famous, the AAA **Durham Bulls,** the popular AAA **Charlotte Knights,** the single-A **Asheville Tourists,** and the entry-level summer league **Kinston Indians,** which serves as the home nine of the Outer Banks. Though it's never hosted a Major League team, many great ballplayers have played ball in North Carolina: Shoeless Joe Jackson played mill-league ball in Rockingham, and an 18-year-old Oriole rookie named George Herman Ruth hit his first professional home run in Fayetteville.

### Professional Soccer

The **Wilmington Hammerheads** play USISL D-3 Pro League soccer, sharing the league with Greensboro's **Carolina Dynamo** and the **Charlotte Eagles.** The **Raleigh Capital Express** plays in the United Soccer League's Atlantic Division.

### Hockey

The National Hockey League's **Carolina Hurricanes** took the ice for Raleigh a few years back, and they're still packing them in. Minor league hockey is big in North Carolina, too: the **Greensboro Generals** and **Charlotte Checkers** battle in the East Coast Hockey League against such teams as the South Carolina Stingrays and the Macon Whoopee (I kid you not). The United Hockey League is home to the **Asheville Smoke.**

## AMUSEMENT PARKS

Located high above Maggie Valley, **Ghost Town in the Sky** is a small, aging amusement park—and a funky, homegrown bit of Americana: think Roy Rogers, Howdy Doody, and wagon wheel chandeliers. For young children and their parents, it can be a real hoot. In the same spirit, just east of Cherokee on US 19, **Santa's Land Park and Zoo** features the kiddie "Rudi Coaster" (with antlers), a miniature steam train, petting zoo (including "reindeer," of course), and Santa's House, where kids can get cheek-to-rosy-cheek with St. Nick himself. The park includes some nods to the mountain culture of the Smokies: a cabin from before the War Between the States, a gristmill, and a moonshine still. Further north, the **Tweetsie Railroad** combines a genuine steam railroad with a ghost town and carnival rides.

Maybe "amusement park" isn't the right term, but **Fields of the Wood,** on U.S. 294 near Murphy, N.C., is a 200-acre Bible park where you can see the Ten Commandments laid out in huge stone letters across an entire mountainside, along with the "All Nations Cross" and

replicas of Golgotha and Jesus' tomb. Along the South Carolina border in Charlotte is **Carowinds,** the state's finest amusement park, and home to its best rollercoasters. Along the coast, particularly around Wilmington, you'll find a handful of small amusement centers with the standard carnival rides.

## MUSIC

### Carolina Beach Music

Outside of the South, beach music is one of the least known and least understood musical genres in America. Part of the confusion lies with those who assume that the term beach music refers to the California vocal surf music of the Beach Boys and Jan and Dean. Carolina beach music is a whole different animal, popular on a whole different coast, and one main difference is that it is not primarily music featuring lyrics about the beach or developed to capture the rhythms of the ocean (as instrumental West Coast surf music was), nor is it music that is necessarily written and performed by Carolinian or even Southern artists. Some of beach music's greatest stars have probably never known that they were making "beach music" at all.

Beach music is blues music; most of the early performers of beach music were black. All that was needed was an easy-flowing song with four beats to the measure, about 120 beats per minute—perfect for dancing the Shag—the subtle yet wild, jitterbug-derived dance that evolved in the beach clubs of the Carolinas in the 1940s and 1950s. Songs like the Drifters' "Under the Boardwalk," the Tams' "What Kinda Fool Do You Think I Am?" and Maurice Williams and the Zodiacs' "Stay" became beach classics. Perhaps the "Johnny B. Goode" of beach music is the Dominoes' "Sixty-Minute Man."

If people found that a jukebox song was good to shag to—even if recorded and/or lyrically set hundreds of miles from the Strand—Bob and Earl's "Harlem Shuffle," for instance—it quickly became absorbed as part of the canon of beach music. Later, in the late 1960s, 1970s, and 1980s, a few regional groups began to record songs that lyrically celebrated the beach music/shagging subculture, including the Em-

Shag Shack, Surf City

bers' anthemic "I Love Beach Music" and General Johnson and Chairmen of the Board's "Carolina Girls".

Of all of the beach-specific songs, the most popular outside the beach music subculture has been the Tams' "There Ain't Nothing Like Shagging," which surprised everyone when it raced up into the top 20 on the British pop charts in the mid-'80s. And then everyone remembered what "shagging" means in British English and got over their surprise. You'll find shagging nightclubs in almost any good-sized coastal town.

Today, any song with the right beat—whether it's country-and-western, gospel, blues, or rock—can make the beach music charts. Such diverse acts as the Cherry Poppin' Daddies, John Fogerty, Tracey Chapman, Alabama, and Patti LaBelle have shared the charts.

You'll find most every kind of live music in North Carolina, from church bell choirs to bluegrass to reggae. Check the local listings in whatever town you're visiting.

## SHOPPING
### Antiques
Because North Carolina was one of the first regions in America settled by Europeans and because much of it was such a relatively wealthy region in antebellum years, it's not surprising that this is a great area for antique hunters You'll find the best prices in smaller towns.

### Factory Outlets
With all the interstates crossing through the state, North Carolina has more than its share of outlet shops. See the destination chapters for specific locations.

# Accommodations

## HOTELS AND MOTELS

The differences between hotels and motels are basically matters of price, amenities, and, in some cases, location. Hotels are usually more expensive than motels, but the increased price is usually—though not always—represented by better facilities. In addition to the pool, ice machine, and soda machine that you'll usually find at a motel, hotels often offer a restaurant or bar, an exercise room, valet parking, and greater proximity to shopping and places of cultural interest.

Another useful distinction for accommodations is proximity to freeways and highways. Sometimes hotels, sometimes motels, these places cater mostly to overnight travelers who need a place to stay while driving to somewhere else, rather than to extended-stay vacationers who want a relaxing place to spend a week or more. Spend the night at a Motel 6, for instance, and you'll find the parking lot nearly deserted at 9 A.M.

By absolutely no means do these descriptions fit in all, or even most, cases. No class of businesses has a copyright on the words "hotel" or "motel," and any business owner in the country has the right to call an establishment whatever he or she wants. A lot of motels are confusing the issue by calling themselves inns, lodges, and so on. If you're already in town, it never hurts to just pull into the parking lot and take a look around.

If you are unsure about staying at a motel because you are afraid it will lack the features you want, or about staying at a hotel because you are afraid it will be too expensive, call ahead. You'll probably call anyway for prices and room availability. Consider also what you are looking for in an accommodation. Do you plan to stay more than two nights? Are you in a hurry to get somewhere else, and just need a place to sleep overnight? Do you want a place where you can "get away from it all" for weeks at a time? If you correctly assess your expectations you should have no problem finding a satisfactory accommodation, from $25-a-night roadside motels to $300-a-night luxury hotels.

Some well-known hotel/motel chains include:

• **Best Western** is a chain with no consistent style; most are clean but strictly stick-to-the-freeway accommodations, while others offer luxurious rooms and prime locations. Call 800/528-1234 in the U.S. and Canada.

• **Days Inn** offers clean rooms, low prices ($29–79, depending on location). Call 800/329-7466 in the U.S. and Canada; website: www.daysinn.com. Often a continental breakfast buffet is served downstairs in the morning.

• **Econo Lodge** has average, low-priced accommodations, usually close to the freeways. Call 800/553-2666 in the U.S.

• **Hilton** offers luxurious rooms, numerous amenities, and great locations. Call 800/445-8667 in the U.S., 800/268-9275 in Canada.

• **Holiday Inn** usually has spacious rooms and quality dining; some offer entertainment, but there is no consistent level of amenities. Call 800/465-4329 in the U.S. and Canada; website: www.holiday-inn.com.

• **Howard Johnson**—a.k.a. "HoJo's"—offers spacious rooms close to the freeways; ask about special prices for seniors and families. Call 800/446-4656 in the U.S. and Canada.

• **Jameson Inn**—has more than a dozen locations in the state. Based out of Calhoun, Georgia, the inns feature work stations, fitness centers, computer-compatible telephone jacks, and continental breakfasts, as well as a Southern Colonial theme. Rooms run $50–60 and up. Call 800/526-3766; website: www.jamesoninns.com.

• **Motel 6** is usually close to the freeway, often in the $20s for a single, and kids stay free. Call 800/466-8356 in the U.S. One caveat: as you check in late to an urban Motel 6, sliding your money in a tray beneath the bulletproof window to the 24-hour front desk clerk, you may wish you'd spent another $10 to get into a more upscale environment. In most smaller towns, there's nothing to be concerned about, but if you're staying in a city with more than one Motel 6, odds are that you'll find the one by the local airport (as opposed to the one downtown) less intriguing, safety-wise.

• **Ramada** is sometimes upscale, sometimes just another hotel. Call 800/228-9898 in the U.S., 800/854-7854 in Canada.

## BED AND BREAKFASTS

Bed and breakfasts are usually someone's house or a portion of their house opened as a guest accommodation. North Carolina enjoys a worthy selection of these, mostly used as weekend getaways but not inappropriate for longer stays. The proprietors provide breakfast in the mornings (hence the name), and some offer lunch and dinner as well. As with hotels and motels, the name is not always indicative of the features. Sometimes older, smaller, rustic hotels call themselves bed and breakfasts to attract a wealthier clientele.

Bed and breakfasts usually offer personal hospitality and atmospheric, often historic homes to stay in. Perhaps because North Carolina is so rich in both of these, its B&B room rates are often cheaper than in a lot of other areas, where the hospitality has to be flown in daily. In many smaller towns, rooms can dip down into the $50 range, which, considering you'll probably spend the same or more for a sanitized, midrange chain with limited cable out on the highway, is quite a bargain.

Many B&Bs offer one or two different meal plans included with the price. They may offer the European-style continental breakfast, a light meal including coffee and orange juice; some combination of toast, English muffin, or Danish; and sometimes fruit. On the other hand, if you're lucky, you may be offered a Southern-style break-

fast and dinner. Expect coffee, eggs or pancakes, grits, biscuits, bacon or ham, and potatoes for breakfast, and fried chicken, steaks, and salads for dinner.

## CABINS

A little-known option for moderate accommodations is to check your destination's local KOA campground to see if they have any of their Kamping Kabins, which can be really quite nice. Call 800/562-5268 or see www.koa.com to make reservations.

## CAMPGROUNDS AND RV PARKS

### North Carolina State Parks

North Carolina has some 16 state parks along its coastal plain. Call 919/733-4181 or see ils.unc.edu/parkproject/ncparks.html for information on the amenities of a specific park.

Unless specified as a tent site, all of the sites have electric hookups. Some tenters pack a portable fan and extension cord with the Coleman gear in the summer.

For many North Carolina parks, you can reserve a site in advance for a minimum of two nights and a maximum of 14 consecutive nights.

### Private Campgrounds and RV Parks

For a listing of North Carolina's privately owned campgrounds and RV parks, contact the N.C. Association of RV Parks and Campgrounds at 893 U.S. U.S. 70 West, Suite 202, Garner, NC 27529, 919/779-5709, website: www.kiz.com/campnet/html/cluborgs/nccoa.

ON THE ROAD

## Food

### SEAFOOD

Along the coast, seafood is king. Carolina **shrimp** are everywhere; you can catch them yourself or buy them right off the boats or nearly as fresh from coastal supermarkets. Ditto for the **Carolina soft-shell crab** used mainly for crab cakes and She Crab Soup. (Along the coast, you'll find lots of places serving crab legs, but these are from imported Alaskan king and Dungeness crabs.) South of Wilmington you'll find a lot of "Calabash seafood," lightly battered and deep-fried. The name comes from the tiny port town of Calabash in the very tip of the southeastern corner of the state, where fishing and shrimping crews used to quickly deep-fry some meals at the end of a long day on the boats. Visitors who came down to the docks to purchase fresh fish from the boats got hungry smelling all this crunchy goodness, and soon they were buying it from quick-thinking vendors, who dubbed the fresh-and-fried style Calabash. Oddly, today most Calabash seafood

© MIKE SIGALAS

restaurants are in South Carolina, along Restaurant Row in Myrtle Beach. Still, there are plenty to choose from in North Carolina.

### CLASSIC CAROLINA EATS
#### Barbecue

> *No man has ever been elected governor of North Carolina without eating more barbecue than was good for him.*
>
> **Raleigh Times** *editor Herbert O'Keefe*

My brother George, who lives not far over the Georgia border in Athens, declared recently that he and his wife had become vegetarians. I asked him how he thought he was going to ever give up barbecue, and he explained matter-of-factly, that he wasn't: in the South, he reminded me, barbecue *is* a vegetable.

Calling a barbecue joint a restaurant is like calling the Grateful Dead a musical group. "Enthusing about 'that great barbecue place,'" asserts UNC-TV reporter Bob Garner, "is one of the honest pleasures of life in North Carolina."

People have various theories as to how to spot a good barbecue joint. Some say that the presence of a pig anywhere on the sign is a good omen. Others claim that anyplace open more than three days a week (normally Thursday through Saturday) should be avoided like a Swedish pizza parlor. I would add only the following amendments: 1) no air-conditioning; 2) the fewer windows, the better.

The ideal barbecue joint is built of bricks or cinder blocks, preferably painted white, usually on a country road where police cruise-bys are weekly events (unless it's mealtime) and where security alarms would only irritate the possums. Therefore, most barbecue owners seem to figure, no windows, no hassle. And who needs windows, anyway? Eating barbecue is a serious business—you're not here to admire the scenery.

A single TV set is allowed—so long as it is set to a Braves game, a Duke, NC State, or Chapel Hill

ON THE ROAD

Bar-B-Q Center, Lexington

sporting event, or a NASCAR race. If you enter a barbecue and find the TV tuned to *Meet the Press,* turn, run, and do not look back. (Of course, that's a purely hypothetical situation: no self-respecting barbecue would be open on Sunday.)

There are exceptions to the above rules. I have once or twice been into a decent barbecue with both windows *and* central air-conditioning—but somehow, it felt like camping on Astroturf.

Now the real question comes—what is barbecue? The answer varies across the country: in the West, "barbecue" is something you do, not something you eat. You *barbecue* some ribs or steaks. To tell a Nevadan you're going to eat some "barbecue" is like telling them you're going to eat some "fried." In the Midwest—and Texas—"barbecued" is an adjective and usually comes before "ribs." Most parts of the deep South agree that "barbecue" (the noun) refers to smoked shredded or pulled pork. Where they can't agree is on how that pork should be prepared, disassembled, and dressed.

On these lofty issues, the populace is squarely divided in North Carolina. If you hear someone talking about "traditional **Eastern North Carolina barbecue,**" they're speaking of the whole-hog, chopped, peppery, vinegar-based variety. Western-style (a.k.a. Lexington, a.k.a. Piedmont) barbecue, on the other hoof, is shoulders only, pulled or sliced, and tomato-based. The coast and the mountains have served as a vacation spot for so many Carolinians from across the state for so long that you'll find a good mix of styles on the well-touristed ends of the state. For an excellent book on North Carolina barbecue, pick up Bob Garner's *North Carolina Barbecue: Flavored by Time.*

## Other Meats

You'll probably also want to try **slaw burgers** and **pimento cheeseburgers,** regional variations on the American artery-clogging favorite. **Slaw dogs** are simply hot dogs with coleslaw on top; you'll also find chili slaw dogs offered at many stands. **Fried chicken** is sold everywhere, from gas stations to Chinese restaurants to drive-up carhop restaurants. And most of it's good.

Fried **chicken livers** are offered at most places that sell fried chicken. If you've always publicly admired Native Americans for using up every bit of the animals they killed, here's a chance to walk your talk.

And of course, **chitlins** will give you another such chance. These are the deep-fried small intestines of a pig.

## Side Dishes

**Brunswick stew,** first cooked up down on St. Simons Island, Georgia, is a much-simmered, tomato-based side dish often eaten with barbecue. **Hush puppies** are deep-fried balls of dough, sometimes seasoned with onions, and they often battle with Brunswick stew for the right to accompany barbecued pork to your plate. Of course, **biscuits** are an important ingredient in Carolina country cooking. One surprising place where you'll find good biscuits is at Hardee's, but maybe that shouldn't be surprising, since Hardee's was founded in North Carolina.

Folks trying to eat healthy in the region are sometimes stymied by the tendency of Carolinians toward **stewed vegetables,** including spinach, okra, and collard greens, throwing in a slab of fatback for good flavor, and **fried vegetables,** which again seems to miss the point of eating vegetables entirely. But in the case of okra, perhaps it's an improvement.

**Grits** have become something like the official food of the South (if you eat at Denny's, you'll know you're in the South when they start including grits on the menu). Most Northerners would mistake them for Cream of Wheat, but don't put sugar and cinnamon on them—while this doesn't taste too bad, the proper way to eat this plain-tasting food is with butter and salt and pepper—or Texas Pete's Hot Sauce—and/or mixed in with eggs, ham, and whatever else is on your plate.

Finally, no trip to the South would be complete without a helping of **black-eyed peas.** These are actually beans, not peas—they're called cowpeas in other parts of the country—and they're not particularly tasty. If they were, you wouldn't have to come to the South (or to a northern "soul food" restaurant) to eat them. They became popular Southern food items because, like collards, they were easy to grow and cheap to buy down here, in a region that only recently has recovered from the Civil War.

## Hot Boiled Peanuts

Take raw, unshelled peanuts. Add water and salt. Boil for about a decade. Now you have hot boiled peanuts, often spelled "hot boil p-nuts" on roadside signs and pronounced "hot bowled peanuts" by most Carolinians. If you've never heard of them, they sound unimaginable, like a fried martini. If you've never eaten them before, they taste a little bit like salted peas. But if you've eaten a handful of them, you're probably hooked for life.

You can find hot boiled peanuts for sale in many convenience stores—usually in a brown paper bag enclosed in a Ziploc resealable bag—outside many Wal-Marts, in front of a flea market, or, best of all, at roadside stands and Minor League baseball games.

## Soul Food

With African-Americans making up nearly 50 percent of the population in many sections of North Carolina, you might think there'd be more "soul food" or overtly African-American restaurants. The truth, of course, is that much of the food you'll find in a soul food restaurant up in New York City is called "homecooking" or "country cooking" down here.

# ALTERNATIVES
## Mexican Food

Used to be that the average Mexican restaurant in Carolina would have to feature phonetic spellings and explanations of its items: "*Burrito:* bur-EE-toe: beans, shredded beef, and cheese, wrapped in a flour *tortilla* (see above)." But over the past 5 or 10 years, coinciding with an increase in the number of Latin American immigrants, numerous Mexican restaurants have opened up in the Carolinas. The influx of people from the south has been much happier for everyone involved than that other invasion from the north a while back. And amazingly, to some degree we have Taco Bell to thank for all this good new spicy food; in many small towns, Taco Bell was the first Mexican food Carolinians had ever eaten. Fortunately, this whetted folks' appetites and has opened the way for more extensive and authentic Mexican restaurants to open, many run by first-generation immigrants. In other towns, chains like Chevy's and Don Pablo's have opened, bringing their experienced Mexican restauranteering into towns that didn't know their *flautas* from a chicken dumpling in 1989.

## More International Cuisine

Asian restaurants—particularly Chinese ones—have a long history in most Carolinian towns, partly a result of the Pacific Theater duty many of the state's men saw in World War II. In bigger cities with tourist districts or large transplant populations—the Triangle, the Triad, Charlotte, Wilmington, Nags Head—you'll find Indian food, Thai food, just about anything you could want.

## Health Food/Vegetarian

If you're dedicated to a low-fat, low-cholesterol diet, you really ought to consider going off it while you're in North Carolina. Otherwise, you'll miss most of the most authentic local cuisine. However, even the most dedicated cultural submersionist may have to come up for some unfried air. You'll find health food stores and restaurants in all the sizeable cities, and wherever non-Southerners have come to live, study, or visit en masse. If nothing else, you can find a Subway or Blimpie's in most every town of any size; these can turn out a pretty good vegetarian sandwich.

## BEVERAGES

### Tea

The terms "sweet tea" and "ice tea" (no *d*) are nearly synonymous here. At some restaurants, it's served as a matter of course, like coffee at a truck stop diner. The sugar in sweet tea is added while the water's still hot, which allows the sugar to melt and blend more fully into the drink.

If you're at a restaurant—particularly in the country—and you want unsweetened tea, ask for it (quietly) and hope they have it.

### Alcohol

The minimum legal age for drinking in North Carolina is 21. A number of North Carolina towns and counties are "dry," but most with any sizeable tourist trade make a point of allowing their visiting guests access to alcohol by passing local variances.

In North Carolina, "hard" alcoholic beverages aren't sold in supermarkets; to buy anything beyond wine and beer, you'll need to visit a package store (also called an ABC or "red dot" store), where sales are permitted Monday through Saturday 9 A.M.–7 P.M. You'll notice that the stores do not have the word "alcohol" or "liquor" displayed on the outside—they are marked by the red dot alone, so that only people in the know will frequent them. It also helps to make certain that even the illiterate can find the package stores.

It's illegal to have an open container of alcohol in a moving vehicle on North Carolina roads.

## SOUTHERN RESTAURANT CHAINS

### Waffle House

Each location of this chain is nearly identical—stools, bright yellow and imitation wood Formica, appalling coffee, a sizzling grill, an order-shouting staff, and a jukebox. A patron of the Waffle House in Orangeburg, S.C., could easily walk into one in Biloxi, Mississippi, blindfolded, sit down, order, play the jukebox, and pay the bill without taking the blindfold off. But the Waffle House serves the needs of Southerners so perfectly that it somehow transcends its chain status.

Founded in an Atlanta suburb in 1955—the same year Disneyland opened—the Waffle House calls itself "America's Place to Eat, America's Place to Work." I've never worked at a Waffle House, other than doing some writing at one, but it does seem to be the one inescapable dining experience in the South. Because it's so common (more than 1,000 locations, seemingly off every other highway exit in the South), and because it's so *available* (open 24 hours every day except Thanksgiving and Christmas), it's become an icon of the South. So beloved is it that the Internet contains several non-official Waffle House sites.

The chain boasts of being the world's leading server of waffles, omelettes, raisin toast, grits, and apple butter. It's also the only place in the world where the jukeboxes play such specially recorded songs as "Waffle Doo-Wop" and "Good Food Fast"—along with standard oldies and country selections.

Try the pork chops and eggs with hash browns and raisin toast. Bert's Chili is also pretty good. Or just order some hash browns with tomatoes, "Scattered, Smothered, Covered, Chunked, Topped, and Diced."

These websites come and go, so if the following link doesn't work, just run a search for "Waffle House" and you're sure to get several hits. The "Waffle House Shrine" at www.geo cities.com/waffleshrine is currently one of the best, particularly for its links and its heartfelt testimonials by hundreds of Waffle House fanatics who post to the site.

One woman explains her Waffle House-related research:

*We started in Naples, Florida, drove 677 miles and saw 42 Waffle Houses along I-75 until we stopped for the night in Calhoun, Georgia. This works out to be one Waffle House for every 16.12 miles. Isn't that great?*

Others tell personal history; how they met their spouse at the Waffle House, or the time they got busted by the cops inside Waffle House or somesuch. "I'm in California" writes one man, "and I'm planning a trip to the westernmost Waffle House, which I understand is in Arizona." It's amazing, but a fitting testimony to an amazing place where the lights are always on, the chili is always good, and the tables are always wood-grain Formica.

## Cracker Barrel

Don't let it keep you away from the mom-and-pop restaurants in town, but if you're out on the interstate and in a hurry, or in dire need of a pullover, this chain is a safe bet for good country cooking along the interstate. With rocking chairs

out front, a fireplace burning, and old-timey photos on the wall, Cracker Barrels have a warm ambience that makes an hour's meal seem like a genuine break away from the highway.

Founded in 1969 in Lebanon, Tennessee, each restaurant contains a little gift shop featuring regional knickknacks reflecting the South in general and often the restaurant's location in particular. Before long I imagine these will spread to every state in the Lower 48, but for now they haven't penetrated the West Coast yet.

## Hardee's

Hardee's was founded in Greenville, North Carolina, and today the chain has more than 2,900 locations in 39 other states. Hardee's is usually the first chain restaurant to infect a small Southern town, opening the way for Ronald McDonald and the rest of the coven.

Some time back, the folks at a consumer magazine rated the fast food mongers of America and named Hardee's food No. 2 among all major fast-food chains, but it's hard to see what all the fuss is about. The two things that are worth getting here are the breakfast sandwiches made with fresh biscuits and the seasonal peach shakes. In 1998, Hardee's was purchased by Carl Karcher Enterprises, owner of the Carl's Jr. chain on the West Coast, and the chain adopted the famous Carl's Jr. star.

## Chick-Fil-A

Don't call it "Chick FIL-uh"; it's pronounced "chick fih-LAY"—"chick *filet*, get it? This is the largest privately owned restaurant chain in America. Georgia's Truett Cathy founded his first restaurant back in 1946; today the company operates nearly 600 restaurants. More than 400 of these are in malls, which means you'll see one in nearly every mall in North Carolina (Cathy pioneered the idea of fast food restaurants in malls). The main thing to get here is a seasoned boneless chicken breast sandwich. Kids love the Chicken Fingers. Closed on Sunday to allow workers to go to church and spend time with their families, Chick-Fil-A remains a true Southern phenomenon. Most non-mall locations feature a playground, a boon to those who need to burn off some energy. Check out the Chick online at www.chickfila.com.

## Bojangles

The dirty rice and Cajun chicken make this Tennessee-based chain a cut above the rest.

## Shoneys

Some people praise Shoneys for its breakfast buffet, but there's no dearth of good breakfast places in North Carolina—I recommend you try one of them instead.

# BUYING GROCERIES

## Farmers' Markets

With all the agriculture in the area, most towns in North Carolina have some sort of farmers' market. Some of the major ones include the **State Farmers Market,** in Raleigh, 919/733-7417; the **Western North Carolina Farmers Market,** in Asheville, 828/253-1691; the **Piedmont Triad Farmers Market** between Greensboro and Winston-Salem in Colfax, 336/605-9401; the **Charlotte Regional Farmers Market,** 704/357-1269; and the **Southeastern North Carolina Agricultural Center Farmers Market,** in Lumberton, 910/618-5699.

ON THE ROAD

## Travel Basics

*Going South always seems to me rather desolate and fatal and uneasy. . . . Going North is a safe dull feeling.*

> F. Scott Fitzgerald, writing to Ernest Hemingway, June 5, 1937

## BY CAR

Far-flung and separated by numerous natural barriers, North Carolina realized early on that the construction of good roads was the key to its future. Today, several federal interstates cross North Carolina, including I-95, the East Coast's primary north-south route, and I-40, which slips into the state over the top of Smoky Mountains National Park from Tennessee and veers across the state clear to Wilmington. I-77 cuts north-south through the state, slicing Charlotte in the process.

But while the heart of the state is easy to get to from most anywhere east of the Mississippi, the coast for many years was a bit trickier. Nowadays, I-40 dead-ends in Wilmington, making that town—and, through a judicious use of US 17, regions north and south—much more accessible than a few years back.

Of course, from New York and other parts north, just head south on I-95 (following the historic Fort Lauderdale Trail blazed by generations of spring breakers) until you hit N.C. 158, then head east to reach the Outer Banks, the Albemarle, and the Central Coast (though US 70 will do well for the latter two). For Wilmington, continue south until you hit I-40, then head east.

### Rentals

You'll find locations for all the major car rental chains throughout North Carolina, and especially around its airports. Contact Alamo at 800/327-9633, website: www.alamo.com, Avis at 800/831-2847, website: www.avis.com, Budget at 800/353-0600, website: www.budget.com, Enterprise at 800/325-8007, website: www .enterprise.com , and Hertz at 800/654-3131, website: www.hertz.com.

### Rules of the Road

Americans drive on the right side of the road, the way God intended. If you forget and drive on the left side of the road, other drivers will remind you by driving straight toward you and honking.

North Carolina requires seat belts for front-seat passengers; if you're in front and you're not wearing one, you'll receive a ticket with a fairly hefty fine. Children under five years of age and weighing less than 40 pounds must ride in an approved child safety seat; if your car has an active airbag, the child must ride in the back seat. Children under 16 must wear a seat belt, no matter where they're sitting in the car.

A driver's license serves as indispensable identification. In America, you need a driver's license for everything from cashing a check to renting movies.

A driver must be 25 years old and have a valid driver's license to rent a car. You will have the chance to buy insurance coverage for the car and yourself; unless your policy back home covers you, you'll want to go ahead and get some now. It's illegal to drive without at least liability coverage in the U.S.

Travelers from outside the U.S. must carry an International Driver's Permit as well as a current valid license from their home country.

Note: It's illegal in North Carolina to drive while drinking alcoholic beverages or while under the influence of alcohol. If you're caught driving with more than an 0.8 blood-alcohol level, you'll be arrested.

## BY AIR

North Carolina's main airports are the **Charlotte-Douglas International Airort,** 5501 Josh Birmingham Blvd., 704/359-4013; Greensboro's **Piedmont Triad International Airport,** 6451 Bryan Blvd., 336/665-5666; **Raleigh-Durham International Airport,** (actually in Morrisville) 1600 Terminal Blvd., 919/840-2123, and **Wilmington International Airport,** 1740 Airport

Blvd., 910/341-4125, all have fairly large airports. If you're hunting for cheap tickets and don't mind a few extra miles on the rental car, check out flights into Columbia, S.C.; Greenville, S.C.; or Norfolk, Va.

## BY TRAIN

Most sizable towns in North Carolina are served by Amtrak. For reservations and schedule information, call 800/872-7245.

## BY BUS

Most towns—sizable or not—are served by Greyhound Bus Lines. For reservations and schedule information, call 800/231-2222.

## BY BOAT

For the nautically endowed—those who own boats—eastern North Carolina is very accessible. The Atlantic Intracoastal Waterway, a 1,095-mile nautical pathway from Norfolk, Va., south to Miami, passes behind the coastal islands of North Carolina.

## VISAS AND OFFICIALDOM

### Entry Requirements

Non-U.S. citizens will need the following for entry to the country:

• Valid passport from a recognized country *or* valid visa

• Roundtrip or return ticket, or proof of sufficient funds to support yourself during your visit and to afford a return ticket. You may be required to purchase a return ticket at the airport before you are given a visa, or you may have to show proof of a return ticket when you are actually applying.

• $13.95 in fees for the services of the immigration, customs, and agricultural inspectors.

### Passports

Passports are the most common type of travel document used as proof of your identity when crossing an international border. A passport is required for travel into the United States and for air travel within the country.

It is always easier to travel with a passport than to try to get by with some other type of photo identification.

If you don't already have a passport, you should start the process for acquiring one as soon as possible. Make sure that it is valid for at least six months, preferably a year, after you plan to return home. If the passport issued to you by the government in your country expires while you are in the U.S., you will have to contact an embassy or consulate of your home country to renew it. U.S. passport offices do not provide services to holders of non-U.S. passports.

For extended stays, bring your birth certificate, extra passport photos, and even a photocopy of the original passport. This will help speed the process of replacing a lost or expired passport. If your passport is stolen, report it to the police immediately and get a copy of the police report, or at least record the important details contained in it (name and title of the officer, the police precinct number, the file number, etc.). This should also help in replacing your passport.

### Visas

Visas are documents, usually a stamp in your passport, that are issued by the government of the country you want to visit. Visas are a precondition for being admitted to a country, but they are not a guarantee of entry. The rules for acquiring a visa are arbitrary and occasionally very strict, but if you plan ahead and follow the rules to the letter, you shouldn't run into any problems.

A very few countries in the world participate with the U.S. in the Visa Waiver Pilot Program. Check with a U.S. embassy or consulate to find out if your country is included in the program. Otherwise, you are required to have a visa. You should always be courteous and respectful to consular, immigration, and customs authorities. If you are applying for a tourist visa to the U.S., you will be required to appear in person at a U.S. consulate or embassy for an interview, as well as meet certain other requirements, including proof that you have a return ticket.

## NORTH CAROLINA PUBLIC FERRIES

North Carolina's ferries are uncomplicated to use, either free or inexpensive, and a scenic, memorable alternative to taking the (often longer) land route, especially since they allow everyone in your car—even the driver—a chance to get out, stretch, feed the seagulls, socialize with other visitors, or maybe catch a few winks. Though they vary in size (the longer the journey, the bigger the boat), they all have bathrooms and some semblance of a lounge, usually with a candy machine, soft drink machine, and road coffee. They can handle just about any kind of vehicle you might be driving; if you're not sure, call ahead and ask. You'll need reservations if your ferry leaves from Cedar Island (800/856-0343 or 252/225-3551), Ocracoke (800/345-1665 or 252/928-3841), or Swan Quarter (800/773-1094 or 252/926-1111). Stop by most any tourist-oriented business and ask for a current schedule of departure times and prices, or call 800/BY-FERRY (800/293-3779) for information.

Departure times vary from season to season. Ferries may close in inclement weather. Try to arrive 15 minutes early to make sure you've got a spot on board, even if you've got a reservation. Below is a list of the state's ferries, with approximate passage times.

**Aurora–Bayview Ferry,** 30 minutes

**Cedar Island–Ocracoke Ferry,** 2 hours, 15 minutes; $10 per car

**Cherry Branch–Minnesott Ferry,** 20 minutes

**Currituck–Knotts Island Ferry,** 40 minutes

**Hatteras–Ocracoke Ferry,** 40 minutes

**Southport–Fort Fisher Ferry,** 30 minutes

**Swan Quarter–Ocracoke Ferry,** 2 hours, 30 minutes; $10 per car

© MIKE SIGALAS

Make sure to find out what the current visa requirements are for travel, or if your country is "officially recognized" by the U.S. government. Visa requirements can change at any time, without notice. If you have already bought nonrefundable air tickets and are denied entry, you'll be out of luck.

The United States charges $13.95 in arrival fees to pay for the services of the customs, immigration, and agricultural inspectors.

## State Border Crossings

Part of the evidence that North Carolina and the rest of the Confederacy lost the argument over state sovereignty is the ease with which one can travel between American states. The only restrictions you're likely to encounter involve transporting certain plants or produce across state lines, or transporting illegal substances or guns across state lines.

Border authorities sometimes forbid produce and plants from entering a state because the flora may contain pests or diseases harmful to the native plants or agricultural products of the state. In some cases, if you are carrying produce in your car and are stopped at a state border, you will be asked to dispose of the produce.

Generally forbidden substances include illegal drugs, explosives, or dangerous chemicals. In most states, transporting illegal drugs across the state line increases the legal penalty for possession from a misdemeanor to a felony.

Many counties also have laws governing the amount of alcohol and number of cartons of cigarettes you can bring across their border. If a county border is also a state border and you are carrying alcohol or cigarettes into that county, check its laws concerning alcohol and cigarettes. A pack of cigarettes and a bottle of beer are not cause for legal action, unless the beer is open. A carton of cigarettes and a bottle of whiskey might raise a few eyebrows, but shouldn't cause you any trouble. Twenty cartons of cigarettes and a case of whiskey will get you into trouble in many counties.

If you are carrying a gun, you must have a valid permit. Check with the embassy or consulate where you got your passport if you plan to buy and carry a gun while traveling in the U.S., and understand that foreign visitors requesting information regarding firearms will be viewed with some suspicion.

## SPECIAL INTERESTS
### Travel with Children

North Carolina is very much a family-oriented state. Many parks feature wide, family-size swings; nearly every community event includes children's activities, and most resorts provide thorough programs for youngsters. The only places where children are unwelcome are in nightclubs and bars, in casinos (no big loss), and in many bed and breakfasts. Still, North Carolina seems to have a higher percentage of "children-welcome" B&Bs than most other states. Where possible, I've noted whenever establishments have stated a preference.

One nice thing about automobile travel in North Carolina is that it's rare you'll find yourself driving very long without the opportunity to stop and let the kids get out and burn off some energy. The enclosed playgrounds now popular at

Old Salem

Chick-Fil-A, Burger King, McDonald's, and some of their competitors make pretty handy pit stops, even on a rainy day.

## Women Travelers

I've never been a woman, despite what my football coach used to yell, so I've asked my wife, Kristin, to help with this section:

Most women find themselves treated especially politely in North Carolina. Doors will be opened, bus seats offered. There are, however, areas still considered male domains—the same places, generally, considered male domains throughout most of the Western world: honkytonk bars, hunting clubs, some golf clubs, sports bars. A woman is in no particular danger in most of these places, but her presence there may be interpreted as a desire for male companionship.

Women traveling alone should be aware of their surroundings. When you head for your car, carry your keys in hand and get to and into the car quickly. Drive with your doors locked and your windows rolled up.

If possible, carry a cellular phone—otherwise, a breakdown on the highway will leave you waiting and hoping the first motorist to stop for assistance has good motives.

A sizable number of crimes each year are committed by people impersonating police officers. If you're pulled over—especially at night—don't open your car door or window more than a crack, and then only to demand that a marked patrol car be called. This is well within your rights.

No matter how authentic the uniform looks, demand to see the marked car. If the officer can't produce a black-and-white, move on. Don't hand over your license, which gives your name and address.

If you feel suspicious, ask the officer to follow you to a more-populated, better-lighted area.

## Gay/Lesbian Travelers

In recent decades, American gays and lesbians have begun to enjoy an increase in tolerance toward same-sex couples. In North Carolina, larger cities like Raleigh, Charlotte, and Wilmington have their share of gay hangouts and nightclubs, many of them private clubs that require a nominal "membership fee" for admittance. In other areas, gay and lesbian travelers not wanting to draw attention to themselves generally avoid public displays of affection.

## Travelers with Disabilities

Though all of the Carolinas' new public buildings provide facilities and access for the physically disabled, many of the state's historic structures and sites have been hard-pressed to do the same. Throughout this book, I've tried to note attractions that may pose special difficulties for the disabled, as well as those that specifically define themselves as wheelchair accessible. If you're uncertain about the accessibility of a specific attraction, be sure to call ahead.

## AA, Al-Anon, Other Recovery Programs

Chapters of **Alcoholics Anonymous** hold meetings throughout the Tar Heel State, and most welcome visitors. Call 252/261-1681 in Kitty Hawk, 252/338-1849 in Elizabeth City, or 910/794-1840 in Wilmington for information and help, 24 hours a day.

**Narcotics Anonymous,** 800/922-5305, specializes in helping those with other drug addictions. **Al-Anon,** 800/750-2666, specializes in providing help for the families of alcoholics.

## Churches

Visiting North Carolina without attending a church service is like going to Thailand and not visiting a temple. Church life and the spiritual life (and sometimes the two intersect) are of major importance to most Carolinians, and it would be hard to get any real grasp on the culture without passing between the white pillars and taking a spot in the pew.

Up in Wilmington, the beautiful First Presbyterian Church downtown not only features sonorous bells, but was once pastored by Woodrow Wilson's father. And up in the Outer Banks, there's the Outer Banks Worship Center, a nondenominational church so devoted to evangelizing Banks visitors that they've built their roadside church in the shape of a huge ark to attract passerby. And then there's the eye-catching

Nags Head Baptist Church, a little white church standing in the shadow of a huge sand dune south of Jockeys Ridge State Park. Up in Old Salem you can still attend services at Home Moravian, one of America's oldest Moravian churches, and home today to one of America's largest Moravian congregation.

Of course, for every large, celebrity church, a couple hundred humble congregations of every stripe meet each Sunday. To get a truly representative feel for the spiritual tempo of Carolina, you might be best off pulling out a Yellow Pages, picking a church that catches your eye, and attending a service.

Compared to most parts of the country, Carolinian churches are still fairly dressy: most women wear dresses or pantsuits (most Carolinian women, visiting a new church, wear a dress or skirt just to play it safe); men wear slacks, shirts, and ties, and often jackets. The general philosophy behind all this finery runs something like this: "You'd dress up to go ask some fellow at the bank for a loan. Doesn't God deserve the same respect?" (Whether it's respectful to treat God as though he thinks as superficially as the average loan officer is another question.) Dress is generally more casual along the coast, and even more so in nondenominational churches.

With the exception of most Pentecostal and Charismatic congregations, very few services are significantly integrated—reminding one of Martin Luther King Jr.'s quote about Sunday morning being the most segregated hours in America. However, very, very few congregations will object to the presence of friendly, respectful visitors of a different race, and most will be quite happy to have you there.

# HEALTH MAINTENANCE
## Insect Repellent
Unless you're planning to spend all of your time on city streets, you'll want insect repellent while you're here. The two critters that will trouble you most are no-see-ums (particularly at the coast) and mosquitoes. No-see-ums are tiny gnats that bite as if it's personal. The best way to

fight them seems to be with Avon's Skin-So-Soft cream. Wear a hat—they'll bite your scalp as well.

Mosquitoes are pleasant companions by comparison, but in swamps and salt marshes they can quickly turn a day hike into purgatory. Skin-So-Soft works with them as well, and so do Deep Woods Off and most Cutter products.

## Sunscreens
Carolina summers can be particularly deceiving; though it's hot, the gray sky overhead can lull you into thinking that your skin's not taking a beating from ultraviolet rays—but it is. To ward off skin cancer, premature wrinkles, and sunburn, use sunscreens with an SPF rating of 15 or more—higher for those with fair skin.

## Adjusting to the Humidity
Stepping off a plane into the middle of a Carolina summer can just about knock you out. If you live in a less humid area and your plans in North Carolina include a lot of physical activity, try to give yourself a day or two to acclimate.

## Local Doctors
North Carolina has no dearth of qualified physicians for those with the money to pay for them. Neither is the state short of walk-in medical clinics where you can stop in without an appointment. Check the local phone book under "Physicians" to find the address and phone number of physicians in your area, or stop into a shop, explain your situation to a clerk, and ask for a recommendation.

# NATURAL HAZARDS

For all its natural beauty, the South does seem to have more than its share of natural hazards— from alligators and poisonous snakes to hurricanes and jellyfish. But 99 percent of the time these hazards can be avoided with a little foresight and caution.

## Lightning Storms
Sociologists throw around a lot of reasons for the fervent spirituality of many Carolinians, but one

overlooked cause may be the prayer-inspiring lightning storms. When the sheet lightning flares across the sky like a flickering fluorescent bar, and the bolts are blasting transformers to either side of the road, even a trip to the local package store can quickly turn into a religious experience.

In a 9.5-year stretch from 1993 to mid-2002, 10 North Carolinians met their maker via lightning—one person zapped to Beulah Land every year and two months. But that's only counting fatalities. No less than 141 people took a bolt during those same 114 months (one every 24.5 days), to varying effect.

It really does happen. So if you're out on the trail or the golf course when a storm rolls in, seek shelter—though not under a tree, since the tree is likely to get hit, in which case you don't want to be anywhere around it. And here's one thing to keep in mind: only a handful of North Carolina's 141 lightning strikes from 1993-2002 took place before noon. None of the fatalities did.

Electrocution is rarely worth risking—especially since the average summer convection storm will be over in less than an hour. Go find a cup of coffee somewhere and enjoy the show from safety.

If you're indoors, do as most Carolinians do—they won't talk on a phone (though cordless phones are okay) or use plumbing when a storm is striking around them, since both phone lines and water can serve as conduits. There are a number of urban legends revolving around someone using the toilet during a lightning storm; almost any Carolinian can fill in the details.

## Hurricanes

Hurricanes—and, more commonly, the threat of hurricanes—are simply a fact of life in coastal North Carolina. Local news teams run ads boasting of their prophetic capabilities, and supermarkets like Piggly Wiggly buy full pages to proclaim themselves "Your Hurricane Stock-Up Store."

> *Sociologists throw around a lot of reasons for the fervent spirituality of many Carolinians, but one overlooked cause may be the prayer-inspiring lightning storms. When the sheet lightning flares across the sky, even a trip to the local package store can quickly turn into a religious experience.*

Pay attention to the public warnings on the radio and television when you're in the state, especially June through October—hurricane season. The mildest warning is a **small craft advisory,** issued when strong winds—up to 38 mph—strike the coastal waters. This is not the day to rent or charter a fishing boat. Next up is a **gale warning,** issued when winds reach 39–54 mph. A **storm warning** means winds 55–73 mph. **Hurricane watches** are issued when hurricane conditions are a real possibility and may threaten coastal or inland areas within 36 hours. A **hurricane warning** means a hurricane is expected to hit an area within 24 hours. If you're visiting the coast and a hurricane warning is issued, it's time to consider visiting North Carolina's historic interior for a few days. One way to stay ahead of the game—or to put off a visit if you haven't left home yet—is to check the National Weather Service website, at www.nws.noaa.gov.

The two things you *don't* want to do are panic or ignore the warnings. If an evacuation is called, you'll hear about it on the radio and TV. But by this point, you as a traveler should be gone already. Save the spot in the relief shelter for a local resident. Get thee to the Smokies.

## Snakebite

Few other states offer the variety of poisonous snakes found in North Carolina. Of North Carolina's 37 known snake species, six of them can make your life complicated in a hurry. And while North Carolina enjoys the highest incidence of poisonous snake bites among U.S. states, the chances of getting bit are still infinitesimal—you're more likely to die from a bee sting or lightning strike. Even if you *wanted* to get bit, you'd have a hard time finding a snake to do the job. Even the woodsiest visitor is unlikely to run across any of them on a visit.

The **copperhead** averages around two to three

feet long and normally lives in damp woods, mountainous regions, or in the high ground in swampy areas—which is to say you'll find it all through coastal North Carolina.

**Canebrake** or **timber rattlesnakes** are also found throughout the state—usually in deciduous forests or swamps on high ground. These snakes average three to four feet in length and can even reach five.

The **Eastern diamondback rattlesnake** runs 3–6 feet and up, with a basic dark brown color and brown-and-yellow diamonds. They mostly keep to the woods of the Lowcountry.

The **pigmy rattlesnake** is rare and only reaches a bit over a foot long. You'll find them in all but the highest lands of the Carolinas. They're dull gray with brown splotches on the back and sides.

The **cottonmouth** or **water moccasin** thrives in wetland areas of the coastal plain.

The beautiful black, red, and yellow **eastern coral snake** is rare, found in woods and fields.

Bring a **snake kit,** wear leather boots to protect your ankles, and watch where you step. Here's the good news: several thousand people are bitten by poisonous snakes each year, but fewer than 10 die in the U.S. annually.

More good news: in most cases, snakebite is preventable. More than 50 percent of poisonous snakebites take place after the victim has seen the snake and had the chance to get away. In fact, most victims are bitten in the attempt to pick up a poisonous snake, harass it, or kill it. The point is simple enough: keep your eyes open when in the woods and stay away from any snake that you're not absolutely certain is nonpoisonous.

If you or somebody in your party is bitten by a snake, try not to panic. Even if the snake is poisonous, odds are nearly even that it was a "dry" bite—meaning that no poison was injected into the victim. Nonetheless, don't allow the victim to engage in strenuous physical activity, since this will get the heart pumping faster, thus spreading the poison quicker. Try to safely identify the breed of snake if it's possible, and if it doesn't take too long to do it. Get the victim to the nearest hospital or emergency medical facility as soon as possible.

If local doctors are unsure of the correct snakebite serum to use to treat the bite, tell them to contact the regional Poison Information Center.

## Yellowjackets

To avoid most stinging insects, the place to start is in your clothing—bright colors attract, dark ones don't. If you notice yellowjackets about and you're drinking or eating something, be sure to keep checking the food or drink (soda cans are notorious) to make sure no yellowjacket has snuck aboard.

Yellowjacket stings are painful—not unlike being burned by a just-extinguished match. The danger comes in when people have allergic reactions.

How can you tell if it's an allergic reaction? A good rule of thumb is that as long as the reaction is around the site of the bite, you can assume it's a local reaction and needs to be treated with something like an antihistamine and maybe a little topical steroid, if anything. But if you get bitten or stung by an insect and you develop symptoms elsewhere on your body, those are signs of an allergic reaction; you need to get in and see a doctor.

Some of the signs of an allergic reaction are hives; swelling of the lips, tongue, eyelids, internal organs; blocked airways; shock; and low blood pressure.

If you're headed in this direction, your doctor will probably administer epipens, which contain epinephrine and quickly reduce the symptoms of an allergic reaction.

## Fire Ants

These ants are extremely aggressive when protecting their nests; if you inadvertently knock over a mound, don't stand around apologizing or you may soon find yourself covered with stinging ants. Stings can cause a severe reaction and even death. Watch for their domed mounds, commonly at least 15 inches wide at the base and about six inches high, usually found in damp areas—which includes most all of the American South—particularly under trees, in lawns, or in flower beds.

Winged fire ants originated in South America and first appeared on U.S. soil in Mobile, Alabama, in 1918. Since then they've spread like the

ON THE ROAD

kudzu of the animal kingdom to 11 Southern states—including North Carolina—and in the last half of the 1990s made their appearance in Southern California, at about the same time as Krispy Kreme doughnuts.

You'll find numerous chemical treatments for ant mounds in any grocery store or hardware store. Some swear that pouring boiling water into the top of an ant mound will do the trick, without harming the local water supply.

Fire ant bites leave a sterile pustule. The urge to scratch or pop the pustule is very tempting, but try not to do it. Scratching or picking at a bite until it becomes open allows it to get infected.

If you're allergic to fire ants, wear shoes and socks—don't go outside barefoot or in sandals.

## Jellyfish

If stung by a jellyfish, clean the area carefully. If you have tentacles still stuck to the wound area, don't just pull them off with your hand—they may still have venom sacs attached. Instead, use a credit card to scrape parallel with the skin, pushing the tentacles off sideways. Try not to break any of the venom sacs.

For pain relief, try meat tenderizer, a baking soda and water paste, or vinegar.

Jellyfish stings very rarely cause allergic reactions, but when they do, they can include hives, itching, and swelling on parts of the body that weren't stung. If any of these symptoms occurs, get to an emergency room.

## Stingrays

Stingray wounds are much more rare than jellyfish stings, but they happen. To avoid them, shuffle your feet as you walk in the water.

If you do happen to step on a stingray, it will let you know—it'll swing its mace of a tail around and send you hopping back to shore. Most stingray victims get it on the foot or ankle.

One treatment is to submerge the wound in the hottest water you can stand for 20 or 30 minutes. This seems to neutralize the poison. Most people enjoy noticeable relief within minutes.

Even so, if you've danced with a stingray and come away stung, you should still see a doctor—you may need an antibiotic.

## Sharks

One of the fatalities during 2001's much-reported "Summer of the Shark" was a Russian national swimming off Avon on Hatteras Island with his girlfriend. The girlfriend was severely attacked, but survived. The man lost a leg and some fingers and bled to death on the shore.

It's horrible, but keep in mind that before this, despite millions of annual visitors, not a single fatal shark attack had occurred along North Carolina's shoreline in 44 years. The odds of being bitten by a shark anywhere in the world are incredibly low; the odds of being bitten in North Carolina's waters are even lower than this. From 1957-2001, the International Shark Attack File counted only 19 shark attacks in North Carolina—20 times fewer than in Florida, half as many as in South Carolina, and even eight fewer than off the coast of Texas.

To make the odds even lower, the experts offer this advice:

• Swim in groups, preferably composed of people better-tasting than you are.

• Don't swim too far out—if you see sharks, you want to be close to shore so you can get out fast.

• Avoid swimming in the late afternoon, at night, or in the early morning. This is when sharks feed the most.

• Lose the flashy jewelry. Sharks can't see well in North Carolina's murky waters, but they'll see the glitter from that belly ring of yours.

Another thing to remember is that sharks don't watch movies, so they don't know that they're supposed to stick their dorsal fins up out of the water as they cruise toward the beach. Most sharks near the shore usually swim on the bottom, so their victims have no advance warning.

Though the whole U.S. East Coast may only see 40 shark attacks a year (and few if any of these fatal), the number of incidents has increased over past decades—presumably because more folks are hitting the surf than ever. Along the East Coast, practically all shark attacks are hit-and-run strikes by black-tipped or spinner sharks, usually no more than six feet long. The shark takes a bite, realizes that the victim tastes bad, and releases. Most bite victims bleed but don't lose any actual tissue.

Of course, sometimes they do. But as others have pointed out, you're still safer in the water than you are driving to it. And vengeance is certainly ours: while sharks kill about 100 people a year worldwide, humans annually kill some 100 million sharks.

## Poison Ivy

If you've been exposed to poison ivy, you have two or three hours to wash it off and avoid a breakout. If you are out and about and can't take a shower, rubbing the skin with alcohol—even beer—will often help. What you *don't* want to do is touch the unwashed, exposed part of your body with any other part, thus spreading the irritating serum.

## Giardia

Ironically, one of the smallest critters in the state causes much more cumulative discomfort than any other. While a lake or stream may appear clean, think twice before taking a sip. You're risking a debilitating sickness by drinking untreated water. The protozoan *Giardia duodenalis* is found in fresh water throughout the state, spread by both humans and animals. Although curable with prescription drugs, giardia's no fun—unless bloating, cramps, and diarrhea are your idea of a good time. Carry safe drinking water on any trip. If your canteen's dry, boiling creek or lake water will kill giardia and other harmful organisms. Some hikers prefer to use water filters made by companies like Mountain Safety Research and Pur, about $50 at most backpacking stores. Cheaper filters may allow the tiny giardia protozoan (as small as 0.2 microns) to pass through; even the best filters may not always filter out other, smaller organisms. Traditional purifying chemicals like chlorine and iodine are unreliable, taste foul, and can be unhealthy. Boiling's really your best bet.

Unfortunately, it's also possible to get giardia while bathing. Be careful not to swallow water while swimming in fresh water; men with mustaches should carefully dry them after leaving the water.

## Lyme Disease

Lyme disease is caused by a bacteria transmitted to humans through the bite of the deer tick. Not all ticks carry the disease, but infection rates in certain areas can be quite high. Don't assume that because you are not in a high-infection area you cannot get Lyme disease. Most cases have been reported in the northeast and upper Midwest, but an increasing number of cases are being seen in southeastern states. If you are bitten by a tick anywhere in the U.S., you should get checked for Lyme disease. The disease can be detected by a blood test, and early treatment can cure the disease or lessen the severity of later symptoms.

An early symptom of Lyme disease is a red, circular rash in the area of the bite that usually develops a few days to a few weeks after being bitten. Other symptoms can feel like the flu: headache, stiff neck, fever, and muscle aches. Sometimes, these symptoms will not show up for months. If any of these symptoms appear, even if you don't remember being bitten by a tick, have a doctor check you. Early detection of Lyme disease provides excellent opportunity for treatment (largely with antibiotics).

The three types of ticks known to carry Lyme disease (not necessarily every individual) are the deer tick (most common) in the northeast and north-central U.S., the lone star tick in the South, and the California black-legged tick in the West. If you are bitten by any tick, save the body for later identification if you can.

Remove a tick as soon as possible after it bites you. The best way is to grab the tick as close to your skin as you can get with a pair of tweezers. The longer a tick has been on your body, the deeper it will bite you to find more blood. The closer to its head you can grab it, the less chance that its mouth parts or head will break off in the wound. If you can't get the whole thing out, go see a doctor. Clean the wound with antiseptic and cover it to avoid infection.

## CRIME

As North Carolina's population has risen, so has its crime rate. By the turn of the 21st century, the state had clawed its way into the top 15 among all states for murders, robberies, and larceny, and had reached the #1 spot for burglaries. It ranked ninth in the Overall Crime Index, and eighteenth for violent crimes.

A friend of mine who grew up around Charlotte says his daddy gave him three rules for staying safe at night, and they seem worth repeating:

- Nothing good ever happened after 2 A.M.
- Don't carry more than you're willing to lose
- There's safety in numbers

Two A.M. is last call at most bars in North Carolina, after which the streets become populated with drunk folk and those who prey upon them. Rule No. 2 is an important one. If you can't immediately hand over your wallet to a robber and know you'll be all right, then you need to go through it and remove the irreplaceable contents. Rule No. 3 also makes sense. Solo walkers get robbed more often than couples, who get robbed more often than trios, who get robbed more often than quartets, and so on. The bigger the crowd, the better the odds.

## How to Protect Yourself

- Don't carry too much money. How much is too much? Too much is so much that you won't gladly give over your wallet to get a robber to leave you and your travel companions alone.
- Don't give carjackers time to size you up.

Walk to your car quickly, with your keys in your hand; get in, lock the doors, start up, and drive off. Fix your hair and/or makeup while you're at a stoplight, like a good American.

- When driving—particularly in urban areas—keep your doors locked and your windows rolled up. Carjackers are generally not the hardest-working individuals you'll ever run across—they're watching for an easy mark.
- Keep your wallet or purse out of sight when you're driving.
- If you're involved in an accident that seems suspicious, signal to the other driver to follow you and then drive to a better-lit, more populated area. A common ploy for carjackers is to bump their victims from behind and then rob them as they get out to inspect the damage to their car.
- If you're traveling with children and get carjacked, tell the carjacker you've got a child in back and ask if you can take him or her out. Many times the carjacker—who doesn't want to add a kidnapping charge to all the others he's racking up—will let you get the child out.
- Park in a central, well-lit area.
- When in public, wear your money and/or purse close to your body—and wallets in your front pocket. This will make it harder for pickpockets/purse snatchers to rob you undetected.

**Edenton Waterfront**

© MIKE SIGALAS

- If you're driving a rental car, make sure there are no identifying markers. Travelers have, in some places in the U.S.—Florida, most famously—become targets. If there are items that indicate your car is rented—license-plate frames emblazoned with the name of the company, for instance—ask the folks at the rental office if you can remove them while you have the car in your possession.

## OTHER ISSUES

### Racism

People have found a number of excuses for not loving each other throughout the centuries. One of the most common is racism.

Members of every imaginable race and combination of races live in North Carolina, but the vast majority—over 90 percent—consider themselves either "white" or "black." And of course, it is between these two groups that most of the racial tension in North Carolina has traditionally existed.

Most of what passes for racism in North Carolina is, instead, largely "classism." What appears as white/black animosity is instead disguised class hatred: in the most common scenario, "racist" whites attribute to blacks all the traits historically attributed to anyone at the bottom of the social ladder—laziness, low intelligence, dishonesty, envy, criminal habits, and reproductive irresponsibility. "Racist" blacks on the other hand, attribute to whites all the traits underclasses generally hang on an upper class: greed, snobbery, condescension, lack of compassion, hedonism, shallowness, spiritual vacuousness, clubbishness. In each case, the "racist" person is probably right to oppose the values they attribute to people they dislike. Where they err is in attributing these values, in blanket fashion, to members of a given race.

If you're "white" or "black," it's possible you'll feel some hostility from "the other" while visiting North Carolina. If you are part of an interracial couple, you'll possibly experience some disapproving looks from members of both races, especially as you venture into the country or into the more homogeneous neighborhoods of the major cities. (If you're Asian or Latino/a, and far from any large town, you may find people scratching their heads, wondering how you ever ended up there.)

To a remarkable degree, a smile and eye contact break down the walls that most people put up between strangers of the "other" and their better selves. Your goal is to show them that you're an exception, that you don't carry the attitudes they expect to find in someone with your pigmentation.

If this doesn't work, the best thing to do is to cut your losses and move on.

### Drugs

North Carolina is not known for its tolerant attitude toward illicit drugs, or for the comfortable nature of its jails. Possession and sale of marijuana are illegal here, as are all the usual mind-altering substances.

### Sexually Transmitted Diseases

AIDS is alive and well in North Carolina, as are numerous other debilitating sexually transmitted diseases (STDs), including a couple flavors of hepatitis and genital herpes. The safest thing to do is to not share hypodermic needles and not have sex with anyone you haven't screened first. If a person tells you he or she is HIV-negative, make sure the person hasn't had sex with another partner since that last screening. And since there's a six-month window during which someone who has contracted HIV may still show negative in a HIV test, to be safe you need to know that a person didn't have sex for six months *before* the screening (although some people with HIV have tested negative as late as five years after contracting the virus).

If, given the irresistible attractiveness of most Carolinians, celibacy seems an impossible task, you should at least reduce the risk by using a latex condom.

## Communications, Media, and Information

### POSTAL SERVICES

Sending mail from the United States to anywhere in the world is pretty easy. Almost every town and city in the U.S. that you are likely to visit has at least one post office, or a local business that acts as the local post office. In larger cities you'll also find the major international delivery companies (UPS, Federal Express, and so on). The U.S. Postal Service and the delivery companies can ship packages for you to many foreign countries.

At publication, a U.S. postal stamp to mail a letter (under 10 ounces) costs 37 cents, and a postcard stamp is 23 cents. Charges for larger letters and packages are based on weight.

The delivery companies and the postal service offer next-day and two-day service to almost anywhere in the world.

If you plan to receive mail in the United States, make sure that the person sending mail addresses the envelope with your name exactly as it appears on your passport. This will help to avoid any questions as to whether the mail is yours. You can also have mail delivered to your hotel. Make sure to provide the person sending you mail with the correct address. Also request that the person sending you mail print or type your address on the envelope to avoid any confusion that might arise because of worldwide differences in writing styles.

Always attach postage yourself to ensure that the proper amount is used.

When shipping large parcels overseas, it's best to pack the item(s) yourself or oversee the job. There are many packaging stores in the United States, offering boxes in various sizes, as well as tape and other packaging material. Many of these stores double as a post office or pickup/dropoff spot for the large delivery companies.

Unfortunately, though the U.S. Postal Service likes to cite Herodotus's quote, "Neither snow, nor rain, nor heat, nor night stays these couriers from the swift completion of their appointed rounds," you'll find that just about any old bank holiday—even Columbus Day—will stay these couriers. Post offices will also close, and any mail you've already sent off will sit for a full day—so be prepared.

### TELEPHONES
#### Public

Public phones are widely available on street corners and outside convenience stores and gas stations. They are maintained by a variety of private companies, which may sometimes charge more than the usual fee of 35–50 cents. Use any combination of coins; however, in the case of a 35-cent local call, if you use two quarters, change will not be provided. Dialing directions are usually provided on the face of the phone, but when in doubt simply dial 0 for an operator, who will direct your call for an added charge of $1 to $3. To place a local or long-distance call, simply dial the number and an automated voice will tell you how much money to deposit. When using a calling card billed to your home account, dial 0 plus the number (including area code) you're calling. You'll hear a tone, then often a voice prompting you to enter your calling card number and Personal Identification Number. For universal calling cards, follow the instructions provided on the back of the card or dial 0 for operator assistance.

Prepaid calling cards are the most hassle-free method of making long-distance calls from a public or private phone. If you purchase a $10 card, you are given $10 of long-distance credit to spend. You can spend it all on one call, or—more likely—on a series of calls throughout your trip. Best of all, if you lose your card—unlike calling cards that give access to your account with your home phone company—you can't lose more than the $10 you spent on it. Stores like Kroger and Wal-Mart sell prepaid calling cards.

Phone books are generally available at public phone booths and normally cover everything within the local area code, though frequently they are vandalized. Besides containing phone listings, phone books also carry maps of the local area, zip codes and post offices, information on public transportation systems, and a listing of community services and events.

## Cellular Phones

It's tragic but true: now that cellphones have gained ground as the verbal communication tool of choice, the pay telephone is going the way of the Greyhound bus. Sure, people still use them, but increasingly only when adverse finances or logistics require it. And as America's abandoned payphone infrastructure increasingly suffers from custodial neglect, even those of us who for years doggedly eschewed cellphones find ourselves throwing in the towel (the same towel that we formerly employed to wipe unknown gummy substances from payphone mouthpieces) and signing up for service plans.

Traveling with a cell phone is convenient; it's often possible, for instance, to sit in the parking lot of a lodging and call for the rates and get a cheaper price than if you walked in and asked at the front desk.

Safety-wise, it makes sense too. North Carolina contains some long stretches between towns, and it makes sense to bring along a cell phone for emergencies if you have the option. As long as you have Sprint, Verizon, or another national plan, you'll find most of the state quite amenable to cell calls, though of course you may run into some trouble weaving in and out between mountain peaks. If you're coming from overseas, make sure your phone is triband so that it'll pick up the U.S. frequency (1900 megahertz), which differs from those overseas.

If you still haven't made the plunge but would like to rent a phone while here, stop in at one of the kiosks at the state's major airports, or check the local phone book from stores for the various cellular carriers.

## Emergency Calls

In an emergency when an ambulance, firefighters, or police are required, you can dial 911 and be instantly connected with an emergency switchboard; otherwise dial 0 for operator. When you dial 911, your number and address are displayed to the person who answers, enabling the authorities to locate you, even if you yourself don't know exactly where you are.

## INTERNET ACCESS

Internet access has spread through North Carolina just as it has everywhere else. Internet cafés seem to be rebounding after nearly disappearing from view. Most public libraries boast Internet access, and most business hotels and B&Bs offer separate modem lines, or at least modem hookups that use your room phone line.

## RADIO

In most of North Carolina, you'll find a wide variety of music, with a heavy emphasis on country but liberal dosings of urban, metal, and pop stations. Contemporary Christian rock music stations have popped up in a many of the bigger cities. As usual, nearly everywhere in the state, the left end of the FM dial is where you'll find gospel stations and the North Carolina Public Radio/NPR affiliate, where faithful listeners will find *All Things Considered, Prairie Home Companion,* and *Car Talk,* along with local shows—a few of which highlight regional music.

The AM dial contains gospel music and preaching, country music—particularly in the mountains—some local news and talk shows, and the sonic strip mall that is American syndicated talk radio today.

## TOURIST INFORMATION
### Statewide Offices

Contact the North Carolina Division of Tourism, Film and Sports Development, 301 N. Wilmington St., 4324 Mail Service Center, Raleigh, NC 27699-4324, 800/847-4862 or 919/733-8372, website: www.visitnc.com.

## Welcome Centers

If you're driving into North Carolina, be sure to stop at one of the state's eight welcome centers, most of them at the state borders. The folks at these offices are generally very knowledgeable and helpful about the state's recreational opportunities and can help you plan to get the most possible from your stay in North Carolina. They also dispense free maps and about a zillion pamphlets from every region of the state. They can even help you set up tee times.

## MONEY

The U.S. dollar is divided into 100 cents. Paper notes include $1, $2, $5, $10, $20, $50, and $100; the $2 bill is rarely seen but perfectly legal. Coin denominations are one cent (penny), five cents (nickel), 10 cents (dime), 25 cents (quarter), 50 cents (the rare half dollar), and the $1 coin (in two seldom-used forms, both with women's faces on them). Most vending machines take only nickels, dimes, and quarters. Unfortunately, there are many counterfeit bills in circulation, usually hundreds or twenties.

In the late 1990s, the old $100, $50, and $20 bills were replaced with new bills featuring much larger portraits on the front side. Tens and fives soon followed. If you're handed one of the earlier forms of bills, rest assured that they're still accepted as legal tender.

## Banks

Most major banks in big cities are open 9 A.M.–5 P.M. Hours for branches in smaller towns vary. Banks are usually closed on Saturday, Sunday, and most national and some religious holidays. Some larger banks open for limited hours on Saturday, frequently 9 A.M.–1 P.M. Branch offices are popping up in grocery stores and shopping malls across the state. But typically, only major commercial banks can exchange foreign currency. Other good places to obtain U.S. dollars include international airports and American Express offices. Check the local phone book Yellow Pages for addresses and phone numbers. Many banks have toll-free numbers answered by an auto-

Patterson's Mill Country Store, outside Durham

mated voice, which gives options for various numbers. Stay on the line or press the appropriate number to speak to a human.

Most businesses accept major credit cards—MasterCard, Visa, and American Express. On occasion, in very small towns and rural areas, cash (US$) will be the only accepted form of money. It's also possible to get cash advances from your credit card at designated automated-teller machines (ATMs). ATM machines are omnipresent in the U.S. You'll see them in grocery stores, shopping malls, sometimes at festivals or fairs, sporting events, street corners, and, of course, at most banks.

In most large supermarkets, it's possible to pay for your groceries with a credit card or a debit card, which deducts the amount directly from your checking or savings account. Often this method incurs a small transaction fee; check with your bank for details. For you to use ATMs and debit cards, your bank must be affiliated with one of the several ATM networks. The most common affiliations are Star, Cirrus, Plus, and Interlink.

If for some reason you can't access your bank account via ATM, you may want to carry traveler's checks in U.S. dollar denominations rather than carrying a lot of cash. Most businesses and tourist-related services accept traveler's checks. Only in very small towns will you run into problems with traveler's checks, or exchanging foreign money. The solution? Drive to a larger town. It's not a very big state.

## Taxes

Expect to pay 6 percent or more—depending on the county—sales tax on anything you buy, except food at the grocery store. You'll also pay a room tax at lodging establishments.

## Tipping

It's standard in North Carolina to tip your waitperson 15 percent of the bill for acceptable service. If you're at a breakfast place, where the bills are lower but the staff is often just as hardworking as those at more expensive dinner spots, you may wish to tip at least 20 percent. Never tip the regular amount to reward rude or inattentive ser-

vice—it only encourages more of the same. The tip is usually not included in the bill—you need to calculate it yourself.

Tip airport skycaps $1 a bag; the same for hotel bellhops.

# ODDS AND ENDS
## Photo Etiquette

You will see quaint homes in North Carolina. You will want to take pictures of them.

If you're in Old Salem, and the house is one of the famous old houses, then go ahead and snap away. If you're up in a tiny Albemarle town and you want to take a picture of a private citizen's house, then you should try to get permission first. It's not a legal requirement, just a courtesy. And courtesy goes a long way in North Carolina.

## Camping Gear

With rain showers so unpredictable—particularly in summer—you'll want a tarp over your tent as well as beneath it. If you're car-camping, consider a screen canopy, inside of which you'll be able to sip your hot cocoa without enduring mosquito and no-see-um bites. If you'll be hiking long distances from a car that can get you to a doctor, bring a snakebite kit.

## Weights and Measures

North Carolina—like all other states in the U.S.—does not use the metric system. The federal government tried to foist it on us in the 1970s while we were still peeved over the 55-mph national speed limit, and it never took. For help converting weights, distances, and temperatures, see the table at the back of this book.

## Electricity

Despite what Hollywood may have led you to believe, it's rare to find anywhere in the South that doesn't vibrate with electrical power. Electrical outlets in the U.S. run on 110 or 120V AC. Most plugs are either two flat prongs or two flat and one round. Adapters for 220V appliances are available in hardware or electronic stores.

## Time Zone

North Carolina rests within the Eastern time zone, the very same time zone used to such good effect in New York City, Boston, and Miami. North Carolina is three hours ahead of Los Angeles.

## Vaccinations

The United States currently has no vaccination requirements for any international traveler. Check with the U.S. embassy or consulate in your country and request an update on this information before you leave.

The International Health Regulations (IHR) adopted by the World Health Organization (WHO) state that countries may require an International Certificate of Vaccination (ICV) against yellow fever. An ICV can also be required if you are traveling from an infected area. For current information, look up the website for WHO, at www.who.ch, or the Centers for Disease Control, at www.cdc.gov.travel/travel.html.

# Nags Head and the Outer Banks

Few stretches of American coastline hold the mystique of North Carolina's Outer Banks. What traveler, studying a map of the American East Coast, hasn't wanted to drive their length? The long tail of land swoops erratically eastward at the Virginia line, missing the mainland's right turn at Sandy Point, a thin shadow of America veering out into the ocean, miles and miles from shore, only gradually, lazily bending back inland after Cape Hatteras. What would life be like *out there,* we wonder, to look to either side of the road and see only water? Surely, we reason, things would be *different.*

In an overcomplicated age, the Outer Banks offer a blessedly scaled-down world. Stuck in the middle of nowhere, if by "somewhere" we mean inhabited land, they are—unlike most other American nowheres, like Baker, California, say, or Shamrock, Texas—also blessed with sandy white beaches and world-renowned outdoor recreation.

And yet, those who loved the Banks first loved them for reasons other than physical beauty.

The aboriginal Croatan on Hatteras and the British settler who later settled on these stormy banks came because access to the ocean meant access to fish. And while the Bankers—the traditional name for the area's independent, rough-and-tumble residents—have often been described as a people who face the ocean, they repeatedly built their villages on the sound side of the islands, doors turned west toward the markets where they'd sell their catch. According to Roger L. Payne's engaging *Place Names of the Outer Banks,* so strong was this inland orientation that if a Banker made reference to the "back of the beach" he or she was clearly referring to the ocean side of the island.

After the tourist trade first boomed in the 1920s, Bankers came to value their sandy beaches as moneymakers, and the term's definition

**Bodie Island Lighthouse**

© MIKE SIGALAS

NAGS HEAD AND THE OUTER BANKS

reversed meanings. Now the ocean side of the island, with its million-dollar homes and pricey hotels, is considered the front of the beach.

The Outer Banks were not an easy place to settle. Sir Walter Raleigh certainly didn't have any luck on Roanoke Island. And though human life here traces back to aboriginal times, so do violent hurricanes. Ironically, many of the early Banks settlers were shipwreck survivors who swam to shore and decided to stay. Even still, Lifesaving Station crews and lighthouse keepers were the only people living along stretches of this brutal coast for many years. Though tourism began in force even in the 1840s, not until roads—and then paved roads—came did the Banks become accessible enough to warrant serious development.

## Orientation

The Outer Banks are really not all that long: only 107 miles separate the Banks' northernmost and southernmost landmarks, Currituck Light at Corolla and Ocracoke Light at Ocracoke—less than the distance between Los Angeles and San Diego.

But neither is driving the Banks just any spin on the interstate. You'll follow two-lane N.C. 12

all the way, take one 40-minute ferry ride (to get off Ocracoke you'll take a second), and pass through more than a dozen towns and villages. In between the settlements, the state and federal governments protect much of the Banks—most of Ocracoke Island, all of undeveloped Hatteras, and a good bit of the Northern Banks.

Though you could drive the Banks in half a day, you can easily spend a week or two just discovering them. Starting at the north, the first widely recognized section of the Banks are the **Northern Beaches,** which include Carova, Corolla, Duck, and Southern Shores—all high-end bedroom communities. Sometimes also included in the Northern Beaches designation but often classified on their own (often simply as "the Nag's Head area") are the three highly developed, touristy towns of Kitty Hawk, Kill Devil Hills, and Nags Head. Due west of Nags Head is Roanoke Island, quieter, more rural, and more historic. South of this—and separated by Oregon Inlet—is **Hatteras Island,** less developed but developed earlier. South of the little village of Hatteras is the northern tip of Ocracoke Island, which is totally undeveloped except for Ocracoke Village at the island's southern end.

# Nags Head and Vicinity

One thing visitors to the Northern Banks notice is the use of milepost designations in denoting locations from the Kitty Hawk Pier (Milepost 1) south through Kill Devil Hills and Nags Head. The higher the number, the further south you are.

## Nags Head

*Planters, merchants, and professional men usually have a snug cottage at Nag's Head, to which they remove their families, with the plainer and more common articles of household furniture, one or more horses, a cow, and such vehicles as are fitted for use on sandy roads. . . . One, two, three, sometimes half a dozen ser-*

*vants accompany the family. . . . Gentlemen who are fond of fox-hunting bring their horse and hounds, and go galloping over the treacherous sands, much to the hazard of both horse and rider.*

**George Higby Throop,** Nags Head, or, Two Months among the 'Bankers, *1849*

Of all the place-names associated with the Outer Banks, perhaps "Nags Head" spurs the imagination more than any other. *From what heinous act could this name possibly derive?* Among locals, you'll hear a number of name creation myths. Here's the one I wish was true: that in days of old, local Bankers used to hang burning lanterns around horses' necks on dark nights and allow the horses to mill about on the shore. These bob-

## OUTER BANKS HIGHLIGHTS

**Cape Hatteras National Seashore,** Hatteras and Ocracoke Islands

**Elizabethan Gardens,** Roanoke Island

**Jockey's Ridge State Park,** Nags Head

*The Lost Colony* **Outdoor Drama,** Roanoke Island

**Manteo waterfront,** Roanoke Island

**Nags Head Woods Ecological Preserve,** Kill Devil Hills

**Ocracoke Village,** Ocracoke

**Roanoke Island Festival Park,** Manteo

**Scarborough Faire, Scarborough Lane, The Waterfront Shops,** Duck

**Weeping Radish Brewery and Bavarian Restaurant,** Roanoke Island

**Wright Brothers National Memorial,** Kill Devil Hills

bing lights, to the eyes of sailors at sea, would resemble the bobbing lights of boats at harbor. Lured to a harbor that was not, the ships would wreck, enabling the rapacious Bankers to practice their homegrown brand of piracy.

Unfortunately, most serious students of local history call this story doubtful. No contemporary accounts or archaeological evidence supports the charge that Bankers, though a rough lot, ever practiced such treachery, and anyway, just you try to hang a searing, smoking lantern around the neck of a nag, they say.

More mundane but likelier theories have it that sailors viewing the area from sea thought Nags Head resembled the head of a horse. Yawn. Or that an Englishman who settled in the area called his spread Nags Head because the region reminded him of Nags Head on England's Scilly Islands—the last bit of England westbound sailors often saw before heading for the Americas.

Maybe so, but I'm still rooting for the story about the lanterns.

Whether they did in the past or not, these days many industrious Bankers certainly do hang out lights—of the electric variety—along the 158 Bypass and the Beach Road, luring in many travelers from afar.

Nags Head is bigger and less quaint than most of us would like to imagine, but still smaller and less busy than you may have heard. Its development reaches nowhere near the level of, say, Myrtle Beach. Population through the winter months still runs around 1,800, though that increases manifold during summer.

## Kitty Hawk

North of both Nags Head and Kill Devil Hills, Kitty Hawk is most famous to schoolchildren of the world as the place where the Wright Brothers tested their new airplane and thus started the aeronautical age—though of course, they really did it over at Kill Devil Hills. This was just the nearest local settlement and post office. The origin of Kitty Hawk's name is disputed; most likely it's the result of English tongues wrestling with Native American words: specifically, Chickehauk, the name of a local Indian settlement, or Etacrewac, the name for the general region. Today, Kitty Hawk seems just a bit more worn than the other towns. Hurricane Fran did a good bit of damage here. The Kitty Hawk Fishing Pier has recently been rebuilt.

## Kill Devil Hills

The word "kill" isn't a real positive one to find in a place name; fortunately, the word "devil" immediately afterwards seems to make it okay. ("Kill People Hills," for instance, might not really draw the tourists.) So where'd the name come from? As usual, the most interesting explanations are the least likely to be true. One theory has it that (1) in yet another soul-for-gold deal gone bad, a

## LIGHTHOUSES: THE OUTER BANKS' FAB FOUR

Of all the lighthouses along the North Carolina coast, the most famous are the four most easily accessible to motorists on the Outer Banks: **Corolla Lighthouse, Bodie Island Lighthouse, Cape Hatteras Lighthouse,** and **Ocracoke Lighthouse.**

It can be hard to remember which is which, but not for Beatles fans: Cape Hatteras is clearly the Paul McCartney of the bunch—the cute, popular, romantic one, the lighthouse made for the cover of magazines. Ocracoke (John Lennon) is the oldest, quite bright, but also visually mellower. No flashy stripes here. Bodie Island Lighthouse (Ringo) is the most social of the bunch, located as it is just south of bustling Nags Head. And the current structure replaces an earlier, pre–Civil War lighthouse (read: Pete Best). Unpainted Corolla Lighthouse (George), long an icon of asceticism far beyond the reach of the paved road, nowadays finds itself very much in the midst of high-dollar developments.

Whether Cape Lookout Lighthouse is Stu Sutcliffe, Billy Preston, or Murray the K is beyond me.

**Cape Hatteras Lighthouse**

© MIKE SIGALAS

Banker dug a hole to the bottom of (then unnamed) Kill Devil Hill and tricked Old Scratch into falling into the hole, where the Banker quickly buried him. A second theory concerns the disappearance of several casks of rum from a shipment beached hereabouts. According to this theory, (2) a Banker named Ike offered to spend the night guarding the rum. When he caught the guilty neighbor returning to steal some more, he chased him off, but (to save his neighbor from prosecution) explained previous thefts as having been performed by the devil himself—whom Ike had dutifully killed. Yet another theory has it that (3) the rum made hereabouts during colonial times was so nasty that people used to say it could "kill the devil," hence the name; and yet another suggests that (4) mariners thought the land mass itself was so treacherous to sail around that the trip itself could "kill the devil." A little more likely theory references the fact that both (5) "kill" and "devil" are Dutch terms referring to, respectively, "stream" and "sand spout," which given the geography makes a kind of sense, but unfortunately there's no evidence that the Dutch had anything to do with naming the area (they probably stayed away, what with all the Satanic apparitions). The dullest, and likely most accurate theory has it that (6) the name references the common shorebird popularly called the killdeer. Killdeer Hills was one of the early names for Kill Devil Hills.

Other than Satan being buried here, the most notable event in local history was one of humanity's most important—here, in 1903, Orville Wright became the first person to fly a propelled craft.

## SIGHTS

### Wright Brothers National Memorial

This 60-foot monument, 800 Colington Rd., 252/441-7430, stands atop the (now) grass-covered 90-foot Kill Devil Hill, from which the Wright Brothers began the world's first controlled (more or less) flight, a wobbly jaunt into 20-mph winds that covered 120 feet in the course of 12 seconds. Meaning that as Orville sputtered his way into history, even the slowest sprinter on a weak junior high track squad could have outpaced him. For that matter, since he flew at an elevation of about 12 feet, a good high school pole-vaulter could have vaulted over him.

From aviation's humble beginnings, the rapidity with which we human beings took to the sky after the Wright Brothers provided the initial boost takes one's breath away: only 66 years after Orville lifted off this dune, Neil Armstrong set his foot on the moon. Within 12 years of the Kill Devil Hills test, men were using airplanes to shoot and bomb each other from the sky.

The monument is really bigger and more impressive in person than it is in pictures, and it's also eye-catching when illuminated at night. A couple times a year it is even opened up and you can walk the stairs inside to the top. Built during the Depression in 1932 of granite from Andy Griffith's hometown in Mount Airy, the obelisk stands far higher than the Wrights ever flew while here. For that matter, so does the roof of the 1960s-styled museum down at the bottom of the hill. The monument's inspiring inscription reads:

> *In commemoration of the conquest of the air by the brothers Wilbur and Orville Wright conceived by Genius, achieved by Dauntless Resolution and Unconquerable Faith.*

The "Genius" line sounds like it's describing Wilbur and Orville's mother, but it's inspiring, nonetheless.

For me, though, the visitors center and the markers at the bottom of the hill are what really bring the historic flight to life. The visitors center (which from the outside resembles a miniature LAX, circa 1969) features various exhibits on early aviation and the Wright Brothers, and a model of the first plane—the Smithsonian holds the original. Check out the marble markers at the bottom of the hill, between the visitors' center and the monument, just after you pass the reconstructed Wright Brothers workshop and living quarters on the way up. The markers note the takeoff and landing spots of the Wrights' four flights on December 17, 1903, the longest (and last) of which was Wilbur's 59-second flight,

the Wright Brothers' barracks

© MIKE SIGALAS

covering 852 feet. After that, a wind gust totaled the world's first airplane, and the two dauntlessly resolute preacher's kids from Dayton, Ohio, packed up and headed home for the holidays. Admission to the park runs $3 per person or $5 a vehicle. Open daily, 9 A.M.–5 P.M.

**Bodie Island Lighthouse,** N.C. 12, 252/441-5711, just north of Oregon Inlet, is named after an island that is no longer an island proper. North of Oregon Inlet (and before Oregon Inlet was cut by a storm), it used to be you'd run across Gunt Inlet. And north of that, at the next narrow spot on the island (south of Washington Baum Bridge), was Roanoke Inlet. Nowadays, folks use "Bodie Island" (pronounced "body" or "bawdy," if you will) to refer to various stretches of land, sometimes from Oregon Inlet north to Kitty Hawk, but usually just from Oregon Inlet north to the site of the old Roanoke Inlet—near the site of the modern-day bridge to Roanoke Island.

The Bodie Island Lighthouse was built in 1872, just after (and by the designer of) Cape

Hatteras Lighthouse. Standing 156 feet tall, the aging lighthouse is closed for climbing, but the bottom is open in summer. Call for details.

If you want to see what Kill Devil Hill looked like in the Wrights' day, before it was planted over with grasses to keep it from blowing away, **Jockey's Ridge State Park,** U.S. 158, Milepost 12, 252/441-7132 gives you a chance. The name sounds like a saddle malady, and some say it comes from the fact that this would have been a great place to sit and watch the local horse races in days of yore. But early maps refer to the place as Jackey Ridge, meaning it was named after the man who owned the ridge and surrounding land. The ridge was doomed for improvement in 1973, when the feisty Carolista Baum planted herself in front of a bulldozer and stopped the march of Progress in its Caterpillar tracks. In 1975 the dune officially became a state park. Jockey's Ridge is home to the East Coast's highest sand dune, rising some 140 feet above the ocean and sound (both of which you can see from the ridge top). Though it's nothing compared to, say, Death Valley, in Death Valley all you can see is other dunes, whereas here you can see the water, sailboats, and many, many rental homes. a fun place to take up hang gliding (Kitty Hawk Kites operates a flight school here) and fun to tumble down. Check out the visitors center, then head over to the dunes. Take off your shoes and enjoy yourself. Summer nights at 8 P.M., head up to the top of the ridge for the ranger-led "Sunset on the Ridge" program. You'll hear about local history and legends, and get to see a beautiful sunset in the west. Also here is the 1.5-mile **Tracks in the Sand Trail,** which begins in the visitors center parking lot and carries you through clumps of live oak, loblolly pine, wax myrtles, and various wildflowers and marsh grasses to the Roanoke Sound.

The Nature Conservancy manages the **Nags Head Woods Ecological Preserve,** 701 W. Ocean Acres Dr., 252/441-2525. Preserving more than 1,400 acres of maritime forest, it's a fine place to disappear from the traffic and crowds at the beaches. Here you'll see ponds, swamps, beech, hickory, oak, and pine, and you couldn't throw a rock without hitting a songbird. Which,

incidentally, don't. Call for hours, and to hear about the various paddling trips the folks here are always putting together.

To get there, turn west at Milepost 9.5, Ocean Acres Drive, off U.S. 158 in Kill Devil Hills. Follow the road until you reach it. After you do, you'll find more than five miles of trails to hike; canoe trips, and a gift shop and visitors center, where you can pick up a trail map. The longest trail, the two mile-long Sweetgum Swamp Trail, climbs a number of ridges and takes you though a variety of plant-life. The shortest—a quarter-mile loop starting at the deck of the visitor center, comes with a separate trail pamphlet interpreting 10 different points of interest. One word of advice—bring insect repellent and boots, if possible, to ward off mosquitoes and deer ticks. The office is open Monday through Friday, 10 A.M.–3 P.M., closed on major holidays; the trail is open everyday—maps are available outside.

## ACCOMMODATIONS

Keep in mind that prices vary greatly between high and low seasons. The lodgings are grouped by their lowest high-season prices for a double room. Come here in the winter and you can stay for a fraction of the cost. Note, too, that you can sometimes save 50 percent by being willing to look out over Virginia Dare Trail rather than the Atlantic Ocean. Certainly it's rough to travel this close to the ocean only to be denied the chance to watch the waves from your balcony, but if saving $100 a night allows you to extend your stay a couple of days—or eat like royalty at oceanfront restaurants every night—you may well decide it's worth it.

### $50–100
On the low end you have **Travelers Inn Motor Lodge,** Milepost 16.5 on Beach Road, Nags Head, 252/441-5242, with a combination of rooms, efficiencies, and cottages, whose rates dip as low as $49 during the off-season, $78.88 high season.

Perhaps cheapest on the oceanfront is **Sandspur Motel & Cottage Court,** Milepost 15.75, Nags Head, 800/522-8486 or 252/441-6993, with rates as low as $42 during the off-season, $84 in high.

The **Owens' Motel,** Milepost 16.5, Beach Road, Nag's Head, 252/441-6361, website: www.owensmotel.com, offers 17 rooms, eight efficiencies, a pool, and a restaurant. Closed winters—call for availability. $55–95, $105–125 for efficiencies.

Next door to the Holiday Inn, you'll find **Miller's Oceanfront Motel** (a.k.a. M.O.M.), Beach Road Milepost 9.5, Kill Devil Hills, 252/441-7404, a recently renovated 1950s family motel with 38 rooms, a cottage, 28 efficiencies, and six suites. It's across from **Miller's Steak and Seafood,** 252/441-7674, which is a good selling point. Open February through December. $59–89-$175. Co-owner Eddie Miller has worked here since the 1950s and bought the place in the 1970s. Ask the manager (Eddie's sister) and maybe you'll hear the story of when a young Eddie backed his car into the motel swimming pool.

### $100–150

Down on the same stretch of beach stands **Beach Haven Motel,** 4104 Virginia Dare Trail, Kity Hawk, 888/559-0506 or 252/261-4785, website: www.beachhavenmotel.com, offering six efficiencies, a restaurant, a pier, canoes, boats, and rafts. Open mid-March through November. $55–114. The **Three Seasons Bed and Breakfast,** 4628 Seascape Dr., Kitty Hawk, 800/847-3373 or 252/261-4791, offers four rooms from $89 low season, $120 high season, golf and tennis privileges, a fireplace, and a full breakfast. It's open from April through November, which explains the name.

### $150 and Up

Steady and chain-regular is the **Days Inn Oceanfront,** 1801 North Virginia Dare Trail, $50–200. South of the Holiday Inn stands the dune-side **Ramada Inn,** 1701 S. Virginia Dare Trail, 800/635-1824 or 252/441-2151, offering 172 rooms, $89–227, low-high season; slightly lower during the week.

The **First Colony Inn,** 6720 S. Virginia Dare Trail, Nags Head, 800/368-9390 or 252/441-2343, website: www.firstcolonyinn.com, is a National Register of Historic Places landmark inn, built as a beach hotel in 1932. Reopened in 1991, it has received four diamonds from AAA. The 26 rooms (all with private baths) and public areas are furnished with antiques. Breakfast buffet, wraparound porches, dunetop gazebo, afternoon tea, heated towel racks (!), and use of the pool all come for the price of the rooms, which can get as high as $265 for an oceanfront in season, and as low as $80 out of season—not that much more than what you'll pay at, say, the Ramada, and the stay here is so perfectly Nags Head that you'll remember it forever. Nonsmoking, no pets. Children are welcome.

A traditional two-story Nags Head house with a picket fence, the **Cypress House Inn,** 500 N. Virginia Dare Trail, Kill Devil Hills, 800/554-2764 or 252/441-6127, has six rooms open year-round, $125 d. Built as a private hunting and fishing lodge in the 1940s, Karen Roos and Leon Faso's inn stands across the road from the Atlantic Ocean, and offers queen size beds, private shower baths, and ceiling fans. Outside you'll find a rocker-rich wraparound porch. Full breakfast included. Bicycles, beach towels, and chairs available. Smoking is forbidden, as are children 13 and under, and pets (smoking or non-) of any age.

Greg Hamby's 1999 **The Cypress Moon Inn,** 1206 Harbor Court, Kitty Hawk, 877/905-5060, website: www.cypressmooninn.com, $125–175, stands within maritime forest on the soundfront; a two-story porch outside the bedrooms offers private access. Not exactly Old Nags Head, but a nice retreat from the hubbub of the main strip.

Also newer is the **The White Egret B&B,** 1045 Colington Rd., Kill Devil Hills, 888/387-7719, website: www.whiteegret.com., $85–110. Its three rooms have a view of the bay, private baths and Jacuzzis, TV, VCR, and private phone with Internet hookup.

### Rentals

The traditional way to stay in Nags Head is in a cottage, usually rented by the week. **Nags Head Fishing Pier Cottages,** Milepost 12, Beach Road, website: www.nagsheadpier.com, 252/441-5141, rents to happy anglers and their families; depending on the time and the cottage you choose, rates can vary anywhere from $350 a week to $1,300. You can often rent for shorter periods too. **Coleman's Cottages** rents a number of locations all the way from Kitty Hawk to Hatteras; rates vary from $395 to over $2,000 a week.

More than 30 rental agencies operate in the North Beach area alone. A couple of the bigger ones include **Ocean Vacations,** 2501 N. Croatan Hwy., 800/548-2033 or 252/441-3127, website: www.oceanfun.com, with 200 cottages and 75 condos. **Sun Realty,** 800/334-4745, website: www.sunrealtync.com., offers more than 1,100 stays on the Outer Banks. See www.outer-banks.org for more information. At **www.carolinadesigns.com, www.resortrealty.com,** and **www.seasiderealty.com**—among others—you can reserve a rental home online, 24 hours a day.

# FOOD
## Seafood and Steaks
**Etheridge's Seafood,** Milepost 9.5, Kill Devil Hills, 252/441-2645, is a place people tend to stumble across (usually by asking a local for the best local seafood) and rave about. *Very* fresh—order something you think you've ordered a hundred times before and you'll be surprised how much better it is at Etheridge's. Items on the menu are named after various members of the Etheridge family, three generations of whom serve and have served the restaurant over the years. Entrées start at $9.95. Full bar, too. If you're here early in the day, stop by for the $14.95 Early Bird Feast, 3:30–5:30 P.M., featuring a seafood cheese crock and crackers, a cup of bouillabaisse or the soup of the day, a salad, and a choice of seafood entrée, as well as dessert—including a good Key lime pie.

While we're in the family way, I'd best mention the restaurants owned by the Miller dynasty, the same family that owns Miller's Oceanfront Motel. The spot with the better location is **Miller's Waterfront Restaurant,** Milepost 16 at the 158 Bypass, Nags Head, 252/441-6151, a fine place for breakfast overlooking the sound during high season (try the

99-cent specials) and an even better place for a sunset dinner (year-round). Serving up year-round 99-cent breakfasts is the original Miller restaurant (since 1978), **Miller's Steak and Seafood,** Milepost 9.5, 252/441-7674, just across from the motel, and a convenient walk from the Holiday Inn or Ramada as well. Along these same lines is **Owens' Restaurant,** Milepost 16.5, Beach Road, Nag's Head, 252/441-7309, website: www.owensmotel.com, founded in 1946, which offers dinners, mostly in the $18.95–23.95 range. **Awful Arthur's,** Milepost 6, Beach Road, Kill Devil Hills, 252/441-5955, is the Hussong's Cantina or Salty Dog Café of the Outer Banks. It features an endless spring break atmosphere, lots of T-shirts for sale, and some of the funniest commercials you'll ever see. The food's not bad, either. Burgers run $3.95–6.95, and dinners—heavy on the seafood but including steaks, pasta, and BBQ—run in the low teens. For a near-identical experience at Milepost 13, Nags Head, go to Awful Arthur's spinoff restaurant, **Bad Barracuda's.** A hip spot with a tropical theme, the **Rundown Café,** Milepost 1, Beach Road, Kitty Hawk, 252/255-0026, features sandwiches ($6 and up) and full dinners like jerk chicken, Jamaican pork, St. Martin shrimp, and a fish burrito, $8.95–11.95, and served with black beans, rice and salsa. Along the same lines, **Tortugas' Lie,** Milepost 11, Beach Road, Nags Head, 252/441-7299, website: www.tortugaslie.com, is a friendly little place across the street from the beach with some creative chow, including a wonderful coconut shrimp, grilled fish and black bean burrito ($6.95), and Coco Loco Chicken—chicken breast rolled in coconut and fried, with lime curry dipping sauce ($5.95). Sushi on late Wednesday nights. You're welcome to join in the pickup volleyball games on the court outside.

**The Wharf,** Milepost 11.5, Beach Road, Nags Head, 252/441-7457, offers a very popular seafood buffet for $15.95. And finally, while I normally stay away from recommending chains, the folks at the **Western Sizzlin Restaurant,** Milepost 8.75, 804 South Croatan Hwy., Kill Devil Hills, 252/441-4594, have really gone out of their way to bring a local feel to their restaurant. They offer up a strong buffet as well. And the quaint **Old Nags Head General Store,** where you'll pay your bill, offers some genuinely engaging items for reasonable prices. The Friday/Saturday seafood buffet is $14.99 for adults; the dinner buffet other nights (which usually includes some seafood) runs $8.99. The popular breakfast buffet is $5.99.

## Barbecue

Who'd think you'd find great barbecue on the Outer Banks? You will, though—in two spots: **Bubba's BBQ** soundside in Frisco, 252/995-5421, and **Pigman's Bar-B-Que,** Milepost 9.5, 1606 S. Croatan Hwy., Kill Devil Hills, 252/441-6803, website: www.pigman.com. Bubba's is the tried-and-true, small-town sort of barbecue joint with the disinterested teenage help (at least the times I was there), the great smoked pulled pork, ribs (also beef and turkey), and the Mason jars full of sauce by the cash register. It's added a second strip-mall location in Avon, 252/995-4385. Sandwiches run around $3.75; most dinners run just under $10. Beer available.

Pigman, on the other hand, is much more. It's a barbecue joint on steroids and maybe some other banned substances—less an example than a *celebration* of barbecue, the result of a mind that takes barbecue to its logical (and not) conclusion, featuring some fascinating takeoffs on this purest of foods: in addition to the pork BBQ and the beef BBQ, Pigman also serves up turkey BBQ, a rare find, tuna-que, and catfish-que. And they all taste great. Sandwiches of the various ques will run you $3.95–4.29; add $1.70 for french fries, hush puppies, and slaw. In further implementation of its Rainbow Coalition of Barbecue-attitude, Pigman also serves barbecued "St. Louie" ribs. They'll sell you anything you want (included whole hams) to go, but try to eat here so you can enjoy the fun atmosphere and watch some of the looped (and loopy) Pigman commercials, which play constantly.

More upscale but also featuring homemade barbecue, **Jockeys Ribs,** Milepost 13, Beach Road, Nag's Head, 252/441-1141, is a little pricier and more of a sit-down place closer to the beach. Great wings.

## More Food

If it's (relatively) late at night, one of the best—and one of the only—alternatives on the Banks is to swing by **Grits Grill,** Outer Banks Mall, Nags Head, 252/449-2888. It used to be called "Grits *24 Hour* Grill," but apparently the sleep deprivation lost its appeal. Now it's open until 10 P.M. in summer, 8 P.M. off-season. To some it's just a wannabe small-town greasy spoon in a shiny shopping center—and one without great food at that. Now that it's open reasonable hours, Grits has lost much of its charm, but it does still feature a surprising array of options including fresh baked breads and rolls, Carvel frozen treats, and (trucked-in) Krispy Kreme donuts.

For a better view than Grits provides, you might head over to the **Kitty Hawk Pier Restaurant,** Milepost 1, 252/261-3151, where the food and décor aren't fancy, but you can eat a good basic breakfast, lunch, or dinner while sitting over the Atlantic. Open 6 A.M.–9 P.M. every day. They once didn't accept credit cards, but they've loosened up on the pier, and will accept your Visa or MasterCard. Down at the Nags Head Fishing Pier, Milepost 12, the **Pier House Restaurant,** 252/441-5141, is a bit fancier (wood chairs, not vinyl). If you're fishing out on the pier, take advantage of the "You Hook 'Em—We Cook 'Em" special ($4.50 for lunch, $5.95 for dinner).

One thing Grits Grill has going for it is a cool name, and you can say the same thing of **Waffle World,** Milepost 9.5, 158 Bypass, 1504 S. Croatan Hwy., 252/449-6973, open 24 hours in summer. The waffles really are fine, as is the "Texas size" french toast. Waffle World also serves lunch.

Down in Frisco on N.C. 12, **Seasons Natural Foods,** 252/995-6986, sells organic foods and herbal supplements.

## ENTERTAINMENT
### Nightlife

The best way to find out who's playing where when you get to the Banks is to pick up a free copy of *Coast* and check out the "Club Hoppin'" section. But here's a brief, necessarily incomplete overview of your nightlife options. If you still primarily consider the word "party" to be a verb, you'll probably like **Awful Arthur's,** Milepost 6, Beach Road, Kill Devil Hills, 252/441-5955, for its drink specials, bar food, and second-story oceanview lounge. Along the same lines is **Carolinian Oceanfront Hotel Restaurant,** Milepost 10.5, Beach Road, Nags Head, 252/441-7171, which also features a deck bar. The Carolinian offers live entertainment, including comedy acts. **George's Junction,** Milepost 11, Beach Road, Nags Head, 252/441-0606, features national country acts, beach music and oldies, and a full-service bar. **Jolly Roger Restaurant,** Milepost 6.75, Beach Road, Kill Devil Hills, 252/441-6530, features nightly entertainment, whether that means hearing a local band or a free-for-all around the karaoke machine. Open year-round.

**Madelines,** at the Holiday Inn, Milepost 9.5, Beach Road, features a number of different acts, sometimes including Carolina beach music and shagging. **Mama Kwan's Grill and Tiki Bar,** Milepost 9.5 on the Bypass, 252/480-0967, is a cozy spot (once you get inside) that features live music and a dance floor until 2 A.M. **Port O'Call Gaslight Saloon,** Milepost 8.5, Beach Road, Kill Devil Hills, 252/441-7484, features reggae and rock acts, and usually hits you with a cover charge if a band's playing. **Red Drum Tap House,** 2412 S. Virginia Dare Trail, Nags Head, 252/480-1095, offers 18 microbrews on tap, plus pub grub and live entertainment. Open year-round. **Run Down Café,** Milepost 1, Beach Road, Kitty Hawk, 252/255-0026, features blues and jazz.

**Comedy Club at the Ramada,** Milepost 9.5, Beach Road, 252/441-7232, features stand-up on Friday, Saturday, and Sunday at 10 P.M. Eat dinner there before the show, and you'll receive preferred seating. If you find that a good fictitious homicide enhances your dining, call for information about the popular **Murder Mystery Dinner Theatre.**

**Kelly's Restaurant & Tavern,** Milepost 10, 158 Bypass, Nags Head, 252/441-4116, has received the *Wine Spectator* Award of Excellence. The tavern doors swing open at 4:30 P.M. Live entertainment. Open all year.

Whether you're a pool shark or just like the

sounds the balls make when they crash together, you'll find no shortage of billiards in town. **Shucker's Pub and Billiards,** Milepost 8.5, Beach Road (Oceanside Plaza), Kill Devil Hills, 252/480-1010, has 12 pool tables and a whole lot of TVs. **Paradise Billiards,** at the Dare Center, Milepost 7, Kill Devil Hills, 252/441-9225, offers Foosball, pool, and big-screen TV.

## Movie Theaters

The coolest theater on the Outer Banks is Manteo's little **Pioneer Theatre,** 113 Budleigh St., 252/473-2216. It's one of the oldest family-owned theaters in America, and it shows one movie, once a day—for three dollars. Other than this, the Outer Banks offers a handful of theaters including the **Kitty Hawk Twin,** Milepost 5, Bypass, 252/441-1808; **Cineplex Four,** Milepost 10, on the Bypass in Nags Head, 252/441-1808; and the **Avon-Hatteras Four,** in the big Food Lion Shopping Center, Avon, 252/995-9060.

## Shopping

The pretty mock-historic **Buccaneer's Walk,** at Milepost 4.5 on the Bypass in Kitty Hawk, features a number of fun stores including **Voyage Books and Treasures,** 252/261-3667, a toy store, and other gift shops. Open Monday–Saturday. Duck, north of Nags Head, also has some good shopping.

# SPORTS AND RECREATION

## Surfing

The Banks have a long and distinguished history of surfing, dating back to the '60s. Stellar local surf shops include **Corolla Surf Shop,** in the Corolla Light Village Shops, 252/453-9283, website: www.corollasurfshop.com, which maintains a surfing museum inside the store. Down on Hatteras you'll find **Ocean Roots,** across from the Avon Pier, 252/995-3369. It offers surf lessons for hodads and gremmies, running $40 for 1.5–2 hours; board rental and other equipment are included.

## Paddling

**Kitty Hawk Sports,** 3933 S. Croatan Hwy., 252/441-6800, website: www.khsports.com, has been in business here since 1981, and runs a variety of creative, quality paddling excursions. From March to December, they'll take you out into Pea Island National Wildlife Refuge, Alligator River National Wildlife Refuge, Cape Hatteras National Seashore, and the Kitty Hawk Maritime Forest on two-hour, four-hour, all-day, and overnight tours that explore the salt marshes, sounds, tidal creeks, and ocean. Megan Jones and the rest of the guides for these trips know their wildlife, and can help you see—depending on the particular trip—black bear, red wolves, deer, otter, dolphins, osprey, heron, ducks, swans, snakes, turtles, crabs, and more.

The most popular tour is the Kitty Hawk Woods Maritime Forest Wildlife Tour, which departs from the kayak center in Kitty Hawk and takes you through a landscape thriving with the critters mentioned above. You'll even pass by a covered bridge deep in the woods and now accessible only from the water. Costs $29 for 2.5 hours ($19 for children 11 and under who share a double boat with adult). Families often favor the mellow and scenic Sunset Tour, and if that's not dark enough for you, if you're here around a full moon, you can sign up for the 2.5-hour, $35 Full Moon Tour, available several nights before and on the full moon. Call for times and prices.

**Kitty Hawk Kites,** 1 877/359-8447, also runs a number of interesting tours. Its sea kayaking and surf kayaking classes generally run $50 for beginners' classes (1.5 hrs) and $49 for three-hour advanced classes. An interesting class perfect for the Outer Banks, the three-hour kayak scuba diving trip ($60), allows you to not only paddle but explore some local shipwrecks. You'll need your c-card, and you'll pay for any dive gear, tanks, or weights. Kitty Hawk Kites also offers adaptive paddling classes for disabled paddlers ($30/hour, $125/day, pre-registration required). You can rent kayaks and canoes starting at $10 an hour and $99 a week.

## Windsurfing

The Outer Banks are the Promised Land for windsurfers; if you'd like to give it a try, call the folks at Kitty Hawk Sports, 800/948-0759 or 252/441-2756. For $49, they promise to have you skimming like a crooked accountant within three hours. If you have the know-how but not the equipment, they also rent boards with rigs for as low as $20 an hour. In season, you'll meet at

hang gliding at Jockey's Ridge State Park

© MIKE SIGALAS

Kitty Hawk Watersports, Milepost 16, at 10 A.M. or 2 P.M., and let the wind blow.

## Hang Gliding

The dunes at Jockey's Ridge are the largest migratory sand dunes in North America, ranging in height from 80 to 140 feet. They're pretty much the sort of place Wilbur and Orville Wright were looking for (and found) in Kill Devil Hill back before it was planted over with grasses: high enough and windy enough to launch from, and soft enough in case the landing doesn't go too well. So it's no surprise perhaps that all the aeronautic ambience in the place where humanity learned to fly would also entice people, even today, to give it a try. Hang gliding has been taught out here for more than 20 years. Kitty Hawk Kites has made a special arrangement with the Park Service to hold hang gliding classes on the dunes. Classes run $55 (lessons and three flights) and up.

## Getting There

Most people drive to the Outer Banks, either coming over on 158 through Point Harbor and into Kitty Hawk, or across through Manteo on U.S. 64/264. Yet another way to access the Banks from the south is to drive north on N.C. 12 from Beaufort until you reach the Cedar Island Ferry. The two-hour ferry ride takes you into the town of Ocracoke. If you want to continue north onto Hatteras Island, you'll need to take a second, shorter ferry. There's a fee for the two-hour Cedar Island Ferry, but the forty-minute Ocracoke/Hatteras ferry is free.

If getting to the Banks for you will include flying, note that by far the closest major airport to the Outer Banks is **Norfolk International Airport,** Norfolk, Va., 804/855-7845. From there you can rent a car and drive down to the Outer Banks.

If you don't want to spend the money for a rental car, consider taking **The Connection,** 252/473-2777, website: www.calltheconnection .com/, a shuttle service that will get you from the Norfolk Airport to anywhere on the Outer Banks. Prices vary depending on the date and your destination, but it'll cost around $90 to get to Nags Head, around $120 to get to Corolla, and $178 for Hatteras. Ocracoke, dead-end trip that it is, runs the most by far: upwards of $250. The good news is that it only costs $10 per additional passenger, so if three or four of you split the fare, things can get downright reasonable. Travel between 6 A.M. and 6 P.M. and you can ask for discount rates, which should save you upwards of $10.

## Getting Around

If you're going to rent a car, presumably you'll rent it in Norfolk or at whatever airport you fly into. However, if you find yourself on the Banks and looking for a rental car, consider **Enterprise Rent-a-Car,** in Manteo at 252/480-1838. If you want a 4x4 for some off-road driving, you might try Junior Suttle's **Outer Banks Jeep,** Milepost 5.5, Route 158 Bypass, Kill Devil Hills, 252/441-1146, ext. 7, website: www.outerbanksjeeep.com. Junior will rent you a Jeep or Dodge Caravan for $100 or $50 a day, respectively, plus 25 cents a mile after 75 miles. You can rent a Dodge Stratus or Plymouth Breeze four-door for $39.95, plus mileage. For a little less you can rent from **U-Save Auto Rental,** at Midgette Auto Sales, 252/491-8500, just over the bridge in Point Harbor. If you're going to be down in Hatteras Island, **Buxton Under the Sun,** 47188 N.C. 12, Buxton, 252/995-6047, rents cars and 4x4s, and provides service to all airports within 250 miles—which includes the one up in Norfolk.

You'll find lots of places eager to rent you a bike on the Outer Banks. In Corolla, try **Ocean Atlantic Rentals,** Corolla Light Village Shops, N.C. 12, 252/453-2440, or **The Bike Barn** in Monteray Plaza, also on US N.C. 12, 252/453-0788. In Duck, try **Ocean Atlantic Rentals,** on N.C. 12, 252/261-4346. In Nags Head, try yet another outlet of **Ocean Atlantic Rentals** at Milepost 10, 252/441-7823. Down on Hatteras, you'll find **Island Cycles** at N.C. 12 in Avon, 800/229-7810 or 252/995-4336, as well as **Kitty Hawk Kites/Outer Banks Outdoors,** at Hatteras Landing, 800/334-4777 or 252/986-1446. On Ocracoke, **Island Rentals** on Silver Lake Road, 252/928-5480, can get you rolling.

## North of Nags Head

The further north you go out of Kitty Hawk (the low point on the Outer Banks, price-wise), the less shabby things become, and the more the homes cost. Houses in Kitty Hawk in early 2000 averaged $118,000 each, Southern Shores' averaged $279,000, Duck's averaged $322,000, and Corolla's averaged $412,000. In a not-unrelated incident, in 2000, just 16 years after the dusty little fishing village of Corolla received its first paved road, the town's first full-service stretch limousine company opened for business, serving the needs of vacationing mainlanders—who come to the Banks, by all accounts, to enjoy the simple things in life. Life has changed everywhere on the Banks over the past twenty years, but perhaps nowhere as much as it has north of Kitty Hawk.

*If Duck has gone from being a sleepy, laid-back village to a posh re-creation of a sleepy, laid-back village, it's one of the rare places where visitors can still experience even a Disneyfied vision of what the Outer Banks were like 30 or 40 years ago. Mansions aside, it's still a cute town.*

### DUCK

Now here's one name that's easy to figure out: Duck was named after all the ducks who frequented the area, though one suspects that if the town was renamed today it'd be called Snowbird.

Up until 1984, Duck was the end of the line for N.C. 12, which north of town turned dirt all the way up the distant village of Corolla. In 1984, however, when the state paved the road clean up to Corolla, the roof ripped off the Northern Banks' real estate market, and Duck went high-end with a fury. Fortunately, the change came late enough that the village's quaint personality had become part of its draw—hence those building developments had an interest in preserving some semblance of an old beach village in Duck.

Nonetheless, the piles of cash haven't exactly rolled off Duck's back. It's lost some of its regional color. One of the village's new condo developments is named Nantucket Village, and this is perhaps instructive: in some ways Duck's become just another take on the laid-back beach village motif of Hilton Head, Kiawah, Bald Head Island, Cape Cod, and most of Eastern Maine, another generic stop on the vacation circuit for the upper classes, with Epicurean restaurants and expensive gift shops out of all proportion to the size of the village.

But if Duck has gone from being a sleepy, laid-back village to a posh re-creation of a sleepy, laid-back village, it's one of the rare places where visitors can still experience even a Disneyfied vision of what the Outer Banks were like 30 or 40 years ago. Mansions aside, it's still a cute town.

And with the shrewdness of its namesake, it's fighting to stay cute. In spring 1999, when a huge Food Lion tried to swagger into town, Duck attacked. The town's 500 residents passed a law limiting future buildings in the area to just 10,000 square feet. The Food Lion stalked away, looking for other prey.

### Accommodations

Donna Black and Nancy Caviness' **Advice 5 Cents, A Bed and Breakfast,** 111 Scarborough Lane, 252/255-1050, website: www.advice5.com, sits in the midst of Duck, in walking distance of the Scarborough Faire shopping center and most restaurants. The ladies also offer their guests casual, home-baked goodies. Five rooms, each with private bath, $95–175. Open February–November.

Outside of town, **Sanderling Inn Resort,** 1461 Duck Rd., 800/701-4111 or 252/261-4111, website: www.sanderlinginn.com, offers 77 rooms, three cottages, 10 suites, golf and tennis, canoes, boats, rafts, a jogging/nature trail, a top-notch restaurant, a spa and fitness center, and access to the 3,400-acre Audubon Preserve next door. Rates run from around $120 in the off-season to nearly $500 a night, in season, for a villa.

## Food

One of the niftiest spots in town is tiny **Tullio's Pastry Shop,** upstairs in the Scarborough Faire, 252/261-7111, email: tullios@beachlink.com, where you can find mouth-watering and mouth-dropping desserts whipped up by award-winning Culinary Institute of America chef Walter T. Viegelmann. In addition to breakfast treats and desserts that may well qualify as narcotics—hot fresh cinnamon buns and other pastries, authentic Key lime and Kentucky bourbon pecan pies—Walter and crew whip up some mean mini-pizzas.

Also in Scarborough Faire is the acclaimed **Fishbone's Raw Bar & Restaurant,** 1171 Duck Blvd., 252-261-6991, email: fishbone@pinn.net, offering local seafood, pork, chicken, pasta, and daily specials, and proud winners of the Outer Banks' Chowder Cookoff a few years back. Good chance to dine with a view of the sound. Dinners run $8.95–25.95.

**Red Sky Café,** actually a part of the Village Wine Shop in the Village Square Shops, 1197 Duck Rd. , 252/261-8646, email: redsky@interpath.com., sells wood-fired pizzas, soups, sandwiches, and a full dinner menu, with dishes from $15.95 on up.

Some argue that the **Sanderling Inn Restaurant,** 1461 Duck Rd., 252/261-3021, is the very top rung of Outer Banks Dining. But vying mightily for that rung is **Elizabeth's Café and Winery,** Scarborough Faire, 252/261-6145, ranked as one of America's Top 100 Restaurants of the 20th Century with 10 or more years of service by the International Restaurant and Hospitality Rating Bureau, and conferred the Best of Award of Excellence by *Wine Spectator.* As at the Sanderling, call ahead for reservations and bring your bravest credit card (the seven-course wine dinner, served at the second seating, runs $125 a person; the six-course wine dinner runs $80). Lunch and à la carte dinners can be more reasonable. Sample items—though they change nightly—include such complicated appetizers as the "leaning tower of duck," stacked sliced roasted duck breast, grilled sweet potatoes, and asparagus over organic greens with bacon balsamic reduction ($8), or a scallop and brie bisque with diced Granny Smith apples ($8); entrées include oven-baked semiboneless duck with a dark cherry,

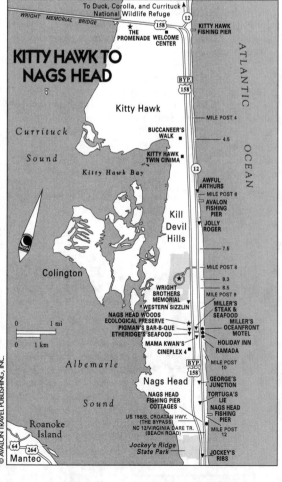

**KITTY HAWK TO NAGS HEAD**

To Duck, Corolla, and Currituck National Wildlife Refuge

WRIGHT MEMORIAL BRIDGE

THE PROMENADE
WELCOME CENTER

KITTY HAWK FISHING PIER

ATLANTIC OCEAN

Kitty Hawk

Currituck Sound

MILE POST 4

BUCCANEER'S WALK

4.5

Kitty Hawk Bay

KITTY HAWK TWIN CINIMA

AWFUL ARTHURS

MILE POST 6

AVALON FISHING PIER

Kill Devil Hills

JOLLY ROGER

7.5

MILE POST 8

8.3

Colington

8.5

MILE POST 9

WRIGHT BROTHERS MEMORIAL

MILLER'S STEAK & SEAFOOD

WESTERN SIZZLIN

NAGS HEAD WOODS ECOLOGICAL PRESERVE

MILLER'S OCEANFRONT MOTEL

PIGMAN'S BAR-B-QUE

ETHERIDGE'S SEAFOOD

HOLIDAY INN

MAMA KWAN'S CINEPLEX 4

RAMADA

0    1 mi

0    1 km

MILE POST 10

BYP. 158

GEORGE'S JUNCTION

Albemarle

Nags Head

TORTUGA'S LIE

NAGS HEAD FISHING PIER

Sound

NAGS HEAD FISHING PIER COTTAGES

US 158/S. CROATAN HWY. (THE BYPASS)

NC 12/VIRGINIA DARE TR. (BEACH ROAD)

MILE POST 12

Roanoke Island

Manteo

Jockey's Ridge State Park

JOCKEY'S RIBS

© AVALON TRAVEL PUBLISHING, INC.

merlot, mango Chambord sauce ($22). A friendly warning: try to save money by ordering an appetizer as an entrée and you'll incur a $12.50 plate charge. Bring in your own wine, and you'll pay a $15 corkage fee. (As of yet, there's no extra charge if you bring your own date, but you might call ahead about a possible escort charge.)

For my money, I'll take the barbecue at north-of-town **Duck Deli** 252/261-3354, anytime. Nice outdoor deck and some pretty good Eastern North Carolina and Kansas City barbecue.

For Duck after dark, try the **Barrier Island Inn Restaurant and Tavern,** 1264 Duck Rd., 252/261-8700, which sometimes offers live entertainment (including comedy) and always has dartboards and a pool table.

### Shopping

**Scarborough Lane** and **Scarborough Faire,** on your right as you drive into the village, combined have around 30 boutiques, shops, and eateries in a pleasant outdoor setting. Faire also includes possibly the Banks' top bookstore, **The Island Bookstore,** 252/261-8981. Across the road on the soundfront, **The Waterfront Shops** feature Duck's General Store, a good place to purchase something with the word "Duck" on it, and the aptly named **Sunset Ice Cream,** along with a handful of other shops. You'll see plenty of ducks here; stop into the general store and you can buy a bag of corn to toss their way.

## COROLLA

Locally pronounced "Cuh-RAWL-uh," the once tiny, roadless village of Corolla is now a more exclusive version of Duck, but with a lighthouse. The paved road ends here at the start of **Currituck National Wildlife Refuge,** but even this hasn't stopped development north of town— homeowners in newly developing Carova north of the refuge merely shift their Broncos into four-wheel drive and plunge onward.

Its out-of-the-way location has kept Corolla out of most history books, but during World War II, with German subs on the prowl, the town suddenly found itself on the front lines of the War in the Atlantic.

In his book *Whalehead: Tales of Corolla, NC,* longtime Corolla postmaster Norris Austin recalls:

Currituck Club, Corolla

© MIKE SIGALAS

*All of the people had blackout shades on their houses and could have only one light per family. We also were not allowed to have headlights on our cars when driving the beach . . . so that the German subs would not see silhouettes of the ships passing by the coast. . . . The [Nazi] subs would get a ship fairly often, and you could see explosions and the sky lit up from the ship burning. . . . After a ship was hit, the Coast Guard told us not to go out on the beach until they picked up the bodies.*

The red-brick 158-foot **Currituck Beach Lighthouse,** on the corner of N.C. 12 and Corolla Village Rd., 252/453-4939, may be my favorite. It first lit up surrounding waters on December 1, 1875. You can climb it for $6 (free for kids under 8), which also gives you admittance to the museum in the keeper's house below. Open 10 A.M.–6 P.M. daily. While the other Banks lighthouses were painted different patterns to help sailors differentiate them from sea, the Currituck light was left unpainted brick for the same reason. Beautiful.

**Historic Corolla,** 877/287-7488, includes three historic buildings from the late 19th century, including a schoolhouse and a post office/general store. The 1885 Corolla Chapel has become a popular spot for weddings—folks from as far away as Russia and Nigeria have come here to tie the knot nautical-style. **Ice Cold Corolla,** also located in the village, sells drinks and North Carolina–style BBQ. All in all, this is a nice, shaded walk that gives folks something to do after taking in the lighthouse, and before the long drive back to Nags Head or Hatteras. Just beyond the shadow of the lighthouse stands the **Whalehead Club,** N.C. 12,

252/453-9040. The building has been under restoration for a while, but the idea is to eventually use the grand old 1920s hunt club as the **Currituck Wildlife Museum.** Call for tours. Outside you'll see a very pretty (and National Historic Register-ed) footbridge. Just over behind the lighthouse on School House Lane and Corolla Village Road you'll find other restored buildings, like the 1895 Lewark Residence, now **The Cottage Collection,** a furniture, antiques, and art boutique. An outbuilding houses a woman's clothing shop. **Island Bookstore** stands where an old general store used to be. **The Lighthouse Garden** is set in a 1920 residence. You'll also find here an old 1878 lifesaving station turned into a tourist shop; plus a barbecue place, a restored schoolhouse, a chapel, and a boathouse. The walk out to the sound-side gazebo is a pleasant one, and it's a good spot to get shots of the lighthouse over the marsh.

Over in the Corolla Light Village Shops, a small but pleasant surprise is the **Nalu Kai Surf Museum,** in the Corolla Surf Shop, 110A Austin Street, Corolla, 252/453-9283. The museum features relics and great old pictures which pay tribute to the early days of surfing. No admission charge—it's just part of the surf shop.

**The Inn at Corolla Light,** 1066 Ocean Trail, 800/215-0772 or 252/453-3340, website: www.corolla-inn.com, offers 43 rooms, tennis privileges, a Jacuzzi, canoes and boats, and a trail for hiking and jogging. Rooms start at $159 in season, and you'll need to book three nights minimum if you're here on a summer weekend. **B&B on the Beach,** 1023 Ocean Trail, 800/962-0201 or 252/453-3033, sounds like a quaint little inn, but it's actually a large realty company specializing in rentals. See www.bandbonthebeach.com for photos of rentals.

NAGS HEAD

## South of Nags Head

### HATTERAS ISLAND

There's nothing like a close call to help you appreciate what you have. So be sure to enjoy this island, because it was almost nuked.

In 1949, the early days of the Cold War, a secret Atomic Energy Commission scouting test sites filed the following report:

> *Cape Hatteras is a possible site for nuclear tests. It is relatively accessible by water, yet could be easily placed "out of bounds" for security control.*

Fortunately, the deserts of the Nevada were easier to acquire, and Hatteras was not annihilated.

What was saved? For starters, the 5,915-acre **Pea Island National Wildlife Refuge** sits south of the fishing-crazed Oregon Inlet on N.C. 12, 708 N. U.S. 64, 252/987-2394. The Pea Island visitors center stands six miles south of the inlet. It's a nice on-the-way spot for wildlife displays, with a pleasant self-guided walk—the Charles Kuralt Trail—for wildlife viewing. The Center is open 9 A.M.–4 P.M.

### Northern Villages

Just south of the refuge, you'll find three little villages of Rodanthe, Waves, and Salvo—none of them likely to inspire a *Southern Living* spread anytime soon, but all of them pleasant enough spots to rent a house and enjoy abundant nature in all directions. In Rodanthe, a great, all-in-one spot to do just this is **Hatteras Island Resort,** Atlantic Drive, 800/331-6541 or 252/987-2345, which offers 34 cottages, 34 rooms, and eight efficiencies at the foot of a fishing pier. Open April 1 through November 15, or until the weather turns bleak. Rooms run $99 in season, and two-bedroom cottages run $799; three- and four-bedroom cottages are also available. On the pier (or, more properly, beneath it) stands **Down Under Restaurant,** N.C. 12, 252/987-2277, another unexpected Outer Banks dining experience—an Australia-themed seafood and steak spot founded by an Aussie. You'll find some great

roo stew, made with real kangaroo, and a long list of imported beer—presumably many best described as "hoppy." Famous for its 15-cent shrimp, served 2–6 P.M. Open for breakfast, lunch, and dinner. Great place for any of them. On the ocean side of N.C. 12 you'll find the **Chicamacomico Lifesaving Station,** founded here in 1874 and under restoration. During the summer, re-enactors run a beach apparatus drill,

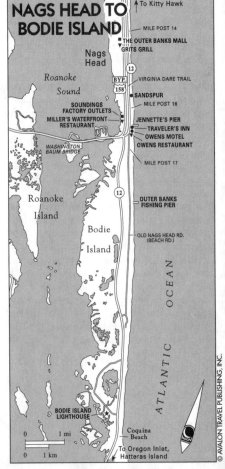

which captures some of the excitement and daring of that time and place. These men, precursors to the Coast Guard, routinely put out in open boats to stormy seas to rescue victims of shipwreck. Call the Chicamacomico Historical Association at 252/987-2626 for more information on the restoration's present status—or ask just about anyone in Rodanthe. They'll know.

Incidentally, the origin of the name Rodanthe is hazy; all anybody knows is it was attached to the place after the U.S. Postal service rejecting the village's first choice—Chicamacomico—as being too hard to spell. And Rodanthe's other claim to fame is the fact that it is one of the few communities in the county which still celebrates Old Christmas, on January 5, a throwback to the pre-Gregorian calendar days before 1752. Certain groups of Protestants, including those in Rodanthe, couldn't accept the change to December 25.

South of Rodanthe comes **Waves,** which also wanted to call itself Chicamacomico but was refused by the U.S. Postal Service. The name apparently refers to the waves at the beach. Waves is home to a lot of vacation homes, as well as **Cecil's Cottages,** on the east and west sides of N.C. 12, 252/987-2673, offering five cottages (bring your own linens) for $450 a month. Open May–September.

Salvo, so far as anyone knows, never wanted to call itself Chicamacomico. In fact, the village here had no name at all until a Federal ship passed during the Civil War and fired a salvo at it. The captain jotted down "Salvo" on a chart to remind himself of the location of the town.

It's home to the **Salvo Inn Motel,** 27357 N.C. 12, 252/987-2240, with nine rooms, three cottages, seven efficiencies, and two cabins, plus a playground and canoes. Rates start at $50. Open April–November.

## Avon

Little Avon was called Kinnakeet until 1873, when people got tired of arguing about how to spell it correctly (I'm serious) and changed the name to Avon, presumably after the river in England, though nobody really knows. One thing we do know for sure—this town is now the busiest on the island. A huge Food Lion pounced

## UNDER THE FLOOR

As you travel the Banks, you'll see numerous examples of the traditional Hatteras-style cottage—a small clapboard house perched high atop stilts to keep it out of storm surfs, with floorboards spaced just far enough apart to allow in a nice breeze. Usually, the large area beneath the house is enclosed in lattice. It gives the homes a quaint look, but its origin is even more colorful.

Lattice became the trend back when people first started building vacation homes on the oceanfront side of Hatteras Island. In the days before ferries, with few amenities out on the Banks, the normally wealthy vacationers would bring along their livestock to provide them and their servants with food and milk through the summer. The livestock roamed the island freely, but on the sandy shore, without any trees to provide shade, the animals tended to huddle in the cool dimness beneath the houses. Before long, fleas, ticks, and other critters would infest the homes. Bite-weary vacationers learned to enclose the stilts in lattice to keep the livestock out.

With the horses and cows long gone, the lattice remains, though often only on three sides of the undercottage: land prices and lot sizes being what they are, many folks have reclaimed the space beneath their homes for parking.

on the island a few years back and now dwells on the Bypass near the village, the peaceful village.

If you'd like to stay in town a night or two and soak up some peace and rays, and try your luck with the shore fishing, you might want to stay at the **Avon Cottages,** located on the ocean side of N.C. 12 at 40279 Younce Rd., 252/995-4123, website: www.avoncottages.com. There are 26 mostly oceanfront cottages that vary from around $640 to $1,300 per week. Those that rent daily run $42–85 per night. Bring your own linens or be prepared to rent them.

**Avon Motel,** N.C. 12, 252/995-5774, website: www.avonmotel.com, has 14 rooms and 29 efficiencies, some with kitchens. A double room runs $90.75 in high season. There's a fishing pier and laundry facility. Open March though mid-December.

To listen to some (possibly live) music and maybe meet yourself a real-live Avon lady (or gentleman), head over to **Lily Pad Lounge,** at the Froggy Dog Restaurant, on N.C. 17, 252/995-4106.

## Buxton

Buxton sits at the broadest point of Hatteras Island and serves as a hub of sorts. Most famous as being the town closest to the **Cape Hatteras Lighthouse,** this is also the place where Swedish scientist Reginald Fessenden first broadcast wireless radio, in 1902, to a receiver set on Roanoke Island, more than 40 miles away. The impressed and fascinated Thomas Edison and Guglielmo Marconi came here to Buxton to investigate. Nine years later, a wireless operator working the late shift in Buxton was the only land operator to receive the *Titanic*'s distress calls. According to legend, the Buxton operator radioed New York but was not believed (the ship was unsinkable, after all) until it was too late. Buxton itself mainly keeps to the sound side of its stretch of island, leaving the beach side to **Cape Hatteras National Seashore.**

This is where Hatteras Island children come to attend the island's one school; this is where many of the island's restaurants, hotels, and stores are. But all in all, it's still a sight less busy than Kitty Hawk.

The **Cape Hatteras Lighthouse,** 252/995-4474, built in 1870, is the tallest of the bunch at 208 feet. This is the light that grabbed a lot of headlines in 1999 (and was the subject of at least one book) by getting moved back from the rapidly eroding shore. And a good thing, too. Within a couple of months a couple serious hurricanes powered through here.

Buxton's other attraction is **Buxton Woods,** home of 500 acres of maritime forest, the largest such preserve in the state. From here you can hike the **Buxton Woods Nature Trail** all the way down to Frisco.

**Cape Hatteras Motel,** 46567 N.C. 12, 800/995-0711 or 252/995-5611, offers six rooms, seven efficiencies, five condos, 18 suites, and a pool, all on the waterfront. The rooms run $52–130 a night. The **Comfort Inn Bux-**

**ton,** on N.C. 12 at Old Lighthouse Road, 800/432-1441 or 252/995-6100, offers 60 rooms and a pool. Rooms go for $130 d. Also on N.C. 12, **Lighthouse View Motel,** N.C. 12, 800/225-7651 or 252/995-5680, website: www.lighthouseview.com, offers 24 rooms and 23 cottages, along with some efficiency apartments and 22 condos on the waterfront. $325–650 a week.

**Cape Hatteras Bed & Breakfast,** run by Cathy Moir on Old Lighthouse Road, P.O. Box 490, 800/252-3316 or 252/995-6004, sits close to the Cape Hatteras Lighthouse and features a full breakfast and seven rooms, all with private baths, $119. The one suite available runs for $139. Open April–November.

Perhaps one of the true joys of Buxton is **Uncle Eddy's Frozen Custard,** on N.C. 12, 252/995-4059, set in an old home that the owners turned in to a commercial enterprise after the town grew up around it, and featuring, out front, a classy little miniature golf course, and some fine homemade frozen custard (which you can buy as a cone, in a sundae, or by the pint). The miniature golf runs $6 for adults, $3 for kids, for unlimited daytime play from 12–6 P.M.

## Frisco

Residents of San Francisco, California, wince whenever somebody uses the contraction "Frisco" to describe the City by the Bay, but there's nothing they can do about the town of Frisco, whose name preserves this linguistic heresy for all time. Frisco was originally named Trent, but an inland village carried the same name, and so in 1898 the island village's first postmaster suggested the name "San Francisco," based on his affection for the California city where he'd spent time before being shipwrecked upon and settling on Hatteras Island. The Postal Service, which had been rejecting Indian name after Indian name as being too difficult to spell, would have none of this new (Spanish!) candidate. But it had no problem with Frisco.

Set (in part) in what was once Frisco's general store, the **Frisco Native American Museum and Natural History Center,** 53536 N.C. 12, 252/995-4440, is a homegrown but heartfelt

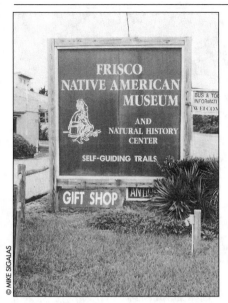

© MIKE SIGALAS

and profound collection of Native American artifacts and exhibits. Outside, a short trail leads through the woods and past some re-created Native American structures. Price runs $5 for a whole family, or $2 for adults.

The natural-grass **Frisco Mini Golf and Go-Karts,** N.C. 12, 252/995-6325, may just be the prettiest miniature golf course you'll ever see. A fun place on a quiet Hatteras summer night. The buzzing Go-Karts, of course, cut though the quiet a bit, but most kids won't mind. Golf runs $6 for everyone over 6. Go-Karts run $5 a ride. Inside you'll find soft-serve ice cream and other fun foods, and a very popular pool room. For a more proper dinner, **Channel Bass,** on N.C. 12, is a very popular seafood and steak spot down on the south side of the island; it's open for dinner, and on the pricey side ($15.95 and up). Nice waterfront view.

### Hatteras

The new 19,000-square-foot **Graveyard of the Atlantic Museum,** beside the Hatteras-Ocracoke Ferry landing in Hatteras, 252/986-2995, brings a welcome chance to study the Banks' unique history and culture in depth. It will feature interactive displays on attempts to colonize the Banks, pirates, Civil War blockade runners, lighthouses and lifesaving stations, and the many shipwrecks that earned Cape Hatteras its gloomy nickname.

The **Lee Robinson General Store,** founded in 1948 (though the current building was built in 1988), is truly a Hatteras tradition.

Some folks can't be around all this water and fish without wanting to get out on the former and start pulling out the latter. If you're one of these people, you may want to talk to **Teach's Lair,** 252/986-2460, which books charters.

If you'd like to stay around Hatteras, **Austin's "1908" Guesthouse,** 57698 N.C. 12, 252/986-2695, offers five efficiencies, with kitchens and bike privileges, for $50–90. **Seaside Inn at Hatteras,** 57303 Monitor Trail, 252/986-2700, website: www.seasidebb.com, has 10 rooms, a lounge, and a shuttle. $75–125 a night.

On the high end is **Cochran's Way,** 54470 N.C. 12, 252/986-1406, website: www.cochrans way.com. Overlooking the Pamlico Sound, it features great sunsets, kayaks, and a big porch. Three rooms, each with private bath, run $125–145. Open April–October.

If camping's an option, **Hatteras Sands Camping Resort,** 252/986-2422, offers more than 100 sites, many with full hookups—including cable TV—for $27–34. Six cabins (sleeping four people) run $37–52.

### Recreation

Brian Patteson leads pelagic birding trips off Hatteras; contact him at www.patteson.com, 252/986-1363.

## OCRACOKE ISLAND

Ocracoke Island is the place where, it's generally agreed, the Outer Banks of the popular imagination—a laid-back, unhurried, largely undeveloped utopia—still lives. It has only one town, and that town has only two streets running its length: Front Street and the Back Road. In a consumer-run, choice-venerating world, Ocracoke provides an invigorating lack of options,

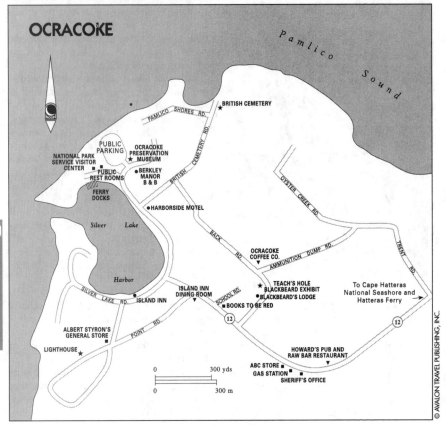

OCRACOKE

*Pamlico Sound*

BRITISH CEMETERY

PAMLICO SHORES RD.

PUBLIC PARKING

OCRACOKE PRESERVATION MUSEUM

NATIONAL PARK SERVICE VISITOR CENTER

PUBLIC REST ROOMS

BERKLEY MANOR B & B

BRITISH CEMETERY RD.

FERRY DOCKS

HARBORSIDE MOTEL

*Silver    Lake*

OYSTER CREEK RD.

BACK RD.

OCRACOKE COFFEE CO.

AMMUNITION DUMP RD.

TRENT RD.

*Harbor*

ISLAND INN DINING ROOM

SCHOOL RD.

TEACH'S HOLE BLACKBEARD EXHIBIT

BLACKBEARD'S LODGE

To Cape Hatteras National Seashore and Hatteras Ferry

SILVER LAKE RD.

ISLAND INN

BOOKS TO BE RED

12

12

ALBERT STYRON'S GENERAL STORE

POINT RD.

LIGHTHOUSE

HOWARD'S PUB AND RAW BAR RESTAURANT

ABC STORE

GAS STATION

SHERIFF'S OFFICE

0        300 yds

0        300 m

© AVALON TRAVEL PUBLISHING, INC.

like a theme park based on Anne Morrow Lindbergh's *A Gift From the Sea.*

But like Duck, Ocracoke isn't stupid. It knows it's cute. But somehow Ocracoke carries it off better than other parts of the Banks. It's home to the smallest school in North Carolina (around 75 students, K–12), and it's the sort of place that people come back to every year—if they remember to make reservations well in advance.

The 1895 David Williams House is now home of the **Ocracoke Preservation Society Museum,** 252/928-7375. Set in a former Coast Garden captain's home, the museum features a number of exhibits on the local dialect, the Confederate Fort Ocracoke, fishing boats, and more.

Open Monday–Friday 10 A.M. to 5 P.M., shorter hours on the weekend. Admission free.

Given the name, a lot of people assume that the **British Cemetery,** British Cemetery Rd., 888/493-3826 or 252/925-5201, website: www .ocracoke-nc.com/cemetery, dates to the colonial era, but in truth it's younger than Elvis. It contains the remains from the HMS *Bedfordshire,* torpedoed off Hatteras by the Germans' *U-558* on May 11, 1942. The cemetery flies a British flag, furnished annually by the Queen herself. An inscription of poet Rupert Brooke, himself killed in World War I, reads, "If I should die, think only this of me / that there's some corner of a foreign field / that is for ever England."

**Teach's Hole Blackbeard Exhibit,** Back Road,

252/928-1718, website: www.teachshole.com, is a unique blending of theater, museum, and gift shop. Several nights a week, old Blackbeard himself—or a local actor portraying him—performs "Blackbeard Lives," a short one-man show delineating the history of local piracy, including the fate of Edward "Blackbeard" Teach himself, who robbed, plundered, extorted, and (indirectly, at least) killed along the Carolina coasts before being decapitated in a sword fight off Ocracoke in 1718. After the show, audience members can have their pictures taken with the rogue (head still attached) both before and after spilling out into a gift shop crammed full of faux pirate gear.

It's a unique stop alive with local history. And yet the whole thing gives one pause: in centuries to come, will vacationers to Olde Los Angeles and Historic Detroit Towne buy their kids plastic guns and crack pipes and enjoy period-costumed re-enactments of carjackings? Probably so. Admission to the small museum and the show runs $3. Entrance to the gift shop is free.

**The Ocracoke Lighthouse** is the oldest one still in use in North Carolina, dating back to

© MIKE SIGALAS

**Ocracoke Lighthouse**

1823, which is a long time for any structure to survive on the Outer Banks. Fortunately, the folks who built the lighthouse—the shortest on the coast, at just 75 feet—built it on one of the highest points on Ocracoke.

About half a block away you'll see the National Register of Historic Places registered **Albert Styron's General Store,** built in 1920, and featuring coffee, ice cream, gifts, beer and wine, and gift baskets.

North of town, the rest of the island is given over to **Cape Hatteras National Seashore,** the first national seashore in the country. Stretching clean from just south of Nags Head all along Hatteras Island and south to Ocracoke Inlet, the park encompasses 75 miles, and 30,000 acres. Here you'll find all sorts of nature-related activities: hiking, biking, camping, boating, birding, fishing, surfing, and shelling.

## Accommodations

Built in 1936, **Blackbeard's Lodge,** 111 Back Rd., 800/892-5314 or 252/928-1101, website: www.blackbeardslodge.com, is the oldest extant hotel in Ocracoke, and probably the kind of old place you'd think of when you think of a lodge on Ocracoke. The 37 rooms are clean and airy, and the use of the bikes and pool (and the option of renting one of six efficiency apartments) makes this a great choice. Under a gradual plan of refurbishment by the owners, Buffy and Ann Warner. The historic **Island Inn,** N.C. 12 and Lighthouse Road, 877/456-3466 or 252/928-4351, website: www.ocracoke islandinn.com set inside a 1901 house, features dining, traditional hotel rooms, and one and two-bedroom condos. Open year-round. $49–89, two-night minimum. Dining.

**Harborside Motel,** Silver Lake Rd., 252/928-4141, offers 14 rooms right across the street from the waterfront. Also offers a meal plan, a shuttle, and a kitchen if you'd like. $55–80; continental breakfast served, featuring baked goods the owner makes herself.

Robert and Amy Attaway's **Berkley Manor Bed and Breakfast,** 800/832-1223 or 252/928-5911, website: www.berkleymanor.com, is a private island estate on three acres, a historic hunting and fishing lodge with a four-story tower. Twelve rooms (with private baths), with full breakfast, run $75–175 a night. Open year-round; nonsmoking.

## Camping

The cheapest way to stay on Ocracoke island is to camp. Most scenic is the $15-a-night **Ocracoke Island Campground,** 919/473-2111, part of Cape Hatteras National Seashore, just north of town on N.C. 12. In town you'll find the private **Beachcomber Campground,** 252/928-4031. It costs $20 a night, and sits behind a convenience store, but it has hot showers. For RVers, it offers electricity and water hookups.

## Food

**Island Inn Dining Room,** N.C. 12 and Lighthouse Road, 877/456-3466 or 252/928-4351, website: www.ocracokeislandinn.com, offers hearty island fare for reasonable prices. **Ocracoke Coffee Co.** on the Back Road, 252/928-7473, opens at 7 A.M., pumping out caffeine to a population of laid-back islanders and lying-back vacationers who you'd think wouldn't really need it. Nonetheless, visiting travel writers are always very grateful to climb up the porch and order a cup of consciousness. Smoothies here as well.

## Nightlife

**Howard's Pub & Raw Bar,** 1175 Irvin Garrish Hwy., 252/928-4441, website: www.howardspub.com, is owned by Buffy and Ann Warner, a former West Virginia state senator and his wife, who moved down here in the early 1990s and quickly became forces to be reckoned with—they also own Blackbeard's Lodge. The food here is made from scratch, and if you like, you can eat it on the deck outside, where you can see the ocean. Howard's also offers jazz and blues on the weekends, karaoke some other nights, and a big ol' TV for watching the game, plus an oceanview rooftop deck, a screened porch, pool table, Foosball, and darts.

> *Ocracoke Island is the place where, it's generally agreed, the Outer Banks of the popular imagination—a laid-back, unhurried, largely undeveloped utopia—still lives. It has only one town, and that town has only two streets.*

## Shopping

It'd be a crime to be caught on Ocracoke for any length of time without a good book to read. **Books to Be Red,** N.C. 12 and School Road, 252/928-3936, though it sounds like the name of a Communist reading course, provides a selection of new and used books for word-hungry Ocracoke residents and visitors. You can buy journals and other items here as well.

# PORTSMOUTH ISLAND

Now home to a deserted village and some houses you can rent from the National Park Service, Portsmouth Island is one of the rarest of battlegrounds in the war between humans and nature: here, nature won. At one time the town was home to more than 1,000 people; the last of them moved off in the early '70s, worn out by having to rebuild after every massive storm. The only way to get here is by private or charter boat. For information on the latter, call 252/928-1111.

# Roanoke Island

Protected from ocean gales by Bodie Island, Roanoke is also separated from the mainland by the Croatan Sound, and thus is considered part of the Outer Banks. The island was home to the first English settlement in North America, Raleigh's ill-fated Lost Colony. The island's two towns, Manteo and Wanchese, reflect the names of the two Native American men taken back to England with the first ships and then returned home again, to differing effects. Manteo became the best friend of the English settlers; Wanchese, the conservative, rebelled against the white peril and is rumored, according to some theories, to have had a hand in the presumed slaughter of the colonists. Though tourism is extending its well-manicured hand across the island, Wanchese is still the rougher, less-commercial fishing village; set on Shallowbag Bay, the town of Manteo is a cute, Elizabethan-style village welcoming tourists from around the world.

## MANTEO

Manteo is a quaint little oceanfront town that reminds you of New England, probably because the first British settlers in this area considered this New England and built accordingly, and partly due to the Elizabethan themes for nearly every motel and B&B on the island. On the whole, the town is as pleasant a stay as you'll find on the Outer Banks.

Settlers in the area originally called this Shallowbag Bay, but the town upgraded to its current name during Reconstruction, when the U.S. Postal Service established an office here. The name comes from the Croatan Indian who, along with the Roanoke Indian Wanchese, was taken from Roanoke to England in 1584 to be presented to Queen Elizabeth I and stir up interest in the colonization of the New World. Later, Manteo was named Lord of Roanoke by Sir Walter Raleigh, and baptized in the first Protestant baptismal service in American history. To the English at least, he was now the ruler of all Native Americans, though of course under the authority of Her

Highness. He also served as middleman between settlers and his none-too-happy Native American brethren, including Wanchese, more conservative and unwilling to see his culture and people changed by the new arrivals and their ways.

One theory as to the colonists' disappearance suggests that they may have left the safety of Fort Raleigh to follow Manteo to live among his people on Croatan (now Hatteras). Whether they made it or not is anyone's guess, though some say they were attacked in transit by a force led by Wanchese and decimated, with only a few survivors.

Manteo laid low throughout most of the rest of history as a sleepy fishing town, but since the arrival of *The Lost Colony* Outdoor Drama in 1937, the town has experienced a thematic adjustment toward all things Elizabethan. The Garden Club of North Carolina helped out in 1951 by building Elizabethan Gardens to capitalize on tourists drawn to the area's early colonial history. More recently, the opening of Roanoke Island Festival Park across the bridge gives folks who might have flown through here on the way to Nags Head another reason to pull over and walk around town awhile. The waterfront's a fine place to spend a morning, afternoon, or evening.

### Sights

**Roanoke Island Festival Park,** across from the waterfront in downtown Manteo, 252/475-1506 or 252/475-1500 (24-hour info line), comes across as a healthy mating of a national historic site and Disneyland. The well-tended park includes the top-notch, interactive Roanoke Adventure Museum, which features a gregarious audio-animatronic pirate, among other Disney-inspired wonders. Before entering the museum, note the rack of Elizabethan garb in the lobby. If you like, you can pick up a costume to wear while on the property. Across the lobby you'll find a theater showing a (no additional charge) short film, *Legend of Two Path,* throughout the day. It tells the story of three local Native Americans, Wanchese, Manteo, and Skyco, who were

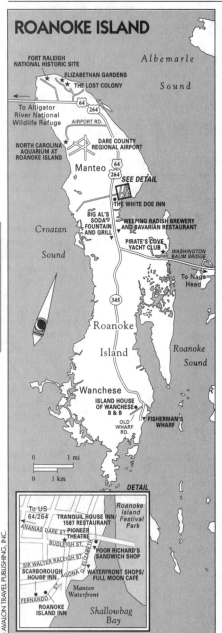

ROANOKE ISLAND

FORT RALEIGH NATIONAL HISTORIC SITE
ELIZABETHAN GARDENS
THE LOST COLONY

Albemarle

Sound

To Alligator River National Wildlife Refuge

AIRPORT RD.

NORTH CAROLINA AQUARIUM AT ROANOKE ISLAND

DARE COUNTY REGIONAL AIRPORT

Manteo

SEE DETAIL

THE WHITE DOE INN

BIG AL'S SODA FOUNTAIN AND GRILL

WEEPING RADISH BREWERY AND BAVARIAN RESTAURANT

Croatan

Sound

PIRATE'S COVE YACHT CLUB

WASHINGTON BAUM BRIDGE

To Nags Head

Roanoke

Island

Roanoke Sound

Wanchese

ISLAND HOUSE OF WANCHESE B & B

FISHERMAN'S WHARF

OLD WHARF RD.

0      1 mi
0      1 km

DETAIL

To US 64/264

TRANQUIL HOUSE INN/ 1587 RESTAURANT

ANANIAS DARE ST

PIONEER THEATRE

BUDLEIGH ST.

SIR WALTER RALEIGH ST.

SCARBOROUGH HOUSE INN

AGONA ST

FERNANDO

ROANOKE ISLAND INN

Roanoke Island Festival Park

POOR RICHARD'S SANDWICH SHOP

WATERFRONT SHOPS/ FULL MOON CAFÉ

Manteo Waterfront

Shallowbag Bay

© AVALON TRAVEL PUBLISHING, INC.

NAGS HEAD

on the front lines when the Old and New Worlds collided, and suffered accordingly. It tells the story completely from the Native American point of view, an interesting counterbalance to the mostly Eurocentric *The Lost Colony.*

Another highlight of the park is its intelligent living history interpretations—be sure to visit the Settlement Site, a re-creation of a 16th-century British landing, complete with reenactors who demonstrate crafts and may even challenge you to a game of ninepins. The Festival Park also includes extensive boardwalks, a Fossil Pit, a strong museum, an art gallery, and occasional concerts.

The park's undeniable star, however, is the *Elizabeth II,* designed after the ships that sailed under Sir Walter Raleigh in the 1500s. A climb aboard (and below) a ship like this is equal to many books' worth of reading for impressing a visitor with the sheer grit of America's first European settlers. The re-enactors who work the ship tell me that the most common question they hear from visitors down in the claustrophobic galley is, "Were the real ships bigger?" No, they weren't. Who would have believed that only four hundred years after the first Europeans crossed the Atlantic to a treacherous life in a strange land in ships smaller than a Greyhound bus, their ancestors would be hurtling back and forth 30,000 feet above the same ocean in padded chairs watching second-rate movies, and complaining that their chicken teriyaki is overdone?

A two-day pass runs $8 for adults and $5 for students. Children under 5 are free.

The **North Carolina Aquarium at Roanoke Island,** Airport Road, 252/473-3494, has a 285,000-gallon tank wherein fish and sharks swim around and through a one-third scale model of the USS *Monitor.* Among all the things you'd expect, you'll find a portrait gallery of U.S. Life Saving Services heroes from the past. Prices run $6 for adults, $4 for children 6–17 years old.

**Elizabethan Gardens,** 1411 U.S. 64/264, 252/473-3234, hasn't been here all that long, but thanks to the good work of the Garden Club of North Carolina, who created it in 1951, it seems as though it has. The 10 acres of grounds include statuary, impatiens, roses, gardenias, hydrangeas, and the sorts of herbs grown by the English settlers. You'll enter by passing through the beautiful circular Gate House, and then move out to visit the Sunken Garden, the Queen's Rose Garden, Shakespeare's Herb Garden, and a number of other plantings, all accented by fountains and statues. One of the most famed (and oft-photographed) of the latter is an interpretation of Virginia Dare as a grown woman, dressed in a fishing net. Sculpted before the Civil War by an American expatriate living in Rome, the statue was shipped to America but sank and spent a couple of years at the bottom of the ocean before it was salvaged and brought to Boston. A New Yorker bought it from the artist and placed it in his studio, but the studio burned, killing the short-lived art collector. Since the New Yorker hadn't paid for the statue yet, the artist, Maria Louisa Ander, got it back. In her will, she gave the statue to the state of North Carolina where, presumably, the Tar Heels would appreciate it. But not long after art supporters placed the statue in Raleigh's Hall of History, the artistic interpretation of the state's best-loved infant as a nude adult drew fire, and Virginia disappeared into a basement for a spell. The state gave Paul Green the hot-potato statue after he wrote *The Lost Colony* for them in 1935. When the North Carolina Garden Club created the Elizabethan Gardens in 1951, Green unloaded the statue on them. So here it is, awaiting its next tribulation. Admission runs $5 for adults, $1 for kids over 5. Open daily, 9 A.M.–6 P.M., earlier in the winter.

If you've been captivated by the story of the Lost Colony, you'll want to be sure to visit the **Fort Raleigh National Historic Site,** U.S. 64, 252/473-5772. The park offers a visitors center, interpretive programs, and a nature trail. The fort was reconstructed for tourists years ago but has since been deconstructed—what you'll see now are berms of grass, the foundations of the original fort. Here too you'll find the Waterside Theatre, home of **The Lost Colony Theatre Under the Stars,** 1409 U.S. 64, 800/488-5012 or 252/473-2127, website: www.thelostcolony.org. This is one of those unique American institutions: *The Lost Colony* has been performed here on this stage

since the 1930s—hence the politics of Paul Green's Pulitzer-winning script, in which the unstoppable determination of the settlers to "civilize" the "untamed" land is offered as encouragement to a Depression-weary audience. The show features a cast and crew of some 125 and runs around $16 for adults and half that for children; Monday nights are "Kids Night," and kids under 12 pay $4 each. Shows Monday–Saturday.

Across Croatan Sound on U.S. 64/264 you'll find the undeveloped 151,000-acre **Alligator River National Wildlife Refuge,** where you may see black bears or a red wolf, recently reintroduced by the Fish and Wildlife Service.

## ACCOMMODATIONS

As always, keep in mind that classifications are based on a lodging's lowest-priced room in high season. You can find cheaper rates (much cheaper, in most cases) in any month that doesn't involve air-conditioning. For a couple of lodgings listed below, you'll find that a water-view room is considerably pricier than the non-view room.

### $50–100

**Duke of Dare Motor Lodge,** 100 U.S. 64/264, 252/473-2175, is a 57-room motel out on the main road; if you want to stay in Manteo, this will keep you in town, though it won't exactly keep you in the Elizabethan mood. Also on the highway at 524 U.S. 64/264, 252/473-3979, scarinn@aol.com, is the 12-room **Scarborough Inn.**

Sally & Phil Scarborough's four-room **Scarborough House Inn,** 323 Fernando St., 252/473-3849, website: www.bbonline.com/nc/scarborough, enjoys a good location in town, just down from the Roanoke Island Inn. Though the building itself is new, it's built along traditional lines and partially furnished with antiques. Rooms run around $89, though a water view can run $109.

### $100–150

The 80-room **Elizabethan Inn,** 814 U.S. 64, 800/346-2466 or 252/473-2101, website: www.elizabethaninn.com, runs as low as $59, depending on the season, and includes a breakfast, bicycles, an indoor and outdoor pool, racquetball court, whirlpool, and gym.

### $150 and Up
The **Roanoke Island Inn,** 305 Fernando St., 877/473-5511 252/473-5511, is a B&B's B&B. It's pretty, pleasant, and within walking distance of the shops and restaurants; it offers bikes for riding around town and features a water view. Eight rooms, open Easter–Thanksgiving. **Tranquil House Inn,** sits right on the Waterfront in the midst of the (mild) waterfront bustle: 800/458-7069, website: www.1587.com, 25 rooms, meal plan, a restaurant, and bikes.

The **White Doe Inn,** run by Bebe and Bob Woody at 319 Sir Walter Raleigh St., 800/473-6091 or 252/473-9851, website: www.white doeinn.com, offers seven rooms with bedside fireplaces, a full breakfast, and private baths.

## FOOD
Manteo's cup runneth over as far as great dining goes. **Poor Richard's Sandwich Shop,** on the waterfront, 252/473-3333, is where a lot of the folks working down here on the waterfront come for lunch. They make some great sandwiches (try the Reuben) and sell them at humane prices. **Full Moon Café,** in the Waterfront Shops in Manteo, 252/473-6666, serves up a beautiful view of Shallowbag Bay and the *Elizabeth II,* and a unique and constantly changing menu with wraps and quesadillas, baked crab dip, hummus, quiches, and salads. Most prices run lower than $16.95. More formal and also delicious in the same plaza is the **1587 Restaurant,** 252/473-1587, website: www.1587.com, serving pricey and smallish dinners from 5–10 P.M. daily. Entrées run $18.95–24.95, and include Cornmeal crusted grouper with wild rice, drizzled with a balsamic reduction, and presented with sautéed wild mushrooms, wilted greens, and fresh strawberries.

**Weeping Radish Brewery and Bavarian Restaurant,** U.S. 64/264 on the way to Nag's Head, 252/473-1157, is an unexpected delight, a bit of Bavaria—including the Outer Banks' first and of this printing only minibrewery. It serves up great sausages (try the knackwurst,

© MIKE SIGALAS

$8.95, served with homemade sauerkraut, mustard, and a pretzel) and smoked pork loin ($13.95), Bavarian goulash, and both authentic and not-so-authentic German sandwiches (including *Ein fleischfreier Hanseat*—das Gardenburger). The restaurant and biergarten sit inside a wooded, village-like plaza that includes a bakery, memorable toy store, and playground. You'll find other locations (though not quite as charming) in Corolla in the Food Lion Plaza, 252/453-6638, and at Milepost 1.5 at Bermuda Green, Kitty Hawk, 252/261-0488. But proprietor Uli Bennewitz, native of Bavaria, is most proud of his beer, which he sells both at the tables ($2.10 for a quarter liter) and at the counter by the bottle.

**Big Al's Soda Fountain and Grill,** 100 Patty Lane (also known as U.S. 64/264), 252/473-5570, plays the nostalgia card, 1950s-style, with the sort of vintage diner food—pork chops, Reubens ($6.95), tuna melts ($6.95), and the then-exotic chicken parmesan ($10.95)—that you'd actually find on the menu of a real diner, circa 1959, as well as the regionally appropriate fresh seafood dinners ($9.95–13.95). Of course, the dinners here feature names like "Leader of the Pack" (a quarter-pound burger with cheese, chili, and slaw, $5.95), and the "Lil' Deuce Scoop" (two chocolate chip cookies sandwiching vanilla ice cream, $2.95). There's also a dance floor and a jukebox. Open 11 A.M.–11 P.M. daily.

## WANCHESE

Wanchese, down on the southern end of Roanoke Island, is named after one of the two Native Americans (with Manteo) taken to England by British explorers in 1584. The Town of Manteo's development and popularity with tourists reflects Manteo's embrace of Christianity and English customs; Wanchese's distrust of—and eventual overt antipathy toward—the English and their culture seems reflected in this fishing village's apparent lack of interest in capitalizing on the tourist boom. Its time will probably come, but as for now, this is still mainly a fishing town without guile. Many folks visiting the Banks make a point of driving over to eat some of the fresh seafood at **Fisherman's Wharf,** Hwy. 345 S., 252/473-5205, where dinners will run you $9.95–17.95, considerably less for lunch. If you'd like to spend the night out here, you might want to book a room at Roy and Jeanne Green's **Island House of Wanchese Bed & Breakfast,** 104 Old Wharf Rd., 252/473-5619, website: www.bbonline.com/nc/island-house, where, in season, a room with breakfast runs $115.

# New Bern and the Central Coast

Let's start with pronunciation. As the region of the state initially settled by Europeans, a lot of firsts come from this part of the state: North Carolina's first towns, its first state capital, even its first Hall of Fame pitcher come from what was known as the Albemarle District. Maybe this is why when approaching the name of a place, locals generally love to plunge in and get the thrust of the word over right away. Pronounce New Bern as one word, "NEWburn," and Beaufort as "BOWferd."

And yet this rush toward the accent is pretty much where the hurry stops along the Central Coast. The Historic Albemarle district, the "Inner Banks," as it were, are in fact the direct opposite of the strip malls in Jacksonville, in greater Wilmington, or up in Nags Head. The Albemarle coast is blessed in that its heyday, its time of regional importance and spurting growth, came when the architectural styles had style. So while Nags Head, largely developed in the 1960s and 1970s, features ugly, car-oriented strips of concrete and neon, towns like Bath, Edenton, Elizabeth City, and New Bern enjoy quiet, narrow, tree-lined streets with classic 18th- and 19th-century homes. Every one of them, it seems, you'll enter by crossing a bridge.

Hope Plantation outside of Windsor

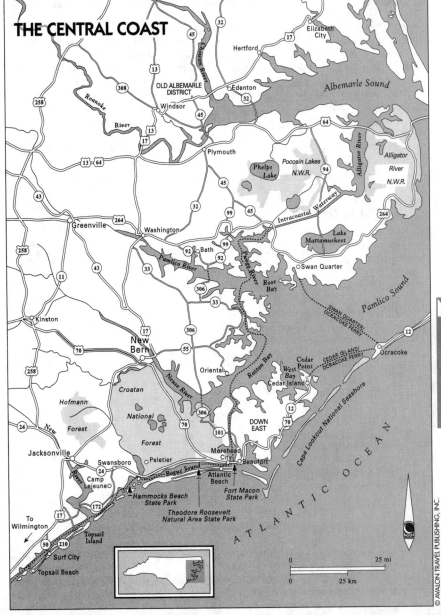

THE CENTRAL COAST

NEW BERN

## New Bern and Vicinity

New Bern (NEWburn, remember) has a lot to brag about. Founded in 1710, it's the second-oldest town in North Carolina, and served as a colonial and early state capital. Unlike most coastal cities, New Bern was founded by a combination of Swiss and Germans—not English—giving it a slightly alpine feel unique to the region. In fact, New Bern is the daughter city to Bern, Switzerland. New Bern is also home to the Tryon Palace, a reconstruction of the 18th-century colonial governor's mansion, which draws thousands of visitors a year.

But New Bern's greatest claim to fame is a local invention that gave its name to a generation, challenged all of America, became a John Belushi punchline in the mid-1970s, and, in the 1980s, indirectly caused Michael Jackson's hair to explode into flame. Turn-of-the-century New Bern pharmacist Caleb Bradham called it Brad's Drink; you and I call it Pepsi-Cola.

But to New Bern's credit, the city doesn't play the Pepsi card very often. The Bear City ("bern" is German for "bear") could choose between high-

NEW BERN

© AVALON TRAVEL PUBLISHING, INC.

## CENTRAL COAST HIGHLIGHTS

**Bath**
**Beaufort waterfront**
**Croatan National Forest**
**Edenton**
**Museum of the Albemarle**, Elizabeth City
**Hertford**
**New Bern's downtown and Pepsi-Cola Museum**
**Oriental**
**Sanitary Restaurant**, Morehead City
**Tryon Palace Historic Sites and Gardens,**
   New Bern

lighting its colonial roots—by reconstructing the Tryon Palace—or slapping Pepsi logos all over everything and opening up a small-town version of Atlanta's World of Coke, and fortunately, thankfully, it chose the former. You will find a couple of Pepsi sights, but they're integrated into the preservationist tone of things here. The true star of the town is the rebuilt Tryon Palace.

## HISTORY

New Bern's post-settlement history, like that of much of the North Carolina coast, starts out with the trumpets of colonial pomp, quiets after the snares of the Civil War, and slowly, slowly begins to build again through the 1900s before flaring into a swing number at the turn of the 21st century, as the town booms with emigrants and their bulging wallets. New Bern was founded in 1710 by Baron Christopher de Graffenried, a Swiss baron leading a group of German Protestants expelled from Catholic Baden and Bavaria. With the blessings of (and £4,000 from) England's Queen Anne, de Graffenried sent out 650 settlers from Gravesend, England, under the direct authority of John Lawson and Christopher Gale, but storms, sickness and French ships thinned them out to less than half that number by the time they reached the Chowan River. There, the wealthy planter Thomas Pollock— for whom Pollock Street is named—took pity

on the survivors and provided them supplies and transportation to the spot where the Trent River meets the Neuse. In September, they were joined by de Graffenried himself, leading a large group of Swiss settlers. He bought 10,000 acres from the Lords Proprietors and John Lawson, who had surveyed the colony. But de Graffenried was smart, and maybe even ethical, so he also paid King Taylor, the chief of the local Tuscarora Indian tribe, for the land. Lawson laid out the town in the shape of a cross, and built fortifications along the transverse road as a defense against Indian uprisings. With the support of his Swiss comrades, De Graffenried named the settlement New Bern, after the Swiss capital.

And everyone lived happily ever after . . . until the outbreak of the vicious Tuscarora War a year later. At war's end, however, the "Indian threat" was largely gone, and the area prospered. Thomas Pollock oversaw the rebuilding of New Bern. Edenton, Beaufort, Brunswick, and eventually Wilmington were founded. These towns and New Bern were showered with trade ships, quickly drawing the curtain on Bath's short reign as North Carolina's primary city. Though Edenton soon became the capital city, and though, as late as 1737, visiting Irishman Dr. John Brickell would describe New Bern as having "but a few Houses or Inhabitants in it at present," by 1771, New Bern's centrality along the coast, and its expanded population, made it the place to be, and Governor William Tryon decided to build a formal, permanent governor's house there. Possibly Tryon guessed that the colonials would respect the Crown more if they saw a little of its grandeur here in the colony, and he built an elaborate governor's mansion in New Bern, considered by most contemporary observers to be the finest government building in America. Local wags called it the "Tryon Palace," as a criticism of the misuse of their taxes. Tryon moved up to New York to become its governor and Josiah Martin moved here until he fled at the beginning of the American Revolution. After the Revolution, the governor of the state of North Carolina was housed here briefly, but by 1798 fire had ravaged the palace and the locals decided they'd always wanted George Street to continue on clear

## DOWN EAST

Head northeast on U.S. 70/U.S. 12 from Beaufort and you'll find the tourism-based 21st-century Carolina coast disappears like a fluorescent memory, leaving you amid green fields and seasoned frame buildings—and with a compulsion to check the road map. Surely, you think, this can't be the way.

But North Carolina's "Down East" area—running generally from north of Beaufort clear to Cedar Island Bay—*is* the way, if you're looking for authentic, unglamorous maritime culture. If it weren't for the ferry to Ocracoke leaving from Cedar Island, few tourists would ever come through here at all.

Turn south at Otway (named for local pirate hero Otway Burns, buried in Beaufort) to get to **Harkers Island.** Harkers is home to a former ship-building village, the most populated area in the region. Down at the southeast corner of Harkers you'll find **Core Sound Waterfowl Museum,** 252/728-1500, worth a stop.

After passing through tiny villages like Davis and Atlantic, toward the northeastern end of the road you'll find the 12,500-acre **Cedar Island National Wildlife Refuge,** largely a salt marsh and home to wild ducks, gulls, geese, ospreys, owls, and red-tailed hawks, along with such earthbound critters as deer, otter, mink, and the occasional black bear. The refuge offers observation area and boat landings. And you can camp there. Call 919/225-2511 for information.

For lodging Down East, check out the inexpensive **Driftwood Motel** in Cedar Island, 252/225-4861, beside the ferry terminal. It's popular with duck hunters and ferry-missers. The **Harkers Island Fishing Center** at 1002 Island Rd., 252/728-3907, also offers 20 rooms. Both it and **Calico Jack's Inn and Marina,** also on Island Road, 252/728-3575, offer efficiencies, fishing access, and ferries to uninhabited Portsmouth Island.

If you're looking to sleep on uninhabited island, **Morris Marina Kabin Kamps,** 1000 Morris Marina Rd., Atlantic, 252/225-4261, will take you across to Core Banks and set you up in a cabin for $100 a night.

birthplace of Pepsi, New Bern

to the river anyway. The building was razed, and remained razed for the next 150 years.

New Bern did well as a trading port through antebellum days, but during the war she was quickly captured by Union forces. This worked in her favor, since the Union needed the town to operate from and thus didn't torch it. The Confederates attempted to retake the town a couple of times but unsuccessfully. After the war, the area's economy dipped with that of the region and not until recently has it truly looked up.

Hence the rebuilding of the palace in the 1940s is truly amazing. In the 1940s, money was still very tight for most people in New Bern, and the city hadn't exactly highlighted the phrase "historical preservation" in their community mission statement—even as late as 1974, the city redevelopment commission was petitioning to have the 1797 Harvey Mansion bulldozed in the name of "progress." Nonetheless, having witnessed the popularity of the outdoor historical drama *The Lost Colony* over on Roanoke Island and the increased interest in colonial sites,

New Bernians rebuilt the Tryon Palace in painstaking detail, giving the city its future tourist draw. In retrospect, New Bern's choice was a miracle of farsightedness and good taste. Most small American communities in the 1950s, confronting the same choices, would probably have spent their tourism dollars building the world's largest Pepsi bottle.

## SIGHTS
### Orientation
New Bern sits at the junction of the Trent and Neuse Rivers; two of its major streets, running in perpendicular directions along different riverfronts, are called Front Street: east/west-running South Front, and north/south-running East Front, also called U.S. 70 Business. Heading north from the Trent River, you'll pass South Front and then Pollock Street, an important street for many of the town's historic attractions (including the Tryon Palace), lodgings, and shopping. The next block up comes Broad Street, also U.S. 70 Business/U.S. 17 Business.

### Tryon Palace Historic Sites and Gardens
This imposing structure at 610 Pollock St., 800/767-1560 or 252/514-4900, website: www .tryonpalace.org, seems a bit grandiose for little New Bern—at least that's what New Bernians have always thought. When the imperial royal governor William Tryon built the imposing structure in 1770, they protested that their taxes were being used for such extravagance. Later, the New Bernians gladly paved it over and pretended it had never been there. The only thing left was the stables.

In the 1940s, wealthy Gertrude Carraway began to think about the glory that had been New Bern's for 28 short years. She spearheaded a drive to bring it back. Finally, in the 1950s, the palace was "restored," as the official

*This imposing structure seems a bit grandiose for little New Bern—at least that's what New Bernians have always thought. They protested that their taxes were being used for such extravagance. Later, the New Bernians gladly paved it over and pretended it had never been there.*

pamphlet puts it—a fairly massive piece of understatement, since when the "restoration" began, Fords and Chevys used to drive to and from the river through the spot where the Georgian mansion now stands. British understatement aside, here it is, a tribute to the grandeur of times past. Sometime in the next ten years, the new Tryon Palace will have stood for twice as many years as the original.

The incredible research and painstaking craftsmanship required to re-create a building and grounds so many years back is a fascinating story in itself. The rebuilders worked using the houses' original blueprints, uncovered in 1939. The house was refurnished based on a detailed inventory of items Tryon and his wife had written out after their new home in New York burned down and they wanted compensation. And the re-creators continue to refine their vision. For instance, the "restored" gardens were laid out in the British style for lack of specific details about their design. Then, in 1991, Tryon Palace researchers searching at Venezuela's Academia Nacional de la Historia found the original garden plan in the collection of 18th-century Venezuelan traveler Francisco de Miranda, who had toured the young United States in 1783. Apparently Palace architect John Hawks had drawn up the plans for Miranda himself, and they revealed a definite French influence the original restorers hadn't known about.

Today, the Tryon Palace bustles with costumed reenactors and tour guides, and includes 14 acres of gardens planted to colonial specifications.

Admission for the guided tour (there are no unguided tours) is fairly steep—about $15 for adults, $6 for students in 1st grade through 12th grade. Tickets are good for two consecutive days. The costumed guides will show you the palace along with three other historic homes from the 18th and 19th centuries, and the New Bern Academy Museum. Open Tuesday–Saturday

NEW BERN

reenactor at Tryon Palace

9 A.M.–5 P.M., Sunday 1–4 P.M. The last guided tour begins at 4 P.M. daily.

## Other Sites

The **Attmore-Oliver House,** 510 Pollock St., 252/638-8558, was built in 1790 by Samuel Chapman. Today it's headquarters for the New Bern Historical Society. You can tour the house, with its period furnishings, Civil War room, and doll collection, for free.

Also free is the art museum set in a pre-WWI bank and aptly renamed **Bank of the Arts,** 317 Middle St., 252/638-2577. True, you can no longer cash your check here, but you'll find plenty of change afoot, what with the ever-changing exhibitions of Southeast paintings, sculptures, photographs, pottery, and fiber arts available for the viewing.

At 256 Middle St., 252/636-5898, you'll see the **Birthplace of Pepsi Cola,** a small museum and gift shop built to celebrate Pepsi, invented here in 1898 by Caleb Bradham. This recreation of an early-1900s drugstore is a nice place to stop in and order a soda. Just don't be a wise guy and ask for a Coke. It's been done. Open Monday–Saturday 10 A.M.–6 P.M.

**Christ Episcopal Church,** 320 Pollock St., 252/633-2109, built in 1752 for a parish that has existed since 1715. It's the third-oldest church in North Carolina and features a communion service donated to the church by King George II. The outdoor chapel was built over the site of the first church in 1873.

Long listed on the National Register of Historic Places (and saved from the wrecker's ball because of it), the 1797 **Harvey Mansion,** 221 S. Front St., 252/638-3205, offers six rooms of artwork and four archaeological exhibits. It's open for free self-guided tours daily 10 A.M.–4 P.M.

The **Firemen's Museum,** 408 Hancock St., 252/636-4087, celebrates the history of one of the nation's oldest continually operating fire companies, and firefighting in general. Here you can see some neat old equipment, including an 1884 horse-drawn steamer. They've even preserved the head of Fred, a valiant firehorse who died pulling a firefighting wagon. Ben Gaskill will tell you Fred's story, and will tell you about the great Fire of 1922, which destroyed every third building in New Bern, and no doubt caused some mean puns in neighboring communities. The museum also features a Civil War display. Open Monday–Saturday 10 A.M.–4:30 P.M., Sunday 1–5 P.M.

Outside of town, the **Bellair Plantation and Restoration,** 1100 Washington Post Rd., (N.C. 43 N), 252/637-3913, was the largest (and is the last remaining) 18th-century century country house in North Carolina. The folks at Bellair give one-hour tours by appointment only, so call ahead.

## Tours

The **Queen Anne Horse and Carriage Co.,** 252/244-1690, offers tours by horse-drawn carriage ($60 for up to seven people for one hour) or omnibus. **New Bern Trolley,** 333 Middle St., 252/637-7316, operates 90-minute guided trolley tours of the historic district. Tours run $12 for adults, $6 for children 12 and under.

# ENTERTAINMENT

## Shopping

New Bern has a colonial feel, and as in any good colonial village, the best goods are to be found near the riverfront and around the Governor's house. Local farmers, canners, bakers, herbalists, and artisans do business down on the waterfront at the **Farmer's Market,** 421 S. Front St., 252/633-0043. Friday 8 A.M.–5 P.M., Saturday 6 A.M.–2 P.M.

You could do a lot of good shopping without ever leaving Pollock Street. **Bern Bear Gifts,** 301 Pollock St., 252/637-2300, seems like a tourist shop in Switzerland, which is exactly the idea. It features European imports, English teapots, lots and lots of bears, beer steins, and of course, Swiss Army knives. It's one of New Bern's little but undeniable delights. Open Monday, Wednesday, Friday, and Saturday 10 A.M.–5:30 P.M., Tuesday and Thursday

**downtown New Bern**

© MIKE SIGALAS

1–5:30 P.M. At the Tryon Palace, **The Craft and Garden Shop,** 610 Pollock St., 252/514-4927, is a great little garden shop with atmosphere to spare. You can get a pass at the gate that will allow you to visit the shop without having to pay admission to the Palace if you don't want to. The **Museum Store** on the corner of Eden and Pollock Streets offers the best place to get various souvenirs of your visit. Diagonally across from the Palace you'll find four converted old residences now branding themselves as the **700 Block of Pollock Street;** they include **Kunstlerhaus,** 720 Pollock St., 252/636-1604, featuring jewelry, pottery, and so on. **Backyard Bears,** 718 Pollock St., 252/637-7122, is literally in the back yard of an old house, and contains bruinous merchandise. Open Tuesday–Saturday 11 A.M.–5 P.M.

Finally, I couldn't describe New Bern's shopping without mentioning **Mitchell Hardware,** 215 Craven St., 252/638-4261, one of those old-fashioned hardware stores packed with everything for the house—including some homey items worth a traveler's browsing—and staffed by people who seem to know everything you'd ever want to know about every item in the store, including where to find it all amid the clutter. Founded in 1898.

## Events

New Bern is a culturally minded town and it's always throwing some sort of event. In January, it's the Garden and History Lecture Series at Tryon Palace, 800/767-1560. In February it's the **Sunday Jazz Showcase** down at the Sheraton, 252/638-2577. The Fourth of July features fireworks over the water. The late-summer **Rotary Cup Regatta** pits cruising-class boats against one another. The Christmas season includes the **Holiday Tour of Historic Inns,** 252/638-8558, a Christmas parade of boats, 252/5781, **Handel's** *Messiah* over at the Centenary United Methodist Church, Middle and New Streets, 252/638-2577, and more. For information on these and the dozens of other annual events in New Bern, call the **Craven County Convention and Visitors Bureau** at 800/437-5767 or 252/637-9400, or visit www.visitnewbern.com.

**NEW BERN**

## Nightlife

**Captain Ratty's Piano Bar,** 330 S. Front St., 252/633-2088, opens at 5 P.M. and offers Friday and Saturday night live sax and piano, plus a jazz party on Thursday nights. Over at the Harvey Mansion, you'll find an atmospheric exposed-beam, low-ceiling, low-key pub in **The Cellar,** 800/638-3205 or 252/638-3205, zuttel@cconnect.net, originally the mansion's kitchen. You'll still see the original fireplace and irons down there, right along with the dartboards and TV. **The Chelsea: A Restaurant and Publick House,** 325 Middle St., 252/637-5469, is a popular place for locals to have a drink downtown. If you'd like to look out over the water as you frolic, try the **ProSail Pub,** at the Sheraton Grand, 100 Middle St., 252/638-3585, with an outside deck overlooking the harbor. On the weekends they also open up the **City Side Café** at the Sheraton, a dance club with a DJ and occasional live performers. If pool's your game, try **Mr. Stix Billiards,** 2724 Neuse Blvd., 252/638-2299, or **Mickey Milligan's,** 3411 Trent Rd., 252/637-3711. Milligan's also has a dance floor and bar food. It opens at 6 P.M.

## ACCOMMODATIONS

New Bern is the sort of town where you'll want to be able to wake up and stroll somewhere for coffee without having to climb in the car or cross a major highway. Leave New Bern's historic downtown and suddenly you're in a not-so-quaint city that you probably don't want to make a part of your vacation. For this reason, if your budget permits, it's worth it to shell out for one of the historic inns downtown, or one of the riverview hotels. Keep in mind too that if you're looking to spend the night in a less-urban spot after spending the day in New Bern, Oriental and Hertford aren't far away.

### $50–100

**New Berne House,** 709 Broad St., 800/842-7688 or 252/636-2250, charges around $88 for a guest room tucked into a 1923 Colonial Revival house beneath magnolia, pecan, and camellia trees. Each of the seven rooms has antique furnishings and its own bath, air-conditioning, and phone. Mystery weekends twice a month, plus full breakfasts. No children or pets. Howard and Marcia, the innkeepers, consider smoking an outdoor occupation. In addition to their fluent English, they speak limited Spanish, French, and German.

Worth a mention on the way out of town on U.S. 70/17 is **Comfort Suites Riverfront Park,** 218 East Front St., 800/228-5150 or 252/636-0022, right next door to the convention center. In exchange for being a fairly far walk from downtown, it offers a fine Neuse riverfront location. It has won its chain's gold Hospitality Award for years, with its whirlpool suites, fitness center, and waterfront balconies as well as a complimentary continental breakfast. All rooms have microwaves, refrigerators, coffeemakers, and hair dryers. Cityview rooms start at $88.95.

Other stays in less central locations include **Days Inn,** 925 Broad St, 252/636-0150, **Economy Inn,** 3465 Clarendon Blvd., 252/638-8166, and **Hampton Inn,** 200 Hotel Drive, 252/637-2111.

### $100–150

Starting at the intersection of Pollock and U.S. 17 Business and working west, you'll find Ed and Sooki Kirkpatrick's friendly (and child-friendly) 1850 **Harmony House Inn Bed & Breakfast,** 215 Pollock St., 800/636-3113 or 252/636-3810, a comfortable B&B set in a large Greek Revival inn decorated with antiques, reproductions, and family mementos. Rates for the 10 rooms (each with private bath) run $99–109 in season (up to $150 for a suite) and include a full breakfast.

Also within walking distance of Tryon Place and the rest of downtown is **Kings Arms: A Colonial Inn,** set in an 1848 home. Guided tours are available through the visitors center, and everywhere you wander you will find a piece of history on a house plaque, historic marker, or mural. $100 per night for the seven guest rooms. The third-floor Mansard Suite features original beadboard walls and a view of the Neuse River, for $145 a night. Innkeepers Richard and Patricia Gulley will bring your breakfast right to your room by candlelight, along with the morning paper.

## FOOD

Set in what used to be inventor of Pepsi Caleb Bradham's *second* drugstore, **The Chelsea: A Restaurant and Publick House,** 325 Middle St., features regional and international cuisine, and larger-than-you'd-expect wine and beer lists. Also on the higher end is **The Henderson House,** 216 Pollock St., 252/637-4784. It serves formal, Southern gourmet lunches and dinners in a converted, historic home. Open Wednesday through Saturday. Call ahead for reservations, and gentlemen, bring your coats and ties.

Less expensive is the **Pollock Street Restaurant & Delicatessen,** 208 Pollock St., 252/637-2480, which offers full breakfasts in addition to the normal deli items. Eat indoors or out. Right next door you'll find another cheap alternative, **Bagels Plus.** Both of these are great places for picking up a lunch that you can tote around while you explore the town.

Out at 3711 U.S. 17, **Moore's Old Tyme Barbecue,** 252/638-3937, offers both chopped pork and chicken barbecue, and even fries up a little seafood as well.

### Coffee and Tea

For coffee and baked goods, you won't find a better spot than **Trent River Coffee Company,** 208 Craven St., 252/514-2030. Owner Ed Ruiz's place offers sandwiches, espresso, flavored coffees, muffins, and other coffeehouse favorites. A very good book selection upstairs. Ed is a friendly former Bay Area flight attendant who's here fulfilling his dream of sharing San Francisco coffee culture with the New Bern area.

## GETTING THERE
### By Car
From I-95, head east on U.S. 70 and you'll come straight into town. From Elizabeth City, Edenton, Windsor, or Washington, just head south on 17. Or, if you'd like, head east at

Washington out on U.S. 264, veer right when it forks onto N.C. 92, and stop over at Bath. Then continue on along N.C. 92 until you come to the Aurora–Bayview Ferry. Ride across the Pamlico River for free (about 20 minutes), take N.C. 306 south to N.C. 55, then take N.C. 55 west to New Bern.

### By Airplane
People coming to the Central Coast from out of state normally fly into Norfolk, Va., Myrtle Beach, S.C., Wilmington, N.C., or even Raleigh/Durham, N.C., and then rent a car and drive the rest of the way. For information on Norfolk International Airport, call 757/857-3200. For Myrtle Beach, S.C., airport information, call 843/448-1589.

### By Bus
**Carolina Trailways** provides bus service to New Bern, at 504 Guion St., 252/633-3100.

## GETTING AROUND

New Bern's rental car spots include **Automotive Rentals of New Bern,** 252/633-6089; **Avis,** 800/831-2847 or 252/637-2130; **Enterprise,** 800/325-8007 or 252/514-2575; **Hertz Rent-a-Car,** 800/654-3131 or 252/637-3021; **National Car Rental,** 800/755-1501 or 252/637-5241.

Taxicab companies include **New Taxi Service,** 252/636-9000, and **Safeway Taxi Co.,** 252/633-2828, and **Tryon Cab Co.** 1018 Pollock St., 252/638-8809 or 252/635-1966.

**Bern Tours,** 333 Middle St., 252/637-7316 offers guided trolley tours that run about 90 minutes; a great way to start your visit here. Or cover much of the same ground to the sound of clopping hooves with **Queen Anne Horse & Carriage,** 675 Weyerhaeuser Rd., 252/633-6101, which offers passengers a horse-drawn carriage or Pennsylvania Dutch Wagon. In either case, call for reservations.

## INFORMATION

For more information on the New Bern area, contact the **New Bern Area Chamber of Com-**

NEW BERN

**merce,** 316 S. Front St., 252/637-3111. Right next door you'll find the **Craven County Convention and Visitors Bureau,** 314 S. Front St., New Bern, NC 28563, 800/437-5767 or 252/637-9400, website: www.visitnewbern.com.

## NORTH ON HIGHWAY 17
### Oriental

If you're looking for Ocracoke-type tranquility, but don't have an Ocracoke-type budget, consider a stay in Oriental. Oriental's a bit of an odd bird hereabouts; founded in the 1880s, it misses out on all the Historic Albemarle Region promotions because it wasn't a colonial-era town. And unlike many of the towns along the Carolina coast, which take their name from the birthplaces of homesick European founders or from various European leaders and benefactors whose favor the founders hoped to enlist, Oriental's naming legend has a California Gold Rush flash to it. Rebecca Midyette, the wife of the unincorporated town's founder and soon-to-be first postmaster "Uncle" Lou Midyette, couldn't really get excited about the prospect of incorporating under the community's placeholder name of Smith's Creek. While in Manteo, Rebecca was taken by the huge wooden sign inside her friend's house, which read "Oriental." The sign, her friend explained, had washed ashore from the wreck of the doomed Union steamship, the USS *Oriental.* The helpful wife smiled widely and that night told her husband she had good news: not only had she come up with a very exotic-sounding name for their isolated town, but she knew where she could get a very large name sign for free.

Television and film writer, director, and producer Kevin Williamson was raised hereabouts. Today, the pragmatically named burg boasts around 1,000 inhabitants and is a popular Sunday-

*Unlike many of the towns along the Carolina coast, which take their name from the birthplaces of homesick European founders or from various European leaders and benefactors whose favor the founders hoped to enlist, Oriental's naming legend has a California Gold Rush flash to it.*

drive destination from New Bern, 20 minutes away. Folks come to Oriental largely for the fresh seafood. The village has taken to calling itself the "Sailing Capital of North Carolina." It's a popular port of call for yachters and sailors using the Intracoastal Waterway. For more information, see www.visitorientalnc.com.

Pillar-of-the-community **Oriental Marina Inn & Restaurant,** Hodges Street, 252/249-1818, is a destination in itself. The inn features 18 waterfront rooms, a laundromat, and a pool. Rates range from $55 a night in low season to $89 in high. The **River Neuse Motel,** at the corner of S. Neuse Drive and Mildred Street, 252/249-1404, is another dockable, cheap waterfront stay, with its own private fishing pier. Rooms start at $65 in high season.

Of course a town with this much atmosphere is bound to spawn some bed and breakfasts. **The Inn at Oriental,** 508 Church St., 252/249-1078, is set in an old 1850s teacher rooming house, but the chalk-wielders of yore wouldn't recognize these 12 rooms today, what with their private baths, antiques and reproductions, and (in three rooms) modern kitchenettes. Full American breakfasts here include Belgian waffles and eggs benedict, if you ask for them. Rooms run $70 on weeknights, $85 on the weekend.

**The Cartwright House,** 301 Freemason St., 888/726-9389 or 252/249-1337, website: www.cartwrighthouse.com, faces the water and offers four bedrooms (starting at $90 d) and one suite. The British accents of hosts Tina and Glyn may make you feel a bit closer to the Albemarle's English Colonial past. Scones and coffee and full breakfast in the morning. Many packages available.

Since the term "Oriental" has gone out of vogue for describing Asian food, this little town may be one of the last places where you can order Oriental cuisine. For coffee, try **The**

**Bean,** 304 Hodges St., 252/249-4918, featuring espresso, bagels, and smoothies. For something more substantial, a local favorite new to the scene is **Oriental Steamer Restaurant and Tavern,** 401 Broad St., 252/249-3557, featuring steaks, seafood, and pasta. At the Marina, the **Oriental Marina Inn & Restaurant,** Hodges Street, 252/249-2204, serves up grilled mahi-mahi, veal marsala, soft shell Cozumel, stuffed lobster, and Raccoon Creek mud pie for dessert. Upstairs, the **Topside Lounge** provides a nice view to admire while sipping a cold one; some nights feature live music up here or downstairs on the Tiki Bar.

## Washington

If you've ever sipped a "cup of Joe," thank Washington. And if you can't read the book of Exodus without picturing a Technicolor Edgar G. Robinson in robes, blame Washington. More on these later.

Washington's bigger than Bath or Oriental. Walk its earnest brick business blocks and you feel its regional importance: this is where local farming and fishing families would come weekdays to sell their produce and buy supplies, and then return on Saturday night to window-shop and maybe catch a vaudeville act over at the Turnage Theater. But because it's always taken the Cinderella's share of the regional economic duties, Washington isn't quite as homey or slow-paced as Oriental or even Elizabeth City. In fact, Washington's importance as a store for naval supplies brought its ruin in the Civil War. Neither army was going to waste a lot of men or ammunition to win, say, Bath. But the Union and the Confederacy fought hard for control of Washington, and finally the Federal troops burnt most of antebellum Washington to keep it out of Confederate hands. It burned again in 1900.

Consequently, Washington features a 1900s, Victorian ambience. Which in most places in America would make it seem old but, in the Albemarle, makes it seem like the new kid on the block. Nonetheless, Washington's trying hard to capture a bigger slice of the boating and tourist trade in these parts.

Washington was the first town in the U.S. named after George Washington. The settlement

downtown Washington

that formed here in the early 1770s initially went by the name Forks of the Tar, but local settlers (wisely) seized the historic moment and renamed their village after the general in 1776. This was a fairly risky maneuver, since the Revolution was far from won at that point, and the British would have wreaked particular havoc on a town bearing the hated Virginian's name.

Having cast its lot with the patriots, Washington did all she could to make sure they won. When the ports at Savannah, Charles Town, and Wilmington were bottled up by British ships, Washington took on the port duties, pulling in ships from other colonies and France to supply the troops. In doing so, by war's end, Washington found itself established as a regional center of commerce and culture. See it online at www.washingtonnctourism.com.

Down on the riverfront you'll find the **Washington/Beaufort County Chamber of Commerce,** 800/999-3857 or 252/946-9168, wash.beauf@coastalnet.com. Here you can pick up a self-guided tour map of the business area. Take a walk up there and you'll see a lot of renovation; a good bit of local effort and money is focused on revitalizing the **Turnage Theater,** 146-154 W. Main St., built 1916. As the only vaudeville stage in Washington, and for a long time the only movie theater, a young Red Skelton and Tex Ritter both tread its floorboards, as did with Roy Rogers and Trigger.

As far as the "cup of Joe," Josephus Daniels, U.S. Secretary of the Navy during World War I and later ambassador to Mexico under FDR, was born in Washington in the early part of the War Between the States. His father was a shipbuilder, but by the end of the war he was, like so many other fathers, a memory.

Nonetheless, the Daniels persevered. Josephus went on to become a famous Raleigh newspaperman. After being named Secretary of Navy under President (and former Wilmington resident) Woodrow Wilson, Daniels appointed a young Franklin Delano Roosevelt his Assistant Secretary. He stressed discipline and preparedness in his sailors, and this included banning consumption of beer and wine aboard ship. Consequently, all through World

War I, disgruntled, begrudgingly sober sailors were forced to sip coffee instead of the grog and ale that had heretofore been their right as sailors. Before long, they took to calling a cup of coffee a "cup of Joe" in honor of their commander.

After he become president, FDR repaid Daniels the favor by naming him Ambassador to Mexico. When Daniels took office, protesters threw rocks at the embassy, paving the way for future generations of North Carolinians to go get stoned in Mexico.

Cecil B. De Mille, who directed the blockbuster Biblical epic *The Ten Commandments,* hailed from Washington as well. You can see the De Mille family grave on the grounds of St. Peter's Episcopal Church, though both Cecil and filmmaker brother William are themselves buried in Hollywood. On the corner of Bonner and Main Streets, and you'll find a historic plaque celebrating Cecil and his father, playwright Henry C. De Mille.

Washington's also home to the **North Carolina Estuarium,** 223 East Water St., 252/948-0000, an aquarium with more than 200 exhibits that focus on marine life in the state's many, many estuaries, and on human interaction with the sea critters. Open Tuesday–Saturday 10 A.M.–4 P.M.; more in the summer. Admission runs $3 adult, $2 for K–12, free for kids under 5. Call for admission fees.

## Bath

Oldest city in North Carolina, Bath was founded in 1705, though French Protestant settlement in the area traces back to the 1690s. With easy river access and the Ocracoke Inlet to sail through on the way to England, this seemed like a good location. John Lawson, surveyor and author of the first history of Carolina (published in 1709) lived here and laid out the original town.

Even before the town's establishment, Carolina's first public library was founded here, consisting of books sent to St. Thomas Parish. Members of the parish established a free school for African-Americans and Native Americans. Bath, though only 50 people lived here in 1708, was the unquestioned social/political center of embryonic North Carolina, and as such, it saw much of the history of the region. The yellow fever epidemics of the early 1700s, political clashes, and the severe drought of 1711 all took their toll on the seedling city. When Tuscarora Indians attacked the Carolinian settlers, the survivors fled to Bath for safety. When piracy bloomed along the North Carolina coast, no less than Blackbeard was said to live here. The colonial General Assembly met in Bath three times in the 1740s and 1750s, and the town's name came up when Carolinians were trying to decide on a capital city, but Bath lost that contest. In 1776, Washington was founded 15 miles up the river and named the seat of Beaufort County government. Bath was drained of most all of its prestige and trade. Through the rest of the 18th, the 19th, and into the 20th, Bath has remained a small, quiet village on the water.

Stop by the **Historic Bath Visitor Center,** 207 Carteret St., 252/923-3971, website: www.pamlico.com/bath, for pamphlets, maps, and a fine 15-minute orientation video. The center's staff leads tours of the 1751 Palmer-Marsh House, the 1830 Bonner House, and the 1790 Van Der Meer House, as well as the 1734 St. Thomas Episcopal Church, the oldest church in North Carolina.

If you'd like to stay here, you'll probably want to do it at the popular **Bath Marina,** 252/923-5711, or at the **Pirate's Den Bed and Breakfast,** 116 S. Main St., 252/923-9571, a newly built (but traditionally styled) home specifically designed to serve as a B&B, run by native Bath residents Lesha and Roger Brooks. Rooms start around $75 in season, which includes a full Southern breakfast.

## Plymouth

Turn right on 64 to visit Plymouth. Civil War buffs know the name of this town well—Plymouth was the site of the largest battle in North Carolina, fought from April 17–20. To learn about the naval vessels involved in the fight, be sure to visit the **Port-O-Plymouth Civil War Museum,** 302 Water St., 252/793-1377, email: wccc@coastalnet.com.

## Windsor

Back on 17 headed north you'll pass through little Windsor, founded in 1768, featuring many antebellum homes and a nice river boardwalk. If you're traveling with kids, you may want to stop by **Livermon Recreational Park and Mini Zoo,** 101 York St., 252/794-5553, where they can see a buffalo and pet donkeys, llamas, goats, sheep, and about 30 other species of foreign and domestic animals. Here too you'll find the start (and finish) of the **Cashie Wetlands Walk,** through natural wetlands cypress and other flora. From the observation deck you should be able to spot a number of species of endangered birds. And if you'd rather paddle than walk, canoes are available at no charge.

North of town, try the delectable country cooking at **Heritage House,** 252/794-4567, North of town on U.S. 17 (a.k.a. "the Edenton Highway"). Pick up a great country breakfast, or a good BBQ sandwich with slaw for $2.85. The high end of the menu (a 10-ounce ribeye) tops out at $10.05. The pecan pie and peach cobbler aren't bad either. And, as with a lot of country restaurants, the folks at Heritage House offer various knickknacks to buy. Last time I was through, the wares included "Evange-Cubes," Rubik's Cubes that, when completed correctly, reveal paintings of various scenes from the Bible.

Outside of Windsor, you're welcome to visit the **Hope Plantation,** 252/794-3140, hope-plantation@coastalnet.com., featuring two National Register homes: the 1763 King Bazemore House and the 1803 Governor David Stone house. Both feature regional period furnishings. On the grounds is the Roanoke-Chowan Heritage Center, honoring the region's original dwellers. Admission is $6.50 for adults, $2 for students with I.D.

# EDENTON

With its sleepy 19th-century waterfront feel, Edenton, former colonial capital, is a nice place to quiet down for a couple of days and absorb the small-town, waterfront tranquility.

Named after Royal governor Charles Eden,

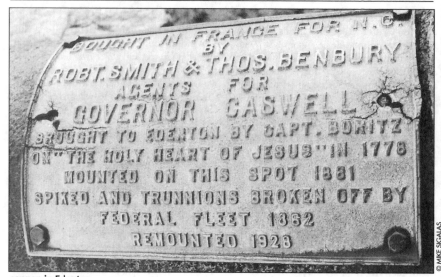

BOUGHT IN FRANCE FOR N.C.
BY
ROBT. SMITH & THOS. BENBURY
AGENTS      FOR
GOVERNOR  CASWELL
BROUGHT TO EDENTON BY CAPT. BORITZ
ON "THE HOLY HEART OF JESUS" IN 1778
MOUNTED ON THIS SPOT 1861
SPIKED AND TRUNNIONS BROKEN OFF BY
FEDERAL FLEET 1862
REMOUNTED 1928

© MIKE SIGALAS

cannon in Edenton

Edenton, founded 1715, nonetheless has something Edenic about it. This is the sort of slow-paced, scenic Southern town most people imagine when they come to explore the South, but often find difficult to locate in the flesh. Shortly after its founding, Edenton stole the limelight from Bath and became the chief city of the young colony. In the early days, when the capital was wherever the governor chose to live, many of the royal governors picked Edenton. The town became internationally famous in 1774 when, in the wake of the Boston Tea Party, local women staged a protest against the new royal taxes and signed a pledge to promise they wouldn't use East India tea. This incident became known as the Edenton Tea Party, and it not only inspired patriotic zeal among Americans, but the fact that fragile women were taking part in politics outraged the British and proved to them that Americans in general were clearly too uneducated and uncivilized to be taken seriously. Many of them still think this.

Depraved or not, Edenton managed to build an impressive collection of structures during the colonial period, many of which are still

standing today. Stop by the **Historic Edenton Visitor Center,** 108 N. Broad St., 252/482-2637, and pick up a guided tour of the distict that will take you through the 1736 St. Paul's Church, the 1758 Cupola House, the 1767 Chowan County Courthouse, and the home of early-19th-century U.S. Supreme Court Justice James Iredell.

Other than historic buildings, Edenton offers the **Emmrich Theatre Production Company,** which presents a variety of musicals—most with Christian themes—year-round at a variety of locations. Tickets run $14 for adults, $8 for kids. Call 252/482-4621 for information or tickets, or website: www.rockyhockplayhouse.com.

## Accommodations

Not quite downtown but a bit more affordable than most of the inns is the $42-a-night, **Coach House Inn,** 823 N. Broad St., 252/482-2107, which offers 38 rooms. The $32-a-night **Colonial Motel and Restaurant** is even further out at 1392 N. Broad St., 252/482-8010. You'll find the $65-a-night, 66-room **Travel Host Inn** at 501 Virginia Rd., 252/482-2017.

At the top of the list both in style and price

## THE EDENTON TEA PARTY

On October 25, 1774, Mrs. Penelope Barker led a tea party at Mrs. Elizabeth King's house in Edenton. There the two women and their 49 female guests signed a decree vowing to support the resolutions of the colonies' First Provisional Congress, which had banned, among other things, the importation of British tea.

That, anyway, is the legend—which has traditionally been accepted as fact in Edenton. A bronze teapot even marks the site of Mrs. King's house on the town's Old Courthouse Green.

The downside of the tea party legend is that it probably never happened. While it's near certain that 51 North Carolinian women signed their names to a protest document sent to England, many historians doubt whether they all ever sat down together—at Mrs. King's house, or anywhere else. The best anyone can figure, it's unlikely that the women, who hailed from at least five counties and represented a number of social classes, would or could have ever arranged a mass meeting. Nonetheless, in what is considered one of the earliest examples of political involvement by American women, the women did manage to sign the same piece of parchment, which likely was circulated petition-style. In part, it declared:

*The Provincial Deputies of North Carolina having resolved not to drink any more tea, nor wear any more British cloth & c., many ladies of this Province have determined to give a memorable proof of their patriotism, and have accordingly entered into the following honourable and spirited association. I sent it to you to shew you faire countrywomen, how zealously and faithfully American Ladies follow the laudable example of their husbands, and what opposition your Ministers may expect to receive from a people thus firmly united against them.*

This audacious show of feminine resolve shocked British sensibilities, confirming their conception of American men as barbarians who couldn't control their women any better than they could handle their liquor. A London cartoonist pictured the female signers gathered for a decadent tea party complete with snifters and paramours. Apparently when the colonials heard about the alleged incident, they decided to go along with the idea that an actual party had taken place, and before long the story of the Edenton Tea Party had settled into its present-day form.

The odd thing, of course, is that the tea party story imagines the women sitting around drinking tea, while the whole point of the resolution was that they vowed not to.

comes Arch and Jane Edwards' landmark **The Lords Proprietors' Inn,** 300 N. Broad St., 800/348-8933, website: www.edentoninn.com. Established in 1982, the inn consists of three restored homes on two acres of grounds in the Historic District. The Edwards moved down here from Washington, D.C., in 1980, convinced Edenton was the "prettiest little town in the South," and set about founding an inn. The three houses here today range in age from 80–200 years old, but they all share the feel of a traditional country inn. Most rooms run $155–190 a night, which includes a full breakfast. One of the new Satterfield Suites will run $225. Each room in the inn features its own private bath with antiques

and reproductions spanning the Federal to Victorian eras. Along with New Bern's The Harmony House, this is the only coastal North Carolina inn named as one of "The Fine Inns of North America," and the only hotel in all the North Carolina Coast listed as one of the National Trust for Historic Preservation's Historic Hotels.

Ask the Edwards about their golf packages; they can also put together a musical evening or an an art gallery viewing, or have an artist come over and teach a class on furniture painting. Tuesday through Saturday you can enjoy dinner at the Inn's **Whedbee House Dining Room and Patio.** Guests pay a "favored" rate of $45 a person. Or you can order à la carte; salads run about $10. Chef Kevin Yokley's entrees might include sautéed scallops and crabmeat sabayon, blue cheese–encrusted beef tenderloin, red snapper en papillote, or smoked pork tenderloin with apricot and Jerusalem artichoke relish (all $25 à la carte); or if a rich dessert is all the bookkeeper ordered, try the Frenched cranberry bread with homemade banana ice cream and butterscotch sauce, or the chocolate extravaganza (each $10 à la carte). The inn features an open wine service throughout the meal: for $10 a person, they'll keep pouring (even changing wines) as long as you keep drinking. Within limits, of course. Non-guests can eat here as well, but they pay $50 a person, plus a one-time $25 "membership" fee.

"Captain" Reuel and Marijane Schappel's **Albemarle House,** 204 West Queen St., 252/482-8204 ($80–125 d), and Bill and Phyllis Pepper's 1907 **Captains Quarters Inn,** 202 West Queen St., 800/482-8945 or 252/482-8945, website: www.captainsquartersinn.com (rooms starting at $95 d), are also popular stays in town.

Finally, you'll find the **Granville Queen Themed Inn,** 108 South Granville St., 252/482-5296, charges $95–120, with full breakfast. Themes in the nine rooms include the Egyptian Queen room, with leopardskin bed, a tomb-mural garden tub, and a bust of Queen Nefertiti. A quirky place with friendly people.

For something outside of town and not particularly historic, but still rich with atmosphere, consider **Trestle House Inn,** 632 Soundside Rd., 800/645-8466 or 252/482-2282, website: www.edenton.com/trestlehouse. Built in 1972 overlooking a wildlife refuge on a private lake, the inn derives its name from the old railroad trestle beams spanning the interior. Canada geese and other waterfowl frequent the lake. The five rooms start at $90 a night, which includes a gourmet breakfast overlooking the lake. Be sure to try innkeeper Peter Bogus' "Peter's Piping Hot Pepper Sauce" on your eggs. Children over the age of 5 are welcome. From Edenton, take Route 32 south 1.8 miles, turn right onto Soundside Road, and continue for 2.8 miles to the Trestle House Inn on the right side.

## Food

For casual but satisfying eating, head out to **Lane's Family BBQ and Seafood,** 421 E. Church Street, 252/482-4008, open 7 days a week 11 A.M.–8 P.M., and featuring a drawing of a pig on the menu—always a good sign. The barbecue's very good and reasonably priced ($2.50 for a sandwich), and so is the French silk pie and banana pudding ($2.50 per serving). Fresh fried or grilled fish runs around $9, and comes (as do all the dinners) with two vegetables, hush puppies, corn bread, or rolls. For something a little fancier downtown, there's **Waterman's Grill,** 427 S. Broad St., 252/482-7733, featuring good fish and homemade desserts.

# HERTFORD

If you're looking for the flavor of the small-town South, you probably couldn't find a better place to taste it than Hertford. As you enter town, you'll see a large mural painted across the side of an old brick building at Church and Grubb Streets. This is a revised version of the mural, which as late as 2000 sported a huge Confederate battle flag, being saluted by a soldier in Confederate gray.

The New York Yankees cap on the mural salutes the late Hall of Fame A's and Yankees pitcher Jim "Catfish" Hunter, who hailed from the Hertford area. In front of the **1828 Perquimans County Courthouse** you'll find a monument to Perquimans County's favorite son, with a detailed listing of his notable professional accomplishments, which started when he leapt from college ball to the Major Leagues without pitching a single game in the Minor Leagues, and later included a perfect game and five straight years winning 20-plus games before arm trouble cut off his career at age 33. Born in 1946, Hunter died in 1999 from Lou Gehrig's disease. Though the monument in front of the courthouse is far more impressive, you can see Hunter's grave at the Cedarwood Cemetery, Hertford, on the east side of Hyde Park Road.

But of course Hertford goes back a lot longer than Catfish Hunter or even the War Between the

Catfish Hunter's grave in Hertford

States. The oldest brick house in North Carolina, the 1730 **Newbold-White House,** 151 Newbold-White Road, off Harvey Point Road, 252/426-7567, is here, available for the viewing. Heck, even Gregory's 5&10 at 119 Church St., 252/426-7659, has been open since 1915. For a handy self-guided walking tour, pick up a tour booklet at the Perquimans County Chamber of Commerce at Hall of Fame Square on Church Street, 252/426-5657, website: www.perquimans.com. You'll also find some good antiquing along Church Street, near the courthouse.

## Accommodations

Hertford is the sort of place where you may well want to stay for the night. If so, you've really got two choices: the Colonial Revival **Covent Garden Inn,** at 107 Covent Garden, 252/426-5945, or the 1820 **Eagle and Anchor Inn,** 215 W. Market St., 252/426-8382. For a unique and private stay outside of town, Ben and Jackie Hobbs' **Beechtree Inn,** 948 Pender Rd.,

252/426-7815, hobbs@inteliport.com, a big spread where you'll stay in one of four small houses. The main house was built in 1710, but you'll be staying in one of four small cottages, each with private bath and fireplace; all 14 buildings on the property were built before 1840. The Hobbses charge $55–90 a night, which includes a full breakfast. If you're interested, Ben offers classes in furniture-making—he's a furniture-maker by trade. Stay from Monday through Saturday, attend class every day, and by the end of the week you'll have built a bedside table with a drawer using hand tools. To see some of Ben's work online, check out www.hobbsfurniture.com. Children are welcome, and so are pets, for a $5 fee. The Hobbs themselves have a cat and a dog, so allergy-sufferers beware. To get there from Hertford, take U.S. 17 toward Edenton, turn left onto Snug Harbor Road, then turn left at Pender Road, the first road on the left. The Beechtree is the first group of buildings. North of town on the way to Elizabeth City, turn right off 17 onto Great Neck Road and you'll find **1812 on the Perquimans,** 385 Old Neck Rd., 252/426-1812. Rooms in this historic old plantation house run $75–125 a night, which includes a full breakfast and full run of five acres of pasture and woodland featuring a private wharf, canoes, fishing, and sailboating.

## Food

For decent home cooking in a cozy environment right downtown, try **Frankies Hertford Café,** 127 N. Church St., 252/426-5593, or head over to **Tommy's Family Restaurant,** 720 Edenton Rd., 252/426-5020, for steaks, seafood, and chicken. For pit-cooked barbecue, head south of town on U.S. 17 to **Captain Bob's BBQ & Seafood,** 252/426-1811.

## ELIZABETH CITY

Called "The Harbor of Hospitality," and often named one of the best small art towns in America, Elizabeth City has five historic districts on the National Register. This town, begun in 1757 and formally founded in 1793, is most famous for the Elizabeth City Rose Buddies, a group of Elizabeth City residents who greet visiting boats at the town marina with a rosebud and a champagne reception. The tradition began in 1983 when retired mail carrier Fred Fearing and his friend Joe Kramer decided to thank the boaters who had chosen to dock at the town's expensive new Mariner's Wharf. Fred got the wine and Joe clipped some rosebuds—one for each of the 17 boats at the wharf—and they held their first reception. The boaters were delighted and vowed they'd return to what had heretofore been a rather unremarkable port. Fred and Joe, sensing they were on to something, threw a reception for the next group of boaters who came to stop in the local slips. Before long, word of Elizabeth City's hospitality had spread up and down the Intracoastal Waterway, and the tradition continues today. In exchange for this hospitality, the generally wealthy boaters spend a lot of money at the town's restaurants and shops—which is at least partly what the town had had in mind when it built the wharf in the first place. So famous are these receptions that even national television weatherman Willard Scott heard of them; he presented Fearing with a golf cart in which to make his rounds. For information on Elizabeth City, stop by the Chamber of Commerce at the corner of McMorrine and E. Ehringhaus Streets, 252/335-4365, website: www.elizcity.com. In keeping with the city's hospitable reputation, the folks there will let you check your email while you're there.

### Sights

The new waterfront home of the **Museum of the Albemarle,** currently at 1116 U.S. 17 S., 252/335-1453, is set to open sometime in 2003. Wherever the museum is when you get there, you'll find exhibits interpreting the human stories of the Albemarle, starting with the Native Americans who settled here first, on through the first English colonists, and the subsequent farmers and fishermen. Free admission.

### Accommodations

For places to sleep, consider the English-style **Elizabeth City Bed & Breakfast,** 108 E. Fearing St., 252/338-2177, $55–85, or the **Culpepper Inn** at 609 W. Main St., 252/335-1993, with 11 rooms, some with fireplaces and king-sized beds, for $65–105.

On the cheaper (around $50) but less charming side are the **Days Inn,** 308 S. Hughes St., 252/338-8900, with 48 rooms. Next door is the **Comfort Inn,** 306 S. Hughes Blvd., 252/338-8900, with 80 rooms and a pool.

### Food

For eats, try to catch a meal at the hip, over-the-water **Mulligan's Grille,** at the Marina, 252/338-2141—clearly less a restaurant in a small Southern town than it is a part of the sun-and-fun international boating scene. But still, the prices are reasonable, especially at lunch, when you can get sautéed shrimp over pasta for $7.95, along with the omnipresent $6 hamburger. Also waterfront is **Arena's Bakery and Deli,** 700 E. Main St., 252/335-2114, a good place to pick up breakfast. At 609 C St. you'll find the less hip but definitely filling **Southern Pig Bar-B-Que,** 252/338-6859.

For a good latte or mocha, see the **Elizabeth City Milling Company,** indoors on the wharf.

## SOUTH ON HIGHWAY 70
### Croatan National Forest

Take U.S. 70 south of New Bern and you'll soon be cutting through the 157,000-acre **Croatan National Forest,** a good place to stop for a picnic or camp, and home to the largest collection of carnivorous plants—including pitcher plants and Venus flytraps—in any national forest. Speaking of carnivorous, this is the northernmost home of the American alligator. But don't let that keep you from enjoying a nice hike—an easy one to start with is the 1.4-mile **Cedar Point Tideland Trail,** which makes a loop through hardwood- and pine-laced estuary and tidal marsh areas. You can hide behind wildlife viewing blinds along the way and take some great nature shots. To get there heading south on U.S. 70, turn right at Roberts Road, left at the T, and right again at Millis Road. Turn left at the next T on to Whithouse Forks Road, then merge onto 48, and turn right on Dudley Rd. Look for the signs to Cedar Point Tideland Trail. You can camp out here too. Or you can camp at **Flanner Beach,** a campground further north and closer to (but still well off) U.S. 70.

## Morehead City

Morehead City was founded in 1857 by John Motley Morehead, former governor of North Carolina, as a land-development scheme. The population got a boost during the Civil War when the crews of several British ships, unable to leave because of the Federal blockade, decided to settle here. It has developed into the state's second largest port. Today, Morehead's historically businesslike waterfront has begun sprucing itself up with a handful of good restaurants, but the town gets most of its attention for two of its fall festivals. Most famous is the annual **Bald Is Beautiful Convention** at the end of September, perennially drawing international media coverage. Founded by Morehead City's John Capps in the early 1970s, the convention celebrates "hairfree" living with big dinners, a deep-sea fishing trip, the traditional "Blessing of the Bald Heads," and several contests, along with motivational speeches and workshops. For further information, call John Capps himself, 252/726-1855.

The second festival is less unique but still very enjoyable. On the first weekend in October, the North Carolina Seafood Festival draws people from across the state, allegedly to "celebrate seafood culture," but mainly to eat lots and lots of seafood. Various events involving said eating include the Opening Ceremonies Luncheon (public invited, $15) and the very popular Habitat Fish Fry at 5 P.M. on the waterfront. Live bands play, sailing boats compete in a regatta, and fisherfolk compete in fishing contests; carnival rides run all weekend, and some 100 street vendors offer seafood snacks of various sorts. You can usually tour a couple of naval ships and Coast Guard cutters as well. And on Sunday there's the Blessing of the Fleet.

As far as permanent eating spots in Morehead: One day I asked an employee down at the Beaufort waterfront which of the many waterfront fish places was her favorite. She pointed at this Beaufort spot and that, but never with much enthusiasm. And then finally, with a look to either side, she whispered, "But really, the *best* fish is up in Morehead City at the Sanitary."

Since 1938, **Sanitary Fish Market & Restaurant,** 501 Evans St., 252/247-3111, has become a landmark around here, a large unpretentious place with views of the water and boats, with the owner walking around greeting everyone and the front register offering T-shirts and bumper stickers to go. And the seafood—prepared a number of ways but fantastic fried—really is wonderful. The hush puppies may be the best around.

Why "Sanitary Restaurant?" Obviously, an earlier generation thought that naming restaurants "sanitary" would make us want to eat there (a second Sanitary lived a long life in Folly Beach, S.C., before closing a few years back). But to most of us living today, it's kind of like calling a place "Roach-Free Diner." We worry when restaurateurs doth protest too much. Fortunately, the Smuckers Effect seems to be in play here: with a name like Sanitary, it has to be good—and it is.

You'll find at least two other eating spots of note on the Morehead City waterfront. First comes the Sanitary's next-door neighbor, **Amos Mosquito's Swampside Cafe,** 509 Evans St., 252/247-6222 (apparently shooting for the Smuckers Effect themselves). Dinners feature seafood and creatively cooked meats. A casual place with a great deck overlooking the boats. For coffee, baked goods, and Internet access, **Coffee Affair,** is a pleasant, classy coffee place right over the water.

Morehead City hosts the **Carteret County Tourism Development Bureau,** where you can pick up information about Beaufort, Atlantic Beach, and Morehead City. Stop by 3409 Arendell St., Morehead City, 252/726-8148.

# Beaufort and Vicinity

First known as Fish Town, Beaufort (BOWferd) is North Carolina's third-oldest city, founded in 1709, though the town wasn't formally laid out until 1722. The local settlers took a lot of grief from the Tuscarora during the Tuscarora War. Blackbeard liked to stay here in Beaufort, and the town even had a certain marital nostalgia for him; he is said to have hung one of his wives here. In 1747, Beaufort residents were booted from their own city by marauding Spanish pirates, though they returned a couple days later with guns and retook the town.

One of the more colorful characters from Beaufort's past would be Captain Otway Burns, a privateer—a government-endorsed pirate—for the U.S. against British ships during the War of 1812. You can see his grave at the Old Town Cemetery. As commander of the *Snapdragon,* Burns terrorized British merchant ships in both hemispheres and caused the British so much grief that they offered $50,000 reward for his capture. Finally, in 1814, the British did capture the *Snapdragon,* only to find that Burns had gone ashore to tend to his rheumatism. Later he served in the General Assembly, and Andrew Jackson appointed him as a lighthouse keeper where, according to all accounts, he lived a raucous good time to the end.

Since the late 1800s, Beaufort has been a popular vacation spot. Today, with its home prices soaring and its downtown restaurants jammed, the town happily lives off its good looks and storied past.

## SIGHTS

The **Mattie King Davis Art Gallery,** at the Old Town Beaufort Restoration Complex, gives local artisans a chance to show their paintings, ceramics, and weavings. Open Monday–Saturday 10 A.M.–4 P.M.

*Blackbeard liked to stay here in Beaufort, and the town even had a certain marital nostalgia for him; he is said to have hung one of his wives here.*

If local history interests you, stop by the **Beaufort Historic Site,** set in the 1825 Josiah Bell House, at 100 Block Turner St., 800/575-7483 or 252/728-5225, website: www.blackbeard thepirate.com. Here you can pick up visitor's information and embark (April–October) on guided tours of Beaufort's historic district via double-decker bus ($5), or on foot. Open Monday–Saturday 8:30 A.M.–4:30 P.M. One of the houses it passes, the 1698 Hammock House (Beaufort's oldest), once served as an inn and was often host to Edward Teach, a.k.a. Blackbeard. One legend even has it that he hung one of his wives from a branch of the large oak tree outside, and that even today, sometimes, *late at night. . . .*

A tour of homes departing from the Bell house also runs $5 and will take you through the interior of an apothecary shop, courthouse, and jail, as well as various historic homes.

The **North Carolina Maritime Museum,** 315 Front St., 252/728-7317, website: www .ah.dcr.state.nc.us/maritime/default.htm, presents in-depth and hands-on exhibits that give visitors a good sense of the region's maritime history, which is to say, its *history,* since Beaufort's past and the men and women who worked and docked at its waterfront are inextricably linked. Some interesting relics from what appears to be *Queen Anne's Revenge,* Blackbeard's flagship, which sank off Ocracoke. Also fascinating is the sealable floating car used in the 1890s for ferrying victims from shipwrecked or sinking vessels. Across the street in the Watercraft Center, you can watch the shipbuilders constructing and restoring traditional wooden boats. Free.

If you look out across the water to the unpopulated islands that face Beaufort, you're looking at the **Rachel Carson National Estuarine Preserve,** 216 Front St. (office), named for the famous author of *Silent Spring,* who based her ecologically groundbreaking book partly on research conducted in the Beaufort area. To get there you'll need to get a boat to take you, but it's worth the trip to explore the marshes and flats that are home to wild horses, 160 species of birds, and various other wildlife. A great place for shelling and clamming. Call 252/728-2170 for information. Volunteers lead field trips to the Reserve during the spring and summer.

## ACCOMMODATIONS

Prices aren't cheap at Beaufort—at least not from late spring to fall. During the winter they drop dramatically, but even in-season you can get a break if you're here during the week, rather than on a weekend.

### $100–150

On paper, the **Inlet Inn,** 601 Front St., 252/728-3600, sounds like another historic B&B, but it's the most modern-looking thing on the waterfront. Still, the location's great, the prices can be reasonable ($65 in the low season, starting at $129 in high), and most of the rooms feature a waterfront view. Some of the rooms have a fireplace; some have porches. Breakfast included in the price of the room.

Often named with North Carolina's top inns, Sam and Linda Dark's 250-year-old **Cedars Inn,** 305 Front St., 252/728-7036, stands back above the waterfront, within easy walking distance of everything. The Cedars offers 12 rooms/suites with private baths, fireplaces, full Southern breakfasts, a wine bar, and bicycles for exploring the boardwalk and historic area. Rates start at $115 a night, in-season. The 1866 **Pecan Tree Inn,** 116 Queen St., 252/728-6733 stands half a block from the Beaufort waterfront and offers seven rooms, two of them suites with Jacuzzis and king-size canopy beds.

A unique place to stay is **The Carteret County Home Bed and Breakfast,** 299 N.C. 101, 252/728-4611, built in 1914, and one of the East Coast's last standing county homes, the place where local residents down on their fortunes would live and work. Now you work else-

where and then pay to stay here. Ah, progress. In return you get double the room—the individual rooms have been combined into two-room suites. To lay on the irony thicker, consider that many people who visit Beaufort are retirees drawing Social Security pensions, and it was the advent of Social Security and welfare that made poorhouses like the Carteret County Home go broke in the first place. The home closed in 1944, and reopened periodically through the years for a variety of uses. Generally its main use was to serve as the local eyesore. Then some folks converted the home into a B&B and got it listed on the National Register of Historic Places. Nowadays owners Terry and Nan O'Pray run the place, and advertise themselves as "the grumpy hosts with the lumpy beds, bad food, and nasty cat," though, they're quick to admit "we like to think that is really false advertising."

### Diving House

If you're in Beaufort to dive, here's a little-known and possibly inexpensive way to stay in town, especially if you're with a larger group. **Discovery Diving Company,** 414 Orange St., 252/728-2265, offers two dormitory-style diving lodges for its customers and their families. Rates run $11 a person to stay in one of the two lodges, with a minimum of $77 a night for your group. The two lodges are divided up to provide four different lodgings, with beds for 8, 10, 14, or 21. Lodges include kitchens, but you'll need to bring your own linens.

## FOOD

**Loughry's Landing,** 510 Front St., 252/728-7541, sits on the boardwalk, serving up steamed crab legs, oysters, clams, fish, and other goodies from the sea.

On a side street, **Beaufort Grocery Co.,** 117 Queen St., 252/728-3899, offers good regional dishes with a gourmet flair in a quaint former market. Easier to find on Front Street is **Clawson's 1905 Restaurant,** 425 Front St., 252/728-2133, another old grocery store with an engaging atmosphere and popular seafood, steaks, and more on the menu. **The Dockhouse Seafood**

Clawson's 1905 Restaurant in Beaufort

© MIKE SIGALAS

**Restaurant,** 500 Front St., 252/728-4872, is usually crowded with suntanned, boat-related people drinking beers and eating fried things. A raucous good time, right on the waterfront. The casual **Finz Grill,** 330 Front St., 252/728-7459, comes with good recommendations and offers deck dining on the water.

The **Royal James Cafe,** 117 Turner St., 252/728-4573, is about as unpretentious as it sounds fancy: a café, poolroom, and bar all in one, where the patty melts and cue sticks give a nod to Beaufort's humbler, fishing village past. Founded about the same time as the Waffle House chain, the Royal James hasn't quite multiplied in the same way, yet people keep coming back for the simple café food and the good company. So too at **Roland's BBQ,** 815 Cedar St., 252/728-1953. It just keeps on doing what it does best, fortifying the air around Beaufort with vitamins P, I, and G.

For ice cream, **The General Store,** 515 Front St., 252/728-7707, offers 32 flavors, along with Matthews coffee, souvenirs, gifts, a laundry room,

and—like a good general store—a little of everything else.

## Nightlife

In addition to the spots mentioned above, add the **BackStreet Pub,** Middle Lane, 252/728-7108, which serves no food, but does offer a wide selection of beer and wines, and often features live entertainment.

## RECREATION AND INFORMATION

### Paddling

People like paddling around the Rachel Carson Reserve, Cape Lookout, and the Shackleford Banks; on the boardwalk you'll find both **AB Kayaks,** 252/728-6330, and **Outer Island Kayak Adventures,** 252/222-3420, ready and willing to get you on the water.

### Diving

**Discovery Diving,** 414 Orange St., 252/728-

2265, website: www.discoverydiving.com/, charges $30 for a full set of gear; $85 for a full day with two dives; or $50 for half a day, not including equipment. Dive sites include the WWII German *U-352* sub, resting 115 feet underwater, the *Proteus* ocean liner, and many more. Call for information and available charters.

## Boat Tours

**Mystery Tours,** Beaufort Waterfront, 252/726-6783, sounds like it gives ghost tours, but it doesn't. It does give scenic harbor tours, and occasionally it's overtaken by "pirates"—but they're flesh-and-blood reenactors, not ghosts. **Lookout Express,** also run by Mystery Tours, 252/728-6997, takes up to 149 passengers out to Cape Lookout, or on morning dolphin cruises or evening sunset cruises. Both the Mystery boat and the Lookout boat can be chartered. Call the numbers above, or see www.mysteryboattours.com for more information.

## Information

For more information about Beaufort, Atlantic Beach, or Morehead City, stop by the **Carteret County Tourism Development Bureau,** 3409 Arendell Street in Morehead City, 252/726-8148, website: www.sunnync.com.

# ATLANTIC BEACH

*Atlantic (685 pop.), on a bluff of a wide peninsula on Core Sound, is a fishing village. Gnarled and stunted water oaks, wind-swept landward, cluster near the highway in the back yards of houses facing the sound. A little wooden church nestles in a grove of moss-grown dwarf oaks. Here and there throughout the village are clumps of myrtle and yaupon.*

*Atlantic Beach, as described in* **North Carolina: The WPA Guide to the Old North State,** *1939*

It doesn't look the way it did in 1939, but even then, Atlantic Beach was a popular summertime vacation spot. Ever since promoters built a large pavilion on the sand in 1887, Atlantic has been

*the* beach fun capital of the Bogue Banks. With a year-round population of 1,900 and a seasonal population much, much larger, Atlantic Beach is typical in spirit and in the flesh of what you'll find up at Nags Head or down at Wrightsville Beach.

## Sights

Head seven miles northwest of Atlantic Beach and you'll find the 298-acre **Theodore Roosevelt Natural Area,** named for patron Alice Hoffman's famous environmentalist ancestor and featuring observation decks, two short nature trails, and the **North Carolina Aquarium at Pine Knoll Shores,** 1 Roosevelt Dr., 252/247-4003, website: www.aquariums.state.nc.us/aquariums. The least-visited and the last of the state's three state aquariums to receive its major overhaul (the planned funds were shunted to hurricane recovery); the Pine Knolls aquarium is still worth a visit for the close-up views it offers of the local marsh and sea life, including the ever-popular shark and alligator exhibits, a shipwreck tank, freshwater tanks, a sea turtle exhibit, and a retooled touch tank. $4 for adults, $2 ages 6–17. Open daily 9 A.M.–5 P.M.

Civil War buffs will want to visit **Fort Macon State Park,** 2300 East Fort Macon Rd., 252/726-3775. Fort Macon was built in 1826–34 and partly designed by a young lieutenant named Robert E. Lee. Later, the Confederate army occupied the fort during the first part of the War Between the States, but they surrendered it to U.S. generals John C. Parke and Ambrose Burnside on April 26, 1862. Free admission and museum. Guided tours available during the summer. Also a good spot for picnicking, fishing, hiking, and swimming.

## Accommodations

A funky find on the causeway is the **Caribbe Inn,** 309 E. Fort Macon Rd., 252/726-0051, website: www.caribbe-inn.com, with 10 rooms, two efficiencies and one suite on the waterfront, plus pier access and a fish-cleaning area, and boat slips if you're coming in by water. Each room is brightly painted with visions of tropical fish. $42–72 a night, $53–83 a night

© MIKE SIGALAS

**Atlantic Beach pier**

for the efficiencies. Ask about weekly rates, as well as fishing and diving packages. **Atlantic Beach-Days Inn,** 602 W. Fort Macon Rd., 800/972-3297 or 252/247-6400 runs $91 in high season, considerably lower in the cold-weather months. At the **Windjammer Inn,** 103 Salter Path Road, 800/233-6466 or 252/247-7123, depending on the room, the day, and the month, prices run $51–120 a night. Every room faces the oceanfront, though, and has a balcony.

Of course, a time-honored way to approach an Atlantic Beach visit is to rent a cottage or condo. Call 800/334-2737 to talk to the people at **Tetterton Management Group.** Or call **Rains Realty and Rentals,** Atlantic Beach Causeway Shopping Center, 252/247-5141, website: www.rainsrealty.com. A house to sleep six to eight should run $600–1,000 a week.

### Food

Mainly it's burgers and fried shrimpville on the island, but **Channel Marker Restaurant,** at the foot of the bridge, 252/247-2344, boasts a waterfront atrium lounge and dining room that overlook Bogue Sound. Fresh seafood, full bar.

For something completely different, **New York Deli,** in the Causeway Shopping Center, 252/726-0111, serves up good South Philly cheesesteaks, subs and salads, deli meats and cheeses, as well as breakfast items all day.

## POINTS SOUTH

### Swansboro

West of the Bogue Banks on N.C. 24, tiny Swansboro, founded ca. 1730, keeps getting mentioned as a place nobody's heard of, but based on the number of restaurants and other traveler-oriented businesses opening up there, clearly it's catching on. Still, this is a relatively quiet and certainly pretty little waterfront town right on the White Oak River. It has some interesting places to catch a meal, including **Yana's Ye Olde Drugstore Restaurant,** 119 Front St., 919/326-5501, a 1950s-styled diner. Get a burger or a piece of homemade pie and enjoy.

### Fort Lejeune

To anyone unaccustomed to military life, it can be sort of ominous driving into Fort Lejeune, what with the signs warning of overhead artillery fire and the little yellow signs reading "Tank Xing." This is the world's most complete amphibious training base, where men practiced for the Normandy invasion. The Few and the Proud are very proud but not so few hereabouts: you'll find a greater concentration of U.S. Marines in Fort Lejeune than anywhere else on the planet—in peacetime. Some 40,000 Marines and sailors live and train here. If you'd like to see what they're up to, stop by the **Fort Lejeune Visitors Center** at the main gate, 910/326-4881, and pick up a Visitors' Day Pass and a self-guided tour brochure.

If you visit on the right day, as you approach the base on N.C. 24, you'll see a long stretch of highway where the side fences are draped with sheets made into touching (and not uncommonly frisky) messages to returning spouses and lovers returning from overseas duty via buses that will pass that way.

## Peletier

Two miles north of N.C. 58's junction with N.C. 24, on N.C. 58, this tiny town is home to the 2,100-seat Crystal Coast Amphitheater, 800/662-5969 or 252/393-8373, where local thespians stage the outdoor three-hour musical Christian passion drama *Worthy Is the Lamb,* said to be the only fully orchestrated musical passion production in the United States. The Easter story gets a full-throttle and, even for most cynics, a moving presentation here: musical numbers, detailed costumes, real horses and chariots, a real river, and even a re-created city of Jerusalem—all out under the stars in a small town in North Carolina. Performances mid-June through August are Thursday–Saturday 8:30 P.M.; September performances Friday and Saturday 7:30 P.M. $14 adults, $6 children 6–12.

## Hammocks Beach State Park

The highlight of Hammocks Beach State Park is that for a small fee you can camp primitively on undeveloped, 892-acre Bear Island. To get there you'll need to paddle over, take a boat taxi, or take the ferry that runs from Memorial Day to Labor Day, Friday–Sunday 9:30 A.M.–4:30 P.M. Pick it up four miles south of Swansboro on N.C. 24. Call 910/326-4881 for information.

## Topsail Island

Pronounced TOPsul, of course. Even if it is on the opposite coast from the one Jan and Dean were singing about, I still get a kick out of driving into **Surf City.** Once there, everything takes on a special importance. How can a person *not* stop in at the Surf City Surf Shop or take a walk along the Surf City Pier?

Surf City is a sun-and-fun, vacation-centered town. I can't tell you about the "two girls for every boy" ratio (I'm married, so maybe some other boy got three) but Surf City is otherwise a traditional North Carolina beach with arcade-fortified fishing piers, lots of rental houses, some seafood joints, and a miniature golf course. With the exception of some Hilton Headesque developments, the rest of Topsail is a lot like Surf City; a great place to rent a beach house with the family or spend a private weekend with that special fishing rod, and maybe not such a great place if you're looking for historic sites and cultural events. For the fishing angle, you might consider a stay in North Topsail at William and Kay Smith's **Seaview Pier and Motel,** 1 New River Inlet Rd., 910/328-3171. They offer a new 1,000-foot pier and 20 rooms at around $60 a night. If it's nightlife you crave, drive your woody to Surf City's **The Original Mermaid,** 1702 N. New River Dr., 910/328-4042, for bar food, drink specials, a deck, and live entertainment on the weekends. For more information on the island, call 800/626-2780, or stop by the Greater Topsail Area Chamber of Commerce and Tourism at 205 S. Topsail Dr., Surf City, website: www.topsailcoc.com.

# Wilmington and the Southern Coast

The lesser-known sister of Southern belles Charleston and Savannah, Wilmington is where the slave-driven antebellum planter culture of the Carolina Lowcountry and Virginia Tidewater had its greatest hold in North Carolina. In the late 1800s, it sported one of the state's largest African-American populations, which allowed Republicans to stay in power here longer than elsewhere in the state. In the 1890s, the Wilmington area was the scene of one of the state's ugliest race riots. In the 1960s, Wilmington would again play host to a divisive racial event.

But if Wilmington has had to wrestle with the challenges of its diversity—the town, after all, produced both Michael Jordan and country fiddler Charlie Daniels in a single generation—it has also been shaped, as all port towns are, by the constant coming and going of ships from distant shores. Even in its most self-reflective years, when the state put its nose to the grindstone and its hands over its ears, North Carolina breathed at Wilmington.

Wilmington is by far the best port in the state; consequently, this is where much of the state's history has been centered, particularly during the Revolution and the War Between the States, when both

Kure Beach Pier

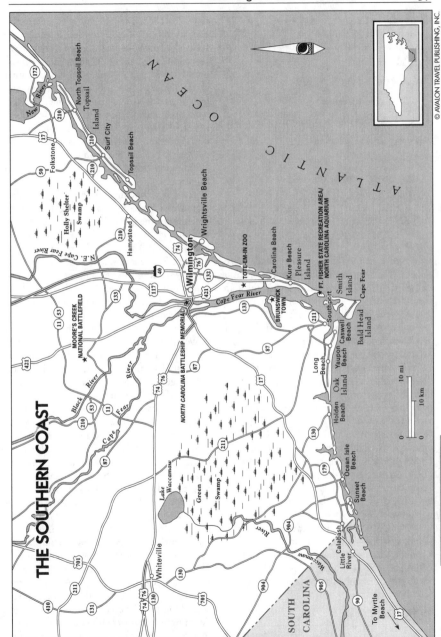

THE SOUTHERN COAST

© AVALON TRAVEL PUBLISHING, INC.

WILMINGTON

## SOUTHERN COAST HIGHLIGHTS

**Calabash**

**Cape Fear Museum,** Wilmington

**Wilmington waterfront**

**Fort Fisher State Recreation Area,** Kure Beach

**Poplar Grove Plantation**

**Southport**

**USS *North Carolina* Memorial**

**Wilmington Railroad Museum**

**Wrightsville Beach**

the British and the Union armies made a bee-line for Wilmington at the commencement of hostilities. If Wilmington is where the state breathes, military enemies wanting to smother the state would naturally head to the port city.

In recent years, anchored by culturally minded Wilmington and featuring a flock of popular coastal islands, the Northern Carolina coast from Wrightsville Beach south to the South Carolina border has come increasingly in vogue as the inland cities of North Carolina balloon with hard-working researchers and computer wonks who want to hit the beach now and again. The southern border across from Little River, S.C., marks the southern edge of this region, but where the north part of the Southern coast ends and where the southern part of the central North Carolina coast begins is purely arbitrary. For our purposes here I've drawn the line below the southern edge of Topsail Island.

Climate in the Wilmington area is mild; it rarely gets above the 80s in the summer and is normally in the 50s during winter months. It rains here a lot—locals can expect 50 inches of rain. Bring an umbrella or be ready to buy one.

## HISTORY

North Carolina's southern coast has winced in the spotlight of American history at least three times. In 1865, after the fall of Charleston to Federal troops, Wilmington remained the one main Confederate port still open along the Atlantic seaboard; blockade runners ducked in and out of Wilmington, hauling cotton and other local produce to the Caribbean and Europe, and bringing back badly needed supplies for local residents and for Robert E. Lee's starving, poorly armed troops up in Virginia. Wilmington quickly became the North's primary focus, and with the fall of Fort Fisher on January 15, 1865, Wilmington closed and the war ended within months.

The federal government's occupation of Wilmington, and its attempts to reconfigure the social structure of the Cape Fear region, led directly to Wilmington's second appearance on history's center stage. In 1898, white Democrats incensed by black/Republican rule marched through the streets wielding torches, killing a number of blacks who stood up to them, chasing out the white Republican mayor, and replacing him with one of their own.

The white Democrats may have recovered power over Wilmington, but Wilmington would not recover its economic momentum for most of a century. In fact, part of the reason Wilmington is such a fine place to visit today is *because* of the Wilmington Riot of 1898. The riot, called by some historians the sole coup d'état in American history, disenfranchised the ascending black middle class in the area and sent many of them packing for Northern climes. This drastic draining of area productivity and morale, combined with exterior factors, turned North Carolina's biggest city into something of a backwater. Hence the building booms of the turn of the century in many Southern towns did not affect Wilmington, preserving her colonial ambience. Things began to look up a bit after World War II, but then in 1960 the Atlantic Coastline Railroad stopped running along the Wilmington-Weldon line. This railroad line, combined with the shipping lane along the Cape Fear River, had brought Wilmington whatever affluence and influence it had known, and now it was gone. Some 4,000 railroad-dependent families transferred

# THE WILMINGTON TEN

If life under the rule of "separate but equal" was rarely equal, it was never cost-efficient. All the duplication of public services—from duplicate regional colleges down to the famed dual drinking fountains—burned a hole through the pocket of Carolinians and other Southerners during the already lean Jim Crow years. When desegregation finally came, this redundancy became doubly apparent. The Wilmington Board of Education, for instance, realized that it now had two high schools within five blocks of each other, and with many white students fleeing to private schools, it had only one campus' worth of students. In 1971, the board decided to demote Williston to a junior high, and move Williston's students to New Haven, which was deemed the better facility.

But the African-American students who'd attended Williston didn't want to switch. After all, with all the white flight, blacks made up the majority in the new combined student body. So why did *they* have to walk the five blocks to attend the "white kids' school"? The African-American students began boycotting classes that winter.

The board refused to be moved by the boycotters, or by their coordinator, the Reverend Benjamin Chavis, a central Carolina native, but then a professional field organizer was sent in by the Ohio-based Commission for Racial Justice of the United Church of Christ. Roused by Chavis's rhetoric and empowered by his organizing, the students staged protests at school headquarters and City Hall. Violence erupted between protesters and white residents.

And then somebody firebombed the white-owned Mike's Grill and Grocery, at Sixth and Nun Streets. Fortunately, no one was killed, but the blast put Wilmington on the edge of hysteria, open race war, or both. Police quickly arrested Chavis and nine others—six of them high school students, and all but one of them black. Three black witnesses testified that the suspects had conspired to burn the store and then shoot at responding police and firefighters. Based on this eyewitness testimony, in October of the following

year all 10 were convicted and sent to prison for long terms—the shortest of which was 23 years.

The appeals began—first in the N.C. Court of Appeals, and then in state Supreme Court. Finally, in January 1976, the appeals of the prisoners reached the U.S. Supreme Court, which turned deaf ears to the case. The Ten had hit the end of the line.

But then something unexpected happened. One of the three key prosecution witnesses, Allen Hall, recanted, signing a sworn affidavit claiming that he'd been coerced to give false testimony in the trial. The following year, the other two main witnesses against the 10 claimed they too had lied to the jury under pressure in 1972—but were now telling the truth.

Those who had always believed in a conspiracy involving a Klansman bomber and an ATF/FBI frame job claimed vindication, and all political heck broke loose. In 1977, author and poet James Baldwin took up the cause, pleading the Ten's case in his widely published "Open Letter to Mr. Carter." The next year, Amnesty International declared that the Wilmington Ten were now being held purely for political motives—making them the USA's first political prisoners.

Finally, in 1979, under not a little pressure himself, Governor Jim Hunt reduced the Ten's sentences, setting most of them free with the five years they'd already served. A year later, based on the witnesses' recanting of their testimonies, a federal appeals court overturned all of the Ten's convictions.

Sprung from his cell, Chavis attacked life with a vengeance. He earned degrees at Duke, UNC Chapel Hill, and Howard University, fathered eight children, penned a number of books, and kept a high profile in the African-American rights movement through his speaking engagements. In 1993, he was elected the youngest-ever executive director of the NAACP, and in 1995 served as national director of Louis Farrakhan's Million-Man March. In 1997, Chavis converted to Islam and changed his name to Minister Benjamin Muhammad.

down to Jacksonville, Florida, and Wilmington was left financially desolate.

Racial conflicts brought Wilmington international recognition for a third time in 1971, after a firebombing and the subsequent arrest of Civil Rights activist the Rev. Benjamin Chavis and nine others. The "Wilmington Ten" made the city's name synonymous with racial division.

But even as the Wilmington Ten were toiling in prison, the town's oldest friend, the Cape Fear River, continued flowing by. And that got some forward-looking people to thinking. As a young Michael Jordan pounded Wilmington's asphalt courts, the city managed to get the decaying wharfs and business blocks downtown declared a National Historic District, and business/community groups like the Downtown Area Revitalization Effort encouraged the refurbishing of old buildings and houses. In addition to successfully preserving more than 200 acres of historic downtown, the effort bolstered Wilmington's sagging civic pride.

Little by little, the rest of the world began to discover the well-preserved colonial buildings, and suddenly Wilmington found itself named as one of America's fastest-growing areas. Its population grew by some 20 percent during the 1990s, thanks in part to the completion of I-40, which made the city much more accessible to the rest of the Eastern seaboard.

And so, as with Charleston, whose riches came in part from slave trading, Wilmington's clouded past has preserved its gleaming future.

# Wilmington

## ORIENTATION

Logistically, Wilmington sprawls. The city began with historic downtown Wilmington, along the Cape Fear River. When things got ugly and dangerous down on the waterfront, the suburbs began expanding, primarily southeast, toward the beach. Nowadays it's pretty much one big strip between Wilmington and Wrightsville Beach. One of the chief issues you'll hear discussed on local talk radio stations is the area's traffic problem: there's just too much land to cover for most Wilmington-area residents driving from work to home and back, and not enough lanes to prevent gridlock.

Highways U.S. 17 (east-west), N.C. 132, and U.S. 74/76 (north-south) are the big ones around here. You'll use one or more of these to get just about anywhere.

### Downtown Wilmington

Historic downtown Wilmington is one of the true gems of North Carolina's coast. The town rose to power as a shipping port with important, early railroad connections. The railroad left, but in the 1980s and 1990s, Hollywood found in Wilmington a friendly, relatively inexpensive place to shoot both interiors and exteriors. Along with the "biz" came money, and with the money came chic restaurants with international cuisine, a vaguely upscale "underground" tone, and a lot of three-dollar coffees. Though at this writing some of the movie money (and excitement) has left for Vancouver and Toronto, things have reached a critical mass here; expensive condos and gourmet eateries continue to blossom here along the Cape Fear, and the riverfront won't be reverting to its 1970s dilapidated state anytime soon.

A main boulevard downtown is Water Street, which fronts the river; a block inland comes the busier and more businesslike **Front Street.** Both of these streets are thriving with cultural and countercultural shops and bistros; local thought has it that the dining places on Water cater to tourists with money to burn. Anchoring the south end of Water Street is a great little shopping complex called **Chandler's Wharf,** which includes both an indoor market and a five-acre outdoor area with a cobblestone street and two well-established waterfront seafood houses, Elijah's and the Pilot House. At the opposite (north) end of the waterfront you'll find the **Cotton Exchange,** 321 N. Front St., 910/343-9896,

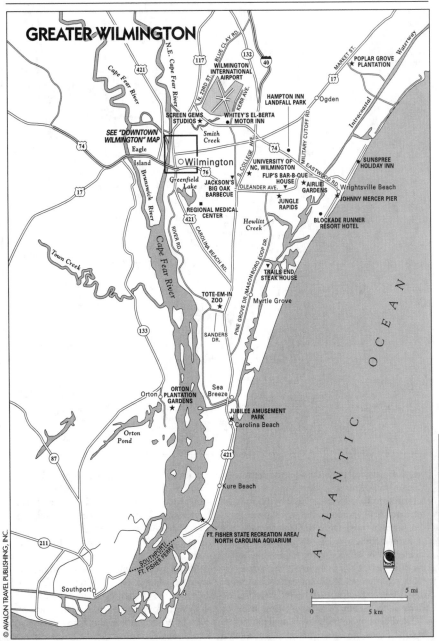

GREATER WILMINGTON

N.E. Cape Fear River
Cape Fear River
117
421
132
40
WILMINGTON INTERNATIONAL AIRPORT
BLUE CLAY RD.
N. 23RD ST.
KERR AVE.
MARKET ST.
POPLAR GROVE PLANTATION
17
Ogden
HAMPTON INN LANDFALL PARK
SCREEN GEMS STUDIOS ★
WHITEY'S EL-BERTA MOTOR INN ●
74
SEE "DOWNTOWN WILMINGTON" MAP
Smith Creek
Eagle
○ Wilmington
Island
76
UNIVERSITY OF NC, WILMINGTON
74
S. COLLEGE AVE.
MILITARY CUTOFF RD.
EASTWOOD RD.
SUNSPREE HOLIDAY INN
Greenfield Lake
JACKSON'S BIG OAK BARBECUE
FLIP'S BAR-B-QUE HOUSE ▼
OLEANDER AVE.
★ AIRLIE GARDENS
Wrightsville Beach
Intracoastal Waterway
JOHNNY MERCER PIER
Brunswick River
■ REGIONAL MEDICAL CENTER
421
JUNGLE RAPIDS
Hewlitt Creek
BLOCKADE RUNNER RESORT HOTEL
Town Creek
Cape Fear River
RIVER RD.
CAROLINA BEACH RD.
TRAILS END STEAK HOUSE
PINE GROVE DR./MASONBORO LOOP DR.
TOTE-EM-IN ZOO
Myrtle Grove
133
SANDERS DR.
Sea Breeze
ORTON PLANTATION GARDENS ★
Orton ○
JUBILEE AMUSEMENT PARK
Carolina Beach
Orton Pond
87
421
ATLANTIC OCEAN
Kure Beach
211
FT. FISHER STATE RECREATION AREA/ NORTH CAROLINA AQUARIUM
SOUTHPORT/ FT. FISHER FERRY
Southport
0        5 mi
0        5 km

N

WILMINGTON

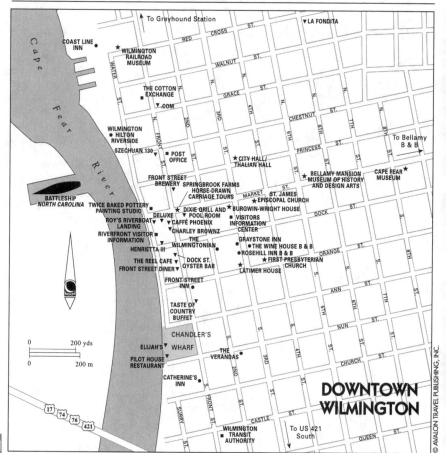

To Greyhound Station

LA FONDITA

COAST LINE INN

★ WILMINGTON RAILROAD MUSEUM

THE COTTON EXCHANGE

.COM

WILMINGTON HILTON RIVERSIDE

SZECHUAN 130

POST OFFICE

★ CITY HALL/ THALIAN HALL

To Bellamy B & B

BELLAMY MANSION MUSEUM OF HISTORY AND DESIGN ARTS

CAPE FEAR MUSEUM

FRONT STREET BREWERY

SPRINGBROOK FARMS HORSE-DRAWN CARRIAGE TOURS

ST. JAMES EPISCOPAL CHURCH

BATTLESHIP NORTH CAROLINA

TWICE BAKED POTTERY PAINTING STUDIO

DELUXE ★ DIXIE GRILL AND ★ POOL ROOM

★ BURGWIN-WRIGHT HOUSE

VISITORS INFORMATION CENTER

ROY'S RIVERBOAT LANDING

CAFFÉ PHOENIX

CHARLEY BROWNZ

RIVERFRONT VISITOR INFORMATION

THE WILMINGTONIAN

GRAYSTONE INN
THE WINE HOUSE B & B
ROSEHILL INN B & B

HENRIETTA III

THE REEL CAFE
FRONT STREET DINER

DOCK ST. OYSTER BAR

★ FIRST PRESBYTERIAN CHURCH

LATIMER HOUSE

FRONT STREET INN

TASTE OF COUNTRY BUFFET

CHANDLER'S

ELIJAH'S WHARF

THE VERANDAS

PILOT HOUSE RESTAURANT

CATHERINE'S INN

17 74 76 421

WILMINGTON TRANSIT AUTHORITY

To US 421 South

DOWNTOWN WILMINGTON

© AVALON TRAVEL PUBLISHING, INC.

0   200 yds
0   200 m

Cape Fear River

WALNUT ST.
RED CROSS ST.
GRACE ST.
CHESTNUT ST.
PRINCESS ST.
MARKET ST.
DOCK ST.
ORANGE ST.
ANN ST.
NUN ST.
CHURCH ST.
CASTLE ST.
QUEEN ST.

WATER ST.
FRONT ST.
2ND ST.
3RD ST.
4TH ST.
5TH ST.
6TH ST.
7TH ST.
8TH ST.
SURRY ST.

website: www.cottonexchange.citysearch.com, a collection of 30 specialty shops and eateries tucked into four historic brick buildings, and featuring a top-notch German restaurant.

Continue north from the Cotton Exchange and you'll come to the Coast Line Convention Center, where folks are trying to make the best of the disappearance of the Atlantic Coast Line railroad, which until 1960 animated this end of town. Over here too is the nifty **Wilmington Railroad Museum.** More on all these below.

Heading away from the river, after Front comes Second Street, and then Third Street, a main thoroughfare. Go north here and you'll leave

town on the Parsley Street Bridge, or U.S. 117. Head south on Third Street and it becomes Carolina Beach Boulevard, heading to the ocean.

A number of delightful side streets cross Water, Front, and Third Streets and dead-end at the river. Just as you'll find down in Charleston, the most important of these is named **Market Street.**

If you turn around at the river and head eastward on Market, you'll discover you're also on U.S. 17, the coastal highway of the Carolinas. This will take you deep into the less enchanting parts of Wilmington as you climb the street signs all the way to 16th and 17th Streets, one-way streets that combine to form another important north-south thoroughfare. If you continue on eastward along Third, it becomes 74 and carries you straight to Wrightsville Beach.

One of the best ways to orient yourself downtown is to take a horse-drawn tour with **Springbrook Farms,** departing from Market Street between Water and Front Streets, 910/251-8889. Owner John Pucci and his period-costumed staff provide a wealth of anecdotes and facts about the many historic buildings in the area.

## Suburban Wilmington

The suburbs between Wilmington proper and the Wilmington-area beaches have the sorts of names that roll off developers' tongues: **Long Leaf Acres, College Acres, Winter Park, Windemere, Landfall,** and so on. These vary some in age and comeliness, but for most travelers, the only interesting thing they offer are a few restaurants, high-end malls, and moderately priced lodgings between downtown Wilmington and the beaches.

## Beaches

**Wrightsville** is the chief beach of the Wilmington Coast, the most-developed beach, and yet, it's not all *that* different from its sister beaches to the south, Carolina and Kure. **Carolina Beach** used to be one of the hot shagging spots along the Carolina coast. It's a pleasure beach, the kind of place Pinocchio might have run away to. Sure enough, the island that holds all three of these beaches is called Pleasure Island. **Kure** used to have the reputation, as some put it, of being the place where the people you see at drag races go to the beach. This is changing somewhat as the expensive townhouses move in and the trailers move out. But at least around the pier and business district, Kure is still a good place to find people wearing blue jeans at the beach.

## Fort Fisher State Recreational Area

South of Kure Beach, just when you begin to despair of sighting natural coastline ever again, you'll discover this pristine area of protected government land. You'll find a lot of history here. The fall of Fort Fisher at the end of the War Between the States caused the fall of Wilmington, which shut off the pipeline of goods to Robert E. Lee's armies and effectively ended the war. Today there's enough of the fort left to get a feeling for what transpired here back in 1865. Also here is

© MIKE SIGALAS

**Fort Fisher**

the **Fort Fisher Aquarium,** a welcome chance to experience the local wildlife, with expert interpretation provided.

## SIGHTS

### Cape Fear Museum

If at all possible, make the **Cape Fear Museum,** 814 Market St., 910/341-4350, your first stop upon arriving in the Wilmington region; it'll give you background for the sites you'll be seeing. This is the kind of lovingly developed midsize museum that puts a lot of larger museums to shame with the sheer force of its desire to interpret for visitors. Be sure to catch the scale model of the Wilmington waterfront, circa 1862, as well as the diorama of the battles for Fort Fisher. Kids will enjoy the chance to crawl through a mock beaver's lodge in the Michael Jordan Discovery Gallery. Outside the gallery you'll find a sprinkling of Michael Jordan paraphernalia, though if that's the only reason you're coming, you may be disappointed. But there's plenty here to entertain adults and kids of all attention spans. Open Tuesday–Saturday 9 A.M.–5 P.M., Sunday 1–5 P.M. $2 for adults, less for kids. Free on the first and third Sundays of the month, and on the first day of each month.

While the Cape Fear Museum is something that new visitors sometimes need pointed out to them; the **USS *North Carolina* Battleship Memorial,** 910/251-5797, website: www.city-info.com/ncbb55.html, is something they can't miss. Located on Battleship Drive on Eagle Island across from the waterfront, the *North Carolina* stands nine decks high and weighs in at more than 35,000 tons. If the Big One ever hits, and the world is reduced to half-savage city-states, Wilmington already has a pretty good head start on its navy. For now though, the *North Carolina* is, among other things, the largest museum in the state. And with its nine 16-inch guns, it's also the best armed. The big guns can fire 2,700-pound shells 23 statute miles, though I imagine a lot of town statutes forbid the firing of 2,700-pound shells within town limits. A host of workers at the Brooklyn Naval Yard finished the ship in 1941.

A tour of the ship gives you some small sense of appreciation for the life of an average sailor in World War II, taken from a small town or urban ghetto and put in menacing situations in cramped quarters far out to sea with strangers from around the country. The ship itself is dedicated to the 10,000 Tar Heels who died on all fronts during World War II.

After serving more than 40 months in WWII combat and enduring at least one direct torpedo hit, the ship lingered in service—a lifer—until 1961, when a flock of tugboats dragged the *North Carolina* out of history and wedged it into Cape Fear mud to serve as a living history lesson. The battleship arrived, in fact, as part of the first wave of today's tourism industry, steaming (okay, being towed) into Wilmington just a year after the Atlantic Coast Line abandoned the town.

Today the most memorable way to get to the ship is to spend a couple bucks a person and take a **Captain J. N. Maffit** water taxi (waterfront, corner of Market and Water Streets, 800/676-0162 or 910/343-1611) from the Wilmington waterfront; to fully appreciate the sheer expanse of the vessel, there's nothing like it. But you can also drive to it.

Once onboard you can tour the ship at your own speed, or pay extra to peek into the engine room, radio center, admiral's cabin, and other interesting rooms. Unfortunately, as you may have guessed, very little of the ship is handicapped-accessible. In fact, make sure you're in good shape before you start climbing up and down the nine flights of steep steps on a hot August day. Once you're over here on this side of the river, you may decide to make a day of it. If so, take advantage of the picnic grounds and keep an eye out for Old Charlie, the local celebrity gator.

Open 8 A.M.–8 P.M. daily during the summer, 8 A.M.–5 P.M. daily the rest of the year. Admission runs $8 for adults, less for children, senior citizens, and (rightfully so) military folks with ID.

### Bellamy Mansion Museum

The **Bellamy Mansion Museum of History and Design,** 503 Market St., 910/251-3700, serves as a good example of the material beauty and refinement the exploitation of slaves brought to the Wilmington region. Four stories tall and 22 rooms large, this 1861 house is Wilmington's best example of (very) late-antebellum extravagance. In 1972 someone attempted to burn down this then-vacant Italianate mansion, presumably as a way of getting back at long-dead slave owners (who, if they received the fate the arsonists presumably wished on them, were already pretty accustomed to flames by then anyway). Fortunately the building wasn't completely destroyed, and was salvaged and turned into a museum of two sorts. First there are the house and restored gardens themselves. The house features Italianate, neoclassical, and Greek Revival styles. The garden has been replanted the way it was planted when the house was still on its first coat of paint. The other part of the museum's story, the slave quarters—though they were only slave quarters for a short time—should be refurbished by the time you read this, a fitting tribute to the people who helped keep this large household running. Rotating exhibits and multimedia presentations spotlight preservation. Forty-five-minute tours begin at the quarter and three-quarter marks each hour, Wednesday–Saturday 10 A.M.–5 P.M., Sunday 1–5 P.M. Adult admission runs $6.

## Cameron Art Museum

In April 2002, the old St. John's Museum of Art on Orange Street changed its name to the **Louise Wells Cameron Art Museum**, a.k.a. the Cameron Art Museum (CAM), and relocated to the intersection of Independence Boulevard and S. 17th Street, 910/395-5999, website: www.cameronart museum.com. The sparkling 42,000-square-foot facility has a 10-gallery permanent collection and runs numerous temporary exhibitions, all dedicated to North Carolina art. It's worth a visit for many reasons, including the extensive collection of Mary Cassatt color prints and the work of Minnie Evans (1892–1987). Evans is something like the Howard Finster of Wilmington, a Christian visionary whose folk works reflected her faith in intensely personal fashion. Here you'll also find a fine display of Jugtown pottery, a unique blending of Asian and traditional Piedmont folk pottery styles, created between 1921 and 1959 by North Carolina craftsman Ben Owen. There are lots of other goodies

here, both locally created and not, including the work of acclaimed North Carolina–raised painter Elliott Daingerfield (1859–1932) and Charlotte artist Romare Beardon (1914–88).

In addition to the museum, a gift shop, and The Forks café, on the museum's 9.6-acre campus you'll also find restored Confederate mounds created before the Battle of Forks Road in the last days of the Civil War, when Wilmington was one of the last two ports still bringing in munitions and other supplies to the faltering Confederacy, while Federal troops were moving in to shut it down. The café serves lunch Tuesday–Saturday 11:30 A.M.–2:30 P.M.; Friday night 5–9 P.M.; and Sunday brunch 10:30 A.M.–3 P.M.

Gallery hours are Tuesday–Thursday 10 A.M.–5 P.M.; Friday 10 A.M.–8 P.M.; Saturday 10 A.M.–5 P.M.; Sunday 10:30 A.M.–4 P.M. Admission is $5 for adults; $8 per family; $2 for children and teens ages 5–18; children under 5 are free. And everybody's free on the first Sunday of each month.

## Wilmington Railroad Museum

Train fans will need to head over to the **Wilmington Railroad Museum**, 501 Nutt St. (corner of Red Cross and Water Streets), 910/763-2634, where the old freight traffic office now plays home to dozens of displays honoring the area's railroad history and celebrating railroads in general. Outside you'll find a steam engine and caboose for the climbing and viewing, always a favorite with kids. Inside the museum they've got a wonderful, massive model railroad diorama upstairs, which kids and not a few adults will enjoy getting a chance to operate. Downstairs you'll find a re-creation of a railroad depot office and other interactive exhibits that help bring to life the Golden Age of rail travel. The museum store carries a good selection of train-related items, including big wooden whistles that sound just like a real steam whistle. Admission for the museum runs $2 for adults, $1 for ages 6–11. Hours are 10 A.M.–5 P.M. Monday–Saturday, 1–5 P.M. Sunday, April–September. Call ahead for winter hours.

## The Burgwin-Wright House

At 224 Market St., 910/762-0570, you'll find perhaps the top Revolutionary home tour in

**Wilmington Railroad Museum**

© MIKE SIGALAS

WILMINGTON

Wilmington. When General Cornwallis traveled throughout the colonies, he brought along his own army of red-coated, musket-wielding travel consultants, who had a way of finding the general the best house in town. In 1781, though Cornwallis was retreating after the costly victory at Guilford Courthouse, and his military career was on the skids (and about to skid to a stop in Virginia), he still managed to find good digs in Wilmington, choosing the Burgwin-Wright house from the 200 available for the seizing. Why this house? Cornwallis was a special-needs traveler. He wanted a spot with a nice dungeon underneath for holding prisoners, and wealthy politician John Burgwin's (Bur-GWIN)10-year-old home had been built over the foundations of the old town jail. The house also featured trapdoors leading to tunnels leading to the river, so that Cornwallis could make a quick exit to the water if necessary. Or so the story goes.

Today the tiered gardens outside have been restored. You can visit these for free, but the preservation group that could have been named by Frank Sinatra—the Colonial Dames—charges $3 for adults to tour the house, open Tuesday–Saturday 10 A.M.–4 P.M.

## Brunswick Town State Historic Site

Located on the Cape Fear River, 19 miles south of Wilmington on N.C. 133, 910/371-6613, Brunswick Town is like Charles Towne Landing at Charleston. Both Brunswick and Charles Towne Landing mark the original English settlements in the area—in both cases, settlements that were abandoned when a second site proved to be safer and more profitable. Unlike Charles Towne, Brunswick Town has not been restored or stocked with buffalo, and this makes the experience all the more ominous. What you will see here are a worthwhile visitors center with exhibits and a slide show to give you some background on what you'll be seeing. Archaeologists have dug up some 60 foundations from the old town, and a number of them have been left open for the viewing. Artifacts on display reveal much of what life was like in the colonial port. You'll also find the earthen remains of the Confederate Fort Anderson, built here in 1862 to help protect the important blockade-running port of Wilmington. Most impressive are the remains of St. Philip's Anglican Church. The 38 outdoor exhibit panels along the self-guided tour makes it easy to get a handle on what used to be where, and who did what there.

Open Monday–Saturday 9 A.M.–5 P.M., Sunday 1–5 P.M. April 1–Oct. 31; Tuesday–Saturday 10 A.M.–4 P.M. and Sunday 1–4 P.M. Nov. 1–March 31. Closed some holidays, so call ahead.

## Fort Fisher State Historic Site

Located south of Kure Beach on U.S. 421 (Fort Fisher Boulevard), 910/458-5538, Fort Fisher is the site of the most important Civil War battle on North Carolina coast; once the Union troops seized Fisher, Wilmington fell easily. And with Wilmington went the last major port open to the Confederacy. Today you'll find a small visitors center and a nice trail around the remaining earthworks. Be sure to catch the diorama of the battle at the Cape Fear Museum before you come out here; it'll make your visit that much more meaningful. Inside the visitors center you'll find artifacts taken from sunken blockade runners, which used to wait behind the fort until nightfall, when they'd make their mad dashes through the net of Union ships. When the North finally got the courage to launch an amphibious assault on the fort on Christmas Eve 1864, the Confederates repulsed them after two bloody days of fighting. But the North had all the time and manpower in the world, and on January 12 they began using a healthier strategy. For days they literally bombed the sand out of the fort; and on the 15th day they launched a surprise attack around the most weakly defended gate of the fort. Northerner or not, you'll find visiting to be a bit easier today. In high season the center's open from 9 A.M.–5 P.M. every day except Sunday, when it doesn't open until 1 P.M. But if you get here after the center closes, you can still take a walk around the largest of the remaining berms, with signs that will explain the logistics of the battles and the history of the fort as you go along.

## Latimer House

At 126 S. Third Street, 810/762-0492, you'll find the carefully preserved late-antebellum (1852) home of prominent Wilmington merchant Zebulon Latimer. You can take a guided tour of the house, which also serves as headquarters of the Lower Cape Fear Historical Society. Walking tours of Wilmington's historical district depart from here Wednesdays and Saturdays at 10 A.M.

## North Carolina Aquarium at Fort Fisher

On the other side of Fort Fisher Boulevard, you'll find the aquarium, 910/458-8257, reopened in early 2002 after a major renovation and expansion. One of North Carolina's modest but informative chain of state aquariums, the Fort Fisher Aquarium tripled in size during its refurbishment, while retaining its focus on the wildlife found in southern North Carolina waters.

A 20,000-gallon shark tank and its occupants are the stars here, and the alligators are also popular. Judiciously, aquarium curators have included neither of these in the touch tank, where little folks (and big folks) can touch horseshoe crabs, hermit crabs, and other nonbiting forms of marine life.

As an example of how dedicated museum curators are to their Cape Fear region focus, even the touch pool is set in a re-creation of the Fort Fisher coquina rock outcropping. Outside you'll find nature trails.

Open Monday–Saturday 9 A.M.–5 P.M. $6 adults, $4 for children 5–17 years of age.

## Historic Churches

Founded in 1729 at old Brunswick Town, the current Gothic Revival home of **St. James Episcopal Church**, 25 S. Third St., 910/763-1628, dates from 1839. The second church building (the first structure built after the move to Wilmington) was gutted by the British when they took over Wilmington during the Revolution; the current version used materials from the first, and enjoyed the same treatment courtesy of the U.S. government during the War Between the States.

Ironically, as Federal troops partook in pew-tossing contests inside the sanctuary, up in Washington D.C., St. James's architect, Thomas U. Walter, was busily completing the addition of the dome atop the U.S. Capitol. Today, fortunately, you'll see that the pews have been put back in place. *Ecce Homo* ("Behold the Man"), the painting of the bound and scourged Jesus that hangs here, was captured from a pirate ship that failed in its attack of Brunswick Town back in 1748.

As with most churches of this vintage, the graveyard is just as interesting as the building itself. Outside of St. James lie a number of colonial figures, including Thomas Godfrey (1736–1763), author of *Prince of Parthia,* the first drama written by a native-born American and professionally produced in the colonies. You're welcome to stop by the grounds anytime during the day, and you can tour the inside of the church any day after 9 A.M. when there are no services underway.

The **First Presbyterian Church,** 121 S. Third St., is a relatively new structure—built in the late 1920s—but the congregation itself dates back to 1785. Moving here after a seminary-teaching position at Columbia, S.C, Dr. Joseph Wilson, "Tommy" Woodrow Wilson's father, took on the pastoring of this church. A mosaic in the vestibule pays tribute to their Pancho Villa–chasing, League-of-Nations-lobbying former church member, who actually lived here only in the summers and holidays during his undergraduate years. In one of his first appearances in print, the future scholar and statesman griped to the Wilmington *Journal* that in Wilm-

## THE BATTLE FOR NORTH CAROLINA

During the Revolutionary War the fate of North Carolina was decided at Wilmington. This was where ousted royal governor Josiah Martin set out to reclaim North Carolina for England. His plan called for Highland Scots to march eastward in February and rendezvous with British general Cornwallis, who would arrive in Wilmington by ship to begin his conquest of the South. He also mustered the Black Pioneers, a group composed of free African-Americans and slaves promised their freedom for service to the Crown. These he assigned to the *Scorpion,* a ship ready to assist General Cornwallis when he arrived. Faced with the simultaneous arrival of these two formidable military thrusts, the rebellious colonials were sure to throw down their arms, throw up their hands, and beg to kiss the nearest Union Jack—if all went well.

It didn't. The Scots got there too early; the Brits got there too late. When General Donald MacDonald's 1,600 Highlanders met at Cross Creek (now Fayetteville) and marched toward Wilmington in February 1776, Patriot minutemen were waiting for them. They thwarted the Loyalists' attempt to cross at Rockfish Creek, and then moved back to dig in around the bridge at Moore's Creek, about 20 miles east of Wilmington. The night before the Scots got there, Patriots snuck down to bridge and pried off the planks of the roadbed. Now the Highlanders would have to walk across the bridge's slippery log runners. These the Patriots

waxed and soaped.

On February 27, 1776, an hour before sunrise, Patriot sharpshooters lay in wait across the creek as an advance party of broadsword-brandishing, bag-pipe-blowing Highlanders attempted to cross the bridge in the cold pre-dawn fog. Most fell from the slippery runners into the icy creek. Those who made it across charged the Patriots' earthworks—and ran right into a storm of deadly musket fire.

Within seconds, the creek thrashed with wounded and drowning Scotsmen; the others—only about half of them armed—turned kilt, running west. The Patriots gave chase and captured more than half of them, along with guns, wagons, and medical supplies.

The Black Pioneers sat patiently upon the *Scorpion,* no doubt wondering where all the action was.

The 30 fallen Highlanders (and single fallen Patriot) had been buried for four months when Cornwallis and his 2,000 troops finally managed to stop by Wilmington in June. He sent scouts ashore to size up the situation and learned that the Patriots now fully controlled the Lower Cape Fear. Rather than attempt a bloody invasion into hostile territory, Cornwallis decided to head south. Fully disheartened, Governor Martin, who had fought so hard to keep eastern North Carolina, finally gave up the coast. He sought asylum aboard Cornwallis' ship. Together, they sailed south to Charleston and the Battle of Sullivan's Island, where the British would suffer another devastating defeat.

ington, "Weeds of the rankest and most un-healthy kind are allowed to grow, and filth of every description to accumulate." However, from all accounts, young Tommy Wilson liked Wilmington; he'd always wanted to be a sailor, and living in the port city was as close as he ever came to it. He enjoyed boating and fishing on the Cape Fear, and liked to bathe in the river, though he never learned to swim and always had a family servant come along for safety's sake. Though the actual church building that was here in during Pastor Wilson's residence is gone, the neo-Gothic church built shortly thereafter in its place is a beauty; its bells ring up and down the historic district on the hour, though they no longer play all night on the hour out of respect for their insomniac neighbors.

## Moores Creek Bridge National Battlefield

The site of this important Revolutionary War battle is preserved as the 86-acre **Moores Creek Bridge National Battlefield**, 200 Moores Creek Rd., 910/283-5591, website: www.nps.gov/mocr, where you can see the bridge site and some reconstructed Patriot earthworks. The visitors center features a diorama re-creation of the bridge as it was on game day, an audio-visual program, and a number of weapons found on the site. The park includes the 0.7-mile History Trail, part of which follows the colonial-era Negro Head Point Road, and the 0.3-mile Tarheel Trail. Both trails begin near the visitors center. To get to the battlefield from Wilmington, take U.S. 421 to N.C. 210, then head west on 210 for five miles.

## Poplar Grove Plantation

Built at the peak of the antebellum period in 1850 and upon the ashes of a former house, the Greek Revival manor at Poplar Grove Plantation, north of town at 10200 U.S. 17, 910/686-9518, made its money underground—growing peanuts. Worked by a team of 60 slaves before the War Between the States and by tenant farmers afterward, Poplar Grove bounced back after the Civil War in a jif, remembering that its roots were in the peanut-friendly soil. Today the plantation has been restored as a living memorial to the lives

and lifestyles lived out here since the mid-19th century. In the house museum you'll see restored bedrooms, parlor, dining room, and library, as well as displays explaining the agriculture of the area. Craftspersons are generally on hand to demonstrate basketmaking, blacksmithing, and other crafts. In Poplar Grove's store you can buy some of the crafts produced here.

This is a worthwhile stop if you're hoping to get more than a home tour and really want to understand a bit of what life was like out here on the plantations. In early 2000 a new Peanut and Agricultural Exhibit Building opened on the grounds, featuring peanut displays and forestry exhibits. Admission to Poplar Grove costs $7 for adults, $4 for children 6 and up. Open Monday–Saturday 9 A.M.–5 P.M. and Sunday noon–5 P.M.

## Airlie Gardens

Located on Airlie Road, off U.S. 74/76, 910/793-7531, Airlie Gardens are what is left from a large rice plantation whose overseers had green thumbs. The extensive gardens are open from March through October, but get here before May if you want to catch the azaleas in bloom (you do). The gardens include a five-mile drive-through section, so bring the convertible and allergy medicine. Horticultural buffs will be interested to see the Topel tree, a hybrid R.A. Topel created by grafting a yaupon on to a different holly. The bright red berries are three times bigger than regular holly berries (but, importantly, still smaller than Halle Berry). The gardens were owned for generations by the Corbett family, but now New Hanover County owns them, and they're managed by the New Hanover County Cooperative Arboretum. Admission is $8 for adults, $2 for ages 3–12.

## Orton Plantation Gardens

South of Wilmington off N.C. 133 to Southport, you'll find these gardens at 9149 Orton Rd. S.E., in Winnabow, 910/371-6851. Orton features 20 acres of gardens with a variety of annuals, perennials, huge oaks, azaleas, and camellias. The home here is still standing, but it's a private residence. Though you can't go inside, it certainly adds to the ambience. Admission to the gardens costs $9 for adults, $8 for seniors, and $3 for kids 6–16.

## Tote-Em-In Zoo

The **Tote-Em-In Zoo,** 5811 Carolina Beach Rd., 910/791-0472, located 10 miles south of Wilmington on U.S. 421, is a throwback to the sort of roadside attraction molded more in the shape of its founder's personality than by an MBA-penciled business plan. After serving in World War II, George Tregembo returned from the Philippines to his home in Maine, bearing a number of artifacts and a newly born interest in tropical wildlife. What George wanted to do was build a zoo to house and display the exotic creatures he'd learned to love, and build a museum to show off his collection of international artifacts. One thing he needed was decent year-round weather. George and his family moved down to their present-day spot on Carolina Beach Road in 1953, bringing along a number of animals he'd already collected. George's Philippine artifacts seeded what would become the uniquely diverse collection of materials in his Museum of Oddities, still an integral part of the Tote-Em-In Zoo (no additional charge).

This Museum of Oddities, with its stream-of-consciousness organization style and hand-written interpretive notes, is like a peek into a young boy's knapsack of found treasures—a monument to an earlier generation's capacity for wonder at the sheer "otherness" of distant places, back before jet planes, satellite television, and the Internet shrank the world. It contains tribal death masks, fossils, foreign currency, WWII relics, arrowheads, mounted animals, weapons, newspaper clippings, and even a fake mummy. Outside, the collection of animals reflects the same kind of whimsical approach; featured are a pair of black leopards, Toby the Mandrill, Clyde the Camel, and a popular pair of Himalayan bears. You'll also find some native turtles and alligators—with all the free food laying around here, you probably couldn't keep them out—but in general the Tote-Em-In is the exact opposite of a museum for local wildlife: it's a collection of exotics.

Running a small zoo requires remembering all the different feeding times and tending to the various illnesses and pregnancies and whatnot, in addition to running the business itself, tending to customers, and keeping the place clean and the gift shop stocked—and working the phones and mailbox to make the trades that would keep his Museum of Oddities fascinating to increasingly TV-dulled visitors. Through the 1950s, '60s, '70s, and '80s, George and his family kept up their vigil. They didn't take many vacations, but they met thousands of interesting visitors every year, and went to sleep each night to the calls of chimps and leopards.

Jerry Brewer went to sleep listening to the same calls—he was five when George's zoo moved in next door to his parents' home. Brewer grew up "just over a sand hill" from the kinds of species most kids only saw on *Mutual of Omaha's Wild Kingdom.* As the 1980s drew to a close and

## SIMBA, THE LION KING OF TOTE-EM-IN ZOO

If you had a mind to, you could make a Disney pilgrimage up and down the Carolina coasts: you'd start out at the Disney resort at Hilton Head, stop by to camp on Hunting Island near Beaufort, S.C., shooting location for the live-action *Jungle Book* of a few years back, and then continue on up to Wilmington and visit the **Tote-Em-In Zoo,** 5811 Carolina Beach Rd., 910/791-0472, to see Simba, the fur-and-blood model for Disney's *The Lion King.* Simba spent his Florida cubhood pouncing about for Disney artists who needed inspiration for the look and movement of the film's singing, talking main character.

Fortunately, unlike that of many child actors, Simba's story has a fairly happy ending. When the Disney gig was over, the cat's Florida owners sold him to Tote-Em-In owner Jerry Brewer, who whisked Simba away from his glitzy movie-star lifestyle faster than you can say "Gary Coleman." Consequently, Simba's spending his young adult years in Wilmington, instead of sitting in a dark apartment somewhere in the Valley, speedballing catnip, waiting for a call from a casting agent that will never come.

George became a little overwhelmed by the task of keeping up the place, he offered it to Jerry and his wife, Sherrie. They've owned it for the past 10 years, though George still lives on the property, close to his beloved animals and relics.

Be forewarned: Though the Brewers clearly care about and for the animals, this *is* an upgraded version of the kind of old-fashioned, cagey zoo that champions of the new generation of barless, "natural habitat" zoos hope to banish from the earth. Yet if changes have been slow to come to Tote-Em-In, guests have not. Even when the zoo was open only during summer and early fall, between 40,000 and 50,000 people visited the zoo each year. With the Brewers' decision to open the zoo year-round, expect that number to increase considerably over the next few years.

Hours are 9 A.M.–5 P.M. daily; after Labor Day 9 A.M.–4 P.M. daily. Admission is $6 for adults, $4 for kids under 12.

## Amusement Parks and Other Activities

The amusement complexes near Wilmington vary between worn beach boardwalks, quaint perma-carnivals, and miniature-golf courses on steroids. In the first category you'll find the **Carolina Beach Boardwalk,** though the city's Vision 2005 revitalization plan seeks to re-create it as, the local Convention Visitors Bureau says, a "cluster of oceanfront boutiques, a coffee and ice cream shop, poster galleries, restaurants, and juice bars." Carolina Beach has brought in consultants from Virginia, and things might be looking up thereabouts.

**Jubilee Amusement Park,** 1000 N. Lake Park Blvd., Carolina Beach, 910/458-9017, falls into the second group; it's the carnival that arrived sometime in 1953 and never left, a great place for kids and teens with energy and money to burn after a day at the beach. Generations of families and teens have enjoyed summer nights here, and Jubilee's survived more storms than the Clinton presidency, so it looks as if it's here to stay. Tickets for individual rides are available; unlimited-use tickets run $11.95 for adults and $8.95 for children five and under on weekdays; $13.95 and $10.95 on weekends.

In the overgrown-miniature-golf category comes **Jungle Rapids Family Fun Park,** 5320 Oleander Dr., 910/791-0666, one of the cleanest places around—and also one of the safest. It's a good bet if you or your kids are looking to kill a roll of quarters (which, of course, must be exchanged for tokens), or if for some reason you'd rather ride chlorine waves instead of the saltwater ones. There's also a climbing wall and a Go-Kart track. In season, it's open Monday–Thursday 10 A.M.–11 P.M., Friday–Saturday 10 A.M.–12 A.M.

Over at 1223 N. 23rd St., **Screen Gems Studios,** 910/675-8479, website: www.screengems studios.com/silverscreentours.html, offers roughly four two-hour guided tours each weekend. You'll need to call ahead to make reservations. Though Screen Gems boasts that it is "the largest and most complete motion picture studio east of California," don't confuse this with the Disney MGM studio tours or Universal Studios. This is a working studio designed to *be* a working studio, with little thought for the tourist trade. Though of course your guides will try to show you all they can, if a film or TV show is in production while you're there, some of the facilities will be closed to you. The films shot here vary in quality but tend (as do the majority of all films produced, to be fair) toward the thumbs-down genre; *King Kong Lives* was shot here; so were *Little Monsters, Exorcist III,* and *Dracula's Widow.* On the upside Screen Gems also saw the making of *Rambling Rose, Road to Wellville, Empire Records, Blue Velvet,* and *Crimes of the Heart.*

For a more sedate and non-movie-related outing, unless you have a *Ghost*-like experience while handling the ceramics, head to 6 Market St., where *Twice Baked Pottery Painting Studio,* 910/343-9886, will let you come in and paint some ceramics, which they'll fire, and which you can then take home. If you live nearby or visit Wilmington a lot, you can even join the Frequent Fire program. Tuesday–Saturday 11 A.M.–7 P.M., Sunday 1–6 P.M. It takes five days for a firing, so make your visit here at the start of your trip or prepare to ship your wares back home to meet you.

The **Fort Fisher–Southport Ferry,** 800/368-8969, website: www.dot.state.nc.us/transit/ferry, serves as a scenic, on-the-way-anyway half-hour boat ride for most anyone traveling north or south through the Cape Fear region. It departs about once an hour from the Southport and Fort Fisher terminals, but times vary, so pick up a ferry schedule at your hotel or at the state Welcome Station. Whenever your departure time, get there a half-hour early to be sure to get a space onboard. Fare runs $3 per car, 50 cents per pedestrian.

# ACCOMMODATIONS

The greater Wilmington area boasts well over 6,000 rooms. As is the case with its restaurants, Wilmington offers an impressive number of memorable stays for a city of its size. There are three fundamental ways to approach a stay in the area: (1) stay downtown on the scenic waterfront, (2) stay on the beach at Wrightsville, Carolina, or Kure Beaches, or (3) stay somewhere in between. Choices 1 and 2 generally run well upward of $100 a night, particularly in high season, and so a lot of folks end up selecting 3. And this is really not such a bad deal since there are a lot of good choices, and the sprawling nature of the region means that being situated in the middle of it all can save you a good bit of driving time as you shuttle back and forth between downtown and the beach.

## Downtown Wilmington
### $100–150
**Coastline Inn,** 503 Nutt St., 800/617-7732 or 910/763-2800, website: www.coastline-inn.com, anchors the Coast Line Center, the old railroad yards that Wilmington has turned into a convention center. Stay down here and you'll have a room right on the river, be within easy walking distance of the Cotton Exchange, and be just yards away from Grouper Nancy's Restaurant. In-season rates start at $89 d on weekdays and $119 d on weekends.

For about the same price, you can stay in antebellum style at the nearby **RoseHill Inn Bed and Breakfast,** 114 S. Third St., 800/815-0250 or 910/815-0250, website: www.rosehill.com. Innkeepers Laurel Jones and Dennis Fietsch run things in the Neo-classic Revival house. Built in

1848 by Wilmington banker Henry Russel Savage, the house later served as home for Henry Bacon Jr., architect of the famed Lincoln Memorial in Washington, D.C. Each room includes a private bath and a mix of antiques, and the breakfasts tend toward the gourmet.

## $150 and Up
You can't miss the nine-story **Wilmington Hilton Riverside,** 301 N. Water St., 910/763-5900, towering over the 19th-century waterfront. The service and amenities are first-rate; it's arguably the city's premier convention facility, and offers some of the best views of the river and the USS *North Carolina,* particularly since the Hilton's are the only views on this stretch of the river that don't have to look *at* the hotel. Rooms are $159 d on weekends in season, less the rest of the week. See the chain online at www.hilton.com.

American Historic Inns, Inc. recently chose **Graystone Inn,** 100 S. Third St., 910/763-2000, website: www.graystoneinn.com, as one of the "Top 10 Most Romantic Inns in the United States." These days Paul and Yolanda Bolda run the huge, atmospheric inn at the corner of S. Third and Dock Streets. It offers seven huge rooms (five with fireplaces) atop a grand oak staircase. The inn is the 1906 former home of Elizabeth Haywood Bridgers, widow and heiress by marriage to the fortune of her father-in-law, Robert Rufus Bridgers, former Confederate congressman, founder of the Wilmington/Weldon Railroad, and president of the Atlantic Coast Line Railway. The charms of this establishment are many, starting with the friendly, unpretentious owners; the house features a hand-carved staircase, a large sunroom, a baby grand piano, and a wonderful 1900s mahogany-paneled sportsman's library—the sort of place where Theodore Roosevelt would have felt right at home, and the perfect spot to read in front of the fire on a cold night. The inn is especially romantic at night when you return home and the huge, illuminated stone front takes on the look of a diplomat's residence; even if you actually spend the night eating wings and watching an Adam Sandler film, you'll feel as if you're an ambassador returning home after a night of high-level intrigue. Each guest room has its own bath with period fixtures—most include a claw-foot tub—and each room has its own phone and PC data port. There's a honeymoon suite on the third floor. Golf packages available. Expect to spend $189– a night in season, which includes breakfast and drinks in the evening.

To be right down on the water, you'll want **Catherine's Inn,** 410 S. Front St., 800/476-0723 or 910/251-0863, set in the 1888 Italianate Forshee-Sprunt House, and featuring a great two-story screened-in porch for eating breakfast, and wonderful views of the sunset over the Cape Fear River. Each of the five bedrooms has a private bath. The gardens are beautiful too.

Dennis Madsen and Charles Pennington's **The Verandas,** 202 Nun St., 910/251-2212, website: www.verandas.com, is set in the 1853 Beery mansion and features four large porches, a screened breakfast patio, and some very large guest rooms. All eight rooms are corner rooms, and four feature fireplaces. Full breakfast. This is the only house in Wilmington with a cupola—you can climb up there and take in a beautiful view of the neighborhood and river below.

The little **Wine House,** 311 Cottage Lane, 910/763-5832, is set in a circa-1863 wine house, a plain, two-room clapboard structure behind a brick-walled courtyard on a small side street in the midst of downtown Wilmington. The two rooms feature heart-pine floors, private baths, and fireplaces. Continental breakfast. Free bikes are available for use.

Unlike those B&Bs that blossomed inside stately old residences, **The Wilmingtonian,** 101 S. Second St., 800/525-0909 or 910/343-1800, set inside what was a century ago an unremarkable business block, has to try a little harder to be quaint. But the Wilmingtonian features a good downtown location and succeeds as a combination small inn and upscale lodge. For longer stays it might be more comfortable (though not much cheaper) than a B&B. The main building is the quaintest, featuring wicker chairs on the porches. The various one-bedroom suites have wooden floors and a variety of themes. Be sure to pick the theme you want. If you're looking for an an-

tebellum experience, for instance, make certain they don't put you into the Southwestern room. Rooms start at $149 d, in season.

Without a doubt, one of the ways you know that an old hard-nosed downtown has been gentrified is when the Salvation Army soup kitchen is reborn as a bed-and-breakfast. That's exactly what's happened at the **Front Street Inn,** 215 S. Front St., 800/336-8184 or 910/762-6442, website: www.frontstreetinn.com. Once, food and shelter were given here to the destitute; nowadays you'll pay upwards of $175 in-season to spend the night and get a single meal. The food now is much better. Featuring good second-story views of the river, the Front Street Inn makes for a less nostalgic, less distinctively Southern stay than most of Wilmington's B&Bs, but Jay and Stefany Rhodes run a friendly place, popular with business travelers (maybe it's the massage therapist and pool table) and with weekenders (maybe it's the free bikes to use). Located close to Chandler's Wharf, the inn features a selection of inn rooms and suites named after various celebrities, from Pearl S. Buck to Molly Brown to Ernest Hemingway (one assumes an extra-large minibar).

Further from the waterfront, you'll find the oak-canopied **Bellamy Bed and Breakfast,** 1417 Market St., 910/763-3081, with four rooms, a suite, and a shared kitchen.

## On the Beach
### $50–100

The **Carolina Temple Apartments,** 550 Waynick Blvd., Wrightsville Beach, 910/256-2773, email: swright168@aol.com, sound as if they would be (a) at Carolina Beach, (b) a church, and (c) a place for permanent residents. No, on all three counts. The "Carolina" is used more generally—the building is located on the south end of Wrightsville Beach, just up the road from the Blockade Runner—and "Temple" refers to the family that built these two cottages nearly 100 years ago. "Apartments" refers to the fact that the units do include private baths and kitchenettes. This time-honored establishment is a good, relatively inexpensive middleground between a hotel and a rental house at Wrightsville

turtle nesting grounds at Fort Fisher

Beach. Here you can stay in an early-1900s former trolley station and experience the family vacation-spot qualities of Wrightsville that might be lost to you staying at one of the big oceanfronts. You'll find the rooms a bit snug but big enough for beach living—two- and three-room suites with private baths and ceiling fans. During high season (June–September) you'll need to rent by the week ($600 for one unit, $750 for two), though you might call to see if you can arrange a shorter stay.

## $100–150

A shell's throw from the Johnny Mercer Pier on Wrightsville Beach stands **The Silver Gull Ocean Front Motel,** 20 East Salisbury Ct., 800/842-8894 or 910/256-3728. Prices for the 32 units run $135 in-season, depending on the apartment you want and the room you choose. This is a solid, if not fancy, place for a family that's not really ready to splurge for a beach house, but wants to have the same sort of beach and pier access.

If you're looking for a suite, a spot with its location to recommend it is **One South Lumina,** 1 South Lumina, Wrightsville Beach, 800/421-3255 or 910/256-9100, with daily, weekly, and monthly rates, washers and dryers, fully equipped kitchens, and a pool.

## $150 and Up

The huge **Blockade Runner Resort Hotel and Conference Center, Wrightsville Beach,** 275 Waynick Blvd., 800/541-1161 or 910/256-2251, website: www.blockade-runner.com, is something of an institution out on the waterfront at Masonboro Inlet at Wrightsville Beach. This is a full-service resort, with more than 150 rooms, activities, kids' programs, and a free breakfast buffet. In-season rooms begin at $193 d.

The **Sunspree Holiday Inn, Wrightsville Beach,** 1706 N. Lumina Dr., 910/256-2231, website: www.wrightsville-sunspree.com, feels much more like a resort than any Holiday Inn you might envision. It's got a great oceanfront location, indoor and outdoor pools, outdoor and indoor dining; even the (good) little gym offers a fine view of the ocean. Thank Fran for this bit of Hilton Head deposited on Wrightsville Beach; the 1996 hurricane destroyed the old Holiday Inn, making room for this welcome, upscale addition. Rooms begin at $199 a night in-season.

## Beach House Rentals

If you know you'll be here for more than a few days, and if you're traveling with a crowd or a family, renting a beach house may well be the best and cheapest way to go. You'll find lots of real estate offices listed in the phone book; some of the more popular ones include **TradeMark Coastal Properties,** 222 Causeway Dr., Wrightsville Beach, 800/529-7653; **Gardner Realty & Management, Inc.,** 1009 N. Lake Park Blvd., Carolina Beach, 800/697-7924; and **United Beach Vacations,** 1001 N. Lake Park Blvd., 800/334-5806, website: www.unitedbeachvacations.com.

## Between Downtown and the Beach
### Under $50

If saving money's all-important, there's a decent **Motel 6** with a pool at 2828 Market St., 800/466-8356 or 910/762-0120.

### $50–100

For some homegrown, midpriced lodging, try the Route 66–ish **Whitey's El-Berta Motor Inn,** 4505 Market St., 800/866-9448 or 910/799-1214, featuring 81 rooms starting at $56 d in-season, a good restaurant serving up comfort food, and a pool. The **Homestay Inn,** at 245 Eastwood Rd., 800/575-6085 or 910/793-1920, website: www.Homestay-inn.com, is corporate all the way, but offers 108 rooms ($69 d and up) with kitchen, a pool, and laundry.

A good fall-back is **Best Western Carolinian,** 2916 Market St., 910/763-4653, which starts at $79 d a night.

### $100–150

For something a little more special but still reasonable, the **Hampton Inn, Inn and Suites, Landfall Park,** 1989 Eastwood Rd., 910/256-9600, draws a fair share of beachgoers, business visitors, and movie types; it's a great crossroads stop for anyone who expects to spend time both in city and on the beach and doesn't necessarily want to plunk down the money for a $200-a-night oceanfront spot or a cute B&B downtown. The main lobby has a huge fireplace and feels more like a well-established lodge than a suburban chain hotel. The pool area has a distinctly resortish feel,

and the staff is truly first-rate, as though they've all personally committed their corporate mission statement to heart. It's no surprise the inn's been winning awards as one of the best of the Hampton Inn chain. You'll find microwaves and Internet hookups in every room.

## FOOD
### Seafood and Steaks

Seafood in a port town? Of course. And where there's surf, there's usually turf. In nature, of course, the two go together like, well, fish and cattle, but in dimly lit restaurants of the credit card variety, the combination claims a certain mystique.

Beginning right on the river over at Chandler's Wharf is the romantic, semi-casual **Pilot House Restaurant,** 2 Ann St., 910/343-0200, serving its nouveau-Southern cuisine by candlelight, both indoors and out. Expect to spend $15–$27 for dinner. Reservations suggested.

Next door on the river is **Elijah's,** 2 Ann St., 910/343-1448, run by the same folks as the Pilot House and priced similarly. It features both an oyster bar (with an outdoor deck) and a dining room with a nautical theme. The crab dip is legendary. Whether observant Jewish diners need to leave an empty chair for Elijah in his own restaurant is one for the theologians.

Note that both the above restaurants close after lunch and don't open again until 5 P.M. for dinner.

A good place to dine outside (or inside) in the midst of things on Water Street is **Water Street Restaurant,** 5 South Water St., 910/343-0042. Set in an 1835 former peanut warehouse bordered in days of yore by a bawdy riverfront and a bawdier red-light district, the restaurant today keeps a casual tone. Not a bad place to pick up a good sandwich for under $8, even at night. If you're hungrier, Water Street's got full dinners—T-bone steaks, good Mediterranean scampi—for $14–18. Kids' menu items run $3–4. Live entertainment.

Another chief downtown eatery is **Roy's Riverboat Landing,** 2 Market St., 910/763-7227, right across from the river, which you can see from your table if you sit upstairs, outside on the balcony. It's been open since 1984, which is forever in Wilmington restaurant history, but the building itself dates far further back, to 1857. The seafood dishes (cioppino $16; shrimp and grits $15) and steaks are all popular, but you'll also find chicken, duck, and other dishes. You may want to save room for such tasty desserts as Miss Margaret's Renowned Four-Layer Coconut Cream Cheese Pie ($5). Not far from there, the determinedly off-beat **Dock St. Oyster Bar,** 12 Dock St., is an informal place for relatively inexpensive shrimp and other seafood. As you sit drinking your gourmet beer, listening to reggae, and reading the T.S. Eliot quotes on the wall, have them whip you up some shrimp Florentine, with spinach, mushrooms, shrimp, and alfredo sauce. Stop by for 25-cent oysters Sunday through Thursday.

Out at Lands End on the way to Wrightsville, the B.Y.O.C. (Bring Your Own Cellphone) crowd eat the fine cuts ($16.95–29.95, much cheaper at lunch) from the **Port City Chop House,** 1981 Eastwood Rd., 910/256-4955.

For another waterfront dining experience, head out on the way to Carolina Beach along the Masonboro Loop Road. **Trails End Steak House,** Trails End Road, 910/791-2034, has been serving up some of the area's most memorable beef platters for more than 30 years. This smallish restaurant, about a quarter-mile south of the Whiskey Creek Bridge, overlooks the Intracoastal Waterway. Expect to pay upwards of $35 for dinner, including salad bar and appetizers. To get there, turn right onto Masonboro Loop Road off Pine Grove Drive, then make a left onto Trails End Road, just over a quarter-mile after the Whiskey Creek bridge. Call for reservations—especially on weekends.

**The Oceanic,** 703 Lumina Ave., Wrightsville Beach, 910/256-5551, provides a great view and some of the best food in the Wilmington area. In fact for a number of years Wilmingtonians voted the Oceanic the overall top restaurant in the area, the best seafood restaurant, and the restaurant with the best water view. For all the hoopla, prepare yourself for a fairly laid-back experience here: historic photos, wood wainscoting, attentive waitfolk in shorts, polo shirts, and ball caps, and some very fresh and thoughtfully prepared seafood. The shrimp, crab, and scallops Oceanic ($18.95)—fresh shrimp, broiled with backfin crabmeat, scallops, and Monterey Jack in sherry cream sauce—will eat up lots of Weight Watchers points, but it sure tastes great.

Out at Kure Beach, **Big Daddy's Seafood Restaurant,** 202 K Ave., 910/458-8622, features quality seafood in a just-growed setting. In whimsical contrast to all the usual nautical paraphernalia on the walls (also here), the owner has hung French poster art. No reason, no marketing strategy—just a quirk of the owner: she went to France, liked the posters, brought them home, and hung them up. Set just a block from the Kure Beach fishing pier, which is perfect for taking a beachfront stroll before or after your meal. Expect to spend about $15–18.95 for dinner. From 2–5 P.M. most nights, Big Daddy's features $8 pecks of oysters, or you can buy the little critters individually for 25 cents.

Many people forget about the dinner cruise option, but on Fridays and Saturdays, April through December, taking one of the dinner/dancing cruises aboard the *Henrietta III* is really a pretty good deal, running $33–$36 per person for the complete evening (except drinks). Call 800/676-0162 or 910/343-1611 for reservations. The Friday night boat features a buffet with baked chicken and roast beef and leaves at 7:30 P.M., returning at 10 P.M. On Saturday, the cruise has a seafood and chicken buffet, and leaves at 6:30, returning at 9:30 P.M. On either night, get there early for a good seat.

## Southern

Set in the antebellum W. G. Fowler house, the **Taste of Country Buffet,** 226 S. Front St., 910/343-9888, puts out like a Sunday pig-pickin' seven days a week, offering up an all-you-can-eat buffet of roasted pig, barbecued pork, fried chicken and fish, baked chicken, and other important Southern church-potluck staples as chicken and pastry, stewed vegetables, biscuits, hush puppies, banana pudding, and chitterlings. On Friday and Saturday nights, there's fried shrimp and clams and roast beef; Sunday they cook up a turkey. Prices, which include tax and a drink, run $6.99 for lunches, Monday–Saturday; $9.50 for dinners and Sunday brunch. Open Monday–Thurday for lunch (11 A.M.–3 P.M.), Friday and Saturday 11 A.M.–9 P.M., and Sunday 11 A.M.–4 P.M.

**The Reel Cafe,** 100 S. Front St., 910/251-1832, website: www.thereelcafe.com, celebrates Wilmington filmmaking with a full bar, a rooftop bar, and lots of nifty relics from the Golden Age of Carolina Film . . . which is to say, just a couple of years ago. Specialties include Louisiana shrimp pasta, sandwiches, and blackened seafood salad. Prices run from $4.99 for the "Royalle with Cheese" quarter-pound cheeseburger to nearly $20 for some of the seafood. Open for lunch and dinner.

**Caffe Phoenix,** 9 S. Front St., Wilmington, 910/343-1395, offers fine food, an indoor balcony, and the overriding sense that somewhere on the reservations log it reads, *Streisand, party of four.* Visiting movie people favor Caffe Phoenix, and so I'm not making a stretch here. It's one of the only places in North Carolina where you can sip a Coppola while sitting *beside* a Coppola. Very pretty at night, more economical during the day. The sandwiches, seafood, and pasta are good anytime. Extensive wine selection. Dinner prices run $12–27 a plate.

For sheer ambience . . . and plenty of it, it's hard to beat **Alleigh's,** 4925 New Centre Dr., 910/793-0999, with its various theme areas, atmospheric outdoor tiki bar, and so on. Live music. Maybe the food's more fun than good, but it's good enough if you're looking for fun.

## Italian

A Italian spot out in downtown Wrightsville Beach, **Clarence Fosters,** 22 N. Lumina Ave., 910/256-0224, serves good seafood, pasta, steaks, and Italian dishes at moderate prices. **Rialto,** in Wrightsville Beach at 530 Causeway Dr., 910/256-1099,

serves a more uptown version of the same genre. Dinner only, with prices at around $9.75–22.

## Mexican

For the best local Mexican food, most folks point to **K-38 Baja Grill,** 5410 Oleander Dr., 910/395-6040, founded and named after the legendary surf spot by Josh Vach, who surfed there and now has found an ingenious way to bring up that fact in conversations for the rest of his life. Gnarly grub, with buku innovative variations including tuna rolls, avocado vinaigrettes, and multicolored tortillas.

## Asian

Former Manhattan restaurant owner Joseph Hou runs two popular spots here. **Szechuan 130,** 130 N. Front St., 910/762-5782, is the very busy downtown descendant of the beloved **Szechuan 132,** University Landing on College Road, 910/799-1426. Both offer atmosphere and a good selection of soups, including a nice velvet corn soup. Entrées ($5.95–12.95) include the delicious (and awe-inspiring), flaming **volcano beef** ($15.95).

**Hiro Japanese Steakhouse,** 419 S. College Rd., 910/452-3097, offers top-grade steaks and chicken for dinner only; average price runs around $16. Communal seating.

## Burgers and Diner Food

As the Mayberry-like ambience of downtown Wilmington works its way from your eyes to your stomach, a chocolate malted or fresh-squeezed lemonade, even a burger or tuna melt, might sound good. If so, look no further than **Hall's Drug Store,** Fifth and Castle Streets, 910/762-5265, the sort of counter and booth spot where Norman Rockwell might have come for inspiration.

In the retro category, **Front Street Diner** offers breakfast and lunch at 118 S. Front St., 910/772-1311. Open every day but Tuesday, from 6:30 A.M. to 2:30 P.M. Cash only. The **Dixie Grill and Pool Room,** 116 Market

> *As the Mayberry-like ambience of downtown Wilmington works its way from your eyes to your stomach, a chocolate malted or fresh-squeezed lemonade, even a burger or tuna melt, might sound good.*

WILMINGTON

**Cape Fear Memorial Bridge, from Chandler's Wharf**

St., 910/762-7280, has been serving up breakfast, lunch, and dinner (including some tasty bean soup) to Wilmingtonians since 1910. To put things in perspective, when you take a seat at the Dixie, you eat in place of earlier regulars who sat guzzling coffee and talking over Teddy Roosevelt's Bull Moose candidacy, the *Titanic* disaster, and the Black Sox scandal. By the time people sat in here discussing the Hindenburg tragedy and the ominous ambitions of Adolph Hitler over their grits, some of them were parents who had themselves grown up coming to the Dixie. And so on, through World War II, Elvis, desegregation, Watergate, September 11, and every point in between.

A recent ownership change, while respectful of its weighty inheritance, has made the Dixie a little more user-friendly to diners who have been spoiled by high-falutin', upstart chains like the Waffle House. New pool tables have been rolled in, the ancient interior got a good scrubbing and a coat of paint, and the menu has been updated to include such finery as apple-cinnamon buttermilk pancakes and homemade sausages. It's a lot of change for a joint that can still remember the first time the owner lugged in a newfangled

radio for the customers' enjoyment, but I expect the Dixie will survive this, and likely outlive us all.

For arguably the best burgers in town, head to the south end of the University of North Carolina's Wilmington campus to find **P.T.'s Grille,** 4544 Fountain Dr., 910/392-2293. Giant burgers and great fries (with the skin on) keep UNCW students coming back after all these years. Chicken breast sandwiches are available for the healthier-minded.

## Brewpubs

The first brewery in this part of the state, **Front Street Brewery,** 9 N. Front St., 910/251-1935, nails the brewpub thing cold. First, though it only got here in 1995, it's set in an old (1883) building with wood floors, old photos on the walls, fish and chips and pot pies (among more commonly available seafood and steak dishes,) a friendly crowd, and some unique, top-notch homemade brews, including a memorable raspberry wheat beer. A lot of locals like it because of the $2.25 pints, all day, every day. **Paddy's Hollow,** in the Cotton Exchange, 910/762-4354, features a similarly stellar location and a Victorian Irish theme. Nice location, friendly folks, good chargrilled steaks, 25-cent wings Monday–Thursday 5–7 P.M., a Friday prime rib dinner for $8.95, and many, many beers. The food's better than your average pub, too.

## Barbecue

**Flip's Bar-B-Que House,** 5818 Oleander Dr., 910/799-6350, is a fine, unself-conscious barbecue place with some great barbecue (you can buy a bottle of the sauce to take home) and a bunch of taxidermied critters all about, including a bear. Closed Sunday. Try some of the lime supreme pie for dessert.

In 1999 **Jackson's Big Oak Barbecue,** 920 S. Kerr Ave., Wilmington, 910/799-1581, was voted the best barbecue in Wilmington by the readers of *Encore* magazine. Good teas, good sides, great barbecue. Closed Sunday. You'll also find good, though not particularly indigenous, ribs at the Wilmington edition of Charleston-based, Memphis-influenced **Sticky Fingers,** 5044 Market St., 910/452-7427. Native or not, these are great ribs.

Cape Fear River from the *Henrietta III*

## ENTERTAINMENT
### Cruises

To really appreciate a port town, you have to approach it at least once from the water. The folks at **Cape Fear Riverboats,** waterfront at Dock Street, 800/676-0162, offer a good way of doing this with their cruises aboard the *Henrietta III.* Salty Vietnam War veteran Carl Marshburn has run his scenic *Henrietta* cruises up and down the Cape Fear River since 1988, early on in the Wilmington renaissance. He named his dinner and dancing paddlewheeler after the *Henrietta,* the first steam paddleboat built in North Carolina, which ran here safely and profitably for 40 years back in the 19th century. After 11 years of service, Carl sold the *Henrietta II,* and then Carl and a skeleton crew flew out to Illinois to his new boat, quickly dubbed the *Henrietta III.* In 16 days of nonstop cruising, the former gambling ship made it down the Ohio and into the Mississippi and then out into the Gulf Coast, around Florida, and up the East Coast until it reached its new home and went, almost imme-

diately, to work. For a long time the inside of the air-conditioned riverboat (not a paddlewheeler) continued to feature a glitzy Las Vegas motif, but the good captain says he'll have it renovated away by the time you read this.

The *Henrietta III* makes narrated sightseeing cruises, a lunch cruise, sunset cruises, dinner dance cruises, and moonlight cruises. Call for information. If you take the cruise (you should), Captain Marshburn will likely be piloting, and you ought to try to talk with him, to draw out some of his interesting stories of life here on the Cape Fear River.

One story concerns a friend of his who works coordinating special effects for local filmmakers. The friend lives in a 1790 home along the river, and after filming was completed for TNT's *The Hunley,* the friend installed two of that film's mock cannons outside his home, facing the river as if they were part of Wilmington's 18th-century civil defense system. The Styrofoam cannons looked real, and they could actually fire their fake charges. One afternoon the friend had a

WILMINGTON

© MIKE SIGALAS

party underway, and as Carl and his shipful of visitors cruised by, the friend decided to open fire on Carl's boat. The partying would-be ambushers, not in the clearest of minds, cut the fuse too long and stuffed too much powder into the cannon. Not only did it fire too late, after the boat had passed, but it blew up the cannon, sending Styrofoam flying everywhere. Which goes to show, alcohol and artillery—even Styrofoam mock-19th-century artillery—just don't mix. Unless the friend has tried a second attack, you should still be able to see the other cannon in front of the old home today. Carl will probably point it out in his narration.

## Nightlife

The Wilmington downtown scene changes so quickly that it's pointless talking about where's hip to go *today*, since today will be, like, ancient history to trendsetting Wilmingtonians six months from now. When you get to town, hunt up a copy of *Encore, The Outrider,* or one of the other local entertainment freebie mags to find out who is playing where. But here's a general rundown: **The Arena,** 6317 Market St., 910/794-1861, features live music and serves late-night food until 2 A.M. Every Sunday night is blues, jazz, or reggae. **Charley Brownz,** 21 S. Front St., 910/245-9499, quickly became an institution downtown, populated by folks in their late twenties and up. You can eat the above-average bar food here as well as drink and watch sports; full menu served until 11 P.M. and "Muncheez" until 2 A.M. The **Paleo-Sun Atomic Bar,** 35 N. Front St., 910/762-7600, website: www.paleoatomic .com, offers (nighttime only) carousing and drinking in a counterculture atmosphere. Costs $2 "Private Membership Fee" to get in. **The Firebelly Lounge,** 265 N. Front St., 910/763-0141, stays open and serves food until 3 A.M. and features live music most nights from Thursday through Saturday. For blues and jazz, head over to the formerly headbanging **Rusty Nail Saloon,** 1310 S. Fifth St., 910/251-1888, website: www.grooveright.com/rustynail. Monday is poetry open mic night, and Sunday is an open jazz jam, starting at 6 P.M. Hip with the collegiate set is **.com,** 121 Grace St., 910/342-0266, a "Cybar

Dance Club," offering a Thursday ladies/college nite, and a Sunday dollar nite.

## Theater and Dance Venues

The premier artsy spot in Wilmington is **Thalian Hall Center for the Performing Arts,** 310 Chestnut St., 910/343-3664. The Opera House Theatre Company performs here, along with traveling artists and troupes. The **Sarah Graham Kenan Memorial Auditorium,** 601 S. College Rd., 910/962-3500, also gets many of the traveling companies that come through town. Each summer the **Cape Fear Shakespeare Festival** gets underway at the Greenfield Lake Amphitheater. Call 910/251-9457. Free. During the summer make your way down to the riverfront at dusk for **Sundown Shindig on the River,** a loose collection of street entertainment, arts and crafts, and food vendors.

## Movie Theaters

The clean, first-run **Carmike 16** over at 111 Cinema Dr., 910/815-0212, gets most of the "hot" movies first. The **Cinema 6** at 5335 Oleander Dr., 910/799-6666, is another place to check for new releases. **Thalian Hall,** 310 Chestnut St., sometimes shows classic old films on the big screen as part of its popular **Cinematique** series. Call for information. The **Fantail Film Festival** in June features top old Hollywood musicals from the 1940s, shown aboard the USS *North Carolina.* A memorable experience, and only fifty cents to get in. Call 910/251-5797 for information. To get a pulse for what's happening in Wilmington filmmaking, try to catch a **Film Nite** at Mollye's Market. Call 910/509-2890 for information and dates.

## Shopping

The **Cotton Exchange,** 321 N. Front St., 910/343-9896, website: www.cottonexchange.city-search.com, features 30 specialty shops and eateries tucked into four historic brick buildings. Much of these are traditional tourist-town niche stores, but among the stained-glass dolphins and Southwestern handicrafts, you'll find the **Celtic Shop,** 910/763-1990, and the atmospheric **Two Sisters Bookery,** 910/762-4444, with a well-chosen collection of local titles. **Fire and Spice,** 910/762-3050, offers hundreds of brands of searing hot sauces and salsas, sporting names like A Woman Scorned and Bayou Viagra.

Out at 1956 Carolina Beach Rd., Harriet Torres runs the funky **Funksters,** 910/762-5990, which advertises itself as "Wilmington's One and Only '50s and '60s Store."

## SPORTS AND RECREATION
### Surfing
The 2000 East Coast Wahine Surfing Championships at Wrightsville Beach got some national press when a female surfer from South Carolina broke away from her heat to save the life of a young boy sucked out by a Hurricane Alberto–churned riptide. A photo of the wet-suited heroine towing in the would-be drowning victim appeared in newspapers around the country.

The southern North Carolina coast enjoys pretty decent surf for this side of the country, and a very active surf scene. East Coast surfers congregate hereabouts for surf contests each summer. The best spot in the region is arguably the Crystal Pier, but it's also often the most crowded. Good spots include the north end of Wrightsville Beach in front of Shell Island Resort; I've seen some great surf off Fort Fisher, and Carolina Beach and Kure Beach can be good under the right conditions. So can Bald Head Island, though it's a pain to get there. As anywhere, stop by a surf shop, strike up a conversation with some local surfers, and find out where they're breaking the day you're there.

Check out www.sncsurf.com before you come; it's a great website for planning your Wilmington-area surfing.

The area is home to some 12 surf shops, but you'll find that one of the best surf shops is one of the first: **Surf City Surf Shop,** 530

*The 2000 East Coast Wahine Surfing Championships at Wrightsville Beach got some national press when a female surfer from South Carolina broke away from her heat to save the life of a young boy sucked out by a Hurricane Alberto–churned riptide.*

Causeway Dr., Wrightsville Beach, 910/256-2265, founded back in 1978 by a couple of surfers, one of whom moved down to North Myrtle Beach to open a couple more stores in the chain, and the other of whom stayed right here. **Sweetwater Surf Shop,** 10 N. Lumina Ave, Wilmington, 910/256-3821—you'll see it just as you cross the second bridge in Wrightsville Beach—is even older (founded 1976), and offers a good selection of new and used boards, including rentals. **Bert's,** U.S. 421, Carolina Beach, **Hot Wax Surf Shop,** 4510 Hoggard Dr., 910/791-9283, and the **Wrightsville Beach Supply Company,** 1 N. Lumina Ave., Wrightsville Beach, 910/256-8821 can also get you in the water.

For **Surf City's Surf Report,** call 910/256-4353.

### Bowling
The Sport of the Gods enjoys a first-rate location at the cleverly named **Ten Pin Alley,** Market Place Mall, 127 S. College Rd., 910/452-5455, featuring 24 lanes, pool tables, good food, and enough arcade games and TV screens to send a lit professor into convulsions. Open every night until 2 A.M. Second in the pecking order is **Cardinal Lanes,** 7026 Market St., 910/686-4223.

## GETTING THERE
### By Car
Most people coming to Wilmington get there by private automobile. If you're coming from the west, just take the I-40 until you reach town. If you're heading south or north along the I-95, turn east when you hit the I-40. And if you're taking U.S. 17, just continue north or south on into town.

### By Air
With a name that perhaps overstates it a bit, the **Wilmington International Airport,** 1740 Airport Blvd., off 23rd Street, two miles north of

Market Street, 910/341-4125, offers daily flights to and from the major domestic hubs. Airlines serving the airport include Delta-affiliated Atlantic Southeast Airlines, 800/282-3424; Midway Corporate Express Airlines, 800/555-6565; USAir, 800/428-4322; and United Airlines Express, 800/241-6522. It's within 10 minutes of downtown Wilmington, fortunately, so even a cab ride won't be too expensive. If you're going to be staying down on the Brunswick Isles, closer to the South Carolina line, try the Myrtle Beach International Airport.

### By Bus

**Greyhound,** 800/231-2222, and **Carolina Trailways,** 910/762-6625, can both get you into Wilmington proper. They'll bring you to the bus terminal at 201 Harnett St.

## GETTING AROUND

### By Bus

The **Wilmington Transit Authority (WTA),** 110 Castle St., 910/343-0106, provides a low-cost alternative to taxis for carless visitors hoping to explore Wilmington and its suburbs. One-way fare runs 75 cents. A transfer will cost you a dime. The buses run until 7:30 P.M. every day but Sundays and most state holidays. Your hotel may well have bus schedules; if not, stop by the Visitors Information Center at 24 N. Third St. to pick one up.

### By Taxi

**Lett's Taxi Service,** 910/458-3999, **Port City Taxi, Inc.,** 910/762-1165, and **Yellow Cab,** 910/762-3322, can all get you where you want to go in the Wilmington area. Most charge around $1.60 per mile.

### Car Rentals

The Wilmington area includes all the usual suspects in the rental car business, including **Budget,** 1740 Airport Blvd., Wilmington, 800/527-0700 or 910/762-8910, website: www.budget.com; and **Enterprise Rentals,** 5601 Market St., 800/736-8222 or 910/799-4042, website: www.enterprise.com.

## INFORMATION

### Tourist Information

Reach the nice folks over at the **Cape Fear Coast Convention Visitors Bureau** at 14 N. Third St., 800/222-4757 or 910/341-4030, fax 910/341-4029, email: info@cape-fear.nc.us.

### Emergencies

Call 911 in any emergency on the Cape Fear coast. If your car breaks down, or you want to call the State Highway Patrol for any other reason from your cell phone, call *HP.

### Hospitals

With luck your visit to Wilmington won't require a hospital trip, but if it does, the **New Hanover Regional Medical Center,** 2131 S. 17th St., 910/343-7000, is the largest hospital in the region, with five ICUs. The **Cape Fear Memorial Hospital,** 5301 Wrightsville Ave., 910/452-8384, is much smaller, but specializes in women's services.

A cheaper alternative for nonemergency care is to visit one of the many walk-in clinics. Two spots to try are **Doctor's Urgent Care Centre,** 4815 Oleander Dr., 910/452-111, open Monday–Saturday until 8 P.M. and Sunday noon–6 P.M.; and **The Pee Dee Clinic,** 1630 Military Cutoff Rd., 910/256-8087, open 9 A.M.–6 P.M. daily.

### Newspapers and Magazines

Owned by the *New York Times,* the *Wilmington Morning Star/Star-News* is the paper of record for Wilmington.

*The Outrider* is a decent little entertainment freebie you'll see around town, with more ads and charts showing who's playing where than articles. A great barometer of one corner of Carolina culture, this may be the only alternative weekly in existence that carries head shop adverts, a "Bar Babe of the Week" feature, *and* the NASCAR scoreboard within its covers. *Encore* is the more professional entertainment weekly, but either will work if all you want to do is plan your evening. You'll likely also spot the *Wilmington Journal* in racks around town. It's been published by and for African-Americans under one name or another since 1927.

*Wilmington Magazine,* a glossy, bimonth-ly publication, began appearing on coffee tables throughout southeastern North Carolina in 1994.

## South of Wilmington

### SOUTHPORT

Solid little Southport rolled up its sleeves, gritted its teeth, and took the brunt of Hurricane Floyd in 1999. Floyd's gone. Solid Southport remains.

Resting on the Intracoastal Waterway and protected from Atlantic storms by Oak and Bald Head Islands, Southport was chartered in 1792, but by then the area already had quite a history. Some argue that the first, ill-fated Spanish explorers bungled through these parts in 1524 and again in 1526. About 200 Native Americans lived in the area in 1715; five years later, none were left. About this time, Stede Bonnet, "The Gentleman Pirate," who admired North Carolina's lax piracy laws (and the state's laxer enforcement of them), operated in the area. He was arrested in the harbor after a fierce battle in 1718. The town itself began forming after the 1748 establishment of the British Fort Johnston.

Just before the Revolution, Josiah Martin, the dogged but not particularly confrontational last royal governor of North Carolina, fled to Fort Johnston hoping for refuge from rebellious colonists, but the horde proved mightier than his men, and he fled on July 18, 1775, to the HMS *Cruizer* offshore. The following night, the colonial Patriots burned the fort to the ground.

After the Revolution, fishermen and river pilots began building homes near the fort's ruins. Wealthy city dwellers also built second (and third and fourth) homes here to take advantage of the coastal breezes during Wilmington's hot summers.

One of the first plots of land planned by the community was "The Grove," now known as Franklin Square Park. The Grove was set aside for public use, and now more than two centuries later it is still being used by the public. Within the park is Franklin Square Gallery, which displays the works of local artists.

The victorious Americans built a new fort on the site after 1794; the "new" officers' quarters, which overlook the river, were constructed in 1805, and it has seen duty in every major American conflict since then. Confederates seized it from the Federals at the start of the War Between the States, and along with other forts in the area, it protected Wilmington's valuable blockade runners. Today it's occupied by the commanding officer of the Sunny Point Military Ocean Terminal.

During all these years, the town went by the name of Smithville, named after revolutionary general Benjamin Smith. In 1887 the town's fathers changed the name to the more place-specific Southport.

In turn-of-the-21st-century Southport, hurricane-tested oak trees still shade Victorian homes, but with 45,000 snowbirds (15,000 permanent residents) living out in the bedroom communities on Oak Island and Bald Head Island, the little town of 2,500 bustles a bit but in a very laid-back way, boasting 15 antique shops, a handful of seafood restaurants and historic sites, the small Southport Maritime Museum, and ample lodgings to make this a nice weekend getaway.

Rand McNally recently named Southport one of the best places in America to retire. It has that kind of pace to it. Today Southport continues to face the Atlantic, even if a couple of islands do somewhat block the view, and so it's fitting that **Waterfront Park** is the most popular spot in town for just sitting and watching life—and mammoth ocean-going vessels—go by. From here you can also see Bald Head Light (1817), 109 feet tall, and the oldest in the state. **Oak Island Light,** built in 1958, stands 168 feet tall and can be seen 24 miles away. By some estimates it's the brightest light in all of the United States.

### Sights

The little **North Carolina Maritime Museum at Southport,** a.k.a. the Southport Maritime

Museum, 116 N. Howe St., 910/457-0003, is a good place to stop in when you first get to town. It tells the Cape Fear region's story with exhibits on the colonial era, pirates, steamboating, fishing, and shipwrecks. You can see a fragment from a 2,000-year-old Native American canoe, a 200-pound pile torpedo pulled from the Cape Fear River, and relics from the shipwrecked *City of Houston*. Admission runs $2 for adults, $1 for senior citizens; children under 16 free. Open Tuesday–Saturday, 10 A.M.–4 P.M.

But really the best thing about Southport is the strolling. Head off some evening (morning will do in a pinch) along Howe and Moore or one of the many residential streets in this historic town. Watch the boats passing by along the Southport **Riverwalk** and just melt into the 19th-century ambience of the town. As you might guess, the locals pull out all the stops for the annual **North Carolina 4th of July Festival.**

### Diving

Wayne Strickland at **Scuba South Diving Company,** 222 South River Dr., 910/457-5201, takes his 52-foot boat (certified for 24 passengers) up to 100 miles offshore to dive sites off Cape Fear's Frying Pan Shoals, including the *City of Houston* steamship and various Civil War wrecks (blockade runners, freighters, and many more). Fortunately Cape Fear has been more than generous in supplying wreck sites for the pleasure of Captain Strickland's clientele. He leaves most mornings at 7 A.M. Walk-ons are welcome if there's room, but call ahead for reservations if possible.

### Accommodations

For most people, Southport's a B&B kind of town. If you want to motel it, try the literally named **Riverside Motel,** 910/457-6986, ($65 a night) which is clean and simple and may remind you of the place where Gere and Winger used to cavort in *An Officer and a Gentleman*. If you're planning to bring in your own fish and need somewhere to cook them, the $80-a-night **Sea Captain Motor Lodge,** 608 W. West St., 910/457-5263, website: www.ncbrunswick.com, offers 12 efficiencies among its 84 rooms.

The stately Federal-style **Brunswick Inn Bed & Breakfast,** 301 E. Bay St., 910/457-5278, website: www.brunswickinn.com, overlooks the Cape Fear River, providing its guests with views of Bald Head Island and the Oak Island Lighthouse. The large bedrooms, furnished with period furniture, have fireplaces and private baths. **Cape Fear Inn,** 317 W. Bay St., 910/457-5989, website: www.ncbrunswick.com, ia also right on the waterfront. Each offers 12 rooms for under $100 a night.

Lois Jane's Riverview Inn, 106 W. Bay St., 800/457-1152 or 910/457-6701, is across the street from the waterfont and offers four rooms and a nice fireplace for under $100 a night.

### Food

Down beside the yacht basin, **Port Charlie's,** 317 W. Bay St., 910/457-0801, is a rustic on-the-water sort of place that you can boat or walk to. Great views of the harbor and very fresh, and not necessarily fried, seafood, along with good steaks, pasta, and so on. The **Marker One Lounge,** in the same building, has a jukebox and dartboards; you'll expect Jimmy Buffett to stumble in at any moment. A good place to start or finish up the evening.

### Information

At the **Southport/Oak Island Chamber of Commerce,** 4848 Longbeach Rd. S.E., 910/457-5787, you'll find maps, pamphlets galore, and self-guided walking tours.

## BALD HEAD ISLAND

Bald Head Island advertises itself as "An Exclusive Sanctuary," which it is. Of course, whether or not the wealthy really need *another* sanctuary is debatable . . . but never mind. The advertisements also point to the island's "Low Key Charm," but of course, nobody needs to be ostentatious here to let others know they're loaded—just being here on the island attests to *that*. The island offers a Hilton Head for people who think Hilton Head is for commoners. You'll find very few short-term stays available; likely you won't be staying here unless you know somebody or are ready to pay for a week's rental at a very expensive home; you can, however, go over on the ferry (no cars) and spend the day on the fairly undeveloped (though not fairly developed) island. If you get over there, stop by the **Bald Head Light** (1817), 109 feet tall, and the oldest in the state. Call the Bald Head Island Information Center at 800/234-2441 for information.

## THE SOUTH BRUNSWICK ISLES

Between the sprouting fingers of Wilmington and Myrtle Beach lie the South Brunswick Isles, where you can still sense the recent rural past of a southern Tar Heel coast as yet uncovered with asphalt and stucco—but you'd best hurry. True, the islands have long been developed in beach-shabby style, in a here-until-the-next-storm sort of way, but as beachfront land becomes more scarce, the realtors and bulldozers seem to have shifted into high gear.

As opposed to the Outer Banks, which have drawn visitors from the North for generations, Holden Beach, Ocean Isle Beach, and Sunset Beach have drawn mostly Carolinians. They've historically functioned as a laid-back, sand-road, regional vacation spot. Carolinians disinterested in the glitz—and higher prices—of Myrtle Beach and the Wilmington beaches would rent a home here each year. But as upstate Carolinians have grown wealthier, more and more of them meander this way looking for condos and summer houses. Prices are rising, and so are the crowds, though this is still a great place for a low-key family getaway.

**Holden Beach,** developed in the 1930s, comes first as you head south from Wilmington on U.S. 17. Because it sets at just the right spot as the coastline sweeps northeasterly to Cape Fear, Holden faces due south; this means you can catch both the sunrise and sunset here without once moving your towel.

Heading south, **Ocean Isle Beach** comes along

*Between the sprouting fingers of Wilmington and Myrtle Beach lie the South Brunswick Isles, where you can still sense the recent rural past of a southern Tar Heel coast as yet uncovered with asphalt and stucco—but you'd best hurry.*

next. Developed in the 1950s, Ocean Isle Beach was a planned community from the start. Odell Williamson returned from World War II with dreams of creating a perfect beach community, with a small commercial quarter and lots of room for family homes. And that's pretty much what Ocean Isle Beach is, even today. You might blink a bit as you cross the causeway and see the **Ocean Isle Beach Water Slide,** 3 Second St., 910/579-9678, but kids won't complain, and that's really about as far as the Myrtlesque developments go on the island. Ocean Isle is also home to the very worthwhile **Museum of Coastal Carolina,** 21 E. Second St., 910/579-1016, with extensive exhibits on both the natural and human history of the Carolina coast. If you're coming to the isles for a few days, stop by here early in your trip to pick up the background information that will make your shell-hunting and tide-watching all the more intriguing.

Little three-mile-long **Sunset Beach** was developed after the other two islands, by Odell Williamson's former partner, Manlon Gore. Sunset feels more remote than the other islands—maybe it's the old-fashioned swing bridge you have to cross to get there—with just a dash of commercialism. Stop by **Bill's Seafood Market,** 310 Sunset Blvd., 910/579-6372, to stock up for the grill.

### Accommodations

If you'd like to stay overnight at Holden Beach you'll find the traditional beachy **Gray Gull Motel** at 3263 Holden Beach Rd. S.W., 910/842-6775. Or try the **Crescent Moon Inn,** 965 Sabbath Home Rd. S.W., 877/727-1866 or 910/842-1190, which offers two rooms and two suites. The **Yardarm Inn,** at 167 Ocean Blvd. W., 910/842-8074, is really a pair of rental houses, one on the oceanfront, one on the second row. Contact **Alan Holden Vacations,** 128 Ocean Blvd. W., 800/720-2200 or 910/842-6061, website: www.holden-beach.com, for information on the Yardarm Inn. Alan Holden can also connect you with a variety of local rental houses on all three of the islands, which is the way most people experience the Brunswick Isles. **Brunswickland Realty,** 123 Ocean Blvd. W., 800/842-6949 or 910/842-6949, website: www.weblync.com/brunswickland, is considered another of the more dependable rental outfits.

For shorter stays, a new and very clean beachfront alternative on Ocean Isle is **The Islander Inn,** 57 W. First St., 888/325-4753, website: www.islanderinn.com. Hard-by is the similar **Ocean Isle Inn,** 37 W. First St., 800/352-5988, website: www.oceanisleinn.com. Down on Sunset you'll find the **Sunset Beach Motel,** at 6 Main St., 910/579-7093, and **Continental Motel & Apartments,** 431 S. Sunset Blvd., 910/579-6772.

### Food

For eats at Ocean Isle Beach, try **Sharky's,** 81 Causeway Dr., 910/579-9177, at the island end of the Ocean Isle Causeway, where you'll discover a great deck (boaters can tie up here) and top-quality beach food: seafood, pizza, and steaks. Located upstairs from Bill's Seafood Market at Sunset Beach is **Crabby Oddwaters,** 310 Sunset Blvd., 910/579-6372, which serves (as you might guess) seafood as well, and enjoys a lot of popularity. Crabby's is a nice place to sip an adult beverage and enjoy the view, but if you're looking for

live music, **Steamers II,** 8 Second St., 910/575-9009, at Ocean Isle Beach offers some of the best nightlife on the Southern Brunswick Isles. Weekends bring live bands, which play the kinds of music most popular hereabouts, from beach music to rock and country.

## CALABASH

Little Calabash, not unlike Lexington, is most famous as a place where a popular type of North Carolina food was first born. Shrimpers returning to Calabash's docks with the daily catch used to deep-fry a pot of shrimp at the end of a long day down by the water. Tourists, who had come to the docks to watch the shrimpers, smelled the shrimp cooking, grew hungry, and started opening up their wallets to see if they could buy some of the fresh, crispy catch. Soon, enterprising Calabash natives found they could make more selling the fried shrimp to outlanders than they could catching it. Today, you'll see scores of "Calabash Seafood Buffets" along the Grand Strand in Myrtle Beach, SC, but you'll also find a number of them right here in Calabash. A couple of the more popular ones are **Calabash Seafood Hut,** 1125 River Rd., 910/579-6723, and **The Coleman's Original Calabash Seafood Restaurant,** 9931 Nance St., 910/579-6875.

# Raleigh and the Triangle

North Carolina's Research Triangle consists of the cities of Raleigh, Durham, and Chapel Hill (along with Cary, Raleigh's adjacent upscale suburb). But while the cities may be considered of a piece today, it was not always so. Raleigh was the first Triangle city founded—way back in the days immediately after the American Revolution, when Tar Heel state legislators eschewed Hillsborough, Fayetteville, and other contenders and decided to create North Carolina's new, centrally located capital from the ground up. Chapel Hill grew up—very slowly—around the state university founded shortly after Raleigh, and was likewise placed in the center of the state to appease North Carolinians east and west with its play-no-favorites location.

If Government and Education established two of the Triangle's three corners by legislative fiat, Durham's ascendancy as the third corner of the state's three-cornered heart came from the Marketplace. The tax dollars and philanthropic grants that Raleigh and Chapel Hill subsisted on came from rough-and-tumble, crude and flagrantly, filthy rich Durham, where the Gilded Age was plated precisely the golden color of bright leaf tobacco, rolled up into Camel cigarettes for the Duke family's American Tobacco Company.

In the midst of these three towns—but closest to Durham—is Research Triangle Park. As with the Triangle itself, it owes its existence to a combination of government planning and commercial savvy; the 7,000 acre, eight-by-

Pullen Park in Raleigh

RALEIGH

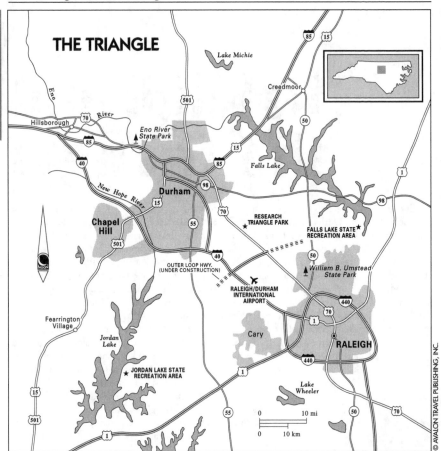

THE TRIANGLE

© AVALON TRAVEL PUBLISHING, INC.

two-mile technological swath in the pine trees southeast of Durham is owned and operated as a private, nonprofit entity by Research Triangle Foundation. The park is home to 100 playgrounds for R&D types, and in addition to the incredible boon to the state's economy, through the years Triangle researchers have brought the region fame by inventing or helping to invent or develop a variety of important technologies, from those that help save lives (3D ultrasound technology, the AIDS fighter AZT, and even the childproof medicine cap) to those that have left mixed footprints on the human culture, including Astroturf, the barcode reader, and digital cellular phones.

The high-paying jobs at Research Triangle Park and the area's universities fill the region with affluent professionals lured from across the state and around the world, whose spending powers a massive service economy that has, in turn, drawn many others.

## HISTORY

In the years after North Carolina first reinvented itself as an American state, one of the first priorities of the founders was to replace New Bern as

© ERIKA HOWSARE

**North Carolina's three presidents, outside the state capitol**

Raleigh was laid out in 1792 and named for North Carolina's most famous admirer from afar, Sir Walter Raleigh. The town plan featured four 99-foot-wide main streets and 66-feet-wide auxiliary streets. Plans called for four public squares of four acres each, and in the middle of these was to be a fifth, six-acre square, home to the state Capitol building. The cornerstone for the first Capitol was laid that year.

Despite a trio of devastating fires, including the 1831 fire that burned down the old statehouse, the town grew rich. Timely intercession by Union General John "Black Jack" Logan prevented the town from burning yet again during the Civil War, and the city went on to prosper as a government center and shipping hub throughout the late 1800s and early 1900s. Triangle Park (RTP) was begun in 1959 when UNC's Dr. Howard Odom, Greensboro developer Romeo Guest, and Governor Luther Hodges put their heads together to solve a problem. The Triangle's universities, it seemed, were educating many of the nation's top medical researchers, which was good. But when they graduated, all these Ph.D.s— many of them Tar Heels born and raised—had

the state capital. Most agreed that the capital needed to be closer to the center of the far-flung state, and farther from the danger of amphibious assault by European invaders.

Hillsborough, Tarboro, and Fayetteville all fought to host the capital; the debate burned so hotly that the State Assembly decided to put the question into the hands of the soon-to-gather Constitutional Convention elected to debate the new Federal Constitution in Hillsborough in 1788. This party of men—and "party" appears to have been the operative term—decided that rather than risk offending the representatives of one town or another, they would choose an entirely new site in the center of the state, within 10 miles of Isaac Hunter's tavern, a popular stop for travelers and generally acknowledged to have the best rum punch for miles. Three years later, the Assembly allocated money to buy 1,000 acres from farmer Joel Lane near the Wake County courthouse.

## TRIANGLE HIGHLIGHTS

**African American Heritage Preservation Cultural Complex (AACC),** Raleigh

**Bennett Place State Historic Site,** Durham

**Brightleaf Square,** Durham

**City Market,** Raleigh

**Durham Bulls Stadium** and **Historic Durham Athletic Park**

**Exploris,** Raleigh

**Historic Hillsborough**

**Mama Dip's Kitchen,** Chapel Hill

**Mordecai Historic Park** and **President Andrew Johnson's Birthplace,** Raleigh

**Pullen Park,** Raleigh

# THE WAR OF REGULATION

One thing that sets the Hillsborough region off from the rest of the state is that it formerly belonged to the Granville District, originally granted to the Earl of Granville, one of the Carolinas' original lords proprietors. Granville resisted selling his tract when all the other proprietors did, so this was the sole slice of North Carolina that did not fall under royal rule after 1729. Thus, the Granville District employed private sheriffs and other political officers, and these were known for their corruption. The citizens of the district complained to the colonial government in the eastern part of the state, but the royal governor and legislators—most of them living on the coast—seemed uninclined to help them. Eventually the citizens formed into a group they called the Regulators, sworn to regulate the governing of the district. They took over county court buildings and captured corrupt officers. When Governor Tryon got wind that even New Bern was at risk, he gathered up a 1,100-man provincial militia and marched deep into Regulator country, confronting 2,000 Regulators at the Battle of Alamance Creek on May 16, 1771.

To his credit, the Irish-born Tryon desperately tried to avoid having to shoot his own subjects. For days he had sent letters demanding the immediate surrender of the Regulators, and the Regulators had responded by demanding that the governor first promise reforms. Tryon saw this as blackmail, and believed that if he gave in now, royal law and order would be forever compromised in the colonies. He was willing to pardon the Regulators if they would put down their arms, but he would not negotiate with them.

Two days later, on the 16th, the Governor ordered his troops to march toward the Regulator camp; the Regulators heard them coming and stood in formation, ready to fire. When the armies were 300 yards apart, Tryon ordered his men to halt. He sent messengers across the no-man's-land to try to convince them to lay down their arms. The Regulators told them to go to Hell. Tryon became convinced that the Regulators, in continuing to make their demands, were actually stalling while

their troops gained better position. He sent a final warning: if the Regulators did not surrender immediately, his troops would open fire.

The white-faced messenger returned with the Regulators' message: "Fire. Fire and be damned."

The militia's six swivel guns and two brass field pieces opened fire. The militiamen opened with musket fire, and the Regulators held their ground and returned fire. After half an hour, they fled to the trees on the perimeter and began firing from there. Tryon's men fought them—standing in the open clearing while the Regulators fired from behind trees—for another hour and a half.

Muskets were not extremely lethal weapons, and both sides were able to continue fighting for some time. Finally, the Regulators stopped shooting as heavily as before and Tryon ordered his troops to charge. They chased the Regulators deep into the woods. In all, it's a testimony to the ineffectiveness of musketfire to note that only nine of Tryon's men were killed, and only 61 wounded. The Regulators, who had by all rights suffered a devastating defeat, lost nine men as well, with 200 wounded.

In addition to the wounded, Tryon took 20 to 30 Regulators prisoner. He hung six of them a month later in Hillsborough on June 19, 1771. Afterwards, hundreds of the surviving Regulators headed over the mountain passes, beyond the reach—temporarily—of the Eastern government. But most of the Regulators and their sympathizers remained here around Hillsborough, and it was probably, suggests historian William S. Powell, for this reason that North Carolina Patriots decided to hold the Third Provincial Congress in Hillsborough. They knew the folks around here were a cantankerous, suspicious lot, and the Patriots wanted to make sure that they would not find themselves fighting both the Regulators—who still wanted local representation and freedom from the dominance of the eastern part of the state—and the English. Hillsborough was also the site of the important Constitutional Convention of 1788, where the North Carolina delegates demanded a Bill of Rights before they would ratify the U.S. Constitution.

to move elsewhere to find work. Meanwhile the rest of the state was steeped in low-paying agricultural jobs, or working at the mills.

It's an interesting conundrum, looked at historically. After all, 1959 was near the height of the Cold War, and over in East Berlin, the Soviets were suffering the same problem, as their well-trained scientists and technicians were also fleeing to places where they could prosper financially.

In Germany, Soviets built the Berlin Wall to keep "defectors" from escaping to greener pastures in West Berlin. In North Carolina, capitalists, assisted by government officials who helped clear the way, built Research Triangle Park between Raleigh, Durham, and Chapel Hill, making the home pasture more green in an attempt to get more research-related professionals to stay and spend in the area. It worked.

## Raleigh and Vicinity

Raleigh has been North Carolina's capital city since its inception; consequently, you'll find a number of interesting (and often free) sites here, from the obvious capital city ones—the Executive Mansion, the Capitol building, the state museums—to quaint neighborhoods and parks.

More than 270,000 people now live in Raleigh proper, with more than 570,000 people in Wake County. Raleigh, once a griddy example of civic pre-planning, has had a tough time keeping up with its exponential growth in recent decades. Traffic—gridlock, if you will—is an issue here, as it is all across the Triangle. In the American Lung Association's 2002 State of the Air report, the Raleigh-Durham-Chapel Hill region tied with Philadelphia for the 10th most-polluted air in the nation. Triangle police and EMTs now receive training in dealing with gang members. With big-city incomes and growth have come big-city problems.

## SIGHTS

### Orientation

The most fundamental geographic distinction in Raleigh is "outside the Beltline" versus "inside the Beltline." If you're "inside the Beltline," you're inside the loop that I-440 makes around the city's center. "Inside" includes most of the best sites in town: the Capitol, the Joel Lane House, Pullen Park, the Capital Area Visitors Center, the Museum of History, the City Market, the State Farmer's Market, walkable Oakwood, and NCSU. If you're "outside the

Beltline" you're in the generally newer area where you'll find the North Carolina Museum of Arts, the AllTel Pavilion, and the Entertainment and Sports Arena. However, it's worth mentioning that the I-540 Northern Wake Expressway, or "Outer Loop," an attempt to lasso and provide freeway access to at least some of the Ral-sprawl, is under construction, and will be for several years. Of course, when it's complete, property values in the areas it serves will skyrocket, and the sprawl will billow out further, until another pragmatist proposes an "*Outer* Outer Loop."

As with any good-sized Southern city, Raleigh has a Five Points District, inside the Beltline along Glenwood Avenue, where within a scone's throw you'll find the city's best theater, pizza parlor, and coffeehouse.

One of the benefits of being the capital city of a state is the museums that collect there. Best of all, many—though not all—are free.

### African American Heritage Preservation Cultural Complex (AACC)

If you think of American culture as a quilt, the AACC, 119 Sunnybrook Rd., 919/212-3598, exists to help point out which of the patches were contributed by African-Americans: egg beaters, for instance, and ice cream cones, peanut oil, and stoplights. The three-acre complex also offers visitors a distinctive group of historical artifacts and documents pertaining to African-Americans in general and black North Carolinians specifically. Displays are housed in several buildings along a nature trail, and include a tribute to Benjamin Spaulding, the founder of the North Carolina Mutual Life Insurance Company—but perhaps the star of the complex is the 50-by-15-foot replica of the *Amistad* slave ship, available for perusing during the day, and at night used in the outdoor drama *The Amistad Saga: Reflections,* which recounts the true story of a slave ship mutiny and the subsequent trial that, the center contends, was "the first Civil Rights Case in America. . . . an early example of people of different cultures, races, faiths, and genders uniting to fight for the same cause of freedom and dignity through the American Democratic Process."

Dr. E.B. Palmer and his wife, Anita, founded the complex as Black Heritage Park back in 1989. It has grown amid the woods behind the Palmers' house principally from the financial and sweat contributions of local friends and organizations. The Complex incorporated in 1994, and by 2000, 140,000 people a year were touring the grounds and exhibits. Admission is still free, but the Com-

plex is struggling to become fully self-sufficient, so if you appreciate what you see, leave a donation. In the meantime, the people here are hoping the publicity from the *Amistad* play—the only outdoor drama in America written, directed, and performed by African-Americans—may well do the trick. The shows are held two weekends in July; call for specific dates. Tickets are $10, adults, $6 children (ages 6–12).

## Artspace

At 201 E. Davie St., 919/821-2787, website: www.artspace.citysearch.com, Artspace is a visual arts center housing more than 25 working studios and two exhibition spaces. You can see artists working and visit whatever exhibitions under way. Hours vary depending on which of the working artists happen to be working. There's no charge for admission, though you won't have to wrestle them to the ground to take your donation.

## Contemporary Art Museum

Now ensconced in its new home at 409 W. Mar-

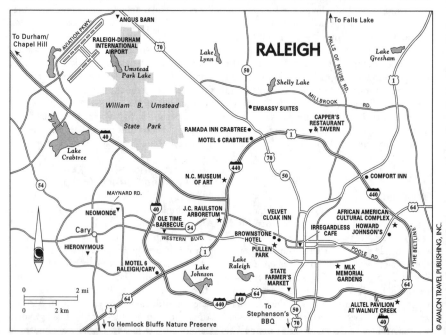

© AVALON TRAVEL PUBLISHING, INC.

tin St., 919/836-0088, the CAM's name pretty much says it. So deep is its commitment to currency that the museum doesn't even collect art—meaning that every exhibit is a visiting exhibit, and when one visit concludes, the next new thing comes along, ensuring that working artists have a place to be seen while they're still alive. Some 60,000 patrons visit the CAM each year, nearly a third of them in schoolbuses. Call ahead for hours and admission prices.

## Exploris

Opened in the final months of the 20th century at 201 E. Hargett St., 919/834-4040, website: www.exploris.org, Raleigh's very own "interactive global learning center" is a shrine to the interconnectedness of the Global Age, a sort of interactive "It's a Small World" for adults and kids alike, without that maddening song. It challenges its visitors to appreciate the relationships and similarities we share with people from around the world, while also encouraging us to respect our differences. This little chapel of humanist optimism is an advisable stop for anyone interested in how the world operates beyond his or her personal horizon. The International Gift Shop is worth a browse; it offers some items you never thought you'd find in the heart of North Carolina. Exploris is open 9 A.M.–5 P.M., Tuesday–Saturday, noon–5 P.M., Sunday; open Monday in the summer (Memorial Day–Labor Day). Admission is $7.95, adults, $5.50, children 4–11, kids under four are free. You can also buy a discount ticket which also allows entrance to one IMAX show: $12.95, adults $8.95, children.

## IMAX Theatre at Exploris

On the same grounds is this 2001 megatheater, an attraction in itself with its own admission charge. IMAX carries a number of films at one time and changes them throughout the year; the spectacular, seven-story-high IMAX films, with their emphasis on exotic natural and cultural landscapes and titles like *Mysteries of Egypt* and *Shackleton's Antarctic Adventure*, complement Exploris well. Tickets are $7.95 for adults, $6.95 for seniors, $5.50 for chil-

dren. You can also buy a discount ticket which also allows entrance to Exploris: $12.95 adults, $8.95 children, under four, free. Open 9 A.M.–5 P.M. Tuesday–Saturday, noon–5 P.M. Sunday; open Monday in the summer (Memorial Day–Labor Day)

## Ray Price Legends of Harley Drag Racing Museum

It's a niche museum if there ever was one, but Harley enthusiasts would do well to stop by Ray Price's Harley-Davidson showroom at 1126 S. Saunders St., 919/832-2261, website: www.rayprice.com—the largest Hog dealership in the Eastern United States. Ray Price (not to be confused with Hank Williams Sr. protégé Ray "Crazy Arms" Price) is famous in leathery circles as a Harley drag racer. He's grasped the heights most weekend riders only dream about: he's a member of the Sturgis Motorcycle Hall of Fame, credited with helping to create the modern racing transmission, and designer of the first wheelie bar. The showroom is downstairs; upstairs you'll find the museum, home to original and restored antique Harleys illustrative of the company's output from 1936 to the present. No admission is charged, and Ray himself is usually on hand to interpret, which is, for Harley racing fans, not unlike visiting Cooperstown and having Babe Ruth show you around. Open 8 A.M.–6 P.M., Monday–Friday, 8 A.M.–4 P.M., Saturday. Hours may vary due to special events, so call ahead.

## North Carolina Museum of Art

At 2110 Blue Ridge Rd., 919/839-6262, website: www.ncartmuseum.org, NCMA is the top art museum in the state and attracts excellent shows; one recent season included a diverse collection of exhibitions featuring works by Audubon, Rubens, Rembrandt, and the apocalyptic paintings of Rev. McKendree Robbins Long. Permanent works include a noted collection of Renaissance and Baroque works by Van Dyck, Raphael, and company, one of strongest collections in the South. American artists Thomas Hart Benton (great-nephew of the Hillsborough-born politician), Winslow Homer, and Georgia O'Keeffe also have works in the permanent collection. Open Tuesday–Saturday 9 A.M.–5 P.M., Friday 9 A.M.–9 P.M., Sunday 10 A.M.–5 P.M.

Incidentally, there's no need to leave the museum hungry; **Blue Ridge, The Museum Restaurant** offers contemporary American cuisine, fresh baked goods, and plenty of nearby art to digest as you eat. Tuesday–Friday 11:30 A.M.–2 P.M., Friday dinner 5:30–10 P.M. (last seating 8:30 P.M.), Saturday brunch 11:30 A.M.–2 P.M., Sunday brunch 10:30 A.M.–2:30 P.M. For reservations, call 919/833-3548.

## North Carolina Museum of History

Founded in 1902, the North Carolina Museum of History, 5 E. Edenton St., Bicentennial Plaza, 919/715-0200, website: ncmuseumofhistory.org, is perhaps not world-class, but it's still a time-saver if you're trying to grasp the state's heritage in a hurry. Devoted to educating Tar Heels about their state's past, the museum's exhibits focus on the broad spectrum of North Carolinian life over the past 500 years. Artifacts include Civil War relics, race cars, railroad memorabilia, and other Caroliniana.

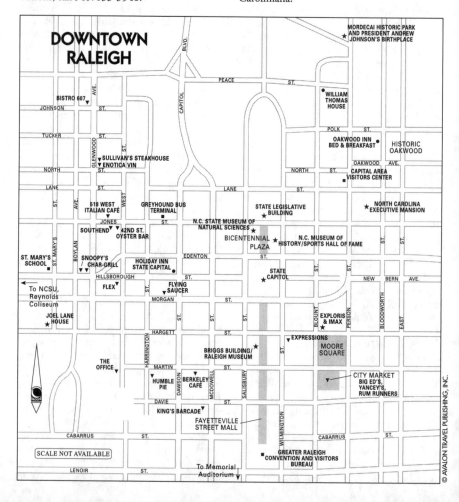

DOWNTOWN RALEIGH

MORDECAI HISTORIC PARK AND PRESIDENT ANDREW JOHNSON'S BIRTHPLACE

SCALE NOT AVAILABLE

© AVALON TRAVEL PUBLISHING, INC.

Historical figures greet visitors to the North Carolina Museum of History.

Here you'll also find the North Carolina Sports Hall of Fame, which pays tribute to more than 200 Tar Heel athletes, and includes such relics as the late Dale Earnhardt's jumpsuit, Jim Valvano's NCSU warmup clothes, Meadowlark Lemon's Harlem Globetrotters basketball uniform, and Charlie "Choo Choo" Justice's UNC football jersey. (They've all been washed and sanitized.)

Free admission. Tuesday–Saturday 9 A.M.–5 P.M., Sunday noon–5 P.M. You can park beneath the museum.

## North Carolina Museum of Natural Sciences

At 102 North Salisbury St. in Bicentennial Plaza, 919/733-7450, website: www.natural sciences.org, the museum's four floors and 70,000 square feet of walk-through exhibits feature four great whales, the world's only acrocanthosaurus, and face-to-face encounters with many residents of North Carolina's wild regions, as well as insights into the state's geology and plant life. Admission to the museum and the permanent exhibits is free, though the museum charges for some special exhibitions. Open 9 A.M.–5 P.M., Monday–Saturday, noon–5 P.M., Sunday; open until 9 P.M. the first Friday of every month but January.

## Mordecai Historic Park and President Andrew Johnson's Birthplace

At the corner of Mimosa Street and Wake Forest Road, 1 Mimosa St., 919/834-4844, email: cappresinc@aol.com, Mordecai Park is probably my favorite historic stop in town. While it's nice to appreciate the well-preserved mansions of the aristocrats of old, the people I find most interesting are those about whom little physical evidence remains. Mordecai Park helps bring the lifestyle of the average Raleigh resident of the early 1800s to life: the park's curators have pulled together a number of local historic structures—including President Andrew Johnson's birthshack (relocated from the end of Fayetteville Street)—and re-created a village street to give a sense of Raleigh in the days when a crack in the sidewalk could be fixed with a hammer and nails, and vehicle pollution was something you had to step around. This is the greatest sort of history

© ERIKA HOWSARE

**President Andrew Johnson's Birthplace**

lesson for kids (and adults), worth any number of CD-ROMs and documentaries. And surely the White House's greatest populist, Andrew Johnson, would smile wide to learn that his lowly birthshack is a more popular attraction than the big plantation house here. Admission is $4 for adults, $2 for ages 7–17, free for children 6 and under. Open Monday and Wednesday–Saturday 10 A.M.–4 P.M., Sunday 1–4 P.M. Hour-long tours begin on the hour, and the last tour begins at 3 P.M.

## Raleigh City Museum

Set in a landmark Gilded Age skyscraper, the 1874 Briggs Building at 220 Fayetteville Street Mall, Suite 100, 919/832-3775, website: www .raleighcitymuseum.org, this 10,000-square-foot museum preserves and interprets the city's past through a host of lovingly rendered temporary and permanent exhibits. Opened in 1993, the museum's focus is strictly (and rightly) local. It's a good chance to pierce through the broad sociological theories and down to the details and faces of real life here in the City of Oaks. Recent displays have shed light on Raleigh's historically

significant businesses and its Civil Rights movement. Open Tuesday–Friday 10 A.M.–4 P.M., Saturday and Sunday 1–4 P.M.

In a city where few historical commercial structures still exist, the Briggs Building is worth a visit all by itself. It began as a successful hardware store during Reconstruction (which, if you think about it, was a good time to open a hardware store); the business continued through the generations until 1994. And that was just on the ground floor: the city's first YMCA, the Raleigh Little Theatre, and the predecessor to the N.C. Museum of Natural History were all born in its upstairs floors.

## City Market

Arguably Raleigh's quaintest commercial quarter, the City Market (intersection of Blount and Martin Streets), 919/828-4555, features cobblestone streets, brick buildings, old-fashioned street lamps, a produce market, restaurants (including popular live music venues **Yancey's Jazz and Blues Café** and **Big Ed's City Market Restaurant**), and specialty shops. It's a stop on the tour trolley routes.

## Haywood Hall House and Gardens

The 1799 Classical Revival–style house and gardens at 211 New Bern Place, 919/832-8357 or 919/832-4158, was home to John Haywood, North Carolina's first elected treasurer. It's worth visiting for the original furnishings, including the table where Lafayette dined during his triumphant 1825 tour of the States. Free admission. Open Thursday 10:30 A.M.–1:30 P.M.

## J.C. Raulston Arboretum

Located on the campus of North Carolina State University, 4301 Beryl Rd., 919/515-3132, website: www.ncsu.edu/jcraulstonarboretum, the eight-acre garden features a visually stunning 350-foot border of perennials, a Japanese garden, and a garden all in white. The arboretum has more than 5,000 annuals, perennials, trees, and shrubs. Be here in the spring for the best blooms.

## Joel Lane House

The oldest house in town is Wakefield, a.k.a. the Joel Lane House, 728 W. Hargett St., 919/833-3431. It's open March–mid-December, Tuesday–Friday 10 A.M.–2 P.M., Saturday 1–4 P.M. Other tours by appointment. Wakefield dates to 1760, meaning that it predates Raleigh itself. In fact, the Lane spread is where Isaac Hunter's tavern once stood, and where legislators met to decide where to place the new city. Lane sold them 1,000 acres, and there, Raleigh was born. Entrance to the site costs $3 for adults, $1 for senior citizens and students, and free for children 6 and younger. Corner of St. Mary's and West Hargett Streets.

## Martin Luther King Jr. Memorial Gardens

The heart of the gardens at 1500 Martin Luther King Jr. Blvd., 919/834-6264, website: www.king-raleigh.org, is a life-sized bronze statue of the Baptist preacher from Georgia who help revive the national conscience. More than 2,400 individuals and families contributed to the building of this memorial, and you'll find their names inscribed on the bricks in the King Memorial Wall, which surrounds the statue. A granite monument honors other Civil Rights pioneers. To view the gardens online, see www.ellis-jones.com/king.html.

© ERIKA HOWSARE

Martin Luther King Jr. Memorial Gardens

RALEIGH

## North Carolina Executive Mansion

Franklin Roosevelt, who spent a few years in the New York governor's mansion before receiving a life sentence to Pennsylvania Avenue, named North Carolina's 1891 executive mansion the tops of all the governors' homes. Located at 200 N. Blount St., 919/733-3456, the mansion is built from all–Tar Heel materials. Take a peek online at www.ah.dcr.state.nc.us/sections/capitol. Guided tours available—contact the Capital Area Visitor Center for information.

## North Carolina State Archives

If you're doing some serious research on North Carolina topics, or maybe looking up ancestors from the Old North State, you'll want to stop by the State Archives, 109 E. Jones St., 919/733-3952, website: www.ah.dcr.state.nc.us. There's no charge; open Tuesday–Saturday 8 A.M.–5 P.M.

## North Carolina State Capitol

It's easy to look at yet another dome (even one with a natty crown, like North Carolina's) and think all capitols are essentially the same. In a way, of course, they are: every state capitol building is the place where the cumulative pride and aspirations of a state's people manifest themselves physically in polished (native) stone. Schoolkids from around the state come to the cruciform Capitol building in Raleigh (Capitol Square, 1 E. Edenton St., 919/733-4994, website: www.ah.dcr.state.nc.us/sections/capitol) to understand something more about people like Andrew Johnson and Governor Vance and brag a little on Michael Jordan and Richard Petty and view the displays that herald the remarkable diversity of North Carolina, county by glorious county.

The present statehouse was built, from 1833 to 1840, with local granite (quarried a mile southeast of the current building) and imported Scottish stonemasons. Horse-drawn tramway cars brought the stones up here along what was called the Raleigh Experimental Railway. This National Historic Landmark replaced a brick 1794 structure that had, as the largest building in the area, doubled as both statehouse and community hall, hosting revivals, balls, and public forums alike. This impressive earlier building featured a marble

© ERIKA HOWSARE

**North Carolina State Capitol**

statue of George Washington by the Italian artist Canova, and some considered it the most precious work of art in the United States. In 1831, a devastating fire burned hot enough to destroy both the fireproof statehouse and George—who, being a statue, was unable to flee.

The current statehouse was begun just two years later, and though it's not the largest capitol you'll see (progress-minded folks at one time suggested destroying it and building a more impressive structure), the North Carolina statehouse is considered one of the nation's best-preserved examples of a Greek Revival public building, with Doric porticoes on the east and west wings. The steps on the west side are chipped, allegedly from the sloppily handled whiskey barrels that used to be run up (full) and down (empty) from the free-flowing, taxpayer-supported wet bar in one of the committee rooms during the corrupt reign of the "carpetbagger" state legislature after the Civil War.

Originally, the entire state government, from governor to the greenest freshman legislator, had offices here, but now the governor and lieutenant governor and their staffs get the whole shebang. Free admission. Open Monday–Friday 9 A.M.– 5 P.M., Saturday 9 A.M.–5 P.M., Sunday 1–5 P.M. You can take a guided tour with advance notice through the Capital Area Visitor Center.

## North Carolina State Legislative Building

Over at the corner of Jones and Salisbury Streets, 16 W. Jones St., 919/733-7928, website: www.ncga.state.nc.us, you'll find where the North Carolina General Assembly came after leaving the capitol. If the mood hits, you're welcome to sit in and watch North Carolina's politicians politick. Open Monday–Friday 8 A.M.– 5 P.M., Saturday 9 A.M.–5 P.M., Sunday 1–5 P.M. If you'd like a guided tour, call the Capital Area Visitor Center in advance.

## Historic Oak View County Park

This 1855 farmstead at 4028 Carya Dr. (intersection of I-440 Beltline and Poole Road), 919/212-7248 or 919/250-1013, offers visitors the chance to experience the days before armies and factories forever altered the Piedmont's rural lifestyle. Free admission. Open Monday–Saturday 8:30 A.M.–5 P.M., Sunday 1–5 P.M.

## Historic Oakwood

Bordered by Franklin, Watauga, Linden, Jones, and Person Streets, the Oakwood neighborhood consists of 20 blocks of vintage Victorian homes listed on the National Register of Historic Places, website: www.historicoakwood.com. It's a pleasant neighborhood to tour by car, but you'd be far better off parking and walking. For information and self-guided walking tours, call the Capital Area Visitor Center at 919/733-3456.

There in Historic Oakwood you'll find **Oakwood Cemetery,** 701 Oakwood Ave., 919/832-6077, home to 40,000 horizontal Carolinians, many of whom passed on to Glory before the surrounding neighborhood was begun in the 1870s. Tour the graves and you'll note some 2,800 Confederate soldiers, including five generals from the Late Unpleasantness, seven governors, and a host of U.S. Senators.

Fans of cemeteries (and I don't mean the ones who sneak in after dark with candles and cats in gunnysacks) will appreciate the Victorian landscape and elaborate statuary here. Stop in at the office and they'll give you a map to show you what's what and who was who and where they are now. Where their bodies are, anyway. If they could tell us where the rest of them is, it'd be a valuable map indeed. For those planning to leave, admission to the cemetery is free. Open daily 8 A.M.–5 P.M.; office hours are more limited.

## Pullen Park

This great old park at 520 Ashe Ave., 919/831-6468, was laid out in 1887 on 80 acres donated by R. Stanhope Pullen. The attractions include a train ride, an indoor aquatics center, six tennis courts, the city's Theatre in the Park, a small lake, pedal boats, and the 1911 hand-carved Dentzel Carousel. It's one of Raleigh's delights, a fine place to take a rest after a busy morning of sightseeing.

## Saint Augustine's College Chapel

Students built this Norman Gothic–style chapel at 1315 Oakwood Ave., 919/516-4189, website: www.st-aug.edu, in 1896 under the direction of Rev. Henry Beard Delany (hopefully they received course credit). The chapel houses the bishop's chair, a memorial of Delany's consecration as the first African-American Episcopal Bishop in North Carolina. Free admission. The chapel stands on the campus of Saint Augustine's College, founded in 1867 by the Episcopal Church to serve the newly freed slaves; it's one of the oldest historically African-American colleges in the nation. According to tradition, Willie Jones, a framer of the state constitution and slave-owning lord of the plantation that included the present-day campus, lies buried somewhere on the campus, in an unmarked grave. The chapel is open in June and July Monday–Friday 9 A.M.–5 P.M.; August–May, there's a Sunday 11 A.M. chapel service.

## Saint Mary's School

This pretty 25-acre campus at 900 Hillsborough St., 800/948-2557 or 919/424-4000; website:

© ERIKA HOWSARE

**Pullen Park**

www.saint-marys.edu, has educated Raleigh's women since 1842, and holds a place on the National Register of Historic Places. A number of the buildings are considered historic sites in their own right; most memorable is the neo-Gothic St. Mary's Chapel, built in 1856. The school still operates today as a college preparatory boarding and day school for high school girls. Free admission.

### Spring Hill House

Colonel Theophilus Hunter Jr. once owned a plantation here, but more recently it was the site of the Dorothea Dix Hospital for Mental Illness, which for many years bore the more to-the-point name North Carolina State Hospital for the Insane. Today, Spring Hill House offers a chance to explore the physical environment and memorabilia of the hospital. Free admission. 705 Barbour Dr., 919/733-5454. Open Monday–Friday 8 A.M.–5 P.M.; guided tours available with advance notice.

### Cary

The city of Cary's theatrical productions and cultural events couldn't hope for a better home than the **Page-Walker Arts and History Center,** set in an early Reconstruction-era railroad hotel at 119 Ambassador Loop, 919/460-4963. The Cary Heritage Museum, located within, is worth a visit if you're in the area and interested in the local heritage. Monday–Wednesday 10 A.M.–9:30 P.M., Thursday 10 A.M.–5 P.M., Friday 10 A.M.–1 P.M. Call ahead if you'd like to visit on the weekend.

**Hemlock Bluffs** is a welcome 150-acre patch of nature amid all the improvements. Hemlock Bluffs Park, in Cary at 2616 Kildaire Farm Rd., 919/387-5980, is a preserve with a nature center, the short (1.2-mile) Chestnut Oak Trail, 100-foot bluffs, and a rare forest of hemlocks that survived the blights that have nearly erased the tree from the state.

### North Carolina Railroad Museum

Train rides are the major draw here. The museum is run by the East Carolina Chapter of the National Railway Historical Society based in New Hill, 919/362-5416, website: www.nhvry.org. Equipment on hand (at press time) includes four diesel engines, two steam engines, and three vintage cabooses. You're always welcome to visit (see the directions below) and view the engines and cars during daylight hours, though due to the volunteer staff, the trains operate and the museum opens only on certain days. Call ahead.

When it *is* open, train buffs (which includes just about any child under 13) will get a thrill out of taking a one-hour, round-trip train ride from Bonsal to New Hill and back. No charge for the museum; small admission (under $10 per adult) for train rides. To get there from Raleigh, take U.S. 1 south to Exit 89 at New Hill. Turn right and go two miles to New Hill. Turn left and go 2.6 miles south on old U.S. 1 Turn left onto Bonsal Road just before going under the two railroad bridges. Parking is on your right. Bonsal is 25 miles from downtown Raleigh.

## Wake Forest College Birthplace Museum

A museum at 414 N. Main St., in Wake Forest, 919/556-2911, interprets the history of both Wake Forest the college and Wake Forest the town. Artifacts and displays celebrate the bygone days before the college moved off to Winston-Salem. The museum building itself was built in 1820, and served as both classroom and home to the college's first president. Free admission. Open March–November, Sunday 3–5 P.M., and by appointment.

# TOURS

There's nothing like walking a town to get a feel for it. **Historic Tours of Raleigh,** 301 N. Blount St., 919/829-4988, offers an hour-long walking tour on Sundays, from spring through fall. During winter the guides may still be willing; call and see if you can work something out. Tours start Sunday 2 P.M. at Capital Area Visitor Center. $9 per person, $25 minimum.

Then again, motorized tours have their advantages, especially on rainy or blistering hot days. That's when you'll want to call **Historic Trolley Tours.** The "trolleys" (gas-powered buses that look like trolleys) offer a narrated 45-minute tour with six stops, which include historic sites, galleries, and museums. You can board at any of

the stops, but the most popular boarding spots seem to be Mordecai Historic Park and City Market. You can pay a little extra for an all-day pass, which allows for unlimited boarding, but generally, unless you're an old Raleigh pro, you'll probably want to do the 45-minute tour to get your bearings, and then begin your explorations. The price is reasonable: around $5 for adults, free for children under 7. March–December, Saturday 11 A.M.–3 P.M. The last trolley of the day leaves from the Old Market at 2 P.M.

# ACCOMMODATIONS

## Under $50

On the low end in Raleigh you'll find yourself in chains: **Motel 6–Crabtree,** 3921 Arrow Dr., 919/782-7071; **Motel 6 Raleigh/Cary,** 1401 Buck Jones Rd., 919/467-6171; **Sleep Inn,** 2617 Appliance Ct., 919/755-6005; **Howard Johnson Lodge,** 3120 New Bern Ave., 919/231-3000; **Microtel Inn & Suites,** 1209 Plainview Rd., 919/231-0002.

## $50–100

Doris and Gary Jurkiewicz's six-room **Oakwood Inn Bed and Breakfast,** 411 N. Bloodworth St., 800/276-9712 or 919/832-9712, website: www.members.aol.com/oakwoodbb/, set in the charming and historic Oakwood district, offers an alternative to standard hotels. Big Southern breakfasts and a great location make this 1871 home a fine choice. Stay here and you'll be able to walk around the Oakwood Historic District without having to hunt for parking.

The 192-room **Brownstone Hotel,** 1707 Hillsborough St., 800/331-7919 or 919/828-0811, website: www.brownstonehotel.com, looks like some "building of the future" from the 1960s—which it is. It's now affiliated with the Holiday Inn, not that you'd guess it. But if you're seeking reasonable prices and a central location directly opposite North Carolina State University and just down from the antiques at the Cameron Village Shopping Center, it's a spot worth considering. It offers a pool, a restaurant, and a lounge, and right next door is the gym at the YMCA. Breakfast buffet comes with the room. A favorite with

Raleigh politicos eager to rub elbows with young voters during lawmaking season.

Right close is the 172-room **Velvet Cloak Inn,** 1505 Hillsborough St., 919/828-0333, website: www.velvetcloakinn.com, whose name may bring visions of Doug Henning but in truth refers to the town's namesake, Sir Walter Raleigh, who in a fit of chivalry flung his velvet cloak down to prevent Queen Elizabeth from having to step in a pool of mud. (Whether the buoyancy of a mud-saturated cloak was sustained under the matriarch's tread is a question left unanswered by history.) The inn's own pool is of water, not mud, and it's indoors.

The 103-room **Days Inn–South,** 3901 S. Wilmington St., 919/772-8900, website: www.the.daysinn.com/raleigh04856, offers a pool and continental breakfast in the morning, and is clean and safe. And the 174-room **Ramada Inn, Crabtree,** 3920 Arrow Dr., 919/782-7525, website: www.ramada.com, is considered a top vessel in the Ramada armada. Restaurant on-site.

## $100–150

The four-room, 1881 **William Thomas House,** 530 North Blount St., 919/755-9400, offers a full Southern breakfast, a wine-and-cheese reception, and a great location within easy walking distance of the museums and the capitol. The 60-room **Capital Inn,** 1625 Capital Blvd., 919/833-1901, is not quite as cozy, but it's a little friendlier than the giants. **Embassy Suites,** 4700 Creedmoor Rd., 919/881-0000, website: www.embassy-suites.com, offers 225 suites, a gym and a sauna, an Italian restaurant, and Embassy Suites' trademark atrium and indoor pool. Across the street from the Crabtree Valley Mall, the hotel is among the best in a good chain; in 1995 it was named *the* top Embassy Suites in the entire world.

## FOOD

### Barbecue

Jerry and Kathy Hart's **Ole Time Barbecue,** 6309 Hillsborough St., 919/859-2544, adver-

**Oakwood Inn Bed and Breakfast**

© ERIKA HOWSARE

tises itself as "A Great Place to Get Porked" (but mercifully, unlike a now-closed Savannah joint that used the same slogan, the décor at Ole Time does not also feature love artwork of two cartoon pigs reenacting the love scene from *Deliverance*). Whatever you may think of their taste in slogans, Ole Time's barbecue surely makes up for it in, well, *taste*. Expect a chopped smoked pork with Eastern North Carolina–style sauce, as well as ribs and chicken. You can get a full meal here for under $10. Monday–Thursday 6 A.M.–8 P.M., Friday 6 A.M.–9 P.M., Saturday 6 A.M.–2 P.M.

Twenty miles south of Raleigh on old N.C. 50 to Willow Spring, you'll find vinegar-based **Stephenson's Barbecue** on the left, 919/894-4530, not long before the intersection with N.C. 210. Closed Sundays.

## Steaks

It may sound and look like a backwoods barbecue joint, but **Angus Barn,** 9401 Glenwood Ave., Route 70 near I-540, Raleigh, 919/781-2444, website: www.angusbarn.com, is probably the biggest culinary star in the Triangle, and has won a siloful of dining awards, bearing more impressive credentials on its wall than an overachiever with MPS. Founded in 1960, Angus Barn is regularly voted the top restaurant in the region by locals, but the Barn's fame spans the nation, having received a jiggle of the snifter from *Wine Spectator*'s reviewers as Best Steakhouse in the United States. Then again, I suppose you'd expect *Wine Spectator* to approve of an establishment whose beer and wine menu is nearly 40 pages long.

The prices reflect the Barn's renown—expect to pay a minimum of $20 for dinner, but more likely $30 and up, plus drinks.

But the Barn that isn't a barn is more than a restaurant. Built around and named for the founder's collection of Wild Turkey decanters, the Wild Turkey Lounge opens daily at 4 P.M. and often features live entertainment. It's a nice place to wait out your table, with complimentary cheese and crackers and a relish plate, 30 wines by the glass, 50 beers, and cappuccino and espresso.

The Country Store, at the front of the restaurant, includes a number of unique local crafts. The west wall of the waiting room is home to one

of the largest collections of single-action Colts on the East Coast, as well as guns and other frontieriana used by cowboys of the stage and screen—including no less than Clint, Tex, and the Duke. Music fans may be interested in the Colt formerly owned by a cowboy of the drifting variety—Hank Williams Sr. If all these gun barrels make you crave a smoke, be sure to visit Angus Barn's walk-in humidor, which carries Angus Barn's own private-label cigar, along with 84 other varieties. To grasp the Barn's exponential growth, keep in mind that the humidor formerly saw use as a 300-bottle wine cellar. Today's wine cellar hosts more than 35,000 bottles.

You might think that **Sullivan's Steakhouse,** 414 Glenwood Ave., 919/833-2888, has a lot of gall to do business in the same town as Angus Barn, but it's carved out a place for itself as a mahogany-walled, Morton's-esque high-end, type-A steakhouse where deals are made, shoulders are clapped, and clouds of cigar smoke waft over the (legendary) martinis. It plays City Cow to Angus Barn's Country Cow.

With dim lighting and jazz, **Cappers Restaurant and Tavern,** in North Hills Plaza, at the corner of Lassiter Mill Road and Six Forks Road, 919/787-8963, website: www.cappersrestaurant.com, offers sophisticated seafood entrées (for instance, a tasty scallops Florentine), as well as beef and other meats, including a New Zealand rack of lamb. But the jazz is what makes Cappers so special: it's widely considered the area's premier live jazz and blues venue, serving up various live acts six nights a week.

## Seafood

The famous **Hieronymous,** 815 W. Chatham St., to the west of town in Cary, 919/468-3336, offers fish caught fresh on the family's own boats, and a nautical, "just-the-fish-ma'am" ambience. The humble **North Carolina Seafood Restaurant,** State Farmer's Market, 1201 Agriculture St., 919/833-4661, features lots of fresh, fried seafood with fries and slaw for roughly five dollars. Also popular is the **42nd Street Oyster Bar & Seafood Grill,** 508 W. Jones St., Raleigh, 919/831-2811. Serving up steamed oysters since Herbert Hoover was in office, 42nd Street is an institution. Over in

*Est Est Est Hargett + Salisbury*
*www.estest.com*

Cary, **Tony's Bourbon Street Oyster Bar,** 107 Edinburgh St., 919/462-6226, serves shrimp, oysters, snow crab, and many other supporting characters from *The Little Mermaid,* all steamed to perfection and ready to eat. Come into the bar late at night—after 10:30 (5 P.M. on Sundays)—and you can eat for a 40 percent discount.

## Hamburgers and Hot Dogs

For hamburgers, you might well try one of the four **Char-Grills** around Raleigh, at 4617 Atlantic Ave., 919/954-9556; 3211 Edwards Mill Rd., 919/781-2945; 618 Hillsborough St., 919/821-7636; and 9601 Strickland Rd., 919/845-8994; website: www.chargrillusa.citysearch.com. It's all charburgers, fries, shakes, iceberg lettuce, wax paper, Styrofoam, and bleached napkins at a Char-grill; they also have hot dogs and decent barbecue. You can order the chicken sandwich for the sake of good health (not the chicken's), but it's probably better to momentarily forget your hopes for a ninetieth birthday and just order whatever your heart . . . er, stomach pleases.

For hot dogs, head over to one of Raleigh's two **Snoopy's,** at 1931 Wake Forest Rd., 919/833-0992, and 919/839-1176, 600 Hillsborough St. Nothing super-fancy, though they do put chili on their dogs as a matter of course. But if you're looking for fancy hot dogs, you're probably the sort of person who buys designer bowling shoes, and there's no help for you.

## Nouvelle Cuisine

**Enotica Vin,** 410 Glenwood Ave., 919/834-3070, website: www.enotecavin.com, features one of the area's top wine lists—bearing some 400 labels, including more than 60 by the glass. Dinner and Sunday brunch only; the intricate dinners include roasted lamb loin with white cornbread pudding, ratatouille, Provencal olives and crispy leeks ($24) and braised veal osso buco with creamy polenta, swiss chard, and oyster mushrooms ($20).

The popular little bistro **Frazier's,** 2418 Hillsborough St., 919/828-6699, is beloved for its appetizers. **Humble Pie,** 317 S. Harrington St., 919/829-9222, website: www.humblpie.com, features art on the walls and not-so-humble dishes like pomegranate roasted rack of New Zealand lamb ($20), Maine lobster with mushrooms, spinach, and pine nuts over linguine, ($18), portobello mushroom ravioli with shallot cream sauce ($12), and spanakopita with rice and asparagus ($12). The popular Sunday brunch includes omelets, sandwiches, bloody Marys, and other drinks.

For something light and quick, **New World Coffeehouse,** 4112 Pleasant Valley Rd., 919/786-0091, features wraps and gourmet coffee.

Inside the North Carolina Museum of Art, **Blue Ridge, The Museum Restaurant** offers contemporary American cuisine, fresh baked goods, and lots of eye candy with your meal. For reservations, call 919/833-3548.

**The Wine Cellar,** 9800 Leesville Rd., 919/845-9665, offers lunch from noon until 3 P.M., and appetizers, entrées, homemade soups, salads, sandwiches, and wraps.

## French

Reminiscent of a French roadhouse, **Bistro 607,** 607 Glenwood Ave., 919/828-0840, is set in an old cottage. A favorite romantic choice for Triangle residents, the French food here is arguably the best in the region. Prices are reasonable, and if you really want to feel as if you're in Paris, you can choose a table on the sidewalk out front.

And while Bistro 607 feels indisputably French, perhaps **Tartines Bistro Provencal,** 1110 Navaho Dr., 919/790-0091, is more so, specializing in Southern French cuisine.

## Italian and Pizza

Known for its reasonable prices and pizza, **Vincent's,** 3911 Capital Blvd., 919/876-6700, is a casual spot to find some good Italian for under $10 a plate.

Family-owned **Daniel's Pizza Pasta Café,** 1430 Highway 55 in Apex, 919/303-1006, offers patio seating. Its goat cheese fondue makes a memorable appetizer, and the lasagna's not bad either. **518 West Italian Café,** 518 W. Jones St., 919/829-2518, serves mouthwatering pastas, including a whole-wheat fettucine, and lemon linguine with shrimp and scallops, as well as pasta-free seafood and steak dinners.

**Romano's Macaroni Grill,** 740 S.E. Maynard Rd., Cary, 919/467-7727, website: www.macaronigrill.com, also offers Italian food in a relaxed setting.

**Lilly's,** 1813 Glenwood Ave., 919/833-0226, and in Five Points at 1813 Glenwood Ave., 919/833-0226, offers a palette of imaginative toppings that give us all the chance to climb out of the sausage-and-mushroom rut. Or try one of the area's **Rudino's** for something more traditional and quite good. **Bella Monica,** 3121 Edwards Mill Rd., 919/881-9778, serves authentic, reasonably priced Italian food by candlelight.

## Japanese and Korean

**Waraji,** 5910 Duraleigh Rd., 919/783-1883, website: www.waraji.citysearch.com, is an upscale restaurant that offers fresh, attractive (which counts for something) sushi in addition to its katsu, shoga-yaki, shabushabu, teriyaki, and tempura dishes. Of the knife-wielding-chefs-at-the-table variety is **The Kanki Japanese House of Steaks,** 4325 Glenwood Ave., 919/782-9708, website: www.kanki.com, one of three locations in the Triangle, and consistently voted as serving up the region's top sushi. Open for lunch until 2 or 2:30 P.M., then closed until dinner at 5 P.M.

**Korean Garden,** in Cary at 748-E E. Chatham St., Chatham Square Shopping Center, 919/388-3615, features Korean beef barbecue.

## Chinese

Set in an old tobacco storehouse, **Five Star,** 511 W. Hargett St., 919/833-3311, puts the chi-chi into Chinese. Don't come in looking for red walls with gold dragons. This is the sort of place Beijing hipsters hang out between house arrests. The food is creative and fresh.

**PF Chang's China Bistro,** at the Crabtree Valley Mall, 4325 Glenwood Ave., 919/787-7754, website: www.pfchangs.com, is one of the Scottsdale, Arizona–born chain's 70 locations nationwide.

## More Asian Food

**Fin's Restaurant,** 7713-19 Lead Mine Rd., Graystone Village in North Raleigh, 919/847-4110,

# WKIX— THE BIG CHANNEL 85

During the 1960s–70s heyday of AM Top 40 radio, 10,000-watt WKIX dominated the airwaves throughout the Triangle and much of the rest of the state. Ask Triangle Tar Heels of a certain vintage and they will tell you how WKIX DJs would broadcast live from the rooftop of a barbecue stand on Downtown (now Capitol) Avenue, causing kids' cars to wrap around the block; or about the beach music bashes with the Tams; or about the wittiest shticks of their radio personalities.

Most intriguing about WKIX's legacy is the number of young, inexperienced, underpaid disc jockeys—usually UNC and NCSU students—who went on to fame and fortune. The most nationally famous of these all worked at WKIX together in the 1970s, when UNC undergrads Rick Dees and Ken Lowe and NC State student John Tesh all took turns on the air. Dees went on to become the "Disco Duck" of the late 1970s and, later, the top disc jockey in Los Angeles in the 1980s and 1990s, a television host, and host of a nationally syndicated countdown program. Ken Lowe (who called himself "Steve Roddy" on the air and was Dees' UNC roommate off it) completed his degree and went on to become CEO of E.W. Scripps Company, which operates Scripps Howard News Service, and United Media, the worldwide licensing and syndication home of *Peanuts* and *Dilbert,* and also runs the Home & Garden Television (HGTV) Food Network and Do It Yourself (DIY). Emmy Award–winning *Entertainment Tonight* host/musician John Tesh read the "WKIX Pacesetter News" and played center on the KIX-Kagers basketball team.

As with so many great old AM powerhouses of the rock-and-roll era, today WKIX AM 850 exists only in the memories of its graying former listeners. Fortunately, you can still hear samples from its glory years at www.reelradio.com.

offers a variety of "Western" dishes given an Asian spin. **Royal India,** 3901 Capital Blvd., 919/981-0849, website: www.royalindia.citysearch.com, cooks its dinners in clay ovens and tries to capture the atmosphere of an Indian palace. In Cary,

RALEIGH

© ERIKA HOWSARE

Yancey's Jazz and Blues Café

**The King and I,** 926 Northeast Maynard Rd., 919/460-9265, is another curry favorite.

With two locations, **Sushi-Thai,** 106 Kilmayne Dr., Cary, 919/467-5747, and 2434 Wycliff Rd., Raleigh, 919/789-8181, website: www.sushithai.citysearch.com, probably sells more sushi than anyone else in the Triangle from its huge, boat-shaped wooden sushi bars, but it also features Thai cuisine as well, hence the name. Bright and sunny during the day, Sushi-Thai serves lunch at moderate prices. The California-sushi-teriyaki plate, a California roll, three sushi, and chicken or fish teriyaki, runs $9.95. Dinners run slightly higher, but generally under $20, and they're worth it: the tasty (an attractively presented) roasted curry shrimp in pineapple, which comes inside a carved-out pineapple half, with red curry sauce, cashew nuts, and bell pepper, runs $17.95.

When the three Saleh brothers moved from the Lebanese mountains to Raleigh in 1977 to open a restaurant specializing in Middle Eastern food, they knew they were facing a whole new world. Fittingly, they named their restaurant **Neomonde** ("**New World**") **Deli.** Though the brothers have gone on to open a successful wholesale bakery, the deli's still located at 3817 Beryl Rd., 919/828-1628, website: www.neomonde.com, and still draws long lines of customers at lunch and dinner. Specialties include pita sandwiches (on fresh-baked white and whole-wheat pitas), but I'd also recommend the meat pies, cheese pies, and the small sampler, which includes hummos, baba ghanouj, tabouli, grape leaves, labneh, and black Calamata olives, along with pita bread.

## More Dining

The Cajun **Yancey's Jazz and Blues Café,** 205 Wolfe St., 919/839-1991, website: www.yanceys jazzandbluescafe.com, offers saucy fare and live jazz and blues five nights a week down at the City Market. Stop in Sunday for a jazz brunch.

Part of a thin chain (54 nationwide) of restaurants born out of Maitland, Florida, the taquitos and carnitas at the highly authentic **El Dorado,** 990 High House Rd., in Cary, 919/461-4900, come highly recommended. The owner is a former resident of East Los Angeles, and knows what he's doing. **Melting Pot,** 3100 Wake Forest Rd., 919/878-0477, website: www.raleighmelting pot.com, offers all sorts of fondues, from the traditional bread and cheese to milk chocolate–based dessert fondues ($12–19), including the nuts-and-berries fondue, milk chocolate blended with Frangelico, cashews, red cherries, and blueberries, and served with fresh strawberries, bananas, fresh pineapple, marshmallows, cheesecake, and chocolate brownies for the dipping. Entrée fondues (with oil or bouillon base) run $48–75 for two persons, and include salads and cheese fondues. Other (non-fondue) entrées available.

**Irregardless Café,** 901 W. Morgan St., 919/833-9920, has been serving up vegetarian grub (but not grubs, fortunately, which wouldn't be vegetarian) since the mid-1970s, and its veggie burgers are praised by some as the best in town. Though the restaurant has widened its menu to include steaks and chicken, if you're eating here you might well want to see what they've learned to do meatless. Nighttime brings live jazz.

The humble **Rockford,** 320 1/2 Glenwood Ave., 919/821-9020, offers vegetarian dishes, hummus, quesadillas, and homemade soups to get you through.

## Delis, Sandwiches
The Kosher **Northern Star Gourmet Deli,** 301 Glenwood Ave., 919/743-0560, is not unlike a small pocket of New York City in the heart of Raleigh, with killer cheesecake (and I don't mean that in a cardiopulmonary way) and knishes in addition to salads and sandwiches. **Village Deli,** 500 Daniels St., 919/828-1428, offers good deli grub and indoor and outdoor seating in Cameron Village.

Former NYC police officer and firefighter Jimmy Schmid owns and runs **The Food Factory,** 211 E. Chatham St., 919/468-1139. Schmid closed on September 11, 2001, when he lost a number of friends, but today (unless it's a Sunday) you'll find him open, serving Boar's Head meats and offering both breakfasts and lunches. Open Monday–Friday 10:30 A.M.–4:30 P.M., Saturday 9 A.M.–3 P.M.

The hoagies at **Sadlacks,** 2116 Hillsborough St., 919/828-9190, taste better than the place looks. But you can always pick up a sandwich and walk across to the clock tower (which looks good) and eat it there.

## Breakfast
The most popular morning spot in town has got to be **Big Ed's City Market Restaurant,** 220 Wolfe St., 919/836-9909. Come down to the City Market on a Saturday morning, order up some country ham, eggs, grits, and biscuits, and when the live Dixieland band starts to play, you'll feel just about as Southern as you can feel in Raleigh.

A favorite of locals and political types doing business at the capitol, **Finch's Family Restaurant,** 401 W. Peace St., 919/834-7396, website: www.4eat.com, offers cheap Southern cuisine. Breakfast served all day, though there's a lunch menu as well.

## Cold Treats
A local favorite, **Cream and Bean,** 2010 Hillsborough St., 919/828-2663, features homemade flavors and a variety of handmade sundae toppings. Or visit a link of the popular local chain, **Goodberry's Frozen Custard,** with Raleigh locations at 11100 Clymer Ct., 919/878-8870; 1407 Garner Station Blvd., 919/772-0205; and 2421 Spring Forest Rd., 919/878-8159; and in Cary at 2325 Davis Dr., 919/387-1877, and 1146 Kildaire Farm Rd., 919/467-2386. In addition to the creamy custard, the Goodberry's people will blend various goodies into your custard upon request. A full fast-food restaurant menu here too.

## Market
**The Fresh Market** has more than 30 locations across the South, and two locations in Raleigh at 400 Woodburn Rd., 919/828-7888, and 6661 Falls of Neuse Rd., 919/676-2939. A pleasant place to shop for top-grade produce and meat.

# ENTERTAINMENT
## Coffeehouses
Cozy and homegrown, **The Third Place Coffeehouse,** 1811 Glenwood Ave., 919/834-6566, offers coffee, teas, sandwiches, and occasionally some captivating people-watching as you sit indoors or out in the heart of Five Points, right next door to Lily's Pizza. **Caribou Coffee** at 4214 N.W. Cary Parkway, Preston Corners, in Cary,

City Market

919/462-0690, offers open folk sessions on Tuesdays and acoustic music on other nights. Call ahead for information. **Hyphen Coffeehouse,** 13 S. Main St. in Fuquay-Varina, 919/567-0303, offers live acoustic music, including an openmike night on Thursdays. (If you're in Fuquay-Varina on a Thursday night, you really ought to also head over to **Richardson's Music,** 501 Broad St., for the live bluegrass.) Both the Raleigh **Barnes and Noble,** 4325 Glenwood Ave., 919/782-0030, and **Borders** in Cary at 1751 Walnut St., 919/469-1930, offer live acoustic music with their books and coffees.

## Nightlife

**The Ale House,** 513 Creekside Dr., 919/835-2222, is simple but sincere. The beer is cold, and the food extends well beyond beer nuts. Great steaks, and a popular place to watch the game. **Baron's,** at the Velvet Cloak Inn (1505 Hillsborough St., 919/828-0333), is where the onetime owner of 1960s–70s powerhouse Top 40 station WKIX AM 850 used to bring his young star disk jockeys and newsmen (who in later years included Rick Dees and John Tesh) to pick their brains and espouse his politics, which one DJ recalled as "far to the right of Jesse Helms." Though Baron's has moved upstairs and now overlooks the pool, the bar still has that sort of smoky feel, where you automatically want to order a martini and keep expecting to see a young Dustin Hoffman waiting nervously for Mrs. Robinson.

An updated version of the hotel lounge, popular with nine-to-fivers, is the Reddenbacher-inspired **Bowties,** the bar at the North Raleigh Hilton, 3415 Wake Forest Rd., 919/2323; a fine place to meet your second spouse. **The Player's Retreat,** 105 Oberlin Rd., 919/755-9589, is a simple, venerable (50-plus years old and counting) drinkers bar, and a popular spot to watch the game of the day. The original location of **Crowleys,** 3071 Medlin Dr., 919/371-3431, is another low-key establishment without guile. Good basic bar food and cold beer.

Over in Cary, **Tony's Bourbon Street Oyster Bar,** 107 Edinburgh St., 919/462-6226, serves mixed drinks and plenty of seafood to go with. Come in late at night—after 10:30 (5 P.M. on Sundays)—and you eat for a 40 percent discount. But the drinks cost the same.

**Vertigo Diner,** 426 S. McDowell St.,

919/832-4477, serves up creative drinks (ever had a Twizzler straw in your cocktail?) and an inspired atmosphere that make this a popular joint with twentysomethings.

In a region where sports are the unofficial religion and the various stadiums and coliseums are de facto cathedrals, sports bars serve as the rocking neighborhood churches where the praising (and not a little cursing) can go on all night long. On a game day, nearly any business offering both beer and satellite television will be packed. Two Raleigh sports bars with the liveliest congregations (and the greatest number of TV screens) are **Playmakers,** 3811 Hillsborough St., 919/743-5544, and **The Ale House,** 513 Creekside Dr., 919/835-2222.

> *In a region where sports are the unofficial religion and the various stadiums and coliseums are de facto cathedrals, sports bars serve as the rocking neighborhood churches where the praising (and not a little cursing) can go on all night long.*

## Live Music and Dancing

These things change quickly; pick up a copy of the *News and Observer*'s "What's Up" insert or a copy of *The Spectator* or *The Independent Weekly* to see who's playing where while you're there.

In general, jazz lovers will want to head to the classy and expensive **Sullivan's,** 414-103 Glenwood Ave., 919/833-2888 in Glenwood South. They have live jazz nightly, baby. **Yancey's Jazz and Blues Café,** 205 Wolfe St., 919/839-1991, website: www.yanceysjazzandbluescafe.com, in addition to evening jazz acts, hosts a jazz brunch Sundays at 11:30 A.M. **Cappers,** 4421 Six Forks Rd., 919/787-8963, also offers live jazz and blues. Call to see who's playing.

**Rum Runners,** 208 E. Martin St. in the City Market, 919/755-6436, website: www.rumrunnersusa.com, is one local branch of a growing chain of dueling piano bars. Nice idea, and usually a good time. **Berkeley Café,** 217 W. Martin St., 919/821-0777, offers live rock and blues. **Expressions** 110 E. Harget St., 919/835-0565, offers a mix of live and DJ music, including jazz and weekly Raleigh reggae.

If you're the sort who frets about Jimmy Carter's sagging eyelids and always thought Mother Teresa really should have tried a little rouge, you'll probably fit right in at **The Office,** 310 West St., 919/828-9994, where, if you're deemed physically attractive and trendy enough and practice good hygiene, you'll be allowed inside to techno-dance with other Grade-A people. What with the "dog-proofed" door, The Office is not surprisingly one of the town's hottest meat markets. The male meat is more seasoned: guys have to be 25 to get in, while women only need to be 21—which means the guys have to stay good-looking four years longer. Hello, ACLU?

Rockers tend toward **Kings Barcade,** 424 S. McDowell St., 919/831-1005, website: www.kingsbarcade.com, where they're more than willing to turn it up to eleven. The annual "Great Cover Up" features local bands in costume covering their favorite stars. The bar was opened by three local musicians who wanted to create a live venue high on decibels, low on pretense, and overflowing with brewskis.

**Five Star,** 511 W. Hargett St., 919/833-3311, metamorphoses from an Asian restaurant into a hip-hop club in the evenings.

**The Hideaway,** 2526 Hillsborough St., 919/821-4955, is a small place with a big jukebox and lots of beer. This is not only a place to hear live country music, it's the sort of place they write country songs *about.*

For country music, try **The Longbranch Saloon,** 600 Creekside Dr., 919/829-1125, website: www.longbranchsaloon.com. Here, they've been country—to quote Barbara Mandrell—since back before country was cool. (Well, actually, since the mid-1980s. At which time it *had* been cool in the early John Denver/Jim Croce/Charlie Rich/Jerry Reed 70s and then was uncool and then cool again after *Urban Cowboy* and then uncool again until the arrival of Randy Travis, George Strait, Dwight Yoakam, and the rest of the New Traditionalists.) The Longbranch is covering its bases: the (ahem)

Longbranch Entertainment Complex now includes a disco dance room and a Top 40 room. To gain entry to any of these bars you need to first become a club member; it's a small fee, but it requires a three-day waiting period.

For blues, try **Yancey's Jazz and Blues Café,** 205 Wolfe St., in the City Market, 919/838-1991, website: www.yanceysjazzandbluescafe.com, especially on Tuesday night when you're welcome to join in the jam.

**East Village Bar and Grill,** 1 Dixie Trail, 919/821-9985, eastvillagegrill.citysearch.com, across from NCSU, caters to college students, specializes in piña coladas, and features a huge patio with a fireplace. **Foster's,** 521 Daniels St., in Cameron Village 919/832-9815, website: www.fostersrestaurant.com, attracts an older crowd; it's one of those classy, dark bars where you can actually have a conversation. Dancing in the evenings.

For something . . . uh . . . different, try European-beer-hall-meets-Hooters-in-space ambience of the **Flying Saucer Draught Emporium,** 328 W. Morgan St., 919/821-7468, website: www.beerknurd.com, the Raleigh location of a small, twisted chain with locations throughout the western reaches of the former Confederacy (yes, there's one in Little Rock). The vast quantity of beers available (more than 200) testify to human culinary evolution, to the fickleness of today's alcoholic, or perhaps to nothing at all. Good bratwurst.

**Southend Brewery,** 505 W. Jones St., 919/832-4604, is similarly the Raleigh location of a small upscale Southern chain, in this case, one begun in Charleston, S.C. Great homemade brews, and fine grilled and smoked meats. A good place to hang out and dance, or watch the game; in summer of 2002 they added eight pool tables.

**Mitch's Tavern,** upstairs at 2426 Hillsborough St., 919/821-7771, sits right across from the library, making it a popular spot for students seeking respite from or inspiration for their studies.

**Slim's,** 237 S. Wilmington St., 919/833-6557, previously known as The Lakeside, is a sofa-stuffed two-story house of drink complete with a private patio. Regulars swear that drinking here

feels just like a party at your friends' house—at least until you have to use the restroom.

Dancing venues include the hip-hop-ocentric **Club Oxygen,** 412 W. Davie St., 919/821-3188, and **Michael Dean's Wood Oven and Bar,** 1705 Millbrook Rd., 919/790-9992, a buttoned-up restaurant that pushes back the chairs on Friday and Saturday nights and cranks up the Top 40.

Gay clubs include **Legends,** 330 W. Hargett St., 919/831-8888, and **Flex,** 2 S. West St., 919/832-8855, the latter of which earned a notoriety a few years back for its "white trash" drag shows.

## Concerts and Shows

Making the Big Time in Raleigh means playing the **AllTel Pavilion at Walnut Creek** (a.k.a. "the Creek") at Rock Quarry Rd., 919/831-6666, website: www.alltelpavilion.com, or the **Entertainment and Sports Arena,** 1400 Edwards Mill Rd., 919/861-2300, website: www.esa-today.com. Acts on either side of the peak of popularity (or ones whose chosen artistic paths don't lead to that particular summit) tend to show up at **The Pourhouse,** 224 S. Blount St., 919/821-1120, where you can drink your beer from a glass instead of a paper cup, and as long as you're on your feet to watch your favorite band, you may as well shoot a game of pool. Minimal membership fee required. Out in Cary, the **Six String Café** at the MacGregor Village Center, 107 Edinburgh St., 919/469-3667, website: www.sixstringcafe.com, is the sort of place Woody Guthrie might have hung out, though he would have had to smoke outside and might have grumbled over the vegetarian chuck. Open Tuesday though Saturday; open-mike nights weekly. The retro **Lincoln Theater,** 126 E. Cabarrus St., 919/821-4111, website: www.lincolntheatre.com, hosts national and local acts of various sorts, with a lean toward the college mainstream.

For classical music, **Meymandi Concert Hall** 2 E. South St., 919/733-2750, is the cutting-edge 1,700-seat home of North Carolina Symphony, all done up in limestone, cherry wood, and maple. Call for information on current performances.

## Local Theater

The 2,300-seat **Memorial Auditorium,** 1 E. South St., 919/831-6060, features a variety of traveling shows through the **Broadway Series South,** website: www.broadwayseriessouth.com, which brings national tours of current Broadway hits to the Triangle. The **North Carolina Theatre** shares the Memorial with the Broadway Series South. The largest musical production company in the entire state, NCT is homegrown and puts on large mainstream musicals. Recent productions have included *A Chorus Line, The Music of Andrew Lloyd Webber,* and *Children of Eden.* See them online at www.nctheatre.com. The **Burning Coal Theatre Company,** 919/388-0066, website: www.burningcoal.org, is more independent and not as well-financed, though at publication it was looking for a permanent performance space. Recent seasons have included a variety of challenging plays, including an adaptation of Ibsen's *A Doll's House,* Lanford Wilson's *The Mound Builders,* and South African playwright Athol Fugard's *The Road to Mecca.*

The experimental **Raleigh Ensemble Players,** at Artspace, 201 E. Davie St., 919/832-9607, website: www.realtheatre.org, have been experimenting since the early days of the Reagan era: one recent show required audience members to remove their shoes and "prepare accordingly" for "unique physicality . . . especially in regard to the interaction between actor and audience." Call for information.

The **Raleigh Little Theatre,** 301 Pogue St., 919/821-3111, website: www.raleighlittletheatre.com, was born under Franklin Roosevelt as a WPA project; the theater building itself, in fact, was built by the WPA. Each season provides five popular musicals from Broadway, four contemporary works, and four shows suitable for kids as well as parents. Pullen Park is home to **Theatre in the Park,** 107 Pullen Rd., 919/831-6058, website: www.theatreinthepark.com, which presents several shows, including Shakespeare and the ever-popular Yuletide rendition of Dickens' *A Christmas Carol* held at Memorial Auditorium. **University Theatre,** at NCSU, 919/515-2405, website: www.fis.ncsu.edu/arts, offers both student and professional productions, including dance and music performances.

## Movie Theaters

In Five Points, **The Rialto,** 1620 Glenwood Ave., 919/856-0111, website: www.therialto.com, is the Triangle's class act when it comes to movies; independent films, re-releases, and foreign titles dominate the screen inside this 1940s-vintage theater. The **Raleigh Grande 16** at Hwy. 70 and Lynn Road, 919/226-2000, website: www.consolidatedmovies.com, is a Robo-Rialto, a 16-screen retro-style cineplex with Dolby digital surround sound. A good place to see the latest *Star Wars* or *Lord of the Rings.* Or, if last month's must-see has become your own personal should-have-seen, you might try to catch it loitering in pre-Blockbuster limbo at the $1.50-a-ticket **Blue Ridge 14,** 600 Blue Ridge Rd., 919/828-9003, website: www.carmike.com.

# SPORTS AND RECREATION

The South, in general, is crazy about sports, and specifically about collegiate sports. The Triangle has more sports than most entire states ever dream of; around here, you'd think "March Madness" was something put on by the local Chamber of Commerce, so firm a hold does it have on the Triangle's consciousness. **North Carolina State University** is a fervent opponent of Duke and Chapel Hill. Games are played at the **Entertainment and Sports Arena,** at 1400 Edwards Mill Rd.; tickets are nigh impossible to find at the door—you're better off calling 919/514-2106, website: www.athletics.ncsu.edu, ahead of time if you want to see a game while you're in town.

To catch a football game at 51,000-seat Carter-Finley Stadium, call ahead to 919/515-2102, website: www.athletics.ncsu.edu. Tickets for each game, if you can get them, normally run $25 and up.

## Parks

**Jordan Lake State Recreation Area,** west of Cary at 280 State Park Rd., Apex, 919/362-0586, website: http://ils.unc.edu/parkproject/jordindex.html, has a 13,900-acre reservoir that's not only popular with boaters, fisherfolk, and swimmers, it's also very popular with bald eagles. In fact, in the summer, Jordan Lake claims the largest population of bald eagles of any similar-sized area in the eastern United States. Open daily 8 A.M.–sunset.

**Falls Lake State Recreation Area** is where all those boats you see parked in the storage yards at the new developments head on the weekends. One of the largest recreational facilities of any kind in the state, Falls Creek offers boating, fishing, hiking, picnicking, swimming, and camping. Located at 13304 Creedmoor Rd., Wake Forest, 919/676-1027, website: http://ils.unc.edu/parkproject/fala index.html. Open daily 8 A.M.–sunset. Admission is $4 during warm weather.

**William B. Umstead State Park** offers visitors 5,400 acres laced with hiking, bike, and bridle trails, and the chance to camp in the Triangle. Canoes and rowboats available to rent during the summer. An ideal place to go for a walk or a picnic if you've had too much of the sprawl. Located at 8801 Glenwood Ave., 919/571-4170, website: www.ils.unc.edu/parkproject/wium.html. Open daily 8 A.M.–sunset.

**Lake Crabtree County Park,** in Morrisville north of Cary, hosts 520-acre Lake Crabtree. You can fish here, or rent a boat. Nice hiking and cycling here as well.

## GETTING THERE
### By Car
Raleigh and the whole Triangle are well-connected with interstates and state highways. From the south, you'll probably be traveling along I-95. Take I-95 to I-40 toward Raleigh. From Pinehurst, head north along U.S. 1 and on to Raleigh. From Chapel Hill, head east on I-40. From Greensboro, head east on I-40/I-85. From the north, take I-85 west to Exit 218; then take U.S. 1 south to Raleigh. From Wilmington, take I-40 west to Raleigh.

In all cases, you'll eventually end up on the Beltway, the I-440 loop, after which your specific destination will decide which exit you'll want to take.

### By Plane
**Raleigh-Durham International Airport (RDU)** is located at Exit 284-B and Exit 285 on I-40. RDU is in the middle of an expansion begun in 2000 and due to run some $500 million before it's completed. As it is, the airport is a midsize hub, offering nonstops to most major US airports. The largest carrier here is Midway—RDU is Midway's base of operations—but other airlines flying to and from RDU include Air Canada, 888/247-2262 (www.aircanada.ca); American Airlines, 800/433-7300 (www.aa.com); Continental Airlines, 800/525-0280 (222.continental.com); Delta, 800/221-1212 (222.delta.com); Northwest Airlines, 800/225-2525 (www.newa.com); Southwest Airlines, 800/435-9792 (www.south west.com); TWA, 800/221-2000 (www.twa.com); United Airlines, 800/241-6522 (www.ual.com); and USAirways, 800/428-4322 (www.usair ways.com), as well as most of the major commuter airlines that derive from these.

### By Train
Amtrak trains service Raleigh and Cary, as well as Durham. Call 800/298-7246 (BY TRAIN) for information.

## GETTING AROUND

During business hours on weekdays, you can take a bus leaving on the half-hour from the airport to the various corners of the Triangle via the Triangle Transit Authority (TTA), 919/549-9999, website: www.ridetta.org. It won't cost you much. You can also catch a ride in one of the local shuttle vans (roughly $25 per person), or taxi ($30). I always have good luck with Alamo when I'm looking for a cheap rental ride: 800/327-9633 or 919/840-0132.

# Durham and Vicinity

*Durham is the New South because there was no Old South there for it to be. When the Civil War ended four miles up the road . . . Durham was three stores, two barrooms, a post office, and a carpenter shop. What has happened there since is not only its history but North Carolina's.*

*Jonathan Daniels*

When the War Between the States began in Charleston, S.C., it made a kind of sense, given that Charleston, beyond all other cities, represented the slave-bought opulence and social stratification of the antebellum South. It's equally fitting then that that same war, for all intents and purposes, ended at Durham, center of the tobacco and textile industries that would keep the Carolinas afloat through the next century, and the apex of the Research Triangle that would catapult North Carolina to the forefront of industry at the start of the new millennium.

Originally a stop on the Great Indian Trading Path in the 1700s, Durham was settled by Scots-Irish and British in the mid-1700s, but not until 1853 was the town incorporated and named for Dr. Bartlett Durham, who had donated four acres of land for a railroad station. "Durham's Station" became, eventually, Durham.

Sherman was camped in nearby Goldsboro, with many of his troops in the streets of Raleigh, when word reached him that Confederate general Joseph Johnston wished to negotiate the surrender of all remaining Confederate troops, thus ending the war. The two generals met to discuss terms at the Bennett Place in modern-day Durham. While waiting for the thing to be decided, both Northern and Southern troops short of chew broke into the storehouse of local tobacco farmer John Green's bright leaf tobacco. After the surrender was settled and the troops all went home, the local postmaster began to receive order after order for "that Bull Durham tobacco." Before long, Bull Durham was the most famous trade name in America, appearing on roadsides, buildings, one of the Great Pyramids of Egypt, and on the wall behind the pitcher's warmup area at Yankee Stadium, where it inspired the new term "bullpen." The Bull Durham name remained, arguably, the most popular trade name in America until the nicotine-rich weed was bumped out of the top spot by then cocaine-laced Coca-Cola.

By the early 1900s, Durham was noted as a powerhouse of tobacco and textile operations, and as a place where African-American businesspeople prospered. Located atop the Research Triangle, Durham is home to the Research Triangle Park, Duke University, and North Carolina Central University. Durham today is also home to many top restaurants and lodgings, to attractive, upscale Brightleaf Square, to the famous Durham Bulls (of *Bull Durham* fame), and to Duke basketball. Gospel great Shirley Caesar and *Late Show with David Letterman* tech Biff Henderson both hail from Durham, as do former San Francisco Giants manager Roger Craig and Hall of Fame catcher Rick Ferrell.

Popular annual events include the **North Carolina International Jazz Festival,** from January to April; February's **Native American Pow Wow,** April's **Old Durham Historic House Tour,** May's **Bimbé Cultural Festival,** June's **Edible Arts Festival of Food and Art** and the **American Dance Festival,** July's **Festival for the Eno,** and September's **World Beer Festival** and the **Bull Durham Blues Festival.**

## SIGHTS

Durham sits at the top of the Triangle, and the **historic downtown** lies directly northwest of the Triangle Park along the Durham Freeway (N.C. 147). Heading west in downtown along Chapel Hill Street, you'll come first to Brightleaf Square, and then to Duke University. Just north of the Durham Freeway is Durham's eclectic Ninth Street District. Most of Durham's rural-themed attractions—Bennett Place, Duke Homestead, and West Point on the Eno—lie north of town.

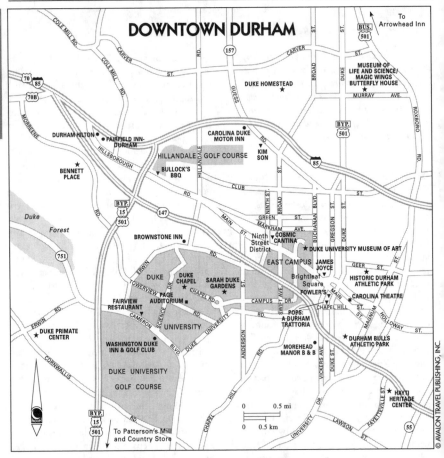

As a whole, Durham isn't really a walkable town, though you can certainly park downtown and spend a day browsing the shops and sights.

## Bennett Place
## State Historic Site

This is where Virginia-born General Joseph Johnston surrendered to Union general William T. Sherman. There's no charge to visit the historic site, which is out at 4409 Bennett Memorial Rd., 919/383-4345. Donations, however, are welcome to help keep up the reconstructed farmhouse and outbuildings, as well as the museum and interpretive center.

## Downtown Durham–
## Brightleaf Square

The Bicentennial did a lot of good things for America. Not only did it bring us tall ships and *Bicentennial Minutes,* but it awakened many to the need for historic preservation across the United States. For instance, it stirred up the Historic Preservation Society of Durham, who the following year succeeded in having downtown Durham named as the first commercial district on the National Register of Historic Places—no small feat, considering that many of the buildings were at that time less than 50 years old. Brightleaf Square and the surrounding neighborhoods are a good spot to take a walk. Pickup one of the Downtown Walking Tour maps at the Durham Visitor Information Center.

## The Carolina Theatre

Encompassing the 1,016-seat Beaux Arts auditorium, which draws nationally known acts ranging from bluegrass to opera; two small cinemas; and an extensive rental library of foreign videos, the 1926 Carolina Theatre, 309 W. Morgan St., 919/560-3030, website: www.carolinatheatre.org, is an art dynamo in Bull City. Call or see the website to find out what's here when you'll be here—it's guaranteed to be worthwhile.

## Duke Homestead State History Site and Tobacco Museum

There are different attitudes with which to approach the Duke Homestead. One is of awed reverence for an American success story. Through hard work, ingenuity, and the addictive qualities of nicotine, the Duke family went from farmers to millionaires, starting right here at this place. Or you might approach it as one approaches any birthplace of a maelstrom, like visiting the starting point of the Cherokee Trail of Tears, or the Munich beer hall where Adolph Hitler first rose to popularity. Or you can visit it as the social historian, the way you might visit a whaling village or gold-mining camp, for a look at what a particular group of people (tobacco farmers in the postwar South) lived like in times gone by. For whatever reason you come, the Duke Homestead is probably worth the trip. This National Historic landmark at 2828 Duke Homestead Rd., 919/477-5498, features the Duke family's mid-19th-century home, tobacco barns, and their original factory. A Tobacco Museum, film, and living history demonstrations bring to life Heartland farm life as it was in the 1800s. No fee charged. Oxygen tanks welcome.

## Duke University

Originally a Christian school, Duke University was still named Trinity College (after the Father, the Son, and the Holy Spirit) when the Duke family dumped $6 million of cigarette money into its lap. Quicker than you could rip open a

the Carolina Theatre

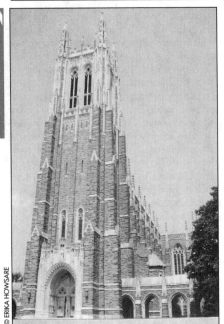

© ERIKA HOWSARE

**Duke University Chapel**

pack of Camels, Trinity came off and the Dukes' name went on.

But James Duke didn't feel fully at ease with this arrangement; and built the campus a "chapel." Though early plans to have stained-glass depictions of the disciples puffing away on their favorite American Tobacco Company products were eventually shelved, the chapel was built per James Duke's specifications on the highest spot on the campus. He intended the building to be the central building of the campus, and sure enough, the 210-foot tower has become Duke's emblem. The neo-Gothic **Duke University Chapel,** Chapel Drive, 919/681-1704, is patterned after the original Canterbury Cathedral, bears 50 bells, and contains more than 800 figures (none smoking) in 77 windows, which consist of a full million pieces of stained glass. The organ has 5,200 pipes, only slightly less than the college's faculty lounge. (I'm joking, of course. Duke University assures me that its faculty lounges are

nonsmoking.) Free organ concerts are held regularly—call ahead for times.

It's hard to pick a bad day at the 55-acre **Sarah P. Duke Gardens** on Duke University's West Campus. The gardens feature more than 2,000 varieties of plants, so that something's nearly always in bloom: April–June, you'll see irises, azaleas, spring wildflowers, dogwood, wisteria, and crabapples. Come a little earlier and you'll catch camellias, cherries, magnolias, and tulips. Come in June or July and you'll see the daylilies, water lilies, and summer annuals. Come in the fall and you'll see the leaves turned, and come in the winter and you'll find blooms on the Japanese apricot and witch hazel.

## Duke University Museum of Art

Featuring extensive collections that encompass Greek and Roman antiquities, pre-Columbian American art, medieval art, Italian and Dutch oils, and African art, the Museum on Duke East Campus draws visitors from around the world.

## North Carolina Central University Art Museum

Over at 1801 Fayetteville St., 919/560-6100, website: www.nccu.edu/campus/index/html, you'll find collections of paintings, sculptures, prints, and African artifacts and art, by both professionals and students.

## North Carolina Museum of Life and Science

Kids love this 78-acre, 55,000-square-foot regional, interactive science technology center at 433 Murry Ave., 919/220-0120, website: www.ncmls.org. Certainly the old rocket outside doesn't hurt. The Ellerbee Creek Railway miniature train ride's popular too, especially as it transverses the Nature Park, giving passengers the chance to see black bears, red wolves, and farm animals. The last of these are also available for a little one-on-one at the petting farm. In all, between the indoor and outdoors exhibits, you'll see some 60 live-and-kicking examples of native North Carolina species, including the ever-frolicking river otters. The highly hands-on science exhibits invite—no, *require*—visitors to learn at least a little something about the subject at hand, whether it be ecology, meteorology, or astronomy. (I especially like the machine that whips up 15-foot whirlwinds.) The **Magic Wings Butterfly House,** largest butterfly house at a museum east of the Mississippi, features Asian, African, and Central and South American species. Admission runs around $5.50 for adults, less for children and seniors. Open Monday–Saturday 10 A.M.–6 P.M., Sunday 1–6 P.M. in the summer; Monday–Saturday 10 A.M.–5 P.M., Sunday noon–5 P.M. the rest of the year.

## Duke University Primate Center

At 3705 Erwin Rd. at U.S. 751, 919/489-3364, you'll find hundreds of prosimian primates: the lorises of Asia, the galagos of Africa, and the lemurs of Madagascar. Visitors—even devoted evolutionists—must make arrangements in advance before dropping by. (You know how family can be.) Given enough notice (two weeks is the minimum), the people here can arrange a guided tour of the outside grounds for you, and they'll also let you visit inside to see the nocturnal prosimians snoozing away.

## Hayti Heritage Center

Located at 804 Old Fayetteville St., 919/683-1709, website:www.hayti.org, the center is set in what was one of America's most prosperous African-American neighborhoods. It features various arts galleries and exhibitions of traditional and contemporary arts, all by African-Americans. Adjacent is the large brick 1891 St. Joseph's AME Church, now a hall for performances, and the former sanctuary for one of the oldest self-governing African-American churches in the South. The congregation was founded in 1869, and its church was built in Richardsonian Romanesque style with funds donated largely by Washington Duke, Julian Carr, W.T. Blackwell, and Eugene Morehead. No charge for admission to the center. Call for information on performances.

## Patterson's Mill Country Store

The Booker family had ancestors who ran the Patterson's Mill store back in the 1870s; in 1973 the Bookers used materials from old stores and houses to build this store, an amalgam of country stores of the late 19th and early 20th century in this part of North Carolina. The reconstructed Reconstruction-era store at 5109 Farrington Rd., 919/493-8149, includes a doctor's office and pharmacy and features the Bookers' famed collection of mercantile and pharmaceutical relics and tobacco marketing memorabilia, such as the billboard outside urging figure-conscious women to "Reach for a LUCKY instead of a sweet." Antiques and locally made crafts for sale.

## Research Triangle Park

This 7,000-acre, eight-by-two-mile technological swath in the pine trees southeast of Durham is owned and operated as a private, nonprofit entity by Research Triangle Foundation, and home to 100 playgrounds for R&D types. If you're here on business, you'll find yourself drifting over to Durham, Raleigh, or Chapel Hill in the evenings. The park was begun in 1959 when local Tar Heels realized that the local Universities were educating many of the nation's top researchers who would then drift away to points north to work, live, and spend. Now the researchers (including not a few former Yankees who were trained at colleges up north) live right here and pump money into the local economy. Stop by at the Durham Visitor Information Center, 101 E. Morgan St., 919/680-8316, for information.

## Historic Stagville

True, the name sounds like it belongs to a gentleman's club, but Stagville, 5825 Old Oxford Hwy., 919/620-0120, website: www.ah.dcr. state.nc.us/sections/do/stagvill/default.htm, was once one of the South's largest plantations. Today, many of the original buildings survive, including some of the original slave dwellings; most interesting are the four two-story slave houses. State-owned, unfortunately they're closed on the weekends (to keep working people from visiting, apparently) but they are open Monday–Friday 9 A.M.–4 P.M. The Open House at Christmas makes this a special time to visit. Admission is free.

RALEIGH

© ERIKA HOWSARE

gristmill at West Point on the Eno

### West Point on the Eno

This city park at 5101 N. Roxboro Rd., 919/471-1623, features the rebuilt 1778 gristmill powered by the Eno River, a blacksmith shop, the 1880s McCown-Mangum House, and the smallish Hugh Mangum Museum of Photography. Hiking trails, picnicking, and rafting are all available. If you're here in early July, be sure to stop by the Festival for the Eno.

## ACCOMMODATIONS

### Under $50

Hey, it's not pretty, but the 181-room **Carolina Duke Motor Inn,** 2517 Guess Rd. at I-85, 800/438-1158 or 919/286-0771, website: www.citysearch.com/rdu/carolinaduke, offers good-sized, clean rooms, along with a pool, free local calls, and free van service to Duke University. **Days Inn–Durham,** 3460 Hillsborough Rd., 800/238-8000 or 383-1551, website: www.daysinn.com, is also right off I-85. It offers 100 rooms, a continental breakfast, and a restaurant next door.

### $50–100

The **Brownestone Inn,** 2424 Erwin Rd., 800/367-0293 or 919/286-7761, has 138 rooms right across from Duke University, and offers a heated indoor pool, Jacuzzi, and sauna. In the morning you'll get a continental breakfast, and in the evenings you can have tea in the colonial-style lobby. The on-site restaurant and pub will get you through the rest of the day. The one-story **Best Western Skyland Inn,** 5400 U.S. 70 West, is just off I-85. It features 31 rooms, breakfast, a playground, and a small pool.

### $100–150

Gloria and Phil Teber's nine-room **Arrowhead Inn,** 106 Mason Rd., 800/528-2207 or 919/477-8430, website: www.arrowheadinn.com, is set in a plantation house built circa 1775 by the Lipscombe family along the historic Great Indian Trading Path traveled by Catawba and Waxhaw Indians between Virginia and the Smokies. The house has been renovated to keep the original moldings, wainscoting, mantelpieces, and heart-of-pine floors, and most of the rooms have a fireplace. All come with a private bath. Amid four acres of magnolias and pecans, the Arrowhead offers tranquility in a fast-paced town. The full breakfasts include fresh-herbed frittatas and baked fruits. If you're staying elsewhere and want to visit, you might call ahead and see if they're having a tea while you're here.

## $150 and Up

Daniel and Monica Edwards' four-bedroom **Morehead Manor Bed & Breakfast,** 888/437-6333 or 919/687-4366, 914 Vickers Ave., Durham, website: www.moreheadmanor.citysearch.com, was built for the CEO of Liggett and Meyers. The massive (8,000-square-feet) Colonial Revival home looms within walking distance of downtown, Durham Bulls Athletic Park, and Brightleaf Square. Each room has a private bath; two have king-size beds, one has a queen, and the other has two full-size beds. With the fare comes beverages in the evenings along with homemade desserts and a full breakfast each morning. Morehouse Manor also offers special weekend packages, including Murder Mystery Weekends. Call for details. Much larger but still historic is the 171-room **Washington Duke Inn & Golf Club,** 3001 Cameron Blvd., 800/443-3853 or 919/490-0999.

# FOOD

Some argue that Durham has the best selection of restaurants in the entire state. To be sure, from barbecue to Chinese, you'll find a little of just about everything here in Bull City.

## Barbecue

Located at 3330 Quebec Dr., 919/383-3211, **Bullock's** is an institution so famous the Sex Pistols immortalized it on an album cover. Okay, maybe not. But you really ought to try it. Pig and complements are available Tuesdays through Saturday. No checks or credit cards.

## American Cuisine

**Nana's,** 2514 University Dr., 919/493-8545, specializes in sophisticated fish dishes and desserts centered around homemade ice cream. Bright and roomy, Nana's attracts locals looking for quality and willing to sacrifice (or pay extra for) quantity. **Fairview Restaurant,** 3001 Cameron Blvd., 919/490-0999, offers huge windowfuls of golf course to look at outside; it's a nice spot for a quiet lunch.

## Asian

**Kim Son,** 2425 Guess Rd., 919/419-9009, is run by a native of Vietnam. The specialty is savory pho dac biet. For authentic, top-shelf Chinese, head to **Neo-China Restaurant,** 4015 University Dr., 919/489-2828. Less traditionally Chinese but still very popular is **Pao Lim Asian Bistro and Bar,** 2505 Chapel Hill Blvd., 919/419-1771, website: www.paolimasianbistro.com, where owner Pao Lim's Chinese food includes Indian influences recipes. The Curry Chicken is a good bet.

## Greek and Italian

Grandpa Sigalas would cut off my ouzo supply if I failed to mention **Taverna Nikos,** in Brightleaf Square, 905 W. Main St., No. 49, 919/682-0043, website: www.tavernanikos.citysearch.com This is a classic Greek restaurant, with the food of the gods available in scads and the owner leaning over your table asking if everything's all right. If you're thinking of something from the other side of the Ionian Sea, **Pop's: A Durham Trattoria,** 810 W. Peabody St., 919/956-7677, has lured fans of northern Italian cuisine for many years, including reviewers from such magazines as *Bon Appétit.* Set in an old tobacco warehouse, Pop's makes for a memorable evening.

## Organic Food

Both a lunch spot and a small grocery store, **Fowler's,** 112 S. Duke St., 919/683-5555, website: www.fowlersfoodandwine.com, offers gourmet sandwiches and espresso drinks as well as a selection of wines and other healthy foods.

## Bakery

**Guglhupf,** 2706 Chapel Hill Blvd., 919/401-2600, website: www.guglhupf.com, is owned by two German immigrants who left the high-tech world to share the elemental joys of baking breads and tarts with skill and enthusiasm.

## Mexican

Besides the Durham location of **El Rodeo,** you'll also find the **Cosmic Cantina,** 1920 Perry St., 919/286-1875, website: www.cosmiccantina.com, popular with students and former students alike. The beans in its organic burritos have never been fried once, much less *refried,* and all of the lettuce and tomatoes have been grown without pesticides. (Bring a can of Black Flag if you miss the taste.) They've got a number of vegetarian and vegan offerings, starting with a $3 veggie burrito. Note: vegetarian burritos feature black beans, while burritos with meat use pinto beans, but you can get whichever you want by asking. Beyond the burritos, key here are the chicken nachos ($6). Drinks include margaritas and Coronas.

## ENTERTAINMENT

### Nightlife

**James Joyce,** 912 W. Main St., 912/683-3022, attempts to be a little bit of Dublin right across the street from Brightleaf Square. Some say that after drinking six pints of Killian's, the meaning of *Ulysses* becomes crystal-clear, but I make no promises.

The Durham location of **Yancey's Jazz and Blues Café,** 115 N. Duke St., 919/667-9821, website: www.yanceysjazzandbluescafe.com, offers live music six days (and nights) a week. **Rum Runners,** 115 North Duke St. in Brightleaf Square, 919/956-5557, website: www.rumrunnersusa.com, is another local outpost of a growing chain of dueling piano bars. **The Green Room,** 1108 Broad St., 919/286-2359, offers beer drinkers 10 pool tables, dartboards, shuffleboards, and other games requiring hand-eye coordination. **Devine's Restaurant and Sports Bar,** 904 W. Main St., 919/682-0228, website:www.devinesrestaurant.com, has been around since 1978, back when Carter was president, Manilow was golden, and I resembled a younger Tony Danza. Now Devine's is 25 and still attracting the young folk with a steady diet of wings and beer and (two to five nights a week) live rock and roll, R&B, and blues. Call to see who's playing. Urban with a capital u, **The Edge,** 108 Morris St., 919/667-1012, offers dancing upstairs and pool downstairs.

**James Joyce at Brightleaf Square**

the Regulator Bookshop

## Coffeehouses

**The Regulator Bookshop,** 720 Ninth St., 919/286-2700, website: www.regbook.com, is also a bookshop, very popular with Duke students of the past, present, and intermittent variety. A fine independent bookstore with a wide selection of magazines and quarterlies, good coffee, and great baked sweets courtesy of the Mad Hatter café. **Duke Coffeehouse,** on the East Campus, 919/684-4069, is popular with nonstudents as well as students. And small wonder: not only does the Coffeehouse offer good live music (often acoustic), but the chance to overhear hypercaffeinated sophomores debating Nietzsche is an experience not to be missed.

## Theater

As the name suggests, the purpose of **Man Bites Dog,** 703 Foster St., 919/682-3343, is to do the unusual, to reverse norms. It has been mounting creative, experimental shows since the mid-1980s. If you're waiting for a revival of *Oklahoma*, look elsewhere, but if the term "lofty" describes your favorite home-decorating style, you're in the right place.

## Movie Theaters

The Streets at Southpoint's 16-screen **Southpoint Cinemas,** 8030 Renaissance Parkway, 919/226-2000, is state of the art—a nice place to see the latest big-screen blockbuster, and a sure place to find the most popular current films.

## Shopping

**Brightleaf Square** at Gregson and West Main Streets, website: www.brightleaf.citysearch.com, was once an old rundown tobacco warehouse district; now it's one of the nicest places to shop in the Triangle. The stores here include a Millennium Music, art galleries, restaurants, and **Wentworth & Leggett Rare Books,** 919/688-5311. **Ninth Street,** website: www.ninthst.com, is the real thing, an actual commercial block with real stores. When it rains, people get wet; when it's hot and humid, people get hot and humid. Actually, in both cases, they usually slip into the Regulator Bookshop for something hot or iced, or into McDonald's Drug Store (no relation), which has been serving ice cream shakes since 1922.

Of course, Durham has its share of shopping centers and malls, but other than the new

**Streets at Southpoint**, they're nothing special. This big (1.3-million-square-foot) shopping, dining, and entertainment complex in south Durham, at 6910 Fayetteville Rd., website: www.thestreetsatsouthpoint.com, is accessible from Hwy. 751 and Renaissance Parkway (Exit 275) or via Fayetteville Road (Exit 276) off I-40. "Imagine 150 stores under one roof!" boasted the promos before the center opened in March 2002, but of course anybody who's ever been to a major American city since 1975 can imagine such a thing. The Streets is, beneath all the dressing, yet another enclosed supermall surrounded by gargantuan parking lots (nothing new). But the Streets does have a slight twist— the center's "Main Street" section is outdoors, with weather and everything. It's meant to suggest the feel of downtown Durham, minus most of its crime and graffiti and all of its vehicular traffic. If you're looking to shop for the sorts of items you can get in upscale malls nation-wide, or if you measure a community's progress by its acquisition of chain stores ("North Carolina's first Nordstrom!"), The Streets at Southpoint is the clean, well-lit place for you. The Streets was developed by Chicago-based Urban Retail Properties Co., who have contributed similar spots to 28 states, including Los Angeles' Century City Shopping Center and Boston's Copley Place. The Streets' 16-screen **Southpoint Cinemas,** 8030 Renaissance Parkway, 919/226-2000, is tops in town.

# SPORTS AND RECREATION
## Durham Baseball
**Historic Durham Athletic Park,** 400 Morris St., 919/956-9555, website: www.durhamamericans.com, is home to the summer college-ball Coastal Plain League **Durham Americans,** who play here in the summers and provide fans with Single-A action. Game or no game, fans of historic Minor League stadiums and/or the film *Bull Durham* (shot here) can stop by and pay a visit, for no charge. The Durham Bulls themselves, made famous by the film, rocketed from Single-A to AAA ball, just a heartbeat away from the bigs, and with this

change came a new stadium, the 10,000-seat **Durham Bulls Stadium** at 409 Blackwell St., 919/687-6500, website: www.durhambulls.com.

It's a wonderful new facility. At publication, the park was being considered as the new home for USA Baseball, the national governing board of amateur baseball. If so selected, Durham could become the training site for the US Olympic and Pan American baseball teams.

## Eno River State Park
At 6101 Cole Mill Rd., 919/383-1686, website: www.enoriver.org, there's rafting, canoeing, kayaking, fishing, and swimming. Primitive camping is available for backpackers along the Fanny's Ford Trail, about a mile up from the parking lot. Check at park headquarters for maps to other trails, which include the half-mile Eno Trace nature trail, with nice wildflower views in the spring, and the more challenging 4.1-mile circuit taking in both the Buckquarter Creek and Holden's Mill trails. For this latter hike you'll want to be sure to get a map at headquarters, but in general, you'll leave from the first parking area beyond park headquarters, follow east along the river bank, and head upland along the right fork through old farmland that's been largely reclaimed by the forest. Some old settlers' homes are still standing. You'll cross a steel and wood bridge over Buckquarter Creek, take the fork to Holden's Mill Trail through pines and hardwoods to rock outcroppings, and continue on to the remains of Holden's Mill.

To get to the park, head northwest of Durham on I-85, and take exit 170 onto U.S. 70 West. Turn right after 0.1 mile onto Pleasant Green Road, State Road 1567. Head 2.2 miles and turn left at State Road 1569, a.k.a. Cole Mill Road. You'll see the park entrance on your right after 0.8 miles. Continue along another mile and you'll come to the park headquarters, where you'll want to stop and get a park map, and sign in if you're planning to hike or camp. A second section of the park holds other wonders; to get there, double back from the park office along Cole Mill Road, cross back over Pleasant Green Road, continue on nearly 1.2 miles, and turn right into the trailhead parking area.

# HILLSBOROUGH

Back in the 1750s, when the Piedmont region figured into the economy of North Carolina primarily as a place to trade with Native Americans, Euro-Americans settled Hillsborough at the site of three successive Indian villages dating back to 1000 A.D., at the point where the Great Indian Trading Path (a.k.a. the Old Occoneechee Trail) crossed the Eno River. Gradually, as the population center of North Carolina shifted inland, Hillsborough grew as an important crossroads town. Until the rise of Raleigh, Hillsborough was one of the colony's most significant inland cities. But with Raleigh came a new order; one in which Hillsborough has not figured prominently. This, however, is good news for travelers; like other towns that had their heydays in the 1700s (New Bern and Edenton, for instance), Hillsborough retains much of its colonial and antebellum feel.

Originally named Orange, and then Corbinton, and later Childsboro, Hillsborough took its present name in 1776 not from its hilly topography but from Irishman William Hill, Earl of Hillsborough, Secretary of State for the American colonies, and—most important in the days after the failed Regulator movement, when Hillsborough was seen as the nest of rebellious backcountrymen—kin to the wife of the current royal governor in New Bern, William Tryon. Governor Tryon himself, and later Governor Martin, along with other wealthy and influential Eastern North Carolinians, soon began to spend their summers in Hillsborough to escape the "fevers" along the coast. Hence, Hillsborough became the summertime capital of Colonial North Carolina.

Famous Hillsborough residents include Declaration of Independence signer William Hooper, who moved out here to the western frontier from the Hertford area; fallen Patriot brigadier general Francis Nash, for whom Nashville, Tennessee, is named; and author and Jacksonian Democratic Party leader Thomas Hart Benton, who, as with many children of the western North Carolina frontier—Andrew Jackson, James K. Polk, Andrew Johnson—ended up spending much of his adulthood further west. Benton, like Raleigh native Johnson, supported the nation's western expansion via land grants to settlers. His son-in-law, John C. Fremont, would trailblaze much of the West and lead troops in the conquest of California; his great-nephew and namesake, painter Thomas Hart Benton, would go on to capture and preserve the grandeur of the quickly vanishing American frontier on canvas. Hillsborough was the site of the hanging of six Regulators by William Tryon in 1771; it was also the site of the important Constitutional Convention of 1788, where the North Carolina delegates demanded a Bill of Rights before they would ratify the U.S. Constitution.

Eighty years later, General Joseph E. Johnston stayed at Hillsborough before riding out to treat with General William T. Sherman and effectively end the Civil War.

Today, Hillsborough has a strong sense of its historical importance and charming ambience, and this is helping it to keep its colonial identity, even as developers turn it into yet another Triangle suburb.

## Sights

The **Old Orange County Courthouse,** on the southeast corner of East King and Churton Streets, was built in 1844–45 by local mason, architect, and legislator Captain John Berry. Be sure to take note of Hillsborough's **Old Town Clock** in the courthouse's octagonal cupola; it was given to the city by the royal government in 1769. It hung a couple of other places before ending up here on the courthouse, but it has been here since 1846. The **William Courtney Yellow House,** 141 E. King St., was already here when the clock arrived in town. Quaker William Courtner bought the house in 1772 and operated a tavern here. Famed circuit-riding Methodist bishop Francis Asbury in 1780 preached to about 200 people here. When British general Cornwallis occupied the town in 1781, he stayed here about half the time—the rest of the time he stayed at another nearby tavern. Apparently he meant to keep would-be assassins guessing. The **Alexander Dickson House,** 150 E. King St., 919/732-7741, website: www.historichillsborough.org, was by some figurings the last headquarters of the Confederacy, though others from towns like Fort Mill, S.C., would disagree. But no one disputes that it is now home to the Alliance for Historic Hillsborough, a good group of people to talk with if you want to see the historic sites of the town—the small city, with still far fewer than 10,000 inhabitants, features more than 100 buildings older than Jesse Helms. The Alliance offers self-guided walking tour maps.

The Dickson House was built in the Washington years and sat about 1.25 miles southeast of here until being moved during the Reagan years to this spot. South Carolinian Confederate General Wade Hampton camped at this home with his troops, and this was where General Joseph E. Johnston would return to discuss issues with other Confederate leaders after conferences with Sherman on April 17 and 18, 1865. Just down at 157 E. King St. you'll see **Seven Hearths,** a huge home dating (part of it, anyway) to the late 18th century. At the end of East King Street, take the lane headed eastward about 200 yards and you'll come to a fenced-in slab with a bronze plaque, marking the spot where the six Regulators were hanged on June 19, 1771, after standing trial in

the Court of the Province of North Carolina. Over at 118 W. Tryon St. stands the former home of General Francis Nash, he for whom Nashville, Tennessee, is named. Nash was killed in battle in 1777; five years later, Declaration of Independence signer William Hooper bought the house. Later, Governor William Graham lived here.

## Accommodations

The 71-room **Microtel Inn & Suites,** 120 Old Dogwood St., 888/771-7171 or 919/245-3102, provides clean, snug accommodations, a free continental breakfast, and free stays for kids up to 18 years old. A room for two (or two, plus kids) will only run you about $50 a night, even in high season. **Hillsborough House Inn,** 209 E. Tryon St., 800/616-1660 or 919/644-1600, website: www.hillsborough-inn.com, offers five rooms and a suite, with a complete breakfast and a pool. Each room is named after a former occupant and decorated as fitting for a particular era, from Miss Eliza's Room (ca. 1790)—wherein Daniel Boone is said to have once slept—with high ceilings, a draped queen canopy bed, and feather couch, to Kate's Room (ca. 1940). Prices begin at $110.

downtown Hillsborough

© ERIKA HOWSARE

## Food

**The Colonial Inn,** located west of the town center at 153 W. King St., 919/732-2461, where they've been serving up fried chicken and other country cooking since '59. That's *1759*. It's one of the 10 oldest inns in the nation—and at press time it had closed down for an ownership change. Its fate is uncertain, but it's such a historically unique location that you might want to take a peek and see if it's reopened yet. If it hasn't, try the

**Village Diner,** 600 W. King St., 919/732-7032. Opened in 1976, this is now the longest continuously operated restaurant in Hillsborough. Traditional Southern cooking here, featuring lunch and dinner buffets with a better salad bar than you might imagine for a country cooking spot. You can also order steaks, seafood, and barbecue off the menu. Whatever you order, be sure to try some of the banana pudding. Open Monday–Friday 6:30 A.M.–8 P.M.; closed major holidays.

# Chapel Hill, Carrboro, and Vicinity

Cuter than cute, Chapel Hill is a nearly ideal college town. As it should be: it was, after all, a town that literally grew up around the State University, which was chartered here in 1789, making this the United States' oldest state-run college.

Chapel Hill today is home year-round to 46,000 people; the University of North Carolina at Chapel Hill adds a student population of 24,000 or so. Neighboring Carrboro grew up around the railroad depot put here to service the college in 1879. While they're still legally separate towns, Chapel Hill and formerly working-class Carrboro today are pretty much one and the same.

Chapel Hill gets a lot of ribbing for its left-of-left politics—some argue that the town, which has drawn so many non-Southerners into its ranks, is as authentically Southern as, say, Birkenstocks and tabouli. Still, folks on all points of the political spectrum agree that Chapel Hill is a pretty little town— "The Southern Part of Heaven," as the Chamber of Commerce likes to say, well worth an afternoon's visit. The town's main drag, Franklin Street, borders the campus and offers shops, coffee houses, cafés, and other college town essentials.

> *Chapel Hill gets a lot of ribbing for its left-of-left politics— some argue that the town, which has drawn so many non-Southerners into its ranks, is as authentically Southern as, say, Birkenstocks and tabouli.*

## SIGHTS

The **Ackland Art Museum,** at the corner of Franklin and Columbia Streets, 919/966-5736, website: www.ackland.org, broadly covers the history of European painting and sculpture, as well as African and Asian art, along with folk art from North Carolina. The 14,000 works include pieces by Rubens, Delacroix, Degas, and Pissarro. The **Chapel Hill Museum,** at 523 E. Franklin St., 919/967-1400, focuses on local history specifically, and southern history and culture in general. No admission charge. **Coker Arboretum,** in the center of the UNC campus, Totten Center, 919/962-0522, website: www.unc.edu/depts/ncbg, is always open and ready to share its wealth of conifers and blooms. **Morehead Planetarium,** 250 E. Franklin St., 919/962-1236, website: www.morehead.unc.edu, is considered the top North Carolina astronomy center. Come visit and you'll see a 30–45-minute Star Theater presentation, along with the oversized sundial, the rose garden, and various art and science exhibits. A small admission fee is charged.

**North Carolina Botanical Garden,** Old Mason Farm Road off the 15/501 and 54 Bypass, 919/962-0522, website: www.unc.edu/depts/ncbg, features 600 acres of nature trails, herbs, aquatics, and carnivorous plants. Plants native to the state are separated by environment. **The North Carolina Collection Gallery,** in the Wilson Library on South Road, 919/962-0522, website: www.lib.unc.edu/ncc/gallery.html, features historic rooms, reassembled here, including the Sir Walter Raleigh room and the original library from Hayes Plantation in Edenton, just the way it was, only farther west.

**The University of North Carolina at Chapel Hill,** 919/962-1630, was chartered in 1789, making it the nation's first state university. Today the school teaches about 24,000 students, approximately two-thirds of them undergraduates. For a free tour of the historic campus, call ahead. Some 82 percent of the university's freshmen come from North Carolina, but in 2002, UNC's students hailed from 42 states and its international students represented 37 countries. Famous graduates include designer of the Intel 386 and 486 chip John Crawford '77; writers Clyde Edgerton '66, Thomas Wolfe '20, Charles Frazier '73, and Jill McCorkle '80; basketball superstar Michael Jor-

dan '84; radio personality Rick Dees '72: *Star Trek Voyager* creator and producer Michael Piller '70; Tom Maxwell '87 of the Squirrel Nut Zippers, *King of the Hill* writers John Altshuler '85 and Dave Krinsky '85; along with TV commentators Roger Mudd '53 and Charles Kuralt '55, former White House communications director Donald Baer '76, and former White House Chief of Staff Erskine Bowles '67; President James K. Polk, Class of 1818; actors Jack Palance '41, Andy Griffith '49, Billy Crudup '90, Louise Fletcher '57, and Sharon Lawrence '83; cartoonist Jeff MacNelly '69; Krispy Kreme's chairman, president and CEO Scott Livengood '74; and Motley Fool founder David Gardner '88. Not bad for a state school.

## ACCOMMODATIONS
### $50–100
Fans of Manteo's *The Lost Colony* outdoor play may want to stay at the four-room **Windy Oaks Inn,** 1164 Old Lystra Church Rd. in Chatham City, 919/942-1001. Playwright Paul

University of North Carolina at Chapel Hill

© ERIKA HOWSARE

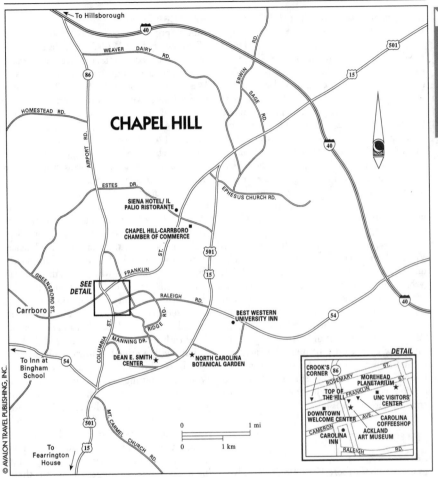

RALEIGH

DETAIL

© AVALON TRAVEL PUBLISHING, INC.

Green once lived here on the 20-plus acres of oaks four miles south of Chapel Hill. All the rooms feature period antiques, and three of the four have their own bathroom. Morning brings big country breakfasts.

## $100–150

**The Inn at Bingham School,** 6720 Mebane Oaks Rd., 800/566-5583 or 919/563-5583, website: www.chapel-hill-inn.com, sets 10 miles west of Chapel Hill at an old preparatory school that closed in 1865. Erase those visions of sleeping in old classrooms or dormitories; the Inn is set in the former headmaster's house. The five rooms each feature fireplaces and private baths. Wine and cheese in the afternoons and a large gourmet breakfast in the morning, served outside on the patio or inside at the formal dining room.

## $150 and Up

**The Carolina Inn,** 211 Pittsboro St., 800/962-8519 or 919/933-2001, website: www.caroli-nainn.com, is an attractive 1924 184-room inn built by John Sprunt Hill, just beside the site of the original New Hope Chapel, from which Chapel Hill got its name (the former chapel stood in the inn's current parking lot). Hill, a UNC grad, deeded the inn to UNC when he died. Besides its comfortable rooms, in-house gym, and location *on* campus and near downtown Chapel Hill, the Carolina Inn is also popular for its in-house Uptown South restaurant, **Carolina Crossroads,** which features an extensive wine list and one of the top breakfasts in all the Triangle. **The Siena Hotel,** 1505 E. Franklin St., 919/929-4000, website: www.sienahotel.com, is meant to remind visitors of graceful European hostelries. The relatively small size of the hotel—just 80 rooms—the balconies, and the smells wafting up from the in-house restaurant, Il Palio, add to the charm.

The **Fearrington House,** 2000 Fearrington Village Center, eight miles south of Chapel Hill on U.S. 15/501 in Pittsboro, 919/542-2121, website: www.fearringtonhouse.com, is the class act in Chapel Hill's stylish accommodations market. Fearrington is a 200-year-old farm that has been reconstructed to resemble a small rural village. The 17 rooms and 16 suites are furnished with period antiques; the in-house restaurant is prix-fixe, offering country-gone-uptown cuisine. Expect to spend $220 and up for two, year-round, which includes breakfast and an afternoon tea.

# FOOD
## Barbecue
In Carrboro's Carrboro Plaza, **Bon's,** 104 Hwy. 54 West, 919/960-7630, serves up lean barbecue every day of the week. Some swear it's tops in the region. Others argue the same about **Allen and Son,** 6203 Millhouse Rd., 919/942-7576, where owner Keith Allen (the "Son," if you're wondering) is known for not only cooking his own pigs on site (as a good barbecue should) but also cutting the hickory trees and splitting the logs by hand. The pecan pie is worth the trip alone, and the Brunswick stew is better than most. **Mama Dip's Kitchen** and **Crook's Corner,** listed below, are popular barbecue destinations with broader menus.

## American Cuisine
Anita "Spring" Council's **City Ways Café,** 405 W. Rosemary St., 919/942-9929, features a lot of freshly baked goodies and ice cream made on the premises. A great place for lunch. **411 West,** 411 W. Franklin St., 919/942-8757, website: www.411west.citysearch.com, offers salads, fish dinners, and some much celebrated pizza. For a casual lunch, **The Grill at Glen Lennox,** 1201 Raleigh Rd. (Hwy. 54), 919/942-1963, website: www.grillatglenlennox.city search.com, offers satisfying salads in addition to more traditional grill items.

Located inside the Southern Season gourmet food and housewares store, **The Weathervane,** 1800 E. Franklin St., Eastgate Shopping Center, 919/929-7133, website: www.southernseason.com, features gourmet dishes with influences from all over the globe, but with a definite Southern inclination. That's why the weathervanes all point south, you know. Dinner specialties include grilled hickory smoked boneless pork chops, served over bacon, corn, and celery cornbread dressing, with broccolini and roasted garlic beurre blanc, and the pan-seared garlicky Gulf shrimp, with a grilled sun-dried tomato-grits cake, black olive tapenade, and wilted spinach. Weather permitting, eat outdoors.

Another favorite with romantics and gourmet fans is **La Residence,** 202 W. Rosemary St., 919/967-2506, website: www.la residence.citysearch.com. Probably the best thing is the outdoor patio in the garden, a delight in brick and white lattice. If it's not raining or scorching, try to get a table out there. Open since 1976, La Residence is older than Britney Spears and has enjoyed better reviews for such dishes as its grilled pork rib chop with cornbread pudding, red Swiss chard, and pomegranate molasses ($23.95); its braised lamb shank with sautéed mushrooms, roasted eggplant, onions, and couscous in a fried potato log au jus ($27.95), and its parsnips, millet, and goat cheese wrapped in swiss chard with a curried red bell pepper and cardamon emulsion ($19.95). The popular desserts include homemade ice cream and a pear tart that goes well with a scoop of same.

## Southern Cooking

The South certainly did have a field day in 1976. Not only did Georgia's Jimmy Carter get elected president and Lynyrd Skynyrd lay down its live version of "Free Bird," but here in Chapel Hill, Mildred Council took $64 and opened up what is today arguably the best Southern cooking eatery in the Triangle. Famous for its fried chicken, **Mama Dip's Kitchen,** 408 W. Rosemary St., 919/942-5837, website: www.mamadips.com, also turns out great ribs. She's won praise from *Southern Living,* has baked a pecan pie on *Good Morning America,* and has published a cookbook, *Mama Dip's Kitchen,* with the University of North Carolina Press. And the tall, lanky Mama Dip enjoys that rarest of pleasures: knowing that Michael Jordan is a fan of *hers.*

**Crook's Corner,** 610 Franklin St., 919/929-7643, website: www.crookscorner.com, has it all when it comes to a good Southern food joint. For starters, it has a pig hoisted high above the entrance, in case you forgot why you came here. Secondly, it has a mystery: Crook's Corner is named for the woman who owned a fish market here just after World War II. She was murdered in the doorway in 1951, the case was never solved, and the building went vacant for years. Finally in 1978 somebody reopened the place as a barbecue stand, and four years later Gene Hamer and the late chef, Bill Neal, took over the operation and pointed the Corner away from home cookin' and toward something called Southern Cuisine. But don't let the seriousness fool you; Crook's is still down-home at heart. It may have the sort of gourmet coffee favored by countercultural types but, in its no-pretense-allowed spirit, Crook's sells it as just that: "Counterculture Coffee." It's listed that way, right on the menu. And while you'll find dishes here over $20 (including the "Scalawag-a filet mignon"), you can also order up a hickory-smoked barbecue pork sandwich and slaw for $6.50. For a full experience (and you will be *full*) you might want to order the Carolina sampler—pork barbecue served with hoppin' John, collard greens, and black pepper cornbread ($14.50). The jalapeño hush puppies (served with cocktail sauce) make a tasty appetizer.

**Top of the Hill Restaurant & Brewery,** 100 E.

Franklin St., 919/929-8676, received national attention in the days immediately following the terrorist bombings of September 11, 2001. Owner Scott Maitland, a Gulf War veteran, hung a large sign on his restaurant window that read, "God Bless America—Woe to Her Enemies." Three members of the Chapel Hill City Council filed complaints, forcing the sign's removal through the use of a little-enforced temporary sign size ordinance. This was more than the shell-shocked nation could stand, and the calls of support poured in from all across the country; eventually the sign was allowed to remain. All that aside, Top of the Hill is one of the top restaurants in Chapel Hill (voted number 1 in town in 1998 by local readers); as popular for its microbrews (voted tops in the Triangle in 2001) and its huge third-floor deck (also voted the Triangle's best), which provides a tremendous view of downtown. The most popular item on the mid-upper-range menu—beyond the beer—is the tuna steak, $18.95.

## Burgers

**Woody's Tar Heel Tavern,** 175 E. Franklin St., 919/968-3809, looks like your average sports bar, but the burgers it puts out—man oh man.

© ERIKA HOWSARE

Crook's Corner

The blue cheese is possibly the best, though the Big Kahuna—guacamole, jalapeños, salsa, sour cream, and cheese—is hard to beat.

## Mexican

Located west of town in Carrboro, **El Chilango,** 506 Jones Ferry Rd., 843/960-0171, features a popular, authentic Mexican buffet. If you're looking for something you can take with you, try a *torta.* Also in Carrboro and also popular, **Carrburritos Taqueria,** 711 Rosemary St., 919/933-8226, offers authentic—and plenteous—Mexican cuisine in an informal setting. Try the fish tacos and massive burritos.

Much less authentic but still very good is the popular Greenwich-Mex **Flying Burrito,** 746 Airport Rd., 919/967-7744, where local art is on the walls and sweet potatoes swell the burritos.

And you can probably guess from its name that **Cosmic Cantina,** is similarly about as authentically Mexican as a tie-dyed serape. But the Cantina, at 128 E. Franklin St., 919/960-3955, website: www.cosmiccantina.com, nonetheless churns out some tasty and healthier-than-the-original Mexico-inspired food.

## Italian

**Vespa,** 306-D W. Franklin St., 919/969-6600, offers a warm, energetic Italian atmosphere, with Italian music, primo pasta, and authentic sorbettos.

## Greek/Mediterranean

Near Vespa is Jamil Kordoura's **Mediterranean Deli,** 410 W. Franklin St., 919/967-2666, website: www.mediterraneandeli.com, popular for its gyros and falafel. Kordoura has owned the deli for more than 10 years now, and he's begun to achieve some regional renown. If you're unfamiliar with or unable to make decisions concerning this sort of cuisine, you can always order a sampler.

## Organic Food

**Spotted Dog,** 111 E. Main St. in Carrboro, 919/933-1117, website: www.spotteddog restaurant.com, makes a fine vegetarian burger, with all the trimmings. **Pyewacket Restaurant,**

431 W. Franklin St., 919/929-0297, offers a more uptown take on vegetarian eating. Seafood here as well.

## Asian

**Akai Hana,** 200 W. Main St. (opposite Chapel Hill Tire), 919/942-6848, is favored by Triangle sushi lovers, though the restaurant offers hot dishes as well.

## Breakfast

Located inside the Carolina Inn, **Carolina Crossroads,** 211 Pittsboro St., 919/918-2777, website: www.crossroads.citysearch.com, offers colorful rooms and a warm setting.

## Pub Grub

**Carolina Brewery,** 460 W. Franklin St., 919/942-1800, website:www.carolinabrew.citysearch.com, filled its first mugs in the mid-1990s and offers half a dozen homebrewed beers, made right inside the massive copper vats that dominate the pub's interior. At one time named the Top Brewpub in the Southeast by *Brewpub Magazine,* Carolina offers delights for beer connoisseurs, which include the malty Anniversary Ale, brewed in the style of the Trappist monks of Europe; California Steamin', a steam beer; and the ever-popular Copperline Amber. People differ on which one of the brews is best, but surely the prize for having the best name goes to the dark lager To Hell n' Bock. Dinners include the pubhouse icon fish and chips, as well as shrimp and grits and some tasty North Carolina barbecue.

## Market

**A Southern Season,** 1800 E. Franklin St., Eastgate Shopping Center, 919/929-7133, website: www.southernseason.com, opened way back in 1975, and it's something like the Plymouth Rock of Epicureanism in the region. The first fresh-roasted coffee in the Triangle was roasted right here.

# ENTERTAINMENT
## Nightlife
**The Dead Mule** (which you can't beat—get it?), 303 W. Franklin St., 919/969-7659, is set in

a converted bungalow. Its porch is a friendly spot on busy Franklin Street. Good spot for a mixed drink. The Chapel Hill installation of **The Mellow Mushroom,** 1502 E. Franklin St., 919/969-8789, books bluegrass acts only, attracting pickers from hereabouts and others that have to travel a far piece.

**The Cat's Cradle,** 300 E. Main St., Carrboro, 919/967-9053, website: www.catscradle.arctic on.com, is just about the perfect size to watch a live act; it's the place where you wish your favorite act was playing as you try to adjust your binoculars while watching them at the AllTel Pavilion. The booking is eclectic, everything from reggae to bluegrass, gospel to hip-hop, and of course, in a college town, lots of college "alternative" rock. **Tyler's Restaurant & Taproom,** 102 E. Main St., Carrboro, 919/929-6881, website: www.tylerstaproom.com, is justly famous for its draft beer and fresh-cut garlic fries.

### Coffeehouses

You just know that a college town like Chapel Hill is going to have some serious coffeehouse action. Two of the best are Caribou Coffee and Coffee Mill Roastery. Set in an old gas station—which to us caffeine addicts, seems fitting somehow—**Caribou Coffee,** 110 W. Franklin St., 919/933-5404, features a stone fireplace, couches, and an outdoor deck. **Coffee Mill Roastery,** 161 E. Franklin St., 919/929-1727, roasts its own beans; a local bakery bakes the Mill's cheesecake and other items, including the bread for its sandwiches. Sometimes they shut off the classical music wafting out of the speakers and a live acoustic music act plays a set. Local artists' works cover the walls.

## INFORMATION
### Newspapers

The Raleigh *News and Observer* is still the main paper, even here in Chapel Hill, but for travelers looking for entertainment options, you'll probably want to pick up a copy of *The Independent Weekly,* or *The Spectator,* for information on what's happening, who's playing where, and so forth.

### Radio

**WNCU 90.7** offers great jazz with an occasional focus on Tar Heels such as John Coltrane, Roberta Flack, Thelonious Sphere Monk, Nina Simone, and Grady Tate. You can also listen online at www.wncu.org. **WUNC 915.** is the local NPR station.

© ERIKA HOWSARE

**mural in downtown Chapel Hill**

## Southeast of Raleigh

### SMITHFIELD

Smithfield is a lot of things, including the childhood home of Frank Sinatra's supposed one true love, actress Ava Gardner (1922–90), youngest of the six children of Mr. and Mrs. J.B. Gardner, who ran a tobacco farm in nearby Brogden. Today you'll find the crammed-to-the-gills **Ava Gardner Museum,** 325 E. Market St., 919/934-5830, website: www.avagardner.org, set in the house where the Gardners operated a guest home for teachers. Ava grew from age 2 to 13 here, before moving up to Newport News, Virginia (briefly), and then to Rock Ridge near Wilson. The 6,000-square-foot museum features theater posters, promotional shots, clothing worn by Ava at notable occasions, her acting awards, and a video documentary. Admission is $5 and under.

Just as important, however, Smithfield is home to **The White Swan,** a barbecue built on the site of a former roadhouse and touring court of sordid reputation, open as a restaurant since the year Ava and Frank got married. Today the barbecue pit is famous for its hot, vinegary barbecue, its fried chicken, and its fried pork skin—which comes gratis with each order, as a garnish. To get there, take I-95 Exit 990 and drive toward Smithfield on U.S. 301 North. It's right there on the highway.

### FAYETTEVILLE

Babe Ruth hit his first professional home run in Fayetteville, in March 1914, and you'll see a historical marker commemorating the fact on Gillespie Street. It was George Herman Ruth's first time out of Baltimore. He'd arrived with the Minor League Baltimore Orioles—and was said to have spent much time watching the trains and riding the elevator in the team hotel. Here in Fayetteville, Ruth got his nickname, Babe, said to have come because of his youth and his wide-eyed "babe in the woods" demeanor when confronted with Fayetteville's wonders.

Other famous folks have visited or lived in Fayetteville. African-American author and anthologist Charles W. Chesnutt taught here in the late 1800s. Oscar-winning actress Julianne Moore (*Boogie Nights, Magnolia, The End of the Affair*) was born here while her father was stationed at Fort Bragg as a military judge. Robert Strange, a U.S. Senator and the author of the first novel about North Carolina, the unremembered *Eoneguski, or Cherokee Chief,* is buried here.

Of course, the town is named after Lafayette, the French hero of the American Revolution, who did the proper thing when he returned to the United States in 1825 and visited the home of the city named for him nearly 30 years previous (Lafayette, Louisiana, enjoyed no such visit). He stayed at the home of Duncan McRae, which was later replaced by the present courthouse.

Fayetteville started out as a Scottish Highlander settlement at the highest navigable point of the Cape Fear River, named Campbelltown in a fit of homesickness. After the Highlanders took a beating while fighting for the Crown in the Revolution, the town was combined with nearby Cross Creek to become Fayetteville. It was named the state capital in 1789 and served as such until 1793. Fayetteville was truly the nexus of the state for many years. Five different wagon roads left from Fayetteville to allow farmers to get their crops to the Cape Fear River, which led to Wilmington, the Tar Heel State's only major port.

During the War Between the States, Fayetteville took as much heat—literally—from Sherman's men as any town in the state. Union general Judson Kilpatrick broke ahead of the rest of Sherman's men with his cavalry, attempting to beat General Wade Hampton to Fayetteville, where Sherman had his sights on the Confederate armory. Kilpatrick and his men took a different road and rode hard until they were sure they were far ahead of Hampton's men. They set up camp, expecting to surprise the Confederates when they came along the road the following morning. But Hampton was riding hard too,

## AVA GARDNER: SMITHFIELD'S SCREEN SIREN

Grabtown-born and Smithfield-raised screen star Ava Gardner's right-place-at-the-right-time story is one of those tales that subverts the Protestant work ethic. While visiting her older sister Beatrice in New York City, the would-be secretary, on break from classes at Atlantic Christian College in Wilson, agreed to pose for some shots for Beatrice's husband, Larry, a professional photographer. Larry made some prints of his comely 18-year-old sister-in-law and hung them in his studio windows to advertise his craft; a movie studio scout noticed the arched eyebrows, cleft chin, and other contortions of interest. He inquired about the model, and set up a screen test with MGM.

Gardner signed a movie contract in 1941 at age 19 and married the 21-year-old Mickey Rooney, the hottest actor in the nation, in January 1942. (Recently, while in town performing a one-man show, Rooney and wife no. 8 paid a visit to the museum devoted to wife no. 1.) A few years later she married bandleader Artie Shaw, but that didn't last long, either. Divorced again, she met Frank Sinatra, and he left his wife and three kids for the woman Ernest Hemingway called "the most beautiful animal in the world." Sinatra's already suffering career suffered even more from the bad publicity, but Gardner pulled strings to get her sore-throated husband the chance to audition for *From Here to Eternity*, which won him a Best Supporting Actor Oscar, and began his comeback. Their marriage, however, only lasted until 1957. Though rich with pursuers—including millionaire Howard Hughes—Gardner never married again.

In MGM's view, Gardner's acting was always secondary to her physical appearance; consequently, she was often given leads in lesser films that needed her presence to make them profitable. Of her mainly B-movie career, she joked, "Nobody ever called it an intellectual profession."

Nonetheless, Gardner went on to make some memorable films, including *On the Beach*, garnering an Oscar nomination for John Ford's *Mogambo* along the way. After playing Lady Brett Ashley in the screen adaptation of Hemingway's *The Sun Also Rises*, she followed Papa's lead and moved to Spain. In later years she turned down a number of films because they required on-screen nudity. "I made it as a star dressed," she explained, "and if it ain't dressed, I don't want it."

Gardner's most famous role, interestingly, had a North Carolina connection. In the same year as Sinatra's turn in *Eternity*, she took a singing-dubbed role in the remake of *Showboat*. The script was based on the novel set along the Mississippi River, but written by New Yorker Edna Ferber after visiting a traveling showboat moored in Bath, North Carolina.

Though Gardner finished out her last decades living in Spain and then London, she kept her ties with North Carolina, and even attended her high school reunion in Rock Ridge in 1978. She visited Smithfield up until strokes incapacitated her, five years before her death from pneumonia in 1990. Gardner is now buried in the Gardner family plot in Sunset Memorial Gardens. Neither of her living husbands showed up for the funeral—but Sinatra sent in the largest flower order the local florist ever filled. The **Ava Gardner Museum** honors Smithfield's most famous resident at 325 E. Market St. in downtown Smithfield, 919/934-5830, website: www.avagardner.org. It's open Monday–Saturday 9 A.M.–5 P.M., 2–5 P.M. Sunday. Around $5 for adults, less for seniors and students.

---

and the Confederates surprised the Northerners, forcing Kilpatrick to leave—so it is said—a female visitor in his tent, leap onto the nearest horse, and ride hell-bent into the swamp in his underwear.

It was a small, tactically inconsequential victory, but it gave Southern hearts one of the few bright spots in the last days of the war. While Hardee's troops crossed the river north of town, Hampton and his men waited in Fayetteville, spreading the story and ready to burn the bridge behind them at the approach of the Yankee troops. The first Union troops to come were some of Sherman's foragers, who clearly didn't expect to find Confederates still in the city. Hampton's cavalry attacked them, killing some

## THE BATTLE OF BENTONVILLE

In early March 1865, General William T. Sherman's 80,000-man Union Army, in hot pursuit of Confederate general Joseph E. Johnston's army, and having just burned the Fayetteville Armory, was headed toward Goldsboro to link up with 40,000 additional Union soldiers and to replenish their stomachs and ammunition stores with the supply wagons that awaited them there.

Johnston had evaded Sherman's army for many miles, engaging in delaying skirmishes but never a full-blown battle—which, given Sherman's greater strength, would have been suicide. But now Johnston had different orders, straight from Robert E. Lee, commanding him to do everything possible to keep the Federals from joining up with Grant and surrounding Lee at Petersburg, Va.

Johnston pieced together the remnants of several shattered armies and dragged the gutters, front porch rocking chairs, and schoolyards of the Carolinas to create a force of 21,000 men to fight the marauding Yankees.

Though Confederate generals Hardee and Hampton had antagonized the army since Georgia with irritating skirmishes, Sherman's men had not encountered a bona fide battle since before Atlanta. Johnston's army caught the Federals by surprise on March 19, when they suddenly turned back and attacked the leading wing of Union troops, under General Henry Slocum, near Bentonville. Sherman later recalled the moment he heard the news:

*When we were within twenty-seven miles of Goldsboro' and five from Bentonville . . . supposing that all danger was over, I crossed over to join Howard's column, to the right, so as to be nearer to Generals Schofield and Terry, known to be approaching Goldsboro'. . . . I had heard some cannonading over about Slocum's head of column, and supposed it to indicate about the same measure of opposition by Hardee's troops and Hampton's cavalry before experienced; but during the day a messenger overtook me, and notified me that near Bentonville General Slocum had run up against Johnston's whole army.*

Johnston's initial assault killed some 304 Union soldiers and wounded 1,112. Sherman ordered Slocum to fight defensively while the senior general rushed in reinforcements from Cog's Bridge. This was easier planned than achieved, however. "The country was very obscure," Sherman noted, "and the maps extremely defective."

Nonetheless, Sherman's men did reach the fray on March 21, at which point Confederate casualties quickly matched and then surpassed the Union's. Still, Sherman was uncertain of the strength of Johnston's army and unwilling to force his hungry men into a general battle when supplies and reinforcements awaited at nearby Goldsboro. Consequently, when Union general Mower pushed through the South's left flank and threatened to fight through clear to Bentonville, Sherman called Mower back. When the Confederates began to withdraw toward Smithfield, Sherman let them. As usual along the Federals' famous march through Georgia and the Carolinas, Sherman fought conservatively, and was roundly criticized for this by politicians in Washington. Later, Sherman admitted,

*I think I made a mistake there, and should rapidly have followed Mower's lead with the whole of the right wing, which would have brought on a general battle, and it could not have resulted otherwise than successfully to us, by reason of our vastly superior numbers.*

According to Sherman's estimate, the Federals lost 1,604 men at Bentonville to the Confederates' 2,343. Having tried their utmost at stopping the enormous Northern army, a month later, Johnston's Confederates surrendered near Durham.

and taking others prisoners. Then they evacuated north, burning the bridge behind them. After Hampton's riders left, more undisciplined foragers overran the city and plundered it until Sherman was able to station troops to protect private property.

Sherman himself took up residence in the Confederate arsenal, formerly the property of the U.S. Government though much expanded by the Confederates. He set his men to building pontoon bridges for the passage north, and on Sunday, March 12, he and his men—long cut off from the rest of the army—received the first mail in many days:

*Sunday, March 12th, was a day of Sabbath stillness in Fayetteville. The people generally attended their churches, for they were a very pious people, descended in a large measure from the old Scotch Covenanters, and our men too were resting from the toils and labors of six weeks of as hard marching as ever fell to the lot of soldiers. Shortly after noon was heard in the distance the shrill whistle of a steamboat, which came nearer and nearer, and soon a shout, long and continuous, was raised down by the river, which spread farther and farther, and we all felt that it meant a messenger from home.*

Fayetteville's **Dogwood Festival**, held each April, pays tribute to the thousands of dogwood trees found in town. Stop by the **Fayetteville Area Convention and Visitors Bureau,** 245 Person St., 800/255-8217 or 910/483-5311, for more information.

## Accommodations

Out on I-95 you'll find a number of chain lodgings, like a **Comfort Inn,** 1957 Cedar Creek Rd., 910/323-8333, where rooms start at around $80. You'll also find a lot of chain lodgings near the Cross Creek Mall, including a **Days Inn,** 1706 Skibo Rd., 910/867-6777, where rooms start at around $50, and a **Courtyard by Marriott,** 4192 Sycamore Dairy Rd., 910/487-5557.

## Food

**King's Kids,** 5520 Murchison Rd., 910/884-3880, offers food for your soul—in the way of Psalms painted on the wall and so forth—to complement your soul food. Open Monday–Saturday 7 A.M.–9 P.M. The King referred to is not the owner (the owners' last name is McMillian) and it's not MLK, though one suspects the Civil Rights–minded preacher would have approved of the Christophilic ambience as well as the Kids' fried chicken, chitterlings, pork chops, barbecued ribs, fresh fish, and pinto beans. This is the real thing, worth a hundred Shoney's. For comfort food of a different kind, see **Cross Creek Brewing Company,** 1895 Skibo Rd., 910/867-9223, serving popular private-label brew and knockwurst near the Mall, next door to the Courtyard by Marriott. Finally, the **Belmont Tea Room and Café,** 1104 Hay St., 910/485-8433, serves soups, sandwiches, salads, desserts, and teas Monday–Friday 11 A.M.–3 P.M. Formal teas are available on weekday afternoons with 24-hour reservations.

# PEMBROKE

**University of North Carolina, Pembroke,** was opened in 1887 as the first four-year college founded for Native Americans. In the 1970s it became part of the UNC system. May brings the **Powwow,** and October brings a second one. The **Indian Wild Game Festival** in November allows you the chance to eat Native American dishes. **North Carolina Indian Cultural Center,** off U.S. 74, on Old Main Street, 910/521-6282, features displays and exhibits depicting Lumbee tribal life. A free 30-minute film provides a brief but interesting look at local Native American lore. But far more evocative is *Strike at the Wind,* an outdoor drama held at the Adolph Dial Amphitheatre that retells the story of Robeson County's Henry Berry Lowrie, a Lumbee Indian (then called the Croatan) who organized a band of outlaws and turned to crime and vengeance after his brother and father were killed by local vigilantes. Call 910/521-2433 for tickets and more information.

# Charlotte and the Southern Heartland

For many people, Charlotte is less a vacation destination than a place to do business. But there are enough attractions here to warrant a visit by the thoughtful traveler, and anyway, if your business is bringing you through the Queen City, there's no reason to stick to business after hours. With a dynamic, transient population, money to burn, and a stronger sense of the future than of the past, Charlotte is in many ways the ideal New South city.

Charlotte is the biggest city in North Carolina, but you wouldn't necessarily know this while talking to a resident of, say, Durham or Raleigh. "It is thought," suggests longtime Charlottean Donna Withrow, "that the Triangle is very jealous of the prosperous Piedmont city." Charlotte is the all-work, no-play sister who has prospered financially far beyond her siblings, who alternately envy her prosperity and scowl at her frumpish clothes and inability to dance. But at Charlotte, a visitor can get beneath the veneer of "tourist" attractions to experience the steady, nononsense heart of this vibrant, Southern dynamo. And just head north of town to Lake Norman or south to Tega Cay to see where many Charlotteans let their hair down and spend large piles of that hard-earned cash.

James K. Polk Memorial

© ERIKA HOWSARE

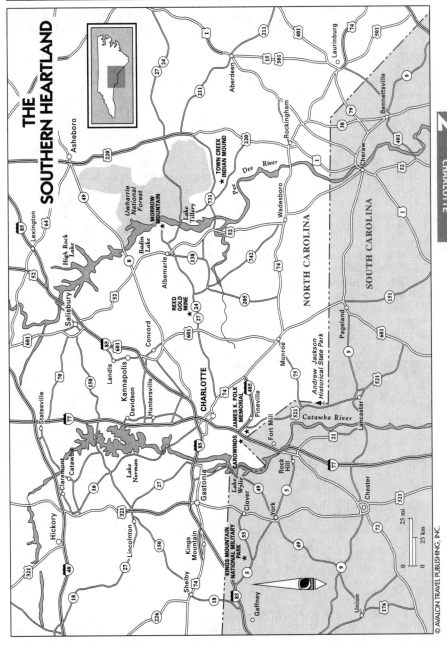

THE SOUTHERN HEARTLAND

CHARLOTTE

NORTH CAROLINA

SOUTH CAROLINA

Uwharrie National Forest

TOWN CREEK INDIAN MOUND

MORROW MOUNTAIN

REED GOLD MINE

JAMES K. POLK MEMORIAL

CAROWINDS

KINGS MOUNTAIN NATIONAL MILITARY PARK

Andrew Jackson Historical State Park

Dee River

Pee

Catawba River

High Rock Lake

Badin Lake

Lake Tillery

Lake Norman

Lake Wylie

Asheboro
Lexington
Salisbury
Landis
Kannapolis
Davidson
Huntersville
Concord
Albemarle
Statesville
Catawba
Claremont
Hickory
Lincolnton
Gastonia
Kings Mountain
Shelby
Gaffney
Clover
York
Rock Hill
Chester
Union
Pineville
Monroe
Fort Mill
Lancaster
Pageland
Cheraw
Bennettsville
Laurinburg
Aberdeen
Rockingham
Wadesboro
Charlotte

Aberdeen
Laurinburg

25 mi
25 km

© AVALON TRAVEL PUBLISHING, INC.

# Charlotte

## HISTORY

In the 1750s, Charlotte's Trade and Tryon Streets were red-dirt Indian trading paths. Scots-Irish surveyor Tom Polk and his wife, Susannah, had traveled with many other Scots-Irish down from Pennsylvania along the Great Wagon Road through the Shenandoah Valley of Virginia, until it merged with the Trading Path. The land here in the Carolinas was free, or nearly so, and it was plentiful. The Indians, since the Tuscarora War of 1711, had been little problem to white settlers. Polk followed the path further and further south, through the little village of Salisbury and into the trees, watching as the homes of other settlers thinned out in the dense wilderness. Where the Trading Path crossed another, lesser trail, Polk built his house on a little ridge at the intersection's southeast corner.

Polk's crossroads became the center of a small cluster of cabins over the next decade. And as the community began to grow out there in the

## HEARTLAND HIGHLIGHTS

**Carowinds,** Fort Mill

**The Coffee Cup,** Charlotte

**Fourth Ward,** Charlotte

**Historic Latta Plantation,** Huntersville

**James K. Polk Memorial,** Pineville

**Lake Norman**

**Lowe's Motor Speedway,** Concord

**Mint Museum of Art,** Charlotte

**Reed Gold Mine State Historic Site,** Stanfield

**Historic Salisbury**

**Town Creek Indian Mound State Historic Site,** Mount Gilead

solitude at the edge of the British-American wilderness, as author Mary Norton Kratt explains in her *Charlotte: Spirit of the New South,* Charlotte Town, as it would come to be known, began to manifest a strong independent streak. When a British surveyor arrived in 1763, he discovered that the pioneers who had come all the way out here into the wilderness to escape from British law were not particularly glad to see it catch up with them, particularly as the surveyor had come to sell them the very land they'd already been farming for years. According to a parchment from England, the land actually belonged to an Englishman who had never even visited the colony.

The settlers ended up buying the land at a discounted rate, but that was hardly the last conflict between the British government and local inhabitants. Scots-Irish Presbyterian minister Alexander Craighead came to the area in 1758, preaching at nearby pioneer churches and espousing a theology deeply influenced by Reformation theologian John Knox. His sermons often focused on the "divine gift of liberty," and he preached that the King who violated his sacred obligations to rule justly could be disobeyed, even "by force." His sermons so stirred up the residents throughout the county that they earned him, in some local histories, the nickname of the area's "father of independence."

The village at Polk's crossroads needed a name, and in 1762, when King George III married 17-year-old German princess Charlotte from Mecklenburg-Strelitz, the town chose to curry Royal favor with a gesture calculated to assert their by now much-questioned loyalty to the Crown: they (like Charlottesville, Virginia) named their village after the new queen, and the newly separate county surrounding the village was dubbed Mecklenburg.

It worked. Charlotte was named the county seat, and a courthouse built there. The county's leaders, believing education was important in

To Carowinds Amusement and Water Park

Coddle Creek Reservoir

To Schiele Museum of Natural History

Lake Norman

**CHARLOTTE**

Huntersville

Concord

UNDER CONSTRUCTION

W.T. HARRIS BLVD.

LOWE'S MOTOR SPEEDWAY

LATTA PLANTATION PARK

Catawba River

BUBBA'S BBQ

Harrisburg

To Reed Gold Mine

GERT'S LI'L DINER

UNIVERSITY OF NORTH CAROLINA AT CHARLOTTE

Mount Holly

MOTEL 6 SOUTH

OLD HICKORY HOUSE

**SEE DOWNTOWN CHARLOTTE MAP**

HISTORIC ROSEDALE

MUSEUM OF HISTORY & HEZEKIAH ALEXANDER HOMESITE

Belmont

**CHARLOTTE**

INDEPENDENCE ARENA

OVENS AUDITORIUM

CHARLOTTE/ DOUGLAS INTERNATIONAL AIRPORT

ELIZABETH BED & BREAKFAST

MINT MUSEUM

FREEDOM PARK

SOUTH 21 DRIVE-IN

SARDIS RD.

SOUTHPARK MALL

BILL SPOON'S BBQ

FAIRVIEW RD.

CAROWINDS

Pineville

JAMES K. POLK MEMORIAL

Lake Wylie

**SOUTH**

**CAROLINA**

To Waxhaw

0        4 mi

0      4 km

© AVALON TRAVEL PUBLISHING, INC.

**CHARLOTTE**

preventing oppression, founded a college for the village's young men and named it Queen's College, for consistency's sake. The King refused to approve its charter, and the founders made changes and tried again. They were refused charter again, so Queen's College went ahead and operated anyway. Later, the main east-west thoroughfare leading toward New Bern and the house of Royal Governor Tryon was named in the governor's honor, but that was one of the last pro-Crown gestures anybody ever saw around Charlotte Town.

By 1775, Polk's village had grown considerably as more fiery, independent-minded Scots-Irish Calvinists had moved into the area. Polk himself was Colonel of Mecklenburg's citizen's militia, and he asked citizens of the county's villages to send representatives to meet at the Charlotte courthouse on May 19 to plan ways to protect their freedom from British rule. As the men met, a messenger arrived with news of the battles of Lexington and Concord, Massachusetts.

Furious, the citizens decided to cut all ties with Britain. The next day, the Mecklenburgers announced their freedom with a proclamation called the Mecklenburg Declaration of Independence, dissolving forever the colonists' bonds with England, declaring, with typical Scots-Irish matter-of-factness:

> *We the Citizens of Mecklenburg County do hereby desolve the political bands which have connected us to the Mother Country & hereby absolve ourselves from all allegiance to the British crown & abjure all political connection, contract or association with that nation who have wantonly trampled on our rights & liberties & inhumanely shed the innocent blood of American patriots at Lexington.*

An 1800 fire burned the courthouse that held the Declaration, and today some historians argue that it never existed. Nonetheless, the May 20 date is commemorated on North Carolina's state flag.

## War Between the States

The Civil War didn't end up doing to Charlotte what it had done to Atlanta and Columbia, S.C., but it might well have if Confederate general Joseph Johnston hadn't notified William T. Sherman, while the latter was encamped over in Durham, that he was ready to discuss the surrender of his troops. When word came to Sherman, he had already ordered his troops stationed in Raleigh to begin marching on Charlotte. When Johnston's message came, Sherman called back his troops.

## Integration

Old-time Charlotteans of both races can tell heartwrenching tales of the humiliation endured by African-Americans during Charlotte's Jim Crow days. But while Charlotte once wielded most of the standard Jim Crow practices, when push came to shove in the 1960s, Charlotte chose civility and civil order over segregation. The Queen City was, after all, growing, and it wanted to continue to grow and prosper. In 1962, work began on a dam at Cowan's Ford north of town, which would create Lake Norman, the state's largest man-made lake, as well as generat-

ing the electrical power necessary for the growing city. And while one dam was rising, another was crumbling. Baptist minister and Civil Rights leader Martin Luther King Jr. spoke in Charlotte in 1963, and was pleased to see that white and black civic leaders had already desegregated the city's lunch counters after organizing a "Friendly Relations Committee" between store proprietors and local black students. Business leaders had also begun desegregating theaters, buses, and lodgings, and members of the all-white Chamber of Commerce had even created a program in which black leaders and white leaders went in mixed pairs to local public restaurants and ate lunch together. By the time the 1964 Civil Rights Act was passed, Charlotte was already largely desegregated.

Schools were another matter. Because most blacks lived in the Second Ward, the logical geography-based school assignments still created schools that were segregated in practice, if not by law. Black parents sued the Charlotte-Mecklenburg Schools in federal court, and UNC graduate U.S. District Court Judge James B. McMillan ruled that Charlotte had to transport students across town until each school's demographics more or less approximated Charlotte's 70–30 percent white-black ratio.

The majority of Charlotteans rebelled against busing, but by 1971 the Supreme Court had affirmed McMillan's order, and Charlotte was told it had only until 1974 to get its school districts in line. To do this logistically, of course, was a nightmare. Students who lived a block from one school might have to spend an hour a day riding the bus to and from a school on the other side of town. Many parents who could afford it tightened their belts and sent their students to private schools, some from racist motives, others out of sheer Mecklenburg distaste for the meddlings of a distant, autocratic government in local affairs.

Charlotte made its 1974 deadline, and by 1979, when Bostonians were battling it out over busing, Charlotte was noted by the *Wall Street Journal* as one of the nation's most thoroughly integrated cities. Of course, few were ever really convinced that there weren't more cons than pros to forced busing, but nobody seemed to have a better idea. Finally, in 1997, a group of white parents sued, claiming that the program unconstitutionally injured white children without having any consistently positive effect on the black children it was designed to help. A lower court judge ruled that the program had accomplished its stated goals and could be ended; a group of black parents appealed, and by 2002, the case ended up on the doorstep of the U.S. Supreme Court, which finally refused to review the case. And so it was that 30-plus years of forced race-based busing came to an end in Charlotte's public schools. Charlotte-Mecklenburg School Board chair Arthur Griffin, himself an African-American graduate of Charlotte's schools and an opponent of forced busing, asserted that the needs of inner-city students needed to be and would be addressed through other, more effective methods.

## Boomtown

Southpark opened in 1972 on more than 100 acres of farmland southeast of downtown Charlotte. The new shopping mall greeted 92,000 visitors its first day, and quickly began its proto-

Wal-Mart destruction of the downtown retail district, which saw a 25 percent drop in sales the first year of Southpark's operation. By the end of the 1970s, downtown Charlotte was somewhere that most people avoided, if they could afford to.

By the late 1970s and into the 1980s, downtown Charlotte, as with so many urban centers in America, had become a run-down, crime-ridden shadow of its former self as the middle and upper classes moved their homes and spending cash to the suburbs. In their perennial can-do spirit, Charlotteans rolled up their sleeves and vowed to create a renaissance of the city center. *Charlotte Observer* writers vowed to refer to the city center as "uptown," rather than "downtown," to help the city's leaders in their quest to create a more positive image of down-...er, uptown. They still do it, even today.

As the '80s dawned, the signs that Charlotte had become a modern American city and a major regional hub came fast and furious. Harvey Gantt, who just 20 years earlier had been the first African-American admitted to Clemson University—or to any state-run South Carolina college—became

**entrance to a Gold Hill mineshaft**

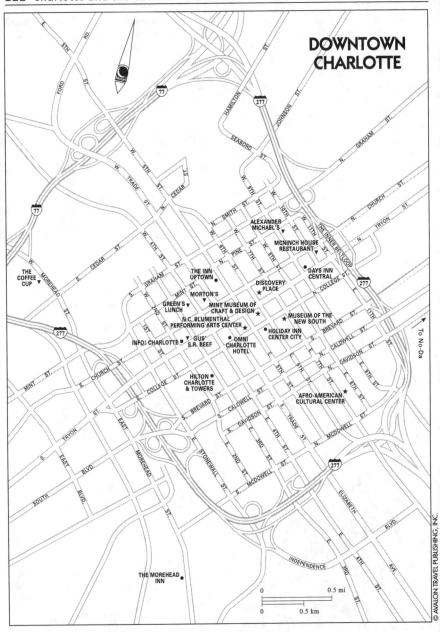

CHARLOTTE

DOWNTOWN CHARLOTTE

the first black mayor of Charlotte, in 1982. Five years later, he was defeated by Sue Myrick, who became the city's first female mayor.

Hurricane Hugo tore through much of Charlotte's beloved old trees and homes, causing nearly as much damage here, 200 miles from the ocean, as it did in Charleston. But while hurricanes changed the treeline and politicos broke the color line, NationsBank cracked Charlotte's skyline. On October 24, 1992, the company completed its $150 million, 60-story NationsBank Corporate Center on the Square at the intersection of Trade and Tryon in the center of Charlotte. The 1990s having been what they were, it's now the Bank of America building.

## Today

Ethnic and religious diversity has become the norm as the Heartland's cities have prospered. And as the world and the world's money have come to the Heartland, with the world (and its money) have come the world's problems. In 2002, nine Charlotte businessmen were arrested in Operation Smokescreen, a wide-ranging federal investigation of a cigarette-smuggling ring that reportedly provided money and supplies to Hezbollah, the anti-Israeli/American terrorist group. And yet the overall prognosis for Charlotte is positive. At press time she was losing her NBA and WNBA teams to New Orleans, but Charlotte's determination to become, and likelihood of becoming, a Major League city is undiminished.

# SIGHTS

Charlotte, traditionally, hasn't been the sort of town that people thought of as a vacation destination. However, as the town has grown, and as efforts have been made to preserve the Queen City's unique history, the list of sights has grown considerably. Here are a few of the most popular.

A good place to start understanding Charlotte is to head to its center, known as the Inner Beltloop, the area of town inside the circle formed by the Brookshire Freeway (I-277) and I-77. It's also known as **Center City,** and the center of

Center City is the bustling intersection of W. Trade and N. Tryon Streets, home of the Marriott City Center and the Bank of American Corporate Center. The southeast corner of this intersection was the spot where Tom Polk built his home, the first building in what would later become Charlotte. Due north of Center City is the resort area of Lake Norman and the rolling farmlands of Mallard Creek.

## Arts and History Museums

Located at 3500 Shamrock Dr., **Charlotte Museum of History/Hezekiah Alexander Homesite,** 704/568-1774, website: www.charlottemuseum.org, includes no less than the oldest existing home in Mecklenburg County, a brick two-story built in 1774 for Revolutionary figure Hezekiah Alexander.

A must for anyone trying to comprehend the story of Charlotte in particular, and of the South in general, the **Levine Museum of the New South,** at the corner of College and Seventh Streets, 324 N. College St., 704/333-1887, is unique among all exhibit halls south of the Mason-Dixon Line (or north of it, for that matter). It focuses solely on the less-romantic but important years since Reconstruction. Museum galleries are open Tuesday–Saturday 11 A.M.–5 P.M. Admission runs $6 for adults, $5 for seniors, students, and children, and $17 per family—which includes two adults and their children under 18 years of age.

At 2730 Randolph Rd., 704/337-2000, the **Mint Museum of Art** is set in a building that originally served as the first branch of the U.S. Mint. The mint closed down in 1861, at the start of the Civil War—when U.S. currency wasn't of much use hereabouts—and converted to a Confederate hospital, which certainly was. During the New Deal the building was dismantled and reassembled here. The collections include American paintings, North Carolina pottery, and pre-Columbian art and artifacts. Open Sunday noon–5 P.M., Saturday–Wednesday 10 A.M.–5 P.M.; it stays open until 10 P.M. on Tuesday, for those who enjoy their Mint after dinner. Adult admission is $6, which includes same-day admission to the Mint Museum of Craft & Design uptown.

Outdoor concerts, dance, and drama performances are held on the grounds in the summer, drawing throngs of culture lovers.

The Art Museum's younger sibling, the **Mint Museum of Craft & Design,** sits uptown at 220 N. Tryon St., 704/337-2000, website: www.mintmuseum.org. If they'd had the space, both exhibitions would still be together—so to keep it simple, they share the name. The Museum of Craft & Design showcases collections of ceramics, fiber, glass, metal, and wood from around the world. Recent exhibitions included "Quilts from the Carolinas" and "The Jewelry of Ramona Solberg." Besides the exhibitions, the museum hosts artist demonstrations, workshops, and various educational opportunities; call or visit the website for current information. Open Sunday noon–5 P.M., Saturday–Wednesday 10 A.M.–5 P.M., and open until 10 P.M. on Tuesdays. Adult admission is $6, which includes same-day admission to the Mint Museum of Art.

## Science Museums

**Charlotte Nature Museum,** adjacent to Freedom Park at 1658 Sterling Rd., 800/935-0553 or 704/372-6261, website: www.discoveryplace.org, focuses its exhibits on Piedmont animals and plants, though the Butterfly Pavilion welcomes exotics as well. The museum's Great Hall is home to an information center, and the gift shop is next door. Kids appreciate the educational but entertaining Dragonfly Puppet Theater, and they love crawling around in the Fiber Fun Hall. The Nature Dome is a clever exhibit; it simulates a night around the campfire, wherein the automated "Grandpa Tree" tells the audience about the various creatures they hear in the forest's night song. Outside, you can hike the user-friendly **Paw Paw Trail** through hardwood forest that, in season, is drenched with wildflowers.

The Nature Museum's sister museum is the highly popular **Discovery Place,** 301 N. Tryon St., 800/935-0553 or 704/372-6261, website: www.discoveryplace.org, considered one of the nation's foremost interactive science museums. As entertaining as anything Disney's cooked up, and as interactive as a bayonet charge, the Discovery Place is a must for kids and anyone else with a healthy interest in the way things work. The Omnimax Theater and planetarium complement the Place's rotating exhibits. Open September–May. Monday–Friday 9 A.M.–5 P.M., Saturday 9 A.M.–6 P.M., Sunday 1–6 P.M. During the summer, hours extend. Entrance costs $6.50 for any one area, $3 for each additional area.

## Sports Museums

Sports fans will be interested in the **Carolina Boxing Hall of Fame,** in Smith Tower at Lowe's Motor Speedway in Concord, 704/455-3203, where you'll find displays honoring the pugilistic arts throughout the history of North and South Carolina. Sugar Ray Leonard and Smokin' Joe Frazier are only two of the inductees. The **North Carolina Auto Racing Hall of Fame,** 119 Knob Hill Rd., Exit 36 off I-77, in Mooresville, 704/663-5331, website: www.ncarhof.com, is home to more than 35 retired race cars, a simulator, and more memorabilia from North Carolina racing. Call ahead for hours and admission prices. The **Memory Lane Motorsports and Historic Automotive Museum,** 769 River Hwy., 704/892-9853, throws its net a little wider, tracing the history of both automobiles and the inevitable racing they inspired. Vintage race cars, automobiles, and motorcycles abound. The **Dale Earnhardt Inc. Showroom,** 1675 Coddle Creek Hwy., Mooresville, 877/334-9663 or 704/662-8000, features a museum dedicated to the late driver, his son, Dale Jr., and other drivers on the Earnhardt team.

## Historic Sites

In 1917, the farmhouse now known as the **Historic Dowd House** became the headquarters of the U.S. Army's Camp Greene, where many young doughboys trained before being sent over to the trenches. Returned Confederate captain James C. Dowd built this home at 2216 Monument Ave., 704/398-2260, in 1879, and raised his family here, including a son, Willis Frank Dowd, a local industrialist of note. The house is open the third Sunday of each month, and by appointment.

Just a couple of blocks from the shimmering skyscrapers and high-powered intersection of

© ERIKA HOWSARE

**Rosedale Plantation**

Trade and Tryon Streets lies the **Fourth Ward,** a serene historic neighborhood of 19th-century and early-20th-century homes. Charlotte's 1960 general development plan contained a crazy idea—to preserve the once prestigious, quickly crumbling Fourth Ward—but it wasn't until the Charlotte Junior League purchased the Berryhill House at 324 W. Ninth St. that momentum began to turn toward preservation. Soon, government renewal funds and special bank loan conditions aided the budding group of preservationists. Since then, many of the other surviving homes from Fourth Ward's 19th-century heyday were restored; other period homes were moved in to replace those that had fallen to the wrecking ball. Pick up a free walking tour map of downtown and the Fourth Ward at the Info!Charlotte Visitor's Center at 330 S. Tryon St. Contact the Charlotte Convention and Visitors Bureau at 800/722-1994, or visit www.charlottecvb.org. Info! Charlotte also has information on downtown and the surrounding area; call 704/331-2700. It's open Monday–Friday 8:30 A.M.–5 P.M., Saturday 10 A.M.–4 P.M., Sunday 1–4 P.M.

Sites in the Fourth Ward include the Gothic Revival **First Presbyterian Church,** 200 W. Trade St., 704/332-5123, behind which you'll find the **Settlers Cemetery,** 704/331-2700, the oldest city-owned graveyard in Charlotte. Charlotteans were buried here from 1776 to 1884, and though the current residents have everything in common now, in life they were a diverse lot: soldiers and planters, slaves, and politicians. **Fourth Ward Park** is a nice spot to take a rest on a busy Charlotte day. **Spirit Square,** 345 N. College St., is set in a former First Baptist church, and now includes a performing arts center and art galleries.

The **Historic Latta Plantation,** 5225 Sample Rd. in Huntersville, 704/875-2312, website: www.lattaplantation.org, was home to pioneer James Latta, and today features reconstructed outbuildings peopled by costumed interpreters. Even the animals here are historically appropriate for the time and place.

North of Center City at 3427 N. Tryon St., 704/335-3325, website: libweb.uncc.edu/archives/crhc/rosedale.htm, **Historic Rosedale Plantation** was formerly a 911-acre plantation, commanded from the master's 1815 manor house. Though 903 acres have slipped off into other uses over the centuries, eight scenic acres of grounds and gardens remain at this National Register landmark. Guided tours are given Thursday and Sunday 1–4 P.M., and the grounds are open 9 A.M.–4 P.M. daily. Adults $4, students and seniors $3, children 8 and under free with an accompanying adult admission.

The original Dark Horse candidate grew up at 308 S. Polk St. in Pineville, which now houses the **James K. Polk Memorial,** 704/889-7145, email: polkmemorial@dasia.net, website: www.ah.dcr.state.nc.us/sections/hs/polk/polk.htm. This North Carolina State Historic Site features the reconstructed homesite of Polk, the man who launched the Mexican-American War and made Manifest Destiny U.S. foreign policy. The visitors' center here features exhibits, a worthwhile 25-minute film, and tours of historic buildings with late-1700s and early-1800s furnishings. No admission charged.

The **McIntyre Historic Site,** 5801 McIntyre

## PINEVILLE'S JAMES K. POLK

Mention the name "James K. Polk" to anybody familiar with American history and three phrases come to mind: "Young Hickory," "dark horse," and "manifest destiny."

Born in Pineville on November 2, 1795, Polk was the descendant of one of Charlotte's first families, and the oldest of ten children born to his prosperous father and his devout Presbyterian mother. After graduating with honors from the University of North Carolina in 1818, Polk followed the westward movement of the nation and moved across the mountains to Tennessee, where he studied law and looked up his father's old friend, war hero Andrew Jackson. Polk and Jackson became allies.

After a couple of terms in the Tennessee legislatures, Polk arrived in Washington as a Jacksonian congressman in 1824, and quickly developed a reputation as a stern, sober, hardworking lawmaker. He kept his mouth closed and his head down, which was convenient, as this allowed him to put his nose to the grindstone.

Polk became Speaker of the House in 1835; he was elected Tennessee governor in 1839. Twice rejected for reelection, Polk was cooling his heels in Tennessee when word came that the Jacksonians were considering running him as the Democratic vice presidential candidate. However, by the end of the eighth ballot for the Democratic *Presidential* nominee, no clear candidate had emerged. In the ninth ballot, Polk was voted the nominee-the first "dark horse" Presidential candidate in U.S. history.

"Who is Polk?" the Whig electioneers asked. Their man, Henry Clay, was nearly as famous as Andrew Jackson, but Clay, the great compromiser, kept wavering on the question of annexing the newly independent nation of Texas, which demanded to be annexed as a slaveholding state. Polk supported the annexation of Texas, of Oregon (which England still claimed), and even of California, and Northern believers in American expansion—which included such otherwise liberals as *Brooklyn Eagle* editor Walt Whitman—were willing to overlook their aversion to slavery in the service of Manifest Destiny. With Clay's votes diluted by those cast for a third-party Abolitionist candidate, Polk beat Clay by 38,000 votes.

At 49, Polk was the youngest man ever elected president. In his inaugural address, Polk asserted—in defiance of British claims—that "our domain extends from ocean to ocean." He noted the rapid expansion of his parents' generation and of his own, and noted that American pioneers were "already engaged in establishing the blessings of self-government in valleys of which the rivers flow to the Pacific."

To Polk, and to most Americans of the time, expansion of American ideals and rule to the West Coast was not only desirable, it was inevitable. Accordingly, as head of government, Polk declared his intention for the U.S. government to play its "proper" role in these proceedings, asserting the government's duty to protect the rights of U.S. citizens, even when they were living outside of the current boundaries of the United States:

*To us belongs the duty of protecting them adequately wherever they may be upon our soil. The jurisdiction of our laws and the benefits of our republican institutions should be extended over them in the distant regions which they have selected for their homes.*

In important ways, Polk was America's first modern president. He was the first president to be photographed. His inaugural address was relayed across the young nation by Samuel Morse on the year-old invention called the telegraph. More importantly, Polk was, to quote historian Bernard De Voto, "the only 'strong' president between Jackson and Lincoln." Most historians agree that Polk's administration was "one of the most eventful single terms in presidential history."

This eventfulness was more than sheer happenstance. Scots-Irish foothills Presbyterian that he was, Polk rolled up his sleeves and got to work. He refused to be bothered with visiting dignitaries after noon. "No president who performs his duties faithfully and conscientiously can have any leisure," he explained.

He annexed modern-day Texas and Oklahoma. He squeezed the British and worked out a treaty for modern-day Oregon and Washington. Then he tried to purchase Alta California and New Mexico for $40 million. Mexico had struggled to effectively settle the area during its 25-year reign over the region and had already lost control of California to the independent-minded Californios themselves, but the Mexican government refused to receive the American diplomats sent to discuss the issue. Covetous of the fine port of San Francisco and concerned about Russian encroachments near Mendocino and suspected British designs on the region, Polk allowed a Mexican-American skirmish in a disputed area in Texas to serve as an excuse to declare war against Mexico. Before it was over, American troops would occupy the streets of Mexico City, and America spanned from coast to coast.

When Polk's four years were finished, he refused to run again. He gave way to Mexican War hero Zachary Taylor and moved back to his home in Tennessee. He died three months later.

James K. Polk Memorial

CHARLOTTE

Ave. in Huntersville, 704/875-1391, was the site of a Revolutionary War skirmish; later, after the Carolina gold rush had begun, gold was mined here.

Charlotte's **Vietnam War Memorial Wall,** a concrete wall telling the history of the Vietnam War and listing names of veterans, stands at Thompson Park, 1129 E. Third St., 704/336-4200.

## More Sites

The 60-story **Bank of America Corporate Center,** 100 N. Tryon St., features a crown top—crown, Queen City, get it?—and Ben Long's three massive frescoes representing making/building, chaos/creativity, and planning/knowledge. Here too are the **North Carolina Blumenthal Performing Arts Center** and numerous restaurants and shops.

**Lazy 5 Ranch,** on N.C. 150 East, 704/663-5100, sounds like a dude ranch, but it's actually a drive-through animal park where you'll see some 600 exotic animals along three miles of road.

The **North Davidson neighborhood** offers a little taste of eclectic Chapel Hill here in businesslike Charlotte. If you've got a loose itinerary, here's a good place to park and walk around and spend an afternoon and evening. This part of town was formerly a fairly rough area known for its leather jackets and porno cinema. However, much has been done to clean up the old mill town area. Some artsy folks, in the spirit of Tribeca and similar names, have taken to calling North Davidson "No Da." As in, there's "No Da" like today.

## ACCOMMODATIONS

Charlotte is a banking town, and its lodgings, by and large, cater to business travelers. This means that, except on the very bottom rung of stays, here you can pretty much count on dataports, conference rooms, fitness centers, and other amenities that matter to those for whom travel is part of a day's—or week's—work. But that's not to say that all is utilitarian in the Queen City: a number of glittering, high-end uptown properties attest to the wonders of the American expense account. Note that, as in any business center, the weekend

rates of Charlotte hotels and inns can sink drastically lower than their weekday rates. At the Holiday Inn–Center City, for instance, you can pay $40 less for a room on Saturday night than you'll pay for the same room on a Monday.

### Under $50

Down on E. Independence Boulevard you'll find **Econo Lodge–Merchandise Mart,** 2721 E. Independence Blvd., 800/553-2666 or 704/375-8444. You'll also find a **Masters Inn** down the road at 2701 E. Independence Blvd., 800/633-3434 or 704/377-6581, website: www.mastersinn.com.

### $50–100

Uptown, the **Days Inn–Central,** 601 N. Tryon St., 800/325-2525 or 704/333-4733, offers 100 rooms, with a restaurant on the premises. For about the same price, you can get into **Travelodge Center City,** 319 Trade St., 800/578-7878 or 704/377-1930, with 101 rooms and all the standard business-traveler amenities.

### $100–150

For something cozy, try the three-guest **Roswell Inn Bed & Breakfast,** 2320 Roswell Ave., 704/332-4915, built in 1927 and featuring full breakfasts and beautiful gardens, with rooms starting at $100 a night. Discounts available for longer stays.

**The Inn Uptown,** 129 N. Poplar St., 800/959-1990 or 704/342-2800, website: www.innuptown.com, is set in an 1890 Victorian within walking distance of the skyscrapers. It looks a little bit out of place out there in the Center City's stark periphery of gated parking lots, but inside it's all rich woods and charm. A full breakfast is included. The 1917, 12-room **Morehead Inn,** 1122 E. Morehead St., 704/376-3357, also offers full breakfasts with your room. Less cozy but far swanker than the name implies, the 298-room **Holiday Inn–Center City,** 230 N. College St., 704/335-5400, website: www.holiday-inn.com/charlotte-ctr.com, features a rooftop swimming pool, fitness center, café, pub, and an impeccable downtown location.

## $150 and Up

The 20-room **Duke Mansion,** 400 Hermitage Rd., 888/202-1009 or 704/714-4400, was once home to James B. Duke. Built in 1915. From $169 a night, year-round, which includes meals. The massive, 407-room, four-diamond **Hilton Charlotte and Towers,** 222 E. Third St., 704/377-1500, website: www.charlotte.hilton.com, has an indoor pool, a health club, and a superb location for anybody in town on business. Located across the street from the Charlotte Convention Center. A rooftop pool and in-the-middle-of-it-all location are the trademarks of the 365-room **Omni Charlotte Hotel,** 132 E. Trade St., 704/377-0400, website: www.omnihotels.com.

# FOOD

## Barbecue

**Bill Spoon's Barbecue,** 5524 South Blvd., 704/525-8865, does what a barbecue is supposed to do, and does it right. Bill serves up a slightly spicy eastern North Carolina–style barbecue, plus Brunswick stew, hush puppies, and banana pudding. The inevitably named **Bubba's Barbecue,** at I-77 and Sunset Road, 704/393-2000, features eastern North Carolina–style barbecue and all the appropriate side dishes. **Greg's Famous B-B-Q,** 233 S. Broad St. in Mooresville, 704/664-4848, and 10915 Monroe Rd. in Matthews, 704/847-5035, features barbecue, of course, but also a number of odd cohabitants—lasagna, for instance. Good and cheap. **Old Hickory House,** 6538 N. Tryon St., 704/596-8014, serves tomato-based *western*-style barbecue in a vintage 1960s western-style barbecue joint.

## American

**South 21 Drive-In,** 3101 E. Independence Blvd., 704/377-4509, is the real thing: an authentic 1955 drive-in. They're still serving up burgers, onion rings, and fries the way they were when the patrons pulled up in much cooler cars. **The Coffee Cup,** downtown at 914 S. Clarkson St., 704/375-8855, open for breakfast and lunch, is famous for its home cooking: peach cobbler, pinto beans, collards, cornbread, fried chicken, and other meat dishes. Closed Sundays.

**Green's Lunch,** 309 W. Fourth St., 704/332-1786, has also been around forever, and it's still a cheap, popular spot for lunch—and breakfast and dinner. **Mr. K's,** 2107 South Blvd., 704/375-4318, is a friendly place that, like South 21, is all about burgers and fries. Most Charlotteans claim Mr. K's burgers are tops in the Queen City. **Price's Chicken Coop,** 1614 Camden Rd., 704/333-9866, has been serving crunchy, tasty fried chicken and fish to Charlotteans (takeout only) since Khruschev and Kennedy were arm-wrestling over Cuba. Worth the calories, if only to taste a bit of the town's history.

**The McNinch House,** 511 N. Church St., 704/332-6159, is pricey and one of a kind. The McNinch House serves five-course meals in a Fourth Ward Victorian that is as warm as the food is special. Big corporate expense accounts buy Charlotte's big wheeler-dealers big porterhouse steaks at **Capital Grille,** 201 N. Tryon St., 704/348-1400. It's the kind of place where an ABSCAM sting might have taken place—dark paneling, quick, respectful staff, martinis, thick steaks lapping over the sides of the plate.

© ERIKA HOWSARE

Note: Charlotte's not the capital of North Carolina, just the banking capital . . . but maybe the folks who eat here regularly know something we don't.

Another type-A carnivorama is **Morton's Of Chicago** at 227 W. Trade St., at The Carillon, 704/333-2602. It's hard to beat Morton's for quality cuts of beef (though some would argue that Capital Grille does just this). Though it's a chain, a lot of Charlotte deals take place under Morton's dim lights.

## Country/Southern Cooking

**Gert's Lil' Diner,** 3658 Beatties Ford Rd., 704/392-0485, doesn't look like much (it's in a trailer), but boy can Gert cook country vittles. Even the okra tastes good. **Mert's Heart & Soul** (no relation to Gert), at 214 N. College St., 704/342-4222, dishes up a healthier sort of uptown comfort food for the nostalgic sophisticate.

**College Place Restaurant,** 300 S. College St., Two First Union Center, 704/343-9268, serves more traditional Southern-style home cooking: breakfasts include grits and livermush, and lunch is a buffet line with some 12 vegetables to choose from. Close to the Convention Center. **Grandma's Country Kitchen,** 6615 N. Tryon St., 704/598-1221, is tiny and tasty; try the fried croaker or deluxe homemade mac and cheese (with half a dozen or more cheeses).

**Gus' Sir Beef Uptown,** 324 S. Tryon St. in the Latta Arcade, 704/347-5741, is popular for its fresher- and less-greasy-than-normal homestyle cooking. **Wellington's,** at the Sheraton–Four Points, 201 S. McDowell St., 704/372-7550, also specializes in high-end Southern cuisine and soul food.

## Asian

**Nikko Japanese Restaurant and Sushi Bar,** 1300-F South Blvd., 704/370-0100, features traditional Japanese dishes, including fresh sushi. Spicy and sophisticated. Another good choice

is **Thai Taste,** 324 East Blvd., 704/332-0001. The name doesn't do the restaurant justice, except to say that it tastes . . . good. Spicy, tangy, with a large number of noodle plates.

## Italian

On the high end downtown is **Bravo! Ristorante,** at the Adam's Mark Hotel, 555 S. McDowell St., 704/372-5440. The waitrons sing, the food hums along.

Near the university, **Amalfi's Pasta and Pizza,** 8542 University City Blvd., 704/547-8651, is low on ambience, moderate on prices, and high on good Italian food. Closed Mondays. Also near the university is **Castaldi's Market & Grill,** at University Place, 704/595-9995, half Italian market, half waterfront restaurant. Creative pasta dishes.

## Cajun and Creole Cuisine

**French Quarter,** 321 S. Church St., 704/377-1715, offers inexpensive New Orleans–style gumbo and jambalaya, while **Tony's Bourbon Street Oyster Bar,** 204 S. Tryon St., Suite 150, 704/343-2400, features seafood. **Dixie's Tavern,** 301 E. Seventh St., 704/374-1700, is a Louisiana-style tavern with live entertainment.

## Brewpubs

The Charlotte location of **Southend Brewery and Smokehouse,** 2100 South Blvd., 704/358-HOPS, serves its own beers along with "brew-b-cue." Both are tasty. **Rheinland Haus,** 2418 Park Rd., 704/376-3836, while not a brewpub, has been known to serve a German beer or two along with some fine German dishes. Something of a landmark in the Queen City.

*A lot of former New Yorkers live in Charlotte nowadays; trading their youse guyses for y'alls. What they don't have to give up is good, New York–style pizza.*

## Latin American

The increase in the percentage of Latin Americans in the Charlotte area has rewarded Charlotteans in many ways, not least of which is in the increase in good Mexican/Latin American dining. Near the university, **Zapata's Cantina,** 8927 J.M. Keynes

McNinch House in the Fourth Ward neighborhood

Dr., in the University Place shopping center, 704/503-1979; and a second location at 1828 Catawba Ave., Lake Norman, 704/987-8890, offers healthy and creative deviations on standard Mexican meals. Downtown, **Latorre's Latin-American Cuisine,** 118 W. Fifth St., 704/377-4448, serves highbrow Nuevo Latino–styled food. Relatively healthy and (especially in central North Carolina) a great change of pace. Dancing on Fridays and Saturdays to a salsa DJ. Cuban cuisine reigns at **La Gran Havana,** 5917 Albemarle Rd., 704/535-0223. Try the chargrilled pork with tamarind sauce. Seafood, seasoned steaks, and the black bean soup are all worthwhile. The no-nonsense **La Canasta Dominicana Restaurant,** 4808 Central Ave., 704/536-0009, dishes up authentic Caribbean cuisine.

## Pizza

A lot of former New Yorkers live in Charlotte nowadays; trading their *youse guys*es for *y'all*s. What they don't have to give up is good, New York–style pizza. **Carlo's,** 5130 N. Tryon St., 704/597-7511, is one purveyor of phenomenal pie, as is **Deano's,** 222 S. Church St., 704/332-3326. The latter is open until 4 A.M.,

and dishes up calzones, hoagies, and even ribs as well as pizza. At 2:30 in the morning, it beats the heck out of IHOP. **Fuel Pizza Café,** 1501 Central Ave., 704/376-3835; 319 W. Trade St., 704/344-1767; and 404 S. Main St., Davidson, 704/896-0200, features New York–style pizza amid old-fashioned gas station memorabilia. Traditional and gourmet pizzas, all on a notable crust. Possibly Charlotte's king of the fancy pizza, the popular and prodigious **Wolfman Pizza,** with locations at McMullen Creek Market, 704/543-9653; Selwyn Corners Shopping Center, 704/377-4695; Cotswold Mall, 704/366-3666; and 10620-A Providence Rd., 704/845-9888, dishes up pizza with shrimp, goat cheese, pineapple, and other Italy-by-way-of-Malibu sorts of toppings. **Brixx Wood-Fired Pizza,** 801 Scott Ave., 704/376-1000, also puts a gourmet spin on its pizzas, and the salads come highly praised. Finally, **Luisa's Brick Oven,** 1730 Abbey Place, 704/522-8782, is worth mentioning for the roasted eggplant pizzas alone.

## Vegetarian

**Berrybrook Farms Natural Foods,** 1257 East

Blvd., 704/334-6528, serves up the kind of food you wish you'd eaten ten minutes after you power down a double cheeseburger and fries: homemade soups, veggie burgers, bean burritos, tofu dogs, smoothies, carrot juice, and healthy sandwiches. **Talley's Café Verde,** 1408 East Blvd., 704/334-9200, is a café in an organic grocery store. Good tasty sandwiches and other entrées.

## More Dining

For French cuisine and ambience, **Bijoux Brasserie and Bar,** 201 N. Tryon St., 704/377-0900, can't be beat. Located in a turn-of-the-century building near the university, **The Melting Pot,** 230 E.W.T. Harris Blvd., 704/548-2432, website: www.raleighmeltingpot.com, is the Charlotte branch of a small nationwide chain. The restaurant offers all sorts of fondues, from the traditional bread and cheese to milk chocolate–based dessert fondues ($12–19) including the nuts-and-berries fondue, milk chocolate blended with Frangelico, cashews, red cherries, and blueberries, and served with fresh strawberries, bananas, fresh pineapple, marshmallows, cheesecake, and chocolate brownies for the dipping. Entrée fondues (with oil or bouillon base) run $48–75 for two persons, and include salads and cheese fondues. Other (non-fondue) entrées available.

## ENTERTAINMENT

### Coffeehouses

With three locations around town, **Caribou Coffee**—1531 East Blvd., 704/334-3570; 731 Providence Rd., 704/332-1512; and 4327 Park Rd., 704/523-6822, plus one up in Davidson at 20619 Torrence Chapel Rd., 704/895-0116—carries a woodsy feel, excellent coffee, and great baked goods. Over 20 types of teas as well. Down at 301 S. College St., Suite 275, 704/338-1505, **Charlotte Coffee Station** provides caffeine-laced beverages to the alertness-deprived. **Dilworth Coffee,** 1235-B East Blvd., Kenilworth Commons, 704/358-8003, roasts gourmet coffees in-house, and serves up tasty desserts and breakfast items.

## Nightlife

When the folks here say that **Ri-Ra,** 208 N. Tryon St., 704/333-5554 or 704/333-5552, is a little bit of Ireland in Charlotte, they aren't spewing blarney. Ri-Ra is an actual old Irish pub that was restored, crated, and shipped to Charlotte for reassembly. Certainly it fits in better here than the poor London Bridge does out in Lake Havasu, Arizona.

**Bopper's Bar & Boogie,** 5237 Albemarle Rd., 704/537-3323, is a nostalgia club; the décor is '50s-early '60s, but the music itself slides around from '60s through today. **Dixie's Tavern,** 301 E. Seventh St., 704/374-1700, has live entertainment some nights, and a fine Louisiana-bar atmosphere every night. **Have a Nice Day Café,** 314 N. College St., 704/373-2233, celebrates '70s and '80s culture, though those of us who remember the '70s and '80s know that most of us were all so busy trying to mimic the '50s and '60s that we didn't really have any time to *have* a '70s or '80s culture. (But don't take my word for it—ask Fonzie.) Nonetheless, HANDC attracts a good mix, from Baby Boomers who can mouth all the words while they dance, to the Gen-Xers wearing silk shirts over their tattoos. Cover charge, generally around $5.

**Jillians Uptown,** 200 E. Bland St., 704/376-1526, is like an arcade for grownups, with virtual games, pool, live music, and dancing. **Latorre's,** 118 W. Fifth St., 704/377-4448, features salsa dancing on Friday and Saturday nights. **Swing 1000,** 1000 Central Ave., 704/334-4443, aims to be the sort of place where Frank Sinatra might have punched a waiter while Dean Martin and Sammy Davis Jr. crooned and Joey Bishop got stuck with the check. Live music and dancing.

**O'Hara's,** at the Holiday Inn–Woodlawn, 212 Woodlawn Rd., 704/525-8350, is a fine place to experience some authentic Carolina beach music and to (try to) shag. Dress code enforced. **Tremont Music Hall,** 400 W. Tremont Ave., 704/343-9494, website: www.tremontmusichall.com, is the Queen City's top alternative/college venue. Tickets run $5 and up; call for information on who's playing when you're in town.

© ERIKA HOWSARE

the Lowe's Motor Speedway

## Shopping

About 45 minutes south of Charlotte on I-85, you'll find Gaffney, S.C., home to **Prime Outlets Gaffney,** 1 Factory Shops Blvd., 888/545-7194 or 864/902-9900. The town once known primarily for its peaches, and its peach-shaped water tower, is now home to some 80 outlet stores, most of them not peach-related. Fans of Paul Harvey and/or great audio will want to visit the **Bose** warehouse, which does business among all the Pottery Barns, Brooks Brothers, Nike, and other freewayside regulars. Yes, many Charlotteans visit Gaffney a dozen times a year. And they aren't coming for the peaches. In Fourth Ward, **Poplar Street Books** does business at 226 W. 10th St., in the old Young-Morrison house.

## SPORTS AND RECREATION

### Auto Racing

The Charlotte Motor Speedway—now the **Lowe's Motor Speedway**, in Concord, 704/455-3200 (tickets), 704/455-3204 (tours), website: www.gospeedway.com, hosts three Winston Cup and two Busch series races every year, as well as numerous other races and car shows. If there's a race while you're in town,

you really ought to experience this bit of Dixiana. Just bring earplugs, seat cushions, and a taste for fried bologna.

If you've misplanned and there's no race when you're here, NASCAR fans can still tour the speedway. Tours run about $5 a person, Monday–Saturday 9 A.M.–3 P.M., Sunday 12:30 P.M.–3 P.M. Nearby you'll find the **NASCAR Silicon Motor Speedway,** at Concord Mills Mall, 8111 Concord Mills Blvd., Suite 202, 704/979-7223, website: www.smsonline.com, full of what are touted as the most realistic racing simulators in the world, as well as NASCAR collectibles and gear.

### Baseball

International League AAA affiliate of the Chicago White Sox, the **Charlotte Knights,** are heirs to more than 100 years of Charlotte professional baseball history, through the decades, on various teams at different levels in different leagues, playing at Old Wearn Field (later renamed Robbie Field, and later still, Hayman Field), at Crockett Park in Dilworth (which burned down in 1985), and now down in Fort Mill, S.C., at 2280 Deerfield Dr., 704/357-8071, website: www.charlotteknights.com. Players passing

**CHARLOTTE**

through Charlotte on their way to the bigs have included Tony Oliva, Eddie Murphy, Cal Ripken Jr., Jim Thome, and Brian Giles. The name of Charlotte's first team, back at the turn of the 20th century? The Hornets. The "Hornet" moniker has always been popular here in the town formerly cursed by the British as the "hornet's nest" of rebellion during the Revolution.

## Basketball

The latter-day **Charlotte Hornets,** 100 Hive Dr., 704/357-0252, website: www.hornets.com, play hoops from November though April, but it seems unlikely, at press time, that they'll still be playing in Charlotte when you get there. The team, which vaulted Charlotte into the ranks of Major League sport in 1988, had signed an agreement to move on to New Orleans, and was only waiting on approval by the NBA Board of Governors. If the deal falls through, or if Charlotte attracts a replacement team—and local officials certainly intend to—they'll likely be playing in the Coliseum off Billy Graham Parkway. If they're not, try the WNBA **Charlotte Sting,** though rumors at press time had them leaving as well, joining the Hornets in New Orleans in 2003. Before the start of the 2002 season, a vice president was quoted as saying, "Despite the uncertainty surrounding our situation beyond the 2002 campaign, we still have the opportunity, with a successful season both on and off the court, to make a statement about the long-term viability of professional women's basketball in Charlotte." Sounds to me like they're leaving. Check www.nba.com and www.wnba .com for up-to-date information. If the Sting's still in Charlotte, they'll be playing at the Charlotte Coliseum; 704/424-9622, website: www.charlottesting.com, June through August.

## Football

The National Football League's **Carolina Panthers** are staying put, so far as anyone knows. They play at 73,000-seat Ericsson Stadium, 800 S. Mint St., from August through December. Tickets for individual games run $40–54. Call 704/358-7800 or 704/522-6500 for tickets, or buy them online at www.panthers.com.

## Lake Cruises

The **Catawba Queen** and **Catawba Belle** run regular luncheon, sightseeing, and dinner cruises on Lake Norman. Boats depart from West Mooresville, 25 miles north of Center City on Highway 150 West. Call 704/663-2628, website: www.queenslanding.com, for reservation information.

## Events

The **Queen's Cup Steeplechase Races,** 112 Somer St., Waxhaw, 704/843-7070, website: www.queenscup.com, were founded not so long ago—in 1995—as an alibi for an all-day festival, some serious tailgating, a hat contest, and fundraising for two worthwhile causes: breast cancer research and preservation of local lands. The festival runs from 10 A.M.–7 P.M. on the last Saturday in April.

# TRANSPORTATION

## Getting There

**Charlotte/Douglas International Airport,** 5501 Josh Birmingham Parkway, 704/359-4027, offers nonstop flights to 150 cities, with a new concourse for commuter aircraft completed in late 2001. At press time, airlines providing service to Charlotte include Delta, Northwest, and US Airways. Charlotte is also easily accessible via I-77, I-85, or a host of smaller roads. Or try **Amtrak,** 1914 N. Tryon St., 704/376-4416.

## Getting Around

Rent-a-car options include **Enterprise,** 100 W. Carson Blvd., 800/736-8222 or 704/334-8575; **Hertz,** 410 Rental Car Rd., 704/359-0114, website: www.hertz.com; **Payless,** 4204 Rental Car Rd., 704/359-4640; and **Triangle,** 3812 Little Rock Rd., 704/399-2601. If you need a taxi, call **Crown Cab Company Inc.,** 1501 St. George St., 704/334-6666, website: www .charlotte.zip2.com/crowncab, or **Yellow Cab Company of Charlotte Inc.,** 5320 Old Pineville Rd., 704/332-6161. In addition to standard cabs, Yellow's Carolina Airport Express, 704/391-1111, can get you in from Charlotte/Douglas.

# North of Charlotte

## LAKE NORMAN AND VICINITY

**Lake Norman State Park,** 800/305-2508 or 704/892-1922, centers around man-made Lake Norman, the largest inland water mass in North Carolina. During the fall, come here on the weekend to take part in the costumes-optional **Carolina Renaissance Festival. Davidson** is home to 1,600-student Davidson College, one of the nation's top small liberal arts colleges. A pie-eyed preacher's son named Thomas Woodrow Wilson attended for a year here in the late 1800s. Today, the town of 7,100 serves Charlotte as a favorite weekend getaway. A few own houses here; others like to stay—or dream about staying—at the 18-room **Davidson Village Inn,** 117 Depot St., 800/892-0796 or 704/892-8044, website:www.davidsoninn.com. The inn's charming in-the-middle-of-town location makes it perfect for anyone with business to do at the college, or with a desire simply to walk the village's streets after dinner. Rooms run around $120; this includes a light breakfast. One of the town's top restaurants, **Jasper's at Davidson,** stands nearby at 127 Depot St., 704/896-1881; other favorites include **Davidson Depot Restaurant & Tap House,** 209 Delburg St., 704/987-8800, and **Knead It? A Bakery Café,** 408 S. Main St., 704/895-2875.

## KANNOPOLIS

A town known for its textiles, Kannapolis is home to the **Fieldcrest Cannon Textile Company,** which churns out enough linens (for sale at **Cannon Village,** 20 West Ave., 704/938-3200) to cover the world in sheets. The Single-A **Kannapolis Intimidators** play their South Atlantic League opponents at Fieldcrest Cannon Stadium, 2888 Moose Rd., 704/932-3267, website: www.intimidatorsbaseball.com. The 67-room **Comfort Inn,** 3100 Cloverleaf Parkway,

© ERIKA HOWSARE

**Davidson College**

704/786-3100, provides a pool and a convenient location if you're here for the linens.

## SALISBURY

Founded in 1753, Salisbury (pronounced "Saulsbury") is one of the oldest towns in this part of the state. In the 1780s, a young law student from down in the Waxhaw region named Andrew Jackson ("the most roaring, rollicking, gamecocking, horse-racing, card-playing, mischievous fellow") used to barrel across town. Jackson and his cronies would steal signposts. They'd relocate outhouses so that in the dark of the night ....

When the leader of a local dancing school Jackson liked to frequent asked the strapping redhead to arrange a Christmas ball for the school, Jackson agreed. He sent out invitations to all of the town's most illustrious residents, and two of its best-known prostitutes. The latter showed up at the ball dressed to kill—or, work—and the dance came to a standstill as people gasped and women went weak in the knees. Jackson reared back and laughed.

But perhaps Jackson's best-remembered prank was the time he and some friends at a local tavern decided to shatter their glasses on the floor, as they had heard was done in sophisticated society. They enjoyed this so much that they decided that smashing the table they sat at would make them seem even more erudite. One thing led to another, and suddenly all was a *Gunsmoke* fight scene, with chairs flying across the room and curtains ripping. As a coup de grace, the young men set the tavern afire.

Imagine the surprise of the people of Salisbury when they found out that Andy Jackson, their town's most notorious hellion, had become the Hero of New Orleans, and later, the president of the United States.

For many years, the seat of Rowan County was a major industrial and trading center. Both Corn-

> *In the 1780s, a young law student named Andrew Jackson ("the most roaring, rollicking, gamecocking, horse-racing, card-playing, mischievous fellow") used to barrel across town. Jackson and his cronies would steal signposts. They'd relocate outhouses so that in the dark of the night....*

wallis and Greene called Salisbury their headquarters at various points during the Revolution.

During the War Between the States, the state built a prison here for Southern deserters; the Confederate army decided to put in some 1,500 troops in March 1862. For some time, the living here was good for Union prisoners, especially compared to other prisons like Andersonville. But in October 1864, 10,000 prisoners were added to the facility, overwhelming the staff and the providers of food for the prisoners. Sanitary practices were barbaric; over the next five months, some 3,400 prisoners died of exposure and disease. Some 2,800 men were ordered transferred a year later to Wilmington in February 1865, but only 1,800 made it. When Union general George Stonemen and his raiders captured the town and prison in 1865, he found it nearly empty of prisoners. He put the captured Confederates into the hellhole, but when he had to leave town he burned the entire prison, as well as the supporting buildings—and, in fact, every other Salisbury building he could get a hand on.

Today, though Salisbury hasn't kept pace with Charlotte and Raleigh, it is home to more than 20,000 people, and it's a tidy, historic town. The sites include **Downtown Salisbury website: momo@ctc.net,** which features the town's 30-square-block historic district, off Fulton Street downtown.

To see the site of the former prison—though it's not identified as such—visit the **Salisbury National Cemetery,** which overlays some of the original prison grounds. Here at the cemetery lie some 11,700 Union Soldiers—5,000 of them unknown, and most of them dead from diseases they caught while imprisoned. The interred are said to include Robert Livingstone, the son of the famous medical missionary to Africa, David Livingstone of "Livingstone, I presume?" fame. Subsequently, **Livingstone College,** a historically African-American,

A.M.E.-affiliated college, was founded here in town, and continues to operate today.

The **Rowan County Museum,** 116 S. Jackson St., set in an 1819 Federal townhouse, examines the lifestyle known by the town's upper class in the early 1800s. For more information about Salisbury, contact the **Salisbury Station Visitors Information Center,** 132 E. Innes St., 704/638-3100.

Lee and Barbara Coombs' **Rowan Oak House,** 208 S. Fulton St., 800/786-0437 or 704/633-2086, website: www.inngetaways.com/nc/features/rowan.html, is a warm, four-room bed-and-breakfast set in an old 1901 Queen Anne home in the West Square historic district, and features period furnishings and such nonperiod amenities as (in one room) a bathroom Jacuzzi.

## South of Salisbury

It is said that the richest gold mining on this side of the Mississippi was done up at **Gold Hill** after the big strike of 1824. This once-bustling, drinking, cussing, and fighting (and mining) town went to California in a handbasket after 1849, but today the folks around here are restoring old buildings and making it a fine place to spend a morning poking around. Already, you can see the Rock Jail, an 1840 store and museum, and a restored general store. All for free. Located on St. Stephen's Church Road via Old N.C. 80 off U.S. 52. Gold Hill closes at sunset.

A half-mile off U.S. 24/27 on Endy Road, just five miles west of Albemarle, **Dennis Vineyards Winery,** 24043 Endy Rd., Albemarle, 800/230-1743 or 704/982-6090, website: www.dennisvineyards.com, offers wine tastings, tours, and sales of its fine wines. Opened in 1997 by Pritchard Dennis and his son, Sandon, Dennis Vineyards has the odd distinction of being an award-winning winery set in a dry county. And speaking of dry, though the wines here are made of Muscadine grapes, if you're tasting, try the dry Carlos white wine, a favorite with locals. Nearby **Morrow Mountain State Park,** 49104 Morrow Mountain Rd., 704/982-4402, email: momo@ctc.net, provides the chance to explore an old—make that ancient—mountain range that has crumbled to humble heights. Miles and miles

of trails for hiking. Also on park grounds is the Historic Kron House, home to an early-19th-century doctor. Camping and cabins are both available in the park. Call for information.

West of U.S. 52 near **Mount Gilead** you'll come upon **Town Creek Indian Mound State Historic Site,** on Town Creek Mound Road between N.C. 731 and N.C. 73. It isn't really on the way to anywhere, but it's a worthwhile side trip; the restored Indian mound and surrounding structures create an instructive, walk-through illustration of Muskogean life and culture in the Sandhills area before the arrival of the British. Reconstructed based on early sketches by John Lawson and 16th-century Spanish explorers, the compound includes two guard towers—something you'll never see still standing in a non-reconstructed Indian mound. The site is open April 1–October 31, Monday–Saturday 9 A.M.–5 P.M. and Sunday 1–5 P.M.; November 1–March 31 it's open Tuesday–Saturday 10 A.M.–4 P.M. and Sunday 1–4 P.M. Closed winter

**Town Creek Indian Mound**

© ERIKA HOWSARE

holidays, but open summer holidays. No charge for admission. Call 910/439-6802 for additional information.

### East of Salisbury

Beyond Statesville on the way east to Hickory you'll come upon Catawba, where you'll find historic **Murray's Mill,** 1489 Murray's Mill Rd., 828/241-4299, one of the state's largest waterwheels, built at the end of the Victorian era. Across the way you'll find **Murray & Minges General Store,** 100 years old and still selling a wide variety of products. Along (but off) U.S. 70, 828/465-0383, you can see one of only two extant covered bridges in the state, the **Bunker Hill Covered Bridge.** The 85-foot span is on

the National Register. It crosses Lyles Creek a couple of miles east of Claremont. No charge.

### Spencer

Set in the buildings and grounds that once were Southern Railroad's largest repair facility, the **North Carolina Transportation Museum,** 411 South Salisbury Ave., 704/636-2889, features exhibits that tell the story of inland transportation from the 1800s to today. Train rides daily April 1–Labor Day, and Saturday and Sunday through mid-December. Open April–October, Monday–Saturday 9 A.M.–5 P.M., Sunday 1–5 P.M.; November–March, Tuesday–Saturday 10 A.M.–4 P.M., Sunday 1–4 P.M. Closed Mondays and major holidays.

## South Carolina's York County

Rock Hill and the rest of York County have become part of greater Charlotte. Residents in Rock Hill, Fort Mill, York, and even Chester listen to the same radio stations, watch the same television stations, attend the same concerts and ballgames, and drive to the same places to work and play. It only makes sense to discuss them here as well.

## ROCK HILL

Established in 1852 as a railway stop between Charlotte and Columbia, and named after the hill of flinty white rock encountered by Charlotte, Columbia, and Augusta Railroad workers, Rock Hill quickly attracted farmers who shipped their produce and cotton to the big cities on the railroad, and counted about 250 residents by the end of the Civil War. As the Industrial Revolution began revolting, locals built water-turned mills to process the area's cotton; before long, the impoverished small farmers who swarmed upstate to fill the mill jobs swelled the town's population to more than 5,500. Downtown Rock Hill sprouted handsome brick business blocks.

Things stayed pretty much status quo until the 1960s, when the business-minded community briefly became center stage for the Civil Rights movement. In 1961, nine black Friend-

ship College students took seats at McCrory's (now Vantell Variety, on Main Street) whites-only lunch counter and refused to leave. When police arrested them, the students were given the choice of paying $200 fines or serving 30 days of hard labor in the York County jail. The "Friendship Nine" chose the latter, becoming the first sit-in protesters of the Civil Rights movement to suffer imprisonment.

As the '60s progressed, supermarkets, suburbs, and shopping malls drained the life of Rock Hill's downtown, just as they did across the country. The city took action and blocked off a two-block area of Main Street to vehicular traffic, creating a pedestrian mall. Unfortunately, as happened to many such efforts in other cities, the pedestrian mall ended up becoming an economic dead spot; downtown continued to spiral. By the 1990s, the city reopened the "mall" to traffic, and—along with other redevelopment efforts—this breathed life back into the district. Today downtown Rock Hill still has a way to go, but good signs, like old buildings under refurbishment, abound. As with York and Fort Mill, Rock Hill is attracting people who are transferring to Charlotte from other large cities but who refuse to get stuck in another big urban area. Some of these folks truly appreciate these small towns for the slower, smaller way of life they offer, and they—more so, in some cases, than the lifetime residents—are making efforts to preserve and to some degree restore traditional Upcountry living to these towns.

## Downtown

Rock Hill's downtown district, though not as old as many in the state, is still a nice place to walk around and get the feel for the town that is, and the town that was.

The first place to stop is the **York County Visitors Center/Tom S. Gettys Center,** 201 E. Main St., 800/866-5200 or 803/329-5200, where you'll find helpful staff and pamphlets galore. It's open Monday–Friday 9 A.M.–5 P.M., Saturday 10 A.M.–4 P.M., and Sunday 1–4 P.M. Look for the blue flyer *Strolling through Historic Downtown Rock Hill, South Carolina.* You'll want this for your walk. If the center's closed or out of maps, here's a shortened version:

Start out at the **Center for the Arts Building,** 121 E. Main St., 803/328-2787. Set in a building completed in 1900, formerly home to a furniture company and dry goods store, Rock Hill's Center for the Arts opened in 1996 with a housing office, classroom, and artist studio spaces for local artisans. The Dalton Gallery, which features local, regional, and national artists, opens to the public for viewing Monday–Friday 9 A.M.–5 P.M. Which is sort of curious, since these hours effectively keep the average employed Rock Hillian from ever seeing the inside of the gallery.

As you stand outside the arts center, facing Main, turn left and walk past the **Peoples Building,** circa 1909, a former bank, and then (still on your left) on into **Vantell Variety,** 135 E. Main St., 803/327-0545. You'll find a lunch counter on your right; go in, sit down at the counter, and order yourself a soda or malt. Enjoy your drink. Linger awhile. And then reflect: For doing exactly the same thing, nine black Friendship College students were dragged off to jail in 1961.

McCrory's, who owned the lunch counter then, sold out a few years ago, and the folks who now own the diner seem like nice people. One of the family was manning the grill when I visited; he said they're always having magazine and

newspaper reporters come down to photograph the famous lunch counter.

When you've finished your soda, head back outside (pay your bill first), turning left again. You'll pass the 1908 Lyric Building and the 1925 Professional Center, now the Citizens Bank. At 154 E. Main St., across the street, you'll find **Central Newsstand and Bookstore,** one of those essential small-town newsstands (with a surprisingly good selection of magazines) where, if you listen hard enough, you can hear the rush of the town's lifeblood as it pumps through the building. You'll also find a cooler of drinks here with, most important, *three* varieties of South Carolina's own Blenheim Ginger Ale.

Cross Caldwell Street and you'll come to the **Tom S. Gettys Center,** 201 E. Main St., 800/866-5200 or 803/329-5200,, circa 1931, at the corner of Main and Caldwell. Once the central post office in town, the building currently houses the **How We Got Here from There** exhibit.

It's more interesting than it sounds, since the exhibit includes Indian dugout canoes used on the Catawba River, a covered wagon, buggy, and, perhaps most fascinating, a genuine Anderson automobile, built here in Rock Hill. Open Monday–Friday 10 A.M.–5 P.M., Saturday 10 A.M.–4 P.M., Sunday 1–4 P.M.

Next door, at 215 E. Main St., you'll see the 1920 **First Baptist Church,** and across Oakland Street is the large **Guardian Building** at 223 E. Main St., originally built in 1926 as the Andrew Jackson Hotel. The spot has hosted countless community receptions and dances in its second-floor ballroom over the years. Now turn left on Oakland. Halfway down the block, you'll pass the 1906 U.S. Post Office building on your right. St. John's Methodist Church, a good-looking brick building completed in 1924, is home to the area's oldest organized church body (1856). Next come two other venerable old churches: on your left, **The Episcopal Church of Our Savior,** built in 1872 and featuring some excellent stained glass, and to your right across White Street, the **First Associate Reformed Presbyterian Church** (1897). Turn right on White Street and then right again on Elizabeth Lane to see **The White House,** at 258 E. White

St. Built in the 1830s, it's one of the oldest homes in the city; it served as a shelter for Lowcountry Carolinians fleeing General Sherman.

Now make your way back down to Main Street, turn right., and head back to your car. Before you drive off to wherever you're going, head over to White Street, turn left, and cross Dave Lyle Boulevard. On your right, you'll see the 1881 **Rock Hill Cotton Factory,** the first steam textile mill in South Carolina, still in use today.

## Winthrop University

You can enter the Winthrop campus from Oakland Avenue. Founded in 1886 as the South Carolina Normal School for Women down in Columbia, the school transferred up to this beautiful shaded brick Georgian campus in 1895. The campus is now a registered U.S. Department of the Interior Historical District, with 5,000 men and women attending. The Winthrop Galleries, in the Rutledge Building and McLaurin Hall, exhibit work by children, Winthrop students, and local and national artists. And, of course, the departments of music, theater, and dance perform regularly throughout the year.

The Winthrop Chapel used to stand in Columbia, where it began as a carriage house at the Robert Mills House, and in the 1870s it was used as the student chapel for Columbia Seminary, where young Thomas Woodrow Wilson's father taught. Tommy Wilson worshipped between these walls, and here became a member of the Presbyterian church. In 1886, Winthrop College was founded in the same old carriage house. Winthrop moved to Rock Hill in 1895, and years later, Winthrop alumni paid to have the building disassembled and moved up here.

To find out what's going on at the university, call the Arts Hotline, 803/323-3000. To set up a campus tour, call 803/323-2211.

## Glencairn Garden

Dr. David and Hazel Bigger began what is now Glencairn Garden when they planted a few azaleas they'd received as a gift. One thing led to another, and by 1940, the garden had grown so large and so beautiful that the Biggers decided to share it with the public. They named it Glencairn Garden in honor of the good doctor's Scottish heritage. Eighteen years later, after Dr. Bigger died (there were apparently no little Biggers), Mrs. Bigger deeded Glencairn to the City of Rock Hill.

Today, Glencairn Garden contains a beautiful fountain, a Japanese footbridge, winding trails, a tiered fountain, and year-round blooms. For the very peak of bloom season, the gardenkeepers recommend a visit from the last week of March through mid-April when you'll likely see blooming azaleas, tulips, pansies, dogwood, periwinkle, wisteria, and other flowers and shrubs. Come in summer for the crepe myrtle, Kwanzan and Yoshino cherry, and various annuals. Fall brings sassanqua and an annual pansy. Winter brings the camellia, Bradford pear, daffodil, and winter honeysuckle.

To get to Glencairn Garden, head along Charlotte Avenue until you reach Edgemont. Open dawn to dusk, every day of the year.

## The Rock Hill Telephone Company Museum

If you have an insatiable curiosity about things in general, or if you just find the subject of telephones and telephone repairs fascinating, then you might want to pay a brief visit here. What makes this place nifty is the work that's gone into some of the displays; clearly, the folks at RHTC are proud of what they do. Lots of interactive displays: use an original magneto telephone to call a friend, or try out an old pay phone in a mockup of a 1930s hotel lobby. At 117 Elk Ave., 803/324-4030, the museum is open Monday, Wednesday, Friday, and Saturday 10 A.M.–2 P.M.

## Museum of York County

This surprising, offbeat, and off-the-beaten-path little museum, at 4621 Mt. Gallant Rd., 803/329-2121, exhibits the largest collection of mounted African mammals anywhere in the world, featuring lifelike dioramas to show what the animals looked like when they were alive and in their native environments. The museum also contains African artifacts, three changing art galleries with work by regional and national artists, and the Vernon Grant Gallery, a permanent exhibit of the Rock Hill artist/illustrator who designed spokes-elves Snap, Crackle, and Pop for Kellogg's Rice Krispies cereal. To get here from downtown Rock Hill, follow the signs: take N.C. 274 northwest to Mt. Gallant Road. Head east until you come to Museum Road. Admission $2 adult, $1 seniors and students. Children under 5 free. York County residents pay half price. Open Tuesday–Saturday 10 A.M.–5 P.M., and Sunday 1–5 P.M. Closed on major holidays.

## Cherry Park

At 1466 Cherry Rd., this landscaped 68-acre park features playgrounds, picnic areas, and a huge statue of Casey, title character of Thayer's famous baseball poem, "Casey at the Bat". Many community picnics take place here, and local softball teams battle it out in the summertime.

## Golf

The **Crystal Lakes Golf Center,** 195 Crystal Ln., 803/327-3231, is a nine-hole lighted course; **Pinetuck Golf Course,** 2578 Tuckaway Rd., 803/327-1141, offers 18 holes.

## Shopping

Out here in textile country, it's no surprise that you can find some good bargains on things made out of cloth. Rock Hill features two outlet stores: **Plej's Textile Mill Outlet,** 215 Chatham Ave., 803/328-5797, where you can find household linens and window treatments, and **Rock Hill Factory Outlet,** at the intersection of Oakland Avenue and Cherry Road, 803/327-7276, which features women's apparel.

If all these old homes have put you in the mood for antique shopping, Rock Hill won't disappoint. Mary Ann Walker's **Vintage Antiques and Collectibles** does business over at 137 E. White St., 803/329-0866, specializing in pre-Depression furniture and home decorations; another specialty is Depression glass. At **Furniture Plus,** 104 S. Oakland Ave., 803/324-1855, Jack Lee specializes in estate items.

## Accommodations

Over by Winthrop University, **The Book & the Spindle,** 626 Oakland Ave., 803/328-1913, is a brick Georgian home overlooking the campus. You can choose between two rooms and two suites here; all boast private baths, cable TV, and coffeemakers; suites include kitchens and a patio. By reservation only, so call ahead.

**East Main Guest House,** 347 Park Ave., 803/366-1161, is set in a renovated circa-1900 Craftsman home in the historic district. Hosts Melba and Jerry Peterson, who oversaw the renovation of the property in 1990, now offer three upstairs rooms. The Honeymoon Suite and the East Bedroom both contain fireplaces and connecting private baths. The bright, airy Garden Room contains twin beds, a private bath, and a view of the back garden. Breakfast is served downstairs in the dining room—or under the patio arbor, weather permitting—and normally includes fresh-baked muffins and breads. Come evening, it's wine and cheese in the parlor.

## Camping

You'll find a number of sites at **Ebenezer Park,** 4490 Boatshore Rd., 803/366-6620. **Chester State Park,** 803/385-2680, has 25 shaded sites, all with electricity and water hookups.

## Food

**Jackson's Cafeteria,** 1735 Heckle Blvd., 803/366-6860, serves basic, though better-than-average, cafeteria-style grub; it's been here forever and is really part of the downtown scene. Another good spot downtown for basic American standards is **Watkins Grill,** 123 Elk Ave., 803/327-4923, a lunch counter with old photos on the walls. Take a peek to see the Rock Hill of yesterday.

For something more upscale, and certainly dimmer, try another old favorite, **Tam's Tavern,** 1027 W. Oakland Ave., 803/329-2226. Tam's serves grilled chicken, burgers, sandwiches, and casseroles for lunch Monday–Saturday 11 A.M.–3 P.M., and fresh seafood, meats, and pasta for dinner Monday–Saturday 5–10 P.M. A strong wine list. If you're looking for something with a little zest to it, try **Tropical Escape Cafe,** 590 N. Anderson Rd., U.S. 21 Bypass, 803/366-3888, where the cooks serve up Filipino and

Chinese foods along with broiled seafood and American dishes. Or head over to the town's best Mexican restaurant, **El Caribe,** 886 S. Anderson Rd., 803/985-7272. For fancy coffee, try **D.C. Stickies,** 113 E. Main St., Suite 10, 803/366-0423.

# FORT MILL

Fort Mill is one of the towns that Charlotte/Rock Hill will someday likely swallow up, but for now the community of 5,931 retains its small-town ambience. The name comes from the town's location: it once stood between a British fort and a gristmill on Steele Creek. Though both the fort, built to protect Catawba women and children when Catawba men were off warring with the Cherokees, and the mill have disappeared, Fort Mill continues, now as home of Springs Industries, one of the country's largest textile manufacturers.

Of course, if the name Fort Mill is familiar to you, you may remember the town as the former home of Jim and Tammy Bakker's famed **Heritage** amusement park and resort complex. Bakker and Bakker have long since lost the park. Members of their PTL ministry sought Jerry Falwell's help to keep the ship afloat, and the park reopened briefly as New Heritage USA before folding again. A couple years later, the Radisson Corporation reopened the park and resort, but this too only lasted a few years before folding. When I was last in Fort Mill, the big news was that four new players had bid on the old Heritage properties. All four deals have since fallen through, and at press time the acreage's future is still uncertain.

## Downtown

Fort Mill has a nice downtown, which includes little **Confederate Park,** home to a Confederate monument, and a very interesting monument to the Catawba Nation. After the initial Indian attacks of the Yamasee War, the Catawbas switched sides and helped save the lives of many back-country Carolinians. The monument also pays tribute to the number of Catawbas who served as Confederate soldiers and officers.

At 205 White St. you'll see the **Founders House,** the refurbished Victorian home of Captain Samuel E. White, now used by Springs Industries as a guest home for visiting business guests. On N.C. 160 stands the two-story brick Georgian home of William Elliott White, where President Jefferson Davis of the Confederate States of America held a final cabinet meeting after the fall of Richmond at the end of the War between the States. Davis had spent the previous night at **Springfield** (on U.S. 21, two and a half miles north of town), a graceful old frame home now employed as center of operations for the Springs Company. Call 803/547-1000 for tour information.

## AAA Baseball

The **Charlotte Knights** play in Fort Mill at, appropriately, the Castle, a very fine stadium on 2280 Deerfield Dr., 803/548-8050. The Knights, a AAA farm team for the Florida Marlins, battle such International League nemeses as the Richmond Braves, Syracuse Sky Chiefs, and Toledo Mud Hens. The season runs from April through early September; if the Knights are in town when you are, try catching a game. Most games start Monday–Saturday 7 P.M., Sunday 2 P.M. Thursday nights are "Thirsty Thursday," offering half-price draft beer and $1 soft drinks. Sunday is Kids Day, with attractions for the younger set, but at any home game the kids will probably light up when they see Homer the Dragon, mascot for the team.

## Christian Epics

Once the main outdoor stage at Jim and Tammy Faye Bakker's theme park Heritage USA, **Kings Arena,** 888/437-7473 or 803/802-2300, email: NarroWay@FMTC.net, is now owned by NarroWay Productions. This non-Bakker-affiliated group produces various Christian musical dramas based on the life of Jesus—huge epics featuring live camels and horses and huge casts. These are reenactments of the Christ story by people who believe that no other chain of events in history has carried such import. They're a unique, non-threatening way to learn more about how many

South Carolinians understand the universe. Tickets run about $12 for adults, less for children.

## Golf

**Fort Mill Golf Course,** 101 Country Club Dr., 803/547-2044, offers 18 holes. Over at the old Bakker/Radisson place you'll find **Regent Park Golf Club,** on Hwy. 21, 803/547-1300, and **Regent Park Practice Complex,** 803/802-2053, a 25-acre lighted facility with practice tees, putting green, chipping area, and on-site golf instruction.

## Accommodations

Whether or not you plan on visiting Paramount's Carowinds amusement park, you might as well benefit from the flood of budget lodging and dining options that have accompanied it. The **Comfort Inn** right at I-77 and Carowinds Boulevard, 3725 Avenue of the Carolinas, 803/548-5200, offers 153 rooms and suites. You'll find it right at the entrance to Carowinds, and right beside the Outlet Marketplace, in case you feel like shopping. **Holiday Inn Express,** located more or less across from Carowinds, at the point where Avenue of the Carolinas tees into Carowinds Boulevard, 3560 Lakemont Blvd., 803/548-0100, is clean, and fancier than you'd think it would be. And right next door you'll see **Sleep Inn,** 3540 Lakemont Blvd., 803/547-2300. It's only a few years old, and a safe bet for a good night's sleep.

Steer clear of the Days Inn–Carowinds: it's too far out from anything worth seeing, the service I received was marginal at best, and the on-the-property restaurant is closed at press time. The rooms were the poorest I've seen in the chain. Days Inn has many fine properties, but this is not one of them.

## Camping

An intriguing place to stay is **Lakeside Lodges,** off I-77 Exit 88 and Gold Hill Road, which not so long ago was known as the New Heritage USA Campground. Lakeside, 940 Gold Hill Rd., 803/547-3505, has 127 sites. A stay at **Lazy Daze Campground,** over on Gold Hill Road, 803/548-1148, is camping South

Carolina–style, which is to say that when you pay for your site (full hookups) you're also paying for a pool, recreation director, miniature golf, game room, and so on. A good place to stay with the family. **Paramount's Carowinds Campground** at 3900 Avenue of the Carolinas, 704/588-3363 or 800/888-4FUN, will get you closest to the park itself; it's a nice, wooded campground, with tent sites and RV sites with full hookups, private showers, a "trading post," and a swimming pool.

## PARAMOUNT'S CAROWINDS

On the I-77, this 83-acre theme park, 800/888-4FUN (4386), is more conceptually interesting than your average Six Flags. Straddling the North Carolina–South Carolina border so that you'll spend the day crisscrossing from North to South and then back again, the park was originally designed to celebrate the history and culture of the Carolinas, with "lands" named Plantation Square, Carolina RFD, Blue Ridge Junction, and so forth.

Then Paramount, the movie company, moved in, bringing along Scooby-Doo, the Flintstones' dog Dino, a host of other Hanna-Barbera characters, and a prerecorded music soundtrack (piped throughout the park via hidden speakers) composed entirely of Muzaked movie themes. When Wayne's World opened up, it was the first land specifically dedicated to a Paramount movie.

Carowinds also includes a water park, featuring waterslides, a wave pool, wading pools for little ones, and even a volleyball court. Not a bad idea on a hot day—be sure to pack a swimsuit, or wear one beneath your clothes. Your admission ticket to the park allows you to use the water park as well.

Some local boosters might tell you that Carowinds is like Disneyland and Walt Disney World, but it's a lot closer to a Six Flags than anything else—more an amusement park than a true "theme" park. At a *theme* park, you need to have some effective theming, not just to separate the inside of the park from the outside world, but to separate the individual themed "lands"

CHARLOTTE

within the park from one another. If you've left Tomorrowland for Frontierland, there had better be no mistaking it.

But at Carowinds, despite the atmospheric names given to different regions of the park, the planners spend little effort or money to make you feel that you're anywhere but at an amusement park. It's easy to step from Wayne's World (supposedly suburban Aurora, Illinois, in the late 1980s) to Blue Ridge Junction and not know you've switched lands.

There's very little to do at parks like this if you're not standing in line, riding a ride, or watching a show, but Carowinds holds one major plus over Six Flags: while Paramount hasn't put much time or money into making the queue areas themselves (where, after all, you spend most of your time) interesting parts of the attractions, the way Disney does on most of its newer rides, at least Paramount doesn't follow the lead of Six Flags over Georgia and have music videos blaring in those areas. At the end of a day at Six Flags over Georgia, you feel as if you've spent 10 hours watching MTV.

What Carowinds *does* have is a bang-up selection of thrill rides. Here are the best the park has to offer:

**The Hurler:** Set in Wayne's World, this ride has a great name and more. The video playing in the boarding station features Mike Myers and Dana Carvey in their roles of Wayne and Garth. This is about as heavily themed as Paramount gets; it adds to the ride and certainly makes the last part of the queue area a lot more fun. The ride itself is a hurtle down an unpainted wooden roller coaster. It *moves.*

**Thunder Road:** Another fine wooden roller coaster, featuring a gutwrenching first drop. The first seat's a good one, but so is the back. Very, very shaky. Put your head against the headrest if you can, or bring aspirin. You can choose between trains that ride forward and those that ride backward. While the latter may sound more daring, a lot of people find that without being able to see where you're going, all the tantalizing anticipation of drops evaporates. If you're only riding once, go forward.

**Carolina Cyclone:** This is a good, fast, violent metal coaster that makes the most of its ride time and does a good job exploiting the possibilities of metal tracks: a nice first drop into two 90-degree loops, then a hard right into a corkscrew, before a big round-up and a final fling into the station. At the end you'll feel so abused you'll be tempted to slap the ride operator.

**Vortex:** This usually has the biggest line; it's a stand-up coaster, which, according to the commercials, is supposed to make it scarier. But while standing up in a sit-down coaster *is* scary (and stupid), the way you're locked in here, it's more like taking a ride while clapped in the village stocks. The other problem I have with this breed of coaster is that if you aren't in the front row, the view never changes. And by the way, stocks or no stocks, you're not really standing—there's a bike-seat thing jammed up into your crotch to keep you from squatting down and out of your overhead shoulder restraint. At best, instead of a "stand-up coaster," they should call this a "coaster with your legs dangling straight under you." Some people swear by this one, but I don't get it. Imagine being in a van you can drive standing up versus a sleek sports car in which you have to slide your legs way forward. Now which vehicle do you think would make the quicker, sharper turns? But if the line's short enough, by all means squat aboard and judge for yourself.

**Drop Zone:** Hop into a chair and get jerked several stories into the air. Then plummet to the ground, slowing just in time to keep from running up Paramount's liability rates. If you're afraid of elevators, this will either cure you or send you into therapy. My favorite moment is those few seconds when the seat carriage stops at the top, all of Carowinds spreads beneath you, the wind ruffles your hair, and you're waiting for the little click that means you're about to plunge back to Earth. Yes, it's very basic and as subtle as a hurricane. But it's a heck of a lot cheaper than skydiving, and you don't have to remember to pull any cords.

**Rip Roaring Rapids:** This ride isn't scary one bit, certainly not compared to a Class IV or above whitewater rafting trip. But it's fun, bumping along in a big wheel of a raft, feeling like a number on a roulette wheel as you face the other passengers, as the boat spins this way and that, bouncing off each artificial rock. Some people get drenched, with a bathtubful of water pouring onto their laps, while others leave the ride relatively dry. That's what makes this a fun ride for me—especially if I'm with a crowd of friends, and it's warm, and I'm not wearing white pants.

**Carolina Goldrusher:** This is just a basic runaway train–type roller coaster, with no big drops but a lot of fast turns as you whoosh around the side of a hill, pines and bridge beams flying past—essentially like watching an old Burt Reynolds chase scene in 3D. A great ride for those who like a little thrill but aren't quite sure if they're ready for the Hurler and Thunder Road.

**Powder Keg Flume:** Carowinds' flume ride is a step above those what-you-see-is-what-you-get flume rides you sometimes find at third- and fourth-rate parks, where the ride essentially consists of a loading area, a lift, and a drop, the latter two connected by about 50 feet of flume track with no theming. Powder Keg Flume (technically not a *log* ride—you're riding in mock wooden barrels) gives you a bit of a ride up there at the top; winding about in the flume among the tops of the pines, you can almost forget for a moment and think you're up in the mountains somewhere. Well, for a few seconds, anyway. Then it's down the final drop with you. Another good one to ride if it's hot—maybe not such a great idea if it's chilly.

When it comes to food, I'm afraid, the best advice is eat outside the park, if possible. You'll see a gas station on your right just as you begin to head onto the Paramount property; it includes a Blimpie's restaurant at the food mart. That's as good a place as any to stock up on sandwiches at a much more reasonable price than you'll find after you pay $30 a person to get into the park.

Usually, when I go to a Disney park, I'm surprised by how decent the food is, and how reasonably priced it is—compared to what they *could* charge if they wanted to. Well, I'm afraid that Carowinds food *is* that poor, and that overpriced. By all means, eat up before you get here. If you *must* eat in the park—and the food lines can get

dreadfully Soviet-esque—then try the Subway, just to the left of the Plantation Entrance.

## SOUTH OF I-85

Tiny **Clover** has no antebellum homes—it was founded in 1874 as a railroad town, though the area had been used as a "preaching point" for itinerant Presbyterian ministers long before that. You'll find some antique shops here on the old main street. Every spring, the town celebrates **Feis Chlobhair, A Clover Kinntra Gatherin'**, a festival honoring the town's Scots-Irish heritage with music, games, and food.

**Kings Mountain State and National Military Parks** mark the spot where in October 1780, a band of Appalachian pioneers—including Joseph Crockett, David's father—surprised the left wing of Lord Cornwallis' army and changed the course of the American Revolution.

Before the battle, British commander Lord Charles Cornwallis, fresh from a victory at Camden, was geared up to invade North Carolina. The defeat at King's Mountain turned popular sentiment against the British, thwarting British hopes of arousing loyalist support in the Carolinas and forcing Cornwallis to split his forces—half to hole up in Charleston and keep an eye on Southern malcontents, and half to march upward toward Washington, Yorktown, and defeat. A film at the visitors center and a 1.5-mile self-guided battlefield trail help to sketch in the rest of the tale. Limited camping; the adjacent Kings Mountain State Park offers more. Kings Mountain National Military Park is near Blacksburg on Hwy. 216, between N.C. 161 and I-85, 12 miles northwest of York, 864/936-7921, fax 864/936-9897. Off I-85, take North Carolina Exit 2. Open daily 9 A.M.–5 P.M. Labor Day to Memorial Day, daily 9 A.M.–6 P.M. Memorial Day to Labor Day. Closed Thanksgiving Day, Christmas Day, New Year's Day.

## YORK

The county seat of York County, York (pop. 7,610) is nicknamed both the "White Rose City" and "The Charleston of the Upcountry." A good place to stop when you get downtown is

**The Historical Center of York County,** 212 E. Jefferson St., 803/684-7262, fax 803/684-7262.

## York Historic District

To start off your tour of this 340-acre historic district, one of the largest in the country—and the second-largest in South Carolina, after Charleston's—you'll want to stop at **Ferguson & Youngblood,** 30 N. Congress St., 803/684-6461. This is a classic general merchandise store, with an emphasis on the word *general*. Tracy Ferguson Jr. sells everything from lock washers to real estate and roasted peanuts here. Stop in, keep an ear open, and you'll soon overhear what's going on in town.

**Ivy Hill Gift Shoppe,** 8 N. Congress St., 803/684-7614, fax 803/628-0847, is one of those stores where you walk in and feel your pulse rate drop immediately. It's that warm and serene inside; all scented candles and garden stones, that sort of thing. Native Yorkers say that this store is such a great place to buy gifts that it's picked bare a week before Christmas. Say hello to Squirrel, the black cat, who lives here.

## Food

Former Cheeseheads Mike and Linda Peavy's **Roadside Grille,** 307 W. Liberty St., 803/628-5415, is a fun place with a road-trip theme: the to-go menu folds like a road map; the food categories include "Start Your Engine" (appetizers), "Light Trips" (salads and soup), "Pick-Ups" (finger food), and "Lubricants" (drinks). The burgers and "freeway fries" are scrumptious, the malts are super-thick. Best of all are the diverse entries from the eateries of roadside America: western caviar from the Big Texan in Amarillo, muffaletta from New Orleans, hot brown (an open-face hot turkey sandwich topped with cream sauce, Parmesan cheese, and a bacon strip) from Louisville, Kentucky, and, of course, Southern barbecue. Karaoke over in the lounge at night.

Wait—*best* of all is the free CD jukebox stuffed with vintage rock, country, and big-band music.

For good steaks, locals point to **The Coal Yard,** set right next to the York Chamber of Commerce at what used to be the train depot, 105 Garner St., 803/684-9653. **The Garden Café,** 8-C N. Congress St., 803/684-7019, offers sandwiches, quiche, pasta, homemade soups, gourmet coffees, and tasty desserts. Come on the weekend for live music and prime rib, chicken, and seafood. For lunch this is a pretty cheap place to go; for dinner, you're looking at the high teens per plate.

# East of Charlotte

## REED GOLD MINE STATE HISTORIC SITE

Located at 9621 Reedmine Rd. in Stanfield, 704/721-4653, this historic site marks the scene of the first gold discovery in America.

I love this story. In the early 1780s, Johannes Rieth, a Hessian soldier fighting for the British in the Revolution, underwent a change of ambition and melted away from his fellow troops and into a small community of German immigrants in the lower Piedmont. Under his anglicized name, John Reed, the deserter joined many other poor British soldiers who took a look around at the land they were seeking to keep under the British thumb and decided they wanted to be a part of its future, no matter who ended up winning it.

By 1799, Reed had established a farm and was raising a family. One day that year, his young son, Conrad, was playing down in the creek—Little Meadow Creek—that traversed Reed's property. He found a large rock that looked like gold, and excitedly showed his father. Reed of course knew better, and proclaimed the rock fool's gold. It was, however, still golden and pretty, so Reed agreed to use it as the doorstop for his house.

By 1802, a houseguest convinced Reed to get the rock examined, just in case the fool's gold might be the genuine item. Reed took it to a Fayetteville jeweler, and said if it was real, he expected to be paid for the gold. And he'd abide no shenanigans—he wanted at least $3.50. The jeweler took a look, went into the other room to dance a jig, came out soberly, and said he guessed the rock was worth $3.50. Reed took the money, walked away, pleased with himself for making $3.50 from selling a doorstop, and the jeweler laughed to think that he'd just bought a 17-pound golden nugget for roughly 1/1000th of its market price.

When Reed found out, he did a smart thing. Rather than riding back to Fayetteville to lynch the jeweler, he formed a partnership with three local men who supplied equipment and workers to dig for gold in Reed's creekbed. They worked part-time at it, balancing their mining time with their farming, but by the end of the first year, according to local lore, a slave named Peter had found another huge nugget—a 28-pound beauty.

Other farmers caught wind of what Reed was doing and began mining their own creeks, and others from surrounding areas heard about it, and the nation's first gold rush ensued. The gold in these parts lasted longer than the gold in California, though perhaps that's partly because not as many people were digging after it. Still, U.S. Government opened the first branch of the U.S. Mint in Charlotte, to help press some of the gold into coins. In fact, until 1848, North Carolina mined more gold than any other region in the U.S., but once the California gold fields were discovered, most of the local miners headed west and things around here settled down quite a bit. It's an important nuance to American history, however, to remember that many of the California '49ers were not, as many believe, inexperienced schoolteachers and plowboys wielding a shovel and pick for the first time. Many of the most successful miners were those who arrived on the scene after years in the Piedmont mines. In fact, much of the colorful mining camp culture of the California Gold Rush, documented by Mark Twain, Bret Harte, and others, was largely imported from the earlier gold rush camps of North Carolina and Georgia.

Today at Reed Gold Mine State Park, you'll find a small museum featuring an orientation film, a guided underground tour, a stamp mill, and walking trails. You can also pan here, for a small charge.

## THE NORTH CAROLINA SANDHILLS

Further along U.S. 74, you'll come across **Rockingham,** established in 1785 and named for the Marquis of Rockingham, who befriended North Carolina before the Revolution. It's the longtime home to the Dixon Brothers, the bluegrass pioneers who came here from Spartanburg to work the mills. Their "Weave Room Blues" is an excellent testimony to the monotony of the life they knew here; their "Wreck on the Highway" was recorded by Bob Dylan.

Under Jim Crow, Rockingham's mills employed only white laborers; African-Americans worked in the peach orchards and cotton fields. The latter produced 75 percent of Rockingham's agricultural income.

To most Carolinians, Rockingham today is better known as home to the *North Carolina Speedway*, 2152 N. U.S. 1, 910/205-1299, website: www.northcarolinaspeedway.com, a.k.a. "the Rock," where NASCAR Busch and Winston Cup racers have been racing since 1965.

In **Laurinburg**, the **Indian Museum of the Carolinas**, 607 Turnpike Rd., 910/276-5880, focuses on archaeological findings from the various Native American tribes that preceded European settlement. The town's **Scottish Heritage Center**, inside the DeTamble Library at St. Andrews Presbyterian College, 910/277-5236, preserves, and illuminates for visitors, the accomplishments and culture of Scottish folks, both in the old country and here in Carolina.

# PINEHURST

A winter resort for more than a hundred years, Pinehurst got its birth when James W. Tufts, of Boston, bought 5,000 acres from the family of Walter Hines Page of Cary. (Page himself was the former editor of the Raleigh *State Chronicle*, just about to be named editor of the *Atlantic Monthly*, and would eventually serve as U.S. ambassador to Great Britain during World War I.) Tufts had millions to spend and wanted to turn the land here into a health resort, but it never came to fruition. Instead, he took the lead from his New York guests, who had taken to driving balls around the cow pastures, and decided to lay out Pinehurst's first golf course. Today, there are no fewer than eight courses in the Pinehurst Resort alone, and 42 between the communities of Pinehurst, Southern Pines, and Aberdeen. Wait—better make that Pinehurst®—the name has been registered. To design the village, Tufts employed no less than Frederick Law Olmsted, who in other days knocked off a couple of projects called the Biltmore Estate and New York's Central Park.

Ohio-born trick shot Phoebe Anne Mozee—a.k.a. Annie Oakley—lived here, where she did service heading up the local gun club. In her day, Pinehurst was not actually a town, but rather a private business enterprise. That's still the case today.

## Sights

The 1772 **House in the Horseshoe,** 324 Alston House Rd., 910/947-2051, 10 miles north of Carthage, was once the main house on a Sandhills cotton plantation. You can still make out the bullet holes from some 1781 musketplay between Carolinian Patriots and Loyalists. No charge for admission, though donations are welcome. Hours vary according to season—call to make sure it's open. Come the first weekend of August for a Revolutionary War Battle Reenactment; the Christmas Open House and Candlelighting in early December is a memorable sight.

The **Pinehurst Harness Track,** on N.C. 5, is the site of the annual spring Matinee Races, polo matches, and various horse shows from May through October. The racetrack, which dates to 1915 and is on the National Register of Historic Places, is open year-round from 8 A.M.–dusk. If you're an equestrian, a horse-lover, or simply the parent of a child going through a *Black Beauty* phase, by all means call 910/295-4446 ahead of time for a guided tour.

The **Tufts Archives,** located within the Given Memorial Library, 150 Cherokee Rd., 910/295-3642, chronicle Pinehurst history, from the early days when millionaire James Walker Tufts strove to build his dream—a resort for his wealthy friends. He did, and the Archives do, and if you get here Monday–Friday 9:30 A.M.–5 P.M., or Saturday 9:30 A.M.–12:30 P.M., you can see them.

The **Sandhills Horticultural Gardens,** 2200 Airport Rd., 910/695-3882, website: normandy.sandhills.cc.nc.us/lsg/hort.html, consists of 10 major gardens cast over 32 acres and maintained by horticultural students at Sandhills Community College. Flora favorites include the formal English Sir Walter Raleigh Garden, and a wetland trail painstakingly contrived to illustrate the flora found in . . . the Carolina Sandhills.

But if you're looking for native flora, head over to the **Weymouth Woods Sandhills Nature Preserve,** 1024 Ft. Bragg Rd., 910/692-2167. Weymouth Woods features 4.5 miles of hiking trails amid 900 acres of pines, wildflowers, streams, and ponds. A museum and on-site naturalist help mightily in introducing flatlanders to the nuances of the distinctive Sandhills ecosystems. Open daily, except for Christmas. Hours: November–March 9 A.M.–6 P.M., and April–October 9 A.M.–7 P.M.

### Where to Golf
For golf info, contact the **Pinehurst, Southern Pines, and Aberdeen Convention Visitors Bureau,** P.O. Box 2270, Southern Pines, NC 28388, 800/346-5362, website: www.homeofgolf.com/cvb.htm. Or try the **North Carolina Division of Tourism, Film and Sports Development,** 301 N. Wilmington St., Raleigh, NC 27601, 800/VISIT NC or 919/733-8372, website: www.visitnc.com, to request the *North Carolina: Official Golf Guide,* updated annually.

### Accommodations
Prices in the Pinehurst area can create something of a challenge for the average traveler. Try the 80-room **Comfort Inn,** 9801 U.S. 15/501, 800/831-0541 or 910/215-5500, website: www.comfort.pmcproperties.com; another possibility, especially if you're traveling in a good-sized group, is **Condotels of Pinehurst,** 305 N. Page Rd., 800/272-8588 or 910/295-8864, website: www.condotelsofpinehurst.com.

But let's say you have money—or an expense account. In this case, you may well want to head to the **The Magnolia Inn,** 65 Magnolia St., right in the middle of Pinehurst Village at the corner of Magnolia and Chinquapin, 910/295-6900. Dating back to Pinehurst's infancy in 1896, this old beauty started out as a duffers' clubhouse but is now a warm, Victorian inn. Fresh, full country breakfasts in the morning, gourmet dinners at night, and a swimming pool, in season.

The 40-room **Pinehurst Resort and Country Club,** Carolina Vista Drive, 910/295-6811, website: www.pinecrestinnpinehurst.com, opened in 1901. The resort itself has some eight golf courses. Guests can also play golf and tennis, as well as enjoying the waters of Lake Pinehurst. Five stories tall and not a little imposing in its Victorian splendor, the **Holly Inn,** at 155 Cherokee Rd., 910/295-6811, is perhaps a little less expensive.

### Food
If just the name—the **Carolina Dining Room,** at the Pinehurst Resort—sounds swanky to you, it's supposed to. The restaurant, 910/235-8433, features dark mahogany paneling and dim lighting; it looks out over the resort's rose gardens and serves up well-prepared and often healthy meals. Open for breakfast, lunch, and dinner. Or you may opt for the steady **John's Barbecue & Seafood Restaurant,** north of town at 1910 U.S. 15/501, 910/692-9474. The authentic, moderately priced dishes at **Theo's Taverna,** 140 Chinquapin Rd., 910/295-0780, include lamb dishes and souvlaki.

## SOUTHERN PINES
Southern Pines is still golf-crazed and resort-like, but it's a real town; Monterey to Pinehurst's Carmel, if you will; Beaufort to Pinehurst's Hilton Head. After lumber interests cut down nearly all the hardwoods hereabouts, Southern Pines was established and marketed as a health resort. The town was incorporated in 1887, and 50 years later the 2,500 population was tripling every winter as snowbirds arrived, many via the New York–Florida Limited on the Seaboard Railroad. A writers colony was founded here by James Boyd, a Pennsylvania-born WWI veteran who moved here after Versailles. Among other works, Boyd authored *Drums* and *Marching On,* both of which contemplate his war experiences, but which are set in the Revolution and Civil War, respectively. Other literary middleweights joined Boyd and his wife here, including novelists Katherine Newlin Burt and Struthers Burt.

### Sights
Today, James Boyd's old home, the **Weymouth Center,** 555 E. Connecticut Ave., 910/692-6261, is home to the **North Carolina Literary Hall of**

© ERIKA HOWSARE

**Southern Pines' Weymouth Center**

**Fame.** Pensmiths honored here include Boyd (which seems only fair), Thomas Wolfe, O. Henry, playwright Paul Green, and others. You'll need to call ahead to schedule a visit, and then you'll need to choose a time from 10 A.M. to 2 P.M. on Tuesday, Wednesday, or Thursday. Small admission charged.

The **Shaw House Property,** at the intersection of Morganton Road and S.W. Broad Street, is home to three historic houses, all on the National Register. Together the three will give you a good idea of what life was like for early settlers in the region. The proud but simple **Shaw House** itself dates to the later antebellum period, around 1840. Charles C. Shaw, father of the first mayor of Southern Pines, built it here, and a thoughtful examination of its straightforward design tells you quite a bit about the difference between Upcountry and Lowcountry Carolina; in other words, between the nose-to-the-plow farmers in the west part of the state and the nose-in-a-Scott-novel plantation owners by the coast.

The other two homes here were imported to the property for preservation. Both were built

in the late colonial period, presumably around 1770. The log **Garner House** has heart pine paneling, original hand-forged hinges, and board doors. The **Britt-Sanders Cabin,** also known as the Loom House, is a simple one-room pioneer home with a loft. The property is operated by the Moore County Historical Society, and is open Tuesday–Saturday 1–4 P.M. 910/692-2051.

The **Taxidermy Hall of Fame of North Carolina Creation Museum,** 156 N.W. Broad St., 910/692-3471, quite unlike most other museums, is set inside a Christian bookstore. The museum's exhibits feature some 200 animals that have gone on to glory and left their corruptible parts behind for taxidermists to render as incorruptible as possible. So if you'd like a good long look at the native North Carolina wildlife that keeps darting into the bushes before you can catch a glimpse, this is the place for you. And not only are these stuffed animals not going anywhere, but you can rest assured that they're among the tops in their mummified fraternity—many have won posthumous state and national ribbons for taxidermic excellence. Open Monday–Saturday 9 A.M.–5 P.M. Admission $1.

## Accommodations

For something quiet and reasonably priced, try the **Days Inn/Resort Center,** 1420 U.S. 1 South, 800/972-3096 or 910/692-7581. Amenities include the on-site J. Albert's lounge with live entertainment. The English-style **Knowllwood House,** 1495 W. Connecticut Ave., 910/692-93990, furnishes its rooms with 18th-century antiques and its guests with a full, 21st-century breakfast. The **Mid-Pines Inn and Golf Club Resort,** 1010 Midland Rd., 910/692-2114, is another excellent old golfer's hotel.

## Food

**Nature's Own,** 1150 Old U.S. 1, 910/692-3811, is the spot in Southern Pines for natural sandwiches (with homemade bread), salads, soups, and other healthy dishes. Open 11 A.M.–3 P.M. for lunch, 5:30–9:30 P.M. for dinner. For the carnivorous, lumber on over to the **Lob Steer Inn,** U.S. 1 North Service Rd., 910/692-3503, where you'll find steak, seafood, and wine. **Russell's Seafood House,** on Route 22 north of downtown, 910/692-7453, is known for its huge portions. If you're looking for non-U.S.A. grub, try **El Chapala,** 1850 U.S. 1, 910/692-5634, for down-home, family-style Mexican. Or try the Scottish-themed **Squires Pub,** 1720 U.S. 1, 910/695-1161, or **Vito's Ristorante & Pizzeria,** 615 Southeast Broad St., 910/692-7815, which serves up authentic Calabrian cuisine.

# ABERDEEN

Originally called Blues Crossing—an excellent name for a jam band, incidentally—this little Scots-Irish Presbyterian farming community centered around the doings at the Bethesda Church, which some nowadays call Bethesda *Presbyterian* Church. But in those days, in these parts, there was no doubt as to the denomination.

Almost as if predestined, the little bastion of Sandhills Calvinism got a boost when A. Frank Page, a miller, moved here from Cary and began

to build a railroad, which eventually turned Aberdeen into an important trading town and shipping station for tobacco and fruit. The town was incorporated in 1893.

A. Frank Page had two sons who went on to some success. Frank (the younger) served as first chairman of the North Carolina Highway Commission, which developed the system of modern highways in the state. But the real high-stepper was Walter Hines Page, born in 1855, who attended Duke, and later John Hopkins, then worked for a number of newspapers and magazines, including the New York *Evening Post* and the *Atlantic Monthly,* as well as the Raleigh *State Chronicle.* In 1900 he worked with publisher Frank Doubleday in founding Doubleday and Company Inc. After supporting his old friend from his days in Atlanta—Woodrow Wilson—Page was rewarded with a post as ambassador to Great Britain. (Wilson, who had attended Davidson for a year and lived with his parents in Wilmington, also anointed Raleigh newspaperman Josephus Daniels for his Secretary of the Navy. Tar Heel boys stick together.) Thus it was Page who pleaded to Wilson's deaf ears—for years—to abandon his policy of neutrality and join the fight against Kaiser Wilhelm's Germany. Page returned to the U.S. in 1918, after Wilson finally committed troops, and died at Pinehurst the same year. He is buried here in the graveyard at Old Bethesda Church.

You'll find said **Bethesda Church** east of Aberdeen on N.C. 5 (Bethesda Road). Built around 1790, it still stands faithfully beside the cemetery filled with many of its former members from pioneer days forward, including the aforementioned Mr. Page. Outside the church, you can make out bullet holes from a minor Civil War skirmish that took place here; inside, the church still retains its old slave gallery, accessed by a separate entrance. Call ahead (910/944-1319) if you'd like to visit.

East of Aberdeen, the well-preserved and National Register of Historic Places–listed **Malcolm Blue Farm,** Bethesda Road, Aberdeen, 910/944-7685, hearkens from 1825 and still features the original farmhouse, barns, a gristmill, and a wooden water tower. The last week of

September brings the Historic Crafts and Skills Festival, and on the second Sunday of December stop by for the Christmas Open House. Otherwise, the farm is open Wednesday–Saturday 1–4 P.M. There's no charge, but you'll probably want to make a donation to the folks who are keeping up this wonderful preservation of rural Sandhills life.

In downtown Aberdeen stands **Union Station,** 910/944-5902, listed in the National Register. The depot, built during the area's boom in the days of Teddy Roosevelt, is a must-see for train buffs. Not only is the Victorian station a delight, but inside you'll find exhibits from the old Aberdeen and Rockfish Railroad that put Aberdeen on the map—even if it did so with very small letters. Outside you'll see one of only two inspection cars still extant in the U.S., as well as an old caboose. Open weekdays 8 A.M.–5 P.M. No charge for admission.

## Accommodations

The **Inn at the Bryant House,** 214 N. Poplar St., 800/453-4019 or 910/944-3300, is a nine-room Colonial Revival Inn built in 1913. The **Pine Crest Inn,** 50 Dogwood Road, 910/295-6121, plants its guests amid some half-dozen golf courses.

# Winston-Salem and the Triad

The Triad suffers from the Dave Clark Five Syndrome. Just as the credibly talented British Invasion rockers suffered from the "rivalry" that music reporters trumped up between them and the legendarily talented Beatles, the Triad of Winston-Salem, Greensboro, and High Point seems a bit lightweight as a destination when plunked down side by side with the Heartland's other three-pointed region, the Triangle. The latter, after all, is home to the state capital and the corresponding state museums, the state's top public (UNC-Chapel Hill) and private (Duke) universities, and Durham, colorful beneficiary of the tobacco industry's 19th- and 20th-century golden era.

But the Triad excels as a representation of heartland North Carolina. Winston-Salem is a real city with a demographic stability—despite its rapid growth—unknown to the Triangle's college towns and research boomtowns. Greensboro, with its arts venues and Civil Rights Museum, is as colorful as Durham in its own way. And while High Point is not as cute as Chapel Hill, it does offer visitors the world's largest chest of drawers, and if you throw in Old Salem and nearby Mount Airy, the Triad arguably wins the charisma award as well.

© MIKE SIGALAS

rooftops in Old Salem

# Winston-Salem and Vicinity

The Moravians who founded Salem descended in both blood and creed from an early Protestant denomination founded in Moravia—what is now the Czech Republic. Fleeing persecution, the Moravians had settled in Germany, where they lived for years in peace and prosperity. They settled under the patronage of a Count Ziszendorf. It is said that John Wesley's experience with the devout, disciplined faith of the Moravians in Europe was what caused the "warming of his spirit" that led to his founding of what his brother Charles dubbed the Methodist movement. And it is Methodism, as much as Baptism, that has produced much of the South's Evangelical culture.

Ziszendorf helped finance and organize the community's immigration to Pennsylvania, as well as the later move southward to North Carolina. It was Ziszendorf who first envisioned and

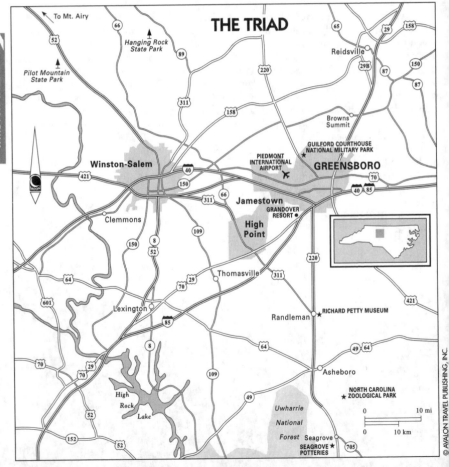

## TRIAD HIGHLIGHTS

**Barbecue,** Lexington

**Guilford Courthouse National Military Park,** Greensboro

**High Point**

**International Civil Rights Center and Museum,** Greensboro

**Mendenhall Plantation,** Jamestown

**Mount Airy**

**North Carolina Zoological Park,** Asheboro

**Pisgah Covered Bridge,** Asheboro

**Old Salem**

**Reynolda House Museum of American Art,** Winston-Salem

**Seagrove pottery studios**

**Uwharrie National Forest**

was under control of the British Crown, the sole holdout Lord Proprietor, Lord Granville, owned the land in this area, and from him the Moravians bought the Wachovia tract and began building the new village of Salem.

The Moravian church owned the land in Salem—individual residents did not. Citizens rented their homes and property one year at a time, allowing for "unsatisfactory" tenants to be removed from the Moravian community without unnecessary trouble. By the time of the American Revolution, Salem had a fair number of homes, but the villagers opposed warfare and did not raise troops, though they contributed financially and logistically to the Patriot cause—allowing British prisoners to be held at Bethsbara, for instance. British general Cornwallis spent one night in Bethania, after which his soldiers burned much of the town.

In 1791, on his presidential tour of the South, George Washington stayed the night in Salem at the new Salem Tavern, and attended a Moravian singing meeting.

In 1849 the state of North Carolina created Forsyth County, and Salem, right in the middle of it, was the logical place to build the county courthouse. The Moravians disagreed, but they did offer to sell land on a nearby hill for a courthouse and surrounding, secular town, under the stipulation that its roads should lead to Salem's. They even allowed the county courts to meet in the Salem concert hall while the courthouse was under construction, though they refused to allow the whipping posts inside town limits. These things were done, and soon the town of Winston was born—named, in 1851, after Revolutionary hero Major Joseph Winston. The Fayetteville-Winston plank road was completed in 1854, connecting Winston-Salem by road to Fayetteville, and from river thence to Wilmington and the European markets. As prosperity came, the towns, built so close together, grew toward each other, and so too the mores of the peoples grew closer together too: when the Civil War broke out, many Moravian young men enlisted alongside their Winston friends to fight the Yankees.

named Salem, though he died in Europe in 1760, shortly before its physical founding.

A team of a dozen highly skilled Moravians traveled down from Bethlehem to found Bethsbara in 1753. Bethsbara—meaning "house of passage"—was a staging village that would allow them to prepare the building of Salem. The village grew as more settlers moved in from Bethlehem, Pennsylvania, and Europe, and it soon became indispensable to many of the local, non-Moravian settlers, who would stop in to do business with its skilled craftsmen. In 1758, local Indians began attacking outlying settlements, and Bethsbara was jammed with people, Moravians and non-Moravians alike. With all the people crammed into such a small village, typhoid soon broke out. Some of the Moravians moved off to found the Moravian but noncommunal Bethania—about six miles from present-day Salem—in 1759.

Though by this time most of North Carolina

The Winston-Salem Tobacco Market opened in 1872, and three years later R.J. Reynolds built his first tobacco factory in Winston. That same year, the railroad arrived in town, making the shipping of tobacco and cotton much easier, and thus the growing of these crops much more profitable. The towns finally joined as one city in 1913.

And so the town grew. A precocious lad named Howard Cosell was born here in 1918. Five years later, a baby girl by the name of Zelma Kathryn Hedrick came into the world in Winston-Salem; years later her physical beauty and coloratura soprano would bring her fame as MGM star Kathryn Grayson, landing her juicy—usually singing—parts opposite Gene Kelly and Frank Sinatra; her greatest roles were in the big-screen version of *Showboat* (where she shared the screen with Smithfield's Ava Gardner) and the 3D version of *Kiss Me, Kate*.

By the 1930s, Winston-Salem was the top manufacturing city in the state, and it remains in the top rank of Tar Heel cities today. The city handled itself pretty well during the days of desegregation; the public schools were integrated as early as 1957.

Sixties and seventies country megastar George Hamilton IV was born here in 1937, and blaxploitation star Pam Grier was born here to an Air Force mechanic and a hospital nurse in 1949. Mark Grace, long-time Chicago Cub but a baseball star nonetheless, was born here in 1964.

If you're visiting town in August in a year that ends with an odd number, you're in luck. The **National Black Theater Festival,** the work of the North Carolina Black Repertory Company, features a number of different productions featuring African-American casts.

## SIGHTS

### Old Salem

This well-preserved Moravian village on Old Salem Road at Academy Street, 888/348-5420 or 336/721-7300, website: www.oldsalem.org, is a state-run historic park that doubles as an actual neighborhood. Even if you've seen similar spots such as Williamsburg, Virginia, Old Salem is still worth a stop. After all, in the 18th century, this was not the average Colonial American community—it was a religious commune, home to the Moravians, who had emigrated from Czechoslovakia by way of Germany. The visitors center here provides good background information on who the Moravians were and how they lived; the rest of the huge historic site serves as one big interactive visual aid.

Some of the best things in Old Salem—the Winkler Bakery, the Salem Tavern, the print shop, the overall ambienc—require no special admission fee. And entrance to the Old Salem Visitor Center costs nothing; the short film on the history of the Moravians is free as well. It's open 9 A.M.–5 P.M. Monday–Saturday, and 2:30–5 P.M. Sunday. (Old Salem is officially closed Easter Sunday, Thanksgiving Day, December 24, and Christmas Day. Truly inhospitable weather can inspire a quick non-holiday closure, too.)

However, to tour most of the historic buildings and participate in the formal Living History exhibits, you'll need to buy a ticket. They come in two varieties the $15 ($8 for children ages 5–16) **Old Salem Visitor Ticket,** which entitles you to two days of unlimited admission to the homes and community buildings on the village's self-guided tour, which at publication included the Single Brothers House, Miksch House, Boys' School, Vierling House and Barn, Vogler House, Shultz Shoemaker Shop, and the Tavern Museum-Barn. It also includes the chance to hear and talk with aforementioned costumed interpreters at various stations throughout the village. However, a much better deal is the **All-in-One Ticket,** ($20 adults, $11 children), since in addition to the Old Salem exhibits, it provides admittance to the Museum of Early Southern Decorative Arts (MESDA), The Children's Museum at Old Salem, and The Gallery at Old Salem during exhibit runs, as well as the use of a recorded audio-walking tour to complement your experience.

Do note, however, that while the Old Salem Visitor Ticket portion of your all-in-one admission is valid for two consecutive days, the MESDA, Audio Walking Tour, The Children's Museum, and The Gallery at Old Salem segments may used

church in Old Salem

© MIKE SIGALAS

for one of the two days only. And while it might be tempting to divvy up a ticket so that you and your friend see different sights, individual segments are not transferable. Still, these all-in-one tickets will save you $11 off the cost of buying each ticket separately. In all cases, kids under age four can accompany a paying adult to every exhibit but The Children's Museum for free. They'll need to ante up $4 to enter the Children's museum, unless they're too young to walk.

Even if you're not willing or able to buy tour tickets, be sure to visit the authentic colonial-era **Winkler Bakery,** where the bakers still cook up Winkler's famous paper-thin Moravian cookies, wonderful ginger bread, and other baked goodies that you'll smell a half block down the street.

In like fashion, the **Salem Tavern,** 736 S. Main St., 336/748-8585, serves meals in its annex building, and you don't have to buy a tour ticket to dine on the authentic Colonial foods served there. You will need to buy one to tour the museum building, though, which is set in the original building, dating to 1784. This building is part of the official tour.

Sure enough, George Washington slept in the Salem Tavern. Twice. In 1791, while touring the Southern part of the then newly United States, the cherry-tree-chopping, silver-dollar-throwing, ivory-toothed Grandaddy of all Founding Fathers spent a couple of nights in Salem, sleeping, like any non-Moravian "stranger," at the Tavern, on what was then the outskirts of town. There, the Moravians could keep an eye on visiting outsiders—or, more specifically, could keep their eyes *off* them. They intentionally forewent windows on the Tavern's first floor to discourage curious Moravian youth from peeking in on the travelers' carryings-on. So popular was the Tavern as a stopping point that the annex was built in 1816 to accommodate the overflow. The Augustus Zevely House

> *George Washington slept in the Salem Tavern. There, the Moravians could keep an eye on visiting outsiders—or, more specifically, could keep their eyes off them. They intentionally forewent windows on the Tavern's first floor to discourage curious Moravian youth from peeking in.*

across the street opened still later (and is still open) to take in additional travelers.

Not all of the village's sites are historic buildings. At 924 S. Main St., inside the Frank L. Horton Center on the southern fringe of Old Salem, 336/721-7300, you'll find a pair of great museums that weren't here when the Moravians were, but are worth a visit nonetheless. The **Museum of Early Southern Decorative Arts (MESDA),** website: www.mesda.org/mesda.html, focuses—as does no other museum in the world—explicitly on the "original decorative arts," the woodwork, metalwork, ceramics, furniture, textiles, and paintings, of the early American South, up through 1820. The museum consists of some 24 reconstructed rooms that show the pieces in their proper setting. The bookstore here has a large collection of books on Old Salem and life in the early South. The first and last tours enter the Museum at 9:30 A.M. and 3:30 P.M., respectively, Monday–Saturday. On Sundays, the first and last tours enter the museum at 1:30 and 3:30 P.M., respectively. Admission for MESDA alone (without touring the village) is $10 for adults, $6 for children ages 5–16. You'll need to leave your camera in one of the lockers out front.

Here too you'll discover the colorful **Children's Museum at Old Salem,** 888/348-5420 or 336/721-7300, website: www.oldsalem.org. Kids will love it. It features a hands-on exhibit they walk through like a funhouse, with things to climb, buttons to push. There's even a kid-size Old Salem house where kids can actually run around and *touch things.* If we replaced all the McDonald's playgrounds in the United States with this sort of educational playground, we'd catch the Japanese in no time.

Here in the real world, Children's Museum is a worthy reward after your children have gritted their teeth all morning and kept their hands to themselves while listening patiently to docents.

And since children of proper age are welcome to go through the exhibit by themselves, it may be a worthy reward for frazzled parents, too. Price for all tickets—kids and adults—is $4. If you're also buying an Old Salem Visitor Ticket or a ticket to MESDA, tickets to the Children's Museum run just $2. Of course, if you're buying the all-in-one ticket, one day's admission is included.

Also in the Frank L. Horton Center is **The Gallery at Old Salem,** presenting self-curated and traveling exhibits focused on art that reflects historical subjects related to the Southern decorative arts and Moravian culture. Entrance to the museum by itself is $5, $3 for children 9–16.

The Fourth of July is a great time in Old Salem. Forget the Black Cat firecrackers and Roman Candles; since the Revolutionary War, Moravians have celebrated American liberties with a candlelit procession, a solemn act of gratitude and remembrance. Christmas is also a pretty time, with wagon rides and music, and Easter is another memorable event, heralded by brass bands that stroll throughout Old Town Salem, waking up folks with the happy news of Jesus' resurrection—for Moravians and other Christians, the ultimate proof of a loving God's power over the forces of death and evil.

There are other fine stays in Winston, but the only lodging in Old Salem—and a good, authentic one—is the 1844 **Augustus T. Zeveley Inn,** 803 S. Main St., 800/928-9299 or 336/748-9299, website: www.winston-salem-inn.com.

## Historic Bethabara Park

If Old Salem isn't old enough for you, head on over to 2147 Bethabara Rd., 336/924-8191, website: www.bethabarapark.org, site of the first Moravian settlement in North Carolina, founded in 1753 and meant to exist only until Salem outgrew it. For nearly 20 years, this village was the chief trading center of this part of Carolina, as well as the spiritual capital for Moravians in the region. Today, this 175-acre park helps bring to life those years of devoted toil in the rough North Carolina wilderness. Sights here include a number of ruins, some restored homes and other reconstructed buildings—including the Gemeinhaus, a 1788 congregation house—and a colonial garden

planted with period varieties. The adjacent wildlife preserve offers a raised boardwalk trail through the wetlands.

The **Diggs Gallery,** at Winston-Salem State University, 601 Martin Luther King Jr. Dr., 336/750-2458, website: www.wssu.edu/diggs, presents 6,500 square feet of African-American artwork.

## Reynolda House

At 2250 Reynolda Rd., 336/725-5325, website: www.reynoldahouse.org, you'll find the Reynolda House Museum of American Art, set in the former home, circa 1917, of Katharine and Richard Joshua (R.J.) Reynolds, they of the tobacco fortune. American paintings are the focus here, dating from the 18th century onward. The home itself is worth the visit, of course; it's on the National Historic Register and features formal gardens. The home's 13.5 acres of old "support buildings" (where I'm from, we call that the tool shed) have been converted into restaurants and shops that go by the name **Reynolda Village.** 2201 Reynolda Rd., 336/758-5584. Open for touring Tuesday–Saturday 9:30 A.M.–4:30 P.M., Sunday 1:30–4:30 P.M., website: www.reynolda house.org.

## Southeastern Center for Contemporary Art (SECCA)

A celebration of contemporary art, SECCA is open to the public and chock-full of visiting exhibits. Located at 750 Marguerite Dr., 336/725-1904, in the former home of pantyhose magnate James G. Hanes of "gentlemen prefer" fame.

## Piedmont Craftsmen Gallery and Shop

Showcasing the work of hundreds of the best craftspeople in the Southeast, the Piedmont Craftsmen Gallery is run by the Piedmont Craftsmen, Inc., a nonprofit group founded back in 1963 to foster public appreciation of traditional Piedmont art. The gallery, at 1204 Reynolda Rd., 336/725-1516, is open Tuesday–Saturday 10 A.M.–6 P.M. The shop here gives you the chance to bring home some of this art while also supporting the artists who keep the tradition going.

**Salem College**

### SciWorks

A 120-seat planetarium, hands-on exhibits, and an outdoor nature trail that winds through a 15-acre environmental park, this 25,000-square-foot museum at 400 W. Hanes Mill Rd., 335/767-6730, can make for a fun day—especially for kids, for whom the museum is especially tailored.

### Tanglewood Park

Located 10 miles west of town off U.S. 158, 4061 Clemmons Rd., 336/778-6300, website: www.tanglewoodpark.org, this 1,100-acre park is home to two 18-hole championship golf courses designed by Robert Trent Jones, Sr., one of which North Carolina golfers have voted the number one public course in the entire state. The park is massive, with room for tennis, horseback riding, paddleboating, hiking, and flower viewing—the rose garden in front of the Manor House, a bed-and-breakfast, is home to more than 800 rose-bushes. But Christmas is when this area really shines; millions of lights glisten on the trees and roadside, creating the Festival of Lights, claimed by some to be the largest drive-through holiday light show in the Southeast.

### Westbend Vineyards

At 5394 Williams Rd. in Lewisville, 336/945-5032, Westbend grows 60 acres of grapes and creates award-winning wines from them. Open for visits and tasting Thursday–Saturday, noon–6 P.M., Sunday 1–6 P.M.

### Winston-Salem Warthogs Baseball

The Carolina League Warthogs play at Ernie Shore Field, 401 Deacon Blvd., 336/759-2233, website: www.warthogs.com. The Single-A affiliate of the Chicago White Sox battle such opponents as the Kinston K-Tribe, the Wilmington, Delaware, Blue Rocks, and the Myrtle Beach Pelicans. Ernie Shore, incidentally, was born in 1891 in tiny Yadkin County and graduated from Guilford College in 1914. He played for the Boston Red Sox in the late 'teens, rooming with a young pitcher named Babe Ruth. Shore is most famous to baseball fans for what he accomplished in 1917: Ruth started a game, walked the first batter, and was immediately ejected from the contest for arguing the umpire's call. Shore came in to pitch. Ruth's runner was thrown out attempting a steal, and the Tar

Heel set down the next 26 batters, becoming the only pitcher in Major League history to pitch a perfect game in relief. After serving in World War I, Shore returned to Winston-Salem where he struggled awhile before being elected Forsyth County Sheriff, a post he held thereafter for 36 years, finally retiring in 1970. He died in 1980.

## Tours

For carriage tours of Old Salem, call **Heritage Carriage Company,** 336/784-5940, for a schedule and information.

# ACCOMMODATIONS

Winston-Salem is a fairly big city and not the best place, safety-wise, to try to save a few bucks on a room. On the other hand, you'll probably be fine down by the Hanes Mall—at one time the largest indoor mall in North Carolina, though you won't be in walking distance of much other than the mall itself and the shops in the parking lot.

## Under $50

Spell it with me: **M-o-t-e-l-6.** In this case, you'll be at 3810 Patterson Ave., 336/661-1588. There's 102 rooms, so as long as you don't come in too late you should be able to find a spot.

## $50–100

On the mid-low end you'll mainly find chains; the 133-room **Days Inn–Hanes Mall,** 3330 Silas Creek Parkway, 336/760-4770, website: www.daysinn.com, offers a pool and a continental breakfast, though they're best if enjoyed separately. The **Sleep Inn,** at Hanes Mall, 1985 Hampton Inn Court, 338/774-8020, has 73 rooms. **Hawthorne Inn and Suites** is closer in; it's at 420 High St. downtown near I-40, with 145 rooms and a restaurant and lounge, and is within reasonable walking distance of Old Salem and the sights downtown.

## $100–150

Spend a little bit more to stay at the 1844 **Augustus T. Zeveley Inn,** 803 S. Main St., 800/928-9299 or 336/748-9299, website:

www.winston-salem-inn.com. It's the only lodging in Old Salem, and my favorite place to stay in all Winston-Salem. You'll find it no surprise to learn that the proprietors have chosen to decorate the inn in Moravian furnishings. I could tell you about the king/queen beds, the private baths, the fireplaces in some rooms and the whirlpool/steam baths, but when it comes down to it, there's just nothing like getting up and taking a walk around the village as it starts to wake up. The Zeveley's crew bakes their own goods fresh daily. A "continental-plus" breakfast included is weekdays, and a full breakfast buffet on Saturday and Sunday. Room rates are $120 in April and October, $80 the rest of the year.

Other Winston-Salem–area lodgings include the brick **Brookstown Inn,** 200 Brookstown Ave., 919/725-1120, built in 1837 as a textile mill. The Brookstown is close to Old Salem though not in it, but it's also adjacent to Winston's downtown, which is a plus come nightfall, since the latter is where all the action is: Old Salem, like most Moravian towns, is not known for its nightlife.

The massive, 579-room **Adams Mark Winston Plaza Hotel,** 425 North Cherry St., 800/444-2326 or 336/725-3500, website: www.adamsmark.com, offers beautiful interiors in the lobby and other public areas, golf privileges at local courses, a pool, a sauna, and a shuttle to Old Salem.

Outside town you'll find **Tanglewood Manor House B&B,** set inside Tanglewood Park, 4061 Clemmons Rd. in Clemmons, 336/778-6300, website: www.tanglewoodpark.org/accommodate.html, 10 miles west of Winston-Salem on Highway 158.

A stay here, in what was once the home of R.J. Reynolds' brother William, gives you the chance to live like a tobacco magnate for a night or two, minus the guilt. Built in 1859—Reynolds later bought it and expanded it—the 28-room manor house offers the perk of being in the midst of a 1,000-acre wonderland of roses, trees, flowery pathways, and (this is North Carolina, after all) golf courses. In fact, the price of a room here gives you a discount on greens fees in the park. The 1809 little Mount Pleasant church on a hilltop in the park is popular for weddings; it's not uncommon for wedding parties to stay here at the inn. The park also rents out cabins and a guest house.

## FOOD

The two must-eats are both in Old Salem, and described above: **Old Salem Tavern** and **Winkler Bakery.** But Winston-Salem has a number of good restaurants. **Zevely House,** 901 W. Fourth St., 336/725-6666, is probably the next in line, though if the weather's good, **The Filling Station,** a renovated old gas station at 871 W. Fourth St., 336/724-7600, is a classy spot with a bar and fireplace-side tables inside and a great big patio outside, heated in winter. Uptown but casual, with a full bar and long wine list. Open for lunch and dinner everyday. Saturday and Sunday brunch. **Little Richards Bar-B-Que,** 4885 Country Club Rd., 336/760-3457, serves up the food of kings. **Pieworks,** at Pavillion Shopping Center, 612 Hanes Mall Blvd., 336/659-0505 churns out some creatively topped pizzas.

## ENTERTAINMENT
### Nightlife

Of all the destination elements that a travel writer covers, nightlife coverage has the shortest shelf-life. What's hot, who's playing where, these things all change out faster than a Venezuelan presidency. If you really want to know who's playing where, check the "What's On" section in the Friday *Winston-Salem Journal.*

If you're looking for folk music, contact the Triad's nonprofit folk music support group, the **Fiddle & Bow Society,** 336/727-1038, website: www.fiddleandbow.org, to find out what songsmiths will be in the area when you are, and where they'll be playing. Irish-themed **Burke Street Pub,** 1110 Burke St., 336/750-0097, offers live music—often of the Celtic variety—and Wednesday-night karaoke. Cover charge for live entertainment. **Club Salsa,** inside McMillan's Cafe, 401 W. Fourth St., 336/750-0855, offers one-hour salsa lessons at 10 P.M.

on Fridays and Saturdays, followed by salsa dancing until 2:30 A.M. There's a charge to get in, but women get discounts until 11:30 P.M. **Eelia's Café,** at the Shattalon Station Shopping Center, 336/922-9099, on the corner of Shattalon Drive and Murray Road, features live, top-ranked folk performers Fridays; cover charge ($10 or so), for live entertainment. Shows start at 8 P.M. **Rubber Soul Music House,** 1148 Burke St., 336/721-0570, is home to eclectic rock/blues/country bands, as well as open jam and open-mike nights; cover charge for live acts. Call for schedule. **Ziggy's,** 433 Baity St., 336/748-0810, is another hot spot for live bands; it gets a lot of the regional and national acts that come to the Triad.

**Thea's House of Blues & Jazz,** at 521 N. Liberty St., 336/722-4195, provides live musicians playing both. For something mellow, try the piano bar at **Paul's Fine Italian Dining,** 3443 Robin Hood Rd., 336/768-2645, which offers live lounge Thursday through Saturday nights. **Icehouse,** 738 E. 28th St., 336/829-7603, offers reggae on Fridays. **The Garage,** 110 W. Seventh St., corner of Trade Street, 336/777-1127, stages live college rock acts on the weekend. **Staley's Charcoal Steak House,** 2000 Reynolda Rd., 336/723-8631, has after-hours lounge music on Thursdays, Fridays, and Saturdays. **Studio 52,** 4240 N. Patterson Ave., 336/744-8252, offers amateur music competitions, disco nights, live jazz, and other lively evenings.

### Coffeehouse

**Morning Dew,** 1140 Burke St., 336/777-0464, offers coffee (of course) and live acoustic music, open-mike nights, and poetry slams on Thursday nights, beginning at 7:30 P.M.

## TRANSPORTATION
### Getting There

Interstates will bring you to the Triad—I-85 and I-40 are the favorites. Coming to Winston-Salem and the rest of the Triad area by air? If so, you'll probably touch down at **Piedmont Triad International Airport,** 800/665-5666 or 336/665-5600, website: www.ptia.org.

Carriers servicing the airport include American, Continental, Delta, Northwest, and United. **Greyhound Bus** serves the Triad; call 800/231-2222 or 336/272-8950 for schedules. **Amtrak** also serves the Triad; call 336/855-3382 or see www.amtrak.org for schedules.

### Getting Around

**Airport Express** will get you to and from the airport; call 800/934-8779 or 336/668-9723 for information. If you want to rent a car at the airport, you'll find nearly all the major companies vying for your business. You might try **Alamo,** 336/665-2540; **Budget,** 336/665-5882, or **Triangle,** 336/668-3400.

## MOUNT AIRY

Mount Airy is Mayberry. Or at least it's as close to being Mayberry as anywhere could be, and that's saying something, because a lot of towns have tried to Mayberryize their downtowns in the 40-plus years since the **Andy Griffith Show** debuted. One of the most popular television shows of all time, and arguably the most beloved, the *Andy Griffith Show* (1960–68) brought Mayberry to life. It was the early 1960s, and television was the medium a popular, nostalgic folk artist like Andy Griffith would naturally use, just as Mark Twain had used the novel and the lyceum to bring to life the Hannibal, Mo., of his childhood; and the way, a generation later, Garrison Keillor would bring to life his Minnesota hometown under the name Lake Wobegon. We Americans are suckers for innocence.

The *Andy Griffith Show,* of course, was a spin-off from Danny Thomas's *Make Room for Daddy,* but Griffith's foothill hayseed act—closer to Gomer Pyle than to Sheriff Taylor—had made him a hit on the *Ed Sullivan Show* and the *Steve Allen Show* in the 1950s, where he'd first appeared in the national spotlight after earning a degree in music at Chapel Hill in 1944 and appearing in summerstock productions of *The Lost Colony* over at Manteo on Roanoke Island. He appeared on Broadway in the comedy *No Time for Sergeants,* where he first met Don Knotts, and for which he received a Tony nomination. After a couple of films—including the classic Elia Kazan film *A Face in the Crowd*—he

© ERIKA HOWSARE

**Mount Airy *is* Mayberry.**

## THE ORIGINAL SIAMESE TWINS

Long before Andy Griffith was born, Mount Airy was home to Chang and Eng Bunker, the conjoined twins whose fame popularized the term "Siamese twins." Born in 1811 in a tiny village on the Mekong Delta in Siam (what is now Thailand), the brothers were linked by a fleshy ligament connecting the bottom of both their breastbones. The superstitious villagers feared their birth was an omen of the end of the world, and the twins berely escaped a premature death by execution. They were discovered years later by Scottish merchants Robert Hunter and Abel Coffin, who paid a large sum of money to the Thai government to introduce the twins to the Western world.

After years on the road, Chang and Eng fired their agents and took up with promoter P.T. Barnum. In 1842, the brothers decided to leave show business behind, and retired to the quiet life in North Carolina. They had let it be known that they were willing to share their wealth with the right kind of girls, who turned out to be twins Sallie and Adelaide Yates (Insert double-dating joke here). The Yates girls came from the Mount Airy area, and persuaded the Bunker boys to move here after they were married. They became members of the Baptist church (yes, it was a double wedding) and reared two large families. Chang and Eng split their time between wives, whom they set up in separate houses on either side of Stewarts Creek in White Plains, five miles outside of Mount Airy. They prospered there until 1874, when they died within an hour of each other. Originally buried in the garden of one of their homes, they were later relocated to the graveyard of the White Plains Baptist Church. You can still see their gravestone today. And yes. . . it's a single gravestone—double-wide.

Author Darin Strauss offers a fictionalized version of the Siamese twins' story in *Chang and Eng: A Novel* (Plume, 2001).

was cast as Sheriff Andy Taylor, the calm, warm-hearted center of an endearing group of small-town eccentrics. The show was set in fictional Mayberry, a ringer for Mount Airy, which, after all, was right close to Mount Pilot (the show's name for the real-life Pilot Mountain), and which included the Snappy Lunch, the local barber-shop, the sheriff's office, and lots and lots of front porches. While a generation of Americans moved away from their hometowns to the big city, from their old neighborhoods to impersonal, unwalkable suburbs, Mayberry became a substitute for the human connections people were missing. In a decade when the world seemed to be coming apart, Mayberry provided a lot of people with a sense of how it should be.

And it still does.

### Sights

If you're here for Mayberry, start at the **Andy Griffith Museum,** 615 N. Main St., 800/576-0231 or 336/789-4636, website: www.visitmayberry.com. You can actually spend the night at Andy Griffith's modest childhood home, **Andy's Homeplace,** 2029 Rockford St., 336/789-5999, website: www.andyshomeplace.com, for $150 a night. The price includes a continental breakfast and use of the recreational facilities at the nearby Hampton Inn. Downtown, you'll still find **Floyd's City Barber Shop** cutting hair. I'm sorry to say that the **Snappy Lunch** has closed—perhaps temporarily—but you can try **Aunt Bea's Barbeque,** U.S. 52 N., 336/789-3050, where they serve up Lexington-style barbecue with specials starting at $3.69.

There are other interesting sites unrelated to the show. For instance, the **Mount Airy Museum of Regional History,** 301 N. Main St., 336/786-4478, website: www.visitmayberry.com, set in the old W.E. Merritt Hardware Company building—look for the copper-roofed clock tower—built in 1904. Inside the museum, exhibits tell the story of the people who settled the foothills of the Blue Ridge Mountains along the Yadkin River. Everyone likes the mockup of a turn-of-the-century general store, and kids especially like the miniature railroad. Nominal admission charge.

## Events

35 years after Andy Griffith left Mayberry, thousands of people pour into town each September for the **Mayberry Festival**; grown men dress up like Barney Fife, Floyd the Barber, and Gomer Pyle, and visiting original cast members are treated like both gods and long-lost kin. Events are held downtown and at the Andy Griffith Playhouse; it's all sponsored by the Surry Arts Council. Call them at 800/286-6193 or 336/786-7998 for information.

But there's more to do in Mount Airy than pretend. There's great music, for one—once a month a live bluegrass and old-time string music show called the **Blue Ridge Jamboree** plays the Andy Griffith Playhouse, 218 Rockford St.; call 800/286-6193 or 336/786-7998 for information. The **Annual Autumn Leaves Festival** comes each October to downtown Mount Airy; old-time and bluegrass music abounds. Call 800/286-6193 or 336/786-7998 for information.

# Greensboro and Vicinity

Greensboro sits amid the lands contained in the original land grant given by the Earl of Granville to the Nottingham Company, a group formed to establish a settlement for Scots-Irish Presbyterians in the New World. Soon the Scots-Irish began to pour in; at the same time, Germans also formed communities in the area, as did Quakers. All of them worked hard to wrest a living from the earth, and nearly all of them had children. The Quaker Payne family in 1768 gave birth to little Dorothea, whom they would affectionately call Dolley. She would go on to marry James Madison and serve as a legendary White House hostess, first to Thomas Jefferson, who was a widower, and then to Madison, as his wife. When the British burned the White House in the War of

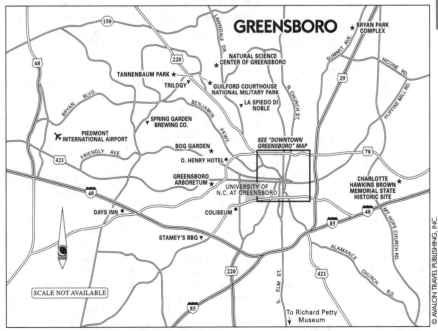

1812, it was Dolley who had the presence of mind to save Gilbert Stuart's famous unfinished portrait of George Washington.

Many years later, when the aged Dolley visited President Martin Van Buren, another widower, she was troubled at the conspicuous absence of a woman's touch in the White House. She sent for her pretty South Carolina cousin Angelica Singleton, who was the perfect age for Van Buren's oldest son, Abraham. The two married, and Singleton charmed Washington society as White House hostess for the remainder of Van Buren's term.

By 1770, the Greensborough area, which consisted of portions of Orange and Rowan Counties, was considered settled enough to become a county in its own right, and was named Guilford County after Lord North, English Prime Minister and Earl of Guilford.

Of course, with a county comes a courthouse, and by 1774, the first Guilford courthouse was built, of logs. A town grew around the courthouse; after the war it was named Martinsville for Alexander Martin, North Carolina delegate to the Constitutional Convention in Philadelphia. Nearby, Greene and Cornwallis' armies fought the famous Battle of Guilford Courthouse, which damaged Cornwallis' army so badly that it effectively ended the Revolution in the Carolinas. But today, nothing remains of Martinsville. County residents, overflowing with Democratic ideals in their new country, wanted the courthouse located at the center of the county so it was equally accessible to all. Accordingly, surveyors pinpointed the exact center of Guilford County, and here, in 1808, was founded Greensboro, named for Patriot general Nathanael Greene, commander of troops at the battle of Guilford Courthouse. The town prospered. Greensboro residents built factories that made chairs, carriages, wool, fur hats, cigars, and snuff. In 1833,

*With its large Quaker population, Greensboro became an important stop on the Underground Railroad. Farmer Vestal Coffin and his cousin Levi sheltered hundreds of escaping slaves in Greensboro, and Levi later moved up to Ohio, where he became known as "President of the Underground Railroad."*

the world's first steam cotton mill creaked, puffed, and rattled its way into operation in Greensboro. In 1851, John Hill Wheeler described Greensboro as "a most flourishing town . . . distinguished for its industry, thrift, and enterprise—for its manufactories and excellent schools." The town was predominantly a cotton town, but also predominantly non–slaveholding; 15,874 whites and 694 free blacks owned just 3,186 slaves.

In fact, a considerable number of Greensboro residents were not only non-slaveholders, but anti-slaveholding. With its large Quaker population, Greensboro became an important stop on the Underground Railroad. Farmer Vestal Coffin and his cousin Levi sheltered hundreds of escaping slaves in Greensboro, and Levi later moved up to Ohio, where he became known in Abolitionist circles as "President of the Underground Railroad," a title which it behooved him to leave off his business cards while still in Dixie.

Though most Greensboro residents opposed secession, once the War Between the States began, they stood beside their fellow Southerners. Though Greensboro men fought elsewhere, the war generally passed the town by until the very end. It was here in April 1865 that Confederate president Jefferson Davis, late of already-captured Richmond, met with General Joseph E. Johnston to discuss the South's military situation now that Robert E. Lee had surrendered at Appomattox. Johnston said he wanted to surrender to avoid any more needless bloodshed. Davis, whom many said would be hung if the Union triumphed, was less enthusiastic about ending the war. Nonetheless, Johnston prevailed, and some 7,000 of his troops were paroled by their Northern conquerors here in Greensboro. After the war, Quaker Yardley Warner purchased 34 acres of farmland, divided it into 68 half-acre lots, and sold the lots for good prices to freed slaves.

Greensboro, like many Piedmont towns, turned into a factory town after Reconstruction. Though William Porter, better known as O. Henry, would remember the Greensboro of his 1870s childhood as "a somnolent little Southern town," fifty years later, Greensboro *Daily News* editor Gerald W. Johnson found Greensboro to be representative of the ugly industrialization of many Piedmont cities. In one essay, he described the city thus:

> *Change is the breath of its nostrils, indeed the very texture of its soul. . . . Where Sherman came up and Grant came down to grind the Confederate armies between them, now Cotton and Tobacco have established their armies of occupation, and Greensboro and a long line of towns like it have sprung up . . . our Chamber of Commerce will fall upon you ecstatically, snowing you under with pamphlets, casting recklessly into the air handfuls of popping statistics like Chinese firecrackers, hustling you into a motor car to exhibit to you endless miles of asphalt and endless rows of unlovely skeletons of houses in process of construction.*

But while Johnson was appalled by the hucksterism of real estate developers and the jingoism of chamber of commerce zealots, he imagined the "refinement" that was to come to Greensboro. A lot of this is due to the five four-year colleges in town: after all, Guilford College—which today is proud of its role as an antebellum Underground Railway depot—had been founded by the Quakers way back in 1837; Greensboro College had come along in 1838; after the war had come the historically African-American Bennett College (opened in 1873 for women); and both the Greensboro branch of the University of North Carolina and North Carolina Agricultural and Technical State University opened in 1891. This last school boasts such alumni as *Challenger* astronaut Ron McNair and onetime presidential candidate Jesse Jackson.

On February 1, 1960, four students from NCA&TSU (then just a college) stopped into Woolworth's on Elm Street to have lunch at the whites-only lunch counter. When asked to leave, the students refused. And thus began the first major Civil Rights sit-in, though a similar protest had taken place, to less effect, at a Durham ice cream parlor in 1957. Today, the Woolworth's is now the International Civil Rights Center and Museum, where you can see the original lunch counter.

Some 200,000 people call Greensboro home today, making it the largest city in the Triad. Famous onetime residents include two-time First Lady Dolley Madison, who served first as a hostess for widowed Thomas Jefferson, then later for her husband, James Madison. The latter, at his 1809 inaugural ball, felt upstaged by his vivacious wife and was quoted as having said, "I would rather be in bed." Short-story writer O. Henry was born and raised here; so was reporter Edward R. Murrow. Two major basketballers, Harlem Globetrotter Fred "Curley" Neal and NBA Hall of Famer Bob McAdoo, were born in Greensboro, as was 19-year Major League pitcher Tom Zachary, most famous as the hurler who served up Ruth's 60th home run in 1927. TV *Survivor* castaway Kelly Wigglesworth, after her appearance on the smash American version of the "reality-based" television show, received a phone call from the Greensboro Police, reminding her that she was wanted on a five-year-old warrant for using a stolen credit card at several different businesses in Greensboro.

Greensboro events include the January–March **African-American Arts Festival,** highlighting the achievements and contributions of African-Americans to American culture. Call 800/668-1764 or 336/292-2211, website: www.uac greensboro.org, for information. The middle of March (the weekend closest to March 15) brings the **Anniversary of the Battle of Guilford Courthouse,** featuring a battle reenactment, a memorial observance, and other appropriate events. Held at Tannenbaum Park. The **Eastern Music Festival,** 200 N. Davie St., 336/333-7450, brings classical music to Greensboro for six weeks each summer. The **Fun Fourth Festival** is an Independence Day celebration held in downtown

**WINSTON-SALEM**

Greensboro that goes all day and into the night. Call 336/274-4595 for information. During the first weekend of October, the streets of downtown Greensboro are blocked off and the CityStage traditional street festival rolls into town, ready to entertain. Free admission; call 336/373-7523 for information, or website: www.uacgreensboro.org.

## SIGHTS
### The Bog Garden
Funny how we start to appreciate things once

they're gone, or almost gone. Such is the case of Greensboro's Bog Garden, on Hobbs Road just north of Friendly Avenue, 336/373-2199. Once the much avoided old town bog, it's no longer referred to as a bog, or even a swamp—it's a "Bog Garden." Whatever it is, it's beautiful. Some 8,000 trees tower over the abundant ferns and wildflowers. The garden's half-mile elevated boardwalk is a great short nature hike, providing an excellent opportunity to view some authentic Piedmont-style nature without leaving town. It's open daily during daylight hours; admission is free.

© ERIKA HOWSARE

**Old Greensborough**

## Old Greensborough

This historical old area gets its Anglicized spelling from Lorde knows where—the buildings here are mostly Victorian-era, not Colonial. (The end of the Colonial period, in fact, antedates the town's naming, which honors General Nathanael Greene, hero of the Battle of Guilford Courthouse, the last major battle in North Carolina.) But be that as it maye, Old Greensborough consists of historic South Elm Street, from the 100 to the 600 block, as well as sections of South Davie and South Greene Streets, and East and West Washington Streets. Stop by the **Greensboro Convention and Visitors Bureau,** 317 S. Greene St., 336/379-0060, where you can pick up a free self-guided tour brochure. Probably the chief attraction in OG is the **International Civil Rights Center and Museum** (covered separately below). After that, you'll want to see the **Blandwood Mansion,** 447 W. Washington St., 336/272-5003, website: www.blandwood.org, a 19th-century Italian villa once owned by governor John Motley Morehead. It was built as a simple Carolina farmhouse, but expanded and villa-ized in 1844 by architect Alexander Jackson Davis. The man-

sion has been restored and contains some of the original Morehead furnishings. Admission runs $5. Open Tuesday–Saturday 11 A.M.–5 P.M., Sunday 2–5 P.M. A little further north on Elm Street, on the west side of the street, you'll see the **Walkway of History,** unveiled on February 1, 1994, the anniversary of the first Woolworth's protest (as you may have guessed, the cross-street here, February 1 Place, memorializes the same event). Sidewalk markers pay homage to famous African-Americans, from the first fugitive "passenger" on the Underground Railroad through the first African-American state Supreme Court justice.

You'll also find more than a dozen antique shops, vintage shops, and bookstores down in Old Greensborough. Ask at any of them for a downtown shopping guide, or if you want one in advance, call Downtown Greensboro Incorporated, 336/379-0060.

## Greensboro Children's Museum

Kids love the hands-on exhibits here. At this colorful museum across from the Greensboro Public Library at 220 North Church St., 336/574-2898, website: www.gcmuseum.com, kids will find displays that allow them to dig for treasure or pretend to fly a plane. One of the neatest displays is the "Our Town" exhibit, a miniaturized town that kids can walk through and explore without parents having to tell them not to touch anything. See the museum's website, www.gcmuseum.com, for admission prices. Open Tuesday, Thursday, and Saturday 9 A.M.–5 P.M., Friday 9 A.M.–9 P.M., and Sunday 1–5 P.M. Also open Mondays in the summer.

### Greensboro Cultural Center at Festival Park/ArtQuest

An "architectural showplace," the center at 200 North Davie St., 336/373-2712, website: www.ci.greensboro.nc.us/culture, features five art galleries, a sculpture garden, and a small restaurant with outdoor seating. ArtQuest is an interactive art gallery for kids. It's open 12:30–5 P.M., Tuesday–Saturday, 2–5 P.M. Sunday, admission is $3. Wednesday is Family Night, with free admission for everyone, 5–7 P.M.

### Greensboro Historical Museum

Located at 130 Summit Ave., 336/373-2043, website: www.greensborohistory.org, the museum offers 12 galleries and two restored houses, all related to local history. From a re-creation of the famed Greensboro Woolworth's counter to the life of Greensboro-born Dolley Madison and the works of O. Henry, the museum does a fine job of bringing Greensboro's past to life for the average visitor. Open 10 A.M.–5 P.M., Tuesday–Saturday, 2–5 P.M., Sunday. Admission is free.

### Guilford Courthouse National Military Park

Located at 2332 New Garden Rd., 336/288-1776, website: www.nps.gov/guco, the 200-acre park features some 30 monuments to soldiers, statesmen, and other participants in the crucial, brutal March 15, 1781, battle here, which helped to shape the outcome of the American Revolution. And though the "long, obstinate and bloody" battle—to quote Patriot general Greene—was an English victory technically, since the Redcoats held their ground, it was so costly to the British that Cornwallis and his troops had to limp northward, where General George Washington was waiting to accept their surrender. Open 8 A.M.–5 P.M. daily; free admission.

© ERIKA HOWSARE

International Civil Rights Center and Museum

## International Civil Rights Center and Museum

Here, back when this old art deco building was Greensboro's Woolworth's, David Richmond, Franklin McCain, Ezell Blair, Jr., and Joseph McNeil, four NCA&TSU students, sat passively at the lunch counter in violation of store policy, which welcomed black retail shoppers but forbade these same people from eating at its luncheonette. The men weren't served, but neither were they forcibly removed. Word spread across campus of what was going on, and black picketers gathered outside with signs bearing such phrases as "GIVE US AMERICAN RIGHTS." The men remained at the counter—hungry, no doubt—until the store closed. They left by a side door.

Soon other black students from A&T and Bennett, as well as white students from Greensboro and Guilford College, arrived to sit-in and picket Woolworth's. Soon they were in front of S.H. Kress, as well. Woolworth's quickly learned that it's not always true that there's no such thing as bad publicity. Soon, the KKK and like-minded whites showed up and tried to take the seats from the blacks sitting on them. Five days later, on February 6, a bomb threat was telephoned in, and Woolworth's was closed to everybody, white and black alike. S.H. Kress closed too. But the bomber was too late—by now the sit-ins were spreading across North Carolina, from Winston-Salem to Charlotte, Durham, Fayetteville, Raleigh, and as far east as Elizabeth City.

Today the famous lunch counter has been preserved, like any other important battlefield. It's the centerpiece of this three-floor African-American cultural center and Civil Rights museum. It's open Monday–Friday 10 A.M.–5 P.M., and Saturday and Sunday by appointment. No admission charge. 134 South Elm St., 336/274-9199, website: www.sitinmovement.org.

## Mendenhall Plantation

Owned by Quakers, the Mendenhall plantation was used as a hiding place for escaping slaves. Here on the grounds, you'll see one of two remaining wagons with false bottoms, used to transport runaway slaves during the time of the Underground Railroad. The plantation is two miles southwest of Greensboro, at 603 W. Main St. in Jamestown, 336/454-3819, website: www.thedepot.com/groups-mendenhall. Open January and February, Friday 11 A.M.–2 P.M., Saturday 1–4 P.M., and Sunday 2–4 P.M.; March through the third week of December, it's open Tuesday–Friday 11 A.M.–2 P.M., Saturday 1–4 P.M., and Sunday 2–4 P.M. Donations are appreciated, but no admission fee required.

## Natural Science Center of Greensboro

Combine a small zoo, a hands-on museum, and a nifty planetarium, and you have the Natural Science Center, 4301 Lawndale Drive, 336/288-3769, website: www.greensboro.com/science center.com, a great place to spend an afternoon—particularly one spent with kids. Inside, the Dinosaur Gallery includes a life-sized T-rex, and the planetarium has multimedia productions that will help you brush up on your knowledge of supernovas and quasars. Other exhibits focus on inventions, gems and minerals, and animals native to the Americas. Outside, children and adults can

© ERIKA HOWSARE

**Mendenhall Plantation**

WINSTON-SALEM

pet small wildlife, feed goats and donkeys, and peer at bison, cougar, and white-tailed deer. Open 9 A.M.–5 P.M., Monday–Saturday, 12:30–5 P.M. Sunday. Admission is $6 for adults, $5 for children 3-13, ages two and under are free.

### Richard Petty Museum

Richard Petty is one of those people Northerners and Westerners may have heard of, but don't realize until coming to the South that they are icons to a lot of Americans. Richard Petty was the king of racing, the seven-time Winston Cup Series Champion. Don't call him the Elvis of racing—Petty raced for 35 years, nearly as long as that other king was even alive, and he will not be forgotten anytime soon. The museum, south of Greensboro at 311 Branson Mill Rd. off Old U.S. 220 S., Randleman, 336/495-1143, website: www.pettyracing.com/main/museum.htm, features awards Petty won, Petty cars, scads of photos involving Petty and statuesque women holding trophies, and a mini-theater replaying highlights from Petty's career. If you don't follow racing, it might be a good idea to stop by here and brush up on your racing trivia so you can blend into local conversations as easily as shifting gears. Open 9 A.M.–5 P.M., Monday–Saturday. Admission $3.50 adults, $2 ages 6–18, free for kids five and under.

### Tannenbaum Park

The exhibits at this 7.5-acre park, which include a number of historic buildings centering around a preserved split-log pioneer farmstead, help the modern-day visitor to experience a little bit of life in the Colonial period. The park, at 2200 New Garden Rd., 336/545-5314, website: www.ci.greensboro.nc.us/leisure/tannenbaum, features living history weekends throughout spring, summer, and fall, and also hosts a Colonial Fair on the second weekend in November. Open spring–fall, Tuesday–Saturday 9 A.M.–5 P.M., Sunday 1–5 P.M.; in winter, it closes a half-hour earlier. Tours of the Hoskins House and other structures are available daily spring through fall. No charge for admission.

### Art Galleries

Greensboro has a large number of art galleries

for a city its size; the following section covers a couple of the most popular. Contact the Greensboro Area Convention and Visitors Bureau at 800/344-2282 for a complete list.

The first place to go is the **Greensboro Cultural Center at Festival Park,** 200 North Davie St., where you'll find **African American Atelier, Inc.,** 336/333-6885, **Green Hill Center for North Carolina Art,** website: www.greenhillcenter.org, featuring exhibitions by Tar Heel painters, sculptors, and other artists, as well as **ArtQuest,** a hands-on children's gallery. Hours vary; admission to the Green Hill Center is free; admission to ArtQuest is free only from 5–7 P.M. on Wednesday, otherwise, the charge is nominal. The **Guilford Native American Art Gallery and Gift Shop,** also at the Greensboro Cultural Center, 336/273-6605, is a welcome venue for Native American artists to show and sell their art and handmade crafts.

**Mattye Reed African Heritage Center,** 1601 E. Market St., 336/334-3209, on the NCA&TSU campus, features one of the larger collections of African art in the entire United States. Visit and you'll be able to examine some 3,500 pieces, imported here from some 30 African nations. It's open Monday–Friday 10 A.M.–5 P.M. The University of North Carolina–Greensboro's **Weatherspoon Art Gallery,** on campus at the corner of Tate and Spring Garden Streets, 336/334-5770, website: www.weatherspoon.uncg.edu, features a sculpture courtyard and six galleries of modern and contemporary art. Worth a visit, if only for the Henri Matisse bronzes. Open Tuesday, Thursday, and Friday 10 A.M.–5 P.M., Wednesday until 8 P.M., and Saturday and Sunday 1–5 P.M. Free admission.

## ACCOMMODATIONS
### $50–100

The **Days Inn-Greensboro Downtown,** offers 122 rooms on two floors, at 120 Senecar Rd., 336/275-9571, website: www.daysinn.com/greensboro06411.

### $100–150

The century-old, three-story, 27-room **Biltmore**

Greensboro Hotel, 111 W. Washington St., 877/374-7067 or 336/274-6350, website: www.biltmorehotelgreensboro.com, has seen better days, but it's still a fine stay if you're looking for a place within walking distance of downtown attractions. The four-room Greek Revival **Troy Bumpas Inn,** 114 South Mendenhall St., 800/370-9070 or 336/370-1660, was built in 1847. Full Southern breakfast and a private bath come with each room. Set in a 1905 Craftsman home, the five-room **Greenwood Bed and Breakfast,** 205 North Park Dr., 336/274-6350, offers gourmet breakfasts and a pool. Younger kids discouraged, smoking forbidden.

## $150 and Up

The 121-room **O. Henry Hotel,** 624 Green Valley Rd., 336/854-2000, website: www.o.henry hotel.com, is a European-style boutique hotel, new but rich with old-fashioned luxuries. On-site is the acclaimed Green Valley Grill. The massive 247-room **Grandover Resort,** 1000 Club Rd., 800/472-6301 or 336/294-1800, website: www.grandover.com, features extensive grounds, including more than 1,500 acres of pine and hardwoods, and stonework imported from Italy and Portugal. A golf course is next door.

## FOOD

Stamey's Barbecue, 2618 Lawndale Dr., 336/299-9888, serves 'Que every day but Sunday. Popular for both lunch and dinner. The **Spring Garden Brewing Company,** 714 Francis King St., 336/299-3649, features Bavarian-style, home-made lagers and better-than-average pub grub. **Paisley Pineapple,** 172 Battleground Ave., 336/333-9833, is set in a Coolidge-era building and features some fine beef, lamb, and fish dishes. If you're a-courtin', you just can't beat the Pineapple's ambience and Old Greensborough location.

Green Valley Grill, at the O. Henry Hotel, 336/854-2015, features early-20th-century ambience, with brick walls and tile mosaics. Dishes tend toward the refined; dinner runs just around $17 a plate. For Italian, try **Soprano's,** 638 W. Academy St., 336/498-4137, or **La Spiedo di Noble's,** 1720 Battleground Ave., 336/333-9833,

which focuses on Northern Italian cuisine, as well as meats and wood-burning oven-cooked pizzas, breads, and other delights. But if you're really looking for high-end eats in Greensboro, you probably can't do better than **Trilogy,** 3722-G Battleground Ave., 336/282-2900, a bistro that won awards from *Wine Spectator* a few years back. The **Barn Dinner Theatre,** 120 Stagecoach Trail, 336/292-2211, offers a show with your meal.

## ENTERTAINMENT

### Coffeehouses

The **Tate Street Coffee House,** 334 S. Tate St., 336/275-2754, offers caffeine and a sophisticated, eclectic air. Usually you'll find Greek music on Tuesday nights, Parisian jazz on Sundays. **Bailey's Coffee & News,** 23 S. Fayetteville St., AB. Pick and Grin open mike, 7 P.M. Tuesday. 625-8451. The coffeehouse inside of **Borders,** 3605 High Point Rd., 336/218-0662, offers live acts some evenings, and open mike nights. **The Master's Loft,** 1724 Battleground Ave., 336/272-0123, is a small coffeehouse set inside a Christian bookstore and featuring live acts on the weekends that vary from Alternative Rock to Urban Gospel and traditional male Southern Gospel quartets. Open mike night on Mondays.

### Nightlife

If there's strength in diversity, then **Montego Bay,** 4536 W. Market St., 336/294-4470, is positively bionic: Tuesdays it offers salsa and merengue lessons; Mondays and Saturdays bring beach music and shag dancing (lessons on Monday); Fridays mean reggae; Sundays is a DJed Latin music party. These things can change; call ahead so you know whether to wear your tie-dye or Weejuns. The bar upstairs at the **Paisley Pineapple,** 345 S. Elm St., 336/279-8488, is a dim, low-key spot where you can sit on the couch, sip something, and talk to your friends without having to shout. The **Spring Garden Brewing Company,** 714 Francis King St., 336/299-3649, features Bavarian-style lagers and pub grub. **Trilogy,** 3722-G Battleground Ave., 336/282-

WINSTON-SALEM

2900, features live jazz and a long wine list. **The Blind Tiger,** 2115 Walker Ave., 336/272-9888, offers cool blues and rock. Warmhearted **Artistika Cafe,** 523 South Elm St., 336/271-2686, provides poetry readings, open-mike nights, and live music.

**The Barn Dance,** 6341 Philippi Rd. off N.C. 62, southeast of Greensboro in nearby Julian, 336/685-9200, offers a family-friendly, alcohol- and tobacco-free old-time country hootenanny on Saturdays, with music provided by the Barnyard Bandits and an occasional guest act. At publication the Barn was experimenting with a Friday night bluegrass gospel night. Adults $7, $5 for children 11 and under.

### Theater

The oldest dinner theater in the entire United States, the Broadway-style **Barn Dinner Theatre,** 120 Stagecoach Trail, 336/292-2211, is an excellent place to spend an evening, especially if you've always thought that a buffet line and a chorus line were a natural combination. Call or see www.barndinner.com, for information on current shows, which run Wednesday–Sunday nights year-round. The **Broach Theatre,** 520 South Elm St., 336/378-9300, was built in 1927 as a Salvation Army. Now it's an excellent location for a dinner-and-theater sort of evening downtown. Half the year—September through June—the Broach runs Children's Theatre, while adult shows (not *that* kind) run February through July and September through December. The **Carolina Theatre,** 310 South Greene St., 336/333-2600, website: www.carolinatheatre.com, also opened in 1927 (as a vaudeville theater); today it's one of Greensboro's top venues. Call or visit the website to see who and what's here when you're in town. The **Greensboro Ballet,** 336/333-7480, website: www.greensboroballet.com, features a variety of dance, from classics to contemporary shows, with a number of productions geared at children as well.

### Shopping

**Replacements Limited,** 1089 Knox Rd., 336/697-3000, website: www.replacements.com, offers hope to anyone who has lost a piece of china or silverware from a discontinued pattern. This 13,000-square-foot showroom contains old and new china, crystal, flatware, and collectibles. More than 6 million items to choose from. This place is so large that tours are actually given every 30 minutes from 8:30 A.M.–8 P.M., seven days a week. Admission is free.

## SPORTS AND RECREATION

The South Atlantic League **Greensboro Bats** battle such foes as the Asheville Tourists and the Hickory Crawdads at War Memorial Stadium, 510 Yanceyville St., 336/333-2287, website: www.greensborobats.com. The stadium was built in 1926, which some (especially the Bats' promoters) claim make it the oldest stadium in American Minor League baseball. It was originally designed for football, and consequently is a little asymmetrical—most of the seating is down the left-field line. The **Greensboro Generals** play in the minor league East Coast Hockey League, against such teams as the Greenville Grrrowl and the Charleston Stingrays. Games are played at the 36,000-square-foot **Ice Chalet of Greensboro,** 6119 Landmark Center Blvd. off W. Wendover Avenue, 336/852-1515, website: www.icechalet.gso.com. Soccer moms and dads and children of same will be pleased to find the **Carolina Dynamo** A-League soccer team plays over at Bryan Park Stadium off Rudd Station Road, 336/316-1266, website: www.carolina dynamo.com.

## NORTH OF GREENSBORO
### Reidsville

The **Chinqua-Penn Plantation,** 2138 Wentworth St., 800/948-0947 or 336/349-4576, website: www.chinquapenn.com, is an elaborate 27-room 1925 English-style home overflowing with decorative artwork. It's set on 22 acres of landscaped gardens. Stays in the area include the friendly and funky **Fairview Farm Bed and Breakfast,** about five miles from Reidsville at 1891 Harrison Crossroads Rd., 336/349-6910, $90 a night. In addition to the full breakfasts, you're welcome to poke around the 135-acre

Elephant sculptures guard the entrance to the North Carolina Zoological Park.

property, exploring the antique autos on site, as well as the antique music machines in the home.

## SOUTH OF GREENSBORO
### Asheboro
Most people know about the San Diego Zoo and the National Zoo in Washington, D.C., but not many know that the nation's third-largest zoo lies just six miles south of the city of Asheboro.

Let me rephrase that: obviously *somebody* knows. Some 1.4 million visitors a year push through the turnstiles at the state-run **North Carolina Zoological Park,** 159 Zoo Parkway, 800/488-0444, website: www.nczoo.org. While older, "cage" zoos have been converting to the more aesthetically pleasing and humane natural-habitat style of exhibit, the North Carolina Zoo lays claim to being the first American zoo designed, from the get-go, as a natural-habitat zoo.

This is a big zoo. The African Plains exhibit alone covers 37 acres; the North American Prairie exhibit provides bison and elk 11 acres of roaming room; even the Sonora Desert exhibit—indoors, for obvious reasons—is big enough for the road-runner to scoot around in, dodging rattlers and

gila monsters along the way. Most zoos this large are the sort you drive through, but while there are trams to take you between many of the exhibits, you can't see much from the trams themselves. You'll walk a lot here; wear good shoes, and if it's warm, plan on drinking a lot of water.

In 1980, Ham, the world's first space chimp, who flew aboard a Mercury rocket in 1961, was transferred to this zoo from the National Zoo in Washington, D.C., and lived here until dying in early 1983 (sadly, just before the gala opening night for *The Right Stuff*).

At the time of printing, the zoo uses only 500 of its 1,400 acres as home to its native North American and African animals; officials have another 900 acres to work with here, and they plan to more than double the zoo's size within a few years, making room for animals from other continents.

In Asheboro you'll also find the **American Classic Motorcycle Museum,** 1170 U.S. 64 W., 336/629-9564, with more than 30 antique bikes on site, dating back to 1936. Out on Pisgah Covered Bridge Road, you'll find the 1910 **Pisgah Covered Bridge,** 800/626-2672 or 336/626-0364, one of only two remaining covered bridges in North Carolina. The surrounding park makes a nice spot for a picnic, and there are hiking trails available.

If you'd like to spend the night here after your day at the zoo, a safe bet is **Best Western–Asheboro,** 242 Lakecrest Rd. off U.S. 64, 800/526-3766 or 336/626-3680, where you'll find 40 clean rooms, a complete breakfast, and a pool. Rooms start at around $60 a night.

Try one of these three barbecue places: **Blue Mist Barbecue Restaurant,** 3409 U.S. 64 E., 336/625-3980; **Henry James Bar B Que,** 2004 S. Fayetteville St., 336/625-1649; or **Hops Bar B Q,** 240 Sunset Ave., 336/629-6240. For non-barbecue but still sufficiently Southern, try **Fran's Chicken Hut,** 1735 S. Fayetteville St., 336/629-1270. Or pick up something not particularly Southern at all at **Olde Towne Deli & Bistro,** 239 White Oak St., 336/625-1973.

## Seagrove

Centered today at the intersection of N.C. 220 and N.C. 705, the pottery village of Seagrove was begun sometime in the late 1700s. Folks around here had a lot of clay at their disposal, and so they turned to making pottery; in the early days, the need was initially purely practical—clay was plentiful, and the money for purchasing store-bought pots, jars, and jugs was not. Around the turn of the century, as glass became more common and moonshining became less popular, many potters packed up their wheels and gave up the art. Others began making their pots more than functional; they added faces, brazen colors, anything to make someone want to buy the jar.

And people wanted to buy them; the wealthy Northerners staying down in Pinehurst found the pottery charming, and were willing to pay good money for it. In 1920, Jacques and Juliana Busbee decided to open up Jugtown Pottery as a way of preserving this great folk art. They brought in skilled potter Ben Owen to re-create traditional Seagrove pottery styles and glazes. Four years later, North State Pottery opened, run by Jonie and Walter Owen.

Today, more than 90 potteries operate in the area. Just take N.C. 220 north from Pinehurst or south from Greensboro to the Seagrove exit (Exit 45), and soon you'll be in downtown Sea-

grove, where you can walk to a number of worthwhile shops. But you'll need to drive to get to most of the original shops, including the one run by original pottery family descendants: **Ben Owen Pottery,** 7.5 miles south of Seagrove at 2199 S. N.C. 705, 910/464-2261. It's open Tuesday–Saturday 10 A.M.–5 P.M. but closed in January. **Jugtown Pottery,** open since 1920, is out at 330 Jugtown Rd., 910/464-3266; take N.C. 705 south to Westmoore and follow the signs to Jugtown Pottery. Open Tuesday–Saturday 8:30 A.M.–5 P.M. Sid Luck, a fifth-generation Seagrove potter, owns **Luck's Ware,** 1606 Adams Rd., 336/879-3261. To get there, drive four miles south on N.C. 705 S. to Adams Road and turn right. The pottery is on the right, three miles ahead; follow the signs. Luck's is open Monday–Saturday 9 A.M.–5 P.M.

In the village, the **North Carolina Pottery Center,** 250 East Ave., at the junction of U.S. 220 and State Road 705, 336/873-8430, Tuesday–Saturday 10 A.M.–4 P.M., offers maps to get you around to the various potteries, and here inside the center you can see examples from most of the potteries before you drive all across the county to visit the shop.

## Uwharrie National Forest

Entered at 789 N.C. 24/27 E. in Troy, 910/576-6391, website: www.cs.unca.edu/nfsnc, the Uwharrie is nearly 47,000 acres large and laced by the Pee Dee, Uwharrie, and Yadkin Rivers. The pristine forest is popular with hikers, equestrians, mountain bikers, and camping. Park admission is free, but there's a small fee for camping. The Uwharrie Trail here covers 20.5 miles, crossing several ridges (and a few roads).

# HIGH POINT

The third and smallest "corner" of the Triad, High Point was the childhood home of both jazz great John Coltrane and baseball great Luke Appling. The town of 70,000 gets its name from its elevation. When the surveyors for the North Carolina Railroad came through here in the 1800s, they marked the area around here as being

## HIGH POINT'S JOHN COLTRANE: JAZZ MUSIC'S PATRON SAINT

John Coltrane was born in 1927 in Hamlet, but his family moved to High Point when he was still an infant, and he was raised there. His grandfather, William Blair, served as presiding elder in the A.M.E. Zion Church, and his father worked as a tailor and played music at night. By the time young John was 12, however, his father and grandparents were dead; that same year, he joined a local band and began playing clarinet and E-flat alto horn. His mother moved north at the start of World War II, and he joined her in Philadelphia in 1943, after graduating high school.

By the time he got to Philadelphia, Coltrane was playing alto sax, but eventually he switched to tenor sax and, later in his career, to soprano. He recorded his first side with a quartet while in the Navy, and went on to play with Cheraw, S.C.–born Dizzy Gillespie, and later with trumpeter Miles Davis, who fired Coltrane in 1956 because of his heroin addiction, hired him back, and fired him again in 1957.

In 1957, Coltrane experienced what he later described as "a spiritual awakening." He wrote later, "I do perceive and have been duly re-informed of His OMNIPOTENCE."

Though he suffered some setbacks, Coltrane successfully kicked heroin and signed as a solo recording artist for the first time. His music, always creative, became more radical— "anti-jazz," *Down Beat* called it. Now traveling with the Thelonious Monk Quartet, Coltrane experimented with sounding several notes simultaneously. He recorded with Miles Davis on the landmark *Kind of Blue*, and in 1961 scored a pop hit record with

his version of "My Favorite Things," which became his signature song. This was Coltrane's most prolific period; he wrote most of his own material, and every year brought several recordings. Perhaps 1965 was his watershed year; he finally reached a happy medium between his experimental leanings and the traditional style with his deeply spiritual album, *A Love Supreme,* which earned two Grammy nominations. The music was divided into four parts titled "Acknowledgment," "Resolution," "Pursuance," "Psalm." It was his best-selling record of all time.

Coltrane died unexpectedly of liver cancer in July 1967, but he has lived on for jazz lovers through the gradual release of his previously recorded work—for which he posthumously has, thus far, earned several Grammy nominations and one Grammy.

But perhaps John Coltrane's greatest impact has been on another level: Coltrane's music has been cited by many listeners for its mystical power—for its ability to convey spiritual truths through sound. The African-Orthodox Church, in fact, sees his music as a conduit to the Divine, a sort of aural equivalent to the traditional painted icon. The church has formally recognized Coltrane as a saint.

Consequently, Coltrane's image is itself the subject of several such painted icons found clear across the country from High Point, in San Francisco, where the congregation of **Saint John Will-I-Am Coltrane African Orthodox Church** worships each Sunday at noon, using the Tar Heel saxophonist's music as a sonic liturgy.

the "high point" between Goldsboro and Charlotte—though its elevation is just 980 feet.

After the original Native American inhabitants died out and/or moved on, Quaker farmers began settling this area in the 1750s, but what's now High Point remained scattered farms until 1853, when the town was laid out just a year before the completion of the 130-mile plank road between Winston-Salem and Fayetteville, which passed through here. This was the state's most important road in those days,

since it connected Winston-Salem (and thus inland North Carolina) with Fayetteville, and thus with the Cape Fear River, Wilmington, and the New England and European markets. The town incorporated in 1859.

The town started out as a trading center for local farm communities, but by 1888, furniture makers industrialized the town by building furniture factories to take advantage of the abundance of local hardwoods. Former dirt farmers began pouring in from the hills and mountains to work in the factories, and the city's population rocketed upwards by 900 percent in the following decades. By the late 1930s, the city boasted of 160 manufacturing plants, including 30 furniture factories and 22 hosiery mills. These factories, incidentally, were nearly all white-only operations. For the most point, blacks were allowed to work in the tobacco plants only.

Today, though the local hardwoods have given out, High Point makes its living on its reputation for great craftsmanship in furniture-making. Oddly, the first chairs, tables, and highboys made hereabouts in the 1880s were crude and poorly built; at that time, High Point furniture makers succeeded simply because of the sheer demand for durable goods during the years of the Industrial Revolution, when many Southerners were beginning to prosper again (or for the first time) and many formerly subsistence farmers began moving to the cities and purchasing their first store-bought or catalogue-bought furniture. By the time High Point's hickories and other hardwoods were depleted, the hard-won skills of local craftspeople, and the efficiency of the factory managers, had increased so that this region was developing a reputation for quality work, and that helped sustain and strengthen High Point's position in the furniture marketplace. Today, North Carolina is known worldwide for its manufacture of top-quality home furnishings, and the capital of this manufacturing is still High Point, whose publicists have dubbed it "The Home Furnishings Capital of the World."

Capital or no, High Point has culture too. Each year, the North Carolina Shakespeare Festival presents top-drawer productions of several of the Bard's works, in a long season running from August through November. In both April and October you'll find all the lodgings packed around here; even if you find a room, you'll pay more for it than the rest of the year. Why? In both of these months, High Point is home to the weeklong Home Furnishings Markets, which draw retailers and journalists from around the country. Contact High Point's Chamber of Commerce/Convention Visitors Bureau, 1101 Main St., 336/889-8151, for information on these events.

the world's largest chest of drawers, High Point

## Sights

Not surprisingly, High Point's attractions mostly center around furniture-making. In fact, a museum dedicated to chronicling the history of furniture manufacturing, **Furniture Discovery Center,** 101 W. Green St., at the corner of Main Street and Green Drive, 336/887-3876, is set in an old factory and designed to give visitors a hands-on experience that leads to a profound understanding of the production flow of a furniture factory. In the first exhibit area, you'll see the creation of a Queen Anne highboy, from its genesis as lumber through its shaping, carving, and joining. Other exhibits spotlight upholstering and other elements of fine furniture. It's more interesting than it may sound; certainly, an understanding of the furniture-making process is integral to understanding the lives of so many foothill residents, both today and over the past hundred and fifty years. And it's also true that, after visiting the Furniture Discovery Center, you'll never sit on your couch ignorantly again. Adults $5, $4 for children 6–15 and seniors. Open Tuesday–

Saturday 10 A.M.–5 P.M., and Sunday 1–5 P.M. Between April and October, it's open Mondays as well. Other worthwhile High Point sights include **High Point Museum and Historical Park,** 1859 E. Lexington Ave., 336/885-1859, website: www.highpointmuseum.org, featuring historic old buildings from the 18th century and costumed living historians, who perform traditional crafts every other weekend. Exhibits inside the museum honor native son John Coltrane and help explain the important links between the manufacture of furniture and other manufacturing processes. Doll lovers will want to visit **Angela Peterson Doll and Miniature Museum,** 101 W. Green Dr., 336/885-3655, where some 1,700 dolls, antique and otherwise, await your visit. If you've come here to buy furniture, try the **Atrium Furniture Mall,** 430 S. Main St., 336/882-5599, website: www.atriumfurniture.com, where you'll find more than 25 stores selling home furnishings and accessories.

Perhaps the most intriguing sight in all High Point is the **World's Largest Chest of Drawers,** 508 Hamilton St., 800/720-5255 or 336/884-5255. It was built in the 1920s, but was then only 20 feet high. Now, after its mid-'90s renovation, it's 40 feet high. In the old days, the bureau served as the local Bureau of Information, later renamed the Chamber of Commerce. Eventually the Chamber moved out, presumably because they were tired of prank callers asking if their drawers were open.

In the 1990s the structure was decaying; the town's Jaycees stepped forward and declared proudly that no matter how shabby its drawers looked, nobody could beat High Point's chest; they subsequently raised the $60,000 needed for an augmentation. But the World's Largest Chest of Drawers, apparently, was not meant for an easy life. Last time I was through town, the Bureau—though still looking sharp—was empty and mothballed, with a For Sale sign in front.

If all of this wood-working piques your desire to observe lumber in its natural habitat, pay a visit to the **Piedmont Environmental Center,** 1220 Penny Rd., 336/883-8531, website: www.piedmontenvironmental.com, featuring hiking trails, a huge walk-on map of the state, and

WINSTON-SALEM

Lexington's Bar-B-Q Center

© ERIKA HOWSARE

other interactive features and nature programs. No charge for admission.

## Accommodations

The **Super 8 Motel,** 400 S. Main St., 336/882-4103, offers 44 rooms for under $70 each. Down the street, just south of the center of town, the **Atrium Inn,** 425 S. Main St., 336/884-8838, isn't overly fancy, but it's fancier than Super 8, and it's hard-by a good lunch spot (see below); rooms go for under $80 a night. The 1918 **J.H. Adams Inn,** 1108 N. Main St., 888/256-1289 or 336/882-3267, website: www.jhadamsinn.com is a 30-room inn set inside the former mansion of hosiery magnate J.H. Adams. Rooms start around $120, breakfast included.

## Food

**Atrium Cafe and Catering,** 336/889-9934, 430 S. Main St., serves lunches for under $10. Specialties include the healthy Oriental tuna plate, on lettuce with baby corn, water chestnuts, bamboo shoots, carrots, onions, and mustard soy vinaigrette ($5.85), the Atrium club sandwich, ($6.05), and a roast pork loin sandwich—pork loin marinated in garlic, cinnamon, cloves, cumin, allspice, oregano and beer, roasted, then sliced and topped with a relish or Dijon mustard, chopped tomatoes, onions, cilantro, and garlic, and served on a toasted French roll ($6.05).

The High Point version of the high-end chain **Liberty Steakhouse & Brewery,** 914 Mall Loop Rd., 336/882-4677, serves up some good beers, steaks, and pizza. Dinners run from the mid-teens through $25 and up. Dinner served until 10 P.M. most nights, until 11 P.M. on Friday and Saturday. A late-night menu is served until 1 A.M.

# LEXINGTON

If High Point is the Home Furnishings Capital of the World, then surely Lexington is the Barbecue Capital of the World—at least if we're talking about hickory-smoked, hand-pulled pork shoulders, which Lexingtonians almost always are. If you've come here for 'Que—and most people who visit Lexington have—it's hard to go wrong, though some would argue that there are some places that serve BBQ more correctly than others. Try Sonny Conrad's **Bar-B-Q Center,** 900 S. Main St., 336/248-4633; **Jimmy's Barbecue,** 1703 Cotton Grove Rd., 336/357-2311; **Lexington Barbecue,** on Business Loop I-85, 336/249-9814; or **Speedy's Barbecue of Lexington,** 1317 Winston Rd., 336/248-2410, and you'll be nearly as right as you can get.

If you need a walk afterwards, stop into **Historic Uptown Lexington,** down on First Avenue, 336/249-0383. You may want to start out at the **Lexington CVB,** 305 N. Main St., 336/236-4218, website: www.visitlexingtonnc.org, to pick up a map of the five-block historic area.

# Asheville and the Northern Mountains

The economic and cultural center of western North Carolina, Asheville never served as a fort or an outpost as Knoxville, its East Tennessee counterpart, did. No, Asheville has by and large made its living off the kindness of strangers. Tourists, to be exact. In fact, so time-honored is Asheville's tradition of tourism that its Minor League baseball team carries the name the Asheville Tourists. The team's bear mascot, Ted E. Tourist, wields a bat in one paw, a suitcase in the other.

Many of the names associated with Asheville—George Vanderbilt, Zelda and F. Scott Fitzgerald—came here only seasonally, or as part of a mountain "cure." Even the most famous Asheville-born novelist, Thomas Wolfe, wrote his best-known novel about his childhood growing up in the home his mother ran for visiting out-of-towners.

## HISTORY

Named for early North Carolina governor Samuel Ashe, Asheville serves as the seat of Buncombe County, one of the few counties in America whose names have passed into the language. In the early 19th century, when pressed to state his point after a rambling, inconclusive speech on a topic only of interest to a few folks back home, Felix Buncombe, a Revolutionary War veteran and early congressman from the area, replied, "I was just talking for Buncombe." Thereafter, whenever a congressman's mouth ran ahead of his thoughts, he might well be asked if he, too, was "talking for Buncombe." By the start of the

Asheville

ASHEVILLE

## ASHEVILLE AND THE NORTHERN MOUNTAINS

North Wilkesboro
Wilkesboro
16
40
16
150
Gastonia
321
321
421
18
64
Lake Hickory
Hickory
Conover
321
27
Lincolnton
150
Kings Mountain
85
18
321
Boone
Blowing Rock
Lenoir
18
64
Lake Rhodhiss
18
Shelby
18
74
Valley Crucis
Beech Mountain
194
Grandfather Mountain
Pisgah National Forest
Morganton
226
NORTH CAROLINA
221
Sugar Mountain
LINVILLE CAVERNS
Lake James
64
Marion
19E
221
Forest City
26
MOUNTAINS
Pisgah National Forest
70
9
64
744
SOUTH
19W
BLUE RIDGE PARKWAY
Mt. Mitchell State Park
9
64
19
23
ZEBULON VANCE BIRTHPLACE
40
BLUE RIDGE
BILTMORE ESTATE
26
Hendersonville
Flat Rock
25
CAROLINA
Mars Hill
25
151
ASHEVILLE
CRADLE OF FORESTRY IN AMERICA
178
TENNESSEE
French Broad River
276
Brevard
64
Hot Springs
25
Pisgah National Forest
276
40

© AVALON TRAVEL PUBLISHING, INC.

## ASHEVILLE HIGHLIGHTS

Biltmore House and Gardens
Biltmore Village
Pack Place: Education, Arts and Science
    Center
Thomas Wolfe Memorial

20th century, the phrase had transmogrified into "talking bunk," and was found in the public statements of Henry Ford and others.

But while the county's name became a household word, Buncombe County's seat, Asheville, remained just a stop on the road from Greeneville, Tenn., to Greenville, S.C.—a place where drovers and their herds of cattle, hogs, or turkeys spent the night before moving on. In 1792, the Buncombe County courthouse was built at the present-day location of Pack Square, and the little country town began to grow around it. In 1797, David Crockett—born over the mountains in Limestone, Tennessee—was married in Asheville to a local woman. Yet long after Crockett lay famous and dead at the Alamo, Asheville lay low, attracting wealthy Charleston and Savannah planters avoiding the malaria-plagued summers back home and enjoying its crisp air and "curative" sulphur springs. Zebulon Vance, North Carolina's beloved Civil War and post-Reconstruction governor and longtime senator, was born and raised in the area, but the War itself largely passed Asheville by. A Confederate armory here manufactured Enfield-type rifles early in the war, but the plant was moved to Columbia, S.C., in 1863. The Battle of Asheville on April 6, 1865, was a minor and fleeting Confederate victory against Union raiders from Tennessee, only a few days before the end of the war.

The coming of the railroad in 1880 marked the period of Asheville's greatest growth, and within 20 years two men came to town who would put Asheville on the map. In 1889, George Vanderbilt rolled into Asheville. Grandson of the steamboat and railroad baron Cornelius Vanderbilt, he proceeded to build the largest pri-

vately owned house in the world—his country house, mind you—which he called Biltmore. About the same time, E.W. Grove, who had made his money in the patent medicine business, moved in from St. Louis; in 1913 he completed construction on the Grove Park Inn, which was and is the finest hotel in the region.

Oddly, a good bit of Asheville's growing prosperity came from others' misfortune. Prominent doctors in the East began recommending Asheville to patients suffering from tuberculosis or any ailment that required fresh air and rest. The new railroad made it easy to get to Asheville, and the health-seekers poured in. The city responded with the construction of hotels, sanitariums, and more than a hundred boardinghouses. One of the latter establishments was run by Julia Wolfe, whose son Thomas was to scandalize the town with his semi-autobiographical novel, *Look Homeward, Angel.*

Many people recovered and decided to stay on. Some call the 1920s Asheville's "Golden Era," and not without reason. Relics from this time include the art deco City Hall, L.B. Jackson's

church in Asheville

Gothic skyscraper, and Edwin Wiley Grove's Arcade. What is now the University of North Carolina at Asheville arrived in 1927.

But the town suffered terribly from the 1929 stock market crash. In a time when everybody was tightening up their purse strings, Asheville—a town built on discretionary spending—was hit hard. Most of the regular vacationers were too broke to visit. And around the same time, advances in medical science eliminated the need for people to come to the mountains to cure tuberculosis.

Predictably, land prices tumbled. Many who had speculated on North Carolina real estate lost all that they had. The city itself fell so deeply that it would take some 40 years to pay off its debts.

Since that low point, however, the city has come back.

In the 1970s, 1980s, and 1990s, fueled partly by students and residual alumni at UNC Asheville, downtown developed into a regional center for the "alternative" subculture. Now, like Athens, GA, Austin, TX, Berkeley, CA, and most other college towns in America, downtown Asheville is known for its nightclubs, galleries, espresso bars, and acupuncturists. For those visiting the region from larger cities, this will either seem comfortingly familiar or too much like home. But for many Easterner alt.types, Asheville's collision of Bohemia and Appalachia strikes a perfect midway point between home and Haight Street.

In addition to those who school here and stick, Asheville, with a population around 62,000, attracts a lot of up-on-Friday/down-on-Sunday tourists. The main draw is by far the Biltmore Estate: though George Vanderbilt is no longer with us, his house still pulls in the crowds. The Blue

*Downtown Asheville is known for its nightclubs, galleries, espresso bars, and acupuncturists. For many Easterner alt.types, Asheville's collision of Bohemia and Appalachia strikes a perfect midway point between home and Haight Street.*

Ridge Parkway also funnels nature lovers of all kinds into the city, and having Great Smoky Mountains National Park just 40 miles away doesn't hurt, either.

However, the high level of tourism—and the city's traditional catering to the out-of-towners who sustain the local economy—doesn't set well with everyone. In May 2001, beating drums and waving signs, scores of Ashevilleans, many of whom had weeks earlier paraded peacefully in a Pro-Hemp rally, marched from Aston Park to the Vance Memorial (without the proper permits) to protest the city's community calendar.

The "Take Back the Streets" marchers claimed that festivals and other events put on by the city unfairly catered to out-of-town tourists. Police and sheriff's deputies intervened and made arrests. Word spread among the deputies that one of the protesters had fired a pistol, and indeed, one protester was shot in the foot, apparently by a pistol he was carrying in a backpack. The remaining protesters marched on the jail until turned back by the Buncombe County sheriff brandishing a riot gun.

Protest marches and gunplay aside, however, *most* Asheville residents are very glad to have visitors, and the town is highly equipped to guide visitors to the city and the region. The Chamber of Commerce Convention and Visitors' Bureau is bursting with brochures, maps, and courteous people. Several signs direct motorists to the bureau, which is located off I-240 at 151 Haywood St. It's open weekdays 8:30 A.M.–5:30 P.M. and weekends 9 A.M.–5 P.M. Open late during heavily touristed months. Call 828/258-3916 for information.

# Asheville and Vicinity

## SIGHTS

### Biltmore House and Gardens

This monument to unbridled spending often affects visitors in one of two ways. Either they lust after the money and power that could build such an edifice, or they decry a system in which one person can accumulate—much less *inherit*—such a fantastic pile of money. Sometimes visitors do both: first lust, then decry.

Others take the historical angle. The Biltmore Estate is, in one sense, a sort of shrine to the industrial-powered American economic explosion in the 19th century. Biltmore sprang from the millions made by Cornelius Vanderbilt in steamboating and railroads, rushing 49ers to the gold fields of California, hauling goods in from the ships of New York City, and pulling natural resources out of the inland areas for shipment overseas. During the post-Civil War Gilded Age, Cornelius' son William greatly expanded the family empire, as did William's older sons, but William's youngest son, George, apparently saw no reason to be an industrial baron when he could be a baron of the more traditional sort here. His fortune assured, he spent his time traveling the world with an eye toward finding the place to create his own kingdom. His travels brought him to the Blue Ridge, and he decided that it would be nice to have a cozy little fiefdom in the mountains. At 26, the same age at which Brian Wilson created *Pet Sounds,* George Vanderbilt began his own masterpiece. Like Brian, George had solid financial backing.

Completed in 1895, the house took five years and the efforts of a thousand workers to build. It has more than 255 rooms. The original estate totaled 130,000 acres, though now it's been whittled down to a mere 8,000, which is cramped, but still enough to provide the house a little privacy. The distance from the front door of the mansion to the street is three miles, which could make getting the morning paper a bit hellacious in cold weather. No wonder these people needed servants.

And these are not just any 8,000 acres: remember 1992's *Last of the Mohicans?* That was filmed here. Remember the scene in *Forrest Gump* where Forrest runs cross-country through the cornfields of the American Midwest? That was filmed here, too. This is a large, diverse place. The grounds were laid out by Frederick Law Olmstead, who, in a less ambitious day, also designed New York's Central Park.

Biltmore is open every day except Thanksgiving and Christmas. The Reception and Ticket Center is open daily 9 A.M.–5 P.M. in January–March, and daily 8:30 A.M.–5 P.M. April–December. Look for online specials at www.biltmore.com, or expect to pay around $31 for one-day adult admission at the Reception and Ticket Center.

If you have but one day to spend at Biltmore, arrive early and well-rested. Spend the extra money and rent one of the little headsets with the recorded audio tour—you've got to part with a good bit of cash to get in, so you might as well know what you're looking at. You'll need around an hour and a half to take in the main floor, second floor, third floor, and downstairs.

Most find the Biltmore experience to be a bit of a cross between touring the Louvre and watching *Citizen Kane* in 3D. There are also "Behind the Scenes" tours for an extra charge.

After leaving the house, check out the mountain view from the South Terrace. Then walk down to the garden and explore the Azalea Garden, Spring Garden, Walled Garden, and the Conservatory, where you'll find **A Gardener's Place,** featuring estate-grown plants, garden accessories, books, and gifts, as well as the seasonally operated **Conservatory Café.**

Over by the stables you'll find **The Stable Shops,** which include a bookshop, Christmas store, candy store, bakery, and ice cream shop.

You'll need to drive to get to the 96,500-square-foot dairy converted into a winery, but the chance to go wine-tasting in the former Confederacy should never be lightly passed by. The Biltmore Winery is, in fact, the most visited winery in all

ASHEVILLE AND VICINITY

© AVALON TRAVEL PUBLISHING, INC.

**Wall Street**

the United States. The wine list is extensive (including nonalcoholic sparkling drinks), as is that of the Wine Shop. **The Bistro,** located here, is open daily 11 A.M.–9 P.M., and features estate-raised beef, lamb, and trout, pizza, pastas, desserts, and Biltmore wines. Children's menu available.

The **Deerpark Restaurant,** open for lunches most of the year, sits between Biltmore House and the winery and offers the chance to dine outside while enjoying a luncheon buffet and Biltmore Estate wines. Children 9 and under dine free when accompanied by a paying adult. Other on-grounds spots to eat include the **Stable Café,** open daily 11 A.M.–5 P.M., which serves lighter meals. For the most formal lunches on the estate, look to the **The Dining Room.** You'll need to make reservations to eat here, and you can do so at the Reception and Ticket Center, the Twelve-Month Pass Desk in the Stable Hallway, and the Winery Passholder Desk.

Other than looking and eating, there's lots more to do here, including hiking, rafting, carriage rides, horseback riding, and mountain biking.

Which is why you'll want to get there early. But if you don't or can't, then come after 3 P.M., and they'll validate your ticket for the next day.

Biltmore received some exciting news in the fall of 2000 when researchers from Appalachian State University, digging at a mound near Biltmore's entrance, found bone, pottery shards, weapons, and other evidence of a 6,000-year-old Connestee trading village. Here, apparently, tribes from the Midwest, southern Ohio, and the Gulf Coast met at the crossroads of two major trading routes and did business. The Connestee people (who predate the Pisgah people, who themselves predate the Cherokee) set up shop here and apparently exchanged mica for imported flint, copper, shells, and pottery.

The village site promises to be one of the most significant findings in this part of the country. At publication, research was only beginning, and it's expected to last at least 10 years.

## Biltmore Village

Beyond the gates of the Biltmore Estate, a village was constructed in 1898 to serve the needs of the Vanderbilts, their servants, and their guests. Twenty-four of the original buildings remain, including three designed by Richard Morris Hunt: All Souls Church, Biltmore Railway Station, and the Biltmore Estate Office. This is a charming

ASHEVILLE

GROVE PARK INN

BOTANICAL GARDENS OF ASHEVILLE ★

AMERICAN COURT MOTEL

BLACK WALNUT B&B ■
RIVERSIDE CEMETERY ■

★ THOMAS WOLFE MEMORIAL

BEAR CREEK RV PARK & CAMPGROUND ■

ASHEVILLE CIVIC CENTER ■

PACK PLACE ■

FOLK ART CENTER ★

CAFÉ ON THE SQUARE ■

DAYS INN PATTON AVE. ■

ASHEVILLE MALL ■

★ SMITH-MCDOWELL HOUSE MUSEUM

WESTERN NORTH CAROLINA NATURE CENTER

ENTRANCE TO BILTMORE ESTATE ■

★ BILTMORE VILLAGE

● BEAUFORT HOUSE INN

BILTMORE

★ BILTMORE HOUSE

ESTATE

★ NC ARBORETUM

**ASHEVILLE**

*Pisgah*

*National*

*Forest*

ASHEVILLE MUNICIPAL AIRPORT

PATTON AVE.

HAYWOOD RD.

MCDOWELL ST.

BROADWAY

MERRIMON AVE.

CHARLOTTE ST.

BILTMORE AVE.

Swannanoa

*French Broad*

HENDERSONVILLE RD.

SWEETEN CREEK RD.

BLUE RIDGE PKWY.

*River*

TUNNEL RD.

LONG SHOALS RD.

PARKWAY

BLUE RIDGE

*River*

251
70
25
19
23
63
26
191
19
23
74
112
40
74A
81
70
40
694
240
25A
25
280
191
26
25
280

0      1 mi
0      1 km

## RACE IN 1885: A NEW ENGLANDER'S VIEW

Massachussetts-born, New York–reared author Charles Dudley Warner, a pal of Samuel Clemens, visited Asheville in post-Reconstruction 1885, and described for readers of the *Atlantic Monthly* the racial politics he found there:

*The negro problem is commonly discussed philosophically and without heat, but there is always discovered, underneath, the determination that the negro shall never again get the legislative upper hand. And the gentleman from South Carolina who has an upland farm, and is heartily glad slavery is gone, and wants the negro educated, when it comes to ascendency in politics—such as the State once experienced—asks you what you would do yourself. This is not the place to enter upon the politico-social question, but the writer may note one impression gathered from much friendly and agreeable conversation. It is that the Southern whites misapprehend and make a scarecrow of "social equality." . . . Well, the negro has his political rights in the North, and there has come no change in the social conditions whatever. And there is no doubt that the social conditions would remain exactly as they are at the South if the negro enjoyed all the civil rights which the Constitution tries to give him.*

*The most sensible view of this whole question was taken by an intelligent colored man, whose brother was formerly a representative in Congress. "Social equality," he said in effect, "is a humbug. We do not expect it, we do not want it. It does not exist among the blacks themselves. We have our own social degrees, and choose our own associates. We simply want the ordinary civil rights, under which we can live and make our way in peace and amity. This is necessary to our self-respect, and if we have not self-respect, it is not to be supposed that the race can improve. I'll tell you what I mean. My wife is a modest, intelligent woman, of good manners, and she is always neat, and tastefully dressed. Now, if she goes to take the cars, she is not permitted to go into a clean car with decent people, but is ordered into one that is repellent, and is forced into company that any refined woman would shrink from. But along comes a flauntingly dressed woman, of known disreputable character, whom my wife would be disgraced to know, and she takes any place that money will buy. It is this sort of thing that hurts."*

place to eat lunch, walk around, and visit the many small, often-touristy shops that surround the historic buildings. The village is located off U.S. 25 E., west of the downtown area.

### Downtown Asheville Historic District

Approximately 170 buildings, some built as early as 1840, make up the largest collection of historic architecture in Asheville. Since the late 1980s, Asheville residents have made a concerted effort to bring the area back to its former glories—and they've largely succeeded. Centering

on Pack Square, the buildings include the Spanish baroque **Church of St. Lawrence,** 97 Haywood St.; the neo-Georgian **Battery Park Hotel,** at Battle Square, and the art deco **S&W Cafeteria,** at 56 Patton Ave.

### Pack Place

Located at 2 S. Pack Square, the **Education, Arts and Science Center** offers museums, galleries, shops, and live performances. The museums include the **Colburn Gem and Mineral Museum; The Health Adventure,** a health and biology museum; the **YMI Cultural Center,** featuring African-American and African exhibits and commissioned by George Vanderbilt in 1893, and **Asheville Art Museum.** The last museum's permanent collection focuses on 20th-century American art, including paintings, sculpture, prints, and handicrafts. Admission $3 to each attraction, or you can get into all the museums in Pack Place for $6.50 adults.

## Botanical Gardens–Asheville

Occupying 10 acres of the campus of the University of North Carolina at Asheville, 151 W.T. Weaver Blvd., 828/252-5190, these gardens contain twenty-six thousand plants native to Appalachia, a sculpture garden for the blind, and a log cabin. Located off U.S. 25 N. near Merrimon Avenue. No admission charged. Open all year.

## Folk Art Center

Located off the Blue Ridge Parkway at Milepost 382, this center, 828/298-7928, features craft demonstrations, exhibits, and the 100-plus-year-old Allanstand Craft Shop, featuring the work of the Southern Highland Craft Guild, who call the center their home, and whose presence guarantees the quality and authenticity of the handcrafted items sold there. No admission charge.

## Riverside Cemetery

As cemeteries go, tree-shrouded Riverside, 58 Birch St., 828/259-5800, is a pleasant place to visit. Locally born author William Sidney Porter, a.k.a. O. Henry, is here. So is Asheville-born Thomas Wolfe, proving that while you actually can go home again, it's not always a healthy thing when you do. Wolfe's famous homeward-looking angel isn't here at Riverside, incidentally. It's at another cemetery over in Hendersonville.

## Smith-McDowell House Museum

Located at 283 Victoria Rd., 828/253-9231, this 1848 brick house is home to a local history museum that illustrates in detail the texture of Victorian-era life in Asheville. The home features a double porch supported by short white columns, and originally faced the old Buncombe Turnpike. Small admission charged. Call for hours.

## Thomas Wolfe Memorial State Historic Site

For anyone who has read the painful story in *Look Homeward, Angel,* this house (52 Market St., 828/253-8304) is a required stop. Though he changed its name to "Dixieland," this was the real boardinghouse, run by his mother, that inspired him. A fire nearly brought the building down a couple of years ago, but at press, plans were well under way to refurbish and re-open the home, which is one of Asheville's top attractions. Just next door, in one of those What-the-$!#!-were-they-thinking? anomalies of modern life, the too-big, too-slick Radisson Hotel Asheville stands here spoiling the ambience like a storm trooper at a hoedown. It clearly belongs out next to an airport somewhere, but here it stands, dwarfing Thomas Wolfe's childhood home.

## The Western North Carolina Nature Center

Western North Carolina used to be the scene of various roadside "See the Bear" exhibits, in which unlucky bruins dwelt in filthy cages. Legislation now forbids such abuse of the state's largest animal, but here at the Nature Center, 75 Gashes Creek Rd., 828/298-5600, you can still see bears—in an environment more like their natural one. Occupying seven acres, the Nature Center is home to a selection of wild and domestic animals, including a bear, a cougar, a golden eagle, deer, skunks, snakes, foxes, and more. Kids will enjoy the small petting zoo. Small admission charged for entrance to the center.

# ENTERTAINMENT

## Nightlife

Downtown has most but not all of the nighttime action in Asheville. The **Asheville Civic Center,** 87 Haywood St., 828/259-5544, features the Thomas Wolfe Auditorium, one of Asheville's largest venues. Folks say that Elvis and Dylan both played here (though never together). The Asheville Symphony plays here throughout the year. Call 828/254-7046 for information.

The much more intimate **Grey Eagle Music**

**Hall,** 185 Clingman Ave., 828/232-5800, features a great mix of nationally and locally renowned artists; previous performers have included folk greats like Arlo Guthrie and Guy Clark, and such bluegrass legends as Del McCoury and Doc Watson. Opens every day but Sunday at 4 P.M., though shows rarely get under way before 9 P.M. To get there from Pack Square, take Patton Avenue west past the Federal Building. Follow the sign that says "To Clingman Ave."; continue across Clingman, make a right and then right again until you've looped around onto Clingman. Head down a half-mile and you're there. Call for information. Tuesdays are open-mike night.

Other local favorites include the family-friendly **Asheville Pizza & Brewing Company,** 675 Merrimon Ave., 828/254-1281; the versatile **Be Here Now,** 5 Biltmore Ave., 828/258-2071; the Irish-themed **Jack of the Wood Pub,** 95 Patton Ave., 828/252-5445; hip **New French Bar,** (a.k.a. NFB), 1 Battery Park Ave., 828/252-3685; and uptown jazzy **Tressa's,** 28 Broadway, 828/254-7072. For the college set, **Vincent's Ear,** 68 N. Lexington Ave., 828/259-9119, is a cut above most of the other student bars, and brings a lot of college-circuit acts to town. Gays and lesbians looking to drink and dance with same favor the well-established, "private" **O. Henry's,** 59 Haywood St., 828/254-1891. Small "membership fee" required.

### Events

Asheville is a town stuffed with people who are thankful they're there, and a town like that just loves to celebrate. Probably Asheville's top annual event, and by some accounts the largest street festival in the Southeast, **Bele Chere** contains road races, mountain music and dancing, cooking, craft demonstrations, games, and lots of other shenanigans, all on the (closed) streets of downtown Asheville in late July. The **North Carolina International Folk Festival/Folkmoot USA** in July offers international dance and music in the Thomas Wolfe Auditorium. August sees the **Mountain Dance and Folk Festival,** 828/258-6107, an event that's been held annually up here since the

1920s, and featuring old-time and bluegrass music and mountain dancing. For a complete listing of events, contact the Asheville Chamber of Commerce at 828/258-3858. Christmas brings a host of events, including **A Dickens Christmas in the Village,** 828/274-8788, and alcohol-free **First Night Asheville,** 828/259-5800, yet another excuse Asheville residents use to celebrate in the streets. Is this a great town, or what?

## ACCOMMODATIONS
### Under $50
**The Wolfe Den,** 22 Ravenscroft Dr., 828/285-0230, is Asheville's cleverly named hostel. Prices vary somewhat, but you'll still come in under $30 a night.

### $50–100
For something inexpensive but still dependable, **American Court Motel,** 85 Merrimon Ave., 828/253-4427, is a reasonably priced non-chain, just $69 in high season. Nothing fancy—it's a basic 1950s motor inn—but you won't get Tom's sort of friendly service at a Motel 6. **Days Inn Patton Avenue,** 120 Patton Ave., 828/254-9661, sits within walking distance of Pack Square Plaza and the Civic Center.

### $150 and Up
If Biltmore House is the place to see in Asheville, **Grove Park Inn and Spa,** 290 Macon Ave., 800/438-5800 or 828/252-2711, is definitely the place to stay. Built in 1913 by E.W. Grove, who served as his own architect and contractor, the inn reflects its mountain setting inside and out. The original portion of the inn was built of massive boulders; the fireplaces inside can easily burn 10-foot logs. F. Scott Fitzgerald used to stay here while visiting his wife/nemesis, Zelda, in a local mental hospital. With later additions, the inn now offers 510 rooms that run $135–425. Suites run into the $625 range.

Open seasonally for years, the Grove Park Inn is nowadays open year-round. In February 2001 the Inn's new 40,000-square-foot spa

ASHEVILLE

opened, providing all manner of luxuriating for those with the time and money. **Beaufort House Victorian Inn,** 61 Liberty St., 800/261-2221 or 828/254-9334, website: www.beaufort house.com, is a historic 1894 bed-and-breakfast with big bay windows and pleasant views of the mountains. Recently ranked number one of all western North Carolina inns. Rooms run $125–235. The **Black Walnut B&B,** 288 Montford Ave., 800/381-3878 or 828/254-3878, website: www.blackwalnut.com, is also more than 100 years old, and sits right in the historic district. You may recognize it from its role in the Sandra Bullock detox epic *28 Days.* Rooms run $95–200, which includes a full gourmet breakfast served by candlelight in the formal dining room.

Outside of town, the **Sourwood Inn,** 810 Elk Mountain Scenic Hwy., 828/255-0690, website: www.sourwoodinn.com, sets on 100 mountainous acres. The hotel has 12 rooms with wood-burning fireplaces, plus a cabin. Rates run $140–175, which includes breakfast.

## Camping

Thirteen miles south of town on State Road 191, the eight-acre **North Mills River** campground, 828/891-3016, is run by the National Forest Service, which means it's both basic and cheap. Sites run $5 a night. No showers or hookups. For more amenities, try **Bear Creek RV Park and Campground,** 81 S. Bear Creek Rd., 828/253-0798 $20–26 a night, with full hookups at most sites, 50 tents sites, and even cable TV hookups.

## FOOD

Asheville contains more good restaurants than you can shake a fat-pincher at; the ones listed here are only a sampling. For starters, **Café on the Square,** 1 Biltmore Ave., 828/251-5565, is in the running for the Most-In-the-Middle-of-It-All Award. Local folks have, in fact, named it "Best Downtown Eatery" repeatedly over the years. It offers pastas, grilled meats, and seafood, with dinner entrées running $15–22. The **Laughing Seed Café,** 40 Wall St., 828/252-5445, is a less

expensive, vegetarian option on an agreeable side street, and it's just upstairs from the Jack of the Wood Pub.

If you've been up in the Smokies and are dying for some good, spicy food, **La Paz,** 10 Biltmore Plaza, 828/277-8779, offers fine Southwestern cooking (with meals around $7–16), margaritas, and patio seating, in season, in the Biltmore Village.

**Malaprop's Bookstore and Café,** 61 Haywood St., 828/254-6734 is something like the Arnold's Diner of the patchouli-and-piercings set. The often-crowded café just adds to the urban feel. Inexpensive sandwiches. Beneath Malaprop's, **Zambra,** 85 Walnut St., 828/232-1060, offers Spanish cuisine, a tapas menu, a large assortment of wines, and a quiet environment.

**Barley's Taproom and Pizzeria,** 42 Biltmore Ave., 828/255-0504, offers live music from Tuesday, Thursday, and Sunday, featuring everything from jazz to folk and even bluegrass. (The experience of eating spinach-and-feta pizza while listening to "Foggy Mountain Breakdown" is quintessentially Ashevillean, and not one to be missed.) The beer selection is tops, with more than 40 to choose from, and all the requisite pizzeria recreational garnishes—darts, pool tables—make an appearance.

The perennial favorite barbecue in these parts is undeniably **Little Pigs BBQ,** 1916 Hendersonville Rd., 828/277-7188, with other locations at 100 Merrimon Ave., 828/253-4633, and 384 McDowell St., 828/254-4253.

If you'd just like to pick something up and picnic or eat as you stroll, head over to Biltmore Avenue, where you'll find **The Asheville Wine Market,** 65 Biltmore Ave., 800/825-7175 or 828/253-0060, website: www.ashevillewine.com, continually voted the top wine shop in Asheville in newspaper reader polls. You'll find a strong selection of wines, cheeses, and all the other ingredients of a pleasant do-it-yourself gourmet meal, including Carolina smoked trout. Open Monday–Saturday 10 A.M.–6 P.M. Next door, **Laurey's** makes sandwiches, soups, and desserts, and will even lend you a picnic basket. Just across the street, the **Blue Moon Bakery** specializes in fine breads and soups, salads, and sandwiches. They also offer a Sunday brunch.

© MIKE SIGALAS

**Laughing Seed Café**

If coffee (and maybe a light breakfast) is all you want, **Beanstreets Coffee,** 3 Broadway, 828/255-8180, is generally considered to brew the best in town.

## SHOPPING

Just walk around Biltmore Village or downtown and you'll find plenty of places with unique crafts and fascinating items just a-beggin' to be purchased. **World Marketplace,** 10 College St., 828/254-8374-8374, website: www.worldmarketplace.org, is a neat, nonprofit shop that tries to funnel some of the disposable income floating around Asheville out to the third world, where it can do wondrous things. The volunteers working there are happy to tell you about the various third-world-made products for sale here. Of local interest is the **Appalachian Craft Center,** 10 N. Spruce Rd., 828/253-8499, where you can buy authentic handicrafts actually made here by local craftspersons. The Asheville location of **Mast General Store,** 15 Biltmore Ave., 828/232-1883, website: www.mastgeneralstore.com, is an authentic, nostalgic shop, with old-time candies and some

honest-to-goodness quality clothing and footwear, perfect for mountain living.

Finding Cherokee-made goods in town is tricky. Local merchants would love to carry them, but to purchase them you'll need to make the drive up to the Qualla Boundary Reservation.

## INFORMATION

**The Asheville Convention and Visitors Center,** 151 Haywood St., 800/257-1300 or 828/258-6111, will load you up with maps, brochures, and other information. Or try the **Asheville Gifts and Welcome Center,** 14 Battery Park. A good information website is www.goasheville.com.

The paper of record in Asheville is the *Citizen-Times,* website: www.citizen-times.com. *Mountain Xpress,* a free weekly, does a good job reporting on the local entertainment scene. You'll find it all over town, or go online at www.mountainx.com.

## BREVARD

Famous for white squirrels, waterfalls, and music, Brevard was incorporated in 1867 with just seven residents—all of whom held public office. Now some 5,400 people live here, and Brevard often shows up on various lists of Best Places to Live in the U.S. And this is some accomplishment, considering that on a subconscious level, at least, some folks must have a hard time feeling at ease in a town that serves as the county seat for (cue eerie music) *Transylvania County.* The name merely means "over (trans) the woods (sylvan)." Or at least that's what they want us to believe.

The squirrels, you'll see scuttling across the lawns and up the trees of the local parks. As for the waterfalls, a good starting point (there are, after all, more than 250 of them hereabouts) is eight miles north of Brevard on U.S. 276: the 85-foot-high **Looking Glass Falls.** Further up U.S. 276 you'll find the very popular **Sliding Rock,** a 60-foot-long smooth rock over which pours a bone-chilling cascade sure to cool you down on the hottest of summer days. The slide is open from Memorial Day to Labor Day, and you'll find lifeguards and bathhouses at the ready.

The folks at the **Transylvania County Tourism Development Authority,** 35 West Main St., 800/648-4523, website: www.visit waterfalls.com, have come up with a handy guide to many of the county's most popular falls. Stop by or call to get a copy.

The Brevard area is also home to the **Cradle of Forestry,** a school founded in 1895 to study the then-new science of forestry. Thought the school closed in 1913, you can view the reconstructed campus about three miles south of the Blue Ridge Parkway on U.S. 276. It's open daily 9 A.M.–5 P.M., and consists of a classroom, a ranger's dwelling, and a lodge in the style of the Black Forest. No admission charge.

Every summer, Brevard hosts 200 to 300 young folks for the **Transylvania Music Camp.** Big-name performers and conductors join these young musicians, and the combination attracts music lovers for daily concerts over a two-month period. For details about performances, call 828/884-2019.

For more information on Brevard in general, call the **Brevard Chamber of Commerce,** 35 West Main St., at 800/648-4523 or 828/883-3700.

If you'd like to stay in Brevard, you couldn't do much better than renting a room at the **Inn at Brevard,** 410 E. Main St., 828/884-2105, website: www.innatbrevard.8m.com. Built in 1885, the inn offers five antique-laden rooms in the main house, as well as 10 cabin-style rooms with private showers in an adjacent annex. A full breakfast is included with the room charge, which runs $110–150 in high season, lower in the off-season. For something more economical, you might try the **Sunset Motel,** 415 S. Broad St., 828/884-9106, where the rooms run $40–70. Be sure to request a nonsmoking room.

# HOT SPRINGS

North of Asheville on U.S. 25/70, just south of the Tennessee line, this small town on the French Broad River has seen better days. Once known as Warm Springs, it was an important stop on the road from Cumberland Gap to the markets of Charleston. In those days, huge droves of cattle, hogs, and even turkeys would come down the road.

With the coming of the railroad, the livestock drives halted, but more and more health seekers began to come to town. People had been coming to the springs since Cherokee days, but now local residents earnestly began to market them. The hot-water-cure business grew exponentially. The local hotel lured flatlanders with promises that the springs would "bring the bloom back to the cheek, the luster to the eye, tone to the languid pulse, strength to the jaded nerves, and vigor to the wasted frame."

Entrepreneur James Patton of Asheville bought the springs and built the massive, 350-room Warm Springs Hotel in 1837. Soon, everyone who was somebody was coming to town. In fact, the daughter of the springs' second owner met her husband, Frank Johnson—son of President Andrew Johnson—in the hotel's majestic ballroom.

The railroad arrived in the early 1880s, but the Warm Springs Hotel burned down shortly thereafter. Northerners moved in and built the Mountain Park Hotel in 1886. They discovered an even hotter spring on their property and shrewdly changed the town's name from Warm Springs to Hot Springs—to advertise both the change in ownership and the upgrade in amenities.

The Mountain Park Hotel was smaller (200 rooms), but it featured 16 marble pools, landscaped lawns, and those Victorian-era standbys, croquet and tennis courts. By the time World War I rolled around, however, hot springs were out of fashion, and the hotel gladly accepted the chance to serve as a prison camp for 517 German officers and 2,300 German merchant marines captured at the start of the war. So pleased were these resort-dwelling POWs with their accommodations and treatment that many of them returned after the war to live around here.

By war's end, the hotel and springs had lost their grasp on the public imagination, and the hotel conveniently burned to the ground in 1920. Two later hotels were built on the springs; neither held a candle to the previous two, and both also burned to the ground.

While nothing remains of the old hotels, and the springs themselves are on private property, the French Broad River still attracts a number of folks to the area, as does the Appalachian Trail, which runs right through town. The privately owned springs have reopened as **Hot Springs Spa & Resort,** 315 Bridge St., 800/462-0933 or 828/622-7676. In keeping with the hyperbolic spirit of the springs' previous promoters, the current owners claim that "the Goddess of Health waved her magic wand" at these springs. It'll cost you and a friend $15–25 an hour for a private soak in the goddess-blessed water. The spa also offers massage. You can rent a two-couple cabin, complete with Jacuzzi, for $125 a night or tent camp for just $10 a night. Setting aside the question of the water's curative powers, this is a nice, reasonably priced spot to enjoy a hot relaxing soak and the company of friends. And this poignant combination can be a blessing in itself.

# The Northern Mountains

Asheville is surrounded by mountains; as you climb the winding two- and four-lane highways to the north and northwest, you reach true southern Appalachia, a verdant, long-isolated land of hollers, shut-ins, and balds, populated mainly by small farmers whose food (and whiskey) came from their own fields, and whose language and faith came from the King James Bible. The people who lived in these former Cherokee lands were independent folks who valued personal freedom above all else. It was Appalachians—not the landed, slaveholding gentry on the coast—who wrote the first constitution penned by American colonists, and who tired of British ineffectiveness and formed the Watauga Association to establish law and order in the mountains. During the war, the Overland men came from the towns around

here, dressed in buckskin, to defeat the redcoats at Kings Mountain, S.C. Daniel Boone grew to manhood here, and so did other men and women who later, driven by the same hunger for land (and the independence it guaranteed) that had led them to settle out here in the first place, carried out the white Euro-American settlement of Tennessee, Kentucky, and the heart of today's United States.

## BLOWING ROCK

Founded in the late 1800s as a vacation village, Blowing Rock is cute by design. Though some folks—1,600 or so—live here year-round, having retired or having decided that seasonal poverty is worth the chance to live here, it's still by and large a community of part-time resi-

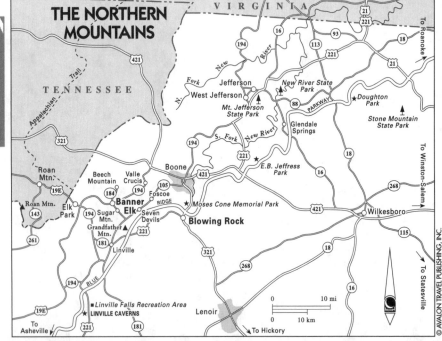

© AVALON TRAVEL PUBLISHING, INC.

dents, folks who make big city money working elsewhere, then come up here to "the village" to while away their free time spending it. It's a Jaycee's dream.

If you're here and it all seems very familiar, you may be having a Mitford flashback; author and Blowing Rock resident Jan Karon set her best-selling, Wobegon-esque series of novels here in Blowing Rock, though she renamed the town Mitford. The inspirations for the small diner and Episcopal parish familiar to Karon's readers are both on Sunset Drive.

## Sights

The thing to do in Blowing Rock, more or less, is walk around and look into the cute shops and maybe—here the Jaycee gets hopeful—buy something. But the ambience is hard to beat, and there's lots of art up here in galleries and in the park; and in the fall, colorful leaves in the trees. Which is why there are lots and lots of people here. If you want to come during leaf-turning season, book far, far in advance.

**Tweetsie Railroad,** on U.S. 321/211, 800/526-5740 or 828/264-9061, website: www.tweetsie-railroad.com, is more than a railroad (which got its name from its shrill whistle); it's a western-themed park *with* a three-mile full-scale steam train ride, and the sorts of rides you'd see at a county fair. It's homegrown Americana, folks. Halloween brings Ghost Train™ Halloween Festival, wherein things get *so spooky* that even the steam train wears a skull mask. The park closes in the winter; it opens beginning early May on Friday, Saturday and Sunday from 9 A.M. to 6 P.M. Starting in late May, Tweetsie opens up every day. On July 4th the park stays open later and shoots off fireworks. The hours contract again to the weekends starting mid-August, and the park closes down for good after the first weekend in November. The Ghost Train™ (I'm not kidding about the trademark) festival takes place over several Halloween nights. Call or see the website for dates.

You can pet the "friendly critters" at Tweetsie's Deer Park; you can pan for gold. You can watch an old medicine show and a can-can act. One of the delights here are the live acts; Tweetsie gets

some good ones. One recent season saw the Cowboy Music Hall of Fame cowboy trio Riders in the Sky—they of "Woody's Roundup" fame—a clogging jamboree, and bluegrass musicians. But clearly, the main attraction here is the railroad; kids love a steam train ride, and so do a few of us adults, I imagine. Even into the late 1930s, the train still ran in the area. The 1939 WPA Guide to North Carolina describes the train:

> *Built in 1886 as a logging railroad, and now a general utility line called "Tweetsie" by the people it serves in this mountain region. "Tweetsie" takes four hours to make her tortuous 66-mile run, barring stops for "critters" to get off the tracks or for delivery of a spool of thread or bottle of medicine to a waiting housewife.*

Admission costs $23 for adults, $16 for children ages 3–12, and free if they're 2 years or under and too young to do much but chortle. Seniors (over 60) pay $19.

**Mystery Hill,** 129 Mystery Hill Lane, 828/264-2792, website: www.mysteryhill -nc.com, is a rural tourist-town essential. You know the drill: the walls are sideways and the floor slanted, and water seems to flow at an angle. When you're a kid, you buy the idea that the one you've seen must be some sort of unique, unexplainable gravitational wrinkle in the universe; with age and traveling comes disillusionment, as you realize that there seem to be unique, unexplainable gravitational wrinkles in every two-bit tourist area across the country. Anyway, Mystery Hill can be fun, particularly if anyone in your party hasn't been through one before. Open year-round, Mystery Hill costs $7 for adults, $5 for children 6 and up, and $6 for seniors; it's not an inconsequential fee, but probably cheaper than the alcohol it would take to reproduce the Hill's effects. Price includes admission to *The Mystery House* and *The Hall of Mystery,* where the attractions are "based on physics and other science and math theories." This includes the Bubble-Rama exhibit, wherein kids can make kid-sized bubbles around themselves; the time-honored "self-pouring" faucet; and a hologram.

ASHEVILLE

# BLOWING ROCK

HILL ST.
RAINEY ST.
SUNFLOWER LN.
MAIN ST.
YONAHLOSSEE RD.
221
321 221 321

PARK AVE. MAPLE ST.
BUS. 321
CHAMBER OF COMMERCE ■
INN AT RAGGED GARDENS ★
ALPINE VILLAGE INN ●
SUNSET
W. CORNISH RD.
E. CORNISH RD.
DR.

SONNY'S GRILL ▼
GREENWAY CT.
GARDEN CIR.
MORRIS ST.
HILL ST.
RANSOM ST.
VALLEY BLVD.

WALLINGFORD ST.
PINE ST.
TIJUANA FATS ▼
MAIN ST.
CHESTNUT ST. CHESTNUT DR.

0       100 yds
0       100 m

S. MAIN ST.
BLOWING ROCK HOSPITAL ■
HENKEL
CHURCH ST.

MOON

**AREA OF DETAIL**

To Foscoe
105
SHULLS MILL RD.
YONAHLOSSEE RESORT
Moses Cone
BLOWING ROCK STABLES ★
Trout Lake
Memorial Park
APPALACHIAN SKI MOUNTAIN ★
To Boone
221 321
WOODLANDS BBQ & PICKIN PARLOR ▼
TWEETSIE RAILROAD ★
MYSTERY HILL ★
Julian Price
Memorial Park
CONE VISITOR CENTER AND PARKWAY CRAFT CENTER ★
SHOPPES ON THE PARKWAY ★
Bass Lake
Mayview Lake
BLUE RIDGE PARKWAY
BUS. 321
LAUREL PARK RD.
RD.
221
0       1 mi
0       1 km
To Linville
BLOWING ROCK ★
321
To Lenoir
SKYLAND DR.
321

© AVALON TRAVEL PUBLISHING, INC.

ASHEVILLE

## A SMOKY MOUNTAIN LINGISTER

Excerpted from *Smoky Mountain Voices, A Lexicon of Southern Appalachian Speech,* edited by Harold F. Farwell Jr. and J. Karl Nicholas.

**Big Ike:** superior; boldly. "He tried to act Big Ike and sass her."

**Foreigner:** anybody from out of the immediate region

**Goozle:** throat

**Jedgmatically:** shrewdly evasive. "Jedgmatically, I don't know if Ray's a blockader."

**Lingister:** an interpreter

**Old Ned:** fat pork. "Jake, hand me some Old Ned."

**Slantdicular:** not perpendicular

**Toothbrush hunt:** to meddle or pry after secrets

The last two quadrants of Mystery Hill aren't really very mysterious, but they are worthwhile: *the Appalachian Heritage Museum* is set in a Victorian-era house built by the founders of Appalachian State University and moved here in the late 1980s. The house has been restored to reflect the lifestyles of middle-class mountain folks in the late 1800s and early 20th century. The *Native American Artifacts Museum* features some 50,000 Native American–related relics, from ceramics and woven pots to arrowheads and hand tools. The museum is worthwhile for anyone interested in the archaeological evidence of the land's first human inhabitants—and/or anybody who feels they need to justify taking the kids to Mystery Hill by making the trip educational

### Events

One Saturday a month, spring through fall, Blowing Rock hosts its **Art in the Park,** a tradition that began in the early 1960s, giving local artists a chance to compete in juried shows in handcrafts and art. A typical show includes 120 exhibitors displaying their basketry, furniture-making, glasswork, jewelry, leatherwork, painting, photography, pottery, quilting, sculpting in metal and wood, weaving, wrought iron, wood carving and turning, and more. After the awards are handed out, the artists and crafters gladly sell their works to visitors. (For more standard items, the **Tanger Shoppes on the Parkway,** U.S. 321, 800/720-6728, website: www.tangeroutlet.com, offers some 30 well-known outlet stores, including The Gap, Ralph Lauren, and the rest of the gang.)

### Accommodations

Leaf-viewing season is high season up here; rooms in October can be double or three times low-season prices. I've come during a cold September and seen plenty of brilliant oranges and reds in the trees, without the grueling traffic I would've faced a month later. But if you want to see foliage, and plugging in a video of Hitchcock's *The Trouble with Harry* just won't do it, then be sure to get rooms far, far in advance, to avoid a startling October Surprise. Or consider camping in the cool fall air, where you can experience the falling leaves in 3D.

On a quiet side road, the 15-room **Alpine Village Inn,** 297 Sunset Dr., 828/295-7206, website: www.alpine-village-inn.com, is about as cute as an old motel can get; it's clean, well-situated in the midst of town, and homey, with quilts and folk art on the walls, real (not motel) furniture, and a pretty outdoor area with a garden and gazebo. Jacuzzi available. Rooms run under $100, and usually closer to $70. For similar prices, the **Hillwinds Inn,** 315 Sunset Dr., 800/821-4908 or 828/295-7660, website: www.hillwindsinn.com, is another motel-gone-a-courting and offers 16 rooms, one cottage, and two efficiencies. William and Judy Horton's **Horton's Lodge,** 190 Morris St., 828/295-0002, website: www.hortons lodge.com, offer clean, less-cute rooms in a motel on a quiet side street off Main Street. Rooms run about $80, and suites run around $100–125, but can save you money if you're up here with a group of people with whom you can share.

© MIKE SIGALAS

**Springhaven Inn, Blowing Rock**

Also on this quiet street you'll find Lee and Jama Hyett's elegant stone six-room, six-suite **Inn at Ragged Gardens,** Sunset Dr., 828/295-9703, website: www.ragged-gardens.com, surrounded by beautiful gardens. Every room is strikingly decorated and features a fireplace. You'll eat breakfast in a glass-enclosed garden room. Rates are premium; $170 and up, in season. Right on Main Street but set off the road with a pretty garden out front, the 1889 **Springhaven Inn,** 828/295-6967, is a quaint old rustic Victorian home with four bedrooms, all with private baths, furnished with antiques and queen or double beds.

## Cabins

The eight cabins at **Timber Cabins,** 120 Apple Ridge Lane, 888/268-4748 or 828/295-6622, website: www.appleridgecabins.com, each have a microwave, refrigerator, and fireplace—and pets are allowed within reason. **Cameron's Country Cabins,** 130 Cameron Dr., 828/295-4836, website: www.cameronscountrycabins.com, offers eight cabins, each with a complete kitchen and fireplace.

## Camping

Local campgrounds include barebones National Park Service campgrounds along the Blue Ridge Parkway: near Falling Rock at the 197-site **Julian Price Campground,** near Blowing Rock, three miles north of the Parkway along U.S. 321, at milepost 297, 828/963-5911; and at **Linville Falls,** one mile north of Linville Falls and the junction with U.S. 221; 829/765-7818. Both cost $12 a night. You'll find private campgrounds, which usually have more amenities, around Boone: **KOA-Boone,** 123 Harmony Mountain Lane, 828/264-7250, open May through October; $28.50 in season; and **Flintlock Campground,** 171 Flintlock Campground Dr., 828/963-5325, costs $18 a night for tents, with water and electricity; $25 a night for full RV hookups.

## Food

If you're planning to eat barbecue up in the Blowing Rock area, you couldn't do better than to visit **Woodlands BBQ and Pickin' Parlor,** 8304 Valley Blvd. (Hwy. 321 Bypass), 828/295-3651, website: www.woodlandsbbq.com. Chopped and sliced beef and pork, ribs and chicken, served with a variety of tangy sauces. The rustic two-story building is a fine place to spend an afternoon or evening, and often it's filled with the sounds of live bluegrass. Widescreen TV and nightly entertainment. Best of all, it's open until midnight, though the kitchen closes at 10 P.M. **Sonny's Grill,** on Main Street, 828/295-7577, has been serving up the goods on Main Street for 43 years; we're talking good ham biscuits, hot cheese sandwiches, fresh soup. But it has never been so busy here as it's been since Jan Karon modeled Mitford's café after Sonny's. Open Monday–Saturday. Down and across Main Street you'll see **Tijuana Fats,** 828/295-9683, where, unlike the real Tijuana, you can drink the table water without fear of amoebic retaliation. The chimichangas and green chile enchiladas are fine; the bar keeps them Coronas a-coming and whips up margaritas and daiquiris like they was sweet tea. The pretty terrace, in good weather, provides an enchanting atmosphere. Eat here and you might momentarily forget you're in Appalachia—which isn't usually why people *come* to Appalachia, of course. But still, we're talking some fine enchiladas.

# BOONE

More than 3,200 feet up, and perched 1,200 feet beneath Howard's Knob, Boone was named for famous Pennsylvania-born explorer Daniel Boone, who lived here from ages 14 to 23 (1760–69) with his parents and siblings near Holeman's Ford on the Yadkin River, about eight miles from Wilkesboro. It was about as much a permanent home as the restless Boone would ever know, though his name is more famously associated with Kentucky, the "raw wilderness" he trailblazed for white settlers. Anyway, Boone never lived in town here, of course—it was named for him after he had risen to fame.

When Boone arrived, the nearest courts lay so far east that no organized government seemed to control the area, even though the settlements theoretically belonged to England as part of the colony of North Carolina. After 1772, John Sevier and James Robertson decided to take things into their own hands. They led their neighbors in forming the Watauga Association, a separate republic with a written constitution. Courts were formed, suspected criminals received trials, and something like European-style government began to settle over the land. In 1776, local Cherokee became disgruntled with whites' treatment of them and decided to throw the settlers out of the country. The ensuing bloodshed bound the Wataugans to their North Carolina neighbors, and by 1778, North Carolina was the recognized governing force here.

Today a town of more than 12,000, Boone is best known as home to **Appalachian State University,** dubbed in 2002 as one of the best colleges in America by *Time* magazine. Boone's sites include the **Appalachian Cultural Museum,** University Hall Drive off U.S. 321, 828/262-3117, website: www.appstate.edu, dedicated to preserving the culture of the mountains. Admission runs around $5. The **Mast General Store** at 630 W. King St., 828/262-0000, is the Boone branch of the "chain" of stores up here, set in an old mercantile building. The original Mast is in Valle Crucis, but if you're not heading that way, you'll want to stop here to take in the authentic 19th-century rural mercantile ambience. The Mast chain had a store in Boone way back in 1923; an advertisement from that year boasted of "Goods for the Living, Coffins and Caskets for the Dead." Today, Mast no longer caters to the departed, but the living can still buy Squirrel Nut Zippers and penny candy from wooden barrels. You'll also find sturdy, traditional clothing and outdoor wear, and an assortment of such essentials as rosebud salves, "courtin' candles," rocking chairs, handmade crafts and baskets, goat's milk soap, and of course, a Radio Flyer wagon.

The ***Horn in the West*** outdoor historic drama, 591 Horn in the West Dr., 888/825-6747 or 828/264-2120, website: www.boonenc.org/saha, is set hereabouts during the Revolutionary War, and it's been performed up here since 1952. It's Boone's answer to Cherokee's *Unto These Hills.* Written by the same author as Manteo's *The Lost Colony, Horn in the West* runs around $12 for adults, less for seniors and children. It's well worth an evening's time. **The Hickory Ridge**

© MIEK SIGALAS

Tweetsie Railroad

**Homestead Museum,** 591 Horn in the West Dr., 888/825-6765 or 828/264-2120, website: www.boonenc.org/saha, is a living history museum with costumed docents who bake in old hearths, make candles, pound tin, and perform other skilled activities the people who originally lived in these cabins would be amazed to see us paying to watch. The Southern Appalachian Historical Association can arrange for groups to actually experience a live-in program at the museum; call for information. The **Daniel Boone Native Gardens,** 651 Horn in the West Dr., 828/264-6390, feature plants native to the area; the log cabin here once belonged to the Boone family—and I don't mean Pat and Debbie's. Admission charged.

## Accommodations

Since Boone is the biggest town in this part of the mountains, you'll find more traffic, more strip-like development (but not much), and more lodging choices here than anywhere else.

The **Boone Trail Motel,** 275 E. King St., 828/264-8839, is about as inexpensive a stay as you can get in town, at under $25 in low season and about $50 in high. It's near ASU and the restaurants of downtown. Not real pretty, but pretty clean, and cheap.

The attractive 47-room **Scottish Inn,** 782 Blowing Rock Rd., 800/524-5214 or 828/264-2483, offers a pool and a location right next to ASU.

Located five miles from Boone, Roy and Martha Barthel's **Window Views B&B,** 204 Stoneleigh Lane, 800/963-4484 or 828/963-8081, website: www.windowviewsb-b.com, provides beautiful views of Grandfather Mountain, Beech Mountain, and others—especially pretty when clad in fall foliage or winter snow. The building itself, with just two rooms for rent, is less fancy than it is comfortable and scenic. When they built it in 1992 Roy and Martha designed the house to capitalize on the view with wallfuls of windows. Breakfasts are tasty and filling, and you'll get an eyeful of mountain scenery while you fill your belly with cinnamon breads and pancakes.

The 120-room **High Country Inn,** 1785 N.C. 105, 800/334-5605 or 828/264-1000, website: www.highcountryinn.com, offers six rooms with fireplaces, two suites with a Jacuzzi, and two three-bedroom cabins for groups.

The **Lovill House Inn,** 404 Old Bristol Rd., 828/264-4204, is set inside an 1875 house on 11 wooded acres. Pertinent facts: wraparound porches, streams criss-crossing the grounds, and fireplaces in three of the six rooms.

## Food

Boone is a college town, and the diversity of the menus available reflect this. For something cheap, see **The Way Cafe** on King Street, a tiny spot with a walk-up window next door to City Hall and featuring baked goods, breakfast items, salads, and healthy sandwiches all day long, as well as Blue Bunny Ice Cream. **Dan'l Boone Inn Restaurant,** 130 Hardin St., 828/264-8657, serves hefty amounts of good fried country food here: fried chicken, fried steak, fried fish, as well as an unfried item or two. It's great stuff if maybe not the healthiest thing in the world; there's probably some connection to the fact that the restaurant is set in an old hospital. If you're had enough fried food and fatback for a while, **Angelica's Vegetarian Restaurant,** 506 West King St., 828/265-0809, will be a godsend. A vegetarian juice bar, with grains and vegetables a-plenty.

**The Bistro,** at New Market Centre, 828/265-0500, falls somewhere in between Dan'l Boone Inn and Angelica. It features a number of vegetarian dishes along with its blackened seafood, filets, and chicken dishes. Open for dinner only, and reservations are a good idea.

## Recreation

The Boone area is fantastic for all sorts of recreational pursuits. **Rock & Roll Sports,** 280 E. King St., 800/977-7625 or 828/264-0765, website: www.rocknrollsports.com, is a good place to stop in if you're interested in biking or climbing while here. They have mountain bike rentals, repairs, parts, accessories, and trail information. Rock & Roll also carries a large selection of rock-climbing gear and has information on local climbs. Open Monday–Saturday 10 A.M.–6 P.M., and Sunday noon–4 P.M.

**Paddling:** Outfitters that can get you out onto the local rivers in a raft or kayak include **Ap-**

**palachian Adventures,** in the tiny town of Todd, 336/877-8800, website: www.appalachianadventures.com; **High Mountain Expeditions,** in Blowing Rock, 800/262-9036; and **Wahoo's Whitewater Rafting and Canoe Outfitters,** 704/262-5774.

**Downhill skiing:** The skiing up here is unspectacular to those jaded by Squaw Valley and Jackson Hole, but it's still good, and it's here all season long—the snowmakers see to that. **Ski Beech,** 1007 Beech Mountain Parkway, 800/438-2093 or 704/387-2011; website: www.skibeech.com, offers 15 slopes, seven chairlifts, and the highest skiing in eastern North American—5,505 feet into the Appalachian sky. Other popular resorts include three-slope, two-chairlift **Appalachian Ski Mountain,** three miles off U.S. 321 north of Blowing Rock on the road to Boone (follow the signs), 704/295-7828, website: www.appskimtn.com, and the state's biggest facility, 18-slope, five-lift **Sugar Mountain,** in Banner Elk, 704/898-4521, website: www.skisugar.com.

**Fishing and hunting:** If it's difficult for you to travel amid all this wildlife without at least trying to kill and eat some of it, you may want to contact **Windmill City Outdoors Guide Service,** 3086 U.S. 421 S., 828/264-0797, which leads full- and half-day trips for anglers and hunters.

**Horseback riding:** The **Yonahlossee Resort Saddle Club,** 223 Pine Hill Rd., 828/963-7856, website: www.yonahlossee.com, offers horseback riding instruction, and has an indoor riding arena for inclement weather. Open year-round.

# NORTH OF BOONE

**Valle Crucis** features the original, 1883 **Mast General Store,** on N.C. 194, 828/963-6511, website: www.mastgeneralstore.com. Set out on its old pine floor is the sort of product diversity that reminds you why these were called "general" stores: besides the candy in wooden barrels— Charleston Chews, Licorice Bullseyes, and many others—you'll also find traditional clothing and

ASHEVILLE

## BOONE AND VALLE CRUCIS IN 1885

In 1885, Massachussetts-born essayist and novelist Charles Dudley Warner, a friend and sometime co-author of Samuel Clemens, traveled through the highlands of Virginia and North Carolina, describing his experiences in a series of articles for the *Atlantic Monthly*, later collected as *On Horseback*.

In general, Warner ("The Professor," in the article) looked upon Carolina with typical Yankee disdain; his description of Boone and Valle Crucis is representative.

*Boone, the county seat of Watauga County, was our destination, and, ever since morning, the guide-boards and the trend of the roads had notified us that everything in this region tends towards Boone as a center of interest. The simple ingenuity of some of the guide-boards impressed us. If, on coming to a fork, the traveler was to turn to the right, the sign read,*

*To BOONE 10 M.*
*If he was to go to the left, it read,*
*.M 01 ENOOB OT*

*A short ride of nine miles, on an ascending road, through an open, unfenced forest region, brought us long before sundown to this capital. When we had ridden into its single street, which wanders over gentle hills, and landed at the most promising of the taverns, the Friend informed his comrade that Boone was 3250 feet above Albemarle Sound, and believed by its inhabitants to be the highest village east of the Rocky Mountains. The Professor said that it might be so, but it was a God-forsaken place. Its inhabitants numbered perhaps two hundred and fifty, a few of them colored. It had a gaunt, shaky court-house and jail, a store or two, and two taverns. The two taverns are needed to accommodate the judges and lawyers and their clients during the session of the court. The court is the only*

*excitement and the only amusement. It is the event from which other events date. Everybody in the county knows exactly when court sits, and when court breaks. During the session the whole county is practically in Boone, men, women, and children. They camp there, they attend the trials, they take sides; half of them, perhaps, are witnesses, for the region is litigious, and the neighborhood quarrels are entered into with spirit. To be fond of lawsuits seems a characteristic of an isolated people in new conditions. The early settlers of New England were.*

*Notwithstanding the elevation of Boone, which insured a pure air, the thermometer that afternoon stood at from 85 to 89 deg[rees]. The flies enjoyed it. How they swarmed in this tavern! They would have carried off all the food from the dining-room table . . . but for the machine with hanging flappers that swept the length of it; and they destroy all possibility of sleep except in the dark. The mountain regions of North Carolina are free from mosquitoes, but the fly has settled there, and is the universal scourge. This tavern, one end of which was a store, had a veranda in front, and a back gallery, where there were evidences of female refinement in pots of plants and flowers. The landlord himself kept tavern very much as a hostler would . . . and it might as well be said here, for it will have to be insisted on later, that the traveler, who has read about the illicit stills till his imagination dwells upon the indulgence of his vitiated tastes in the mountains of North Carolina, is doomed to disappointment. If he wants to make himself an exception to the sober people whose cooking will make him long for the maddening bowl, he must bring his poison with him. We had found no bread since we left Virginia; we had seen cornmeal and water, slack-baked; we had seen potatoes fried in grease, and bacon incrusted with salt (all thirst-provokers), but nothing to drink stronger than buttermilk. And we can say that, so far as our example is concerned, we left the country as temperate as we found it. How can there be mint juleps (to go into details) without ice? and in the summer there is probably not a pound of ice in all the State north of Buncombe County.*

*There is nothing special to be said about Boone. We were anxious to reach it, we were glad to leave it; we note as to all these places that our joy at departing always exceeds that on arriving, which is a merciful provision of nature for people who must keep moving. This country is settled by genuine Americans, who have the aboriginal primitive traits of the universal Yankee nation. The front porch in the morning resembled a carpenter's shop; it was literally covered with the whittlings of the row of natives who had spent the evening there in the sedative occupation of whittling.*

*We took that morning a forest road to Valle Crusis, seven miles, through noble growths of oaks, chestnuts, hemlocks, rhododendrons,—a charming wood road, leading to a place that, as usual, did not keep the promise of its name. Valle Crusis has a blacksmith shop and a dirty, flyblown store. While the Professor consulted the blacksmith about a loose shoe, the Friend carried his weariness of life without provisions up to a white house on the hill, and negotiated for boiled milk. This house was occupied by flies. They must have numbered millions, settled in black swarms, covering tables, beds, walls, the veranda; the kitchen was simply a hive of them. The only book in sight, Whewell's "Elements of Morality," seemed to attract flies. A white house,—a pleasant-looking house at a distance,—amiable, kindly people in it,—why should we have arrived there on its dirty day? Alas! if we had been starving, Valle Crusis had nothing to offer us.*

ASHEVILLE

outerwear, and an assortment of such mercantile essentials as stone-ground meal, porch swings, handmade crafts and baskets, lye soap, and of course, a Radio Flyer wagon.

## SOUTH OF BOONE

The **Toecane Ranger District** ranges south of Boone and to the north and east of Asheville. It extends to the Tennessee state line and includes Mount Mitchell State Park, home of the highest peak in the eastern United States, a popular hike. You'll see large bursts of rhododendrons in the area in the spring. Craggy Mountain Scenic Area is near Craggy Gardens, a stop on the Blue Ridge Parkway, and Roan Mountain is on the Tennessee state line. The District

Ranger's office is in Burnsville on the U.S. 19 E. Bypass, 828/682-6146.

### Grandfather Mountain Park

The Pisgah National Forest's northernmost quadrant is the **Grandfather Ranger District,** which includes Grandfather Mountain, U.S. 221 and the Blue Ridge Parkway, Linville, 800/468-7325 or 828/733-4337. Grandfather Mountain is the only private park in the world designated a United Nations International Biosphere Reserve.

The mountain's trademark is its Mile High Swinging Bridge, but don't expect to look 5,280 feet straight down from it. Grandfather is the highest point in the Blue Ridge Mountains, and when you're on the bridge you're a mile above *sea level,* but only *90 feet* above the actual ground.

Still, at the top of that 0.017-mile drop is a spectacular, 360-degree view. And as far as the thrill goes, at 90 feet, as Kim at the Grandfather Mountain office points out, "If you fell, it still wouldn't be pretty." The park offers a nature museum and animal wildlife habitats that give you the chance to see representative local animals—black bears, deer, eagles, panthers, and otters—up close. Hiking trails abound.

Admission to the park costs $12 for anyone over 12 years of age, $6 for kids 4–12. The park is home to several annual events, including the "Singing on the Mountain" All-Day Gospel Sing (the fourth Sunday in June) and the Highland Games & Gathering of the Scottish Clans (on the second weekend in July). For information call 800/468-7325, website: www.grandfather.com.

Here too are the Linville Gorge Wilderness Area and a handful of uncrowded campgrounds. The District Ranger's office is in the public library building in Marion. Contact the District Ranger at 828/652-4841.

The **French Broad Ranger District** is on the French Broad River northwest of Asheville. The District Ranger's office is located on the main street in downtown Hot Springs. Contact the District Ranger at 828/622-3202.

## Linville Caverns

Deep inside Humpback Mountain lie North Carolina's only caverns developed for tours. From the Blue Ridge Parkway, exit at the Linville Falls Village marker and turn left on U.S. 221. Four miles along, you'll come to Linville Caverns, 800/419-0540 or 828/756-4171, website: www.linville caverns.com. They're not going to make you forget Carlsbad Caverns or the Great Bat Cave, but there's still a lot of time-molded beauty down there: stalactites and stalagmites, some of them older than Jesse Helms and Strom Thurmond combined, forming all sorts of beautiful shapes that nobody knew about until 1822, when fishermen noticed that some of the trout they were trying to catch seemed to be disappearing straight *into* the mountain. They found torches, lit them, and spelunked their way inside.

Now the need for spelunking is through, a fortunate thing since most people never felt real comfortable with the verb. The limestone cavern is open for half-hour, well-lit, guided tours through the paved viewing area. In addition to the formations, you may spot bats, crayfish, and crickets; you will most certainly see some of the trout, who still like to hide out down there in the cool water. It's a great destination on a hot day—winter and summer, the temperature is always in the 50s. Admission runs around $6 for adults, $4 for children 5–12 years old, $5 for seniors.

# EAST OF BOONE

## Hickory

Hickory has been famous for years for its furniture warehouses and showrooms, most of which you'll find along U.S. 321 between Hickory and Blowing Rock. Sites include the **Catawba Furniture Museum,** 2220 U.S. 70 S.E., 828/322-3510, which features exhibits covering the region's long history of furniture-making; and the **Hickory Furniture Mart,** 2220 U.S. 70 S.E., 828/322-3510, website: www.hickoryfurniture.com, open since 1984 and full of 20 acres of furniture for sale and ogling.

## Wilkesboro/North Wilkesboro

Home to an Apple Festival in the fall and the Bluegrass Merlefest each spring, North Wilkesboro is home to the **Wilkes Art Gallery,** 800 Elizabeth St., 336/667-2841, website: www .northwilkesboro.com/wilkart.htm, featuring monthly exhibits of local and regional artists. Wilkesboro is home to the **Old Wilkes Jail Museum,** 203 N. Bridge St., 336/667-3712, website: www.wilkesboro.com/OldWilkesInc, which saw service as the county jail from 1860 through 1915, and once held returned Confederate Thomas Dula, jailed for the murder of Laura Foster, convicted after two trials, and hung in Statesville on May 1, 1868. The sensational trial was held in Wilkesboro, and Dula was represented by his former military commander, former and future governor Zebulon Vance. He was hung—as anyone who has ever heard the song "Hang Down Your Head, Tom Dooley" knows—in Statesville.

# Cherokee and the Gateway to the Smokies

Just south of Great Smoky Mountains National Park on U.S. 441, the parkland whose every use is closely supervised by the U.S. Federal Government bumps directly against a land where Uncle Sam holds little sway—the Qualla Boundary Cherokee Reservation.

The reservation lies in the Southwestern section of North Carolina, arguably the most unspoiled section of the southern Appalachians. The millions of visitors to the Great Smoky Mountains National Park do not clog the roads here. The inns in the mountains are quiet, and in some places you can view landscapes that have not changed since before the Cherokee themselves arrived.

The Cherokee reservation's residents—formally known as the Eastern Band of the Cherokee to distinguish them from their exiled cousins in Oklahoma—descend from the 1,000 or so who refused to leave their homeland. Through sheer willpower, they keep their ancient culture alive, even today. One of the most inspirational tracts of virgin timber in the East, the Joyce Kilmer Memorial Forest—named for the man who wrote "Poems are made by fools like me / But only God can make a tree"—is found here. The waterfalls in the area are the most striking in the region, and nowhere else in the country can you try your luck at finding so many kinds of precious stones. For those seeking natural beauty, outdoor activities such as whitewater rafting and hiking, or simply some relief from the pressures of modern life, the Cherokee region is hard to beat.

Ghost Town in the Sky, Maggie Valley

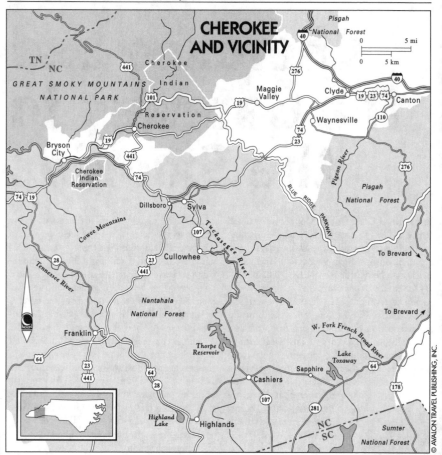

**CHEROKEE AND VICINITY**

TN
NC
Cherokee

GREAT SMOKY MOUNTAINS
NATIONAL PARK

Pisgah
National Forest

0      5 mi
0      5 km

Cherokee     Indian

Maggie
Valley

Clyde

Canton

Reservation
Cherokee

Waynesville

Bryson
City

Cherokee
Indian
Reservation

BLUE RIDGE PARKWAY

Pigeon River

Pisgah
National Forest

Dillsboro     Sylva

Cowee Mountains

Tuckasegee River

Cullowhee

To Brevard

Tennessee River

Nantahala
National Forest

To Brevard

W. Fork French Broad River

Franklin

Thorpe
Reservoir

Lake
Toxaway

Sapphire

Cashiers

Highland
Lake     Highlands

NC
SC

Sumter
National Forest

© AVALON TRAVEL PUBLISHING, INC.

## HISTORY

Despite its glittery casino future and recent cement-teepee past, Cherokee's deepest roots reach back centuries, through the ages when this was the Cherokees' *world*. The Cherokee thrived in the richly forested land where towering chestnut trees covered mountains spilling with waterfalls and laced with trout-rich streams. Bison, bear, and deer roamed the valleys. With a language that would outlive their dominance, the Cherokees gave names to the mountains and rivers that reflected the beauty they saw.

Then the outsiders came. Searching for a city of gold that the Indians kept telling him was farther away, Hernando De Soto and more than 600 soldiers filed through this area in 1540, plundering Cherokee crops and forcing Indians to carry the Spaniards' gear as they pushed onward. Euro-Indian relations hit a low point in 1838 when United States troops sent by Andrew Jackson entered the area, rounded up every Cherokee they could find—more than 15,000—and forced them and their 1,000 African-American slaves to walk and/or take boats to Oklahoma. The four different trails the groups of Cherokee took to the new

## CHEROKEE AREA HIGHLIGHTS

**Museum of the Cherokee Indian,** Cherokee
**Great Smoky Mountains Railroad,** Dillsboro
**Harrah's Cherokee Casino**
**Highlands**
**Maggie Valley Opry House,** Maggie Valley
**Oconaluftee Indian Village,** Cherokee
**Rafting the Nantahala Gorge**
*Unto These Hills* **Outdoor Drama**

These were the planters from places like Charleston and Savannah who had come to the mountains to escape the summertime heat and fevers of the Lowcountry. They bought large pieces of land and built second homes, most of them larger than the homes the local folks used all year. Their high churches and their society ways came with them, setting sophisticated architectural standards that still hold sway in such towns as Highlands. During this time, certain villages began to experience a seasonal variance in population, a common circumstance nowadays, but a novel one then.

The Civil War impoverished the Southern planters and curbed the summer-long mountain pilgrimages. But the subsequent arrival of the railroad brought another wave of outsiders who had done a little better in the war financially—Northerners. And they were determined to make more money from the natural resources they found in the region. As the timber and minerals rode the rails out, money flowed in, enabling the mountain people to prosper a little themselves. Naturalists and tourists began to visit in greater numbers, and the locals scurried

"Indian Territory" are now spoken of collectively as the Trail of Tears. Some 4,000 Cherokees—mostly the elderly and children—died in the move, as did many of their African-American slaves and the tribe's dedicated Baptist missionaries.

Heartened by the virtual disappearance of the "savage" Indians, a different type of people began to arrive in southwestern North Carolina. The men wore high boots, the women wore silk dresses, and most families brought slaves.

© MIKE SIGALAS

Canton

CHEROKEE

## SHADES OF GRAY: SLAVEHOLDING AND REBELLION IN THE CHEROKEE NATION

From the Colonial period through the 1838 forced removal to Oklahoma, most members of the "Five Civilized Tribes"—the Cherokee, Seminole, Creek, Choctaw, and Chickasaw—blended steadily with the white society around them, adopting the Christian faith, European-style clothing, and the white American lifestyle. Intermarriage was common.

Roughly 10 percent of all Cherokees owned African-American slaves. An estimated 1,000 slaves traveled the Trail of Tears along with their Cherokee masters. A few used the opportunity to escape, but most did not. Many Cherokee who chose to evade removal and hide out high in the Smokies did so with their slaves.

Members of both the Western and Eastern Cherokee grew wealthy through slavery and came to side with fellow southerners on such issues as states' sovereignty and "property" rights. At the commencement of the Civil War, like other Carolinians and Tennesseans, many Eastern Cherokee took up arms in defense of their homeland. Out west in Oklahoma, the Western Cherokee—after much heated debate—also sided with the Confederacy. Some 7,000 Cherokee (approximately 25 to 33 percent of the fighting Cherokee population) would die in the war, most of them wearing Confederate gray. No state suffered a higher death rate than the Cherokee Nation.

Today, two miles north of Cherokee on U.S. 441, a plaque erected by the United Daughters of the Confederacy honors the Cherokee men who served in the Confederate army. You can also see a small display on Cherokee Confederates in the Museum of the Cherokee Indian in Cherokee.

about building inns and mountain hotels to make them comfortable.

In the 20th century, as more and more Americans moved off the farms and into the cities, they began to miss their connection with nature. Feeling the need to preserve the natural beauty of areas as remote as southwestern North Carolina, they took steps to ensure that the mountains and forests would remain places of enjoyment and activity for a growing number of visitors. In the 1930s and 1940s, the TVA constructed a series of dams on the rivers, providing electrical power as well as beautiful lakes. The Great Smoky Mountains National Park set aside the highest of the mountains, and the creation of the Nantahala and Pisgah National Forests ensured that the resources of the area would be managed more carefully. Up to 70 percent of the land in some counties fell into the hands of Washington, D.C., preserving manifold delights for visitors.

## ORIENTATION

Like well-defined characters in a good play, the towns on this side of the park all have their specialties: **Cherokee** has the gambling and the Indian heritage sites. **Maggie Valley** offers the most lodging and the best Appalachian music. **Waynesville** is the biggest town this side of Asheville, and is small-town cosmopolitan, with its walkable Main Street and numerous bed and breakfasts. **Dillsboro** is the quaint train town, home to the historic Jarrett House Inn and a depot for the Great Smoky Mountains Railroad. And **Bryson City** serves as gateway to the best whitewater action in the entire Smokies region.

# Cherokee

The Eastern Band of the Cherokee, who populate the Qualla Boundary reservation, descend from the 1,000 or so Cherokee who evaded President Andrew Jackson's 1838 removal of Native Americans from the path of "American progress." About 300 of them held U.S. citizenships and demanded their rights as American citizens; the rest laid low in Tennessee and North Carolina towns or hid out in the mountains. Today's population within the boundary is over 6,300, and tribal enrollment is 10,000.

The Cherokee who live here today, like some other Indian nations across the country, have moved in recent years to take advantage of their tribe's unique status by legalizing high-stakes gambling within their reservations. Few other reservations, though, enjoy the proximity to American tourists that Cherokee does. It's no wonder that Harrah's gladly moved in to build and operate the casino. Next to having a casino outside the gates of Walt Disney World in Orlando, this is about as good a location as Harrah's could ask for.

An effort has been made in recent decades to move away from the town's tacky, "rain dance for a dollar" trappings. If you're interested in Cherokee culture and history, you'll want to take in the Museum of the Cherokee Indian, the Oconaluftee Indian Village re-creation, and perhaps the outdoor drama *Unto These Hills*. But be prepared for some disheartening roadside scenes, including the much-lamented presence of Plains Indians teepees and headdresses, Injun-theme miniature golf, and war dances for hire. The folks up here need to make a living somehow, and it'll be a while before every last rubber tomahawk has been beaten into a slot machine.

For information, stop by the **Cherokee Visitor Center,** P.O. Box 460, Cherokee, NC 28719, 800/438-1601, website: www.Cherokee-nc.com. It's on U.S. 441 North, on the right near The Ponderosa Restaurant, as you head toward the National Park.

## SIGHTS

Located on U.S. 441 at Drama Road in downtown Cherokee, the newly renovated **Museum of the Cherokee Indian,** 828/497-3481, houses a great collection of artifacts, covering the nation's history from prehistory to the present. Fascinating multimedia exhibits tell the Cherokee story. Open year-round. Admission is $3.50 for adults.

**Oconaluftee Indian Village,** on Drama Road off U.S. 441, near the Mountainside Theatre, 828/497-2315 or 828/497-2111, is also very worthwhile—a replica of a Cherokee community, ca. 1750. Your guided tour includes live demonstrations of Cherokee crafts and skills, including beading and the proper use of a blowgun. You'll also be able to see replicas of the sorts of buildings found in Cherokee life of the period, including typical homes and the political center of the village, the Council House. Presented by the nonprofit Cherokee Historical Association, the village is open May 15–October 25, 9 A.M.–5:30 P.M. daily. Admission is $12 for adults, $5 for children 6–12 years. Ages 6 and under get in free. You can buy a package ticket that includes entrance to the village and the museum and a discount on your tickets to *Unto These Hills*. You'll see the head of the pleasant **Cherokee Botanical Garden and Nature Trail** as you exit the village.

## ENTERTAINMENT
### Unto These Hills

During the summers at the Qualla reservation, a cast of 130 puts on the stirring *Unto These Hills* Outdoor Drama at the Mountainside Theatre, U.S. 441 N. at Drama Road, Cherokee Indian Reservation, 866/554-4557 or 828/497-2111, website: www.untothesehills.com. The show depicts the history of the Cherokee people from the point of first contact with Europeans to their 1838 deportation along the Trail of Tears. The script was written by Kermit Hunter, author of *Horn in the West,* the outdoor drama in Boone.

*Unto These Hills* saw its first performance here way back in 1950, and more than six million folks have experienced the show in the half-century since. As with *The Lost Colony* out at Roanoke Island, *Unto These Hills* contains a compelling combination of elements: a powerful historical story, a powerful script, a beautiful and enigmatic theater, a strong, devoted cast, and the powerful novelty of knowing that the events on stage took place right here, on this same soil, under these same stars, with the same scent of pines and hemlock in the air. Many of the castmembers are direct descendants of the men and women they portray, lending poignancy as they depict the history of the Cherokee people from their first meeting with Spanish explorer Hernando De Soto to the forced march to Oklahoma. Shows run from mid-June through late August, Monday–Saturday 8:30 P.M. Pre-show entertainment begins at 7:45 P.M. The reserved seats at the front of theater run $16, with no discount for children. General-admission seats in the rear of the theater run only a couple of bucks shorter for adults, but kids 6–13 cost only $6. Children under 6 get in free with adult paid admission. Group discounts available for 20 or more.

Incidentally, if you're buying a combination ticket for Oconaluftee Indian Village and Museum of the Cherokee, you'll receive a discount for *Unto These Hills* tickets.

## Smoky Mountain Jamboree

The Smoky Mountain Jamboree, located on Acquoni Road opposite the Best Western, 828/497-5521, mounts an alcohol-free "country music extravaganza" for $12.50 a ticket. Children 12 and under enter free with a paying adult. The show starts nightly at 8 P.M. June through October, and on weekends only during April, May, and November. Closed the rest of the year.

## Harrah's Cherokee Casino

Most Indian casinos across America offer all the depressing aspects of Las Vegas without offering any of its glitzy visual hyperbole or $5.95 lobster dinners in trade. No matter what the billboards claim, they all tend to resemble the most smoke-filled, godforsaken corner of the seediest one-off casino in Reno.

Harrah's Cherokee Casino, 800/427-7247 (HAR-RAHS), is several cuts above those

Harrah's Cherokee Casino

© MIKE SIGALAS

CHEROKEE

# THE SPEECH OF SPECKLED SNAKE

The Savannah *Mercury* published the following article in 1829. It is rumored to have been written by John Ridge, a young Cherokee named Speckled Snake who had been educated in Connecticut, in protest of Andrew Jackson's proposed moving of the Creeks, Cherokees, and other tribes to the Indian Territory west of the Mississippi.

*BROTHERS! We have heard the talk of our great father; it is very kind, he says he loves his red children.*

*BROTHERS! I have listened to many talks from our great father. When he first came over the wide waters, he was but a little man, and wore a red coat.—Our chiefs met him on the banks of the river Savannah, and smoked with him the pipe of peace. He was then very little. His legs were cramped by sitting long in his big boat, and he begged for a little land to light his fire on. He said he had come over the wide waters to teach Indians new things, and to make them happy. He said he loved his red brothers; he was very kind.*

*The Muscogees gave the white man land, and kindled him a fire, that he might warm himself; and when his ene-*

*mies, the pale faces of the south, made war on him, their young men drew the tomahawk, and protected his head from the scalping knife. But when the white man had warmed himself before the Indian's fire, and filled himself with their hominy, he became very large. With a step he bestrode the mountains, and his feet covered the plains and the valleys. His hands grasped the eastern and the western sea, and his head rested on the moon. Then he became our Great Father. He loved his red children, and he said, "Get a little further, lest I tread on thee." With one foot he pushed the red man over the Oconee, and with the other he trampled down the graves of his fathers, and the forests where he had so long hunted the deer.—But our Great Father still loved his red children, and he soon made them another talk. He said, "Get a little further; you are too near me." But there were now some bad men among the Muscogees then, as there are now. They lingered around the graves of their ancestors,*

*(continued on next page)*

casinos—largely because the Cherokee wisely selected Harrah's experienced and well-financed casino makers to build and run the whole show. Harrah's offers vacationers a place to help compensate Cherokees for taking their land, one roll of quarters at a time. The $80 million facility houses a 60,000-square-foot museum, 2,300 video games, including video poker, blackjack, craps, and others—and you can learn to play games for free. Great food—Market Square Buffet, the Range Steak House, Midwestern Beef. And Vegas-style childcare—video games, free pizza—is thoughtfully provided at "Planet for Kids."

If you want to see some big-name stars, the 1,500-seat **Cherokee Pavilion Theatre** offers the strongest lineup this side of Dollywood. Former performers have included Loretta Lynn, BB King, Charlie Daniels, Wynonna Judd, Bill Cosby, Brooks and Dunn, Kenny Rogers, and that patron saint of pit bosses, Mr. Wayne Newton.

## Shopping

Across Drama Road from the Museum of the Cherokee, **Qualla Arts and Crafts,** U.S. 441 at Drama Road, 828/497-3103, ranks as, arguably, the best market in the world for authentic Cherokee crafts. First opened in 1946, the co-operative features the baskets, masks, pottery, finger weaving, wood carving and other crafts of more than 300 Cherokee craftspersons. Open year-round: 8 A.M.–8 P.M. daily June–August; 8 A.M.–6 P.M.

CHEROKEE

## THE SPEECH OF SPECKLED SNAKE (Cont'd)

*until they were crushed beneath the heavy tread of our Great Father. Their teeth pierced his feet, and made him angry. Yet he continued to love his red children; and when he found them too slow in moving, he sent his great guns before him to sweep his path.*

*BROTHERS! I have listened to a great many talks from our great father. But they have always began and ended in this—"Get a little further; you are too near me."*

*BROTHERS! Our great father says that "where we now are, our white brothers have always claimed the land." He speaks with a strait tongue, and cannot lie. But when he first came over the wide waters, while he was yet small, and stood before the great chief at the council on Yamacraw Bluff, he said— "Give me a little land, which you can spare, and I will pay you for it."*

*BROTHERS! When our great father made us a talk, on a former occasion, and said, "Get a little further; go beyond the Oconee, the Ocmulgee; there is a pleasant country," he also said, "It shall be yours forever." I have listened*

*to his present talk. HE says the land where you now live is not yours. Go beyond the Mississippi; there is game; and you may remain while the grass grows or the water runs. BROTHERS! Will not our great father come there also? He loves his red children. He speaks with a strait tongue, and will not lie.*

*BROTHERS! Our great father says that our bad men have made his heart bleed, for the murder of one of his white children. Yet where are the red children which he loves, once as numerous as the leaves of the forest? How many have been murdered by his warriors? How many have been crushed beneath his own footsteps?*

*BROTHERS! Our great father says we must go beyond the Mississippi. We shall there be under his care, and experience his kindness. He is very good! We have felt it all before.*

*BROTHERS! I have done.*

Ten years later, the removal was completed along the "Trail of Tears." Shortly after the removal, Ridge was assassinated by Cherokees for his role in the treaties that gave away their lands.

---

daily September through October; and 8 A.M.–4:30 P.M. daily November–May.

## ACCOMMODATIONS

The 15-story **Harrah's Hotel and Conference Center,** on U.S. 19, opened in May 2002 across from the Casino on the other side of Soco Creek.

Yes, you read that correctly—*15 stories.*

But don't worry—even before the hotel was begun, Harrah's assured us that this charming Smoky Mountain skyscraper would actually *"highlight"* the beautiful mountain setting" [italics mine], which to a lot of people sounded like a

doctor informing parents that a two-inch scar will hereafter "highlight" their child's face.

Truth be told, it's an attractive building, and it has its charms, including an elevated walkway high over the creek connecting the casino with the hotel. When it's snowy outside, the views are phenomenal. The hotel's main lobby incorporates traditional Cherokee art, and offers an indoor pool, spa and workout room, 15,000-square-foot conference center, a 24-hour restaurant, and Club Cappuccino, a coffee bar. **Seven Sisters** restaurant serves up steaks, seafood, pasta dishes, and desserts.

Cherokee has benefited financially from this huge boost to its bed count. And the casino and reservation's restaurants and shops will make even more money as travelers linger longer in the immediate vicinity. Fittingly for a casino hotel, room prices are a bit of a crapshoot: the price of a given room can vary from $49 to $200 depending on availability, though if you book far ahead, you should be able to get in at under $80 a night. Most rooms offer a view of the creek, but you may save a few dollars by opting for a parking-lot view. See www.harrahs.com for special packages, which can save you a good bit of money.

Nearby, in Sylva, Patrick and Mary Ellen Montague's 1914 bungalow, the **Freeze House,** 71 Sylvan Hts., 828/586-8161, fax 828/631-0714, offers three rooms, $75–100. The house was built by Patrick's maternal grandfather (Mr. Freeze) during the first World War, and used initially as a private home that doubled during summers as a guesthouse for outlanders seeking the cooler mountain air. When the train stopped bringing up guests after World War II, the Freeze family took in boarders year-round, and eventually the house became a fully private home. In the mid-1990s, Patrick's son refurbished it. Two private guest houses—equipped with kitchens and great for larger families or groups—are also available for $400 and $600 a week.

## CAMPGROUNDS

Cherokee offers no less than 13 campgrounds. **Indian Creek Campground,** nine miles north of town on Big Cove Road, 828/497-4361, is a favorite with tenters, who appreciate the secluded tent sites. It offers 75 sites for $16–17 a night.

Notable among the other sites is the cartoon-related **Yogi in the Smokies,** eight miles north of town on Big Cove Road, 828/497-9151, with more than 200 sites for tenting or RV-ing, three rental cabins, and programs for the kids.

# Maggie Valley

Maggie Valley is more a strip of tourist-related businesses than it is a true, walkable old-time mountain community in the mold of a Dillsboro or Waynesville. Unlike those towns, founded in horse-drawn centuries and designed to accommodate foot traffic, Maggie Valley didn't get a post office until 1904, and didn't *really* get going until after World War II. It was shaped by the automobile, and by the needs and wants of those who drove up here to be near the national park. Even today, for all its hundreds of rooms, Maggie is home to just 350 year-round residents.

But this is not necessarily a bad thing. The charm of Maggie Valley is that, for all its attempts to gussy itself up, the town seems always about one step away from being pure country. Just travel a couple of hundred yards from U.S. 19's restaurants and motels and suddenly you'll find yourself in a beautiful, rural Appalachian valley. In fact, a number of outfits in Maggie Valley rent brookside cabins amid the mountain laurel and hemlocks, but within walking distance of the restaurants and shops.

Maggie also offers some good BBQ, a home-grown amusement park or two, and a couple of must-sees for any enthusiast of Appalachian culture: **The Maggie Valley Opry House** and **The Stompin' Grounds.** For more information, contact the **Maggie Valley Area Chamber of Commerce,** 2487 Soco Rd., 800/785-8259 or 828/926-1686.

One note: Maggie has just one main street, but that main street has two names: U.S. 19 and "Soco Road." Most locals use the former, and give directions by landmark (e.g., "It's on 19 past Ghost Town"). Where possible, however, we've taken the post office's lead and included the Soco Road street address as well.

## SIGHTS

### Ghost Town in the Sky

Located on U.S. 19, high above Maggie Valley, Ghost Town in the Sky, 800/446-7886 or 828/926-1140, website: www.ghosttowninthesky.com, is not a true, abandoned old town but a small, aging amusement park—and a funky, homegrown bit of Americana. Built in 1960 at the height of the *Gunsmoke-Bonanza* era, Ghost Town is a tribute to the East's fascination with the West as delineated in dime novels, Saturday-morning serials, and early television: think Roy Rogers, Howdy Doody, and wagon-wheel chandeliers.

For young children and their parents, it can be a real hoot.

Admission, like the mountain itself, is a bit steep: $22.95 for everyone over 10 years of age, and $13.95 for kids 3–10 (kids two and under get in free)—though this includes unlimited use of the carnival-like rides and shows. It's open daily in the summertime, weekends only September–October. Getting *up there* is half the adventure. You can take the minivan tram, a 3,364-foot double incline railway (with grades up to 76.9 percent), or a two-seat 1962 Italian chairlift—for non-skiers, at least, a dramatic and novel way to arrive anywhere, much less a Western ghost town. Once you get to the park itself you'll be in the Mining Town area, but to hit the bulk of the park, you've still got some climbing to do, or you can take another tram.

Ghost Town is divided into four themed areas: Mining Town (the lowest), Western Town, Indian Village (with Cherokee dancers), and Mountain Town. For older kids, the Red Devil roller coaster is the big draw—a short, looping metal coaster that seems all the higher by being some 5,000 feet up a mountain. Not a bad one, though it's the only real thrill ride up here. There's also a small train and a kiddie area and a handful of carnival rides that nobody's troubled to re-theme for the park. Thus, you can find yourself deep in Appalachia, swinging back and forth in a huge Viking ship, high above a re-created Kansas town.

Parents, depending on their philosophies, will either want to be sure to catch or avoid

> *Built in 1960 at the height of the* **Gunsmoke-Bonanza** *era, Ghost Town is a tribute to the East's fascination with the West as delineated in dime novels, Saturday-morning serials, and early television: think Roy Rogers, Howdy Doody, and wagon-wheel chandeliers.*

the hourly gunfights on Main Street. Double, I suppose, for the can-can shows in the saloons. The park considerately allows guests to bring in coolers packed with picnic goodies, and they'll even transport your cooler to the park's picnic area, where it'll be waiting for you when you're ready to eat. If all else fails, parents can enjoy the views of the surrounding mountains. The Town itself dishes up some fair grub, including ice cream, funnel cakes, and that staple of the 19th-century American frontier diet, pizza.

## Soco Gardens Zoo

The animals you'll find at Soco Gardens Zoo, 3758 Soco Rd., Maggie Valley, 828/926-1746, aren't specific to the Smokies region, but are rather largely exotics: a jaguar, alligators, llamas, monkeys, ostriches, and so on, including a number of species who haven't seen the top of a mountain since working their ways down Mount Ararat.

As at every zoo, the reptile shows are very popular at Soco. If you're planning to hike the Smokies, this'll give you a chance to have a good, safe eye-to-eye with a cottonmouth and a copperhead ahead of time, to better identify them in the wild. Years ago, somebody lost a leg here to one of the park's alligators. Fortunately—for the zoo's insurance company, at least—the victim was another alligator, theretofore known as Tripod. You can still see him today, unless things have taken a grimmer turn and he's now known as Pogo.

Open 10 A.M.–6 P.M. during spring and fall, 9 A.M. to 7:30 P.M. daily during the summer. Closed winters. Admission is reasonable: $6 for adults 13–65, $5 for seniors, and $3 for kids 12 and under. Wheelchair accessible.

## Santa's Land Park and Zoo

Like Ghost Town in the Sky, Santa's Land Park and Zoo, 2.5 miles east of Cherokee on U.S. 19, 828/497-9191, seems like something out of

entrance to Ghost Town in the Sky, Maggie Valley

© MIKE SIGALAS

a simpler, less cynical era. It's a Christmas-themed park featuring old-fashioned amusement park rides painted green and red. But young kids will love the kiddy Rudi Coaster (with antlers), the miniature steam train, the petting zoo (including "reindeer," of course), the juggling and magic-making elves over at the Jingle Bell Theater, and Santa's House, where they can get cheek-to-rosy-cheek with St. Nick himself. The park includes some nods to the mountain culture of the Smokies: a cabin from before the War Between the States, a gristmill, and a moonshine still. If you're up here anyway, you might want to take in the pleasant **Fall Harvest Festival** on weekends in October, featuring mountain craft exhibits, fresh apple cider and apple butter, and more. Open Monday–Friday 9 A.M.–5 P.M., Saturday–Sunday 9 A.M.–6 P.M., May–October and Thanksgiving week, Saturday–Sunday 9 A.M.–6 P.M. in November. Starting in December, Santa's away overseeing operations further north. Admission runs around $14.72 for everybody 3 and up.

## ENTERTAINMENT

### Maggie Valley Opry House

If you're here to experience Appalachian folk culture and music, be sure to catch the Maggie Valley Opry House, 3605 Soco Rd., 828/926-9336, featuring Maggie Valley's unqualified bluegrass star, Raymond Fairchild, considered by aficionados to be among the best living banjo pickers. Cherokee-born (and part Cherokee-blooded) Fairchild, famed for a deadpan concentration as he picks, recorded his first albums in the early 1960s. Nowadays, after 40 years of festivals and different touring bands—including his famed Maggie Valley Boys, with son Zane on lead guitar—Fairchild runs his Opry House and plays for appreciative fans with a backup band. If at all possible, get over to the Opry House at 8 P.M. on any night April–October, and catch this man in action. To get familiar with his work before you arrive, pick up his classic *31 Banjo Favorites* CD, on the Rhythm label. It's a great trove of Smoky Mountain music.

CHEROKEE

## The Stompin' Ground

And speaking of mountain music, the Stompin' Ground, 828/926-1288, may look like a big old barn on U.S. 19, but it just may be the Studio 54 of clogging. The Stompin' Ground throws open its doors nightly from May to October. Stomp inside and you'll find some top-notch clogging afoot. And if you get the itch, you can give it a go yourself.

## Diamond K Dance Ranch

This family-oriented nightspot (1 Playhouse Dr., Maggie Valley, 828/926-7735) offers live country music every Saturday night (adults $7, kids $4), teen nights, Friday-night fish fries ($5.95), and award-winning chili. No alcohol allowed on premises.

## Carolina Nights

After the casino, the next best bet for "resorters" is to head to the 300-seat Carolina Nights on U.S. 19 across from Microtel in Maggie Valley, 828/926-8822. The theater offers a prime rib dinner and a show that stakes a claim some- where between Nashville and Vegas; count on Blues Brothers imitators and a magic act along with your country and homespun comedy.

# RECREATION

## Cataloochee Ski Area

If you've come to North Carolina in search of the world's best ski slopes, you have been criminally misled. However, Cataloochee, 1080 Ski Lodge Rd., 828/926-0285, website: www .cataloochee.com, has nine slopes (seven with snowmaking equipment), three ski lifts, and a rope tow. At publication, the park is in the midst of a three-year, $2.1-million infrastructure-improvement project. Rates run roughly $23 for adults on a weekday, $36 on a weekend, with discounts for kids and juniors, seniors, students, and members of the military. If you're coming here during the week, ask about the "Kids Ski Free" arrangement with various local lodgings, which can save parents considerable amounts of money. Night skiing is available too, at $18/$21.

# ACCOMMODATIONS

Maggie Valley, with just around 350 full-time residents, offers the most rooms in the area. To rent an individually owned cabin or vacation home in the Maggie Valley/Cherokee region, call **Vacation Rental Cabins,** 800/338-8228 or 828/926-3164.

## $50–100

If you're looking to try to re-create the sort of down-to-earth, agrarian lifestyle that existed up here before the tourists came, you'll find a good semblance outside of town at the five-bedroom **Ketner Inn & Farm,** 1954 Jonathan Creek Rd., 800/714-1397 or 828/926-1511. Built in 1898 and resting on 27 acres of rolling farmland, the house is full of country and Victorian antiques, plus porches and full country breakfasts. Innkeeper Mary Anderson welcomes children. Rates run $55–75.

Up 1,000 feet above the town proper, clinging to the side of Setzer Mountain, you'll find the **Abbey Inn,** 6375 Soco Gap Rd., 800/545-5853, a friendly motor court built in 1952 and featuring wooden furniture, separated rooms, great views, and moderate prices, along with free gourmet coffee in the lobby. See it online at www.abbeyinn.com. On a case-by-case basis, the Abbey Inn allows dogs, for a small fee.

The 21-unit **Riverlet Motel & Restaurant,** 4102 Soco Rd./U.S. 19, 800/691-9952 or 828/926-1900, is a humble little motor inn beside a creek. To the right of the motel you'll find a little picnic area that narrows to an end where two little riverlets rejoin each other. My brother proposed to his wife, Susan, on this spot in 1994. Joe says the coffee shop's pretty good, too— breakfast only. Open April through October. Close by you'll find a **Comfort Inn.** 3282 Soco Rd., 828/926-9106, hugging the same creek.

Maggie Valley's **Microtel,** 3777 Soco Rd./U.S. 19, 828/926-8554, website: www.microtel maggie.com, a 58-unit motel, feels almost European—or shiplike—in its utilitarian classiness. The Micro features a picnic area, mountain view, and covered pool. The motel's open year-round, unlike some of its competitors.

## $100–150

Located beside a quiet creek, **Country Cabins,** 171 Bradley St., 828/926-0612, website: www.countrycabins.mv.com, are just the sort of cute, hand-hewn cabins you want to see. They seem much more out of the way than they are, just off Maggie's main drag. Each of the log cabins offers a wood-burning fireplace, a kitchen, and a porch, and you can walk to a number of shops and restaurants. Cabins run $105–120 d a night. **Mountain Joy Cottages,** a block off the main road at 121 Setzer Cove Rd., 888/926-1257, website: www.mountainjoycottages.com, feature similar cabins, and a covered pool. Cabins, including some with Jacuzzis, start at $130.

## $150 and Up

The **Timberwolf Creek Bed & Breakfast,** 391 Johnson Branch, 828/926-2608, is a large gray and white building folded into the side of the mountain. It features three rooms; the most deluxe is the Timberwolf Retreat, a suite with a king-sized bed, vaulted red oak ceilings, a spa tub for two, and a balcony overlooking the stream outside. The other two rooms are the Woodland and the Streamsong, and the names pretty much tell you what view each provides. Both feature queen beds, whirlpool tubs-for-two, private decks, and private entrances. The Streamsong's double French doors open to a private deck over the stream.

Hosts Sandee and Larry Wright serve up a full gourmet fireside breakfast (sometimes featuring French custard toast with spiked apples, and baked omelettes)—or you can take your breakfast outside by the waterwheel. In the evenings the Wrights dish up some fresh baked goods and mugs of steaming hot cider in front of the fireplace—just the sort of treat that makes you feel like a well-loved nine-year-old. However, no actual nine-year-olds are allowed to stay here, as kids, like pets, are officially deemed "inappropriate" at the Timberwolf. Smokers will need to practice their craft outside on the porch. $195–245 a night. Wednesday is Dinner and Jazz night. Contact innkeeper@timberwolf creek.com for more information.

The **Cataloochee Ranch,** 119 Ranch Dr.,

**M**

**CHEROKEE**

Maggie Valley, 800/868-1401 or 828/926-1401, website: www.cataloochee-ranch.com, was founded in 1933 by Tom and Judy Alexander on an old Cataloochee Valley farm inside the national park. In 1938, fleeing the stringent land-use limitations within the park proper, the Alexanders moved the ranch to its current location bordering the park at the top of Fie Top Mountain, elevation 5,000 feet.

Today, the Alexanders' children and grandchildren run the ranch, which can host up to 65 guests in its cabins, suites, and rooms. Meals, as you might guess, come filling and family-style. Activities in the 1,000- acre spread include horseback riding (extra fee), pack trips (ditto), hikes, singalongs, fishing, wagon rides, a swimming pool, tennis courts, and the time-honored marshmallow roast. Three private entrances to the park provide ranch guests with another very significant amenity, and if you're here in the winter (open holidays and weekends only), you're as close to the Cataloochee Ski Area (also owned by the Alexander family) as you can get.

Rooms in the ranch's big lodge run $145–275, April–November. The big breakfasts and the dinners (often grill-outs, when weather permits) come with your room fee. Lunches are available at an extra charge.

You'll find Fie Top Road off U.S. 19 at Ghost Town in the Sky. Drive up the road for three miles, and you're there.

Interested in horseback riding but staying elsewhere? You can still book a horse at the Cataloochee, for only a bit more than ranch guests pay.

**The Swag,** 2300 Swag Rd., 828/926-0430, website: www.theswag.com, really *is* out of the way—by design. Built of hand-hewn logs, and sitting on 250 acres bordering the national park, the Swag is expensive, but popular with hikers who appreciate the lodge's private entrance to the park. First opened in 1981, the Swag offers 12 guest rooms furnished with antiques and patchwork quilts. Six of the rooms have fireplaces, and all have private baths.

This is one of the few inns in the region to offer a racquetball court. The five-star dining room serves three meals a day to guests and the public.

The name, incidentally, refers to the dip in the mountains here: the private, 2.5-mile-long driveway to the lodge begins at the bottom of

Maggie Valley accommodations

the Swag and rises 1,100 feet to the inn's location at the peak. Consequently, the folks at the lodge will tell you, spring arrives at the bottom of the driveway three weeks before it reaches the lodge at the top. Open from Memorial Day to the end of October, the Swag is located off I-40 at Exit 20; head 2.8 miles south on U.S. 276 to Hemphill Road and follow the signs. Rates run $265–510 a night. If you're only coming up for a meal, lunch runs $16.50 per person and dinner runs $30–45.

## Campgrounds

Maggie Valley offers more than 600 campsites, all of them with electricity and water, and some with sewer as well. The biggest campground is **Presley's Campground,** 1786 Soco Rd., 828/926-1904, which features about 30 tent sites to go with its more than 200 RV sites. Prices run $17–20 a night; open April through October. Others include the **Creekwood Farm RV Park,** 40 Happy Valley Circle, 828/926-7977 ($18–20), and the tidy **Hillbilly Campground and RV Park,** 4115 Soco Rd., 828/926-3353 ($18–20).

## FOOD

Don't let the name keep you away: **Butts on the Creek,** 1584 Soco Rd., Maggie Valley, 828/926-7885, may sound (at best) like a waterfront smokers' club, but it provides arguably the finest barbecue in the area. Inarguably, it offers the nicest location, with lots of windows and a back porch looking out over Jonathan Creek. Butts dishes up great smoked pork and chicken ($6.25 for a sandwich), as well as full dinners—St. Louis ribs, chicken, Texas beef brisket—with two sides and hush puppies for $7.95–16.95. They also

offer some fine desserts made from scratch, including a great Key lime pie and some tasty cobblers. Closed Mondays.

And yet, a lot of local folks prefer the **Bar-B-Que Shak,** on U.S. 19 below Ghost Town in the Sky, 828/926-0560, which plays Loretta Lynn to Butts' Faith Hill. Here, the waitresses still call you "hon," and you can still pick up a great BBQ pork sandwich for $2.50.

Set in a rustic cedar cabin, **J Arthur's,** 2843 Soco Rd., 828/926-1817, offers fresh local mountain trout ($15.50), prime rib ($15.95), and a great gorgonzola cheese salad ($7.50). The "Left Bank–style" French onion soup makes a great appetizer on a cool mountain night. There's a better-than-average kids menu ($6.95) and a toy-equipped "kids corner" for tykes. Dinner only.

If you're looking for Italian, Maggie Valley's **Snappy's Italian Restaurant and Pizzeria,** 2769 Soco Rd., 828/926-6126, provides worthwhile Italian fare. **Mountaineer Buffet,** 6490 Soco Rd., 828/926-1730, offers all-you-can-eat comfort food, outdoor dining on a large screened porch, and beautiful views.

And you can't visit these parts and miss taking in at least one big country breakfast, the kind with the checkered tablecloth and stacks of pancakes and apron-wearing waitresses and such. Some argue that the best is **Joey's Pancake House,** 4309 Soco Rd., 828/926-0212, where you can pile on Belgian waffles cinnamon French toast, eggs benedict, slow-cooked oatmeal, creamy chipped beef, and blueberry, chocolate chip, and banana nut pancakes beneath wagon-wheel chandeliers. The pancakes are the true stars here—you can buy Joey's pancake batter by the sackful at the checkout. Winter discounts. **Country Vittles,** 3589 Soco Rd., 828/926-1820, also gets good reviews.

# Waynesville

Waynesville was originally founded by Patriot officers and soldiers who received land grants following the American Revolution. Many had served under General "Mad" Anthony Wayne, and they named their settlement in his honor.

A couple of generations later, at the end of the War Between the States, Waynesville witnessed the surrender of the last Confederate force in North Carolina—the bedraggled Army of Western North Carolina—on May 6, 1865. In fact, for a long time, Tar Heels argued that the very last shot of the Civil War fired on land was fired here on May 10, 1865, but later records determined that the Confederates down in Brownsville, Texas, had held out three days longer, so Waynesville was stripped of this particular glory. The railroad reached here in 1883 and brought up some of the first tourists.

Today, this pretty town (pop. 10,000) features a pleasant downtown area with brick sidewalks and several small shops in the old buildings.

## SIGHTS

The **Shelton House Museum of North Carolina Handicrafts,** 49 Shelton St., 828/452-1551, is set in the old Shelton House, a two-story home built between 1876 and 1880 and now listed on the National Register of Historic Places. The museum contains Civil War and Native American artifacts, and displays of such hand-crafted goods as woodcarvings, quilts, pottery, musical instruments, and weavings. Located at the corner of Shelton and Pigeon Streets, the museum stays open for the tourist season, May through October, Wednesday–Saturday 10 A.M.–5 P.M., Sunday 2—5 P.M. No admission charged.

### Old Pressley Sapphire Mine

Just east of Waynesville, in **Canton** (Exit 33 off I-40), you'll find the Old Pressley Sapphire Mine, 240 Pressley Mine Rd., 828/648-6320. The Old

downtown Waynesville

Pressley is a favorite of rock hounds, and the storied source of one of the largest sapphires ever plucked from the earth, the 1,445-carat "Star of the Carolina." Today you can mine a bit yourself ($10), or just enjoy the picnic area and browse the rock shop.

### Lindsey Gardens and Miniature Village & Mini-Apolis Grand Prix Park

Popular with the younger set, this complex, at 1110 Soco Rd., 828/926-1685/926-6277, features miniature racecar tracks, bumper boats, miniature golf, a gem mine, and a diminutive train that meanders through the gardens and a village of more than 90 miniature buildings.

## ENTERTAINMENT
### HART: Haywood Arts Repertory Theatre

Beside the Shelton House in Waynesville stands the 250-seat **Performing Arts Center, 250 Pigeon St.**, where the Haywood Arts Repertory Theatre (HART) produces two mainstage musicals, five mainstage plays, and up to six Studio Theater shows every season. This means that they'll probably be performing something when you're up here. The mainstage plays and musicals tend toward mainstream classics: a recent season included *Our Town, The Sound of Music,* and *Antigone.* Tickets for plays and musicals run $12–15 for adults. The box office is located at **Mast General Store** on Main Street, or call 828/456-6322 for show information and reservations.

### Shopping

In Waynesville, as in any good mountain town, you'll find just about everything there is to do on Main Street. For instance, on Main Street stands the Waynesville location of **Mast General Store,** 63 N. Main St., 828/452-2101,

**Mast General Store**

website: www.mastgeneralstore.com. Though this store only opened in 1991, both the Mast business and the building itself are much older than that. The first Mast store, in fact, opened up in Valle Crucis back in 1883. With its old oak floors and early 1900s tin ceilings and fixtures, the Waynesville store feels as though it dates from the same era. It still offers an antique feel and the sort of product diversity that reminds you why these were called "general" stores. A 1923 advertisement for the Mast store in Boone boasted of "Goods for the Living, Coffins and Caskets for the Dead." Today, Mast no longer caters to the departed, but the living can still buy Squirrel Nut Zippers, Charleston Chews, and Licorice Bullseyes from wooden barrels. You'll also find sturdy, traditional clothing and outdoor wear, and an assortment of such mercantile essentials as rosebud salves, stone-ground meal, "courtin' candles," porch swings, rocking chairs, handmade crafts and baskets, goat's milk and lye soap, and of

> *With its old oak floors and early 1900s tin ceilings and fixtures, the Waynesville store feels as though it dates from the same era. It still offers an antique feel and the sort of product diversity that reminds you why these were called "general" stores.*

CHEROKEE

course, a Radio Flyer wagon. To get to the Waynesville store, take U.S. 276 south to Main Street, turn right, and then turn right into the parking lot.

Open on Main Street since 1945, **Whitman's Bakery and Sandwich Shop,** 18 N. Main St., 828/456-8271, serves luscious breads, pies, pastries, cookies, and cakes. They make sandwiches, too—a good spot for lunch. Open Tuesday–Saturday at 6 A.M.

The **T. Pennington Art Gallery** features the drawings of Teresa Pennington, a self-taught artist whose personal takes on Western North Carolina (including a recent series on the Blue Ridge Parkway) have won her national acclaim.

The **Open Air Market** on Main Street strikes an interesting balance between a newsstand and a grocery store. At the **Twigs & Leaves Gallery** in the center of town you'll find nature-related handcrafts, photography, and paintings as well as a pottery studio manned by Kaaren Stoner.

Every Wednesday and Saturday during the summer, you'll find local farmers on the north end of Main Street for the **Farmers Tailgate Market.** If you're staying somewhere with an efficiency kitchen, this is a great place to pick up fresh mountain produce, including berries, new potatoes, cucumbers, green beans, tomatoes, squash, onions, and carrots.

## ACCOMMODATIONS

### $100–150

If you're looking for a B&B within walking distance of the shops on Waynesville's Main Street, take a look at Judith and Dennis Frampton's **Prospect Hill Inn,** 274 S. Main St., 800/219-6147 or 828/456-5980, website: www.prospecthillnc.com. $95–135. This turn-of-the-century, seven-bedroom Victorian stands right on Main Street at the top of Prospect Hill, at the edge of downtown. A pleasant stay, with an enormous front porch manned with rockers and wicker furniture. Breakfasts are upscale—

served on the porch on fine china and silver—and gourmet. The living room provides a good view of the Smokies. Though they discourage kids staying in the house proper, the Framptons offer two efficiency apartments in the old carriage house behind the main House for $450 a week. They overlook a quiet street and face Eagle's Nest Mountain.

### Campgrounds

Camping near Waynesville comes cheaply at the **Sunburst** public campground, 828/877-3265, adjacent to the Shining Rock Wilderness Area. Head seven miles east of town on U.S. 276, and then six miles south on N.C. 215. None of the 14 sites have hookups, but the area offers flush toilets, and campsites run just $4 a night.

## FOOD

Over toward Waynesville you'll find **Eddie's Bar-B-Que,** 3028 Jonathan Creek Rd., 828/926-5353, a very friendly, down-home spot with a mascot who looks not a little like our friend Piggly-Wiggly. Here, a pork sandwich will run you $4.25, or a platter (with hush puppies, cole slaw, and fried apples) for $7.45. Combo rib platters run up to $11.45. All-you-can-eat chicken on Thursday night, and prime rib on Saturday. Closed Monday–Wednesday. East of Waynesville on U.S. 74, you'll come upon the town of Canton, home to **Skeeter's Barbecue,** 828/648-8595. Skeeter's doesn't look like much from the outside, but it's the real thing. Down-eastern pit-smoked in hickory, tangy vinegar-red pepper sauce, or traditional Southern tomato-based sauce. Unlike most barbecue joints, they serve breakfast, lunch, and dinner, and you can find grilled chicken salads and sandwiches here as well. Open Monday–Saturday 7 A.M.–9 P.M. **Antipasto's,** in the Waynesville Shopping Plaza, 828/452-0218, provides good Italian fare (closed Monday).

# Dillsboro

Known as the home depot for the **Great Smoky Mountains Railroad** and as a cute mountain village (pop. 100) loaded with local crafts, Dillsboro is a child of the old Western North Carolina Railway, which arrived hereabouts in 1882. William Allen Dills founded the town as a stopover for travelers up from Asheville. He built the Mt. Beulah Hotel on Main Street, which exists today as the Jarrett House, still a worthwhile lodging and restaurant. For more information about Dillsboro, contact the **Jackson County Chamber of Commerce** at 828/586-2155.

For more information, contact the **Jackson County Travel and Tourism Authority,** 116 Central St., Sylva, 800/962-1911 or 828/586-2155.

## SIGHTS

### Great Smoky Mountains Railroad

With stops in Dillsboro, Bryson City, and Andrews, the Great Smoky Mountains Railroad, 800/872-4681, is a classy and creative operation.

You remember the railroad, in fact, from its role in the Harrison Ford/Tommy Lee Jones film *The Fugitive.* Though none of the current trips include collisions with busfuls of convicts, the railroad does offer a number of different trips with a variety of themes. The GSMR operates both steam and diesel trains on most routes, with the steam trips running about five dollars more than the diesel trips. (The prices quoted below, unless otherwise noted, are for the steam trips.) Kids 2 and under ride free; those 3–12 ride for roughly half the adult fare.

The **Tuckasegee River** trip ($31) leaves from Dillsboro Depot, heads west to Bryson City, lays over for an hour there, then returns to Dillsboro. Along the way, you'll thread the pitch-black 836-foot Cowee tunnel.

Other trips include ones taking in the Nantahala Gorge (Bryson City departure, $31), Red Marble Gap (Andrews departure, $26, diesel only), and the Fontana Trestle (Dillsboro departure, $31). You can even take a

**Great Smoky Mountains Railroad car**

CHEROKEE

© MIKE SIGALAS

Olde Towne Inn

seven-hour "Raft 'n' Rail" trip that includes rafting (Bryson City departure, $64), and gourmet dinner trips (Dillsboro departure, $54, diesel only). For youngsters and parents of same, every summer for a week or so, the railroad swings a deal with Sir Topham Hatt and brings in that oft-cheeky tank engine, Thomas, direct from the Isle of Sodor and the VCRs of every parent in America. These 30-minute trips (Dillsboro departure, and steam only, of course) cost $10 a ticket (for both adults and children). Be sure to call ahead to reserve for this one. The gift shop at the GSMR station at Dillsboro, incidentally, offers one of the world's largest selections of Thomas items.

## SHOPPING

Dillsboro's Front Street and Haywood Road (or U.S. 19 Business) host a number of shops worth a browse. Front Street's **Mountain Pottery** is a working studio where you can watch artisans creating raku pottery, handmade porcelain, and stoneware. Up on Haywood Road you'll find a

handful of other shops, including the countriana **Corn Crib,** 828/586-9626. And quiltophiles won't want to miss **Apron Shop,** between Haywood and Front on Webster Street, 828/586-9391, featuring locally handmade quilts, as well as aprons, pillows, and baskets.

## ACCOMMODATIONS
### $50–100

For sheer tradition and pretense-free mountain hospitality, the **Jarrett House,** 800/972-5623 or 828/586-0265, is hard to beat. The Jarrett House has been renting rooms and feeding hungry visitors since 1884, when it was opened by no less than Mr. Dills himself, founder of the town of Dillsboro, just two years after the coming of the Western North Carolina Railway in 1882.

Dills christened the inn the Mount Beulah Hotel, named after his daughter, Beulah. Some may tell you that the hotel's original name came from the fact that the inn faces Mount Beulah, and that's true as well. Dills, you see, named the *mountain* after his daughter, too. Ah, the privileges of founderhood. Beulah's daughter lives next door to the hotel, even today.

A significant portion of the town's income used to derive from the passengers who piled out of the daily train up from Asheville for a noontime "dinner" at the hotel. Within a couple of years—beginning with a pair of scandalously cigarette-wielding women from Edenton in 1884—outlanders had begun to come up and stay for the summer.

The hotel's second owners were Frank and Sallie Jarrett, who changed the name to Jarrett Springs Hotel to take advantage of a sulphur spring out back of the hotel, and operated it from the 1890s through the 1950s—an amazing run. Sallie's country-cured ham, red-eye gravy, and hot biscuits became the stuff of legend, and a definite Jarrett House tradition. Today you can still pick up a ham dinner here, even if you're not a hotel guest, for $12.50. When the hot springs craze abated, the next owners changed the name to its current incarnation. Though the hotel changed owners a number of times in the 1950s, all told, the hotel has had only four owners for 110 of its 120 years. The current owners, the Hartbargers, have owned and operated the Jarrett House since 1975, and clearly honor the mantle they've assumed.

Rooms run $85 year-round; price includes breakfast. No pets, no kids under 11, no credit cards.

Also in Dillsboro, Lera Chitwood's **Olde Towne Inn,** at 300 Haywood Rd. (U.S. 23/74), 888/528-8840 or 828/586-3461, is a friendly spot just across from the Great Smoky Mountain Railroad depot. The five rooms in this 1878 home are named after colors, and they run $75–135. All but the least expensive, the Yellow Room, have their own baths. If you choose that room, you'll be sharing with Mrs. Chitwood.

## Campgrounds

Just east of Dillsboro, the town of Sylva offers a number of pleasant cafés. If you'd like to camp in the Sylva area, the privately owned **Fort Tatham**

**Campsites,** 175 Tatham's Creek Rd., 828/586-6662, offer shaded sites on a stream. You'll find the campground six miles south of the junction of U.S. 441, U.S. 23, and U.S. 74. Sites—most with hookups—run $15–18 a night. Open between May and October.

## FOOD

For country ham, Southern-fried chicken, or hand-battered mountain trout, head over to the **Jarrett House,** 800/972-5623 or 828/586-0265, in Dillsboro, where they've been serving huge platters of good cooking, family-style since 1884. You will not leave here hungry; your meal comes with cole slaw, candied apples, buttered potatoes, green beans, pickled beets, hot biscuits, and a drink. Dinners run $12.50. Kids eat for $5. Open Monday–Saturday 4–8 P.M., and Sunday 11:30 A.M.–2:30 P.M. and 4–8 P.M. No credit cards.

## GETTING THERE
### By Car

The biggest road in these parts is I-40, which from the west leads out of Knoxville, Tenn., over the top of the national park, skirting its eastern edge. Take U.S. 276 south, then get onto U.S. 19 and head west. From the Raleigh area or Wilmington, simply head west on I-40 Asheville, then take U.S. 19/23 west.

From Greenville, S.C., take I-85 to I-26, and then head north to asheville and I-40.and U.S. 19/23 west. As an alternate route, you can take U.S. 25 to I-26 to I-40.

Visitors from Chattanooga usually enter this region on U.S. 65, one of the more scenic highways in the area. It crosses the lower portion of southwestern North Carolina, passing through such towns as Franklin, Highlands, and Hendersonville. Very pretty, but plan on a long trip, and bring the Dramamine.

If you're starting from Atlanta, a favorite route is to take the Atlanta Highway (U.S. 78) to Athens, Georgia (a great stopover), and then head north on U.S. 441 off the loop highway and take it all the way to Franklin.

## By Air

The closest airports to the Cherokee region are in Asheville, Chattanooga, Tenn., and Knoxville, Tenn. Greenville, S.C., isn't much further, so if you find a cheap flight there, take it.

## By Bus

Driving on these mountain roads in the back of a huge bus sounds gut-wrenching to me, but it is, technically, possible to get to, say, Waynesville via Greyhound bus. Of course, routes are everything, and while it'll only cost you $21 and an hour and a half to get from Knoxville to Waynesville (because it's a direct route), it'll take you far longer to bus from Atlanta, since the

first thing your bus driver will do after leaving Atlanta is head toward Knoxville, where you'll have to transfer to the Knoxville-Waynesville line. The moral of the story? If you're going to let the dog do the driving, fly into Knoxville or Asheville. Of course, when you get to Waynesville, you'll be without transportation to get you into the park or nearby towns. But if this is your best option, call 800/229-9424.

## Car Rentals

If you're flying into the area and need to rent a car, you'll want to rent it at the airport. Contact Alamo at 800/327-9633, website: www.alamo.com, Avis at 800/831-2847, website: www.avis.com, Budget

# THE BATTLE FOR DUPONT STATE FOREST

DuPont State Forest, off U.S. 64 between Brevard and Hendersonville, offers visitors 10,400 acres of forest featuring four major waterfalls on the Little River and several on Grassy Creek. But it was not always so. People visited this spectacular, formerly corporate-owned land for generations (by permission and not) and wondered why it wasn't protected and made more accessible to the citizenry. In 1995, after much legal wrangling, threats of development and the invocation of eminent domain, and the timely intercessions of the nonprofit Conservation Fund and state government, it's finally been done.

The forest was named for the corporation that made the initial 7,600 acres available to the Conservation Fund at bargain prices in 1996. For a time, the now-central 2,200-acre section encompassing High Falls, Triple Falls, and Bridal Veil Falls seemed doomed to become yet another exclusive 100- to 200-home golf paradise at the hands of developer Jim "the Cliffs" Anthony—famous for developing the storied course, the Cliffs of Glassy. Fortunately, in late October 2000, Governor Jim Hunt and the elected Council of State voted 9–0 to use the law of eminent domain to preserve this area for all North Carolinians—and for all visitors to the state.

What with all the headlines over the months, the general public couldn't wait to explore the land once it was theirs. From the very start, hikers and

bikers enjoyed the broad gravel roads laid out by The Cliffs to bring in the construction trucks that never came. In November 2000, volunteers swept in to prepare the would-be fairways and golf cart paths for hikers, bikers, and equestrians.

The property features more than 90 trails, most of them set on DuPont's old gravel roads; mountain bikes are welcome on several. Fishing and horseback riding are also permitted here. Thus far, camping is not. Hunting is, so be sure to wear fluorescent colors in season.

The elevation here ranges from 2,300 feet (below Hooker Falls on the Little River) to the 3,600-foot, exposed granite dome of Stone Mountain. The land includes the smallish Lake Julia. Most of it is forested with young to middle-aged hardwoods and white pine dating back to the middle 1900s.

Besides the beautiful waterfalls—several of which appeared in the 1990s film version of *Last of the Mohicans*—it's the eight or so miles of unpaved roads on the property that have kept DuPont's popularity growing. Most of the roads are closed to motor vehicles but provide tremendous opportunities for hikers, cyclists, and equestrians.

You can get to the DuPont State Forest from Hendersonville via Kanuga/Crab Creek Road, from Asheville and Brevard via U.S. 64 and Little River Road, or from Greenville, S.C., via Cedar Mountain and Cascade Lake Road.

at 800/353-0600, website: www.budget.com, Enterprise at 800/325-8007, website: enterprise .com, and Hertz at 800/654-3131, website: www .hertz.com.

### Emergencies

Call 911 for any emergency in this region. The local hospitals are **Cherokee Indian Hospital,** Hospital Road, Cherokee, 828/497-9163; **Harris Regional Hospital,** 68 Hospital Rd. in Sylva, 828/586-7000; and the **Haywood Regional Medical Center,** 262 Leroy George Dr., 828/452-8559, in Clyde. To access the biggest hospital in the region, call the **Mission and St. Joseph's Hospital Health Line,** Asheville, 800/321-6877 or 828/255-3000.

## CULLOWHEE

Home to a campus of Western Carolina University, Cullowhee (pop. 5,700) is a good place for students of Smoky Mountain culture. For travelers, one possible destination here is the **Mountain Heritage Center** in the H.F. Robinson Administration Building on campus. It tells the story of the Scots-Irish, the principal settlers in this region. Open Monday–Friday 8 A.M.–5 P.M., Sunday 2–5 P.M.

Outside of town is **Judaculla Rock,** a huge soapstone carved with ancient Native American images. Call 828/586-2155 for directions.

For more information, contact the **Jackson County Travel and Tourism Authority,** 116 Central St., Sylva, 800/962-1911 or 828/586-2155.

# Bryson City

Rightly dubbed "The Outdoor Adventure Capital of the Smokies," Bryson City (pop. 1,100) offers great, uncrowded access to the park and yet plenty of shops and restaurants to keep you from feeling deprived. It's also close to the Nantahala River Gorge, the most popular area in the region for whitewater rafting, most often with outfitters at the Nantahala Outdoor Center, Nantahala Rafts, or Wildwater Ltd. Rafting. Call the **Swain County Chamber of Commerce,** 800/867-9246 or 828/488-3681, for more information on Bryson City and vicinity.

## RECREATION
### Rafting the Nantahala Gorge

Southwest of Bryson City, the Nantahala River flows parallel to U.S. 19 from Topton to Wesser, about 10 miles from Robbinsville. The gorge walls vary in height from 500 to 1,500 feet, and the river between them offers excellent opportunities for whitewater rafting, canoeing, and kayaking. Along the road you'll find several picnic areas and places with access to the rushing water. Guided whitewater trips are offered by **Wildwater Ltd. Rafting,** 12 miles west of

Bryson City on U.S. 19, 800/451-9972; **Nantahala Outdoor Center,** another mile along at 13077 U.S. 19 W., 800/232-7238 or 828/488-6900, website: www.noc.com; and **Nantahala Rafts,** Gorgarama Park, 14260 U.S. 19 W., about a mile after that, 828/488-2325. Of the three, Nantahala Outdoor Center is the largest, founded in 1972. Rates to run the Nantahala with a guide—a fairly mild, family-friendly run—range from $22–28 per person. If you're looking for whiter water, the Outdoor Center also leads trips of various lengths and skill levels on the Ocoee, Nolichucky, Pigeon, and Chattooga.

On most of these rivers, be prepared to see a lot of other rafts as you go along.

If you'd like to stay close to the river, the Nantahala Outdoor Center has a large lodge that includes simple motel rooms ($55–65), co-ed bunkhouse-style beds ($14 a person), and two- to ten-bedroom cabins, starting at $110 a night. Across from the Wildwater Ltd. Rafting center, you'll find its 22-acre **Falling Waters Adventure Resort,** 10345 U.S. 74 W., 800/451-9972, with roomy, elegant yurts featuring French doors, tongue-and-groove pine floors, decks, and skylights for $64–79 a night.

# NANTAHALA NATIONAL FOREST

Visitors often confuse the purposes of a national park and a national forest, and are horrified when they see logging, hunting, and private building going on in the latter. Whereas a national park is set aside for preservation and recreation, a national forest encompasses recreation, forestry, hunting, and various other uses of the land. National forests are often bigger than national parks, and islands of private land may exist within them.

Perhaps due to a lack of publicity, many travelers in search of natural beauty zoom through national forests on their way to national parks. In the parks they sometimes find clogged roads, crowded campgrounds and picnic areas, and too many other people. Many national forests offer the same wild beauty, hiking trails, and campsites as the parks do, but with a lot less human competition for resources.

Case in point is the Nantahala National Forest, which at 515 thousand acres is almost as large as the better-known Great Smoky Mountains National Park. Nantahala offers many more camping areas than the national park, and it includes the most rugged section of the entire Appalachian Trail—80 miles in all. Here also is the *Joyce Kilmer Memorial Forest,* an awe-inspiring 3,800-acre tract of virgin forest with trees that tower more than a hundred feet high. Above the town of Sapphire, Whitewater Falls drops 3,411 feet in a horizontal distance of 500 feet. It's the highest waterfall in the eastern United States, and the nearby national park has nothing like it.

You'll find the central administrative offices for the Nantahala National Forest at 50 S. French Broad Ave. in Asheville, 828/258-2850. Call or stop by for maps and other information.

The forest is formally divided up into four districts. The **Cheoah Ranger District,** just south of the national park, contains the Joyce Kilmer Memorial Forest. No camping is permitted in the Kilmer area, but other campgrounds are close

## LAND OF THE WATERFALLS

Not everyone can raft a river or hike to the top of a mountain, but everyone can enjoy a waterfall. If you do nothing else in the Nantahala, be sure to visit a few of the falls.

The town of Highlands is the center of North Carolina waterfall country. From west to east, here are the major falls. From Franklin to Highlands, U.S. 64 follows the Cullasaja River, which offers more falls than a *Dick Van Dyke Show* marathon. The first is **Lower Cullasaja Falls,** more of a cascade, really, in which the river falls for more than 300 feet in a quarter of a mile. Next comes **Dry Falls,** so named because visitors can walk behind the deluge and view the backside of the water without getting wet. Then comes **Bridal Veil Falls,** which splash down 120 feet, landing partly on the road. You can get a free car wash here. (How did they ever get the asphalt to set?)

Once you get to Highlands, take N.C. 106 south for two miles to the **Glen Falls Scenic Area,** where the water plummets 50 feet. Or you can continue east on U.S. 64 through **Cashiers,** then take State Road 107 south into South Carolina. Turn left on Wigington Road (S.C. 37/413), then when it tees two miles later, turn left on S.C. 130, which will rename itself N.C. 281 on the other side of the line. Once this happens, keep an eye on your right for the developed viewing area for **Whitewater Falls.**

Whitewater Falls is the tallest waterfall in the eastern United States. It is actually a pair of falls that fall sequentially on either side of the North Carolina/South Carolina state line. North Carolina claims the upper falls, which cascade 411 feet; South Carolina's lower falls come in at an even 400 feet.

Whichever falls you visit, be careful: people injure themselves, and sometimes die, due to the slippery rocks and long drops.

by. The **Highlands Ranger District** is the one with the most waterfalls, and it's an excellent place for picnicking. It runs from the Sylva area to the border with Georgia and South Carolina. The **Tusquitee Ranger District** extends all the way to the western tip of North Carolina, and includes some small Tennessee Valley Authority–born lakes nestled in the mountains. It's a good place for fishing and camping. The **Wayah Ranger District** reaches from the Cowee Bald to the Georgia border. It includes the *Wayah Bald,* a mountaintop covered with wild azaleas that bloom spectacularly in May and June.

# FRANKLIN

Franklin, the seat of Macon County, rests on an old Cherokee settlement. It also sits over some of the more unusual geological deposits in the United States.

North Carolina is rare in that it is the only state where all four of the "major" gems–diamonds, rubies, sapphires, and emeralds–have been found. Though the diamonds have been few and far between (maybe a dozen in recorded history), the area around Franklin (pop. 3,000) abounds in emeralds, rubies, and sapphires, as well as garnets and amethyst. Some call it the "Gem Capital of the World." Tiffany's once owned an emerald mine in the area, and now rockhounds from novice to expert flock here to see what the earth brings forth. Nearly all of the mines hereabouts are located in the Cowee Valley north of town, off N.C. 28.

Here's how it usually works. For a set fee—often around $10—mine proprietors provide you with a bucket of mud alleged to contain wondrous stones, though some allow the independent-minded to dig their own bucket's worth of mud themselves. Then the miners head over to the flume and have at it. Do it long enough and you'll probably find gemstones, and possibly one that's worth more than you paid for the bucket of mud. But obviously, if the mines paid off that well, the owners would be sifting through their own mud. But you knew that.

And you probably also know that this'd be a memorable afternoon for kids. If you want to

better your odds, pay extra for a "concentrated" bucket. In fact, most of the mines are "enriched" to begin with.

About a mile north of Franklin on U.S. 441, you'll come across **Gem City Mine,** 828/524-3967, which includes a sheltered flume line, allowing you to mine even if the rain's coming down in sheets. Open May 15–October 15. Call for hours. **Gold City Gem Mine,** 9410 Sylva Rd., 828/369-3905, includes a large covered flume for rainy-day mining, wheelchair access, and even special kid-sized mining buckets. The **Jackson Hole,** 828/524-5850, also with a covered flume, sits on N.C. 28 and U.S. 64, halfway between Franklin and Highlands. It offers an on-site snack bar and gem shop. The **Jacobs Ruby Mine,** 269 DeForest Lane, 828/524-7022, features only native stones. Or try the **Rose Creek Mine,** 115 Terrace Ridge Dr., 828/349-3774. Camping available.

In Franklin, a lot of people like to shop for local arts and crafts at such shops as **Cowee Creek Pottery,** 20 West Mills Rd., 828/524-3324, the **MACO Crafts Co-op,** 2846 Georgia Rd., 828/524-7878, and Michael M. Rogers Gallery, 18 W. Palmer St., 828/524-6709.

If you'd like to stay in Franklin, you might consider **Summit Inn,** 210 East Rogers St., 828/524-2006, a 14-room 1898 house atop Franklin's highest hill. Ornately carved high-boy beds, armoires, and other antiques warm the rooms. Rates run $59–99 based on room, occupancy, and season. Only six of the fourteen rooms offer a private bathroom, so if privacy is important to you, be sure to ask for one of these when you make reservations. Children and even infants are welcome; the inn has a special children's room. Children under 6 stay free in the parent's room, and cribs are available. Children 7–16 can stay in a parent's room for an additional $10. Rollaway beds available.

The Summit also serves some of the best meals in Franklin—which can include lobster, steak, trout, and baked chicken. The soup and bread are homemade. Dinners are served family-style on tables lit by kerosene lamps. And this inn offers one amenity lacking in most B&Bs: pool tables. The inn is open year-round, though in the

M

CHEROKEE

winter months the dining room is open only on weekends.

## HIGHLANDS

At 3,835 feet, Highlands is North Carolina's second highest town, and it's in many ways the perfect example of a resort town. In fact, when it was originally laid out in 1875 (by two natives of Kansas), it was planned as a resort community. The tale goes that the two Jayhawkers drew a line on a map from Baltimore to New Orleans, and another from Chicago to Savannah. They built Highlands at the point where these lines intersected. In the 1920s, with the development of the Highlands Country Club, the prestige factor reached new heights. Today, the town supports just 2,000 year-round residents and upwards of 25,000 residents in the summer.

As evidenced by the marker on Main Street, Spanish explorers under Juan Pardo passed through this area back in 1567 as part of Spain's aborted conquest of North America. Had Spain kept its grasp on this continent, Pardo's name would no doubt be as well known as those of Lewis and Clark. He and his men walked all the way up here from the Spanish Fort San Felipe on modern-day Parris Island, S.C. His job was both to explore Spain's new dominion and, in doing so, establish an overland route to the silver mines of western Mexico. He and his 300 men built blockhouses along the way and left small detachments of soldiers to man them and evangelize the local Indians. After passing through here, Pardo and his men tramped all the way to modern-day Alabama before finally heading back to San Felipe.

The Highlands area is also the wettest in the eastern U.S.: it gets 80 inches of precipitation in an average year. The plant life, from trees to lichens, is splendid. When the French botanist Andre Michaux came through in 1788, he noted the *shortia,* a plant whose only other known habitat was Japan. Asa Gray rediscovered the plant a hundred years later, and botanists still drive up to research it in Highlands.

Most people, however, come to relax. Highlands has a fine collection of houses belonging to summer people and retirees. The quaint houses in town start at around $500,000. It's no wonder that the small grocery store here carries caviar along with its bacon and eggs. Travelers delight in the lake at the west end of town and the waterfalls along U.S. 64 from Highlands to Franklin.

The most popular thing to do in Highlands is to walk the small town, browsing into the many downtown shops and galleries as you go. But you may also want to drive out to the **Highlands Biological Station,** on Horse Cove Road, founded in 1927.

In fact, if you were visiting the Smokies primarily to understand its plant life, you probably couldn't find a better place to start off your journeys than here. Now overseen by the University of North Carolina, this 16-acre research center offers facilities for use by qualified scientists researching Southern Appalachian biota and environments. On the station's land you'll find the kid-friendly **Highlands Nature Center,** 828/526-2623, in the chestnut Clark Foreman Museum Building, featuring displays on the natural history and biodiversity of the region. Kids and grownups can view a live beehive, peer through a microscope, and examine the rings in a cross-section of a pre-Columbian hemlock.

Back outside, you'll find a number of trails threading the station's **Highlands Botanical Garden,** which borders Lake Ravenel. Along these trails, you'll find an incredible real-life primer on southern Appalachian plant life—so far, researchers here have labeled some 450 specimens of plants native to the region. The garden is open year-round.

The Biological Station is open from late May through Labor Day, Monday–Friday 10 A.M.– 5 P.M., Sundays 1–5 P.M. No admission charged.

### Events

Highlands has enough seasonal visitors with enough free time on their hands to support quite a summer arts community. The **Chamber Music Festival,** all during July, offers chamber music concerts at the Episcopal church (yes, there's high church in Highlands). Performances on Tuesday nights and Sunday afternoons. For details, call or visit the Highlands Chamber of

Commerce, 396 Oak St., 828/526-2112. The **High Country Arts and Crafts Fair** in early June features a hundred or so craftspeople who gather at Mountain Hillbilly Crafts, seven miles south of Highlands on N.C. 106. Call the Chamber of Commerce for more details. **Helen's Barn,** on West Main Street, is where locals and visitors meet on Friday and Saturday nights for a hoedown wherein beginning and expert cloggers and square dancers send the hay a-flying. Food and drinks available. Call 828/526-2790.

The **Highlands Playhouse,** 828/526-2695, has presented dramas and musicals to the summertime audiences every summer since 1932. Call for information and tickets.

For theater with a lighter touch, the **Highlands Studio for the Arts,** 828/526-9482, may be the way to go. Improvisational acting and one-acts are the specialties, offered from July–September, with performances on Tuesday, Thursday, and Friday nights.

## Accommodations and Food

The **Highlands Inn,** corner of Fourth and Main Streets, 828/526-9380, website: www.highlandsinn-nc.com, was built in 1881, and even today, the inn and its restaurant—the **Kelsey Place Restaurant**—are the prime spots to stay and eat in Highlands. The inn offers 46 guest rooms, open from May through October. Standard double rooms run $94–134 a night. "Extended continental breakfast" included.

Frank Lloyd Wright and Associates designed **Skyline Lodge and Restaurant,** Flat Mountain Road, 800/575-9546 or 828/526-2121, as a casino in the 1920s, and construction began in the 1930s. But the Depression turned more depressing than the project's backers had anticipated, and work halted. For decades, the building remained unfinished, until it was completed in the 1960s as a lodge. Located four miles east of Highlands on Flat Mountain Road, Skyline sits atop a 4,300-foot mountain on 55 acres of grounds that include old-growth conifers, a pond and a 30-foot waterfall, tennis courts, and a swimming pool. Rooms run $79–169 a night, which includes a continental breakfast. There

are also some new rental cabins. Call for prices and availability.

If you know Wright, you know that this is no rustic hand-hewn log cabin tucked into the trees. The rooms are modern, with telephones and, in some cases, king-size beds. Rooms on one side of the lodge hear and look out on the waterfall; rooms on the other side get a mountain view. The lodge offers fine **dining.** Non-guests are welcome here as well for the dinners. Plates include locally raised trout sautéed with lemon, white wine, and butter ($18.95) and jumbo sea scallops tossed with fresh spinach, ginger root, and garlic in Jamaican tomato sauce ($19.95). Take note: here across the Macon County line, you're in a dry county, so you'll need to bring your own wine or hard liquor. The restaurant will charge a setup and/or corkage fee. The lodge is open May–October. To get there from Highlands, take U.S. 64 east to Flat Mountain Road. Turn left and follow the signs.

A budget-friendlier stay inside town is the **Mountain High Inn,** Second Street and Main Street, 800/445-7293 or 828/526-2790, website: www.mountainhighinn.com, with rooms running $48–119.

The **Central House,** Fourth and Main Streets, 828/526-9319, is a traditional, moderately priced country restaurant set in an 1878 inn. Dinners run around $19; you may want to start off with the inn's beloved blue crab soup. The inn's grounds include a waterfall and a pond. For something down-home and easy on the pocketbook, try some barbecue at **Carolina Smokehouse,** on U.S. 64 northeast of town in Cashiers, 828/743-3200; or a sandwich and chocolate malt at **Brigitte's Soda Fountain,** on East Main Street in the Blue Ridge Pharmacy Building, 828/526-9451.

In honor of sore-footed Juan Pardo, you might choose to eat at **Pescado's Highland Burrito** on N. Fourth Street, 828/526-9313. Pescado's offers fresh, health-conscious Mexican food that's more Century City than Mexico City. If you've been overdoing the barbecue, here's a great place to take a break.

CHEROKEE

# East of Bryson City

The region east of Bryson City bills itself as "the peaceful side of the Smokies," and, compared to Tennessee's Gatlinburg and Pigeon Forge, that's certainly the truth. Townsend lies in a cove—a flat area in mountain parlance—called Tuckaleechee Cove. Tourists have been visiting since 1904, when the railroad came through, but recent excavations show that this area has been popular with people for more than 2,500 years.

When road crews began widening Hwy. 321 in 1999, they uncovered evidence of extensive Indian habitation, so work was halted while archeologists studied the newly exposed ground. Scientists found what was left of a big Cherokee town, as well as evidence of habitation dating back to 200 A.D. Human remains were found as well, and the Eastern Band of the Cherokee and Seminoles from Oklahoma, the presumed descendants of those who lived here, helped make the decision to leave the 70 graves intact. Each was covered with a layer of concrete before the road was paved over.

## FONTANA

Below the North Carolina line and east on N.C. 28, Fontana Lake is a child of the Depression-era Tennessee Valley Authority. The TVA built Fontana Dam to generate power for a Tennessee aluminum plant, just in time for the demands of World War II. Fontana Village arose to house the construction crews.

When the war was over, existentialist Jean-Paul Sartre, on a tour of the United States, visited Fontana Village. Writing in *Le Figaro,* he waxed rhapsodic about what he saw: "The striking thing is the lightness, the fragility of these buildings. The village has no weight, it seems barely to rest upon the soil; it has not managed to leave a human imprint on the reddish earth and the dark forest; it is a temporary thing."

He was wrong about the temporary part. When the 480-foot dam—for a long time the highest in the eastern United States—was completed, it may just have been the last hard day's work anyone's ever put in around Fontana; the town has been a resort since then. Unlike Norris, Tennessee—a village built under similar circumstances and eventually sold house-by-house—Fontana Village was leased in one piece from the government and turned into a resort when the construction workers left. Due to its out-of-the-way location, it's less crowded and less expensive than most of the other amenity areas circling the national park.

The **Fontana Village** resort consists of 250 cabins and a modern hotel. Rooms at the hotel run $49–149; cabins cost $69–209; camp cabins run $49–59. A campsite costs around $20 a night. A 16-bunk hostel offers even cheaper, if less private, digs. Outdoor activities are the name of the game here, including tennis, golf, hiking, horseback riding, fishing, and boating. For information, call 800/849-2258 or go to www.fontanavillage.com on the web.

The **Log Cabin Museum,** set in an 1875 cabin, documents the history of the village. Also on N.C. 28—inside the Fontana Motel, of all places—is the **Graham County Museum of Prehistoric Relics,** 828/479-3677. Therein you'll find thousands of prehistoric Amerind stone weapons, tools, and other artifacts.

## ROBBINSVILLE

South on Route 1147, Robbinsville is the seat of Graham County, about 60 percent of which resides within the Nantahala National Forest. Before the current town was founded, the Snowbird Indians—Cherokee who lived in the Snowbird Mountains—dwelled here. Cherokee chief Junaluska, who commanded his warriors in an alliance with General Andrew Jackson against the Creek Indians in the 1814 Battle of Horseshoe Bend, was one inhabitant. According to tradition, Chief Junaluska saved Jackson's life when Old Hickory was attacked by a Creek warrior. The good chief received American citizenship and a good bit of Graham County as a reward. He's buried off N.C. 143 Business; you can view the grave for free.

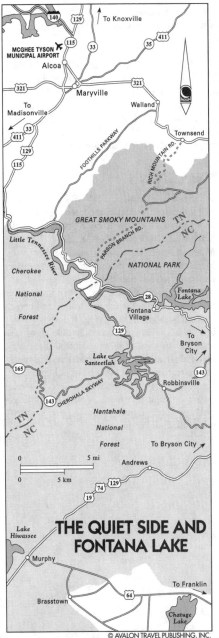

THE QUIET SIDE AND
FONTANA LAKE

© AVALON TRAVEL PUBLISHING, INC.

Today, Robbinsville serves as the southern starting point for the **Cherohala Skyway,** one of only 20-some national scenic byways in the nation, first opened in 1996. Robbinsville is also home to **Tapoco Lodge Resort,** 14981 Tapoco Rd., 800/822-5083 or 828/498-2435, website: www.tapocolodge.com. It offers an American meal plan, which provides three full southern meals a day. Rates start at $69 a person, but you can rent just a room (no meals) starting at $79 d. Other local lodgings include the **Phillips Motel,** 290 Main St., 828/479-3370, which offers efficiency rooms.

## MURPHY

This little town on U.S. 19 is the seat of Cherokee County and one of the oldest settlements in far western North Carolina. Set where the Hiwassee and Valley Rivers meet, Murphy was founded in 1830 as an Indian trading post, but the Cherokee were here long before that. A mile and a half north of town, in Tomotla, settlers found an old mine shaft containing a cannon barrel, picks, and other mining tools apparently used by De Soto and his gold-hungry Spaniards when they passed through here in 1540. In 1567 Juan Pardo followed in De Soto's tracks, leading an expedition up from St. Augustine via the South Carolina Lowcountry.

In 1715 British major George Chicken of South Carolina led an expedition against the local Cherokee here. In 1817, Baptist missionaries to the Cherokee founded a school about three miles northeast of the town site. The town itself was originally named Huntersville, for the colonel who founded it, but it was renamed for Archibald Murphey, a politician and much-admired advocate of free popular education. As fate would have it, the town leaders misspelled Murphey's name. Fort Butler was built nearby in 1837 by General Winfield Scott's men as one of the staging grounds for the Cherokee removal to Oklahoma.

In spring of 1865, at the tail end of the War Between the States, a band of local men deserted the Confederate army for a Federal unit. Charges of treason were filed against them in the Cherokee County courthouse. In those days before shredders, the scalawags destroyed the case documents the old-fashioned way—they burned down the courthouse. Confederates led by Major Stephen Whitaker caught up with the deserters at Hanging Dog Creek, about four miles northwest of town, on May 6, 1865. Today the town, with fewer than 2,000 citizens, still centers around the old courthouse square, which features a "new" (1926) courthouse of local blue marble and a Confederate monument.

## Sights

Murphy is home to a pair of interesting sites. The **Cherokee Historical Museum,** 87 Peachtree St., 828/837-6792, contains artifacts from the Cherokee era and the early white settlements in this area. In the eclectic spirit of small-town museums, it also contains an extensive doll collection. There is no charge for admission.

**Fields of the Wood** on N.C. 294, 828/494-7855, is a 200-acre Bible park where you can see the Ten Commandments laid out in huge stone letters across an entire mountainside, powerful visual testimony to the Bible's vital place in Appalachian culture, as well as an ethical reminder to birds and airplane passengers. For fun, you can have your picture taken beside your favorite commandment (or perhaps the one you most enjoy breaking). Also here are the All Nations Cross and replicas of Golgotha, the hill where Jesus was executed, and Jesus' tomb. There is no charge for admission. The

park is open dawn to dusk daily. Go there at www.cogop.org/fow on the Web.

## Accommodations

The **Hilltop House,** 94 Campbell St., 828/837-8661, is a bed-and-breakfast that offers three rooms and a meal plan. **Huntington Hall Bed and Breakfast,** 500 Valley River Ave., is another B&B option. **Park Place Bed and Breakfast,** 54 Hill St., 828/837-8842, offers three rooms, meal plans, private golfing, and tennis privileges.

# BRASSTOWN

Brasstown is just down U.S. 29/19 from Murphy, and it's mainly known as the home of the 380-acre **John C. Campbell Folk School,** 1 Folk School Rd., 800/365-5724 or 828/837-8637. Modeled after Danish schools, the school was founded in 1925 to preserve the crafts, music, dances, and other traditions of the Appalachian people. It makes a wonderful day trip from the park. You can visit the school's history center for free and browse the craft shop, a founding member of the Southern Highland Craft Guild, which features the work of more than 300 local and regional artists. You can also take the local trails and visit artists' studios to watch work in progress. For a longer stay, the school offers 3- to 12-week classes in mountain music, dance, and crafts. Call for information or go on the Web to www.folkschool.com.

# Great Smoky Mountains National Park

*ALWAYS enwrapped in the illusory mists, always touching the evasive clouds, the peaks of the Great Smoky Mountains are like some barren ideal, that has bartered for the vague isolations of a higher atmosphere the material values of the warm world below. Upon those mighty and majestic domes no tree strikes root, no hearth is alight; humanity is an alien thing, and utility set at naught. Below, dense forests cover the massive, precipitous slopes of the range, and in the midst of the wilderness a clearing shows, here and there, and the roof of a humble log cabin; in the valley, far, far lower still, a red spark at dusk may suggest a home, nestling in the cove. Grain grows apace in these scanty clearings, for the soil in certain favored spots is mellow; and the weeds grow, too, and in a wet season the ploughs are fain to be active. They are of the bull-tongue variety, and are sometimes drawn by oxen. As often as otherwise they are followed by women.*

**Craddock, Charles Egbert (Mary Murfree),**
**The Prophet of the Great Smoky**
**Mountains, 1885**

Forget the Grand Canyon, Yellowstone, and Yosemite: Great Smoky Mountains National Park attracts more visitors than any other national park in the country—more than 10 million guests visit every year.

Since this 520,000-acre, 800-square-mile park appeals to so many people, if you're looking for some quality time with Mother Nature, you'll need to get off the beaten path. Fortunately, doing this is easy for the most part: Simply get out of the car. Roughly 95 percent

view from Newfound Gap Road

SMOKY MOUNTAINS

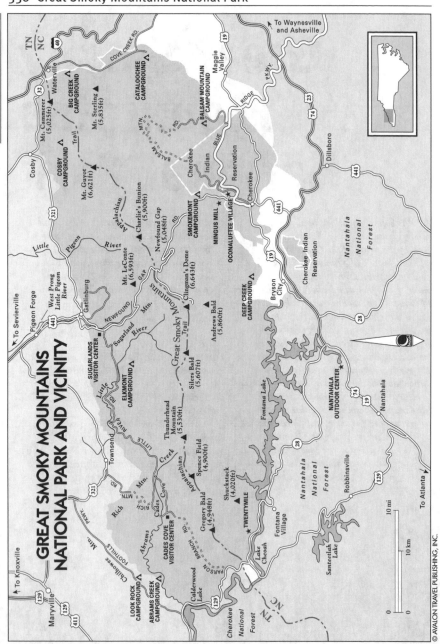

GREAT SMOKY MOUNTAINS
NATIONAL PARK AND VICINITY

© AVALON TRAVEL PUBLISHING, INC.

## SMOKY MOUNTAIN HIGHLIGHTS

**Appalachian Trail**

**Cades Cove**

**Clingmans Dome**

**Cataloochee Valley**

**LeConte Lodge**

**Mount LeConte**

**Newfound Gap**

falls and smell the pines but also want HBO and a Jacuzzi at night. And the region's schizophrenic personality also makes it just right for families mixed in their interests. How many other vacation spots offer both a Ripley's Believe It or Not! *and* the Appalachian Trail as local attractions?

And then there's the park itself. Unlike most other parks, Great Smoky Mountains National Park preserves a considerable amount of historical structures along with its natural splendor. At preserved settlement sites like Cades Cove and Cataloochee, 21st-century visitors can view a 19th-century lifestyle caught in amber. Meanwhile, the park's natural beauty continues to charm the masses. The Smokies feature more different flowering plants than any other national park in the United States— or Canada for that matter. The total stood around 1,500 at publication time, but botanists seem to discover new species in the park every year.

of all visitors to the Smokies never venture more than 100 yards from their vehicles. Hike 101 yards down the nearest trail, and you have escaped nearly 9.5 million of those 10 million visitors. And the remaining half million, fortunately, don't all come at once.

Why do so many people visit here? Accessibility is one important factor. Even with the prevailing southwestern migration patterns, one-third of all Americans still live within a day's drive of the park. For Easterners, other than the very-out-of-the-way Everglades National Park at the tail end of Florida, the Smokies are the largest natural area available. To Westerners and international visitors touring the country in a car or RV, the Smokies make a reasonable midpoint destination. And the park is closer to a major airport (in Knoxville) than most other national parks. The original park charter forever forbid the charging of an admission fee. So even today, you won't pay a dime to enter the park.

And then, for better or worse, there's the park's proximity to all the buffets, motel rooms, and miniature golf courses in Pigeon Forge and Gatlinburg. These human-made attractions and amenities make the park a good destination for tepid nature enthusiasts—those who want to see the water-

## HISTORY
### Before the Park

The sanctuary that is Great Smoky Mountains National Park was, like most sanctuaries, born of necessity. The devastation that led to the birth of the park came at the sharp end of an ax—by way of the railroads. Once railroads gave eastern lumber interests access to long-undisturbed areas of timber, the trees began falling at a disturbing rate.

Influential Knoxville businessman Willis P. Davis and his wife returned from a trip to the western national parks in 1923 and suggested that the Park Service make a park in the Smokies before it was too late. Fortunately, as lumbermen decimated the area's forests in the 1920s, the same trains that hauled out lumber began to haul in tourists, an important (if inadvertent) step in raising public support for a park.

The early visitors to the Smokies were so

> *The sanctuary that is Great Smoky Mountains National Park was, like most sanctuaries, born of necessity. The devastation that led to the birth of the park came at the sharp end of an ax—by way of the railroads.*

SMOKY MOUNTAINS

impressed with what they saw—and so mortified by the encroaching devastation from logging—that they joined the Davises and their Knoxville friends in asking Washington to step in and declare the area a national park.

The Coolidge administration was willing to talk. The large national parks in the West had proved popular, but for the vast majority of Americans, these parks were a thousand or more miles away. In practice, these "parks for the people" served mainly moneyed folks like the Davises who had the leisure time and funds to travel to, say, Yellowstone or Yosemite. The Department of the Interior was looking to create new, more accessible parks in the East.

However, the government had run into problems. Creating parks in the trans-Mississippi region had mostly involved setting aside lands already owned by the federal government. But the East had been settled earlier and more thoroughly than the West. Most areas of natural beauty in the East had long histories as summer or winter playgrounds for the upper classes, who held expensive deeds on their vacation properties and sway with those in power. Thus, it would not do to turn, say, the Poconos, Cape Cod, or Miami Beach into a national park. What was needed instead was an eastern area of scenic beauty, sparsely populated with people of negligible political power—people who could be bought out cheaply and forced out quietly.

## Making Room

In the Smokies, the National Park Service found its prize. Some subsistence Appalachian farmers would undoubtedly be happy to sell for what seemed like a good price, and those who weren't would not be well-connected enough to stand up against the pro-park forces. Though many wealthy Knoxvillians owned vacation homes in the area, many were willing to allow—and even supported—the creation of a national park as a way to protect the scenic beauty around their weekend cabins and lodges. Once all the proper donations had been made and strings had been pulled, the National Park Service allowed these people to lease for as long as they, and in some cases their children, were alive.

## THE NATION'S MOST VISITED NATIONAL PARKS

1. **Great Smoky Mountains National Park,** 10.1 million visits annually, on 521,621 acres (19.4 visits per acre)

2. **Grand Canyon National Park,** 4.4 million visits annually, on 1,217,403 acres (3.6 visits per acre)

3. **Yosemite National Park,** 3.4 million visits annually, on 761,266 acres (4.5 visits per acre)

4. **Olympic National Park,** 3.3 million visits annually, on 922,650 acres (3.6 visits per acre)

5. **Rocky Mountain National Park,** 3.1 million visits annually, on 265,722 acres (11.7 visits per acre)

6. **Yellowstone National Park,** 2.8 million visits annually, on 2,219,790 acres (1.3 visits per acre)

Even still, the farmers and lumber companies who owned land in the Smokies did have to be paid *something*. Congress balked at footing the bill. However, the states of North Carolina and Tennessee, which had been working to build their economies through increased tourism and improved roads, willingly contributed. Both state governments hoped to rope the park within their borders. The present-day border-straddling location of the park serves as a nice compromise.

In 1926, President Calvin Coolidge—himself a flinty son of the Appalachians of southern Vermont—signed the bill that authorized and protected the area as a federal park, but it could not be created until the NPS had acquired 150,000 acres in the area.

Private citizens and companies gave land and money, but it would take nearly $12 million to acquire all the desired parcels. North Carolina finally gave up its quest to have the park completely within its borders and agreed to donate $2,162,283 toward a park straddling the Tennessee line—but only if Tennessee coughed up $2 million of its own. Tennessee's legislature raced into session and came out with $2,345,330, and Congress eventually came through with $2,293,265 from Washington. Then a couple of major park supporters buttonholed John D. Rockefeller Jr. and persuaded him to cut a check for $5 million. Suddenly, the fund-raising portion of the venture was over.

But having the money and owning the land were two separate things. More than 6,000 parcels had to be purchased, including some 1,200 small farms owned by mountain families, many of whom had lived on the land for generations. Eventually, the 150,000 acres—and more—would come: All the money suddenly floating around the mountains mollified most of the park's opponents quickly enough. The lumber companies, which had initially led the opposition to the park on economic grounds, could be and were bought out. Entire lumber company towns such as Smokemont were evacuated and dissembled. The companies were compensated for their losses.

More sustained opposition came from some of the area's 7,300 farmers. Roughly half gladly took the money and moved to cities or more fertile farming lands, but the other half wanted to stay. They became the biggest obstacle to the park's founding. In the days before Social Security cards, most mountain people had experienced little if any contact with the federal government. They found it outrageous that flatlanders in business suits were suddenly going to take their land—to make, of all things, a park for flatlanders. Some gave up, bewildered, but others stood up courageously to the strange, powerful forces that had come for their land. Courage, however, doesn't buy good attorneys, and nearly all of these opponents ended up expelled from the park's boundaries within the next several years. By 1939, the *WPA Guide to North Carolina* would describe the park as "largely deserted by its inhabitants."

In a humane gesture, the government allowed a few elderly and sick mountain people lifetime leases to their own land. But they couldn't hunt and fish, cut firewood, or farm using the old ways. Many who had permission to stay ended

up leaving anyway, out of frustration. Others, over the next decades, saw their ex-neighbors making a good living providing tourist amenities in the gateway towns and moved outside the park to share in the bonanza.

One last group of park opponents consisted of local conservationists who favored national forest rather than national park status for the Smokies. They believed that a national park would attract huge crowds of visitors, compromising the mountains' peaceful atmosphere and threatening its distinct vegetation and wildlife. They lost the battle, of course, but you can't fault this group for a lack of foresight.

## A Park Is Born

By 1934 the governments of Tennessee and North Carolina had purchased more than double the required acreage—more than 300,000 of the park's present-day 520,000 acres—and signed it over to the Department of the Interior. On June 15, 1934, the U.S. Congress formally bequeathed national park status to the Smokies, freeing up the Park Service to develop the area for visitors. The Depression was on, but the Civilian Conservation Corps (CCC) was at full throttle. The corps went on to build the park a strong infrastructure—roads, bridges, trails, and campgrounds—and other sturdy, often inspired, amenities.

Although as late as 1939 not a single campground had yet opened for business, on September 2, 1940, President Franklin D. Roosevelt bumped along in a caravan up the dirt road to Newfound Gap for a dedication ceremony. Thousands of others arrived in hundreds of cars to attend. Thus, from the beginning, traffic and crowds have been part of the park scene.

## Humans and Nature

Great Smoky Mountains National Park, as it appeared in those days, would shock us today. Under private ownership, whole sections had been clear-cut; large gullies ran down the hillsides, and many streams were filled with silt and nearly devoid of life. Bear, deer, and other game had been hunted to the edge of extinction and were only slowly beginning to reassert themselves in the area. Left alone, however, nature quietly reclaimed the land. Now towering trees grow along roads that were once railbeds, and the vegetation is so lush that most folks drive blissfully by what they assume to be virgin forest.

Visitation has steadily increased in the Smokies over time. The interstate highway system soon put the park within a day's drive of an estimated one-third of the U.S. population, and a great portion of that one-third made the trip. While the number of visitors has doubled and doubled and doubled again, the roads in the park have largely stayed the same size, causing congestion during summer and even worse traffic during the fall foliage season. The Park Service has resisted efforts to widen the roads and ignored other schemes meant to increase accessibility at the expense of ecology, among them a suggestion to run a chairlift from Gatlinburg to Clingmans Dome. In doing so, the Park Service has preserved a wonderful wilderness area, one that continues to provide inspiration and joy to those who come to see it.

### Recent Developments

In October 2000, Mike Tollefson became the park's new superintendent. A Seattle native, the new chief came straight from the head position at Sequoia and Kings Canyon National Parks in central California, where he had overseen the removal of nearly 300 park buildings as part of an effort to protect ancient sequoias. His announced priorities at the Smokies included improving air quality and, not unrelated, reducing traffic in the Cades Cove area. By 2002, debate was still underway concerning proposals to replace private vehicular traffic in Cades Cove with a shuttle or rail system. Plans were also being discussed to destroy and remove the buildings in the Elkmont area so that the Victorian-era logging and resort community could be returned to its natural state.

## ORIENTATION

### Getting In

For now at least, nearly everyone who visits the park arrives by car, usually via one of three roads. More than one-third enter via the **Gatlinburg entrance,** on the Tennessee side, making this the park's de facto main entrance—a reality that has its good side and its bad side. On the good side,

view from the Smokies

the Park Service has sensibly loaded up most of its best visitor amenities near this entrance, including the Sugarlands Visitor Center and Park Headquarters. From here, you can either head up the Newfound Gap Road over the mountains or turn right and head for the Cades Cove area along Little River Road.

The downsides of the "main" entrance are the crowds and the tourism gauntlet you'll have to run in Pigeon Forge and Gatlinburg just to get into the park. If you've come to the Smokies to get away from it all, accessing the park via Sevierville, Pigeon Forge, and Gatlinburg may bring to mind the old Steve Miller line about having to go through hell before you get to heaven.

At the reservation outside of North Carolina's **Cherokee entrance,** the trend seems, thankfully, to be away from the concrete tepees and Sioux headdresses of the past and toward lower-key, Cherokee-respecting attractions—and a modern-day, Cherokee-enriching casino. Once inside the park, you'll find the interesting Oconaluftee Visitor Center and Pioneer Farmstead and the photogenic Mingus Mill—but then you've got to continue on up Newfound Gap Road (U.S. 441) for about 10 curvy miles before you hit the next roadside pullover at Newfound Gap.

**Townsend** is the least-used of the three main entrances to the park. It leads to an intersection of the Little River Road, which heads toward the Sugarlands Visitor Center and Gatlinburg, and Laurel Creek Road, which goes to Cades Cove.

## Major Roads

**Newfound Gap Road,** a.k.a. **U.S. 441,** crosses the park and the park's namesake mountains at Newfound Gap. This is the road you'll travel if you enter the park by either the Gatlinburg or Cherokee entrances.

During the push to establish Great Smoky Mountains National Park in the 1920s and 1930s, supporters cultivated public interest in the project by including an over-mountain road in the plan. A direct route between east Tennessee and North Carolina, the supporters argued, would stimulate trade and help both areas' economies.

The route they chose largely followed the existing dirt path over Newfound Gap, first blazed as

early as the 1850s. Until its discovery, travelers over the main range of the Smokies had to use the higher Indian Gap. This "new-found gap" was lower and hence more passable later into the winter and earlier in the spring. It soon replaced Indian Gap as the primary crossing point in this region.

Newfound Gap Road was paved, and the supporters were right about the economic development—probably more right than they knew. Today, Newfound Gap Road crosses the park from one tourist town to another, climbing from 1,465 to 5,048 feet at its highest point. Motorists sense that they're seeing most of the park, since they're crossing from one side to the other and even changing states along the way. Unfortunately, on most warm-weather days, what you'll mostly see traveling Newfound Gap Road is traffic, sometimes of the bumper-to-bumper variety.

For many, the highlight of the drive lies at the gap itself, where you'll find breathtaking views, the state line sign (a popular picture spot), a crossing point for the Appalachian Trail, and a monument where Franklin D. Roosevelt formally dedicated the park in 1940.

## Clingmans Dome Road

Named after its endpoint, the highest mountain in the park, this road spurs off the Newfound Gap Road at Newfound Gap. Clingmans Dome was named for the man who first measured it accurately—a little-known, part-Cherokee, Confederate brigadier general, Thomas Lanier Clingman. Before that, the Cherokee knew the dome as Ku wa' hi—"Mulberry Place." They believed that bears had great "townhouses" under this and three nearby mountains. The Great White Bear, chief and doctor to the rest, lived at Mulberry Place. The bears would come here to chat it up and dance before heading downstairs to hibernate for the winter.

Reaching 6,300 feet in elevation, the dead-end, six-mile road (a.k.a. Skyland Drive), which leads to an observation tower, is the highest paved road east of the Mississippi.

## Roaring Fork Motor Nature Trail

This road is a one-way, five-mile loop just outside of Gatlinburg. It'll take you into the park and uphill to the **Grotto Falls** parking area, then downhill back to town along a rushing stream. The water cavorts over rocks, cooling the air and providing moisture for luxurious ferns and mosses. A great place for photographers, the road is off-limits to RVs and closed in winter.

## Little River Road

One of two main roads in the park, Little River Road leaves from the Sugarlands Visitor Center over Sugarlands Mountain, descends to the Little River, and follows it toward the Cades Cove area. Some of this 18-mile road was constructed on the remains of the Little River Railroad, which was used to bring logs out of the mountains in the early 20th century.

A turnoff to the left leads to the **Elkmont** community, a group of cabins long occupied by families who owned them when the park came into existence. Back on the road, a turnoff to the right leads to **Metcalf Bottoms,** where you'll see a log schoolhouse and several old cabins.

The Little River grows in volume the further it goes. It plunges over a small waterfall at **The Sinks,** a popular if bone-chilling swimming hole. Further downstream, you'll see people tubing on the river. The National Park Service takes a dim view of this sport, since it's hazardous, especially when the water is high. But it's allowed and people do it. Little River Road ends at an intersection with Laurel Creek Road, which leads to Cades Cove and the road out of the park to Townsend. **Laurel Creek Road** is a pleasant drive, but you won't see much but trees.

## Cherokee Orchard Road

Here's a true back road, lying just outside Gatlinburg. Follow the Historic Nature Trail Road to Gatlinburg to Cherokee Orchard Road. It runs three and a half miles through an old orchard and past the site of several log cabins. In season, it's a great drive for wildflower viewing.

## Cades Cove Roads

You can read about the Cades Cove Loop Road below, but here are a couple of good roads that lead *out* of the area. Cades Cove residents used to take **Rich Mountain Road** to do their shopping, trading, and hollering down in Maryville. Today this seven-mile road starts out one-way as it winds out of the cove, offering several views of farmland, and crosses Rich Mountain at the park boundary. Outside the park it becomes a two-way road and descends to U.S. 321 near Townsend. The one-way, eight-mile **Parson Branch Road** is even prettier; it leaves the cove just beyond the Cable Mill parking area and wanders down to U.S. 129 between Fontana and Chilhowee. Beautiful, lush mountain laurel and fern surround the road, and it fords a creek several times. If Cades Cove is crowded—and it often is in summer—this is an excellent escape from the crowds. Both Rich Mountain Road and Parson Branch Road are closed in winter.

# Sights

Consider this: Of the 10.1 million people who visit Great Smoky Mountains National Park each year, some 2.5 million of them visit **Cades Cove,** a large, relatively flat area first settled in 1821. If Cades Cove were a national park all by itself, it would be one of the top 10 most visited national parks in the country.

Thousands of small-scale farmers once worked 1,200 farms within the boundaries of today's Great Smoky Mountains National Park. Although most of the farm buildings have fallen, the few that remain can help you get an idea of life before the park. The biggest collection of ante-park structures lies in Cades Cove. At its peak, the 5,000-acre valley supported 685 residents, who kept several churches and mills in operation. Today the park permits cattle grazing to keep the pastures from returning to forest, and it also maintains the farm buildings, churches, and a mill. A narrow, 11-mile, one-way road circles the cove, with 19 interpretational stops that explain the old ways of life here.

The restored and preserved buildings and farms of Cades Cove are well worth seeing. Bring or rent a bike, and you'll be able to pass up the motorized masses on the often RV-crammed one-lane road. Even better, on Saturdays and Wednesdays from May to September, the road is open to bicyclists and pedestrians only until 10 A.M.

Along the road you'll see **Tipton Place,** which features a cantilevered barn. This sort of structure is an example of mountain ingenuity: The building spreads out at its second story to provide shelter for outdoor chores and for animals.

The best part of the cove, however, centers on **Cable Mill,** a working mill alongside a frame house and several farm buildings. During visiting season, crafts and farming demonstrations take place. One weekend in October, re-enactors at the mill make sorghum molasses the old-fashioned way.

The Cherokee called this area Tsiyahi, meaning "Otter's Place," but the settlers renamed it, presumably after a human, though nobody is quite sure whom. To many students of the subject, the name most likely refers to a Cherokee chief named Cade, or Kade, who once held land in the cove. Another story says that the cove is named for Kate, the settlers' name for the wife of Cherokee chief Abram. Others argue that the cove was named after an early settler family named Cade, and yet another story says that the name was originally Cage Cove, referring to the "cage" created by the mountains surrounding the cove.

One popular hike out of the area leads to 20-foot-high Abrams Falls, a worthwhile trek. And the Cades Cove campground, though often crowded, offers the only camp store in the park.

# ELKMONT

Pennsylvanians Colonel W.B. Townsend, J.W. Wrigley, and F.H. McCormick acquired more than 75,000 acres of Smokies timberland in 1902 and formed the Little River Lumber Company, headquartered outside current park boundaries in the little community of Tuckaleechee (renamed Townsend). The company built the Little River Railroad to span the 18 miles between Townsend and Elkmont, from where Shays—geared locomotives designed for steeper grades—climbed

even higher into the mountains to pick up the prized lumber. Before long, sportsmen were riding up from Knoxville to Townsend on the Southern Railroad Line and then switching over to the Little River Railroad to be carried deeper in the mountains than they'd ever ventured before. Making a base camp in Elkmont, they headed up further to hunt and fish. Shrewdly, Colonel Townsend, the LRLC's president, quickly added passenger and observation cars to the train and raised the passenger fare.

By 1907, many of Townsend's regular customers, men who came up on weekends from Knoxville, Maryville, and Chattanooga to hunt, fish, and rub dirty elbows with the loggers, had founded the Appalachian Club. To show its appreciation for their business, in 1910 the Little River Lumber Company deeded the club a 50-acre tract for a clubhouse. The company also agreed to lease hunting and fishing privileges on some 40,000 acres above Elkmont exclusively to the Appalachian Club for 10 years. In exchange, the club was expected to manage the fish and game and to patrol the area for poachers.

Of course, once the large, comfortable clubhouse went up, the tough logging camp went the way of Crane's Yellow Sky. A less sports-minded breed of flatlander soon wanted to join the club. Men began bringing their wives for the weekend. The whiskey and games of dice and five-card stud were replaced by teas and dances and bridge tournaments. Soon the town had a post office, boarding house, theater, and church. Men of leisure began building cottages and bringing their families not just for the weekend but for the entire summer. With ruggedness and stamina no longer requirements for admission in the Appalachian Club, wealth and connections became key factors to admission. And the club denied access to its facilities and functions to all nonmembers.

Elkmont continued to grow. Though it no longer felt like a lumber town, timber was still the town's chief industry, and the trees continued to fall. As the trees were clear-cut, the lumber company had no more interest in the land and sold it for good prices. In 1912, three brothers bought 65 acres and built the two-story, white clapboard

Wonderland Park Hotel. A couple of years later, a group of men from Knoxville who hadn't made the cut at the Appalachian Club bought the Wonderland and formed their own club. They reserved some rooms for club members, but left others open to the public.

The Little River Railroad shut down in 1926. The railroad bed became the base for today's Elkmont Road, and as the automobiles rolled into town, a greater boom seemed on the horizon. But then the government came calling. Despite the best legal efforts of some Appalachian Club members, the land became a national park. However, though the members lost their land, their lawyer was able to get them long-term leases to their cabins. The leases were renewed in 1972, but most of them expired in 1992, the same year the Wonderland finally closed its doors.

Nowadays, Elkmont is home to the park's largest campground and to a very rare phenomenon—**synchronized fireflies** (lightning bugs). For some reason, at only this elevation (2,200 feet) the fireflies light up and black out in sync with one another, creating a memorable sight. Look for them in May, June, and July (and sometimes early August) in the late evening— 9–10 P.M.—on the nature trail past the campground and across the stone bridge.

flume at Mingus Mill

© MIKE SIGALAS

## CATALOOCHEE

If you want to see historic structures but find Cades Cove too congested, the hard-to-get-to Cataloochee Valley may offer you the Smokies experience you were hoping for. The Cataloochee Historic District sits about 11 winding miles from I-40 and 16 twisting miles south of Big Creek. The upper Smokies were one of the last areas in the Southeast to be settled, and Cataloochee Valley was one of the last areas in the Smokies to be settled—just before the Civil War.

In the early 20th century, the Cataloochee Valley was home to two prosperous villages, Big Cataloochee and Little Cataloochee, with more than 200 buildings and more than 1,200 residents between them. It was the largest settlement in all of the Smokies, roughly twice as populous as Cades Cove.

Today, a thin, carefully preserved human residue lingers over the Cataloochee region. An old school, churches, and quite a few houses and barns still stand. While Cataloochee's restored structures can't compare to Cades Cove's, neither do its traffic and crowds. In fact, you can't even *get* to Little Cataloochee by car—that requires a two-mile hike. For some folks, the sheer quiet of the 29-square-mile area makes the entire experience superior to that found at Cades Cove. The spot is so remote that when bears run into trouble with visitors elsewhere in the park, they're hauled up here and released so that they won't be able to find their way back.

The name Cataloochee, incidentally, comes from the Cherokee term for "waves of mountains," an accurate description of the view, even now. There's camping up here, including a very popular camp for equestrians.

Back on the beaten path—Newfound Gap

Road—you'll find **Oconaluftee Mountain Farm Museum** right beside the visitors center near the Cherokee entrance. It offers periodic demonstrations of old-time farming methods.

Nearby **Mingus Mill** is also worth a stop—especially if you're tired of the same old grind. That is to say, don't expect the vertical waterwheel usually found in the region's other mills. The Mingus Mill, a "tub" or "turbine" mill, features a wheel that lies on its side. And the old

spattering wooden flume that scoops water out of the creek to feed the mill is worth a couple of snapshots all by itself.

The mill grinds corn and wheat. In fact, you'll find cornmeal and flour on sale inside the mill, packaged in miniature sacks. Unfortunately, these products aren't actually ground there at the mill—they're ground in a modern facility in Tennessee. Blame the newfangled health codes.

# Recreation

## HIKING

Whether it's a stroll in the woods or a multiday trek in the backcountry, hiking ranks high on the list of things to do in the Smokies, where more than 800 miles of trails await the walker. Below is a selection of good **day hikes** in the park. Most are on well-marked trails, but it's never a bad idea to carry a good map. An excellent guidebook for hiking is *Hiking Trails of the Smokies*. Printed on lightweight paper, it's easy for hikers to carry. It costs $16.95 and is available at visitors center gift shops.

Anyone wanting to hike for longer than a day and to camp along any trail in the park needs a permit, available from ranger stations.

### Appalachian Trail Hikes

The most famous trail in America runs through the Smokies, along the 68-mile mountain crest that makes up the Tennessee–North Carolina border. Here, Maine-to-Georgia hikers tramp alongside weekend hikers, who mingle with daytrippers who want to experience the famous trail. As a result, the section of the trail near Newfound Gap can be very crowded.

Leave the Newfound Gap parking lot and head east four miles to **Charlies Bunion,** a sheer drop of 1,000 feet. A spectacular view awaits. The trail climbs 980 feet in the first three miles.

**Newfound Gap to Clingmans Dome,** a 7.5-mile, one-way trek along a section of the Appalachian Trail, is the highest trail in the park and

the highest stretch along all of the Appalachian Trail's 2,100-mile length. The trail offers superb views as the elevation rises 1,600 feet.

### Cades Cove Hikes

The five-mile round-trip **Abrams Falls** hike is a good one for kids; they love to play in the water at Abrams Creek, which drains Cades Cove. Begin along the Cades Cove Loop Road

the Appalachian Trail

© MIKE SIGALAS

and hike down to the falls, or go to the Abrams Creek Ranger Station off the Foothills Parkway on the west side of the park and hike upstream to the falls. The latter is the prettier route, even if it's a bit out of the way.

Two trails lead to **Gregory Bald,** a former summer pasture. The Gregory Ridge Trail, 11 miles round-trip, begins at the turnaround at the start of Parson Branch Road and climbs 2,600 feet up Gregory Ridge. The Gregory Bald Trail, nine miles round-trip, begins farther down the Parson Branch Road and climbs 2,100 feet. Keep in mind that Parson Branch Road is a one-way road leading out of the park. Hikers camping in Cades Cove are in for a long drive to get back to their sleeping bags.

The **Rich Mountain** trail begins on another of those one-way roads out of Cades Cove. Once motorists get to the boundary of the park—Rich Mountain Gap—traffic runs in both directions. Walk east from here along a fire road until the trail takes off to the left. Follow it to the top of the mountain and the intersection with the Indian Grave Gap Road. A good view of the mountains and Cades Cove awaits.

Hikers can reach the beautiful mountain bald of **Spence Field** by two trails. The first is the **Bote Mountain Trail,** a jeep road that begins on Laurel Creek Road, which leads into Cades Cove. Spence Field lies 13 miles ahead, a climb of 2,900 feet. The shortest trail is also the steepest. Begin at the Cades Cove Picnic Area and follow the **Anthony Creek Trail** to its intersection with the Bote Mountain Trail. Prepare to walk nine miles and gain 3,200 feet in elevation.

## Mount LeConte Hikes

Mount LeConte is the third highest mountain in the eastern United States if you measure from sea level to each mountain's peak. But if you measure from the valley floor below each mountain to that mountain's uppermost point, LeConte ranks as the tallest mountain east of the Mississippi. Consequently, it offers some of the park's most striking views.

These views, and the lodge they inspired, have made Mount LeConte very popular with park

---

## SMOKIES HIKING REMINDERS

**Y**ou've heard these rules before, and you'll see them on signs throughout the park, but here are a few points to keep in mind as you hike through the Smokies:

**1. Stash a windbreaker or sweater in your pack.** The higher you go, the colder it gets, so a shirt that feels cool and comfortable at the bottom of a mountain trail may prove inadequate for the cold weather at the mountaintop. Getting chilled is rarely any fun, and in bad weather it can be life-threatening.

**2. Never drink from streams or creeks.** Yes, you're getting "back to nature," but there's no reason to bring some of that nature home in your digestive tract. Carry your own drinking water or take a filtering device with you.

**3. Keep kids close.** Because of the park's dense foliage, kids can bolt ahead and get lost faster than you can say "Hansel and Gretel." Consider equipping young folk with a whistle, provided they use it only if necessary.

**4. Bring bug repellent.** Unless, of course, you want to walk along doing a Leonard Bernstein-at-the-podium impersonation.

**5. Carry a poncho.** The Smoky Mountains get an average of 40 inches of rain per year.

---

visitors. In fact, in the late 1920s and 1930s, when the Great Smoky Mountains Conservation Association was trying to win support for a park, it used to bring influential people to a special camp on the top of the mountain to let the views work their magic.

The old Masonic argument that "all roads lead to the mountaintop" may or may not be true, but at least five trails lead to the top of Mount LeConte. If you're making the climb, you might want to spice things up by hiking up one trail and down another, though depending on which trails you choose, you may need two vehicles to pull it off.

One popular trail for the ascent is the **Boulevard Trail.** It begins at Newfound Gap, thus eliminating a good deal of the climb. To get to the trail, park at Newfound Gap and head east on the Appalachian Trail. The Boulevard Trail will turn off to the left. The total distance is eight miles one way, with an elevation gain of 1,545 feet. Since the trail follows a ridge top, with lots of ups and downs, you'll feel like you're climbing much more.

The **Alum Cave Trail** is a steep, 2,800-foot, 5.5-mile climb that offers a lot to see. If your knees are sturdy, it's a good choice for the downward trek. Along the way, as you might guess, you'll pass Alum Cave, which incidentally was named all wrong. The spot is not a true cave, but really a large overhang. The alum—a mineral found in the overhang—is not truly an alum, but actually a pseudo-alum.

Miners came up here starting in the 1830s to remove the pseudo-cave's deposits of pseudo-alum, used for dyeing fabric and stopping external bleeding. They also mined other non-pseudo-minerals up here, including Epsom salts and saltpeter (used in gunpowder). During the Civil War, with medicine and munitions in short supply, the Confederacy mined here extensively.

In addition to the un-cave, the trail also offers a rock arch and other great scenery. The trail begins at the Alum Cave Bluffs parking lot off Newfound Gap Road.

The next three Mount LeConte trails leave from the Gatlinburg area. They'll come in handy if the park is jammed with cars that make it difficult to get to the other trails.

So named because the mountain it crosses resembles the head of a bull, **Bullhead Trail** begins in the Cherokee Orchard parking lot near Gatlinburg. The elevation gain is 4,017 feet, and the hike is 7.25 miles one-way.

**Rainbow Falls Trail,** another trail setting off from the Cherokee Orchard parking lot, is a 6.75-mile, one-way hike that passes an 80-foot waterfall and gains 4,017 feet. Some hikers avoid this trail because it's rocky and steep with lots of gullies.

Hikers coming from the Gatlinburg area can save 700 feet of elevation gain by taking the **Tril-**

> *The Ramsay Cascades trail offers quite a finale. The 100-foot Ramsay Cascades, while not a straight drop, is the highest waterfall in the park.*

**lium Gap** trail, which begins along the Roaring Fork Motor Nature Trail at the Grotto Falls parking lot. The elevation gain is 3,473 feet over seven miles one-way.

## More Trails on the Tennessee Side

Right outside of Gatlinburg on the Newfound Gap Road and one of the more popular trails in the park, **Chimney Tops** is only two miles one-way, with an elevation gain of 1,335 feet. By the end most people are using hands and feet, but the view is worth it.

The 1.5-mile, one-way **Grotto Falls** hike is cool on even the hottest days. Leave the Roaring Fork Motor Nature Trail at the Grotto Falls parking area and walk upstream to this waterfall. Hikers gain only 500 feet in elevation and can look for salamanders on the way. The park shelters 23 species of them.

The **Hen Wallow Falls** hike leaves from a less crowded area. Drive to the Cosby Picnic Area on the northeast end of the park for a two-mile, one-way hike. The elevation gain is 600 feet through a forest with magnificent poplars and hemlocks. The falls are two feet wide at the top and 20 feet wide at the bottom.

The **Ramsay Cascades** trail offers quite a finale. The 100-foot Ramsay Cascades, while not a straight drop, is the highest waterfall in the park. The trail begins in Greenbrier Cove, about six miles due east of Gatlinburg on U.S. 321. Four miles one-way, the trail gains 1,600 feet in elevation. Hikers should be careful at the falls; several people have fallen to their deaths.

## More Hikes on the North Carolina Side

At Cataloochee you'll find the remote but popular, 7.4-mile **Boogerman Loop Trail,** which climbs around 800 feet to a peak elevation of around 3,600 feet. As Allen R. Coggins recounts in his delightful book *Place Names of the Smokies,* the trail is named for Robert

"Boogerman" Palmer, whose abandoned cabin you'll pass on the trail. Asked in school what he wanted to be when he grew up, the bashful Palmer supposedly put his head down, laughed, and answered, "the Boogerman." His friends laughed along and began using the name. The older Palmer got, the more his neighbors realized that he hadn't been kidding about his chosen vocation. He withdrew more and more from his mountain neighbors. He grew his beard long and enjoyed frightening children with his appearance. They rewarded him by creating tall tales about their encounters with "the Boogerman." When the lumber companies came around and bought up his neighbors' land, Palmer refused to sell—which is why his namesake trail threads in part through all-too-rare virgin Appalachian forest.

In addition to old-growth forest, the Boogerman Loop Trail also offers some wonderful color in autumn, remnants of settlers' cabins, and pretty views of *cataloochee*—"waves of mountains." To get there, take Cove Creek Road to the Caldwell Fork Trail and follow the signs.

## BIKING

Mountain bikes are prohibited on all Smokies trails—as are all vehicles—but a few unimproved roads make good riding. You might try the Cataloochee Valley on the eastern end of the park. Or try the Parson Branch Road out of Cades Cove—but keep in mind that even for bicycles, this is a one-way road.

In the more populated areas of the park, the roads can get quite busy with distracted drivers. So if you're going to bike the park, get out there early. The best place to ride is Cades Cove. A concessionaire at the campground store there rents bikes. When the Cove is jammed with cars, you'll be glad to be on your bike.

---

## SMOKY MOUNTAIN BALDS

None of the Smoky Mountains—indeed, none of the Appalachians south of New Hampshire—extend above the tree line. Heavy forests cover the highest peaks in the park. How then does one explain the balds—ridge-top areas where there are no trees? Some of these 10-plus-acre balds are covered with grass, while others are covered with heath (the family containing mountain laurels, rhododendrons, and azaleas). Theories as to the origin of the balds involve lightning fires, plant disease, or some sort of action by Indian residents.

Whatever created the grass balds, early European settlers put them to use as summer pastures for cattle and sheep. Since settlers usually had to carve every pasture or garden out of virgin hardwood forest, having a ready-made pasture was a godsend. In the spring of each year, men and boys would drive cattle to the mountain heights, always wary of marauding bears and mountain lions. All summer the animals would graze on the grass under the watchful eye of boys or an old man.

Meanwhile, down on the farms, families could raise gardens and fields of corn, free of trampling livestock that might knock down fences to get at the grain. In fall, when the weather began to turn cold and all the crops were in, the animals, fattened by summer grass, were driven home.

The balds make satisfying hiking destinations. Coming out of the woods and onto a wildflower-bedecked grass bald with a stunning mountain vista is enough to make persons of a certain vintage burst out singing "The Sound of Music."

The park contains eight named balds. Andrew's Bald, near Clingmans Dome, is the closest to a road, about a mile and half each way. To get there, go to the Clingmans Dome parking lot and look for the signs. Spence Field and Gregory's Bald can be reached from Cades Cove.

When people stopped grazing cattle on the balds, the surrounding forests slowly began to reclaim them, and the Park Service was faced with a quandary: Should officials let nature take its course and eventually cover the balds, or should the forest be restrained? Luckily for hikers, the park chose the latter course. The balds remain.

# FISHING

Approximately 730 miles of streams thread through the park, and Fontana Lake lies on the southern border. Except for Fontana, which harbors smallmouth and rock bass, trout is the name of the game here. The park is one of the last refuges of the brook trout, the only species native to these parts; anglers who catch one must release it. Efforts to restore brook trout populations have led to the closing of some streams, and rangers can tell you which ones. Rainbow trout are the interlopers whose exploding populations have made the brook trout so rare, so they are fair game.

Trout season never stops in the Smokies. A Tennessee or North Carolina fishing license enables you to fish all over the park year-round, and you'll find licenses for sale in the gateway towns. Trout stamps are not required, but you're only allowed to use one-hook artificial lures—no bait of any sort is allowed.

You can fish right beside the road or, if you're serious about it, backpack deep in to the most remote streams in the park. You can even hire a guide to take you to the best places. A good book for anglers is Don Kirk's *Smoky Mountains Trout Fishing Guide,* available for $11.95 at local bookshops and tackle stores.

# HORSEBACK RIDING

Horse owners can ride in the park and even take overnight equestrian camping trips with Park Service permission. The park limits the number of horse camps, and you'll need to bring your own horse feed. For a complete set of guidelines for horseback riding, call 865/436-1200 or write to Superintendent, Great Smoky Mountains National Park, 107 Park Headquarters Rd., Gatlinburg, TN 37738.

Horses are available to rent from several places in the park, generally for about $15 for a short ride. All rides are guided, usually at a sedate pace,

and children under 6 have to ride with an adult. On the Tennessee side, visitors can rent horses near Park Headquarters, 865/436-5354; at Cades Cove Riding Stables, 865/448-6286; and east of Gatlinburg on U.S. 321, 865/436-5634. On the North Carolina side, try Smokemont, 828/497-2373; or Deep Creek, 828/488-8504.

May through October you can tour Cades Cove in a truck-drawn hay wagon in the evening. The rides costs $6 a person or $8 for a ranger-led trips. No reservations are required. The wagons depart from the Cades Cove Stables. If you've got a group of 15 or more, you can reserve your own wagon for day trips. For group reservations, call 865/448-6286.

# WATER SPORTS

Except in spring and after torrential downpours, you'll have a bear of a time trying to canoe, raft, or even kayak the park's rivers and streams. You may spot some intrepid, experienced kayakers (or some foolish, inexperienced ones) within the park, but for true white water you'll probably need to go outside, preferably to the French Broad or Nantahala River.

If you're seeking a milder experience and don't mind taking a cool dip, you can ride **inner tubes** at the Sinks area of Little River Road. Use caution, though. Rocks—both underwater and not—can make this activity hazardous. Lots of people tube this area every year, and you'll probably be fine if you keep your head about you—specifically if you keep it away from the rocks.

# SKIING

The park offers no downhill skiing, but during winter cross-country skiers practice various forms of their sport on roads and trails. Clingmans Dome Road, the Cherokee Orchard Road, and the Roaring Fork Motor Nature Trail provide excellent skiing when the weather cooperates.

## Accommodations

When it comes to a place to stay inside the most visited national park in the country, **Mount LeConte Lodge** is the only game around—and it's 5.5 miles from the nearest road. Jack Huff built LeConte Lodge in the 1920s, and when the park came into existence the lodge was allowed to remain. Various environmental hardliners have argued for the demise of the venerable lodge, but public sentiment has overwhelmed them every time.

LeConte Lodge holds about 50 guests, either in cabins or private rooms within cabins. Rooms run $79 a night *per person*, and accommodations are extremely rustic: no electricity, hot water, or telephones. The flush toilets stop working in cold weather, so you may have to use a pit toilet. Most of dinner and breakfast comes out of cans carried up the mountain by pack llamas—used because they damage the trails less than horses. The staff serves hearty meals family-style, a great chance to mingle and swap stories with other travelers. The sunset over Clingmans Dome is the evening's sole planned entertainment, and guests retire to their toolshed-sized cabins with wool blankets and kerosene heaters to beat back the cold.

And most guests wouldn't have it any other way.

LeConte Lodge enjoys more demand for its rooms than any other hostelry in the region. Open from late March through November, the lodge accepts reservations for the following year beginning on October 1 (or the following business day if October 1 falls on a weekend). Call 865/429-5704 or write Wilderness Lodging, 250 Apple Valley Rd., Sevierville, TN 37862. Reservations for the entire year are usually snatched up completely within two weeks. But folks have been known to cancel—it won't hurt to call at the last minute to see if a bunk's opened up.

An alternate way to get a bunk at the lodge is to sign up for a Smoky Mountain Field School hike. The lodge reserves three Saturdays a year for these hikes—one each in the spring, summer, and fall. Call 800/284-8885 for dates.

## CAMPGROUNDS

The National Park Service takes a rather stoic stance toward campers: Tent here and you're going to rough it, like it or not. You'll find no sissy pay showers here, and only when the numbers overwhelm pit toilets do the flush toilets open up. Neither will RVers find electrical or water umbilical cords.

Sites run $12–17. You can reserve one up to five months in advance at the park's three most popular campgrounds, Cades Cove, Smokemont, and Elkmont, from May 15 through October 31. Just call 800/365-2267 and type in the park code, GREA, at the prompt. All sites at the park's other campgrounds, and any unreserved campsites at the campgrounds listed above, are available on a first-come, first-served basis. No more than six people can occupy one site, either in two tents or one RV and one tent. During summer and fall campers can stay only seven days; the rest of the year they can stay 14 days. Pets are permitted in campgrounds but you'll have to restrain them.

Overall, the park offers 1,008 campsites at 10 developed campgrounds: five in Tennessee and five in North Carolina. The larger campgrounds offer campfire programs in the evenings. Call 865/436-1200 for information.

### Tennessee Campgrounds

**Cades Cove,** with 161 sites, lies in a part of the Smokies rich in things to do. Besides the cabins and the Cable Mill, trails lead to a bald and a waterfall. This is the only campground with a store, and the Cades Cove Loop Road is the best place in the park to ride a bike. The campground can handle 35-foot RVs, is wheelchair-accessible, and is open year-round.

**Cosby,** with 175 sites, features smaller crowds. It's also more convenient if you're planning to see the Greenbrier area and hike to Ramsay Cascade. Tubing Cosby Creek is a favorite activity here. Cosby can handle 25-foot RVs and is open late March through October.

**Elkmont,** with 220 sites, is the biggest campground in the entire park. It's close to the Metcalf Bottoms Historic Area and the delightful Little River. In late May, June, and early July, you can see the amazing synchronized fireflies along the nature trail past the campground. Laurel Falls is nearby, and Elkmont is also the campground closest to the worldly pleasures of Gatlinburg. It can handle all sizes of RVs, is wheelchair-accessible, and is open year-round.

**Look Rock** offers 92 sites on the extreme western edge of the park. Since it's out of the way, it's a good place to look for a spot when other campgrounds are full. Look Rock offers access to Abrams Creek. It can handle 25-foot RVs and is open late March through October.

**Abrams Creek,** with 16 sites, is the smallest park campground in Tennessee. This gem lies in a forest of huge conifers that lend it a cathedral effect. It is the trailhead for a hike up to Abrams

## LEARNING IN THE SMOKIES

D uring the peak visiting season—roughly June through August—the Park Service provides daily walks, hikes, and talks involving various aspects of the Smokies. Some are geared for children, while others can be enjoyed by all ages. Check the visitors centers for information on what is happening when you're there.

Two groups provide educational experiences in the Smokies for teachers, children, families, or individuals who wish to immerse themselves in some aspect of this park.

The **Smoky Mountain Field School,** 800/284-8885, offers courses ranging from two days to one week involving topics such as geology, stream life, waterfalls, hiking, birds, insects, mammals, bears, and mushrooms. Classes are run in conjunction with the University of Tennessee, and tuition is $36–295. Participants are responsible for arranging their own lodging and meals.

By contrast, the **Great Smoky Mountains Institute at Tremont,** 9275 Tremont Rd., Townsend, TN 37882, 865/448-6709, offers a package deal—program, lodging, and food all in one price. The institute, on the Middle Prong of the Little River in Walker Valley, offers days filled with geology, wildflowers, forest ecology, or cultural history. Evenings include Appalachian music, guest speakers, night hikes, and other activities. The institute has a dormitory with 125 beds, and participants sleep Shaker-style—males on one side and females on the other. It serves hearty, family-style meals. Typical programs include a summer adult backpack trip, $110; a naturalist-led LeConte trip, $230; and a women's backpack trip, $110. Other programs include photography workshops,

grandparent-grandchild weeks, and teacher escape weekends.

In Gatlinburg, the **Arrowmont School of Arts and Crafts** brings 1,500 students and 150 instructors together each summer to a 70-acre campus to work on carving, weaving, pottery, and more than 15 other media. The school originated in 1912 when Pi Beta Phi opened a settlement school in what was then the economically depressed Appalachian town of Gatlinburg. Noting the high value people put on local crafts, the school added crafts instruction along with the other subjects. When improved public schools eliminated the need for the settlement school, the emphasis was shifted entirely to crafts. Those seeking information on the crafts programs should write the school: Arrowmont School of Arts and Crafts, P.O. Box 567, Gatlinburg, TN 37738.

Outside the park's western perimeter, just down U.S. 129/19 from Murphy, Brasstown is home to the 380-acre **John C. Campbell Folk School,** 1 Folk School Rd., 800/365-5724 or 828/837-8637, founded in 1925 and modeled after Danish schools to preserve the crafts, music, dances, and other traditions of the Appalachian people by teaching outlanders about them. It's a wonderful day trip from the park; you can visit the school's History Center free and browse the craft shop, a founding member of the Southern Highland Craft Guild, which features the work of more than 300 local and regional artists. You can also take the local trails and visit artists' studios to watch work in progress. For a longer stay, the school offers three- to twelve-week classes in mountain music, dance, and crafts.

Falls and is also wheelchair-accessible. It can handle 16-foot RVs and is open late March through October.

## North Carolina Campgrounds

**Balsam Mountain,** with 46 sites, is a good base for exploring the Cherokee Reservation; Mingo Falls is a good day trip from here. The campground can handle 30-foot RVs and is open mid-May through October 18.

**Deep Creek,** with 108 sites, lies three miles north of Bryson City and within two miles of three waterfalls: Juneywhank Falls, Indian Creek Falls, and Toms Branch Falls. The campground can handle 25-foot RVs and is open mid-April through October.

**Smokemont,** with 140 sites, is the largest campground on the North Carolina side and a good place to take in the Mountain Farm Museum at Oconoluftee and Mingus Mill. It's also the park campground closest to Cherokee, North Carolina. Open year-round and wheelchair-accessible, it can take all RV sizes.

**Big Creek,** with nine sites, is the smallest campground in the park. It lies on the far eastern end of the Smokies. It's open May 1 to November 2 and can take 26-foot RVs.

**Cataloochee,** with 27 sites, also on the eastern end of the park, lies at the end of a rough, unpaved road that will guarantee campers freedom from crowds. The Cataloochee area contains several old buildings left behind by a community of 1,200 settlers. The campground is open late March through October.

## Trail Shelters

Shelters, most of them on the Appalachian Trail, offer accommodations for hikers who do not want to carry tents or sleep under the stars. Each shelter has three walls and a chain-link fence across the front. Inside you'll find 8 to 14 beds made of wire mesh strung between logs. Outside you'll find a pit toilet. The good news is that shelters are dry and bear-proof, with beds up off the ground. The bad news for some folks is that you may find yourself in close quarters with up to 13 total strangers, any of whom may be champion snorers or Amway enthusiasts.

Sugarlands Visitor Center

You don't have to pay to stay in one of the shelters, but you do need to reserve your bunk in advance. Call Park Headquarters at 865/436-1231 up to one month before your visit.

## Backcountry Camping

Despite all the talk of crowding in the park, it offers close to 100 backcountry sites where, some contend, the ultimate camping experience takes place. Park workers have established backcountry sites all over the park; they shift the locations from time to time to minimize the wear and tear on the land. A site can accommodate from 8 to 20 campers, who can stay up to three days before moving on. Reservations are required for some sites, but there is no charge. Write to Backcountry Permits, Great Smoky Mountains National Park, Gatlinburg, TN 37738 or call 865/436-1231. If you're already in the park, stop by one of the visitors centers—at Sugarlands, Cades Cove, or Oconaluftee—or one of the ranger stations.

To keep things as pristine as possible, the park requires backpackers to pack out all garbage.

Don't bury it or throw it in a pit toilet. In general, practice zero-impact camping: Tents should not be trenched, and hand-dug toilets must lie well away from the campsite and any water sources. Campers can build fires in established fire rings, but park officials prefer that you use a portable stove to lessen the impact on the land.

A final note: Park rangers are very strict about camping in unauthorized places. You can't spend the night in a parking area or picnic area or on the side of the road, even if all the campgrounds are full. The same holds true for the backcountry. Be sure to reserve ahead and allow enough time to get to your destination.

## INFORMATION

The best place to get oriented to the park and to find out what's happening is the **Sugarlands Visitor Center,** just outside Gatlinburg. It includes a small natural history museum, a slide show, free maps, and people who can answer questions. A bookstore offers helpful volumes and films. The **Oconaluftee Visitor Center** sits on the North Carolina side of the park. Both centers are open daily 8 A.M.–7 P.M. Rangers at stations scattered throughout the park can also answer questions and deal with problems.

### Emergencies

In case of trouble, call **Park Headquarters,** 865/436-1230; **Gatlinburg police,** 865/436-5181; or **Cherokee police,** 704/497-4131. Sevier County Hospital on Middle Creek Road in Sevierville, 865/453-7111, is 15 miles from Gatlinburg. Blount Memorial Hospital on U.S. 321 in Maryville, 865/983-7211, is 25 miles from Cades Cove, and Swain County Hospital in Bryson City, N.C., 704/488-2155, is 16 miles from Smokemont.

# Resources

# Suggested Reading

## History

Anderson, Eric. *Race and Politics in North Carolina, 1872-1901: The Black Second.* Baton Rouge, LA: Louisiana State University Press, 1981. A compelling look into North Carolina race relations in the post-Reconstruction era.

Battaile, Andrew Chandler, Arthur W. Bergernon Jr., et. al. *Black Southerners in Gray: Essays on Afro-Americans in Confederate Armies.* Edited by Richard Rollins. Redondo Beach, CA: Rank and File, 1994. Fascinating studies on this little-known minority group in the Civil War.

Frome, Michael, *Strangers in High Places.* Knoxville, TN: University of Tennessee Press, 1994. This book details the 40-year effort to bring the Great Smoky Mountains National Park into existence.

Godwin, John L. *Black Wilmington and the North Carolina Way: Portrait of a Community in the Era of Civil Rights Protest.* Lanham, MD: Univerioty Press of America, 2000. The definitive resource on the story of Benjamin Chavis, the Wilmington Ten, and the birth of the 20th-century Civil Rights movement in North Carolina.

Hudson, Charles, and Carmen Chaves Tesser, eds. *Forgotten Centuries: The Indians and Europeans in the American South, 1521-1704.* Athens, GA: UGA Press, 1994.

Hurmence, Belinda, ed. *My Parents Don't Want Me to Talk About Slavery.* Winston-Salem, NC: John F. Blair, 1989. Absolutely fascinating accounts of life under slavery and during Reconstruction.

Kephart, Horace and Ralph Roberts, *Our Southern Highlanders: A Narrative of Adventure in the Southern Appalachians and a Study of Life Among the Mountaineers.* Knoxville, TN: University of Tennessee Press, 1977. Originally published in 1913, this classic was the first ethnographic look at the people who lived in what is now the Great Smoky Mountains National Park.

Lee, Jr. Robert E., ed. *Recollections and Letters of Robert E. Lee.* New York: Garden City, 1904.

McPherson, James. *Battle Cry of Freedom.* Oxford: Oxford University Press, 1988. A one-volume history of the Civil War.

Pollard, Edward A. *The Southern History of the War.* New York: Charles B. Richardson Publishers, 1866. A revealing account of the War Between the States as it appeared to one contemporary Southerner.

Powell, William S. *North Carolina: A History.* Chapel Hill, NC: UNC Press, 1988. A reprint of the 1976 book written as part of a series honoring the U.S. bicentennial. A good, well-balanced survey of the state's past.

Sherman, General William T. *Personal Memoirs.* New York: Webster, 1892.

Simpson, Lewis P. *Mind and the American Civil War.* Baton Rouge, LA: LSU, 1989. Studies American history's foremost conflict in terms of the collision of two distinct philosophies and the cultures that spawned from them.

Stick, David, ed. *An Outer Banks Reader.* Chapel Hill, NC: UNC, 1998. Concise, compelling first-person accounts of the Outer Banks, written by an assortment of explorers, sailors, soldiers, scientists, and plain-old civilians—from 1524 through today. Compiled by David Stick, a legendary Banks historian.

Ward, Geoffrey. *The Civil War.* New York: Alfred A. Knopf, 1990. The companion volume to Ken Burns' Civil War documentary.

Woodward, C. Vann, ed. *Mary Chesnut's Civil War.* New Haven, CT: Yale, 1982. The Pulitzer Prize-winning collection of letters by a witty, shrewd eyewitness to the inner workings of the Confederacy, with references to the events in North Carolina.

## Description and Travel

Kuralt, Charles and Loonis McGlohon. *North Carolina is My Home.* Guilford, CT: Globe Pequot, 1998. In prose, poetry, and pictures, the native Wilmingtonian expresses his life-long love affair with the state.

Kuralt, Charles. *On the Road With Charles Kuralt.* New York: Putnam, 1985. A cadre of evocative glimpses at 1970s–1980s America (including a handful of North Carolina) seen through the eye of native Wilmingtonian Charles Kuralt.

*North Carolina: The WPA Guide to Old North State.* Federal Works Project, 1939. The definitive old-time guide, created during the New Deal era.

Stick, David. *North Carolina Lighthouses.* Raleigh, NC: North Carolina Department of Cultural Resources, 1980. Everything you ever wanted to know about the state's famous and not-so-famous coastal beacons.

## Music

Bryan, Bo. *Shag: The Legendary Dance of the South.* Beaufort, SC: Foundation Books, 1995. The single best reference on the dance, the music, and the surrounding subculture.

Gale, Jack. *Same Time, Same Station.* Palm City, FL: Gala, 1999. Great anecdotes of the days of early rock and roll radio in North Carolina.

Henry, O. *The Best of O. Henry.* Philadelphia, PA: Courage Books, 1992. A good introduction to Asheville's most famous short story writer.

McCloud, Barry. *Definitive Country: The Ultimate Encyclopedia of Country Music and Its Performers.* New York: Perigee, 1995. A wonderful if increasingly dated reference for the student of country music.

## Fiction and Literature

Haley, Alex. *Roots.* New York: Doubleday, 1976. The fascinating tale of this writer's ancestors, beginning at the time of slavery and moving onward throught the Civil War and emancipation.

Marshall, Catherine. *Christy.* New York: McGraw Hill, 1967. The inspiring story of a young woman who goes to teach school in a remote East Tennessee town. It later became a television show and a musical performed in the Smokies.

Wolfe, Thomas. *Look Homeward, Angel.* New York: Scribner's, 1929. The epic coming-of-age novel, first published in 1929, tells the story of a restless young man who longs to escape his chaotic family life in little Altamont (near Asheville).

## Biography

Remini, Robert Vincent. *Andrew Jackson.* New York: Harper Perennial, 1999. A concise, celebratory but unsweetened treatment of the former Salisbury barrister and hellion whose election as president ushered in the age of the "common man," and whose domestic policies ushered most Cherokee out of the Tar Heel State.

Trefousse, Hans L. *Andrew Johnson: a Biography.* New York: Norton, 1989. A fine recounting of the underappreciated president born in Raleigh.

## The Outdoors

Moore, Harry H. *A Roadside Guide to the Geology of the Great Smoky Mountains National Park.* Knoxville: University of Tennessee Press, 1988. Even if in many places you can't see the rocks for the trees, this book will tell you what is there.

Rhyne, Nancy. *Carolina Seashells.* Orangeburg, SC: Sandlapper Publishing, 1989. Learn to know your conch from your limpet.

Smith, Richard. *Wildflowers of the Southern Mountains.* Knoxville: University of Tennessee Press, 2001. This filed guide to wildflowers is a delight, whether you're walking through a mountain meadow in May or sitting in front of a fire and wishing you were in the Smokies.

## Odds and Ends

Egerton, John, et al. *Southern Food.* Chapel Hill: University of North Carolina Press, 1987. Combining recipes, fine writing, and great photos, this book takes a satisfying look at country cooking.

Garner, Bob. *North Carolina Barbecue: Flavored by Time.* Winston-Salem, NC: John F. Blair, 1996. Not so much a guidebook as a celebration of the vinegary manna of the mountains. Other North Carolina regions (and barbecue styles) are covered as well.

Wilson, Charles Reagan, and William Ferris. *Encyclopedia of Southern Culture.* Chapel Hill, NC: University of North Carolina Press, 1989. This stupendous book—1,634 pages long—addresses mint juleps, sacred harp singing, kudzu, and other Southern items with scholarship and wit.

# Internet Resources

## General Information

**www.ncgov.com**
   The official government site for visitors.

**www.visitnc.com**
   North Carolina Department of Commerce, Division of Tourism, Film, and Sports Development. Good general information on NC attractions.

## Newspapers

**www.charlotteobserver.com**
   Online homepage of the *Charlotte Observer.*

**www.citizen-times.com**
   Online homepage of Asheville's largest daily.

**news-observer.com**
   Online homepage of the Raleigh *News & Observer.*

**www.news-record.com**
   Online homepage of the Greensboro *News & Record.*

## Radio

Unfortunately, recent lawsuits by ad firms have stopped and reversed the proliferation of online local radio programming, which would have enabled you to listen to Tar Heel radio stations live, from anywhere on earth. All the parties involved—broadcasters, recording artists, advertisers, advertising companies—are trying to work out some sort of arrangement that will enable broadcasts to resume, for everyone's benefit (including the listeners). In the meantime, you can hear older broadcasts at the site below.

**www.airchecks.com**
   Offers radio broadcasts from the 1950s–2000 from Raleigh and Charlotte stations, and from other stations all around the country.

## Parks and Recreation

**ils.unc.edu/parkproject**
   Information on every park in the North Carolina state system.

**www.nps.gov**
   This National Parks Service site includes information on all Federal lands in the region, including Fort Sumter, Fort Moultrie, Fort Pulaski, and Cumberland Island.

**www.campingnc.com**
   Information on camping sites across the state.

**www.corollasurfshop.com**
   Current surf conditions on the Outer Banks.

**www.sncsurf.com**
   Current surf conditions in the Wilmington area.

**www.mtbikewnc.com**
   Information on bike trails in Western North Carolina.

**www.oldsmoky.com**
   Find a fishing guide in the Smokies.

**www.paddlenorthcarolina.org**
   Information on rafting and kayaking in the Tar Heel state.

**www.state.nc.us/wildlife**
   Online fishing licenses and angling information from the North Carolina Wildlife Resources Commission.

# Index

**A**

Aberdeen: 251–252
abolitionist movement: 31–32
Abrams Falls: 49, 347
accommodations: 56–57; *see also specific place*
Ackland Art Museum: 205*f*
A Dickens Christmas in the Village: 291
African-American Arts Festival: 267
African American Atelier, Inc.: 272
African American Heritage Preservation Cultural
    Complex: 171–172
Airlie Gardens: 149
air travel: 64–65
Albemarle Region: 3, 18–19, 21, 22
Albert Styron's General Store: 103
alcohol: 61
Alexander Dickson House: 203–204
Alligator River National Wildlife Refuge: 92,
    107
Alum Cave Trail: 49, 349
American Classic Motorcycle Museum: 275
American Dance Festival: 193
American Revolution: *see* Revolutionary War
amusement parks: 54, 151, 243–245, 315–316
Anderson, Robert: 33
Andrew's Bald: 350
Andy Griffith Museum: 264
*Andy Griffith Show*: 263–264
Angela Peterson Doll and Miniature Museum:
    279
animals: 10, 12, 13
Anne, Queen (of England): 22, 113
Anniversary of the Battle of Guilford Court-
    house: 267
Annual Autumn Leaves Festival: 265
Anthony Creek Trail: 348
antiques: 55, 97
Appalachian Cultural Museum: 301
Appalachian Heritage Museum: 299
Appalachian State University: 301
Appalachian Trail: 49, 347
aquariums: Fort Fisher Aquarium 144; North
    Carolina Aquarium at Fort Fisher 147; North
    Carolina Aquarium at Pine Knoll Shores 133;
    North Carolina Aquarium at Roanoke Island
    106
archaeological sites: 146

architecture: 145, 179, 203–204, 225, 239, 289,
    344–345
Arrowmont School of Arts and Crafts: 353
Art in the Park: 299
ArtQuest: 270, 272
Artspace: 172
Asheboro: 275–276
Ashe, Samuel: 281
Asheville: 281–293
Asheville Art Museum: 290
Asheville Smoke: 54
Asheville Tourists: 53
Ashley-Cooper, Anthony: 18
Atlantic Beach: 133–134
Attmore-Oliver House: 116
auto racing: 52–53, 233, 248
Ava Gardner Museum: 212, 213
Avon: 99–100

**B**

Bald Head Island: 164–165
Bald Head Light: 163, 165
Bald is Beautiful Convention: 129
balds: 350
Bank of America Corporate Center: 228
Bank of the Arts: 116
Barbadians: 19–21
barbecue: 58–59, 90, 159, 182–183, 199, 229,
    280, 324
Barker, Penelope: 125
baseball: 53–54, 202, 233–234, 242, 260–261
Bath: 23, 122–123
Battery Park Hotel: 289
Battle for North Carolina: 148
Battle of Alamance: 26, 170
Battle of Bentonville: 214
bays: 5
beaches: 83, 143; *see also specific place*
beach music: 54–55
Beaufort: 130–133
Beaufort Historic Site: 130
bed and breakfasts: 57; *see also specific place*
Bele Chere: 291
Bellair Plantation and Restoration: 116
Bellamy Mansion Museum of History and De-
    sign: 144–145
Bennett Place State Historic Site: 34, 35, 194

Benton, Thomas Hart: 203
Bentonville: 214
Berkeley, John: 18
Berkeley, William: 18
Bethabara Park: 259
Bethesda Church: 251
beverages: 61
bicycling: 50, 350
Biltmore House and Gardens: 285, 287
Biltmore Village: 287
Biltmore Winery: 52
Bimbé Cultural Festival: 193
birds: 13–14
Birthplace of Pepsi-Cola: 116
Birthplace of President Andrew Johnson: 175–176
Black Pioneers: 26, 148
Blandwood Mansion: 269
Blowing Rock: 296–301
blue crab: 48
Blue Ridge Jamboree: 265
boating: 65, 91–92, 133
Bodie Island: 98
Bodie Island Lighthouse: 85, 86–87
Bog Garden: 268
Bojangles: 63
boll weevil: 40
Bonnet, Stede: 163
Boogerman Loop Trail: 349
Boone: 301–303, 304–305
Boone, Daniel: 301
border crossings: 67
Botanical Gardens — Asheville: 290
Bote Mountain Trail: 348
Boulevard Trail: 49, 348–349
bowling: 161
Boyd, James: 249
Bradham, Caleb: 112
Brasstown: 336
Brevard: 293–294
Brewer, Jerry: 150–151
brewpubs: 158, 210
Bridal Veil Falls: 330
Brightleaf Square: 194
British Cemetery: 102
British proprietary period: 18–23
Britt-Sanders Cabin: 250
Brunswick Isles: 4
Brunswick Town State Historic Site: 146–147
Bryson City: 329–333

Bull Durham Blues Festival: 193
Bullhead Trail: 49, 349
Buncombe, Felix: 281
Bunker, Chang and Eng: 264
Bunker Hill Covered Bridge: 238
Burgwin-Wright House: 145–146
Burns, Otway: 130
bus travel: 65
Buxton: 100
Buxton Woods Maritime Forest: 17, 100
Buxton Woods Nature Trail: 100

C
cabins: 57
Cable Mill: 345
Cades Cove: 50, 344–345, 347–348
Cades Cove Roads: 344–345
Calabash: 166
Calhoun, John C.: 30–31, 32–33
Cameron Art Museum: 145
camping/campgrounds: 51, 57, 79; see also specific place
canoeing and kayaking: 46, 132, 303, 351
Cape Fear Coast: 4
Cape Fear Museum: 144
Cape Fear River: 19, 25, 159
Cape Fear Shakespeare Festival: 160
Cape Hatteras Beach Trail: 48
Cape Hatteras Lighthouse: 85, 100
Cape Hatteras National Seashore: 92, 100, 103
Capps, Joe: 129
Captain J. N. Maffit water taxi: 144
Carolina Beach Boardwalk: 151
Carolina Boxing Hall of Fame: 224
Carolina Dynamo: 54
Carolina Hurricanes: 54
Carolina Nights: 318
Carolina Renaissance Festival: 235
Carolina soft-shell crab: 58
Carolina Theater: 195
Carowinds: 54, 243–245
Carraway, Gertrude: 115
car rentals: 64; see also specific place
Carteret, George: 18
Carteret, Nicholas: 19
car travel: 64, 93
Cary: 180
Cashiers: 330
Cashie Wetlands Walk: 123
Cataloochee: 346–347

**Index**

Cataloochee Ski Area: 318
Catawba Furniture Museum: 306
Cedar Island National Wildlife Refuge: 114
cell phones: 77
Cedar Point Tideland Trail: 48, 128
Center City: 223
Center for the Arts Building: 239
Central Coast: 4, 111–135
Chamber Music Festival: 332
Chapel Hill: 205–211
Chapel Hill Museum: 205
Charles I, King: 18
Charles II, King: 18
Charles Kuralt Trail: 98
Charles Town: 19, 20, 21, 22, 25, 26, 27
Charlies Bunion: 49, 347
Charlotte: 216–234; accommodations 228–229;
    entertainment 232–233; food 229–232; histo-
    ry 218–223; North Davidson neighborhood
    228; recreation 233–234; sightseeing
    223–228; transportation 234
Charlotte Checkers: 54
Charlotte Eagles: 54
Charlotte Hornets: 234
Charlotte Knights: 53, 233, 242
Charlotte Museum of History: 223
Charlotte Nature Museum: 224
Charlotte Sting: 234
Chavis, Benjamin: 139, 140
Cherohala Skyway: 335
Cherokee: 307–315
Cherokee Botanical Garden and Nature Trail:
    311
Cherokee Historical Museum: 336
Cherokee Indians: 17, 32, 301, 307–311, 335
Cherokee Orchard Road: 344
Cherry Park: 241
Chesnut, Mary Boykin: 31
Chesnutt, Charles W.: 212
Chick-Fil-A: 63
Children's Museum at Old Salem: 258–259
Chimney Tops: 49, 349
Chinqua-Penn Plantation: 274
Christ Episcopal Church: 116
churches: 68–69; *see also* historic churches
Church of St. Lawrence: 289
City Market: 176, 188
Civil Rights: 40–41, 138–140, 220–221, 238,
    267
Civil War: 33–38, 212–215, 220, 310

Clarendon, Edward, Earl of: 18
Clay, Henry: 31
climate: 7–9
Clingman, Thomas L.: 37, 343
Clingmans Dome: 49, 347, 350
Clingmans Dome Road: 343
Clinton, Henry: 27
Clover: 245
Coastal Plain: 4–5
Coffin, Abel: 264
Coffin, Levi: 33, 36, 266
Coffin, Vestal: 33, 36, 266
Coker Arboretum: 205
Colburn Gem and Mineral Museum: 289
colleges: Livingston College 236–237; Saint Au-
    gustine's College Chapel 179; Wake Forest
    College Birthplace Museum 181
Colleton, John: 18
Coltrane, John: 277
communications: 76–77
Contemporary Art Museum: 172–173
Coolidge, Calvin: 340
Cornwallis, Charles: 26–27, 28–29, 148, 245
Corolla: 96–97
Corolla Lighthouse: 85
Corolla Surf Shop: 45, 91
Cosell, Howard: 256
cotton: 30, 39, 40
covered bridge: 238, 275
crabbing: 47–48
Cracker Barrel: 62–63
Cradle of Forestry: 294
Craggy Mountain Scenic Area: 305
Craighead, Alexander: 218
Cram, George F.: 38
Craven, William, Earl of: 18
crime: 73–75
Croatan Indians: 17
Croatan National Forest: 128
Crockett, David: 283
Cromwell, Oliver: 18
cruising: 159–160
Cullowhee: 329
Culpeper Rebellion: 21
Currituck Beach Lighthouse: 97
Currituck National Wildlife Refuge: 96
Currituck Wildlife Museum: 97

**D**
Dale Earnhardt Inc. Showroom: 224

Daniel Boone Native Gardens: 302
Daniels, Josephus: 40, 122
Davidson: 235
Davis, Jefferson: 36, 266
Davis, Willis P.: 339–340
de Graffenried, Christopher: 113
De Mille, Cecil B.: 122
De Mille, Henry C.: 122
Dennis Vineyards Winery: 237
desegregation: 40–41
De Soto, Hernando: 308
Diamond K Dance Ranch: 318
Diggs Gallery: 259
Dillsboro: 325–329
disabled travelers: 68
Discovery Place: 224
doctors: 69
diving: 46, 132–133, 164
Douglas, Stephen A.: 37
Dowd House: 224
Down East: 114
drugs: 75
Dry Falls: 330
Duck: 94–96
Duke Homestead State History Site and Tobacco
    Museum: 195
Duke, James: 39
Duke University: 195–196
Duke University Museum of Art: 196
Duke University Primate Center: 197
Dula, Thomas: 306
DuPont State Park: 50, 328
Durham: 193–205
Durham Americans: 202
Durham, Bartlett: 193
Durham Bulls: 53

E
Eastern Music Festival: 267
Eden, Charles: 123
Edenton: 123–126
Edenton Tea Party: 125
Edible Arts Festival of Food and Art: 193
Edison, Thomas: 100
Edisto Indians: 19–20
Education, Arts and Science Center: 289
1828 Perquimans County Courthouse: 126
electricity: 79
Elizabethan Gardens: 106–107
Elizabeth City: 127–128

Elizabeth I, Queen (of England): 105
Elkmont: 345–346
Ellis, John: 37
Eno River State Park: 202
entertainment: see specific place
environmental issues: 14
etiquette: 42–43
events: see specific place
Episcopal Church of Our Savior, The: 239
Exploris: 173

F
factory outlets: 55
Fall Harvest Festival: 317
Falls Lake State Recreation Area: 192
family travel: 67–68
farmers' markets: 63; see also specific place
fauna: 10–14
Fayetteville: 212–213, 215
Fearing, Fred: 128
Feis Chlobhair, A Clover Kinntra Gatherin': 245
ferries: 66, 93, 151–152
Festival for the Eno: 193
festivals: see specific place
Fieldcrest Cannon Textile Company: 235
Fields of the Wood: 54, 336
fire ants: 71–72
fireflies: 346
Firemen's Museum: 116
First Associate Reformed Presbyterian Church:
    239
First Baptist Church: 239
First Night Asheville: 291
First Presbyterian Church (Charlotte): 225
First Presbyterian Church (Wilmington):
    148–149
fish/fishing: 12, 46–47, 72–73, 303, 351
Fitzhugh, George: 32
flora: 10, 11
Flytrap Trail: 48
Folk Art Center: 290
Fontana: 334
Fontana Lake: 335
food: 58–63; see also specific place
football: 52
Fort Fisher Aquarium: 144
Fort Fisher State Historic Site: 147
Fort Fisher State Recreational Area: 143–144
Fort Lejeune: 134–135
Fort Macon State Park: 133

Index

Index

Fort Mill: 242–243
Fort Raleigh National Historic Site: 107
Fourth Ward: 225
Fourth Ward Park: 225
Franklin: 331
Fressenden, Reginald: 100
Frisco: 100–101
Frisco Native American Museum and Natural History Center: 100–101
Fun Fourth Festival: 267
Furniture Discovery Center: 278

**G**

Gale, Christopher: 113
Gallery at Old Salem, The: 259
Gantt, Harvey: 221
gardens: Airlie Gardens 149; Biltmore House and Gardens 285, 287; Bog Garden 268; Botanical Gardens — Asheville 290; Cherokee Botanical Garden and Nature Trail 311; Coker Arboretum 205; Daniel Boone Native Gardens 302; Elizabethan Gardens 106–107; Glencairn Garden 240; Haywood Hall House and Gardens 177; Highlands Botanical Garden 332;

J. C. Raulston Arboretum 177; Lindsey Gardens and Miniature Village 323; Martin Luther King Jr. Memorial Gardens 177; North Carolina Botanical Garden 205; Orton Plantation Gardens 149; Sandhills Horticultural Gardens 248; Sarah P. Duke Gardens 196
Gardner, Ava: 213
Garner House: 250
gay and lesbian travelers: 68
gem mines: 322–323, 331
geography: see land
George II, King: 23
George III, King: 218
Ghost Town in the Sky: 54, 315–316
giardia: 73
Gibbs, John: 22
Glencairn Garden: 240
Glen Falls Scenic Area: 330
gold: 247
Gold Hill: 237
golf: 51 see also specific place
Grace, Mark: 257
Grady, Henry W.: 39
Graham County Museum of Prehistoric Relics: 334

## Galleries and Art Centers

Ackland Art Museum: 205
African-American Arts Festival: 267
Arrowmont School of Arts and Crafts: 353
Art in the Park: 299
ArtQuest: 270, 272
Artspace: 172
Asheville Art Museum: 290
Bank of the Arts: 116
Cameron Art Museum: 145
Center for the Arts Building: 239
Contemporary Art Museum: 172–173
Diggs Gallery: 259
Duke University Museum of Art: 196
Edible Arts Festival of Food and Art: 193
Education, Arts and Science Center: 289
Folk Art Center: 290
Gallery at Old Salem, The: 259
Green Hill Center for North Carolina Art: 272
Guilford Native American Art Gallery and Gift Shop: 272
High Country Arts and Crafts Fair: 333

John C. Campbell Folk School: 336, 353
Louise Wells Cameron Art Museum: 145
Mattie King Davis Art Gallery: 130
Mint Museum of Art: 223
Museum of Early Southern Decorative Arts (MESDA): 258
Native American Artifacts Museum: 299
North Carolina Central University Art Museum: 196
North Carolina Collection Gallery: 206
North Carolina Museum of Art: 173–174
Page-Walker Arts and History Center: 180
Piedmont Craftsmen Gallery: 259
Reynolda House Museum of American Art: 259
Southeastern Center for Contemporary Art (SECCA): 259
T. Pennington Art Gallery: 324
Twigs & Leaves Gallery: 324
Weatherspoon Art Gallery: 272
Wilkes Art Gallery: 306

Grandfather Mountain Park: 305–306
Graveyard of the Atlantic Museum: 101
Grayson, Kathryn: 256
Great Dismal Swamp Canal: 6–7
Great Smoky Mountain balds: 350
Great Smoky Mountains: 5
Great Smoky Mountains Institute at Tremont: 353
Great Smoky Mountains National Park: 50, 337–355; accommodations 352–355; camping/campgrounds 352–355; entrances 342–343; hiking 347–350; history 339–342; roads 342–344; sightseeing 344–347
Great Smoky Mountains Railroad: 325–326
Greene, Nathanael: 28–29, 266
Green Hill Center for North Carolina Art: 272
Greensboro: 265–274
Greensboro Children's Museum: 269–270
Greensboro Cultural Center at Festival Park: 270, 272
Greensboro Generals: 54
Greensboro Historical Museum: 270
Gregory Bald: 348, 350
Gregory Bald Trail: 348
Gregory Ridge Trail: 348
Grier, Pam: 257
Griffith, Andy: 263–264
Grotto Falls: 50, 344, 349
Grove, E. W.: 283, 291
Guardian Building: 239
Guest, Romeo: 169
Guilford Courthouse National Military Park: 270
Guilford Native American Art Gallery and Gift Shop: 272

**H**
Hamilton, George: 257
Hammocks Beach State Park: 135
handicapped travelers: 68
hang gliding: 93
Hardee's: 63
Harkers Island: 114
Harper, Thomas: 32
Harrah's Cherokee Casino: 312–313
Harvey Mansion: 116
Hatteras: 101
Hatteras Island: 17, 83, 98–101
Hayti Heritage Center: 197
Haywood Arts Repertory Theatre: 323

Haywood Hall House and Gardens: 177
Health Adventure: 289
health and safety: 69–75
Heath Charter: 18
Heath, Robert: 18
Hedrick, Zelma Kathryn: 256
Helms, Jesse: 41
Helper, Rowan: 36
Hemlock Bluffs: 180
Henderson, James Pinckney: 32
Hen Wallow Falls: 50, 349
Hertford: 126–127
Hezekiah Alexander Homesite: 223
Hickory: 306
Hickory Ridge Homestead Museum: 302
High Country Arts and Crafts Fair: 333
Highlands: 332–333
Highlands Biological Station: 332
Highlands Botanical Garden: 332
Highlands Nature Center: 332
High Point: 276–280
High Point Museum and Historical Park: 279
hiking: 48–50, 347–350; *see also specific place*

## Hiking Trails

Alum Cave Trail: 49, 349
Anthony Creek Trail: 348
Appalachian Trail: 49, 347
Boogerman Loop Trail: 349
Bote Mountain Trail: 348
Boulevard Trail: 49, 348–349
Bullhead Trail: 49, 349
Buxton Woods Nature Trail: 100
Cape Hatteras Beach Trail: 48
Cedar Point Tideland Trail: 48, 128
Charles Kuralt Trail: 98
Cherokee Botanical Garden and Nature Trail: 311
Flytrap Trail: 48
Gregory Bald Trail: 348
Gregory Ridge Trail: 348
Paw Paw Trail: 224
Rainbow Falls Trail: 349
Rich Mountain Trail: 348
Roaring Fork Motor Nature Trail: 343–344
Tracks in the Sand Trail: 48, 87
Trillium Gap Trail: 349

## Historic Churches

Bethesda Church: 251
Christ Episcopal Church: 116
Church of St. Lawrence: 289
Episcopal Church of Our Savior, The: 239
First Associate Reformed Presbyterian
    Church: 239
First Baptist Church: 239
First Presbyterian Church (Charlotte): 225
First Presbyterian Church (Wilmington):
    148–149
St. James Episcopal Church: 147–148
St. Thomas Episcopal Church: 123

Hillsborough: 203
Hill, William: 203
Hilton Head Island: 19
Hilton, William: 19
historic drama: 301, 311–312
history: 2–3, 15–41; abolitionist movement
    31–32; British proprietary period 18–23;
    Civil Rights 40–41, 138–140; Civil War
    33–38, 212–215, 220, 310; early antebellum
    Old South 29–33; integration 220–221; Mex-
    ican War 32–33; Native Americans 15–17;
    New South 39–40; nullification crisis 30; Re-
    construction 38–39; Revolutionary War
    25–29, 148; see also specific place
hockey: 54
Hodges, Luther: 169
Holden Beach: 165
Holden, William: 39
Holshouser, James E.: 41
Hooper, William: 203
Hope Plantation: 123
horseback riding: 303, 351
hospitals: 162
hotels: 56–57; see also specific place
Hot Springs: 294–295
House in the Horseshoe: 248
humidity: 69
Hugh Mangum Museum of Photography: 198
Hunter, Jim "Catfish": 126
Hunter, Robert: 264
Hunter, Theophilus, Jr.: 180
hunting: 51, 303
hurricanes: 8–9, 70

## I

Indian Museum of the Carolinas: 248
Indian Wild Game Festival: 215
insects: 14, 69, 71–72
integration: 220–221
International Civil Rights Center and Museum:
    271
Internet access: 77
Intracoastal Waterway: 7

## J

Jackson, Andrew: 25, 30, 203, 226, 236, 308,
    334
Jackson, Jesse: 267
James K. Polk Memorial: 225
J. C. Raulston Arboretum: 177
jellyfish: 72
Jockey's Ridge State Park: 87
Joel Lane House: 177
John C. Campbell Folk School: 336, 353
Johnson, Andrew: 25, 29, 35, 175–176, 203
Johnson, Gerald: 267
Johnson, Robert: 23
Johnson, Samuel: 24
Johnston, Joseph, E.: 34, 38, 193, 203, 214, 266
Jordan Lake State Recreation Area: 191–192
Joyce Kilmer Memorial Forest: 330
Jubilee Amusement Park: 151
Judaculla Rock: 329
Junaluska: 334
Jungle Rapids Family Fun Park: 151

## K

Kannapolis: 235
Kannapolis Intimidators: 235
kayaking: see canoeing and kayaking
Kiawah Indians: 20
Kill Devil Hills: 84–85
King, Elizabeth: 125
King, Martin Luther, Jr.: 220
Kings Arena: 242
Kings Mountain State and National Military
    Parks: 245
Kinston Indians: 53
Kitty Hawk: 84
Kitty Hawk Maritime Forest: 92
Kramer, Joe: 128
kudzu: 11
Ku Klux Klan: 39

**L**

Lafayette, Marquis de: 212
Lake Crabtree County Park: 192
Lake Norman State Park: 235
lakes: 6
land: 2–9
language: 42
Latimer House: 147
Latta Plantation: 225
lattice: 99
Laurinburg: 248
Lawson, John: 13, 113, 122
Lazy 5 Ranch: 228
Lee Robinson General Store: 101
Levine Museum of the New South: 223
Lexington: 280
lighthouses: Bald Head Light 163, 165; Bodie Island Lighthouse 85, 86–87; Cape Hatteras Lighthouse 85, 100; Corolla Lighthouse 85; Currituck Beach Lighthouse 97; Oak Island Light 163; Ocracoke Lighthouse 85, 103
lightning storms: 69–70
lightning bugs: see fireflies
Lincoln, Abraham: 33, 35–37
Lindsey Gardens and Miniature Village: 323
Linville Caverns: 306
Little River Road: 344
Livermon Recreational Park and Mini Zoo: 123
Livingston College: 236–237
Logan, John "Black Jack": 38, 169
Log Cabin Museum: 334
Looking Glass Falls: 294
Lost Colony Theatre Under the Stars: 107
Louise Wells Cameron Art Museum: 145
Lower Cullasaja Falls: 330
Ludwell, Phillip: 22
Lyme disease: 73

**M**

MacDonald, Donald: 27, 148
Madison, Dorothea (Dolley) Payne: 265–266, 267
Madison, James: 265, 267
magazines: 162–163
Maggie Valley: 315–321
Maggie Valley Opry House: 317
Magic Wings Butterfly House: 197
Malcolm Blue Farm: 251–252
mammals: 10, 12
manners: 42–43
Manteo: 105–109

Marconi, Guglielmo: 100
Martin, Alexander: 266
Martin, Josiah: 26, 27, 29, 113, 148, 163
Martin Luther King Jr. Memorial Gardens: 177
Mast General Store: 301, 303, 323
Mattie King Davis Art Gallery: 130
Mattye Reed African Heritage Center: 272
McAdoo, Bob: 267
McIntyre Historic Site: 225, 228
McNair, Ron: 267
Memory Lane Motorsports and Historic Automotive Museum: 224
Mendenhall Plantation: 271
Mexican War: 32–33
Midyette, Rebecca: 120
Mingus Mill: 347
Mini-Apolis Grand Prix Park: 323
Mint Museum of Art: 223
Mint Museum of Craft & Design: 224
Mississippian Indians: 16–17
Mitchell Hardware: 117
Monck, George: 18
money: 78–79
Moore, James: 23
Moores Creek Bridge National Battlefield: 149
Moravians: 254–255
Mordecai Historic Park: 175–176
Morehead City: 129
Morehead, John Motley: 129
Morehead Planetarium: 205
Morgan, Daniel: 28
Morrow Mountain State Park: 237
Morton, Joseph: 22
motels: 56–57; see also specific place
Moultrie, William: 27
Mountain Dance and Folk Festival: 291
Mountain Heritage Center: 329
Mountain Valley Vineyards: 52
Mount Airy: 263–265
Mount Airy Museum of Regional History: 264
Mount Gilead: 237
Mount LeConte: 49, 348–349
Mount Mitchell State Park: 305
Mozee, Phoebe Anne: 248
Muhammad, Benjamin: 139
Murphy: 335–336
Murray's Mill: 238
Murrow, Edward R.: 267
music: 54–55
Museum of Coastal Carolina: 165

Museum of Early Southern Decorative Arts
   (MESDA): 258
Museum of Oddities: 150
Museum of the Albemarle: 128
Museum of the Cherokee Indian: 311
Museum of York County: 240–241
Myrick, Sue: 223
Mystery Hill: 297, 299

**N**
Nags Head: 83–93
Nags Head Woods Ecological Preserve: 87
Nalu Kai Surf Museum: 97
Nantahala Gorge: 329
Nantahala National Forest: 330–331
Nash, Francis: 203
National Black Theater Festival: 257
Native American Artifacts Museum: 299
Native American Pow Wow: 193
Native Americans: 15–17, 20, 215, 218, 242,
   301, 313–314; *see also specific Indian tribes*
Natural Science Center of Greensboro: 271–272
Neal, Fred "Curley": 267
New Bern: 112–120
Newbold-White House: 127
Newfound Gap Road: 343
New South: 39–40
newspapers: 162, 211
North Carolina Aquarium at Fort Fisher: 147
North Carolina Aquarium at Pine Knoll Shores:
   133
North Carolina Aquarium at Roanoke Island:
   106
North Carolina Auto Racing Hall of Fame: 224
North Carolina Blumenthal Performing Arts
   Center: 228
North Carolina Botanical Garden: 205
North Carolina Central University Art Museum:
   196
North Carolina Collection Gallery: 206
North Carolina Estuarium: 122
North Carolina Executive Mansion: 178
North Carolina 4th of July Festival: 164
North Carolina Indian Cultural Center: 215
North Carolina International Folk Festival/Folk-
   moot USA: 291
North Carolina International Jazz Festival: 193
North Carolina Literary Hall of Fame: 249–250
North Carolina Maritime Museum: 130
North Carolina Maritime Museum at Southport:
   163–164
North Carolina Museum of Art: 173–174
North Carolina Museum of History: 174–175
North Carolina Museum of Life and Science:
   196–197
North Carolina Museum of Natural Sciences:
   175
North Carolina Railroad Museum: 180–181
North Carolina Seafood Festival: 129
North Carolina State Archives: 178
North Carolina State Capitol: 178–179
North Carolina State Legislative Building: 179
North Carolina Transportation Museum: 238
North Carolina Zoological Park: 275
Northern Mountains: 296–306
Northern Villages: 98–99
North Wilkesboro: 306
nullification crisis: 30, 33

**O**
Oak Island Light: 163
Oakley, Annie: 248
Oak View County Park: 179
Oakwood: 179
Ocean Isle Beach: 165
Ocean Roots: 45, 91
Oconaluftee Indian Village: 311
Oconaluftee Mountain Farm Museum: 347
Ocracoke Island: 101–104
Ocracoke Lighthouse: 85, 103
Ocracoke Option: 50
Ocracoke Preservation Society Museum: 102
Odom, Howard: 169
Old Durham Historic House Tour: 193
Old Greensborough: 269
Old Orange County Courthouse: 203
Old Pressley Sapphire Mine: 322–323
Old Salem: 257–259
Old Town Clock: 203
Old Wilkes Jail Museum: 306
Olmsted, Frederick Law: 248, 285
Oriental: 120–121
Orton Plantation Gardens: 149
Outer Banks: 3–4, 17, 81–109

**P**
Page, A. Frank: 251
Page-Walker Arts and History Center: 180
Page, Walter Hines: 40, 248, 251
Paleo-Indians: 15–16

Palmer, E. B.: 172
Palmer, Robert "Boogerman": 349–350
Pardo, Juan: 332, 335
Pack Place: 289–290
passports: 65
Patterson's Mill Country Store: 197
Paw Paw Trail: 224
Pea Island National Wildlife Refuge: 92, 98
Peletier: 135
Pembroke: 215
people: 41–43
Peoples Building: 239
Pepsi-Cola: 116
photo etiquette: 79
Pickens, Andrew: 28
Piedmont: 5
Piedmont Craftsmen Gallery: 259
Piedmont Environmental Center: 279
Pinehurst: 248–249
piracy: 130
Pinehurst Harness Track: 248
Pisgah Covered Bridge: 275
plants: 10, 11
Plymouth: 123
poison ivy: 73
Polk, James K.: 32, 203, 225, 226–227
Polk, Leonidas LaFayette: 40
Polk, Tom: 218–219
Pollock, Thomas: 113
Poplar Grove Plantation: 149
Porter, William (O. Henry): 267
Port-O-Plymouth Civil War Museum: 123
Port Royal: 19–20, 22
Portsmouth Island: 104
postal services: 76
pottery: 276
Powwow: 215

## Plantations

Bellair Plantation and Restoration: 116
Chinqua-Penn Plantation: 274
Hope Plantation: 123
Latta Plantation: 225
Mendenhall Plantation: 271
Orton Plantation Gardens: 149
Poplar Grove Plantation: 149
Rosedale Plantation: 225

precipitation: 8
Pryor, Roger: 35
Pullen Park: 179

QR
Quiet Side: 335
Rachel Carson National Estuarine Preserve:
    130–131
racism: 75, 138–140, 289
radio: 77, 185, 211
rafting: see whitewater rafting
rain: see precipitation
Rainbow Falls: 349
Rainbow Falls Trail: 349
Raleigh: 167–192; accommodations 181–182;
    entertainment 187–191; food 182–187; recre-
    ation 191–192; sightseeing 171–181; trans-
    portation 192
Raleigh Capital Express: 54
Raleigh City Museum: 176
Raleigh, Sir Walter: 105
rattlesnakes: see snakes
Ramsay Cascades: 50, 349
Ray Price Legends of Harley Drag Racing Muse-
    um: 173
Reconstruction: 38–39
recreation: see sports and recreation
Reed Gold Mine State Historic Site: 247
Reed, John: 247
Regulators: 26, 170
Reidsville: 274
reptiles: 12–13, 70–71
Research Triangle Park: 197
Revolutionary War: 25–29, 148
Reynolda House: 259
Reynolda House Museum of American Art: 259
Reynolds, R. J.: 256
Richard Petty Museum: 272
Rich Mountain: 49, 348
Rich Mountain Trail: 348
rivers: 5–6; see also specific place
Riverside Cemetery: 290
Roanoke Island: 105–109
Roanoke Island Festival Park: 105–106
Roaring Fork Motor Nature Trail: 343–344
Robbinsville: 334–335
Robertson, James: 301
Rockefeller, John D., Jr.: 341
Rock Hill: 238–242
Rock Hill Cotton Factory: 240

Rock Hill Telephone Company Museum: 240
Rockingham: 247–248
Rodanthe: 98–99
roller coasters: 244–245
Rollins, Richard: 32
Roosevelt, Franklin D.: 341
Rosedale Plantation: 225
Rotary City Regatta: 117
Rowan County Museum: 237
Russell, William Howard: 32, 36
Ruth, George Herman "Babe": 212

**S**

S&W Cafeteria: 289
Saint Augustine's College Chapel: 179
Saint Mary's School: 179–180
Salem Tavern: 258
Salisbury: 236–238
Salisbury National Cemetery: 236
Salvo: 99
Sandford, Robert: 19
Sandhills: 4–5, 247–248
Sandhills Horticultural Gardens: 248
Santa's Land Park and Zoo: 54, 316–317
Sarah P. Duke Gardens: 196
Saunder, Hiram: 28
Sayle, William: 19
SciWorks: 260
Scots-Irish: 24–25, 26–27, 148, 218–219
Scottish Heritage Center: 248
Screen Gems Studio: 151
seafood: 58, 89, 155–156, 183–184
Seagrove: 276
Sea Islands: 17
secessionism: 33, 35
Settlers Cemetery: 225
Seven Hearths: 204
Sevier, John: 301
sexually transmitted diseases: 75
sharks: 72–73
Shaw House: 250
Shelton House Museum of North Carolina
    Handicrafts: 322
Sherman, William T.: 34, 38, 193, 203, 214
Shoneys: 63
Shore, Ernie: 260
shrimp/shrimping: 47, 58
sightseeing highlights: 45; *see also specific place*
Singleton, Angelica: 266
Sinks, The: 344

## State Parks

DuPont State Park: 50, 328
Eno River State Park: 202
Falls Lake State Recreation Area: 192
Fort Fisher State Recreational Area: 143–144
Fort Macon State Park: 133
Hammocks Beach State Park: 135
Jockey's Ridge State Park: 87
Jordan Lake State Recreation Area: 191–192
Lake Norman State Park: 235
Morrow Mountain State Park: 237
Mount Mitchell State Park: 305
William B. Umstead State Park: 192

skiing: 51, 303, 318, 351
slavery: 19, 20–21, 30–32, 310
Sliding Rock: 294
Smithfield: 212
Smith-McDowell House Museum: 290
Smoky Mountain Field School: 353
Smoky Mountain Jamboree: 312
snakes: 70–71
soccer: 54
Soco Gardens Zoo: 316
Sothel, Seth: 22
Soto, Hernando de: 17
South Brunswick Isles: 165–166
South Carolina Revolution: 23
Southeastern Center for Contemporary Art
    (SECCA): 259
Southern Coast: 137–166
southern cooking: 156–157, 209, 230
Southern Heartland: 216–252
Southern Pines: 249–251
Southport: 163
Speech of Speckled Snake: 313–314
Spence Field: 348, 350
Spencer: 238
Spirit Square: 225
sports and recreation: 45–55
Spring Hill House: 180
Stagville: 197
state's rights: 30, 32, 37
state symbols and emblems: 48
stingrays: 72
St. James Episcopal Church: 147–148
Stompin' Grounds: 318
St. Thomas Episcopal Church: 123

Sunday Jazz Showcase: 117
sunscreen: 69
Sunset Beach: 165
Surf City: 135
surfing: 45–46, 91, 161
Swansboro: 134
sweet tea: 61

**T**

Tanglewood Park: 260
Tannenbaum Park: 272
Tarleton, Banastre: 28
taxes: 79
Taxidermy Hall of Fame of North Carolina Creation Museum: 250
Taylor, Marble Nash: 37
tea: 61
Teach, Edward "Blackbeard": 103, 130
Teach's Hole Blackbeard Exhibit: 102–103
telephones: 76–77
terms of address: 42–43
theaters: 160, 191, 201, 333
Theodore Roosevelt Natural Area: 133
Thomas Wolfe Memorial State Historic Site: 290
thunderstorms: see precipitation
time zone: 80
tipping: 79
Tipton Place: 345
tobacco: 39, 40
Tollefson, Mike: 342
Topsail Island: 135
Tote-Em-In Zoo: 150
tourist information: 77–78; see also specific place
tours: see specific place
Town Creek Indian Mound State Historic Site: 237
Townsend Acts: 26
T. Pennington Art Gallery: 324
Tracks in the Sand Trail: 48, 87
Trail of Tears: 309, 310
trails: Alum Cave Trail 49, 349; Anthony Creek Trail 348; Appalachian Trail 49, 347; Boogerman Loop Trail 349; Bote Mountain Trail 348; Boulevard Trail 49, 348–349; Bullhead Trail 49, 349; Buxton Woods Nature Trail 100; Cape Hatteras Beach Trail 48; Cedar Point Tideland Trail 48, 128; Charles Kuralt Trail 98; Cherokee Botanical Garden and Nature Trail 311; Flytrap Trail 48; Gregory Bald Trail 348; Gregory Ridge Trail 348; Paw Paw Trail 224; Rainbow Falls Trail 349; Rich Mountain Trail 348; Roaring Fork Motor Nature Trail 343–344; Tracks in the Sand Trail 48, 87; Trillium Gap Trail 349
train travel: 65
transportation: 64–68
Transylvania Music Camp: 294
Tregembo, George: 150
Triad: 254, 254–260
Triangle: 167–215
Trillium Gap Trail: 349
Tryon Palace: 112, 113, 115
Tryon, William: 26, 113, 115, 170, 203
Tsali area: 50
Tufts Archives: 248
Tufts, James W.: 248
Turnage Theater: 122
Tuscarora Indians: 17, 113, 123
Tweetsie Railroad: 54, 297
Twigs & Leaves Gallery: 324

**U**

Underground Railroad: 33, 36, 266
Union Station: 252
universities: Appalachian State University 301; Duke University 195–196; Duke University Museum of Art 196; Duke University Primate Center 197; North Carolina Central University Art Museum 196; University of North Carolina at Chapel Hill 206; University of North Carolina at Pembroke 215; Western Carolina University 329; Winthrop University 240
USS North Carolina Battleship Memorial: 144
Uwharrie National Forest: 276

**V**

vaccinations: 80
Valle Crucis: 303–305
Van Buren, Martin: 266
Vance, Zebulon B.: 38, 39, 283, 306
Vanderbilt, George: 283, 285
Vietnam Memorial Wall: 228
Virginia to Florida Bicycle Route: 50
visas: 67
visitor centers: see specific place

**W**

Waffle House: 61–62
Wake Forest College Birthplace Museum: 181
Walkway of History: 269
Wanchese: 109
Warner, Charles Dudley: 289, 304–305

Warner, Yardley: 266
War of 1812: 30
Washington: 121–122
Washington, George: 28
Waterfront Park: 163
water taxi: 144
Waves: 99
Waynesville: 322–324
weather: *see* climate
Weatherspoon Art Gallery: 272
weights and measures: 79
Westbend Vineyards: 260
Western Carolina University: 329
Western North Carolina Nature Center: 290
West, Joseph: 20
West Point on the Eno: 198
Weymouth Center: 249
Weymouth Woods Sandhills Nature Preserve: 249
Whalehead Club: 97
White House, The: 239–240
Whitewater Falls: 330
whitewater rafting: 46, 329
Whitman, George Washington: 37
Wilkes Art Gallery: 306
Wilkesboro: 306
William B. Umstead State Park: 192
William Courtney Yellow House: 203
Williamson, Hugh: 29
Wilmington: 136–163; accommodations 152–155; entertainment 159–161; food 155–159; recreation 161; sightseeing 144–152; transportation 161–162
Wilmington Hammerheads: 54
Wilmington Railroad Museum: 142, 145
Wilmington Ten: 139, 140
Wilmot Proviso: 32

Wilson, Thomas Woodrow: 40, 148–149, 235, 240
Windsor: 123
windsurfing: 92
wine-tasting: Biltmore Winery 52; Dennis Vineyards Winery 237; Mountain Valley Vineyards 52; Westbend Vineyards 260
Winkler Bakery: 258
Winston, Joseph: 255
Winston-Salem: 254–263
Winston-Salem Warthogs: 260–261
Winthrop University: 240
WKIX: 185
women travelers: 68
Woodward, Henry: 19, 20
World Beer Festival: 193
World's Largest Chest of Drawers: 279
Wright Brothers National Memorial: 85–86

**Y**
Yamasee Indians: 17
Yates, Adelaide: 264
Yates, Sallie: 264
Yeamans, John: 20
yellowjackets: 71
YMI Cultural Center: 290
York: 245–246
York County: 238–246

**Z**
Zachary, Tom: 267
Ziszendorf, Count: 254–255
zoos: Livermon Recreational Park and Mini Zoo 123; North Carolina Zoological Park 275; Santa's Land Park and Zoo 54, 316–317; Soco Gardens Zoo 316; Tote-Em-In Zoo 150

# Acknowledgments

Thank you to my wife, Kristin Sigalas, for the encouragement and counsel. And to my sons, Noah and Ben.

Thanks also to Connie Nelson of the Cape Fear Coast Convention and Visitors Bureau; Quinn E. Capps of the Dare County Tourist Bureau; the folks at Kitty Hawk Kayaks; Captain Carl Marshburn of the *Henrietta III;* Joel Young and the rest of the staff and volunteers at the Maggie Valley Chamber of Commerce & Visitors & Convention Bureau; David Redman, director of the Cherokee Tribal Travel and Promotion Office; Marla Tambellini and Erin Guill of the Asheville Convention and Visitors Bureau. Thanks also to my brother, sometime research associate and photographer Joe Sigalas, PhD. And to Joel Venable for introducing me to Floyd the Barber.

Thanks to my ever encouraging editor, Kevin McLain, and to copy editor Emily McManus, for getting me to do one more set of windsprints. This book has also benefited from the professionalism of Naomi Dancis, Melissa Sherowski, Robin Clewley, Sarah Coglianese, Aimee Larsen, Donna Galassi, Bill Newlin, and the rest of the crew on both sides of the Avalon Travel Publishing empire. Thanks also to Pauli Galin, Karen Bleske, and Amanda Bleakley, for their years of support and friendship.

Much is owed also to Leslie Anderson for the inspiration.

And to my parents, who always pulled over to read the plaques.

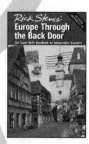

# ƒOGHORN OUTDOORS®

Campers, hikers, boaters, and anglers agree:
With Foghorn, you'll spend less time planning
and more time enjoying the outdoors.

**www.foghorn.com**

# ROAD TRIP USA

Road Trip USA guides take you off
the beaten path, onto classic blacktop,
and into the soul of America.

**www.roadtripusa.com**

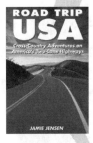

# THE DOG LOVER'S COMPANION

A special breed of guidebook for
travelers and residents who don't want
to leave their canine pals behind.

**www.dogloverscompanion.com**

# ADAPTER KIT

Adapter Kit helps travelers extend their journey
and live like the locals, with the help of authors
who have taken the plunge themselves.

**www.adapterkit.com**

# AVALON TRAVEL PUBLISHING
## www.travelmatters.com

Avalon Travel Publishing guides are available at your favorite book or travel store.

# U.S. ~ Metric Conversion

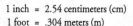

| | | |
|---:|:--:|:---|
| 1 inch | = | 2.54 centimeters (cm) |
| 1 foot | = | .304 meters (m) |
| 1 yard | = | 0.914 meters |
| 1 mile | = | 1.6093 kilometers (km) |
| 1 km | = | .6214 miles |
| 1 fathom | = | 1.8288 m |
| 1 chain | = | 20.1168 m |
| 1 furlong | = | 201.168 m |
| 1 acre | = | .4047 hectares |
| 1 sq km | = | 100 hectares |
| 1 sq mile | = | 2.59 square km |
| 1 ounce | = | 28.35 grams |
| 1 pound | = | .4536 kilograms |
| 1 short ton | = | .90718 metric ton |
| 1 short ton | = | 2000 pounds |
| 1 long ton | = | 1.016 metric tons |
| 1 long ton | = | 2240 pounds |
| 1 metric ton | = | 1000 kilograms |
| 1 quart | = | .94635 liters |
| 1 US gallon | = | 3.7854 liters |
| 1 Imperial gallon | = | 4.5459 liters |
| 1 nautical mile | = | 1.852 km |

To compute celsius temperatures, subtract 32 from Fahrenheit and divide by 1.8. To go the other way, multiply celsius by 1.8 and add 32.

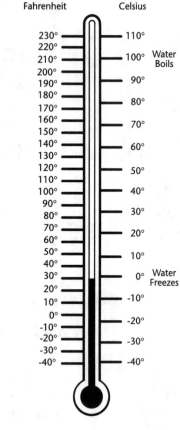

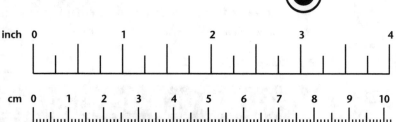